Encyclopedia of Physical Education, Fitness, and Sports

Sports, Dance, and Related Activities

Reuben B. Frost
Volume Editor

Thomas K. Cureton, Jr.
Series Editor

Sponsored by
The American Alliance for Health,
Physical Education, and Recreation

ADDISON-WESLEY PUBLISHING COMPANY
Reading, Massachusetts
Menlo Park, California · London · Amsterdam · Don Mills, Ontario · Sydney

ISBN 0-201-01077-1
ABCDEFGHIJ-HA-7987

About the Alliance

Since 1885 when the original organization was founded by a group of people interested in "physical training," the American Alliance for Health, Physical Education, and Recreation has been the professional home of educators concerned with physical activity, health, and fitness.

Alliance sponsorship of the publication of this five-volume *Encyclopedia* crowns more than 90 years of program efforts devoted to professional development, research, and scholarship.

In that time the Alliance has provided numerous vehicles for the growth and dissemination of the knowledge base of the profession. These include an Alliance network of periodicals reaching all members and many segments of the public; professional meetings and conventions; professional books and reports; and collaboration with the professions, government, business, and media.

The Alliance has been attentive to the responsibility of providing reference materials representative of the profession. These materials have helped members to initiate, develop, and conduct programs in health, leisure, and movement-related activities for the enrichment of human life.

The AAHPER *Journal of Physical Education and Recreation* has been the major journal of the profession for nearly 50 years. The *Research Quarterly* has been published since 1929. *Completed Research in Health, Physical Education, and Recreation,* an annual publication, is now in its 18th year. *Health Education* has been published since 1969. The annual convention of the Alliance provides continuous reporting of current research, with abstracts available in an annual volume since 1970.

The educational world is just awakening to the importance of motor behavior. For eons the cognitive aspects of scholarship were explored with great emphasis upon the history and heritage of knowledge. As the world recognizes greater responsibility for affective and motor behaviors as well, the area of physical activity assumes its rightful place in the education of human beings.

For many years the Alliance has recognized the growing need for a compendium of knowledge related to physical education, sport, and fitness. Students, teachers, leaders from other disciplines, the Alliance Research Council, the American Academy of Physical Education—all have encouraged the development and publication of such a reference.

Yet, perhaps like most achievements realized through group effort, one individual can be pointed out as primarily responsible for bringing this *Encyclopedia* into being. Dr. Thomas K. Cureton, professor emeritus of physical education, University of Illinois at Champaign, has been the conscience of the profession in promoting, preparing, and urging its publication. Under his determined and persevering leadership, the idea of the *Encyclopedia of Physical Education, Fitness, and Sports* was initiated and the volumes organized and published.

As meaning and ideas are gleaned from this work, future scholars will be in debt to Dr. Cureton and to the hundreds of other professional women and men who have contributed to these volumes. It is with a sense of great achievement that the American Alliance for Health, Physical Education, and Recreation joins with the publisher in the presentation of a reference unique in the annals of education.

With the publication of these volumes, at long last an inclusive analysis of the areas represented by the art and science of movement-oriented activities will be available for use. It should be a valuable asset to the professional libraries of Alliance members and will undoubtedly become part of the professional collections of most university, school, and city libraries.

The American Alliance for Health, Physical Education, and Recreation is a voluntary, professional organization presently made up of the following seven associations: Association for the Advancement of Health Education (AAHE), American Association for Leisure and Recreation (AALR), the American School and Community Safety Association (ASCSA), Association for Research, Administration, Professional Councils and Societies (ARAPCS), National Association for Girls' and Women's Sport (NAGWS), National Association for Sport and Physical Education (NASPE), and National Dance Association (NDA).

Purposes of the Alliance are to support, encourage, and assist member groups as they seek to initiate, develop, and conduct programs in health, leisure, and movement-related activities for the enrichment of human life. Headquarters are in the National Education Association Center, 1201 Sixteenth Street, N.W., Washington, D.C. 20036.

Series Editor

Thomas Kirk Cureton, Jr., series editor of the five-volume *Encyclopedia of Physical Education, Fitness, and Sports,* is professor emeritus of physical education at the University of Illinois, having retired in 1969. He has, however, continued to speak, write, study, work, and spread the gospel of physical fitness.

Educated at Yale University, Springfield College, and Columbia University, Dr. Cureton's contributions to his profession and his influence on the lives of those with whom he has come in contact are immeasurable. His inspirational teaching, his passion for research, and his untiring pursuit of knowledge have brought him fame and appreciation. During his long professional career, thousands of graduate students have come under his guidance. Through their accomplishments as well as his own, his influence in the field of physical education and fitness is felt worldwide.

Dr. Cureton has contributed over fifty books and monographs and at least 600 articles to the professional literature of his field.

He has been honored by many organizations in the areas of health, fitness, and youth leadership. He has served as consultant on fitness to the Council on Physical Fitness and Sports under three United States presidents. He is a Founding Fellow of the American College of Sports Medicine. His contributions to the program of the YMCA have been recognized by the Roberts-Gulick Award for Distinguished Leadership. The American Alliance for Health, Physical Education, and Recreation has accorded him its highest honor—the Gulick Award.

Dr. Cureton is still a vigorous participant in physical activities. In 1973, he broke four national meet records for his age class in the National AAU Masters' Swimming Championships. He continues his active professional life as Director of the Physical Fitness Institute at the University of Illinois.

Volume Editor

Dr. Reuben B. Frost is Buxton Professor Emeritus at Springfield College, Springfield, Massachusetts, at which he was Director of Health, Physical Education, and Recreation from 1960 to 1972. He continued to teach at Springfield College until his retirement in 1974. He received his A.B. from Luther College in 1928, his M.A. from the University of Iowa in 1938, and his Ph.D. from the University of Oregon in 1958. He has taught, coached, and served as administrator at the high school, college, and university levels for over 40 years.

Dr. Frost has held many offices in state, district, and national Associations of Health, Physical Education, and Recreation, serving as president of the Central District Association in 1954–55, and the American Association in 1965–66. Active in the YMCA, he was chairman of the New England Physical Education Committee, co-chairman of the National Health and Physical Education Committee, and president of the National YMCA Health and Physical Education Assembly.

Dr. Frost has lectured throughout the United States and in numerous other countries. He directed the Peace Corps Training Program at Springfield College in 1963 and represented the United States at the International Olympic Academy in Greece in 1965. He has authored over thirty-five articles and two books, with a third in press.

Dr. Frost's many honors include the following: Honor awards from the Massachusetts, the Central District, the Eastern District, and the American Association for Health, Physical Education and Recreation; the Distinguished Service Award and an Honorary Doctor of Humane Letters from Luther College; election to the North Central Conference Hall of Fame and the Helms Foundation Hall of Fame; and election as a Fellow of the American Academy of Physical Education. He is listed in *Who's Who in America, Who's Who in*

American Education, Leaders in Education, and *Community Leaders of America.* South Dakota State University recently named its new basketball arena in his honor. In May 1976, Dr. Frost was awarded the honorary Doctor of Humanics degree from Springfield College.

Preface

This volume of the *Encyclopedia of Physical Education, Fitness, and Sports* deals with the very essence of physical education—activity itself. For those who are primarily engaged in the movement phase of physical education, a large portion of what they do will consist of sports, dance, and related activities. It is essential, therefore, that some attention be given to the origin, nature, terminology, performance, and pedagogy of activities in these categories. As the title suggests, this is the prime object of this volume.

The term *sport* defies absolute definition. Even when used to characterize a game or other physical education activity there is considerable disagreement as to the exact bounds of meaning. Sport means many different things to many different people. Sport is utter concentration, deep involvement, a challenge met, a game won or lost. It may consist of shooting an arrow, sailing a boat, kicking a goal, serving an ace, bowling a strike, or clearing a crossbar. Sport is fun, disappointment, triumph, and defeat. It is a means of testing one's strength, courage, and stamina.

There is far from complete agreement as to which activities should, and should not, be considered sports. The categorization of sports is usually nebulous. Those presenting classification schemes generally use terms such as aquatics, team sports, individual and dual sports, lifetime sports, carry-over sports, combatives, self-testing activities. Because many sports fit more than one category and others do not readily fall into any of them, a rigid classification scheme is not presented here.

Dance, as one of the oldest art forms, is also found in most physical education programs. It is recognized by anthropologists as an important cultural force. It is an excellent means of communication and self-expression. As indicated in the Dance Section (see article 50), dance is an art form in which "the body is the instrument and movement the medium used for purposes of human expression." The various forms of dance together with its history, cultural significance, and contributions to education are presented here.

Related Activities are those which are included in most good programs of physical education but which technically are neither dance nor sport. There are those who classify some of these activities as sport and may have good reasons for doing so. For purposes of this volume they have, however, been grouped separately. These activities are developmental and, in most cases, challenging. They may also be relaxing and/or useful in everyday living.

The selection of activities for inclusion in this volume has required many somewhat arbitrary decisions. The criteria on which selection was based are:

1. Has the activity been included somewhat extensively in physical education programs?
2. Is it generally considered an educational and developmental experience, rather than one which is highly commercialized and which has entertainment as its principal objective?

Because each author was granted considerable leeway with regard to format and because a number of articles originally written for other publications were included, there is considerable inconsistency in style and organization. Nevertheless it is believed that the purposes of the book, to describe and explain, have been adequately served and that those who seek a concise, authoritative source of information will find it here.

While the large number of people who made significant contributions to this volume cannot possibly be identified individually, it seems appropriate to mention a few. Deep appreciation is expressed to Dr. Thomas K. Cureton, Jr., Series Editor, for his perseverance and constant assistance; to the section editors, Dr. Frank Sills and Dr. Frances Dougherty; to Lyle Welser; and to the authors* who gave unstintingly of their time and knowledge. To the Addison-Wesley staff and Raymond Ciszek for their cooperation and ever-ready counsel go heartfelt thanks. And affection and gratitude to Jean Frost for her unwavering support and assistance in editing and typing. To the many other unnamed persons whose hard work and talents have made this volume possible, a sincere thank you.

Wilbraham, Mass.   R.B.F.
January 1977

---

* Background information on the accomplishments and affiliations of most of the contributing authors will be found in the Biographical Appendix alphabetized by authors' surnames.

Contents

CONTENTS

CONTENTS

Section 2

DANCE

CONTENTS

Introduction

Section 1 contains sixty-four articles which deal with forty-seven sports. Eighty-one authors have made contributions to the discussions. The subject matter ranges from football to shuffleboard, Nordic skiing to synchronized swimming, boxing to cricket. Authors come from all sections of the United States, from England and from Canada. Writers include coaches from universities, colleges and secondary schools; participants in small town programs and the Olympic Games; and physical education teachers from camps and educational institutions, both large and small.

Most of the articles deal with the origin of the sport, its scope and significance, the nature of the game, the fundamental skills, the tactics and strategies, appropriate facilities and equipment, and the terminology and etiquette peculiar to the sport. References and other sources of information are usually added.

The sports are arranged alphabetically with no attempt at classification. Illustrative material is included to enhance interest and to help inform.

Some reprints from professional publications have been used to supplement the articles by the authors, to present another point of view, or to cover a sport for which no available author was found.

RBF

1
Archery

Maryanne M. Schumm

Did you know that

☐ Despite the fact that the bow and arrow was the principal weapon of war for over 300 years . . .

☐ and in 16th-century England it was mandatory that every physically able male own and use a bow . . .

☐ and before gunpowder was invented the bow was the main hunting implement in nearly every society in the world . . .

☐ there are now more archers in the world than at any time before in history! (Gannon 1964, p. 7)

FROM SLINGSHOTS—OR MUSICAL INSTRUMENTS?

Many authorities have attempted to list the most important events in human evolution. Most agree that speech, the control and use of fire, the discovery of the wheel, and the invention of the bow and arrow, were prime achievements in the life of humans. It would be difficult to argue which of these was most important—but it cannot be overlooked that early people, struggling to stay alive, might not have survived without the development of the bow and arrow (Fig. 1.1).

The exact origins of archery are unknown. Through the use of cave drawings and other artifacts, archeologists estimate that the bow and arrow were in use between 25,000 and 100,000 years ago. The cave dwellers may have started off with rock throwing, worked up to lashing a stone on a stick, sharpened the stone to form a spear, and then discovered a form of slingshot from which they could project a rock or small spear with greater force than

Fig. 1.1 Archer at full draw position. Courtesy of *JOPER.*

they could throw it. Or the bow may have evolved from a rudimentary musical instrument. Some tribes still "play" the bow, placing one end in the mouth, while squeezing the middle of the string against the handle of the bow, then humming and plucking the taut string at the same time.

Whatever its origin, archery was a method of procuring food for early people and later developed into a weapon of war for many different societies. East and West Indian natives depended on bows, as did the Eskimos and nearly all African tribes. The ancient Egyptians, Chinese, Israelites, Greeks, Romans, Persians, Babylonians, and Assyrians fought with the bow and arrow. The Cretans were especially well-known archers. At age seventeen youths became apprentice warriors and devoted their whole lives toward perfecting military skills. They placed particular emphasis on archery because Apollo, the archer god, was the patron of Crete. When generals and kings wanted archers, they sent to Crete for the "Cream of the Crop."

The English, Welsh, French, and Italians perfected the use of the crossbow and longbow for war, and fought many famous battles, including those at Hastings, Crécy, Poitiers, and Agincourt. In the Americas, the Indians also developed the use of the bow for hunting and as a weapon of war.

CUSTOMS AND LEGENDS

It is still possible to find many old archery customs, legends and ideas linked to names, speech, songs, and folklore in evidence today. For example, Apollo, the archer god, had a tremendous influence on ancient civilizations and their reverence for the ability to shoot straight and true. In 1969, *Apollo II* was the first ship to hit a prime target—the moon. Its name implies knowledge and recognition of the legend of Apollo's accuracy. Indirectly, archery could be considered the first sport represented on the moon.

It is interesting to note a phase of archery still practiced by the Stone Age Bushmen of South Africa. When a young warrior feels attracted to one of the women in his tribe, he carves a small lover's bow out of antelope horn, and makes tiny matching arrows. At the appropriate time, he shoots a shaft toward the girl, and watches for her reaction. If she keeps the small arrow, it is a sign that she accepts him as a mate; if she rejects the arrow, it is a sign that she does not favor him. By using the bow, he avoids chancing public humiliation. This practice is reminiscent of the legend of Cupid and his bow!

England is given credit for popularizing archery for war. It is from England that we gain much of the romantic bow lore. One of the most famous names in all English legend was *Robin Hood,* a character known to a great many children today. Robin lived in Sherwood Forest with faithful followers, all excellent archers. He passed the time by stealing from the wealthy and giving to the poor, and staying out of the clutches of the Sheriff of Nottingham.

Another legendary figure is *Sir William Tell.* Every year, in the village square in Altdorf, Switzerland, there is a reenactment of the story of Tell, who shot an apple off his son's head with a crossbow to prove himself innocent of an accusation.

ADVENT OF A SPORT

It was probably soon after the advent of gunpowder that archery could generally be classified as a sport. As soon as countries switched to the more efficient firearms for hunting and defense, anyone who pursued the art of shooting with bow and arrow did so for enjoyment or challenge rather than for food or defense. Archery clubs were eventually formed in England, and tournaments were held in which archers shot at fixed targets.

The first archery club, the English Royal Toxophilite Society, was formed in 1781. The first United States club, the United Bowmen of Philadelphia, was organized in 1828. Both contributed greatly to the development of archery as a sport in their respective countries, and they are still active today. The National Archery Association, formed in 1879, sponsored the first United States National Tournament. With the accelerated growth of the sport over the years, the tremendous changes in equipment, forms of archery, and the varied interests of the participants, many different organizations have been formed to control it. The world governing body, the *Fédération Internationale de Tir à l'Arc* (FITA) was formed in 1931, the National Field Archery Association in 1939, Archery Manufacturers Organization (AMO) in 1954, the Professional Archery Association (PAA) in 1961, and the Junior Olympic Development Program (JOAD) and College Division of the NAA(CD) about

1970. The World Championships of archery are held every two years in selected countries, and the sport was officially added to the Olympics in 1972.

EQUIPMENT AND TECHNOLOGICAL ADVANCEMENTS

Changes and advancements in the equipment with which an archer must work are probably most responsible for the growth in popularity of the sport. To shoot, an archer should have a bow, arrows, arrow-holder (quiver), arm-guard, finger tab, target mat, stand, and target face.

The old, straight-limb wooden bow (English style) has given way to the highly efficient recurve bow (first used by the Turks) which is most commonly made of a composite of laminated woods and fiberglass, or magnesium and fiberglass. (Fig. 1.2). The bow may be a single unit or may be snapped apart into two or three pieces for easier transportation. The bow is usually equipped with a cutout sight window, a mechanical aiming device (sight), an arrow rest or holder, one to four metal stabilizing rods to reduce the twisting of the bow as it is shot, and a comfortable built-in or custom-made handle. Bows usually range in length from 62 to 70″ and in pull from 20 to 60 lbs.

Arrows, too, have been modernized. The cedar arrow has been replaced by the durable fiberglass and highly efficient aluminum arrow. Most tournament archers use aluminum arrows as they are exactly matched in spine

Fig. 1.2 Archers using modern recurve bow. Courtesy of *JOPER*.

(stiffness) and weight. Feathers are slowly being replaced by plastic vanes which are not as affected by weather conditions and are more durable.

Another major advancement contributing to archery's popularity is the mechanical indoor shooting range. The lanes at the range are 60 feet long, as in bowling, and are, in fact, often constructed on old bowling lanes. After shooting, the archer presses a button and the target moves up to the shooting line so the arrows may be withdrawn. The target may then be reset at any distance up to 20 yards.

ARCHERY TODAY

Archery and archers come in all shapes and sizes. There seems to be something for everyone, regardless of age or experience or taste. Some of the different events include:

World and Olympic contests. Each country's best archers shoot long distances measured in meters (90, 70, 50, and 30 meters for men, 70, 60, 50, and 30 meters for women) at a ten-ring face scored 10 through 1.

National, state, and local shoots. These are for all ages, professional and amateur, freestyle or barebow (with or without sight), indoors and out, featuring varying rounds (different distances and number of arrows), for both target and field archers. A standard field archery course is laid out like a golf course in the woods, with targets set at varying distances, 20–80 yards, using a two-ring face scored 5 and 3. The natural terrain is utilized to make the different shots more challenging.

Archery bowling. This comparatively new event features a special target face, on which the archer attempts to "strike" with one shot, or "spare out" with two. A perfect score would be 300.

Flight. Shooting for distance (the modern record is over one mile!).

Clout. Shooting at a 48-foot target on the ground at distances of 120–180 yards.

Archery golf. Played on a golf course. The object is to knock a 4″ rubber ball off a stake, which is one foot off the ground, in as few shots as possible.

Bow birds. Shooting at cardboard Frisbee©-like targets tossed into the air.

Archery skiing and horseback archery. Moving through a course in a certain time limit, shooting at targets along the way.

Bowfishing. Shooting at fish with a reel mounted on the bow.

Hunting.

Crossbow competition.

Wheelchair archery. The Para-Olympics, held in conjunction with the Olympic Games, include this sport event.

There are about 7.5 to 8.5 million Americans who participate in archery in some form, and they spend about $40 million each year on equipment. There are nearly 10,000 registered Field Archery Tournaments and almost the same number of Target Tournaments held each year.

There are between 3000 and 4000 archery clubs (target, field and combination) as well as some specialized clubs for archery golf, flight and crossbow.

THE LURE OF THE BOW

As far as one can judge from recorded history, there has never been a total discontinuation of archery since its inception. With the growing emphasis on sports and relaxation, the current trend toward participation sports rather than spectator sports, and the present booming popularity of archery, it looks as though the sport may be around for at least a few thousand more years!

REFERENCES

Bear, F. 1968. *The archer's bible.* New York: Doubleday.

Burke, E. 1957. *The history of archery.* New York: William Morrow.

Gannon, R. 1964. *The complete book of archery.* New York: Coward-McCann.

Grimley, G. 1958. *The book of the bow.* London: Ebenezer Baylis and Son.

Haugen, A., and H. Metcalf 1963. *Field archery and bowhunting.* New York: Ronald.

Klann, M. 1971. *Target archery.* Reading, Mass.: Addison-Wesley.

Witt, J. 1969. Which way is the target? *Archery World Magazine* (March).

2
Badminton

Arne L. Olson

ORIGIN AND GENERAL DESCRIPTION

Among most investigators who have studied the question, it is agreed that badminton probably originated in India as a game called "poona" in which a light object was batted back and forth over an obstruction somewhat resembling a net. It is documented (Brumbach and Ballou 1963, p. 169) that a similar game was played in England at the Duke of Beaufort's country home, "Badminton." Because guests from several parts of the world were introduced to the game there, players began calling the game *badminton*. At the "Badminton House" the game was played with four players on a side on an hourglass-shaped court. It is believed that the narrow area at the net on this court was simply a convenience so that nonplaying guests could move in and out of the room without interfering with play. The game became standardized on a 44 × 20′ court (doubles) with a 5′, 1″ net about 1893. Singles matches are played on a 44 × 17′ court. International competition was organized in 1936.

The basic purpose of the game is to win either the serve or points by hitting the bird (shuttlecock) to the opponent's court so that it cannot be returned. Play is started with an *underhand* serve (Fig. 2.1) which must go over the net into the opposite court in a diagonal pattern into a marked area 6′6″ away from the net. It is then returned with any "clearly hit" strokes back and forth until it touches the floor. If it lands on or inside the boundary lines, the side hitting the bird wins the volley. If it lands outside, the side hitting loses the volley. Points are scored only by the side which has served. Matches normally consist of two out of three games with all matches played to 15 points. In women's singles the winner is the first player to gain 11 points. A method of "setting" the contest to a higher point level is available under certain conditions when the game is tied just before the terminal point level.

SKILLS AND STRATEGY

In order to describe play, it is important to understand the basic flight patterns of the bird. A "clear" is a shot hit so that it cannot be reached by an opponent until it comes down near the back boundary line. A "drop" is a

Fig. 2.1 Play is started with an underhand serve. Courtesy of Frank Fu.

shot hit so that it drops to the court just after it crosses the net. A "smash" is a shot that is hit from an overhead position downward toward the opponent's court. A "drive" is a flat shot parallel to the floor which is used occasionally as a surprise in an attempt to pass an opponent at the net or get the bird so close to an opponent's body that it cannot be returned forcefully.

The fundamental serves and return strokes are used from any position on the opponent's court. Overhead strokes (except on the serve) are preferred because it is easier to hit the different areas of the opponent's court with varieties of shots. Forehand strokes are also preferred because most players are more powerful with this stroke action. Occasionally players must use a backhand stroke if they cannot get in position but an overhead "round the head" shot is usually chosen by advanced players because of its greater power potential.

Although the singles and doubles games dictate general court positions in various situations, basic singles strategy would consist of running opponents to keep them off balance as well as trying to keep them at the rear of the court because of the adjustment time possible while the bird is returned from this deep position. If the bird can be propelled so that it is coming down behind your opponent, it is advantageous since it is more difficult to return the bird to a deep location on the court and a weak shot will often result. The general principle in singles is waiting for an opponent's error.

The doubles game differs in that players try to hit the bird on a downward trajectory or at least force opponents to hit upward on each shot. The emphasis is on offense. Positions of partners on the court vary according to the flight of the bird. If the bird is received high and short on one side of the net, one player should hit the bird downward while the partner goes to the front of the court to "finish off" any weakly hit returns. In contrast, if the bird is likely to be returned in a smash from the opponents, a side-by-side defensive position should be assumed.

EQUIPMENT

The equipment necessary for play includes a racket for each player, a bird (shuttlecock), a net, and court boundary lines. Badminton is frequently played in the backyard without lines, but this activity is entirely different from the game played in official competition. The rackets can be made of wood or metal and the birds of feathers or plastic. Feathered birds do not last long and because of consequent expense, plastic birds are used by the average player. Advanced players prefer feathers because of the more consistent bird flight and also because they have greater air resistance and therefore slow down as they fly.

COMPETITION

Competition in badminton ranges from local club to regional, national (governed by the American Badminton Association [ABA]), and international competition. Different regions conduct high school and college competition. National competition is available for women at the college level under the sponsorship of the Association of Intercollegiate Athletics for Women. Tournaments are usually conducted over a short period of time except for international competition leading to the Thomas Cup for men and the Uber Cup for women. This competition is played in zone playoffs similar to the Davis Cup in tennis and results in a team championship determined every four or three years, respectively. Tournament structures are usually divided by age and also by sex. Junior (under 17) and senior (over 40) competition is available in many areas and matches are divided into men's singles, women's singles, men's doubles, women's doubles and mixed doubles.

Benefits and Requirements for Participation

Badminton can be played on a recreational basis with inexpensive equipment and only the dividing net if the ceiling height is sufficient. The activity can be played indoors or outdoors if it is not windy. Competition requires a lined court with a smooth surface. Good traction is important.

Competitive badminton is a very explosive game and requires quickness and ability to control one's body as well as to control a small light object with the racket. If played on a regular basis (especially singles at a competitive level), it can contribute to power development of arms and legs as well as cardiovascular fitness. For most players, however, badminton provides a sport outlet for moderate competition to satisfy a general recreational need. It is very easy to get a satisfying performance level and therefore badminton quickly becomes a popular activity among the athletically as well as the non-athletically inclined. The sport (or game) readily adapts to the skill and experience of the individuals playing.

REFERENCES

Brown, E. 1969. *The complete book of badminton.* Harrisburg, Pa.: Stackpole Books.

Brumbach, W. B., and R. B. Ballou, Jr. 1963. A brief outline of background material on the sport of badminton. *The Physical Educator* (December) **20:** 169–170.

Davidson, K. R., and L. R. Gustafson 1964. *Winning badminton.* New York: Ronald.

Devlin, J. F. 1937. *Badminton for all.* New York: Doubleday.

Devlin, J. F., and R. Lardner 1967. *Sports illustrated book of badminton.* Philadelphia: Lippincott.

Friedrich, J., and A. Rutledge 1962. *Beginning badminton,* Belmont, Calif.: Wadsworth.

Grant, D. 1950. *Badminton.* Montreal: Graphic.

Pelton, B. C. 1971. *Badminton.* Englewood Cliffs, N.J.: Prentice-Hall.

Poole, J. 1969. *Badminton.* Pacific Palisades, Calif.: Goodyear.

Sullivan, G. 1968. *Guide to badminton.* New York: Fleet.

3
Baseball
Carl W. Selin

ORIGINS AND DEVELOPMENT

As with many other modern ball games, the evolution of baseball probably began with ancient religious rites stressing fertility of crops or people. The first recorded "batting contest" took place in Egypt some 5000 years ago (Henderson 1947). "Poison Ball" in France and the British games of "Rounders" and "Cricket" are generally recognized as the source of the

American game of baseball. The legend that Abner Doubleday was the originator, and Cooperstown, New York, was the birthplace of baseball in 1839, has long been discredited (Coffin 1971).

In 1845, a surveyor, Alexander Cartwright, systematized the rules and regulations of baseball including laying the bases 90′ apart in a square, limiting the defensive players to nine, and placing them in the standard positions known today. He eliminated hitting the runner with the ball for an out and instituted a nine-inning game with teams switching from offense to defense after three outs.

The first intercollegiate baseball game was played between Williams and Amherst in 1859. The first professional baseball association was organized in 1871 and five years later the National League was formed.

In 1901 the Western League became the American League. After several years of fighting, the leagues banded together as "Organized Baseball" with the National, American, and minor leagues. The modern World Series began in 1905. For boys aged 17 and under, American Legion baseball started in 1925 in South Dakota. Little League baseball for boys aged 12 and under began in Williamsport, Pennsylvania, in 1939. For graduates of the Little League, the Pony League began in 1951 in Washington, Pennsylvania. The Babe Ruth League, also for boys 13 to 15 years of age, was founded in 1952.

THE GAME

Nine players constitute a baseball team. Playing at any one time are nine defensive players, a batter, and any runners on base. The pitcher attempts to throw the baseball over the plate and through the batter's strike zone, while the batter attempts to hit the ball to safely get on base and/or advance any other runners.

The other defensive players include a catcher, first baseman, second baseman, shortstop, third baseman, left fielder, center fielder and right fielder. The objective of the defensive team is to prevent offensive players from becoming runners or to prevent their advance around the bases.

The objective of the offensive team is to have its batters become runners and its runners advance around the bases to home plate at which they score a run. The team's objective is to score more runs than its opponent.

A game consists of nine innings, unless the score is tied, forcing the game into extra innings. Each inning includes three outs for each team. An out is made in a number of ways: (1) by the batter striking out (three strikes), (2) by hitting a fly ball which is caught by a defensive player, (3) by a defensive player who fields a ground ball and throws it to a base ahead of the runner, forcing him out, or (4) by tagging a runner who is off the base when the ball is in play. Most of the outs will be in one of the four categories above; there are others which occur less frequently. (See current official baseball rules.)

THE PLAYING FIELD

The playing field—often referred to as a diamond—is uniquely laid out in a square with home plate (Fig. 3.1) as the focal point and first and third bases 90′ away.

Second base is across the diamond from home plate and 90′ from first or third bases (Fig. 3.2). The foul lines extend from home plate through first and third bases to the outfield fence. The outfield consists of the area beyond the bases and yet between the foul lines. A fair ball must land on the playing field within the foul lines. The pitcher's mound is equidistant from first and third base and 60′, 6″ from home plate.

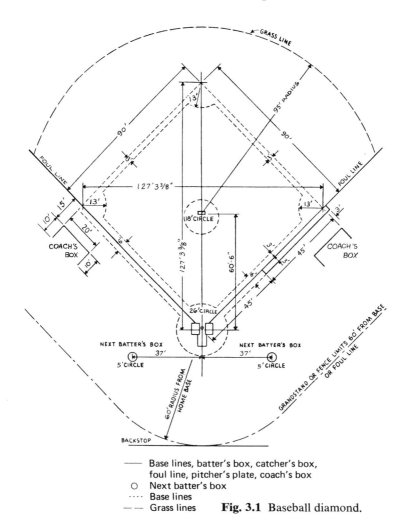

——— Base lines, batter's box, catcher's box,
        foul line, pitcher's plate, coach's box
 O   Next batter's box
···· Base lines
— — Grass lines   **Fig. 3.1** Baseball diamond.

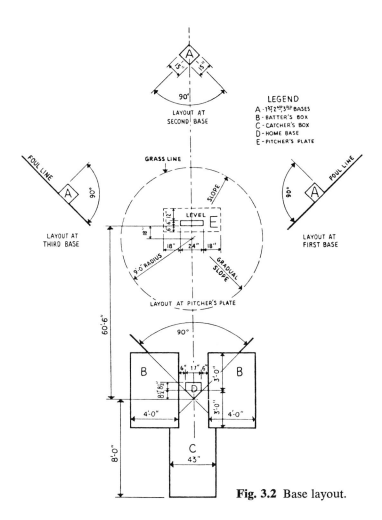

LEGEND
A - 1ST 2ND 3RD BASES
B - BATTER'S BOX
C - CATCHER'S BOX
D - HOME BASE
E - PITCHER'S PLATE

Fig. 3.2 Base layout.

EQUIPMENT

The baseball is a sphere weighing between 5 and 5¼ ounces and measures between 9 and 9¼ inches in circumference. It is formed by winding yarn around a small core of rubber, cork, or a combination of both, and is covered by two pieces of white, stitched horsehide.

The bat must be round and not over 2¾″ in diameter at its thickest part, nor more than 42″ in length. It must be made of hardwood, although recent rule changes allow an aluminum bat at some levels of competition.

Each player uses a leather glove or mitt. The first baseman generally wears a special glove to receive the many throws for putouts at first base. The catcher may wear any type of mitt, but generally wears a thicker mitt designed to receive the faster thrown balls of the pitcher and to protect the fingers of the catching hand.

It is now required that players wear protective helmets when batting or running bases.

TACTICS AND STRATEGY

Perhaps the heart of the game of baseball is the unique confrontation between the pitcher and the batter. Batters are trying to reach first base or beyond by getting a fair hit or by receiving a walk. He may also reach first base on an error by a defensive player or by being hit by a pitched ball. Pitchers attempt to strike out the batters or make them hit the ball into a "put-out" situation. Branch Rickey (1971) writes:

> The unique strength in the game of baseball as a team sport lies in the ingenious geometry of the diamond. It is really a game of individuals; nine men and a batsman play out the drama on separate stages as the action unfolds. To be sure, the game has the double play, the hit and run, the squeeze bunt, the relay, but the ten men on the field perform uniquely alone and face their responsibilties alone most of the time. The pitch, the hit, the catch, the throw, the run—again and again. It is almost impossible to find any other team sport that so critically and clearly tests the mettle of each man alone on almost every play and yet fuses them all together into a group working in team competition.

In addition to the players, each team is allowed to have two base coaches, who are confined to the coaching "boxes" behind first and third base. Their purpose is to aid the baserunners as they advance or return to base.

RULES AND REGULATIONS

Enforcement of the baseball rules is the duty of the umpires. Games include from two to four umpires, one of whom is umpire-in-chief, while the others are field umpires. The umpire behind the plate calls balls and strikes in addition to making calls on plays at home plate and often at third base. The field umpires may take any position desired, and their chief function is to make all decisions on the bases.

An experimental move has added a new player to the offensive team in some leagues. The "designated hitter" takes the turn at bat for the pitcher to eliminate the weakest hitter on most teams and to speed up the game. This batter does not play with the defensive team. Other experimental rules are being tried occasionally to speed up the game or to improve playing conditions.

Many professional teams—and some colleges—now play their games on artificial turf rather than grass fields. While eliminating much field maintenance and improving play in bad weather, the batted balls seem to travel faster and accelerate as they skip through the infield.

RECENT DEVELOPMENTS

Recent years have seen a host of franchise shifts among major league teams. Since the move of the Brooklyn Dodgers to Los Angeles, a number of teams have moved to new locations in an effort to improve their economic position. In addition, there has been an enlargement of both leagues by adding new franchises.

Attendance has been growing at baseball games and television has had a major influence in shifting a number of World Series games to night games so that they may be viewed by a greater audience.

Today's professional baseball leagues are guided by the Commissioner of Baseball who, with team owners and league officials, establishes baseball policies and rules, and arbitrates disputes. Player associations are growing stronger and are utilizing collective bargaining in dealing with owners.

Although controversy swirls over which sport is America's "National Pastime," baseball still reigns as the number one participant game in the United States. As spring arrives, flying baseballs fill the air in nearly every community from coast to coast and border to border, as teams from the level of Little League (or even Sweatshirt League) to the Major Leagues begin practice. The long summer season is ideally suited to the game of baseball.

BASIC INSTRUCTION

I. Skills needed by the pitcher

- ☐ Position of the foot on the pitching rubber before and during the delivery.
- ☐ Proper wind-up and follow-through position.
- ☐ Stretch position and delivery.
- ☐ Delivery of fast ball, curve, and change-up—including position of hand and release.
- ☐ Holding runners on base—and throwing to various bases.
- ☐ Fielding ground balls.
- ☐ Covering bunts in various situations.
- ☐ Backing-up bases.

II. Skills needed by the catcher

- ☐ Basic stance for receiving a pitch.
- ☐ Footwork on pitched balls to left or right.

Fig. 3.3 The "follow-through" is important in pitching. Courtesy of *JOPER*.

☐ Blocking pitched balls which are in the dirt.

☐ Blocking the plate against runners.

☐ Catching foul pop-ups.

☐ Throwing to bases—including holding runners on base.

☐ Fielding bunts and throwing properly.

☐ Giving signs, assisting pitcher, and selecting of pitches.

III. **Skills needed by infielders**

☐ Fielding ground balls to the left, right, in front and behind.

☐ Catching line drives and pop-ups.

☐ Coordinating catches with infielders and/or outfielders on pop-ups or fly balls.

☐ Tagging runners.

☐ Holding runners on base.

☐ Throwing to various bases.

☐ Double-play throws and footwork.

☐ Proper position and technique of cutoff plays.

☐ Proper positioning for covering bunts.

☐ Run-down plays.

☐ Special skills for first basemen regarding footwork and stretch.

IV. Skills needed by outfielders

☐ Proper stance to get jump on the ball.

☐ Catching fly balls, line drives, and ground balls (right, left, in front, and behind).

☐ Throwing to bases, or plate—throw overhand and keep ball low.

☐ Using cutoff men on throws—throw the ball at the head of cutoff man.

☐ Special situations:
1. Ball in sun.
2. Ball that could be caught by two outfielders—call for catch to avoid collisions.

☐ Backing-up bases where passed balls are possible.

V. Skills required for batting

☐ Grip.

☐ Stance.

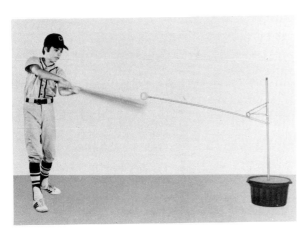

Fig. 3.4 Artificial devices are often used to teach youngsters how to hit. Courtesy of *JOPER*.

Fig. 3.5 The "headfirst" slide is an effective way of returning to first base when the pitcher throws there to hold the runner on. Courtesy of the University of North Dakota.

    ☐ Stride—including balance and timing.

    ☐ Swing—keeping bat level.

    ☐ Bunt.
        1. Safety bunt.
        2. Drag bunt.

    ☐ Hit and run.

VI. **Base running**

    ☐ Rounding individual bases.

    ☐ Stealing bases—taking a lead.

    ☐ Stealing base—start and pivot.

    ☐ Sliding into bases:
        1. Hook slide.
        2. Bent leg slide.
        3. Headfirst slide.
        4. Breaking up the double play.

    ☐ Run-down techniques (avoiding the tag).

    ☐ Heeding coaches' instructions.

REFERENCES

Allen, A. P. 1964. *Baseball coach's handbook of offensive strategy and techniques.* Englewood Cliffs, N.J.: Prentice-Hall.

Alston, W., and D. Weiskopf 1972. *The complete baseball handbook*. Boston: Allyn and Bacon.

Coffin, T. P. 1971. *The old ball game*. New York: Herder and Herder.

Combs, J. W. 1939. *Baseball—individual play and team strategy*. Englewood Cliffs, N.J.: Prentice-Hall.

Dugan, K. 1971. *How to organize and coach winning baseball*. West Nyack, N.Y.: Parker.

Henderson, R. W. 1947. *Ball, bat, and bishop*. New York: Rockport Press.

NCAA Baseball Guide.

Rickey, B. with R. Rigert 1965. *The American diamond*. New York: Simon and Schuster.

Spackman, R. R. 1963. *Baseball*. Annapolis: United States Naval Institute.

4
Basketball

Three authors have contributed to the material on basketball. Jerry Wrenn and Burris Husman wrote about men's basketball and Judy Devine discussed women's basketball. Complete coverage was thus obtained, whereas either article by itself would have left too many things unsaid. RBF

Men's Basketball
Jerry Wrenn and Burris Husman

HISTORY

It was in December of 1891 that Luther Gulick, Dean of the Physical Education Department at *The School for Christian Workers* (now Springfield College), asked James Naismith and his class to invent a game that (1) could be played indoors, (2) would be as interesting as lacrosse and football, and (3) would provide plenty of exercise.

Naismith (later to become a Doctor of both Divinity and of Medicine) decided that the ball should be large and soft, and opted for a goal that could not be rushed and that the ball could not be "slammed through."

Naismith wrote the rules in pencil and gathered his class for the first game. The place was the school's gymnasium at the corner of State and Sherman streets in Springfield, Massachusetts, the goals were peach baskets brought in by the janitor, and the uniforms were the usual gym costumes of black, full-sleeve woolen jerseys and long gray trousers. The rules excluded running with the ball or holding it against the body and made holding, pushing, and tripping illegal.

The game was an immediate success and the first public contest was played on March 11, 1892. While the original principles of the game were maintained, the rules have been changed and expanded from year to year. Improvement and regulation of equipment kept pace with the rapid growth of the game. The fact that a girls' game played at Smith College in 1893 was described in the *Springfield Republican* attests to the popularity and rapid expansion of the sport.

When basketball was first played, nine players were on each team. Within three years, the number was reduced to five: two forwards, a center, and two guards. The original rules allowed little body contact, placing full concentration on the ball. Players were prohibited from rushing the ball toward the goal, as in football, but were allowed "steps" if the ball was caught while running full speed. Later the dribble was developed.

Originally the two forwards were selected for their shooting and offensive ability, the center for skill in passing and maneuvering, and the two guards for their defensive prowess. The guards stayed in the defensive end of the court to guard the goal. The center, originally a midcourt player, soon joined the two forwards for improved offensive play. Later a fourth man, one of the guards, was included in the offense. This style of play featured the standing guard for defense. During this time, the center jump, required after each goal, was a major part of the offense. It featured a tall center who could control the tip for a quick basket. The next step in the evolution of the game was to move the standing guard into the offense. This forced teams to move the "sleeper" forward back on defense. Thus developed the present systematized screening offenses and the pick-up, or assigned, man-for-man defense.

The success of screens against the man-for-man defense forced the use of the zone defense. The zone defense, which had to be approached cautiously and against which one had to take only good shots, led to a stalling, or a "come to me" type of offense. To combat this slow, uninteresting game, the ten-second rule which forced opponents to advance the ball offensively, and a rule eliminating the center jump were initiated. This resulted in a much faster game, featuring the fast break.

In recent years there have been several rules restricting the movements of the tall player. The three-second rule, widening of the free-throw lane, and the "goal-tending" rule are examples.

The history of shooting in basketball deserves consideration. In earlier years the major shot in basketball was the "scoop" shot. The ball was held in both hands, brought back between the legs, almost touching the floor, and scooped toward the basket. Since this shot was easy to block, the two-hand push shot was created. As the game was speeded up, players learned to shoot with one hand when close to the basket. This led to the development of the one-hand push shot, which in the West soon became the one-hand set shot. In the past few years the one-hand set shot has practically disappeared. The game now features one-hand driving shots, hook shots, and the one-hand jump shot.

GENERAL DESCRIPTION

Basketball is played on an area called a court. The team consists of five players. The object of the game is to place the ball in the opponent's goal and to keep the opponent from putting the ball in your goal. The game is started by tossing the ball up between two players in the center of the court. The team gaining possession of the ball becomes the offensive team; the other, the defensive team. On offense the ball may be rolled, passed, bounced, or batted from one player to another. The ball may also be advanced by drib-

Fig. 4.1 The object of the game is to shoot the ball into the opponents' basket. Courtesy of Luther College.

bling. A dribble is executed by throwing or tapping the ball on the floor and bouncing it once or several times. The dribble ends when the player touches the ball with both hands simultaneously, loses control of it, or when the ball comes to rest while the player is in contact with it. A player is permitted to take as many steps as he desires between dribbles. A score is made by either throwing a field goal, which scores two points, or making a free throw (a penalty shot) which scores one point.

BASIC SKILLS

Catching

Catching is dependent upon the speed of the ball, the direction and height as it approaches, the location of the defense, and the next anticipated offensive maneuver. A player in position to receive a pass has his head up, his back

Fig. 4.2 Rebounding is an important aspect of successful basketball. Courtesy of Eastern Kentucky State University.

straight, and feet slightly spread. He is ready to move in any direction. If possible, the receiver should always move toward the ball. Moving toward the ball helps the receiver keep his body between the ball and the defensive man, thus reducing the chances of an interception. His body should be relaxed, hands advanced with fingers spread, elbows in, and weight forward. First contact should be made with the pads of the fingers. The speed and spin of the ball are stopped by the give of the arms toward the body, and a gradual tightening of the fingers around the ball. It is essential that the receiver keep the ball from falling back on the heel of the hands. His eyes should watch the ball until he has it in complete control. To speed up the offense, it is important that the receiver bring the ball toward his body so he is in position for the next pass, shot, or dribble.

Passing

A good player can analyze the situation and pass accurately, deceptively, and instantly to an open teammate. Accuracy is more important than speed, although a slow deliberate pass will permit the defense to maneuver and stop the attack.

Most passes should be thrown between the waist and the shoulders. If a player is stationary or moving toward you, the pass should be thrown waist high. Good passing requires judgment, deception, split vision, speed, and accuracy.

The two basic passes are the two-hand chest pass and the one-hand underhand pass. Two rules to be observed in passing are: (1) see the defensive man and anticipate his movements, and (2) throw the ball away from the defense.

Two-hand chest pass. This pass is important in that it can be thrown from either a stationary or running position. It also affords the player opportunity to feint, protect the ball, and still be in a position to make one of four fundamental offensive maneuvers: pivot, pass, shoot, or dribble. The ball is held in front of the body, chest high, elbows in, with the fingers spread over the sides and slightly behind the ball. The axis of the ball passes through or near the ends of the fingers, not the middle of the hand. Figure 4.3 shows the ball being passed by stepping forward with one foot, snapping the wrist, and pushing the ball with a sharp extension of the fingers. The pass should be level or as nearly so as possible, and should be passed with slight reverse "English" or spin to make the ball easy to catch.

One-hand underhand pass. The one-hand underhand pass developed from the two-hand underhand pass which was one of the early passes in basketball. The one-hand underhand pass is basically a close-order pass used for short distances, such as two men crossing, as in a weave, or by the post man feeding a player who is cutting to the basket.

Fig. 4.3 Two-hand chest pass. Courtesy of the University of Maryland.

To execute a right-hand pass, the ball is held at the right side with the left foot forward and the right foot back. The right hand is behind the ball, fingers spread, with the thumb pointing out, and the left hand is in front of the ball as a guide. The ball is passed by carrying it back to the hip, and then swinging it forward in an arc. The follow-through is made with the palm of the hand up and the fingers pointing in the direction of the pass. This pass may also be made left-handed. A good basketball player will learn to pass with either hand since it is advisable to give the ball maximum protection by passing with the hand next to the player receiving the ball.

For certain situations the bounce pass, the hook pass, the baseball pass, the two-handed overhead, and the off–shoulder passes are utilized. A discussion of these passes as well as certain other advanced skills may be found in the references listed in the bibliography.

Dribble

If a pass opportunity exists, the pass should be made before the dribble. This does not mean that the dribble is not important. The dribble is useful to clear the ball after a rebound, to move away from an eager defensive man who may tie up the ball, to drive around a man for a goal, to set up an offensive play, and to freeze the ball in the stalling game.

There are two main types of dribbles: the low driving dribble and the high hard dribble. The low driving dribble is used when maneuvering near defensive opponents; the high hard dribble is used when a player makes a clear break for the basket with all of the defensive men behind him.

The low driving dribble is executed from a crouched position with either the left or right hand. The player has his weight forward on the balls of his feet, his knees are bent slightly, with his head and eyes up scanning the floor for possible pass opportunities. The fingers are spread over the top of the ball and, with a relaxed, flowing wrist movement, the ball is pushed toward the floor. The ideal height of the dribble is about knee high. The low dribbled ball contacts the floor to the right or left (depending upon which hand the dribbler uses) and not in front of the dribbler.

In the high dribble the ball is dribbled in front of the body, about waist high. The dribbler should use his stronger hand, since speed is essential and defensive men are not in a position to steal the ball. The crouch is not as extreme as that used in the low dribble, however. The player moves at top speed, pushing the ball out in front of him with a flowing wrist motion.

Stopping, Pivoting, Cutting, and Feinting

There are two basic stops made in basketball, the jump or two-foot stop, and the stride or shuffle stop. A good basketball player stops suddenly and will be on balance after he stops, ready to pass, shoot, pivot, or cut. The two-foot or jump stop is executed by keeping the body low, taking a short jump and stopping on both feet with one foot in advance of the other 15 to 18 inches. The stride or shuffle stop is the more common and is executed in two counts. On the first count, the rear foot comes in contact with the floor. On the second count, the front foot is carried forward well out in front of the body for balance and support.

Pivoting is the footwork used along with stops to change or reverse direction of the body. One foot, called the pivot foot, must be kept in contact with the floor at all times. To execute the player should be on the ball of his pivot foot with weight forward, and then by lifting the opposite foot and turning on the pivot point, he may step in any direction. This allows the opportunity for a player to protect the ball and move opposite the defensive man whenever he is closely guarded. This is a very important skill once the dribble has been completed.

Cutting or maneuvering without the ball is another essential skill. Inexperienced players run continuously at the same speed in order to get free for a pass. Short bursts of speed, stops, and quick changes of direction are more effective than merely running at the same speed. Every movement has meaning. A short step or two toward the ball to draw the opponent close and then a quick cut to the goal may result in an easy basket.

Sometimes it is best to cut toward the blind side of the defensive man, especially if his eyes follow the ball in flight. On the other hand, a cut in front of the defensive man may position him behind you, making it difficult for him to cover you defensively.

Feinting is any movement made to draw an opponent off balance or out of position. It may be used to advantage by both an offensive player and a defensive player. A feint may employ the ball, the feet, the hands, the eyes, the head, the shoulders or any combination of these. A feint may be used to get free to shoot, to dribble around an opponent, to elude the defensive man in order to receive a pass from a teammate, or used defensively to throw the opponent off balance.

The defensive man must be guarding closely if a feint or fake is to be successful. To bring the defensive man close it is necessary to look at the basket or fake a shot. Looking at the basket with the ball in shooting position is one of the most neglected fakes in basketball.

Shooting

Shooting is important because the ultimate purpose of the other techniques is to get in a good position to shoot. It is, therefore, best not to shoot from an off-balance position or when closely guarded.

Successful shooting can be learned by every player, although some players have a natural ability to "hit." In all shooting it is important that the player have a good base and be on balance. The ball must be controlled with the pads and tips of the fingers. The shooter should strive for a medium or high trajectory (arch) of the ball, since a ball with a low arch has less chance of rebounding off the rim or backboard into the basket, and is also more easily blocked by the defense. In shooting, the eyes should be fixed on the rim or the "spot" on the backboard. Many shooters fail to follow through to the rim, because they follow the flight of the ball with the eyes. Even after the ball is released, it is important to concentrate with the eyes on the "target."

Lay-up shot. This shot is perhaps the easiest to make since it is taken close to the basket. The lay-up shot may be taken from either the right, left, or directly in front of the basket. In shooting the ball from the right side of the basket, the ball is shot with the right hand, keeping the body between the defensive man and the ball. To shoot the lay-up on the right side, the inside or left foot is used for the takeoff. The right foot is used to get height and maintain body balance. The ball is held in the left hand, with the right hand spread behind the ball. The ball, resting on the pads of the fingers, is carried over the right shoulder. At the height of the jump, the right arm is extended, and the ball is laid up against a spot on the backboard to the right and above the rim. The eyes are focused on this spot throughout the shot. The jump should be a high jump, not a broad jump. After the release of the ball, the player should land on both feet, facing toward the court, on balance, and ready to rebound.

One-hand set shot. For a right-handed shooter the right leg is forward, and pointing toward the basket. The left leg is back, weight being forward on the ball of the right foot. The ball is supported on the left hand, with the right hand behind the ball, fingers spread. As the shot is taken, the ball is carried forward and over the right shoulder. The knees bend slightly as the ball is pushed off the left hand by the right hand, and the eyes are on the rim of the basket. In the follow-through, the arm is extended with the back of the hand toward the basket, the fingers pointing toward the floor. This shot is a lead-up to the jump shot, and should be learned for this purpose if not for outside shooting.

Jump shot. It should be noted that this is one of the best shots in basketball today, and is used by every successful high school, college, and professional player since it is hard to block.

This shot is executed by coming to a quick stop, and bringing both feet together in a jumping position with the knees bent. A right-handed shooter should carry the ball as high as possible over his right shoulder with his left hand supporting the ball. At the height of the jump the wrist and hand should flip the ball toward the basket. The eyes should be on the front edge of the rim, with the follow-through toward the basket (Fig. 4.4).

In addition to the aforementioned, there are other shots that are effective. The post man, with his back to the basket, must develop turning shots, such as the step-away turning push or hook shot, the turning jump shot, and the step-back and turn shot. With the exception of the hook shot these shots are similar to those previously described. The hook shot is similar to the hook pass. The ball is carried on the pads of the fingers, and guided by the

Fig. 4.4 The jump shot. Courtesy of the University of Maryland.

left hand. The almost straight right arm is swung in an arc away from the defensive man.

Defense

Defenses vary so much that coaches do not agree on the basic principles of defense, nor do they accept a basic defensive stance. Most coaches agree, however, that defensive play is more consistent than offensive play, and that a good defense will win games when the team has an off night.

The man-for-man and zone defenses or a combination of these two plus many variations of each have been developed. Regardless of the type of defense used, the individual defensive play involved in playing a man-for-man defense is basic for playing the other types of defense.

Hints to the individual on playing man-for-man defense:

☐ Keep your weight on the balls of the feet. Be low and on balance ready to move in any direction.

☐ Concentrate on the hips and midsection of your opponent when he has the ball.

☐ Be alert for screens. Watch not only your opponent, but also the other players in the area and the ball.

Fig. 4.5 Basic defensive stance. Courtesy of the University of Maryland.

□ Stay between your man and the basket; when in close to the basket, however, be on the side of your opponent next to the ball.

□ Talk to your teammates. Let them know what the opposition is doing, and what you are going to do.

□ Don't cross your feet, but use a shuffle movement to stay with your opponent.

□ Never stand flat-footed. Try to feint your opponent into making the move you want.

□ Stay loose on a player with the ball who has not dribbled; tighten up and rush a player after he has dribbled.

□ Never rest on defense. Rest on offense while two or three of your teammates are running an option.

□ Study your opponent. Learn his strengths and weaknesses.

□ Do not lunge at your opponent's fake or leave your feet.

□ Check your opponent when a shot is taken. Keep him behind you so you can rebound the ball.

When playing an opponent in a straight man-for-man defense, the defensive player must always *stay* with his man wherever he goes. If, for example, he is confronted by a screening situation, an attempt must be made to go over-the-top of the screen (Fig. 4.6).

Regardless of the effort made by the defensive player, however, there will be situations when he cannot get over-the-top of a screen and, therefore,

X = Defensive player
O = Offensive player
⌇⌇➤ = Dribble
──➤ = Player movement without ball
──┤ = Screen

Fig. 4.6 Player O_1 moves in a position to screen player X_2. Player X_2 must step forward and go over the screen in order to stay with his man.

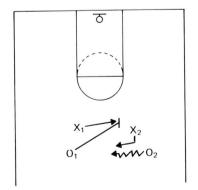

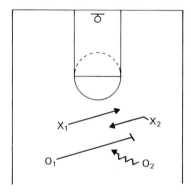

Fig. 4.7 Player O_1 moves in a position to screen player X_2. Player X_2 must slide behind the screen in order to stay with his man. Player X_1 must allow him sufficient room to make this move.

Fig. 4.8 Player O_1 moves in a position to screen player X_2. Player O_2 starts a dribble around the screen, and O_1 rolls toward the basket leaving player X_2 out of the play. Player X_1 must then switch from guarding O_1 and attempt to stop player O_2 from going in for an easy shot.

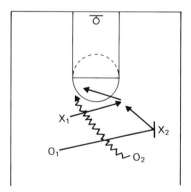

must slide behind the screen. This move is illustrated in Fig. 4.7. In this situation the defensive player slides behind the man setting the screen in an attempt to recover and gain a good defensive position on his opponent.

In certain situations it will be impossible to *stay* or *slide* with the opponent and when it will be necessary for the defensive player guarding the man setting the screen to leave his man and continue his defensive play by guarding the man with the ball. This is called a *switch* and is depicted in Fig. 4.8. Since the switch often creates a two-on-one situation in favor of the offense, it should be avoided whenever possible.

This brief presentation of basketball is at best only an introduction to one of the most popular sport activities in the world today.

REFERENCES

Auerbach, A. 1957. *Basketball for the player, the fan, and the coach.* New York: Pocket Books.

Baisi, N. 1961. *Coaching the zone and man-to-man pressing defenses.* Englewood Cliffs, N.J.: Prentice-Hall.

Bates, J. D. Daddy of the cage game. In *Basketball was born here.* Springfield, Mass.: Naismith Basketball Hall of Fame.

Brown, L. 1965. *Offensive and defensive drills for winning basketball.* Englewood Cliffs, N.J.: Prentice-Hall.

Ceravalo, J. J. 1970. *The modern 1–4 basketball offense.* West Nyack, N.Y.: Parker.

Cousy, B. 1970. *Basketball concepts and techniques.* Boston, Mass.: Allyn and Bacon.

Julian, A. F. 1960. Doggie. In *Bread-and-butter basketball.* Englewood Cliffs, N.J.: Prentice-Hall.

Knudson, T. A. 1972. The evolution of men's amateur basketball rules and the effect upon the game. Unpublished doctor of physical education dissertation. Springfield, Mass.: Springfield College.

McGuire, F. 1959. *Defensive basketball.* Englewood Cliffs, N.J.: Prentice-Hall.

————— 1959. *Offensive basketball.* Englewood Cliffs, N.J.: Prentice-Hall.

Pinholster, G. F. 1958. *Encyclopedia of basketball drills.* Englewood Cliffs, N.J.: Prentice-Hall.

Rupp, A. F. 1967. *Rupp's basketball guide book.* New York: McGraw-Hill.

————— 1957. *Rupp's championship basketball.* (2nd ed.) Englewood Cliffs, N.J.: Prentice-Hall.

Steitz, E. S. (ed.). *The official national collegiate athletic association basketball rules.* Phoenix, Arizona: College Athletics Publishing Service, Annual Publication.

Wilkes, G. 1963. *Basketball coach's complete handbook.* Englewood Cliffs, N.J.: Prentice-Hall.

————— 1959. *Winning basketball strategy.* Englewood Cliffs, N.J.: Prentice-Hall.

Winter, F. 1962. *The triple-post offense.* Englewood Cliffs, N.J.: Prentice-Hall.

Wooden, J. 1966. *Practical modern basketball.* New York: Ronald.

Women's Basketball

Judith K. Devine

THE GAME

Women's basketball is a court game played between two teams of five players each. The object of the game is for the members of one team to maneuver a standard-sized ball among them until such time as any one of the players feels she is close enough to put the ball into the appropriate basket. The opposing team members attempt to prevent the scoring of a goal by placing themselves in strategic positions to intercept passes, guard free players, block tries for goals or by forcing the offensive or attacking team into making ball-control errors or rule infractions.

An official begins the game at center court by throwing the ball upward between two opposing players. Each player attempts to tap the ball to a teammate. If the team which gains possession of the ball is successful in maneuvering the ball toward its opponents' goal and scoring, two points are awarded that team and play is restarted by giving the ball to the nonscoring team out of bounds at the end line. Bodily contact during play is penalized by awarding the fouled player one or two free throws. Each successful conversion of such an attempt scores one point.

The number and length of playing periods vary according to the level of play. College level players play two twenty-minute periods while at the secondary level there are four periods of eight minutes each.

Fig. 4.9 An official begins the game at center court by throwing the ball upward between two opposing players. Courtesy of *JOPER.*

Although once vastly different, the rules for men's and women's basketball are almost identical today. Current women's rules may be obtained from the National Association for Girls and Women in Sport, the AAU, or the National Federation of High School Athletic Associations.

Basketball is a popular game with girls and women throughout the nation and the world. It requires minimum facilities and equipment, can be played by any number of participants, is easily adapted to varying age or ability groups, demands only a basic understanding of rules, and contains skills which may be quickly learned. There are few Americans today who do not have some familiarity with the game.

Basketball is among the more vigorous of the sports engaged in by women. The continuous movement and action require players to achieve and maintain high levels of muscular strength and cardiorespiratory endurance. Contrary to the historic belief that women could not handle the physiological or emotional stress of basketball, modern research has shown the female athlete to be as capable as her male counterpart in adapting to the demands of the game.

EARLY BEGINNINGS

Within weeks after Dr. James Naismith invented and introduced the new athletic activity of basketball to the young men of Springfield College, a small group of college women began to play the game. In spite of the handicaps of long dresses and bustles, typical of the 1890s, the women were equally enthralled with the challenge of shooting a ball into a peach basket. March of 1892 marked the date of the first scheduled competition in women's basketball as a group of young teachers, stenographers, and faculty wives met for a contest at Springfield following a men's tournament (Naismith 1941, p. 162).

The game's popularity spread quickly when directors of physical training for women introduced basketball as a substitute activity for dumbbell exercises and rowing-machine programs. Berenson (1894, p. 6), in expressing a common opinion of the time, wrote that "women have long felt the need of some sport that would combine both the physical development of gymnastics and the abandon and delight of true play." At the turn of the century, basketball had become the most popular sport activity for American college women (Ainsworth 1930, pp. 29–30; Thompson 1903, p. 241).

Almost immediately, basketball for women began to differ from basketball for men. The men's rules were thought to allow too much roughness and to encourage the development of undesirable characteristics such as aggressiveness.

From the beginning, rules were a point of contention among leaders of the women's game. Each locality and normal school adopted its own set of rule modifications, making interschool competition almost impossible. In 1898, an attempt was made to standardize the rules.

Modifications reflected the philosophy that in addition to causing roughness, the original rules placed too much emotional strain on players and overstressed physiological limitations. Hence, the court was divided into three equal areas with one to three players assigned to each area, players were no longer allowed to bat or snatch the ball from the hands of an opposing player, a player could not use more than a three-bounce dribble, and no one was permitted to hold the ball longer than three seconds (Naismith 1941, pp. 162–166).

In spite of the early attempt to standardize rules, variations still exist. A major controversy erupted in the 1920s between the two main governing organizations for women's basketball, the AAU and the Division of Girls' and Women's Sports (DGWS). The "philosophical" differences between the leaders of the two organizations concerning standards related to the welfare of the participants stifled the growth of basketball for women for the next four decades. It was not until the late 1950s that the two groups considered reconciliation, and not until the 1964–65 basketball season that identical rules were finally adopted. The joint efforts of the AAU and DGWS have had the greatest impact on the continuing evolution of women's basketball. From a static nine-player game, basketball has been transformed into a highly mobile five-player activity characterized by high levels of individual skill and finesse. The advanced and sophisticated techniques and strategies evidenced in men's basketball have now become an integral part of women's basketball. As an additional step in enhancing basketball's popularity and universal appeal, the early 1970s saw the adoption of identical rules for boys and girls at the interscholastic level and, with only a few minor exceptions, the adoption of identical rules for men and women at the college level. As both a spectator and participant sport, basketball in general and women's basketball in particular is experiencing unparalleled growth.

TERMINOLOGY

Assist A pass to a teammate which leads to an immediate score.

Backboard The rectangular or fan-shaped surface to which the rim is attached. It is usually made of fiberglass.

Backcourt The half court area containing the goal for which the opponents are shooting.

Backdoor An offensive maneuver involving a cut behind the defender toward the basket.

Baselines The shorter or end boundary lines.

Blocking A foul involving body contact which impedes the progress of an opponent with or without the ball.

Blocking out A body positioning maneuver by defensive players to keep offensive players behind them and away from good rebounding position.

Charging A foul involving body contact resulting from a player with the ball moving into an opponent whose position is established.

Cut A quick movement, often following a fake in the opposite direction into an unguarded area.

Defense The team not in possession of the ball.

Dribble A skill in which the player gives impetus to the ball one or more times causing it to rebound from the floor. Since the ball cannot be carried while moving, the dribble provides a legal manner of moving the ball to various locations on the court.

Drive An offensive maneuver involving quick acceleration while dribbling toward the basket.

Fake or feint A pretense of one movement, followed by a different movement or direction.

Fast break An offensive maneuver requiring rapid movement of ball and players from the defensive to the offensive end of the floor with the intent of scoring before the defensive players can position themselves.

Foul A rule infringement for which one or more free throws are awarded.

Free lance A nonpatterned style of offense giving players complete freedom of choice in play development.

Free throw An unguarded shot at goal from immediately behind the free-throw line. Free throws are awarded to the opposing team after fouls have been committed against them.

Frontcourt The half court area containing the goal for which the team is shooting.

Give and go An offensive maneuver involving two players; one player passes to her teammate, then cuts for the basket, anticipating a return pass.

Goal A successful scoring attempt; also the 10' high rim and attached net through which the ball must pass.

Jump ball or tie ball Tossing the ball up between two opponents to start play initially or to restart play after neither or both teams gain possession of it.

Man-to-man defense A defensive system in which each player is assigned to guard a specific opposing player.

Offense The team in possession of the ball; also, a pattern of play used by a team in an attempt to score.

One-on-one An example of the ratio of offensive players to defensive players. An advantage is gained by one team when the ratio becomes uneven, like two-on-one, three-on-two, etc.

Outlet pass The initial clearing pass away from the goal area following a rebound. The pass is usually directed toward the sideline.

Pattern play A preplanned system of offensive play development.

Pick-screen A legal method of blocking or delaying the progress of an opponent on the defending team.

Point An area of the court just outside the restraining circle at either end of the court.

Post-pivot An offensive player who plays nearest the free-throw lane.

Press Aggressive defensive maneuver of continued and unyielding harassment over the space of a half, three-quarter, or full court area. The purpose of a press is to force opponents into committing errors.

Rebound The act of catching a ball which misses the goal but strikes the rim or backboard and caroms back toward the floor.

Switch A momentary reassignment of defensive responsibility.

Traveling Illegal movement while in possession of the ball.

Turnover Loss of ball possession due to an error or violation.

Violation An infraction of the rules for which the ball is awarded to the opposing team out of bounds.

Wing An area of the court just beyond the free-throw line extended.

Zone defense A defensive system which makes covering assignments for specific court areas.

FUNDAMENTALS

Since basketball is a continuous action game, players must constantly make the transition between offensive and defensive play. Attention to the proper body stance is the first step in attaining proficiency with either individual offensive or defensive fundamentals.

Offensive Stance

The basic offensive stance suggests that the head be up, body and feet facing the goal with knees flexed. The body should be balanced with feet shoulder-width apart and the ball held in front of the body using the fleshy pads of the fingers and thumbs on both hands. This position allows the offensive player three options: to pass, to dribble, to shoot.

Defensive Stance

The basic defensive stance suggests that the head be up, body and feet facing the player being guarded. The knees should be flexed to such a degree that the body is in a low crouch position, hips tucked under (more commonly referenced as "tail down"), weight evenly distributed over both feet which are shoulder-width apart and staggered with one foot forward. Arms are positioned so that one is usually up and forward while the other is either down and forward or extended to one side. Movement is possible while maintaining this position through utilization of a side-stride "shuffle-and-close" step. Correct defensive footwork eliminates the fundamental error of crossing the feet and legs while moving.

If a defender is guarding an opponent with the ball, the proximity to that opponent is determined by court position and the opponent's unused offensive options. An opponent in scoring position is guarded more closely than one out of shooting range. A player who has not used the dribbling option should be guarded more loosely than one who has completed the dribble so as to prevent the offensive player from driving in for an easy score. A player who has already dribbled should be defended tightly in hopes of preventing a shot or causing the player to throw a poor pass.

If a defender is guarding an opponent without the ball, she should try to minimize that player's offensive contribution. Her first task is to establish a position which will allow her to focus in all instances on both the ball and her opponent. Next she should continually readjust that position so that she remains between the offensive player and the goal at all times. By keeping an arm extended in front of the player as she moves about the court, the passing lane to that player is closed and the defender has been successful in negating the offensive player's effectiveness.

Passing—Receiving

Maneuvering the ball around the court by throwing or passing it among teammates is one of the rudimentary elements of basketball. Successful passes depend on the choice of pass and execution of the skill as well as the teammates' ability to receive the ball successfully.

Passes should generally be aimed at the receiver's chest level, and directed to the side of the body away from the defender. Passes to moving teammates should be directed ahead of the player so no hesitation in movement results. A player should usually be encouraged to face in the direction of the intended pass, regardless of preceding moves. Passing effectiveness is increased if the player is capable of executing several types of passes, and is adept at faking which may further deceive the opponent.

In anticipation of receiving a thrown ball, the hands and arms should extend forward toward the ball, the fingers should be slightly flexed, spread and relaxed, and hands should be held parallel to one another. To absorb force at impact, one should "give" with the ball by allowing the hands to be pushed slightly back toward the body as the arms bend at the elbows and shoulders.

Chest pass. From the offensive stance, the ball is moved to chest height with fingers spread along the side of the ball and thumbs behind the ball. A simultaneous action then occurs involving a step onto the forward foot as the arms begin extending forward toward the target. The hands rotate inward and downward as the arms reach full extension and the wrists uncock. While this pass is one of the more basic passing options, women possessing little arm strength will enjoy only minimal success when trying to pass at a distance of more than ten to fifteen feet.

Bounce pass. The bounce pass is a chest pass variation. From the chest pass ready position, the ball is angled in a sharp, downward direction toward the floor at such an angle that it will rebound upward into the hands of a teammate. This pass adds variety to the passing options, while contributing deceptiveness in technique.

Two-hand overhead pass. From the basic offensive stance, the ball is moved overhead by extending the arms upward at the shoulder, bending the elbows and cocking the wrists by drawing the fingers back. The pass is executed as the elbows extend, the wrists snap forward, and a forward step is taken in the direction of the pass. The overhead pass has particular use for taller players, or for any player desiring to pass over the head of an opponent.

Dribbling

When there are no passing options open, a player may use the dribble to move the ball down court. The dribble is also used when driving toward the basket for a score, when trying to "outposition" an opponent, or when trying to clear from a congested area. Aimless use of the dribble interferes with the offensive tempo of the game, wastes valuable time and effort.

From the basic offensive stance, the ball is bounced repeatedly from the floor with one hand. The opposite arm is held up and away from the body to protect the ball from a defender. The dribbling hand and forearm work in a pumping action against the ball to cause and control the continuous bouncing action. Only the fingers contact the ball. The palm should be kept off the ball.

The height of the dribble is dependent upon the task at hand. A low or control dribble is used in instances when one is trying to protect the ball while maneuvering for a shot or pass. A high or speed dribble is used when one is not in close proximity to defenders and there is a need to cover distance rapidly. In the high dribble the ball may be pushed forward and downward, thus enabling the player to take several running steps between bounces. The effectiveness of dribbling may be increased by learning to use either hand, by not watching the ball, and by becoming proficient in changing pace and direction.

Shooting

The primary objective on offense is to score. The type of shot a player selects will be determined by that player's proximity to the basket, the position of defenders, and the player's proficiency with various shooting skills. The successful shooter is one who masters the technique of shooting, remains relaxed and confident and lets nothing interfere with her concentration.

Lay-up. The lay-up is a shot completed while moving towards the basket at an angle following a drive, and one which is intentionally "banked" or rebounded off the backboard and into the basket. Following the completion of the last dribble, the weight is shifted to the foot opposite the shooting hand, and a jump is initiated from this leg. The opposite knee is driven upward to provide added height. The ball is carried with both hands to a position above and in front of the head. From here the ball is released to the shooting hand which continues carrying the ball upward through full arm extension. From this one-arm support position, the wrist uncocks providing the needed force to propel the ball to a point on the backboard three to four inches above the rim. The exact ball placement is determined by the angle of approach and the fact that the ball will rebound at the same angle at which it is placed. As the ball is released, the entire body should be fully extended.

One-hand set shot. To perform the most fundamental of basketball shots, the fingertips of both hands are placed on the ball with the preferred shooting hand behind the ball and the supporting hand positioned on the side of the ball. The shot is executed from a stationary position with knees flexed, feet shoulder-width apart, the foot on the side of the preferred shooting hand slightly forward, and eyes focused on the rim. The ball is moved to a position between chin and shoulder height with the shooting elbow pointing toward the basket. As the knees straighten from their flexed position, the ball starts

Fig. 4.10 The jump shot is probably the most commonly used shot in basketball. Courtesy of Luther College.

upward and the wrist of the shooting hand cocks. The supporting hand is withdrawn, the shooting arm fully extends, the wrist uncocks and backspin is created as the ball is released from the tips of the fingers. The total body follows through in upward extension, being careful not to fall or lean forward into potential defenders.

Jump shot. The jump shot, because of the versatility it permits, is probably the most commonly used shot in basketball. The shot is similar to the one-hand set shot except that the ball normally is held slightly higher initially and the release of the ball is delayed until the player has jumped into the air. From a deep knee bend crouch position, the player springs upward off the balls of the feet while simultaneously raising the ball and cocking the wrist. Just after the feet leave the floor, the supporting hand is withdrawn and the shooting hand positions the ball above the head. At the height of the jump, the arm straightens and the wrist uncocks thus pushing the ball upward and forward toward the goal. The body is fully extended at the release.

The jump shot has revolutionized the game of basketball. It has provided a means of shooting over an opponent, and can be executed immediately following almost any body motion such as a fake, dribble, pivot, or pass reception. The level of release of the shot, the immediacy with which the shot may be executed, and the lack of preparatory movement necessary to complete the skill all make the jump shot most difficult to defend.

Hook shot. A player with her back to the basket who receives a pass within scoring range may opt to use a hook shot which is almost impossible to defend. From the offensive stance the player drops one foot back toward the goal while simultaneously sighting the rim. As the body rotates, the weight is shifted over the back foot and the ball is raised with both hands from waist level to shoulder height. The ball is then rolled over onto the shooting hand. The supporting hand withdraws from the ball as the shooting arm and hand extend outward while balancing the ball. As the body continues its rotation toward the goal, the knee of the nontakeoff leg is raised forward and upward causing the player to spring into the air. The straightened shooting arm lifts directly overhead in a pendular or circular motion. The ball is released off the fingertips when the arm, in its forward swing, nears the side of the head. The wrist flexes on the follow-through and the continued body rotation places the player in a position facing the basket. The high level of release and position of the ball on the side of the body away from the defender throughout the execution of the shot make this shot very effective.

Pivot

A pivot is a fundamental skill which enhances player movement options by providing a legal method of turning in place while holding the ball. The pivot or turn is executed by keeping one foot in contact with the floor. The nonpivot foot may step in any direction to complete the desired turn. The pivot is most frequently utilized to turn away from a defender by placing the offensive player's body between the ball and the opponent.

Fake or Feint

A fake or feint is a deceptive move which precedes another move of a different pace or in a different direction. The purpose of a fake is to tempt the opponent to react or commit herself. Hopefully this reaction will momentarily draw the opponent out of position permitting unhindered execution of any chosen maneuver. Fakes may be made with the eyes, hands and arms, head, foot or with the ball.

Blocking Out

Effectiveness as a rebounder may be enhanced if an individual can position herself in a more advantageous rebounding position than her opponent. After each scoring attempt and anticipated rebound, all defensive players should make a conscientious effort to alter or eliminate the offensive player's pathway to the basket. This is accomplished by determining the direction the player has chosen and pivoting into that pathway. The defender's objective is to remain between the opponent and the goal while maintaining the most advantageous rebounding position. After the pathway has been blocked, the defender should prepare herself for the rebound.

Rebound

The ability to out-rebound opponents is considered a most essential contribution to a team's success. Individual rebounding skill is a combination of proper technique, timing, and positioning. After blocking out, the body is readied for the rebound. The knees are flexed with weight balanced over both feet, the arms are up and the eyes are focused on the goal. As the ball begins its downward fall, the player should jump high into the air assisted by a lifting upward arm swing. In full body extension, the player reaches for the ball with fingers spread and ready to grasp the ball firmly at a position above and in front of the head. As one descends from the jump, the ball is pulled downward to chest level. The player should land with feet at least shoulder-width apart, and body in a partially piked position. For additional ball protection, the elbows are held out away from the body. Immediately the player should proceed with one of the three appropriate options which follow a rebound. She should try to shoot if on offense, look for an available receiver for an outlet pass, or dribble to a less congested area.

TACTICS AND STRATEGY

Offense

The best offense is one which is simple enough to be thoroughly understood and mastered by the players, yet effective enough to combat the opponent's defense. The goal of all offensive strategy is to create scoring opportunities for oneself or others. Whether the chosen offense is a free-lance style of play in which there are no preestablished patterns of play development or a pattern offense in which players follow a preplanned system of play development, there are basic principles of offense which deserve attention. A combination of proficient execution of offensive fundamentals and adherence to the offensive principles which follow form the basis for effective maneuvering while a team is attempting to score.

Any strategy must consider the strengths and weaknesses of the individuals involved and plan to make the best use of the personnel. Of the five players on a team, two are usually designated as guards, two as forwards, and one as a pivot player. The guards are usually the two shorter players and are most often the ones who possess the greatest amounts of quickness, agility, and speed. A guard should be an excellent dribbler and ball handler and should have the ability to cut, fake, drive, and score. The guards are usually the players who bring the ball downcourt from the defensive end and the ones who initiate the offensive plays. Forwards are taller, stronger players who

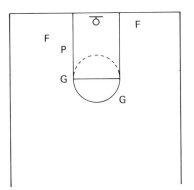

Fig. 4.11 The goal of all offensive strategy is to create scoring opportunities for oneself and others. Courtesy of Southern Connecticut State College.

must be good passers and receivers, be able to drive and cut, possess good outside and corner shots, and be aggressive in rebounding. The pivot player is usually the tallest player and best jumper on the team, is strong but mobile, is not easily intimidated by the pressure and congestion in the lane area while shooting, passing or receiving, is a strong rebounder, and has mastery of the hook shot and a one- or two-handed "tip in" shot. Figures 4.12–4.14 show the deployment of the guards, forwards, and pivot players in each of the three most common initial offensive alignments seen today.

From any of these offensive alignments, play commences. If possible the offensive player tries to maneuver about the court until she has created a

Fig. 4.12 Single post (2 guards, 2 forwards, 1 pivot).

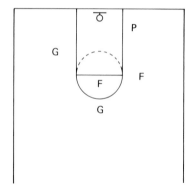

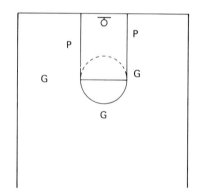

Fig. 4.13 Tandem or 1-3-1 (1 point guard, 2 wings, 1 guard and 1 forward, 2 pivots—1 high, 1 low).

Fig. 4.14 Double post (3 guards, 2 pivots).

situation where only one defender stands in her pathway to the goal. If this one-on-one situation is achieved, the offensive player uses any combination of fakes and other individual offensive fundamentals to outmaneuver her defender and attempt to score. Quite often the ability of the defender prohibits this offensive maneuverability and help must be sought. The aforementioned dilemma has given rise to a series of two-player patterns which form the basis for almost all offensive strategy.

The "give-and-go" play is a two-player tactic utilizing the fundamental skills of passing, receiving, faking, and cutting. In Fig. 4.15, 1 passes or "gives" the ball to 2, fakes and cuts or "goes" behind X, and receives a

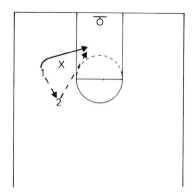

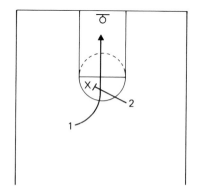

Fig. 4.15 Give-and-go play.

Fig. 4.16 Screen or pick technique.

return pass from 2. This simple technique may be executed by any two team-mates from any position on the court.

A "screen or pick" is a noncontact technique used to block the progress of a defender by utilizing the body as a partition between a teammate with the ball and her opponent. The momentary impediment gives the teammate an opportunity for an unhindered shot or an unobstructed drive toward the goal. In Fig. 4.16, 2 passes to 1, then moves to set a screen on 1's defender. After the screen is set, 1 drives past 2 toward the goal leaving the defender blocked out of position to interfere. Like the give and go, screens may be set by any player against any teammate's defender.

The "split-the-post" play involves three members of the offensive team. In Fig. 4.17, the pivot, in a high-post position, receives a pass from 3 who

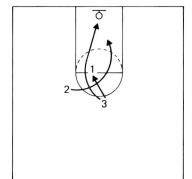

Fig. 4.17 Split-the-post play.

immediately cuts in front of the pivot and toward the basket. Player 2 imme-diately follows by cutting in front of the pivot to the opposite side. As these two players complete a scissors pattern around the pivot player, four options become available. The pivot may pass to 2, pass to 3, turn and shoot or drive down the lane herself.

Any style of offensive play, even the most highly structured, should allow players to take advantage of any scoring opportunity which is created. It is not necessary to complete the entire sequence of a patterned play if a player recognizes or creates a defensive error which will permit an open shot.

Players should also be encouraged to pass the ball rapidly when on of-fense. Good defensive players shift on every pass of the ball, and since the ball can be moved more rapidly than a player can, a succession of quick passes will ultimately catch a defender out of position.

A spread offense is a more effective means of overcoming the opponents' defense than one which places players in close proximity to one another. "Bunching" allows a single defender to guard more than one player and lets the defense assist one another in covering tactics. Players who remain spread force the defense into a one-on-one situation thereby allowing the employment of offensive cutting, driving, and screening maneuvers.

As with all game strategies, there are tactics which should be avoided in basketball as well as ones which should be utilized: (1) Cross-court passes are risky at any time because they are easy to intercept. (2) Coming to a stationary position after dribbling but before passing allows the defender to close in and guard the passing attempt also, so players must be taught to pass off a dribble. (3) Players who lose sight of the ball by turning their back on it become momentarily uninvolved in the action. A player should be taught to position herself in such a way that she always has her opponent *and* the ball in view. (4) Unnecessary dribbling stagnates the offense. Dribbling should be permitted only when no passing options are open. (5) When without the ball on offense, a player should use fakes and cuts to keep her defender occupied and unavailable to assist other defenders.

Defense

A good defensive effort provides relentless harassment of opponents, forces the offense to take poor shots, and tries to cause numerous offensive errors or turnovers. There are two systems of defense, man-to-man which is player-oriented, and zone which is ball- and area-oriented. Once players become proficient with individual defensive fundamentals, the man-to-man system seems to be the less permeable defense. In man-to-man defense, each player is assigned to guard a specific opponent. The assignments should be made carefully with consideration being given to comparable height, position, style, and ability. After the transition to the defensive end of the court, defensive players "pick up" their assigned opponent with active defense when the opponent reaches a position about three feet outside the defensive restraining circle. The defender then attempts to maintain a position no greater than three feet from her opponent regardless of the offensive player's maneuverability. Since the offense's weapons against a man-to-man defense are composed of screens, cuts, and drives, the defender must be cognizant of these tactics and able to minimize her opponent's effectiveness.

Two variations of the man-to-man defense are the pressing man-to-man and the sagging man-to-man. A pressing man-to-man requires pressure on the offensive players over a greater area of the court such as a half-court press, three-quarter-court press or full-court press. These are risky defenses in that they offer the offense much more room for maneuvering, but when a team is behind, the pressure and change of tempo may be effective in causing a great many offensive turnovers.

The sagging man-to-man defense is a means of providing help to those defenders nearest the ball by those defenders farthest away from the ball. In Fig. 4.18, defenders 1 and 3 are playing on the side opposite the ball's location. They have "sagged" into the middle to provide a second line of

Fig. 4.18 Sagging defense.

defense should an offensive player successfully drive around defender 2, 4, or 5.

Another type of defense is the zone defense. In a zone each player is assigned responsibility for a specific court area. Any offensive player who enters that zone is defended man-to-man, but when the offensive player leaves that zone, the defender has no further responsibility for her.

Several different patterns of zone defense may be seen in basketball today. Each has its own areas of strong coverage and weak coverage and should be selected on the basis of its ability to minimize the opponent's offensive effectiveness. Figures 4.19–4.23 depict the initial positions of defensive players for some of the more common zone defenses.

Man-to-man defense is the preferred defense for most advanced-level players. Its advantages are immediate player accountability, the opportunity to match players of similar attributes, and the fact that no one area of the court is ever left momentarily uncovered. The disadvantage lies in the fact that if a defender is outmaneuvered there is little if any help to prevent the opponent from scoring.

Zone defenses may be played effectively by players of lesser ability, may be used readily against poor passing teams, provide the best rebounding

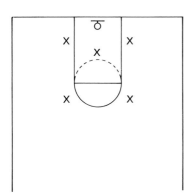

Fig. 4.19 Zone defense: 2-1-2.

Fig. 4.20 Zone defense: 1-2-2.

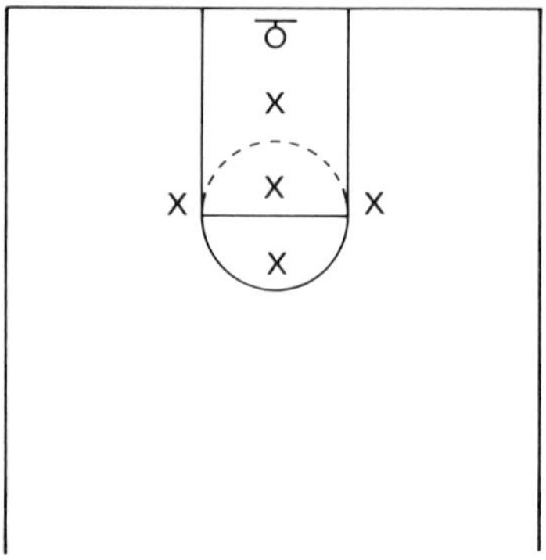

Fig. 4.21 Zone defense: 1-3-1.

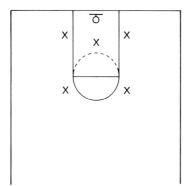

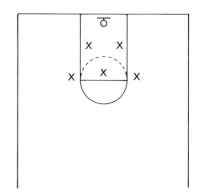

Fig. 4.22 Zone defense: 2-3.

Fig. 4.23 Zone defense: 3-2.

strength because of player positioning, provide a system of coverage for out-maneuvered defenders, and can be adjusted or altered according to the offense's preferred shooting areas. The disadvantages are its ineffectiveness against strong outside shooters, the possible mismatches of taller players playing against shorter players, and the inherent lack of coverage in the "suture" area between each player's zone.

As with offense there are some basic principles of defensive play. In addition to proper stance and footwork, the hands should be kept up to discourage overhead passes, defenders must be encouraged to talk to team-mates signalling screens or player movement behind a defender, and all must learn to anticipate the offensive team's actions. Each defender should close in quickly on an opponent with the ball, should sag off toward the basket when the ball is thrown, and should be ready and willing to cover for players who have been outmaneuvered. Like the offense, a team's defense is only as strong as the individual talents of its members.

TEACHING EFFECTIVENESS

Teaching the elements of basketball, like teaching any physical skill, can be challenging and rewarding. The most successful teacher is the one who is well versed in the game's repertoire of skills, has the ability to critically analyze skill performance, is cognizant of the strategies which may be employed and can anticipate the problems of beginners.

Familiarity with all the skills of the game aids the teacher in providing learning experiences for all students regardless of their previous progress. A typical class may be found to contain many different psychomotor proficiencies, and a good teacher can adjust the class environment to reflect those differences in achievement. The entire class may be subgrouped into beginning, intermediate, and advanced levels within each lesson and all students challenged and motivated by the material presented.

A teacher adept at skill analysis can do much to speed the progress of a student's learning. One who can focus on errors in performance and provide corrective measures can be an invaluable contributor to the overall task of skill development.

A thorough understanding of the game's strategies enables the teacher to introduce team play concomitant with individual skill. As players become more proficient in individual fundamentals, their ability to utilize more complex strategy also increases. A good teacher can recognize this student readiness and can plan for the appropriate blend.

Fig. 4.24 A teacher adept at skill analysis can do much to speed the progress of a student's learning. Courtesy of California State College at Fullerton.

Those who have had considerable experience teaching beginners have recognized a variety of problems which may be anticipated. Awareness of these problems prior to the instructional presentation may enhance the teaching by providing guidance during lesson planning. Problems one should expect are excessive use of the dribble, poor passing, poor shooting in terms of technique and choice of shot, poor body balance and footwork leading to poor defensive positioning, little if any movement by players on offense, poor timing overall, and excessive fouling.

Classroom Organization and Teaching Techniques

Attention to the following may enhance the learning environment during the presentation of basketball.

1. An attempt should be made to provide for some method of individualized instruction. It would seem that utmost satisfaction might be gained if students are allowed to progress at their own rate.

2. Enough equipment should be provided so that there is at least one ball for every two students. If it is impossible to provide this many basketballs, any ball of similar size will suffice in the initial learning stages. One might supplement the available basketballs with volleyballs, soccer balls, or playground balls.

3. Groups should be kept small enough so that students are afforded maximum practice opportunities. Limit groups to three or four students. This helps to ensure adequate use of practice time and enables students to avoid standing in line waiting for a turn.

4. Drills should focus on the fundamentals of the game and should be as gamelike as possible. A one-on-one situation is much more desirable for practicing offensive maneuvers than are uncontested individual movement and shooting.

5. Limited facilities should not alter the amount of material which may be covered in the presentation. Lanes and restraining circles may be drawn or taped on any floor space and wall targets or artificial goals (wastebaskets, hula hoops, rope) will suffice if official goals are not available.

6. To ask players to know and understand the play of the pivot, forward, and guard positions is unrealistic. Even the most talented student will need instruction to achieve this goal. Students should be permitted to select the position of their choice early in the learning experience, then should be given practice drills specific to that position. Switching of position should occur only when a student is unsuccessful in the position of her initial choice.

7. Rules should be presented only as they are required by the level of play or for the maintenance of safety. Detailed rules should be omitted unless understanding them is vital to the desired performance. It seems unnecessary to ask beginning basketball students to learn court dimensions, officiating techniques, specific timing regulations, or the complex procedural aspects following some rule infractions.

8. Initial instructions in team offense should be completed without the presence of an opposing defense and vice versa. When the opposing team members are finally added, they should act in a passive rather than active role until their counterparts experience success with the lesson.

9. Teaching man-to-man defense before introducing any other type stresses to players that it is people who need to be guarded, not floor area. Individual defensive fundamentals are given considerably more attention in man-to-man defense than in zone defense, and it is these fundamentals which serve as the basis for all defensive play.

10. The use of various audiovisual aids should not be overlooked in teaching basketball. Of particular help are films, film loops, and videotapes.

11. Student progress should be measured and recorded continually throughout the unit. A determination needs to be made concerning the appropriateness of self-evaluation, peer-evaluation, or instructor-evaluation techniques, or any combination of these. The intent of the evaluation should be to measure each student's progress against the total amount of material to be learned, not to measure her progress against that of her peers.

12. Establishing a progression for presentation of skills should take into account these three questions:
    a) What are the essential skills one must learn before being able to play the most elementary form of a game? (Pass, catch, simple shot)
    b) What skills serve as foundational techniques for other skills? (One-hand set shot should precede a jump shot)
    c) What skills can be learned by students at this level? (All students could be taught the dribble while only very advanced students should be taught a behind-the-back dribble.)

13. Except for some contribution to conditioning and for practice of the fast-break offense, one must question the value of exclusive full-court scrimmage. Half-court scrimmage allows more time to be spent on the two main elements of basketball, offense and defense, and dispenses with the considerable time spent on the less important transition phase between the two.

Unusual Features

The overall intent of the philosophy which established basketball as essentially a noncontact sport is generally accepted by competitors in the game. In formal competition, players who are found to be guilty of causing more than incidental contact raise one hand overhead to clarify for scorers, teams, and spectators to whom the foul should be charged. In informal play, the custom is for the player who commits a contact foul to verbally admit the error, in which case the ball is automatically awarded to the opposing team. In both formal and informal play participants are encouraged to utilize "honor calls" on out-of-bounds balls.

The start of each playing period is usually preceded by a handshake between opponents. Ideal sportsmanship may be exhibited during a game when both teams make acknowledgment of an unusually fine play. The conclusion of a women's game is almost always characterized by a complimentary team cheer for the opponents and an expression of appreciation to the officials. Players and coaches from opposing teams usually intermingle informally after the contest, then adjourn from the playing court to a lounge or reception area for a planned but casual social. The practice of socializing with opposing teams has contributed greatly toward establishing many warm and rewarding friendships among competitors.

Equipment

An official basketball court measures 94' by 50' with an overhead requirement of at least 22' and an out of bounds clearance of at least 10'. Figure 4.25 provides information on court markings.

Backboards are usually made of glass but wood and metal are also commonly used. The backboard must be either rectangular in shape or fan shaped.

The basket or goal is attached to the center of the backboard so that the rim projects outward ten feet above the floor. A two-foot-long white net is suspended from the 18" diameter rim.

The ball is round with a leather or rubber covering. The weight of the ball should be between 20 and 22 ounces, and should measure 29½ to 30¼" in circumference.

Electric timing and scoring devices are required for official play. The 30 second shot timer is a requirement for women's collegiate level play.

The majority of basketball players participate without any extraneous equipment. Some may choose to wear knee pads or wrist bands.

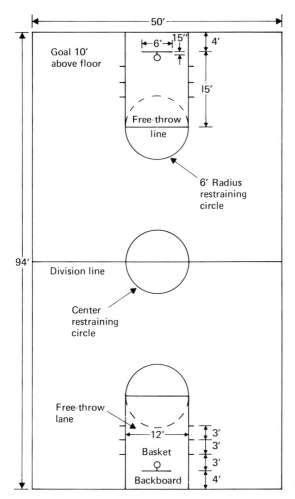

Fig. 4.25 Official court for women's basketball.

REFERENCES

Ainsworth, D. S. 1930. *The history of physical education in colleges for women.* New York: A. S. Barnes.

Barnes, M. J. 1972. *Women's basketball.* Boston: Allyn and Bacon.

Bell, M. M. 1964. *Women's basketball.* Dubuque, Iowa: William C. Brown.

Berenson, S. 1894. Basketball for women. *Physical Education* **3,** September.

Cousy, B., and F. Power 1970. *Basketball concepts and techniques.* Boston: Allyn and Bacon.

Ebert, F. H., and B. A. Cheatum 1972. *Basketball—five player.* Philadelphia: Saunders.

Miller, K. D., and R. J. Horky 1970. *Modern basketball for women.* Columbus, Ohio: Merrill.

Naismith, J. 1941. *Basketball, its origin and development.* New York: Association Press.

Neal, P. 1966. *Basketball techniques for women.* New York: Ronald.

Newell, P., and J. Benington 1962. *Basketball methods.* New York: Ronald.

Schaafsma, F. 1971. *Basketball for women.* (2nd ed.) Dubuque, Iowa: William C. Brown.

Sharman, W. 1965. *Sharman on basketball shooting.* Englewood Cliffs, N.J.: Prentice-Hall.

Women's basketball 1972. Chicago: The Athletic Institute, Merchandise Mart.

Wooden, J. R. 1966. *Practical modern basketball.* New York: Ronald.

5
Bowling

Two articles on this subject were necessary. Marie R. Liba wrote about the nature and scope of bowling, the number of participants, the scores attained by various classes of bowlers, and other facts of interest pertaining to this sport. The presentation by D. C. Seaton and others stresses basic rules, performance of basic skills, playing strategy, and terminology. The illustrations enhance the exposition of techniques and the "helpful hints" and "playing courtesies" add needed information. RBF

Bowling: General Information
Marie R. Liba

DEFINITION AND SCOPE

Bowling is a challenging and intriguing activity, participated in by a great many individuals of all ages and of varying physical capabilities. Bowling is a sport that can be enjoyed at a wide range of ability levels from the novice rolling a first line on a Sunday afternoon, to the highly skilled bowler in a classic league, to the bowler on the professional tour.

The game of bowling has diverse origins and forms. (See Pluckhahn, Encyclopaedia Britannica, 1970, for an excellent description.) In this article, however, only the indoor, tenpin game will be discussed. This is the most popular form of bowling in the United States. The game is bowled indoors on lanes and consists of ten frames. Equipment consists of special shoes and a ball which can be rented for a nominal fee. Most bowling establishments are now equipped with automatic pin-setting machines and have well-cared-for lanes with marks for spot bowling.

WHO BOWLS AND WHEN?

Individuals, families, and groups can be found almost any time of day and every day of the week bowling for fun and relaxation. The number of persons who participate in this type of informal bowling is impossible to estimate. Informal bowling is scheduled around the formal, organized league bowling most of which is conducted under the auspices of the recognized governing bodies of the sport: The American Bowling Congress (ABC) established in 1895, the Women's International Bowling Congress (WIBC) established in 1916, and the American Junior Bowling Congress established in 1946. The membership in the ABC has grown from a mere 251,000 in the 1895–96 season to well over 4 million at the present time (Abbot 1975, p. 90). The growth in membership in the WIBC has been even more phenomenal, from 40 members in the 1916–17 season to more than 3 million at present. The junior bowlers have increased from a membership of 93,767 in the 1946–47 season to almost 700,000 at this time.

The 1971–72 annual reports of the ABC (1972) and the WIBC (1972) contain some interesting facts. Detroit leads all cities in the number of members (ABC, 142,268–WIBC, 100,614) and the number of leagues (ABC, 3,395–WIBC, 3,006). Second place for the cities was held by Chicago with a membership of 112,272 and 2,917 leagues for the ABC and 76,167 and 2,623 leagues for the WIBC. New York leads the states in the number of members (417,676), and California had the greatest number of leagues (ABC, 12,224–WIBC, 15,669). Second place for the states in the number of members was held by Ohio with a membership of 369,368 reported by the ABC and a membership of 304,284 reported by the WIBC. Second place for the states in the number of leagues was held by New York with 11,082 leagues reported by the ABC and 10,868 reported by the WIBC.

Twenty-one women and 1000 men bowled a perfect game in the 1971–72 season. High individual performances for three games were 771 for the women and 864 for the men. The highest individual league average for the women was 211 and nine women averaged 200 or more for the season. (This information was not included in the ABC report.)

The bowling season for both men and women culminates in an annual tournament. These tournaments are somewhat unique in the number of participants, variety in events and the length of the competition. A total of 4732 teams competed for more than $600,000 in the 1972 ABC tournament, which, incidentally, was won by a team of five left-handed bowlers, *a first*. A total of 5898 teams competed for more than $350,000 in prize money in the 1972 WIBC tournaments.

A third, large category of bowlers is students in the schools. Instruction in bowling is offered as part of the curriculum in a large number of high schools, colleges and universities in the United States. Many of the educational institutions also offer an opportunity for students to participate competitively in bowling both at the intramural level and at the interscholastic and inter-collegiate level. It is impossible to even estimate the number of bowlers in this category.

SKILL AND STRATEGY

Bowling skill and strategy involve first the development of a good movement pattern that enables the bowler to roll the ball at a consistent and optimum speed and in the desired direction so that maximum pinfall can be obtained. Casady and Liba (1968) suggest that an optimum bowling speed for men is about 2.25 seconds and for women about 2.5 seconds. Most proficient bowlers choose to throw a hook or curve ball in preference to the straight ball. For example, Klatt (1965) found that 85 percent of her superior women

Fig. 5.1 Bowling skill involves the development of a good movement pattern. Courtesy of *JOPER*.

bowlers rolled a hook or curve ball. Her superior bowlers had an average of at least 170 in league play. Observation of men on the professional bowlers' tour indicates that most of them use the hook or curve ball. Characteristic of their skill level, of course, is the ability to adjust the amount of "break" according to the particular lane being bowled.

Klatt (1965) reported the following findings in comparing two groups of women in league bowling: superior bowlers (averaged 182 and were in the top one percent of the league) and above average bowlers (averaged 145 and were about one standard deviation above the league average). Superior bowlers had 3.7 strikes per game compared to 1.85 for the above average; had 6.4 pocket hits compared to 3.9; averaged 8.8 on the first ball pinfall compared to 7.9; had only 2 open frames compared to 4. Both groups had about the same number of spares per line, 4.3 and 4.0 and splits per line, 1.3 and 1.3. Webster (1940) in a similar study of men reported that a bowler averaging 180–189 would have 3.5 strikes, 4.2 spares, 0.9 splits and 1.3 open frames whereas a bowler averaging 120–129 would have 1.6 strikes, 2.9 spares, 1.10 splits and 4.4 misses. His results are similar to Klatt's except for spares.

These findings compare favorably with a guide suggested by Wilman. His 180-average bowler has 6 pocket hits, 4–5 strikes and 1 miss or blow or error; his 150-average bowler has 4 pocket hits, 3–4 strikes, and 2 misses; his 130-average bowler (lowest given) has 2 pocket hits, 2 strikes, and 3 errors.

The national average for men reported by the ABC for the 1960–61 season was 154 and is probably quite representative since it changed only one point from the 1954–55 season and remained stable through 1963–64. The WIBC reported a national average of 132 for women for the 1971–72 season. The ABC survey for the 1960–61 season also showed that 10 percent of the membership had a league average of better than 175 and an additional 29 percent averaged 160 and 174.

Martin (1960, pp. 113–116) and Martin and Keogh (1964, pp. 325–327) report bowling norms for college students. Males who were beginners averaged 111, intermediates averaged 134 and the advanced groups averaged 154, the latter figure being about that of the national average for men. Women who were beginners averaged 97, intermediates averaged 117 and an average of 129 is reported for a group of experienced women bowlers, a figure somewhat comparable to the national average for women.

Other Facts of Interest. Walters (1959, pp. 94–100) reported that the above average woman bowler is better in general motor ability than the below average bowler. Liba, Harris, and Sabol (1965, pp. 113–120) reported that 16 percent of the women in their study were able to swing a 15-lb. ball easily and 29 percent found it difficult to swing a 10- to 11-lb. ball. Thompson (1958, pp. 231–246), Singer and Beaver (1969, pp. 372–375), and Liba

(1962, pp. 245–248) all report a warm-up effect in bowling. A significant difference in pinfall in favor of bowlers having a formal warm-up was reported by Thompson. Best performances were recorded in frames 5 and 10 as well as a significant improvement from game 1 to game 3 in the Singer and Beaver study. In contrast to Thompson's findings, however, no significant change occurred from game 1 to game 2. A significant trend over five trials was reported for bowling speed by Liba.

REFERENCES

Abbott, J., 2d, 1975. *The Oxford companion to sports and games.* London–New York–Toronto: Oxford University Press, p. 90.

American Bowling Congress 1972. *1971–72 annual report.* The Congress, Milwaukee, Wisc.

Casady, D. R., and M. R. Liba 1968. *Beginning bowling.* Belmont, Calif.: Wadsworth.

Klatt, L. A. 1965. A comparison of factors related to force and direction of force in the performance of above average and superior women bowlers. Unpublished master's thesis. Madison Wisc.: University of Wisconsin.

Lehman, H. C. 1938. The most proficient years at sports and games. *Res. Quart.* **9,** 3:3–19 (October).

Liba, M. R., C. W. Harris, and B. Sabol 1965. Relationship of selected variables to ability to handle a bowling ball. *Am. Educ. Res. J.* **2,** 2 (March).

Liba, M. R. 1962. A trend test as a preliminary to reliability estimation. *Res. Quart.* **33,** 2 (May).

Martin, J. L., and J. Keogh 1964. Bowling norms for college students in elective bowling classes. *Res. Quart.* **35,** 3, Pt. 1 (October).

Martin, J. L. 1960. Bowling norms for college men and women. *Res. Quart.* **31.**

Pluckhahn, B. 1970. Bowling. *Encyclopaedia Britannica.*

Singer, R. N., and R. Beaver 1969. Bowling and the warm-up effect. *Res. Quart.* **40,** 2 (May).

Thompson, H. 1958. Effects of warm-up upon physical performance in selected activities. *Res. Quart.* **29,** 2 (May).

Walters, C. E. 1959. Motor ability and educability factors of high and low scoring beginning bowlers. *Res. Quart.* **30,** 1 (March).

Webster, R. W. 1940. Psychological and pedagogical factors involved in motor skill performance as exemplified in bowling. *Res. Quart.* **11,** (4):42–52 (December).

Women's International Bowling Congress 1972. *1971–72 annual report.* The Congress, Greendale, Wisc.

Bowling: Basic Instruction*

D. C. Seaton, I. A. Clayton, H. L. Liebee, and L. Messersmith

ORIGIN AND DEVELOPMENT

Existing records indicate that a form of bowling may be traced back as far as 7000 years. Archeological studies of ancient Egyptians provide us with evidence of implements for playing a game similar in some respects to our modern game of bowling. Variations of the modern game were developed in Europe around 1000 to 1500 years ago, with alleys consisting of outdoor areas on open greens. The original bowls were spherical stones, probably not equipped with holes for the fingers as we find in modern equipment, but held in the open hand. The ninepin game was developed in Germany. Martin Luther was an enthusiastic bowler and is credited with having standardized the number of pins at nine. The game was brought to America by the early settlers, who utilized the sport as a recreational activity in the colonies.

The ninepin game became increasingly popular with the colonists, and in 1840 the Knickerbocker Alleys were built in New York City. The game lost favor with governmental authorities when gamblers began wagering on the outcome of matches, and in 1841 the game was outlawed in Connecticut. In order to circumvent the law and continue the game of bowling, a tenth pin was added, thus changing the name of the game to tenpins. Tenpins soon became popular all over the country, but there was a wide variation in size of pins, length of alleys, rules of play, and general regulations governing the game. The American Bowling Congress (ABC) was organized in 1895 and was given the task of establishing a standardized set of rules governing play, equipment, and tournament competition. The Woman's International Bowling Congress (WIBC) was organized in 1916 and was followed soon afterwards by the American Junior Bowling Congress. Bowling is now one of the fastest growing indoor sports in America; it is estimated that over 30,000,000 persons engage in the sport with varying degrees of regularity.

In addition to tenpin bowling there are two other forms of bowling played in various sections of the country and promoted by national organizations. Duckpin bowling is governed by the National Duckpin Bowling Congress, and lawn bowling is under the direction of the American Lawn Bowling Association. In duckpin bowling the pins and balls are smaller than in regulation

---

*   Reprinted by permission from D. C. Seaton, I. A. Clayton, H. L. Liebee, and L. Messersmith, *Physical education handbook.* (6th ed.) Englewood Cliffs, N.J.: Prentice-Hall, 1974.

tenpin bowling; as its name implies, lawn bowling is played on an outdoor surface.

NATURE OF THE GAME

The modern game of tenpins is played on indoor wooden lanes, 60 feet long from foul line to number one pin, and 41 or 42 inches wide (Fig. 5.2). The tenpins are located in diamond formation on pin spots 12 inches apart, center to center (Fig. 5.3). A regulation tenpin is 15 inches high with a diameter at the base of 2¼ inches, and is constructed of clear, hard maple (Fig. 5.4). A bowling ball is constructed of a mixture of natural and synthetic rubber, cotton, sulphur, and carbon black, which acts as a softener to accelerate the mixing process. Balls may not exceed 27 inches in circumference and weigh more than a maximum of 16 pounds. Balls are bored with two or three holes in which the player places his fingers to hold the ball in preparing to deliver it on the lane. The game is played by rolling the balls down a wooden lane in

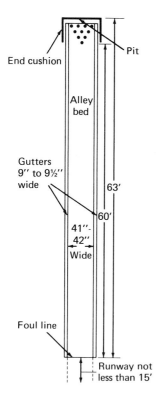

Fig. 5.2 Alley dimensions.

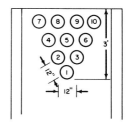

Fig. 5.3 Position and number of pins.

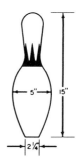

Fig. 5.4 Dimensions and shape of bowling pin.

an effort to knock down the pins stationed at the end of the lane opposite the bowler.

Bowling is an excellent recreational activity for all ages and both sexes. Because of the relatively small expenditure of energy required to participate in the game, it may be played for years after more strenuous activities have been abandoned.

BASIC RULES

Two lanes immediately adjoining each other are used in all games of league or tournament play, and the bowling of ten complete frames on these lanes constitutes an official game. Members of contesting teams successively and in regular order bowl one frame on one lane, and for the next frame alternate and use the other lane, so alternating each frame until the game is completed. Each player bowls two balls in each frame unless a strike is made on the first ball, in which case the second ball is not rolled (with the exception that in the tenth frame if a strike or spare is made, the player immediately rolls on the same lane the additional balls or ball to which the strike or spare entitles him).

In case of a tie game, each team bowls one complete frame on the same lane in which the tenth frame was bowled, bowling and scoring said extra frame in exactly the same manner as the tenth frame. If, at the completion of the first extra frame, a tie still exists, teams must change lanes for additional frames that may be required to determine the winner.

It is a foul if a bowler permits any part of his foot, hand, or arm, while in contact with the lanes or runways, to rest upon or extend beyond the foul line at any time after the ball leaves the bowler's hands and passes beyond the foul line. No count is made on a foul ball, and any pins knocked down are immediately respotted. A foul ball counts as a ball bowled by the player. If a player commits a foul which is apparent to both captains or one or more members of each of the opposing teams competing in a league or tournament on the same pair of lanes where the foul is committed, and the foul is not seen by the foul judge or umpire, or recorded by an automatic foul detecting device, a foul shall nevertheless be declared and so recorded.

Pinfall—Legal

Every ball delivered by the player shall count unless declared a dead ball. Pins must then be respotted after the cause for declaring such dead ball has been removed.

☐ Pins knocked down by another pin or pins rebounding in play from side partition or rear cushion are counted as pins down.

☐ If, when rolling at a full setup or in order to make a spare, it is discovered immediately after the ball has been delivered that one or more pins are improperly set, although not missing, the ball and resulting pinfall shall be counted. It is each player's responsibility to detect any misplacement of pins and have the setup corrected before he bowls.

☐ Pins knocked down by a fair ball, and which remain lying on the lane or in the gutters, or which lean so as to touch kickbacks or side partitions, are termed dead wood and counted as pins down, and must be removed before the next ball is bowled.

Pinfall—Illegal

When any of the following incidents occur, the ball counts as a ball rolled, but pins knocked down shall not count.

☐ When pins are knocked down or displaced by a ball which leaves the lane before reaching the pins.

☐ When a ball rebounds from the rear cushion.

☐ When pins come in contact with the body, arms, or legs of a pinsetter and rebound.

☐ A standing pin which falls upon removing dead wood or which is knocked down by a pin setter or mechanical pinsetting equipment shall not count and must be replaced on the pin spot where it originally stood before delivery of the ball.

☐ Pins which are bowled off the lane, rebound, and remain standing on the lane must be counted as pins standing.

☐ If in delivering the ball a foul is committed, any pins knocked down by such delivery shall not be counted.

Bowling on Wrong Lane

When only one player or the leadoff men on both teams bowl on the wrong lane and the error is discovered before another player has bowled, a dead ball shall be declared and the player, or players, required to bowl on the correct lane. When more than one player on the same team has rolled on the wrong lane, the game shall be completed without adjustment, and the next game shall be started on the correctly scheduled lane.

Scoring

All players should learn how to score because it adds considerably to the enjoyment of the game if the player can keep an accurate record of the score as it progresses throughout a game. As indicated earlier, a complete game consists of ten frames. If a player does not get a strike or spare in any frame, scoring is just a matter of adding the number of pins knocked down in each frame, and carrying the cumulative total in each succeeding frame. If all pins are knocked down with the first ball, it is called a strike and a cross (X) is marked in the small square in the upper right-hand corner of the frame on the scoresheet. If all pins are knocked down with two balls, it is a spare and is indicated by a diagonal mark (/). A strike means that the bowler is credited with ten pins in the frame in which he obtained the strike, plus the number of pins knocked down on two successive balls. Hence no numerical score is marked down when a strike is made, but is delayed until the player has again taken his turn and bowled two more balls. A spare means that a player is entitled to ten pins in the frame in which he obtained the spare, plus the number of pins knocked down on his next ball.

In order to illustrate scoring we shall score a hypothetical game (Fig. 5.5). A bowler starts a game by getting 7 pins on his first ball and 2 of the remaining 3 pins on his second ball in frame one, giving him a score of 9, which is marked down immediately on the scoresheet in frame one. In frame two, the bowler knocks down 5 pins on his first ball. This number is marked down immediately in the left-hand box of the small boxes located in the upper right-hand corner of the frame area. If he happens to be using a score pad

Fig. 5.5 Scoresheet showing method of indicating score.

with only one small box, he writes the results of the first ball to the left of the small box. On his second ball in frame two, the bowler gets 3 of the remaining 5 pins. This number is written in the right-hand box and the total of the two, 8 pins, is the bowler's score for frame two. This number is added to his total for frame one, 9 pins, which gives a cumulative total of 17 pins to be marked down in frame two. In frame three, he rolls a strike, so no score is recorded, only a strike mark (X) in the small box in the upper right-hand corner. In frame four, he rolls another strike and still no score is recorded in frame three because he has not yet rolled two additional balls after the strike in frame three. In frame five, he hits 9 pins on his first ball, so this number is immediately recorded in the upper box. Now the score may be computed for frame three, because he has rolled two balls after his strike in that frame. We obtain the score for frame three by totaling the score of two strikes and 9 pins, or 29 pins, which is added to his total of 17 pins in frame two, making a total score of 46 pins for frame three.

On his second ball in frame five, he misses the single pin, for an error, so his score may be totaled for frames four and five. The score in frame four is obtained by adding 19 pins (10 for the strike and 9 for the two additional balls in frame five) to the score of 46 in frame three, for a total of 65 in frame four. Since he did not strike or spare in frame five, his score is increased by 9, the number of pins obtained in this frame, making a total of 74 pins through frame five. On his first ball in frame six, he obtains 8 pins, so this number is marked down in the upper box. On the second ball, he gets the remaining 2 pins for a spare, so a mark (/) indicating this is marked down in the upper box. This means that his score in frame six is 10, plus the number of pins that he obtains on his first ball in frame seven. On his first ball in frame seven, he obtains 5 pins, which gives him a total of 15 pins to be added to his previous total of 74 in frame five, or a total of 89 in frame six. On his second ball in frame seven he obtains 4 of the remaining 5 pins for a total of 9 pins, giving him a total of 98 pins through frame seven. In frame eight he obtains 9 pins on two balls, which added to 98 gives a total of 107 pins through frame eight. In frame nine, 7 pins are knocked down on two balls, giving a score of 114 through frame nine. In frame ten our bowler gets a strike, which entitles him to roll two additional balls. He obtains strikes on both additional balls, giving him a score of 30 pins for frame ten, or a total of 144 for the complete game. A careful study of these directions and the accompanying scoresheet should enable anyone to learn the fundamentals of scoring in a short time.

Automatic scoring machines have been developed which record the score immediately after a person bowls, but the machines are rather expensive and it will probably be some time before they are in general use. Knowing how to score adds to the interest and enjoyment of the game, so all students should acquire this knowledge and skill.

Tabulation of Marks

Bowling teams usually consist of four or five members, so it is difficult to determine the relative standing of two teams during a match by looking at the scores of individual team members. Utilization of the "mark" system will show at a glance the relative position of each team. Each strike or spare is considered as a "mark" and is generally considered to add a ten-pin total to the value of a team's score. A double is worth two marks since its value is more than a single strike or spare. The marks for each team are tabulated for each frame, and the cumulative total is recorded on a line at the bottom of the scoresheet. Since a mark is worth a possible ten pins, a mark is lost and should be deducted from the team's mark total each time a bowler fails to score at least five pins in the situations listed in the summary below.

Summary of mark system

1. One mark for each single strike or spare.

2. Two marks for consecutive strikes (a double).

3. Loss of marks—one mark is deducted from a team's cumulative total when a bowler fails to get as many as five pins in the following situations:
   a) with the first ball after a spare.
   b) with the first ball after consecutive strikes (a double).
   c) with both balls in any frame not preceded by a mark.
   d) Two marks are lost in any frame in which a bowler fails to get as many as five pins, following a double, strike, or spare.

Computing Team Handicaps

In most bowling leagues an effort is made to equalize competition between teams by giving the weaker team a handicap based on scores of individual team members. To compute the handicap, the bowling averages are totaled for each team, and the smaller total is subtracted from the larger. A percentage (usually 70 to 80) of this difference is given to the team with the lower total. Thus, using a 70 percent handicap, if team A has a total of 700 and team B has 800, A would receive a handicap of 70 pins, which would represent 7 marks to be credited to A at the start of the match. The 70 pins are added to the total pins that members of A actually score in each game; this total is compared with the total scored by members of B in order to determine the winner. Obviously, if bowlers do not have established averages at the start of a match, the handicap cannot be figured at that time. In such a case, team members may agree to "scratch bowl" (the team with the highest total pins wins the match) or to compute a handicap after the match, based on the scores that were bowled during the match.

TECHNIQUES AND FUNDAMENTALS

If one is to become proficient at bowling, he must give proper attention to such fundamentals as selection of correct equipment, employment of the proper stance, and adoption of a standard number of steps in the approach which will enable him to move toward the foul line with a smooth, rhythmical movement.

Equipment

It is important to select a ball equipped with holes that fit the fingers. Balls are bored with either two or three holes. One should try both and determine which feels more comfortable and which can be controlled with the least effort. If a bowler's fingers are weak, he may feel the need to use three fingers in order to properly control the ball; however, many expert bowlers who have strong fingers use the two-hole ball because they feel it can be handled with greater accuracy. The holes should be large enough for the fingers to slip in and out easily. The thumb hole should be comfortably loose, the finger holes comfortably snug. To determine the correct fit of a bowling ball, place thumb completely in thumb hole, fingers relaxed and spread over finger holes. The crease of the second joint of the fingers should extend a quarter of an inch beyond the inside edge of the finger holes. The holes should not be too large, as extra pressure will have to be exerted to hold the ball in the act of delivery. As one progresses in bowling, he may wish to own his own ball, in which event he should purchase one with holes bored to fit his particular needs. Women generally use balls lighter in weight than those used by men. Most modern lanes have an adequate supply of both types of balls for use by bowlers (Fig. 5.6).

Another important item in the bowler's list of equipment is proper footwear. Most commercial lanes will not permit bowlers on the lanes unless they are wearing regulation bowling shoes. The righthanded bowler should use a shoe with a leather sole on the left foot (to facilitate sliding at the release) and a rubber sole on the right shoe. The left-handed bowler reverses this order. While bowling establishments have shoes to rent, it is more economical for a person to own his own shoes if he bowls regularly. Shoes are available in a variety of colors and styles and vary in price.

Stance

There is no definite or prescribed stance assumed by all bowlers in preparation for the start of their delivery movement. Whether one stands erect or crouched, the feet should be slightly spread and the ball held in a comfortable

Fig. 5.6 Position of fingers in a three-hole ball.

position in front of the body. The ball should be held with both hands, some-where between the waist and chin, the left hand giving major support to the weight of the ball until the right arm is lowered as a part of the approach and delivery. On the backswing, the ball should not be raised higher than a plane parallel with the shoulders.

Approach

Bowlers vary in the number of steps taken in the approach. The number of steps ranges from three to five, with more bowlers using four steps than any other number. One should experiment with the delivery and decide upon a definite number of steps—it is not advisable to be continually changing delivery form. Using a four-step approach, the right-handed bowler will take his first step with the right foot, following with the left, then right, and com-pleting the delivery with the left foot forward. If three or five steps are used in the approach, the first step will be taken with the left foot. In proper execution of the approach, the bowler should move from his starting position toward the foul line in a smooth, rhythmical motion that will allow him to keep control of his body and the ball, both while in motion and at the com-pletion of the last step when the ball is released on the lane.

Starting from a comfortable standing position, either erect or crouched, with ball held in both hands in front of the body, step first with the right foot (in four-step delivery) and at the same time prepare to push the ball forward in front of the body (see Fig. 5.7). As the second step is taken the ball is continued on the downward and backward swing, reaching the peak of the backswing as the right foot is planted on the floor in completion of the third step. While taking the fourth and last step, the bowler starts the ball forward and releases it as he completes the fourth step. The first and second steps should be short, natural steps, with momentum and step length increasing on the last two steps. The last step is the longest, and forward momentum should

Fig. 5.7 Beginning stance and steps used in the four-step approach.

be checked by a slide on the left foot at completion of the approach. The toe of the left foot should be pointed toward the target and the right leg and foot should be behind the body.

Release of Ball

The ball should be released out in front of the body and laid, not dropped, on the lane. The bowling ball, when properly delivered, has a double motion. When first released it slides and revolves, sliding in the direction toward the pins and revolving toward the left gutter in the case of a right-handed bowler throwing a hook ball. After sliding a certain distance, friction decreases the slide action and the revolving effect takes over, causing the ball to hook, back up, or roll straight forward, depending upon the direction of the rotation movement. A hook ball breaks toward the left and a backup ball toward the right for a right-handed bowler.

The Straight Ball

Beginning bowlers should concentrate on perfecting the straight ball before attempting to roll a hook or curve. In rolling a straight ball, the thumb should

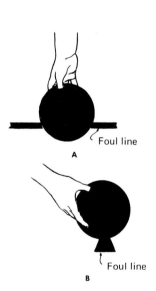

Fig. 5.8 (Left) Front view of grip for straight ball. (Right) Side view of grip for straight ball.

Fig. 5.9 Path of straight ball.

be held in the twelve o'clock position with the fingers underneath the ball. This position should be maintained throughout the delivery, with no rotation of the arm during the release of the ball (Fig. 5.8). The ball should be started from the right side of the lane and directed so that it will strike in the 1-3 pocket (Fig. 5.9).

The Hook Ball

Most good bowlers use a hook ball; beginning bowlers will want to learn this delivery as soon as possible. To obtain maximum pin action, the ball should strike the pins at an angle, but the angle of the straight ball is limited by the width of the alley. The straight ball revolves forward, but the hook ball revolves at an angle, thus giving it greater pin splash or action by imparting a revolving action to the pins themselves. To obtain a hook on the ball, the bowler should release the ball with the V formed by the thumb and first finger pointing toward the target. The thumb is released first and as the ball leaves the fingers a rotation effect is imparted to the ball (Fig. 5.10). This delivery is sometimes called the "handshake" delivery because the position of the hand is similar to that used in an ordinary handshake. After releasing the ball, the hand should be carried upward and forward toward the pins in the follow-through. Some bowlers obtain an increased hook on the ball by rotat-

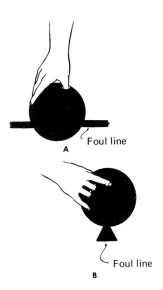

Foul line

A

Foul line

B

Fig. 5.10 (Left) Front view of hook grip. (Right) Side view of hook grip.

ing the arm in the counterclockwise direction as the ball is released. Other bowlers increase the hook by forcefully lifting the fingers upward as the ball is released. In this delivery the fingers leave the ball last and impart a vigorous lift to the ball, which gives it a strong counter-clockwise spin. Many professional bowlers combine arm rotation and forceful lift of the fingers in order to obtain maximum hook on the ball. This is perhaps the most difficult of hook ball deliveries to master and should be used only by bowlers who bowl regularly (Fig. 5.10).

The Curve Ball

The curve ball is difficult to control and is not recommended for beginning bowlers. In this type of delivery the ball travels more slowly and the ball follows a wide curve in approaching the pins (Fig. 5.11).

The Backup or Reverse Hook Delivery

In a backup delivery the ball travels first straight forward or to the left, and then breaks to the right for a right-handed bowler (Fig. 5.13). This type of

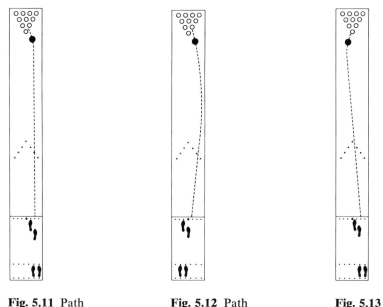

Fig. 5.11 Path of curve ball.

Fig. 5.12 Path of hook ball.

Fig. 5.13 Path of backup ball.

Fig. 5.14 Release of backup ball.

delivery is not recommended because it is difficult to control, gives fewer strikes than the hook ball because of reduced pin-mixing action, produces more splits than other deliveries, and often results in difficult pin leaves. A backup ball results when the forearm is rotated clockwise, or the thumb comes out of the ball late, imparting a lift to the ball, instead of the lift coming from the fingers (Figs. 5.13 and 5.14).

PLAYING STRATEGY

An individual sport, bowling has no complicated playing strategies similar to those found in many team sports. One should plan his game so as to knock down the greatest number of pins possible. This is accomplished by individual control and accuracy, rather than cooperation with teammates in the execution of plays.

Playing strategy should include, first, a mastery of a definite approach and delivery style. The good bowler will settle upon a definite pattern as early as possible, making every effort to throw each ball with the same motion. Most bowlers are classified as "spot" or "pin" bowlers. The spot bowler selects a spot on the alley a few feet from the foul line over which he attempts to roll his first ball in each frame. The pin bowler looks at the pins while approaching and making his delivery. Whether throwing a hook or a straight ball, the bowler should follow his selected style on all balls and concentrate on developing accuracy with a smooth and rhythmical delivery. To make a decent score, the bowler must pick up spares consistently. Accuracy is essential for good spare bowling.

SAFETY

Bowling is about as safe an activity as is found in our list of recreational activities. Accidents have been caused by bowlers releasing the ball on the backswing and permitting it to strike spectators or fellow bowlers in the rear

73

of the lane. Obviously, this may be prevented by having the ball well under control at all times. Slippery or rough surfaces on the approach may cause the bowler to fall, so it is wise to test the approaches and become aware of any irregularities before beginning competition. Pinsetters have been injured when bowlers rolled the ball into pits before the pins were spotted. See that workers are ready before rolling and this danger element can be eliminated. Bowlers have been known to have their fingers crushed by improperly removing the ball from the retaining rack. In order to eliminate the possibility of injury, the bowler should always pick up the ball with the palms of the hands parallel to the sides of the bowling rack (Fig. 5.15).

HELPFUL HINTS

- ☐ Select a ball that fits your hand.
- ☐ Practice your approach at home; some object such as an old flat iron may be carried to simulate the bowling ball.
- ☐ Dress properly for bowling. Wear loose-fitting clothing and, if bowling on a strange lane for the first time, find out the requirements regarding the use of bowling shoes. Managers in most lanes require that regulation bowling shoes be worn.
- ☐ Having taken your stance, concentrate on your delivery and ignore any remarks that may come your way from the spectators.
- ☐ Control your temper. Public exhibition of anger disturbs fellow bowlers and detracts from your efficiency.
- ☐ Bowl, do not throw the ball.

PLAYING COURTESIES

- ☐ Do not talk or otherwise disturb a bowler who is on the approach and ready to bowl.

Fig. 5.15 Lifting ball from ball rack.

☐ Do not walk in front of a bowler to secure your ball from the rack when the bowler is ready to bowl. Use one ball only—wait for its return.

☐ When bowlers on adjacent lanes are both ready to bowl, the one on the right should always be permitted to bowl first.

☐ Do not use a ball that is the personal property of some individual unless given permission to do so by the owner.

☐ Be at your post, ready to bowl when your turn comes.

☐ After delivering the ball and noting the result, turn and walk back immediately to the rear of the runway, being careful to stay in your approach lane.

☐ Do not argue with the foul line judge over decisions even though you think an unjust call has been made against you.

☐ Be punctual when scheduled to bowl. Nothing upsets a team more than having to wait for a late member.

TERMINOLOGY

Anchor The person who shoots last on a team. An anchor is the symbol of hope.

Baby split The 1-7 or 3-10 railroads.

Backup A reverse hook. A backup rotates toward the right for a right-handed bowler.

Bed posts The 7-10 railroad.

Blow An error; missing a spare that is not a split.

Box The same as a frame.

Brooklyn A cross-over ball, one that strikes in the 1-2 pocket.

Bucket The 2-4-5-8 or 3-5-6-9 leaves.

Cherry Chopping off the front pin on a spare.

Crossover Same as a Brooklyn.

Double Two strikes in succession.

Double pinochle The 7-6 and 4-10 split.

Dutch 200 or Dutchman A score of 200 made by alternating strikes and spares for entire game.

Error Same as a "blow." Failure to make a spare that is not a split.

Foul To touch or go beyond the foul line in delivering the ball.

Frame The box in which scores are registered. There are ten frames to each game.

Gutterball A ball that drops into either gutter.

Handicap A bonus score or score adjustment awarded to individual or team based on averages.

Headpin The number one pin.

High hit Hitting the headpin full in the face or head-on.

Hook A ball that breaks to the left for a right-handed bowler.

Jersey side Same as a Brooklyn.

Kegler Synonym for bowler, derived from the German "kegel."

Lane A bowling alley.

Light hit Hitting the headpin lightly to the right or left side.

Line A complete game as recorded on the scoresheet.

Mark Obtaining a strike or spare.

Open frame A frame in which no mark is made; at least one pin remains standing after rolling both balls in a frame.

Pocket Space between the headpin and pins on either side.

Railroad Terms used by some for a split. There are several kinds.

Sleeper A hidden pin.

Spare All pins knocked down on two balls.

Split A leave after the first ball has been thrown in which the number one pin is down and an intervening pin is down between pins that remain standing. Indicated by 0 on scoresheet.

Spot A place on the alley at which a bowler aims.

Strike All pins knocked down on the first ball.

Striking out Obtaining three strikes in the last frame.

Tap When a pin is left standing on an apparently perfect hit.

Turkey Three strikes in a row.

REFERENCES

American Association for Health, Physical Education and Recreation, Division for Girls' and Women's Sports. *Official bowling, fencing, and golf guide.* (Current ed.) Washington, D.C.

American Bowling Congress. *ABC bowling guide.* (Current ed.) Milwaukee: American Bowling Congress.

Andsley, J. 1964. *Bowling for women.* New York: Sterling Publishing.

Archibald, J. J. 1963. *Bowling for boys and girls.* Chicago: Follett.

Casady, D., and M. Liba 1962. *Beginning bowling.* Belmont, Calif.: Wadsworth.

Clause, F. 1962. *How to win at bowling.* New York: Fleet.

Day, N. 1960. *How to bowl better.* New York: Arco.

Dawson, T. 1960. *The secret of bowling strikes.* New York: A. S. Barnes.

Forslund, E. M. 1964. *Bowling for women.* New York: Ronald.

Martin, J. L. 1971. *Bowling.* Dubuque, Iowa: William C. Brown.

Vannier, M., and H. B. Poindexter 1968. *Individual and team sports for girls and women.* (2nd ed.) Philadelphia: W. B. Saunders.

6

Boxing

Henry J. Eichin

HISTORY OF BOXING

The connection between boxing as a military training technique and war is as old as warfare itself. Western civilization was founded upon Grecian and Roman military might. These great empires utilized various forms of boxing to toughen soldiers. Boxing during military training is used today as it was centuries ago. The branches of the Armed Forces of the United States use boxing as one of the means of teaching its fighting men such attributes as self-discipline and aggressiveness.

The modern form of boxing was developed in England at about the time of the American Revolution. The modern armies of Allied and Axis powers during World War I and II trained men for combat with boxing, despite advanced technology. Even with the advent of the Jet-Nuclear Age, soldiers, sailors, and airmen train for hand-to-hand combat by boxing as well as with some of the oriental martial arts.

People throughout the various social strata and geographical areas of this country have engaged in boxing. Since their inception, prize fighting and professional boxing have been rejected as well as accepted. The recent refusal of Muhammed Ali (Cassius Clay) to be inducted into the Armed Forces during the Vietnam conflict brought controversy to a struggling sport. On the other hand, the aftermath of World War II brought the rise of Joe Louis, a soldier, and an upsurge in the fistic enterprises.

The television productions of boxing which followed the Korean War brought the professional sport to unparalleled heights with weekly bouts nationally telecast, and nightly fights broadcast to some of the larger cities of the country. Because of television, interest in boxing increased in the United States during the 1950s and the sport flourished at all levels. Amateur, AAU, Golden Gloves, and collegiate boxing activities were increased by soldiers who had trained using these techniques.

Intercollegiate boxing began after World War I upon the return of the doughboys to institutions of higher education. The first recorded intercollegiate match was between Penn State College and the University of Pennsylvania in 1919. Prior to this, colleges and universities had offered boxing as an intramural activity. The NCAA recognized champions from 1924 to 1960 when at the University of Wisconsin the fatal injury of an intercollegiate boxer brought a waning collegiate sport to a tragic halt.

Only a few boxing programs at the two- and four-year institutions throughout the country remain. The nation's three largest military academies,

Fig. 6.1 Boxing is part of the training of all cadets at the United States Military Academy. Courtesy of the United States Military Academy.

Air Force, Navy, and Army, are the remaining bastions of collegiate boxing with some matches being reported at the University of Nevada at Reno, University of California at Berkeley, and California State University at Chico.

Boxing skills with their thrusts and parries were akin to those of fencing and dueling in the Middle Ages. Bayonet training of infantry soldiers of World Wars I and II was also likened to that of boxing. One can appreciate the desires of the military leaders of Rome and Greece to acquaint their legions with boxing skills to improve the effectiveness of their lancers and swordsmen.

What value, then, do military leaders attribute to the fistic arts in present day training when thermonuclear weapons and lasers are available? According to officials at the Air Force Academy, two major purposes are served by requiring each fourth-class cadet to box:

☐ Boxing is taught in order to develop an understanding of the psysiological aspects of boxing. In addition to physical conditioning, boxing will also develop and intensify the military leadership attributes of quick reaction, coordination, accurate timing, cool judgment, aggressiveness, and determination.

☐ The boxing course teaches the cadet to think and react under pressure. It teaches how to use all mental and physical resources in accomplishing an objective in the most elemental of combatives. It develops self-confidence, courage, stamina, and agility. It also teaches the ability to keep calm and poised under pressure, thus developing emotional control. This is one of the most valuable contributions to the course since this calmness under pressure can mean the difference between a right or wrong decision to an Air Force officer.

BOXING SKILLS

Stance. A right-handed boxer will have his left foot slightly forward of his right. The feet should be comfortably spread, hip to shoulderwidth apart. The balance should be on the balls of the feet enabling the boxer to move in any direction. The knees will be comfortably flexed. The right hip and shoulder are at a 45° angle to the opponent. In this manner, when the hands are raised the boxer will be looking between his left shoulder and hands at his opponent.

The key to good stance is balance. The body must be balanced with the fighter constantly prepared to take the offensive. He should never be standing on his heels or leaning back, but always on balance, ready to move forward, backward, or to either side, and remain on balance ready to strike, block, or retaliate immediately.

On-guard position. After positioning the body, position the hands. For a right-handed person, the right hand should come up with the thumb close to the right corner of the mouth. The elbow should be pointing directly at the floor and the elbow and forearm should be close to the body. The elbow and forearm of the left should be parallel with the right, the elbow down, and the hand turned with the palm facing to the right. The hands should be open to afford a larger surface area when close to the body and not punching. The chin should be close to the pocket formed in the left shoulder.

Footwork. The boxer should step with his lead foot in the direction he wishes to go and slide the trailing foot into the new "on-balance" position. Using this shuffling or gliding method, he can move "on balance" in any direction. At no time should the feet come close together; neither should they be too far apart.

Left jab. From the basic stance and on-guard position, the left jab is delivered by extending the left hand forward and rotating the palm toward the floor. There should be a straight line from the knuckles to the wrist, to the elbow, to the shoulder. This "power line" should extend back to the anchor point where the right foot touches the floor. This ensures a solid punch with the weight of the fighter being delivered into a small compact area. The left jab should be delivered with as much velocity as possible. It is a fast punch which may hurt an opponent and should occasionally be aimed to the midsection, as well as the head. As the punch is delivered, the chin should automatically drop down into the protected pocket formed by the hollow in the left shoulder, and the right hand should move forward in front of the face for protection.

Defense of left jab
From the basic on-guard position, with the right hand at the corner of the mouth, left hand halfway out, both elbows down, there are several blocks that can be used:

☐ Catch—One of the basic blocks is to catch with the open right hand. Rotate the right hand up and over until the hand is exposed to the opponent's glove which is caught in the palm of the right hand. The right hand should not be extended to make this block. Rather, the fighter should wait until the left lead of his opponent touches his right hand, then the glove can be moved to absorb the shock.

☐ Parry—Another block is to move the right hand to the right as though parrying. By making this slight motion to the right with the open hand facing his chin, the fighter can absorb the shock from a left lead without harm. As in the case of the catch, the hand should not be extended to the punch but rather the punch should be taken, and then the head may roll away from the shock. In both of these basic blocks, the right elbow is down and held close to the body and the movement is primarily with the wrist and forearm.

Straight-right-to-head. Step to the left and forward with the left foot; maintain balance. Drive the right hand "through" the opponent's chin. At the moment of contact, the right arm should be fully extended and level with the shoulder (corkscrew punch, palm down). The principle of a "power line" is as important for the straight right as it is for the jab. The left hand should come back in front of the face for protection and to block the opponent's right-hand counter.

Defenses. Block with palm of left hand. Step back quickly, causing blow to fall short or slip to the side.

One-two combination

The one-two combination is a rapid delivery of first the left and then the right hand. The purpose of the left lead is to make the opening. The purpose of the right is to cross with power to try to put the opponent down. The success of the one-two combination depends upon first scoring with the left hand on the nose and eyes of the opponent, then rapidly replacing the left hand with the right hand. If the jab is delivered correctly, with the elbow down when the punch is started, the arm extended to its full length, with a straight line from the knuckles to the shoulder, into the face—nose or mouth —of the opponent, the fighter is ready to deliver the straight right. In the on-guard position, the right hand is at the corner of the mouth, elbows against the body. From this position, the right hand is delivered with a piston-like motion, letting the right hand rotate slightly so the palm is facing the floor at the point of impact.

Fakes and feints

Fakes and feints are the hallmarks of an expert boxer. A fake or feint is best described as making the opponent think he is going to be hit when he isn't. To execute an effective feint a boxer uses the eyes, body and hands to convince his opponent he's going to be struck. The purpose of the feint is to make an opening for another punch. Feinting creates momentary openings, so combinations must be learned in order to take advantage of the opening created.

Left hook. The left hook is a power punch which requires a pivoting of the fighter's weight for its power. From the on-guard position shift the weight to the left foot with the left elbow up, keeping the left arm bent at a right angle. From this position the weight is pivoted back to the right foot using a twisting motion. The left hand travels parallel to the floor, elbow high, to the opponent. The punch should be of high velocity. As the fighter shifts his weight to his left foot, he is in effect cocking himself. All of his weight and power are delivered in one quick motion. At no time should the fighter's left arm be extended past a 90° position. The elbow should always be high and parallel to the floor, and the punches delivered with high velocity to the point of impact. The right hand is kept in the on-guard position, while delivering the punch, and inside of the left hand, ready to defend any punches delivered by the opponent. The hooking arm never straightens.

Right hook. The right hook is delivered in much the same manner as the left hook, except in the case of the right hook the weight is first shifted to the right foot at which time the right elbow is raised parallel to the floor. The right arm is kept at right angles, and then the weight is pivoted back to the left foot with a twisting motion, striking the opponent. This is a power punch, to be delivered with the same quick motion that makes the left hook a success. A roll of the weight to the right followed by a quick move to the left is most important. Throughout, the right elbow must be high, the right arm must be in a 90° position. The left arm is held in position of on-guard inside of the right. The hooking arm never straightens.

Defense of hooks
Step back quickly. Catch the oncoming blow with the right glove or right forearm. Do not reach out for the hook. Keep elbows and arms as close to the body as possible. Raise arms and hands to the side of the head and step forward (partial cover). Bend slightly at the waist (pivot left) causing blow to pass around the shoulders. Roll with the punch.

Left uppercut. Assume the "on-guard" position. Bend directly to the left and slightly forward until the left elbow is almost touching the hip bone. The left arm is in a half-bent position (90° angle), forearm parallel to the floor, palm up. The right elbow is close to the side, forearm covering the right side of the body and face. Allow the left shoulder and hip to swing forward, shift the weight quickly to the right and carry the left arm to the center line of the body. When the center line of the body is reached, extend the legs and whip the left arm upward in an arc for the solar plexus, hoping to hit the opponent's head as well as his body.

Right uppercut. Assume the "on-guard" position. Bend to the right and slightly forward so that the right elbow is almost touching the hip and the right arm is in the half-bent (90° angle) position, parallel to the floor, palm up. Rotate the body to the left, turning the right hip and shoulder to the center line, then suddenly straighten the body and whip the right hand upward to the solar plexus or chin. The left arm covers the left side of the body and face throughout.

Defense against uppercuts
The most effective defense for an uppercut is merely moving a few inches backward out of range. One may also drop the open glove across the opponent's wrist (shoulder to shoulder).

Infighting. The inside position must be obtained through slipping, weaving, and ducking. Place the forehead on the opponent's breastbone. Force forward with the head, pushing the opponent off balance. Keep driving both hands to the opponent's midsection. Maintain the inside position at all times. Shift with the opponent. If the opponent drops his arms, switch the attack to the head. Use shortarm jolts.

Clinching. Clinching is that which occurs when one or both fighters lead, and momentarily their arms become locked together. However, it is known from experience that clinching is often used in defense. For example, it is common practice for a fighter who has been stunned to clinch or hold his opponent to protect himself from further damage while he clears his head. The best way to clinch is to come from the inside of a man's guard and to place one's hands over his elbows and clamp down with both hands at the point of each elbow. However, a fighter is still required to break and take one step back at the referee's command of "break." It is important also that as the fighter breaks and steps back he keeps his hands up for protection.

7

Club Sports in Colleges and Universities

Jay Arnold, Carl Erickson, Harry Fritz, and Frank Spechalske

Club sports are generally recognized as forerunners of the intercollegiate sports movement in America. As Mueller and Mitchell (1960, pp. 17–18) write:

> Students interested in a particular sport or activity banded together in activity clubs, somewhat in the manner of the sport clubs in English universities. (Indeed, the English influence upon American sports in the early 1860s was so strong that almost all the sports participated in were of English origin. Only gradually were rules of some of the games or sports adapted or changed, or new sports invented such that they took on peculiarly American characteristics.) Later on these student groups began to expend time and energy in developing specialized teams to represent their groups, in colleges, schools, or municipalities, as the case happened to be. This, then, was the beginning of a varsity-like program.

Club sports have also had a profound influence on the intramural sports movement in this country.

During the past decade, many weaknesses and deficiencies in varsity athletic programs, plus increasing student demands for participation in the decision-making process at the collegiate and even the secondary levels, have led to a revival of club sports. Increased sport opportunities, improved physical education programs, greater awareness resulting from television, and increased mobility have made students much more interested in doing their own thing. Wise administrators and leaders see great benefits in this renaissance, and they seek to avoid some of the problems that appeared in the earlier club movements. (Various institutions gradually shifted control of early athletics programs from the students to the faculty and administration because of the need for care and prevention of football injuries.) These are among the concerns that must be considered in a well-planned club sports program.

*   Reprinted by permission of *JOPER* **46,** (8), (October 1975), pp. 19–22.

Varsity competition in athletics by civilized people attempts to satisfy competitive urges in a socially acceptable manner. But varsity athletics programs may drive potential participants away from activity by failing to fulfill other basic human needs. The emphasis on winning in sports often deprives participants of other important personal benefits—simple enjoyment of the sport, development of team spirit, and other physical, social, and emotional benefits.

Varsity sports often fail to provide personal benefits for a variety of reasons. *Enjoyment* is not always achieved at the varsity level because of overemphasis on winning, leading to overly long practice sessions. Restrictions which allow students to play only one varsity sport may also cause boredom. *Physical fitness* is often approached from a punishment, or highly specific, point of view rather than positively, with humanistic and self-actualization goals. Many varsity-level programs may not be oriented toward lifetime sports. *Self-discipline* may be replaced by the coaches' disciplinarianism approach. Modern practices in intercollegiate athletics, e.g., padding schedules and violating recruiting eligibility and playing rules are frequently antithetical to the *development of sportsmanship.*

In addition, students have developed strong interest in such ecologically oriented activities as cycling, packpacking, and kayaking. Generally, only the club sports program provides students an organized means for learning about and participating in such activities. Properly organized club sports and intramural programs provide potential settings for achieving the previously mentioned values.

Offering students the opportunity to take part in intercollegiate competition is a major goal for club sports programs. Club sport teams attract a variety of students—those whose skills are not of varsity caliber, students who don't want to devote the time and energy demanded by modern varsity sports, those who prefer a more relaxed approach to competition, ones interested in a sport for which there is not a varsity team, and students who for academic or other reasons cannot conform to varsity intercollegiate regulations (chiefly, graduate, professional, and part-time students and staff). Judicious guidance of interested students, long-range planning, and an efficient program will hasten the day we achieve the goal of sports participation for all who want it.

OPERATIONAL GUIDELINES

State and local regulations delegate to the schools and/or their agents responsibility for preventing unsafe practices and conditions. Athletic competition at the club sports level may be as ferocious, as intense, and as potentially dangerous and frustrating as competition at the varsity level. Though many club sports teams want as little formalized structure as possible, guidelines and safeguards are needed to protect the safety of the participants, the spectators, and the reputation of the institution. When guidelines for club sports competitions are established, the welfare of the individual must be a primary consideration.

CRITERIA FOR ADMINISTRATORS

In club sports groups of people gather to engage in competitive physical activity. Success in a club sport may depend upon physical prowess and athletic skill. Frequently, the varsity intercollegiate competition format is employed in the club sports program. Therefore, club sports should be housed in the physical education, intramural, and/or intercollegiate athletic unit. The chief administrative officer of the club sports program should be the administrative officer of the department of physical education, intramurals, or intercollegiate athletics because:

☐ Professional preparation to handle the club sports program should include a bachelor's and/or master's degree with an academic emphasis in physical education or recreation and in administration.

☐ Campus sport and recreation facilities and equipment should be under the administrator's supervision.

☐ The administrator should be responsible for the organized, structured, and scheduled athletic contests for the student body of the club sports program.

☐ The administrator should have a broad background in sports and other related athletic activities.

☐ The specialist should be knowledgeable in appropriate areas of responsibility, including the place of athletics in education; sponsorship of clubs; financing; eligibility; facilities, equipment, and instruction; rules for participation; intercollegiate competition; priorities regarding use of facilities; scheduling of games; first aid and emergency care; prevention and care of athletic injuries; selection, assignment, and evaluation of coaches; legal liability for the institution and participants; insurance coverage for participants; travel, meals, and lodging for participants; public relations; assignment of staff.

Within the unit, either a professional physical educator, recreation professional, or sports administrator should be designated director of the club sports program. The director should work cooperatively with the college or university administration, coaches, and the student affairs unit. The rationale:

☐ Participants on the club sports teams participate in vigorous physical activity. There should be adequate health and medical safeguards and insurance coverage.

☐ A physical education or recreation professional should have the expertise to provide the necessary instruction, organization, and leadership abilities to supervise the club sports programs.

☐ Other personnel working directly with club sports programs should be professionally prepared in the area of physical education and recreation.

The club sports program should be appropriately supported financially from general university funds, student fees, club sports dues, and/or gate receipts. The director of physical education, intramurals, and/or athletics should be the budgeting officer because of expertise.

Each club sport should have an advisor who is either a full-time staff member or a qualified graduate assistant (not necessarily a physical educator). The ability to participate in the decision-making process without domination is one of the most important traits that should be sought in this individual. The advisor must be acceptable to the membership of the club sport and preferably should be chosen by that group.

ORGANIZATION OF THE CLUB SPORTS PROGRAM

The following procedures are suggested as guidelines for organizing the club sports program and providing a framework within which it should function. The department should determine load compensation for the advisors. Commercially sponsored club sports teams should be subject to all applicable institutional and program operating regulations.

A club sports advisory council should be established as an advisor to the administrator of the club sports program. Its functions should include:

☐ Recommending club sports policies.

☐ Serving as the liaison between the club sports program and the director.

☐ Recommending scheduling policies and approving schedules submitted by the program director.

☐ Recommending budgetary procedures and approving budgets submitted by the program director.

☐ Evaluating the club sports program.

☐ Recommending regulations and operating procedures pertaining to all club sports.

☐ Recommending and approving new club sports and new club sports programs.

The club sports advisory council should be representative of the campus community. The membership should be elected or selected from the following groups: club sports representatives, student athletic board, student government association, student affairs, student fees board, intramural governing board, class presidents or other class officers, and faculty athletic committee or other faculty committees.

Generally, eligibility to participate in club sports should be open to all undergraduate and graduate students, faculty, and staff. However, because club competition in certain sports may be chiefly with varsity teams, participation in these activities may have to be restricted to eligible full-time undergraduates. Specific scholastic requirements are not recommended; academic stipulations are imposed only when certain club sports participate basically with varsity teams from other institutions, or when institutional requirements govern the eligibility of such participation. In some situations, basic funding for club sports is derived from general undergraduate fees, which implies that faculty, staff, and graduate students may not be eligible unless they pay an appropriate fee. Subject to institutional regulations, the approval of the club sports advisory council, and the program director, each club sport would recommend its eligibility requirements for membership and/or participation. Additional participation requirements may pertain to special safety or skill requirements of the activity. For example, a basic swimming skills test might be a requirement for an aquatics-oriented club. On occasion, and within prescribed parameters, noncollege personnel may be permitted to participate in certain collegiate-based club sports.

In some instances, club sports provide a short-term steppingstone to varsity status. This is particularly true in sports in which the competition is predominantly varsity in nature, and this evolution may be encouraged for such sports. It should be understood, however, that participants in many club sports prefer the less structured atmosphere of club sports, as contrasted with the more formal varsity approach, and aspire only to provide expanded competitive opportunities for interested student participants.

In many situations, it is suggested that the attainment of varsity status for a sport follow a procedure determined by the varsity intercollegiate athletic unit. It may be appropriate and desirable to have the club sports advisory council work cooperatively with other affected units or administrators to expedite the transition from a club sport to a varsity sport. Among the considerations basic to changing status from a club sport to a varsity sport are:

☐ Demonstrated stability and continuity of the club sport over several seasons.

☐ Willingness of the participants of the club sport to adhere to eligibility standards required by regulating bodies controlling varsity programs.

☐ Geographic availability of competition that is basically varsity in nature.

☐ Adequate eligible undergraduate membership to ensure continued interest.

☐ Availability of professional coaching staff.

☐ Committed available funding to support varsity-level program.

☐ Official varsity designation by appropriate college or university officials, such as the athletic council and the director of intercollegiate athletics.

☐ Adequate facilities for the sport to function at the varsity level.

ADMINISTRATIVE PROCEDURES

How should a club sports program be managed as far as funding, legal liability, eligibility, scheduling, and other related administrative procedures?

Funding is a major consideration in both the planning and the operation of any club sports program. Ideally, the money for travel, equipment, insurance, and other related expenses should come from the general funds and/or student fees, dues, and gate receipts. However, in many institutions, because of the philosophy of the administration or state regulations governing the expenditure of tax revenues, monies from the general fund may not be used. Other means of funding may include a variety of fund-raising activities. Fees may be established to cover the use of lockers, equipment, and facilities. While these means of funding club sports programs are not ideal, they do make possible a highly worthwhile program. Student involvement in the financing process may broaden the educational experience and help students feel they have a vested interest in the program.

A program is only as strong as its leadership. The previously mentioned competencies desirable for club sports administrators and sponsors would be possessed only by highly trained individuals. Some club sport coaches may be full-time faculty; others may be graduate assistants or possess expertise and interest in a desired area. Compensation for individual services to the program—release time, stipend, salary, or recognition for voluntary service—should be available. Guidelines for compensating personnel should be the same as those for related kinds of activities, such as club sponsorship, band direction, varsity coaching, and theatrical direction.

Most athletic programs are constantly striving to overcome problems related to inadequate facilities. This lack of facilities causes some administrators not to be receptive to club sports. Increasing the scope of the athletic program to include club sports provides a strong justification for increasing and improving existing facilities. Additional student involvement resulting from this approach should appreciably improve student support for the club sports and athletic program, thereby adding a potentially powerful lobby to assist in acquiring funding for additional facilities.

As the club sports program develops at an institution, the number of different clubs and the number of participants may continually increase. Program funding, coaching compensation, and other related areas need to be coordinated between clubs as this occurs. It is recommended that the director of the club sports program serve as the budget coordinator to provide efficiency of supervision and administration for the total program. The program director can supply valuable expertise to the various clubs and relieve them of certain financial administrative duties and responsibilities for which their members and sponsors may have little skill or knowledge.

An institution sponsoring a club sport assumes a degree of responsibility and, therefore, legal liability. The same procedures and policies designed to protect participants in school programs should be followed for club sports. These should include:

☐ Insurance for all participants, including appropriate coverage for athletic injuries and any other illness or injury related to participation in the program. A combination insurance package comprised of faculty/student/family and college or university required or provided insurance is acceptable.

☐ Annual medical examinations for participants in contact and vigorous activities designated by the institution.

☐ Regulations guaranteeing that a participant has experienced a sufficient amount of preseason practice time to assure a sufficient level of physical conditioning and skill acquisition to make participation reasonably safe. The guidelines for varsity programs for each individual sport should be consulted in establishing these regulations.

☐ A planned and supervised program for the care and prevention of athletic injuries. Included within this program should be a provision for a qualified person to be available or on call during all games or contests. Provision should also be made for adequate emergency transportation.

☐ Regulations detailing approved emergency care and procedures for treatment of those injured while participating in club sports. A planned method for reporting all such injuries should also be included.

☐ Established policies governing procedures to be followed when traveling, making overnight stops, etc. These should include such considerations as types of vehicles to be used, who can drive them, age of driver, how many riders per vehicle, who is allowed to travel, how much distance can be traveled in a day, hours of travel, conduct while traveling, insurance required, and type of supervision required.

☐ Regulations detailing appropriate equipment for each activity.

☐ Parental permission or other appropriate waiver forms for participation, when applicable.

☐ Facilities that are safe and that by their nature do not create any undue hazard for the participant.

Whether legal liability rests with the institution, with the sponsor, or with a combination of the two depends upon the laws of a particular state. Adherence to the above recommendations will go a long way toward eliminating suits due to negligence. Negligence has generally been defined as "failure to act as a reasonably prudent individual would under the prevailing circumstances." It is the negligence consideration that strongly suggests the need for a tighter structuring of the club sports program and direct institutional management.

SCHEDULING THE PROGRAM

A final important concern centers around the scheduling of the club sports program, including the necessity for coordinating indoor and outdoor athletic facilities with the athletic, intramural, physical education, and recreation programs. The limitations, if any, on the number of contests to be scheduled, and such matters as the distances to be traveled, should be the responsibilities of the club sports director.

Few colleges and universities have sufficient space and facilities to handle all of the needs of regularly scheduled physical education classes, intramurals, varsity athletic teams, and the club sports program. It is imperative, therefore, that all facilities receive optimal use. This can be best achieved by having a coordinator for scheduling facilities who is responsible only to the administrator of the unit. It is highly recommended that a standard procedure be initiated by which all interested groups are allowed to apply for the opportunity to use the facilities appropriate to their activity. The coordinator of scheduling must establish priorities for use, based on circumstances at the particular institution. Club sports should be included in these priorities. Optimal efficiency of use implies the scheduling of an appropriate activity in every facility at every hour, allowing for cleaning and maintenance requirements. Consideration should be given to hours during which facilities are not normally used. Bowling boomed during World War II because proprietors recognized the need for recreation for workers on the swing shift from 4:00 p.m. to midnight. Morning bowling leagues were also developed for use by those who worked from midnight to 8:00 a.m. Colleges have extended the use of their facilities throughout the evening and weekends. In the future, schools may find it necessary to schedule activities all night to meet student needs and to achieve maximum use of limited facilities.

When it becomes apparent that existing facilities will not accommodate the program, the wise administrator works toward expanding the facilities. The effort to acquire new facilities must be coordinated with all facility users participating. Individual groups such as the athletic department, the physical education department, the intramural department, or the recreation department that try to secure facilities for themselves frequently fail because individual user groups do not swing enough weight. If, however, all groups coordinate their efforts to acquire facilities, success is possible. The chief administrator, who coordinates the facilities and represents all the units using them, is the logical person to organize a concerted effort to acquire additional facilities. This person should be the most knowledgeable as to the facility needs of various units.

Rules and regulations governing class attendance and distances to be traveled by participants or club sports teams should be established and must be consistent with institutional regulations for students participating in other extracurricular activities.

It is hoped that all institutions will realize the tremendous potential club sports have for increasing the number of students involved in a dynamic competitive program. Once an institution makes this commitment to its students, it is strongly recommended that all policies and procedures governing its club sports program be published in a handbook that is readily accessible to all members of both the student body and the faculty.

REFERENCE

Mueller, P., and E. D. Mitchell 1960. *Intramural sports.* New York: Ronald.

8
Cricket

K. J. Fisher

INTRODUCTION

To any foreign visitor to the United Kingdom or Commonwealth countries, newspaper headlines carrying words such as "England in Trouble," "West Indies in Run Riot," or "Australia Slump" may be very misleading. They do not refer to geographical or sociopolitical disturbances, but to the situation in the current international cricket match between the national team and the visitors.

As the most English of all English games, cricket has a peculiar appeal to the British which fascinates and infuriates strangers and followers alike. From scattered origins it has evolved to a modern game uniquely combining athleticism, strategy, and skill.

Although firmly rooted in Britain, Australia, South Africa, the West Indies, New Zealand, India, and Pakistan, it is played in a score of other countries including the United States. Although the laws of the game are still the responsibility of the Marylebone Cricket Club (better known as the MCC) in London, each country has established its own administrative body or board of control.

In this article it is not the writer's intention to give a detailed technical analysis of cricket but merely to provide some explanation of some of the game's unfamiliar aspects. With this in mind this chapter is divided into sections as follows:

☐ Historical background

☐ Mode of play

☐ Laws of cricket

☐ Terminology

☐ Methods of instruction

☐ Clothing and equipment

☐ Recent trends and developments

HISTORY AND DEVELOPMENT

Although there were many games played in early times which bore some resemblance to cricket, the first written evidence that cricket was popular has been traced to the first quarter of the seventeenth century (Bowen 1970, p. 28). The word cricket was most probably derived from the word "creag" or "creaget," which was an old Celtic game. In support of this claim Bradman points out that "creag" is very close to the Saxon "cricce" or "cric" which was a crooked stick. Cricket bats were curved in shape well into the 18th century. (Bradman 1958, p. 226.)

Despite regal opposition to sports and games, cricket grew in popularity in the British Isles through the 17th century. In fact, games, sports, and pastimes were so indigenous to British culture that it would have taken much more than royal decree to dampen the enthusiasm of the people for their recreation. On the Continent, however, cricket did not become popular ". . . because the social and legal reasons did not exist there to give it tacit or overt encouragement" (Bowen 1970, p. 39).

The 18th century saw rapid growth of the game. This was due almost entirely to the patronage of noblemen, innkeepers, and brewers, who arranged games and cricket competitions between towns and villages. Betting was rife. There seems little doubt that betting on matches was the factor which contributed most to the need for the establishment of a set of rules or code of ethics. The first known such rules of cricket date from 1744 and the administrative body established to supervise these laws was founded some 30 years later in 1774. This body is still responsible for any changes in the laws today and is the famous Marylebone Cricket Club, or simply MCC.

The game spread to other countries owing to the influence of three factors:

☐ by colonization—immigrants and free settlers imported their social habits and customs.

☐ military presence—cricket provided ideal recreation for troops and sailors far from home.

☐ tours by representative teams—teams consisting of great players of the time played exhibition and challenge matches against local teams. This was the forerunner of modern Test Cricket equivalent to World Series Baseball.

Prior to 1835 all bowling was underarm and, although the 1835 laws permitted a round arm delivery, it was not until 1864 that the modern over-arm form of bowling became legalized. This is possibly the greatest single change in the development of cricket for, as Bradman (1958, p. 229) points out, "modern cricket without overarm bowling cannot be imagined."

MODE OF PLAY

The game is played on a grass pitch between two teams of eleven players, one captain having been appointed for each team.

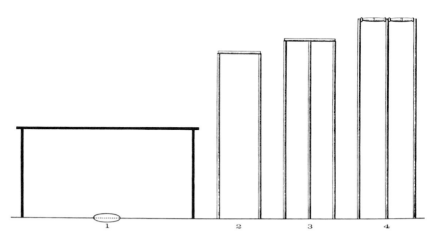

Fig. 8.1 Diagram of wickets. Wicket 1, with the hole in the center, was 2′ wide and 1′ high. It is not known exactly when wicket 2 displaced the primitive size with its more elegant proportions of 6″ × 22″. Nor is it quite certain when wicket 3 made its first appearance with an increase of 2″ in height and 1″ in breadth. Wicket 4 is the present day wicket. From C. Box 1877, *The English Game of Cricket,* London: The Field Office, p. 382.

The object of the game is to bowl out your opponents for fewer runs than your own team score. Games (or matches) may comprise one innings (the word is both singular and plural) each or a maximum of two innings for each team. Unlike baseball, ten of the eleven players must be dismissed before an innings is concluded. (As batsmen bat in pairs, one batsman will always be left "not out.")

Prior to the commencement of the game both captains toss a coin to decide which team will bat or take the field. The toss normally takes place in the center of the playing area, near the actual pitch. The fielding teams come out on to the field first, take up their positions as designated by the captain and await the entry of the first two batsmen (often called "opening batsmen" because they are opening the innings).

In most cases the "opening" bowlers of the fielding team are fast bowlers. The fields set out by a captain for fast bowlers are somewhat different from those set for slower or spin bowlers. (This is unlike the fielders in baseball who for the most part have set positions.)

Both batsmen attempt to score runs when, after striking the ball, they each make good their ground behind the popping crease (or batting crease).

If a batsman hits the ball so that it crosses over the boundary line, four runs are scored; but if the boundary line is cleared by the ball, six runs are scored. A batsman is not compelled to hit or strike at every ball. He may attempt runs even when he does not hit the ball. Furthermore, when he does hit the ball, he isn't compelled to run.

When one bowler finishes his 6- or 8-ball over, another bowler resumes from the other end of the pitch. If a bowler bowls a ball so wide or so high that the batsman cannot reach it, the umpire calls "wide" and gives the appropriate signal (Fig. 8.3). Similarly the umpires will call and signal "no-ball" if they consider that the bowler has delivered the ball with an unacceptable action or has contravened the front foot law in his delivery stride (Fig. 8.3).

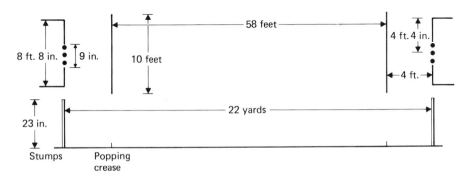

Fig. 8.2. The dimensions of a cricket pitch (that area between the two sets of stump is more commonly called *The Wicket*).

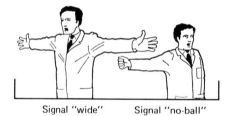

Signal "wide"   Signal "no-ball"

Fig. 8.3 Officials' signals for "wide" and "no ball."

The only ways that a batsman can be out off a "no-ball" are run out, handled the ball, obstructed the field, and hit the ball twice.

The captain of the fielding side may decide to use only two bowlers, but most commonly four or five bowlers are needed to dismiss the batting team, sometimes more. When the fielding side has dismissed ten batsmen (one always remains "not out"), the batting side is *all out*. The batting side now takes the field and vice versa.

Declarations

If the captain of the batting team feels that his team has made enough runs and/or he wants more time to bowl at his opponents (the pitch may be awkward for batting!) then he may *declare* his innings closed. This he does by summoning his two current batsmen from the field.

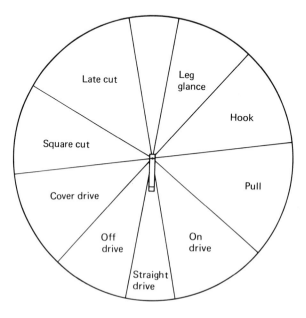

Fig. 8.4 Titles and directions of batting strokes for right-handed batsmen.

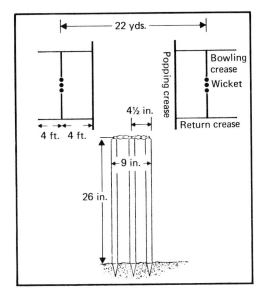

Fig. 8.5 The pitch and the wicket.

THE LAWS OF CRICKET

The Pitch and Playing Area

The pitch is normally situated near the centre of the playing field and is marked out as shown in Fig. 8.4. The boundaries are normally indicated by a line, rope or picket fence and are situated about 75 yards from the pitch on

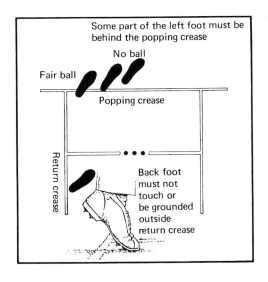

Fig. 8.6 The "no ball" rule.

either side of the wickets. This sometimes varies with the size of the ground. In England many small grounds restrict the length of the boundaries.

The batsman. The batsman may ask for a guard from the umpire and will be given necessary information regarding the bowler and his arm action.

A batsman shall play the ball with his bat, in order:

- ☐ to score runs or
- ☐ to defend his wicket.

He can be given out in the following ways:

- ☐ bowled (Law 34)
- ☐ caught (Law 35)
- ☐ stumped (Law 42)
- ☐ run out (Law 41)
- ☐ LBW (Law 39)
- ☐ hit wicket (Law 38)
- ☐ obstruction (Law 40), i.e., deliberately preventing a fielder from catching the ball.
- ☐ handled ball (Law 36)
- ☐ hit the ball twice (except for the sole purpose of guarding his wicket) (Law 37)

A batsman may retire at any time, and only return with the consent of the opposing captain, and then only on the fall of a wicket. An injured batsman may have a runner.

Fig. 8.7 The author batting in a club cricket game. Courtesy of K. John Fisher.

Runs awarded to the batsman are made from the bat, which includes the hands holding the bat, i.e., batting gloves. Runs made in other ways are known as byes, leg byes, no balls, and wides.

A batsman must be within his popping crease when the ball is in play in order to safeguard his innings, i.e., when the ball is in play and his wicket is "broken" while he is outside his popping crease, he will be given out. Any part of the batsman's person or his bat is sufficient to be given "not out," providing that part is within the popping (i.e., batting) crease.

The batsman is allowed to defend his wicket with any part of his person except his hands, providing he has hit the ball with his bat first. (Otherwise the LBW Law may apply.)

If a batsman is injured, he can ask for one of his own team to act as a "runner," who will then act for the batsman other than the actual playing of the ball.

The bowler. A bowler shall bowl an "over" of 6 or 8 balls from one end, after which another player of his team shall bowl an over of similar number of balls from the opposite end. (Overs of either 6 or 8 balls are bowled according to the agreed conditions of play—in Great Britain it is 6 balls per over.)

The bowler *must* indicate whether he intends to bowl over or round the wicket, and which arm he shall use.

Balls bowled as a "wide" (Law 28) or a "no ball" (Law 26) do not count towards an over of 6 balls, but each add one run to the opponent's score.

A bowler must complete an over unless injured or suspended for unfair play. He cannot bowl two overs consecutively in one innings.

A delivery is fair only if the ball is bowled, not thrown or jerked.

If a "no ball" is called, either (a) for bowling from outside the return crease or from placing the front foot over the popping crease, or (b) from throwing or changing mode of delivery, one run is added to the opponent's score, only if no other runs are scored from it.

A throw is deemed if the bowler's arm, being bent just prior to the delivery, is straightened on delivery.

The bowler may run out the nonstriker for "backing up" too far, and if in doing so, he throws the ball at the wicket, it shall not be deemed a "no ball" unless overthrows result.

The bowler may also attempt to run out the striker, if he is "coming down the wicket," in which case a "no ball" is called.

The ball is considered dead (Law 25) when, in the opinion of the umpire, it is finally settled in the hands of the bowler. The ball ceases to be dead on the bowler starting his run or bowling action.

The bowler bowls a wide if, in the opinion of the umpire, the ball passes out of reach of the striker and would not have been within his reach when taking guard in the normal position.

The fielder. Law 44. The fielder's task is to prevent runs from being scored, by stopping the ball when struck, with any part of his person. If he willfully stops it otherwise, e.g., with his cap or sweater, five runs shall be added to the run or runs already made.

The fielder may attempt to "run out" a batsman at any time other than when the ball is dead.

The fielder can catch the ball when struck by a batsman, in which case the batsman is deemed caught. The catcher must be inside the field of play at the time he makes the catch.

The substitute. A team consists of eleven players on the field of play. A substitute can replace an injured player but only in order to field.

The wicketkeeper. Law 43. The wicketkeeper must not interfere with the batsman in any way. He must remain behind the wicket until the ball either has been played by the striker, or has passed the wicket.

If the wicketkeeper takes the ball in front of the wicket (the batsman having not played it), no stumping may be given.

The wicketkeeper "stumps" a batsman by taking the ball behind the stumps, and then removing the bails or bail, providing the batsman is outside the return or popping crease.

The wicketkeeper can stump the batsman if the ball is not gathered, but rebounds off his person—equally he can throw down the wicket.

The umpires. Laws, 45, 46, and 47. The umpires should ensure that the wickets are properly pitched, and which watch or clock is to be followed (Law 45).

Fig. 8.8 Wicketkeeping stance.

They are the sole judges of fair play, and the final judges of the fitness of the ground, the weather, and the light for play in the event of the decision being left to them. The umpires shall change ends after each side has had one innings.

The umpires should stand where they can best observe the play, and see the actual events of each ball and action in play. The umpire standing normally behind the wicket gives the batsman his guard.

The umpires shall not order a batsman out unless appealed to by the other side which shall be done prior to the delivery of the next ball and before time is called (Law 18). An "appeal" to the umpire is really a question: "How was that?"

The umpire at the bowler's wicket shall answer the following appeals:

- ☐ when a batsman is bowled
- ☐ when a batsman is caught
- ☐ when a batsman is LBW
- ☐ when a batsman is run out at the bowler's end
- ☐ when a batsman is guilty of obstruction
- ☐ when a batsman handles the ball
- ☐ when a batsman hits the ball twice

Signal boundary "four"   Signal boundary "six"

Signal "one short"   Signal "out"   Signal "leg-bye"   Signal "bye"

Fig. 8.9 Officials' signals.

The umpire at the striker's end answers the following appeals:

- ☐ when a batsman is stumped
- ☐ when a batsman hits his own wicket
- ☐ when a batsman is run out at the striker's end
- ☐ when a batsman takes a "short-run" between wickets

In any case in which an umpire is unable to give a decision, he shall appeal to the other umpire whose decision shall be final.

The umpire signals "out" by raising the index finger above his head. If the batsman is not out, the umpire calls "not out."

An umpire may alter his decision, if he does it promptly. The umpire also:

- ☐ Counts the number of balls played in an over
- ☐ Calls and signals "no balls," wides, short runs at his end
- ☐ Signals boundaries, byes, and leg-byes

The LBW Law (Law 39). Because this law is the most controversial in the game, a proper understanding of it is essential. The initials LBW stand for "leg before wicket" and, as it implies, the batsman's leg has (unfairly) prevented the ball from hitting the wicket. In fact, *any* part of the batsman's body is considered to be his leg regarding this law, except the hand holding the bat.

Before giving a batsman "out" LBW, the umpire must be able to answer (with certainty) yes to three questions.

1. Did the ball pitch straight, or on the *off* side of the wicket?
2. Would the ball have hit the wicket if the batsman had not stopped it with any part of his legs or body, except his hand? and
3. Was the part that was hit, *when* it was hit, in line between the two wickets?

If the answer to any of these questions is no, the decision is "not out."

TERMINOLOGY

The terms associated with cricket have become part of the game's tradition. They may refer to peculiarities such as the playing surface, a type of ball delivered by a bowler, or the position of a batsman in the batting lineup. The extent of cricket terminology is so wide and varies so from one cricket-playing nation to another that it is impossible to include them all here. On the next page are some of the best-known terms categorized for easy reference.

Terms Related to the Laws of Cricket

LBW Leg before wicket. Occurs when any part of batsman's body prevents a ball from hitting the wicket.

No ball An illegal delivery by the bowler, a throw.

Wicketkeeper Equivalent to the catcher in baseball, he stands behind the stumps.

Terms Related to Dismissing a Batsman

Run out Stumped, but in open play and by any fielder after the batsman has hit the ball.

Snicked or edged When the ball lightly touches the edge of the bat.

Stumped A batsman is stumped by a wicketkeeper breaking the wickets with ball in hand when the batsman is out of his ground. The batsman in this case has missed the ball.

Yorked A batsman is yorked when the ball passes under the bottom edge of his bat.

Terms Related to Bowling a Cricket Ball

Beamer A head-high ball, quite dangerous and unsettling for a batsman.

Bouncer or bumper A short-pitched fastball aimed to intimidate the batsman.

Full toss A ball which reaches the batsman without bouncing (normally easy to hit and score runs from).

Inswinger A ball which curves in toward the batsman.

Leg break Spin imparted to a ball so that on pitching the ball runs counter-clockwise (or from leg-side to off-side).

Long hop A short-pitched ball, slow and very easy to hit.

Off break Spin imparted to a ball so that on pitching the ball turns clockwise (i.e., from the off-side to the leg-side).

Outswinger A ball which swings or curves in the air away from the batsman.
Wrong 'un, googly, or bosie An off-break bowled with a leg break action.

Yorker A ball so directed that it passes *under* the (swinging) bat.

Other Common Terms

All-rounder A player equally good at batting and bowling (often fielding as well).

Collapse A sudden fall of wickets seriously affecting the batting side.

Dolly An easy catch.

Duck A score of zero.

Hat-trick A rare feat in which a bowler captures three wickets with consecutive balls.

Rabbits Normally the last ones in the batting lineup, almost always a bowler.

Shooter A ball which skids through after pitching.

Sticky wicket A drying wicket which causes the ball to bounce and turn awkwardly for the batsmen.

Stonewalling Batting, the sole aim of which is defensive.

Tail or tail-enders The last few batsmen in the order.

METHODS OF INSTRUCTION

In general coaches and instructors agree that the three main "departments" in cricket are batting, bowling, and fielding.

As far as batting and bowling are concerned much the best form of instruction is carried out in "nets." These are special practice cricket pitches, which are surrounded, except for the bowler's end, by netting which will catch the balls that the batsmen hit or miss. Net practice affords a teacher or coach the opportunity to be at close quarters with batsmen and bowlers, to observe faults, to correct technique and so on.

To teach the basic principles of cricket at an early age, group coaching has proved to be the most effective. Group coaching merely refers to constant practice in a group situation. By using the whole-part-whole method, instructors attempt to "groove" a physical movement. In most cases the instructor demonstrates the action and the class or group complete a number of repetitions. Group coaching provides only the *basis* for all cricket instruction: it is only when augmented by net practice that it becomes really meaningful.

Fielding in cricket, as in baseball, involves catching, running, ground fielding, and throwing. With the exception of the wicketkeeper, however, no fielder is permitted to wear gloves or any other similar implement in the field.

Practice*

Practice is usually conducted by the coach, teacher or captain, and when possible, should be made enjoyable.

---

* This section is condensed from MCC coaching books.

Close to the wicket fielders. Fielders in these positions (see Fig. 8.9) need quick reactions, reflexes and "safe" hands. A slip "cradle" or plastic net can be used, but much the best practice is directly off the bat. This demands accurate full-pitched throwing to a batsman who skillfully steers or edges the ball to the waiting fielders.

Moving fielders. Fielders further away from the bat should always move in as the bowler is running up to bowl in a match. In practice sessions, much attention is given to ground fielding, running and catching from different ranges, and throwing returns in to the wicketkeeper.

Wicketkeeping. The wicketkeeper is often the focus of a team's fielding as any hits made by the batsmen are normally returned to the wicketkeeper. He stands either right up to the stumps or well back according to the pace of the bowler and the type of pitch.

Wicketkeepers can practice by getting bowlers to bowl at a set of stumps, gradually increasing pace, introducing spin or swerve and so on. However,

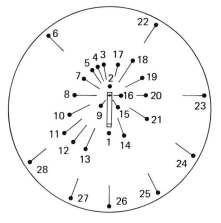

Fig. 8.10 Diagram showing the various fielding positions for right-handed batsmen.

1. Bowler
2. Wicketkeeper
3. First slip
4. Second slip
5. Third slip
6. Third man
7. Gully
8. Point
9. Short mid-off or silly point
10. Cover
11. Extra cover
12. Second extra cover or extra mid-off
13. Mid-off
14. Mid-on
15. Forward short leg or silly mid-on or silly leg
16. Short leg
17. Leg slip
18. Short fine leg
19. Backward square leg
20. Square leg
21. Midwicket
22. Deep fine leg
23. Deep square leg
24. Deep midfield or extra long-on
25. Long-on
26. Straight hit
27. Long-off
28. Deep extra cover or long-off.

wicketkeepers (as with all cricketers!) will receive their best practice during an actual game since there is no real substitute for match conditions.

CLOTHING AND EQUIPMENT

For batsmen. In order to play certain shots in cricket it is essential to get behind the line of the ball, so it is not surprising that batsmen are allowed to wear certain protective equipment. The amount and type of protective equipment have grown rapidly in the 1970s due to the increasing incidence of short-pitched fast bowling. As former international cricketer, Trevor Bailey (1975, p. 23), points out, protective gear for batsmen is not obligatory, but became necessary over the years as bowling became faster and overarm.

Standard batting equipment includes pads or leg-guards, batting gloves (which have protective padding for the fingers and thumbs), a thigh pad and an abdominal protector or box which protects the genital area.

For bowlers. There is no protective or special gear for bowlers, or fieldsmen, with the possible exception of a steel-reinforced toe on the boots of "fastish" bowlers. This prevents their boots wearing out too quickly from the "drag" evidenced in many fast bowlers' delivery stride.

For wicketkeepers. In addition to leg-guards and abdominal protector, wicketkeepers wear special gloves or gauntlets. Inside the gloves, the wicketkeepers also wear inner gloves made from chamois leather.

General. The bat consists of a cane handle (often reinforced with rubber splices to minimize jarring), which is fitted into a V formed by the actual blade of the bat. Most bats are made from selected English willow, and are given a light coating of linseed oil or special bat oil to preserve them. The size of the bat varies, but a full size one stands about 35 inches long and weighs about 2 lb, 4 ozs (Bradman 1958, p. 9).

Fig. 8.11 The stance: as seen by the bowler.

Fig. 8.12 The stance: feet comfortably apart and parallel with crease; left shoulder pointing down the wicket and eyes looking squarely at the ball.

Fig. 8.13 The forward stroke: head and eyes full on the line of the ball, left shoulder, arm, and hand in control, presenting full face of the bat: left knee slightly bent to 'shut the gate'.

Fig. 8.14 The forward stroke: the batsman has made full use of his reach: bat meets ball just in front of the left foot and virtually below the eyes

107

Fig. 8.15 Basic bowling action.

Cricket balls vary in composition from compressed cork, molded plastic and rubberized composition to the more common red leather ball with a seam of six stitches. Whatever the composition, the Laws are quite clear about its weight and circumference. Law 5 reads:

> The ball shall weigh not less than 5 1/2 ounces, nor more than 5 3/4 ounces. It shall measure not less than 8 13/16 inches, nor more than 9 inches in circumference.

RECENT TRENDS AND DEVELOPMENTS

The 1970s have witnessed a newfound interest in cricket, especially in Britain, where dwindling attendances at County Cricket matches were threatening the game with financial ruin. This reawakening of interest resulting in partisan following and vociferous spectator support has been almost entirely due to the introduction of "limited overs cricket."

This differs from the normal country game (which is scheduled to last for 3 days with no certainty of a result) in that both sides bat for a set number of overs (45 or 60 six-ball overs). The team scoring the most number of runs at the end of the overs limitation is the winner.

There are prizes and awards for big hitters "man of the match" and awards for bowlers who get four or more wickets in a game. The first World Cup held in England in June 1975 on the limited-overs basis was a great success. The West Indies players emerged the victors.

Betting and gambling, for decades banned from being associated with cricket, has now returned with a vengeance. On most county grounds licensed betting offices will take any bet one would care to offer!

The presence of the world's fastest bowlers in the current Australian and West Indies national teams has prompted the England captain to consider wearing a protective hat or helmet for batting, similar to those used by baseball players in North America. If the helmet were adopted, it would be some departure from the rather feeble felt cap in current use.

DEFINITION OF CRICKET

Concerning the definition of cricket, Sir Frederick Toone wrote:

It is a science, the study of a lifetime, in which you may exhaust yourself, but never your subject. It is a contest, a duel or melee, calling for courage, skill, strategy and self-control.

It is a contest of temper, a trial of honour, a revealer of character. It affords a chance to play the man and act the gentleman. It means going into God's out-of-doors, getting close to nature, fresh air, exercise, a sweeping away of mental cobwebs, genuine recreation of tired tissues. It is a cure for care, an antidote to worry. It includes companionship with friends, social intercourse, opportunities for courtesy, kindliness and generosity to an opponent. It promotes not only physical health, but mental force.

REFERENCES

General

Bailey, T. 1975. The human target. *Daily Telegraph Magazine* **551,** June 20.

Bowen, R. 1970. *Cricket: a history of its growth and development throughout the world.* London: Eyre and Spottiswoode.

Bradman, D. G. 1958. *The art of cricket.* London: Hodder & Stoughton.

McCool, C. 1961. *The best way to play cricket.* England: Taylor Garnett Evans, Hertfordshire.

MCC cricket coaching book 1972. London: William Heinemann.

The laws of cricket (1947 Code) 1968. (4th ed.) London: Marylebone Cricket Club.

Wright, B. 1971. *Rules of the game.* London: Stanley Paul.

Equipment

Harpers Sports and Games 1970. Cricket balls in the making. *Harpers Sports and Games* **1799,** April 9:209–212.

Morris, A. 1975. The bat with the flattering centre. *Sportsworld* **4,** 3:25.

Sherwin, W. H. 1970. Willow and cricket bats. *Harpers Sports and Games* **1801** (May): 283.

Simpson, R. T. 1970. Selection and care of cricket bats. *Harpers Sports and Games* **1791** (March): 133, 141.

9
Cross Country
Harry R. Groves

INTRODUCTION AND BRIEF HISTORY

Running over the countryside is among the oldest of physical activities. As a competitive athletic activity, it dates back only to 1837 with the Crick Run at Rugby School in England.

In prehistoric times, people ran what would be similar to modern day cross-country running to escape enemies and wild beasts.

Runners were used as messengers in ancient civilizations. The most famous runner was the Greek soldier who in 490 B.C. ran from the Plains of Marathon to inform the populace of Athens of the Greek victory over the Persians. This was the beginning of the modern day marathon race.

One of the most widely known "runs over the countryside" in early American history was attributed to the scheming of Thomas Penn, brother of William Penn, in 1737. The time-honored Indian method of dividing land equitably was to walk from sunup to sundown. All of the land covered in a day would belong to the "white man." Thomas Penn conditioned three rugged colonists for this cross-country race for two years. Instead of walking the three colonists ran from sunup to sundown much to the surprise of the Indians. The distance covered was approximately 70 miles from the suburbs of Philadelphia to presentday Jim Thorpe, Pa. (Lucas 1975).

The competitive sport of cross country developed in the late 1880s on the east coast but really did not develop nationally until the 1950s and 1960s. It has become an interscholastic, intercollegiate, and "open" amateur activity for all ages, both male and female. Due to the flexibility inherent in the activity, it is now widespread and may be found almost anywhere—in city parks, at the beach, in the mountains, or even on the roads and highways. There are "jogger" activities for fitness and health for everyone which probably evolved from the competitive programs. The terms "Run for Fun" and "Run for Your Life" have been standard slogans for the front of running shirts. The future should bring not only an increased participation at all levels but also a more rapid development of public supported specialized running areas—over the countryside, in public parks, and on wooded trails.

All references in this treatise will be to the competitive sport of cross-country running.

Fig. 9.1 A national cross-country race may involve a large number of entries. Courtesy of Penn State University.

DESCRIPTION OF THE EVENT

A competitive cross-country race may be conducted between two or more teams. The number of individuals involved in a single race may be as few as 10 in dual meets or upwards of 1000 as conducted annually in England.

The precise rules governing competition vary from scholastic or collegiate to open amateur races. There are separate rule books for each group.

Scoring. Seven participants figure in the scoring of a single race. The low scoring team is the winner. A perfect score in dual competition is 15 points to 50 points. The winner's score, 15 points, is obtained by adding the numbers of the places garnered by the first five finishers on that team as follows: 1st + 2nd + 3rd + 4th + 5th places equal 15 points. A team cannot score lower than 15 points and win. If there are fewer than five finishers on any team, that team loses by default.

The loser's score, 50 points, is obtained by adding 8th + 9th + 10th + 11th + 12th places equal 50 points.

What happened to 6th and 7th places? In a "perfect score" situation these places would be garnered by the winning team. The 6th and 7th place runners are called "pushers." Although they are not added into the score of the winner, they nevertheless prevent the loser from getting them.

Another possible score would be 15 to 40. The winner has 15 points while the loser has 40 points, having gotten 6th + 7th + 8th + 9th + 10th which equals 40 points.

The closest possible score is 27–28. Ties are possible with winners being declared according to the particular rule book followed. Ties may be broken by awarding the victory to the team with the highest finisher or by totalling the scores of the top four finishers on each team, etc.

The course. Cross-country courses vary in length from 1¼ miles to 9 miles depending on the age level of the competitors. In Europe, races are run over the countryside or over whatever terrain is available and may involve the hopping of creeks, fences, or fallen trees on various types of footing.

In the United States these races are conducted largely in parks, on golf courses, on wooded trails, and occasionally on hardtop roads. There are fewer hazards than there are in European cross country.

The course should be 30 feet wide with no bottlenecks so that there is ample running room for all competitors.

For large races, a starting area is essential to permit all competitors a "fair chance." Three hundred feet is required to line up 250 runners on a single starting line. The starting line should be a surveyed arc, with the radius measured from a point in the middle of the track about one-quarter of a mile from the start. All runners on the starting line should be the same distance from the point a quarter mile down the course, while the running area should not narrow to 30' for the first half mile and should be as straight as possible for this distance. All turns should be as gradual as possible. Right-angle turns should be avoided entirely.

The best course design would be a figure eight with the start and the finish at the crossover. Single loop courses are the most impractical from the standpoint of competitive running and spectator interest. The final course layout, however, will be determined by the available area.

Other rules. Since there is a team involved, *uniforms* are required. All runners must run over the same course without taking shortcuts. The course may be marked by a continuous line on the ground with lime or paint and shall indicate all turns and changes of direction. Flags or stakes using the following color code are acceptable: yellow for right turns, red for left turns, and blue for straight ahead.

TERMINOLOGY

Aerobic running Running is done at a pace where oxygen supply to the working muscles is sufficient to maintain a constant environment. This type of running will cause the greatest improvement in the cardiovascular system. Long, easy running is usually aerobic.

"Fartlek" This is a Swedish word meaning "speed play." It was developed by Gosta Holmer in the late 1930s and early 1940s in Sweden. Speed play was conducted on soft forest trails with striding, sprinting, jogging, and walking of various distances intermingled over a predetermined course. This concept, with slight variations, is used by coaches throughout the world. Most American coaches conduct Fartlek training in parks and on golf courses.

Finish chute A large Y-shaped funnel used at the finish line to keep runners in proper order so that finish places may be recorded. The open end of the Y should be approximately 50' with 60' to 90' distance from the actual finish line to the stem or openings (Fig. 9.2).

The stem of the Y should be 100' to 130' long with one to five channels each about 30″ wide to accommodate large numbers of finishers. It is impossible to record competitors' numbers by hand at the finish line as runners cross in rapid succession. There are photo timers which have been helpful in this endeavor, but the "chute" has been the only method of recording results which comes even close to being accurate.

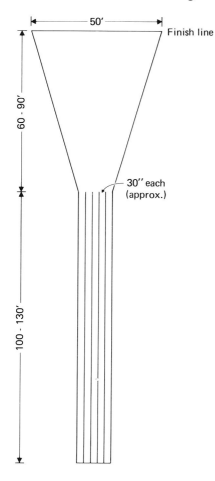

Finish line   **Fig. 9.2** Finish chute.

Flexibility exercises Normal joint flexibility should be maintained through daily stretching exercises. Joints must be exercised through a full range of movement. Running alone tends to restrict flexibility.

Harrier Runners in cross country are referred to as "harriers" (from England). An early form of cross-country running was called paper chasing or "hare and hounds." In these races one group started and as they ran dropped paper scraps to leave a trail. A parallel was drawn between these runners and the hounddog that was used in England at the time (1830s) to chase hares. Eventually the term harrier evolved to describe all cross-country runners.

Hill and dale This is another term for cross-country running.

Hill repeats If run at a rapid pace, uphill repeated runs cause oxygen debt. The hill should be 300 yards to 600 yards in length at a 20 percent (or approximately 11.5°) to 30 percent (or approximately 16.5°) incline. Runners run several times up the hill at race pace or faster and jog down. Repeated runs downhill should be avoided since they seem to cause injuries.

Interval running Originally interval running took place on the track but it may also be accomplished over a measured cross-country course. It is a system of taking runs of measured 440s, 880s, or miles on the track or over the cross-country course at race pace or faster with short recovery jogs between each run. An example is 8–10 × 880 yards with a two- to three-minute jog between each. The time of the run will vary depending upon terrain. Another workout is 10–15 × 440 yards with a 220-yard jog.

Marathon training Distance runs of 10 to 20 miles at a session can be advantageous for the advanced cross-country runner. A continuous program of distances of this type is called marathon training.

Perfect score A 15 to 50 score as described above.

Pushers A "pusher," as has already been described in the scoring procedure, is the 6th or 7th placer on the winning team. These places are not added into the total of the winner but act as displacers to the losers. A team that totaled 15 points also garners 6th and 7th place. The losing team then has 8, 9, 10, 11, 12th places totaling 50 points. This is a perfect score. In the event that a team has more than seven competitors, these athletes do not act as "pushers" and, for the purpose of scoring, are disregarded entirely.

Quick score In large meets, when the chute is used to record finishing places, quick scoring of the meet is accomplished in the chute. Scorecards (scoring places) are given runners who are on the teams. (Individuals who compete with less than a five-man team are also permitted to run.) Representatives of a given team have the same color numbers or some other identification. The individual (nonteam) competitors have another. This allows officials to give a scorecard to team members only as they leave the chute. Each coach of a scoring team collects the scorecards from his entire team. The coach adds up the total of his best five finishers, indicating his 6th and 7th placers, and turns his scorecards in at the scorer's table for checking.

Weight training There are several weight-training machines on the commercial market. For cross-country and distance runners, these machines have advantages over barbells in that they serve as time savers and have specific stations useful to runners. It is important to increase muscular strength, develop muscular endurance, and maintain joint strength so that frequent breakdowns from training and competition do not occur. Weight training should be done in sets of 10 repetitions for one or more sets.

SKILLS

A cross-country runner must develop cardiovascular endurance from daily runs, strength and muscular endurance from weight training and calisthenics, and flexibility from stretching exercises on a daily basis.

A sincere love of running is essential for happy participation in the sport of cross country. Cross country is a fall sport in the United States and serves as a part of the total year-round training program of distance runners.

In cross country, 8 to 10 competitions in September, October, and November will permit sound training and a competitive program to progress simultaneously. The idea of intense training days followed by easy or moderate training days is a sound approach to long-term development. Most advanced runners train two sessions per day.

To develop groups of runners to handle "hills and dales," it is essential

Fig. 9.3 Cross-country runners usually run in packs in the early parts of the race. Courtesy of Luther College.

that a balanced program be developed in both aerobic and anaerobic running.

A sample training program for an advanced runner in October is listed as follows:

Sunday		15–18 miles easy to moderate
Monday	AM	6 to 10 miles
	PM	10 miles steady at better than 6 min per mile
Tuesday	AM	6 to 10 miles
	PM	3-mile jog—10 × 880 yards (2.5–3 min jog) run at race pace or faster on cross-country course
		3-mile jog or 15 × 440 yards (220-yard jog) or 3–4 × 1½ or 2 miles over cross-country course
Wednesday	AM	6 to 10 miles
	PM	10 miles easy
Thursday	AM	6 to 10 miles
	PM	3 miles job or *Fartlek* run on golf course 10 × hill repeat 3 miles
Friday	AM	4–6 miles
	PM	4–6 miles with 5–8 × 110 strides on grass
Saturday	AM	1–2 miles on way to breakfast
	PM	race 5–6 miles

Total mileage is 80 to 110 miles per week.

The following is a weight-training program that can be conducted throughout the year after the initial two weeks of a beginner:

A weight machine or loose weights are needed. All lifts except situps are done with 10 repetitions.

Upper body. Military press, curls, standing rowers, lats, bench press. Situps, 30 reps, then move up to the next level. These should be bent leg.

Legs. Leg press, quads or knee extensions, hamstring curls, toe raisers, toe hops with a light weight on the shoulders. Leg lifts after situp will add strength to the thighs as well as to the abdomen.

This program continues three times a week until competition starts and then is done twice a week. It is best done just before showering. On in-between-days, push-ups, pull-ups, and dips constitute the program. Begin with one set and progress to one set plus whatever can be done a second time. "Skin the cats" on a horizontal bar can be helpful in the area of flexibility and strength.

The progression on weights should be gradual. When a person can handle 10 reps, he should try for 5 reps of the next highest weight or add 5 lbs or 2½ lbs of the small moveable weights that fit the weight machine.

While this entire training program is in effect, flexibilities (hurdler's types) should be performed daily.

It is not fair to distance runners to train them on a seasonal basis. They must love training and derive benefit from practice efforts. Proper training in realistic proportions can be fun. There would be no world champions without a sensible and long-term approach.

Mileage per week can vary greatly depending on the amount of interval running, fast work, or meets. The following is merely a recommended guide:

First two weeks   Beginners, 10 miles per week
Next month   20–30 miles per week
After one year   50 miles per week and up

TACTICS AND STRATEGY: BASIC PRINCIPLES

The most efficient way to run a distance race is to pace the miles evenly. However, this is not practical in large meets since it would require catching up to many runners on a crowded course.

From the point of view of energy distribution, the runners should run the hills as if "they are not there," trying to maintain an even pace. This means, of course, that energy output must be increased on the hills. Since a team output is important, group running can be a very positive weapon. Pace variations at different points in the race can likewise be a positive tactic and tend to discourage opponents.

Some basic principles of cross-country running are:

☐ A complete medical examination once a year is essential.

☐ Running should be frequent and moderate. It is far more important to stay on a regular program than to work so hard that it becomes necessary to stop due to fatigue or injury.

☐ The greater portion of one's running should be aerobic (slow, where oxygen is in constant supply to the body processes).

☐ Interval running should be started gradually and carried on gradually throughout the year on a once a week or once every two weeks basis.

☐ Beginners should jog a mile a day for two weeks and follow this with calisthenics. The mileage should then be increased and a weight training and running program instituted.

☐ Two-a-day runs will bring development more quickly and, if done easily, add to the longevity of the athlete. Morning runs of 30–35 minutes are ideal. Two-a-day should not be started until six months of running have elapsed. Two easy runs a day are better than one hard one.

☐ A weight development program should be started after the first two weeks and continued throughout the year.

☐ Along with strength development of the upper body, specific attention should be paid to foot, ankle, knee, and hip strength. Proper shoes can assist in preventing injuries to these areas. The posture of the athlete can also be the intial cause of such injuries.

☐ Flexibility training should be carried out on a daily basis. Ground hurdling, toe touching, and splits will stretch the hamstrings, thighs, hips, back, and neck.

ETIQUETTE

The most important point of etiquette in cross country is helping opposing runners stay on the cross-country course. Also in close finishes in big meets, it is common for athletes to assist in providing the proper order of finish and assuring that no one is displaced.

EQUIPMENT

Running shorts and shirt must be worn in accordance with rules. Training requires proper shoes ("flats") since protection of the feet is basic to injury-free running. There are several outstanding shoes now sold commercially (*Runner's World* 1975).

In competition, regular track spikes are worn with ⅜ to ⅝" length spikes.

Spikes and flats with a substantial arch support and heel cushion are essential equipment.

RESEARCH AND BIOMECHANICAL PRINCIPLES OF DISTANCE AND CROSS-COUNTRY RUNNING

It is important to understand the running mechanics which accompany the athlete's technique as he advances from season to season and from year to year. As a result of a project conducted at the Biomechanics Laboratory at Pennsylvania State University by R. C. Nelson, it was learned that five distance runners tested over 2- and 3-year periods followed the pattern of a slight decrease in stride length and a slight increase in stride rate. This same trend occurred with the sixth man in his third year of the training program. The change in stride occurred without special work or drills as actual performance improved. There was no significant measurable physiological change which would have a bearing on improved performance during this same period. It may be concluded that improved performance is related to mechanical improvement in running technique.

Besides this, Nelson (1969–1972) also measured maximum running speed of all five men.

Below are leg speeds and mile times of five athletes tested:

Runner A 30.96 feet per sec 4:11.0
Runner B 29.42 feet per sec 4:15.7
Runner C 27.45 feet per sec 4:20.0
Runner D 26.92 feet per sec 4:23.0
Runner E 25.28 feet per sec 4:31.0

The correlation on leg speed is not as high for cross-country runners. As the distance of the race increases, it becomes less important.

The foot landing of cross-country runners is on the ball of the foot with dropping to the heel. A good heel cushion for injury prevention is essential.

The mechanics for running up and down hills differ from those for running on flat areas. In fact, adaptability of one's running technique is essential for best performance.

Uphills are accomplished with a slight increase of body lean and a somewhat shorter stride. Rhythm should be consistent on hills with no burst or speeding up of tempo. Downhill running will cause less body lean and a slight lifting on the ball of the feet. Downhill should be neither a "breaking" nor a "letting go."

Breathing must be deep from the diaphragm area. It is important to condition the abdomen with situps and leg lifts. "Side stickers" and pains are related to shallow breathing.

REFERENCES

Doherty, K. J. 1971. *Track and field omnibook*. Swarthmore, Pa.: TAFMOP Publishers 347, pp. 296–367.

Lucas, J. A. 1975. The NCAA Cross-Country Championships 1938–1975. A paper presented at United States Track Coaches Association Workshop, November 23–24.

Nelson, R. C. 1969–1972. *Stride length studies*. Biomechanics Laboratory, Penn State University.

Runner's World 1975. Study on shoes. October.

10
Curling
Ruth A. Howe

Curling, a lesser known team sport, is considered the "ageless" game because it can be played and enjoyed equally by men, women, old and young. The concept of curling being the "Old Man's Game" or the "Gentleman's Game" is changing as spectators and participants learn more about the skill, strategy, and the stamina required to participate at various levels of competition. Today "bonspiels" or tournaments are hosted for men, women, senior men, and mixed teams.

Curling is played on a sheet of ice by two opposing teams, each consisting of four players: a lead who shoots first rocks; a second; a third or vice skip; and a skip, the master strategist who most often shoots last rocks for a team. Throughout the game, there will be a shooter, two sweepers, and a player in the house signaling with the broom the shots to be made and indicating a point of aim to make the shot. The skip calls for the shots to be made, the shooter attempts to make the shot by varying the weight or force placed on the rock, the sweepers sweep if the rock needs to travel further, or if sweeping is needed to make the shot because of irregularities in ice conditions. The sweepers are responsible for judging the rock's distance, while the skip is responsible for calling sweeping for the rock's movement laterally. The number of ends (length of the game) to be played is determined prior to play. A game can consist of 6, 8, 10, or 12 ends. A toss of a coin determines which team shoots first, the loser shooting first. The rocks, or 42.5-pound stones, to be shot by each team can be identified by the handles. One team plays the red-handled rocks, while the other team shoots the black- or white-handled rocks. A target, called a house, is composed of concentric circles 1, 4, 8, and 12 feet in diameter and located at each end of the rink. (This can be seen in Fig. 10.1.)

The object of each team is to propel its rocks closer to the center of the house than its opposition does. Each player shoots two rocks. Teams alternate shooting with the scoring team, after the first end, shooting first. It is considered a real advantage to shoot the last rock. Each rock is a potential point as long as it rests on or touches the rings that make up the house. To count, a rock must be closer than any of those of the opposing team. With

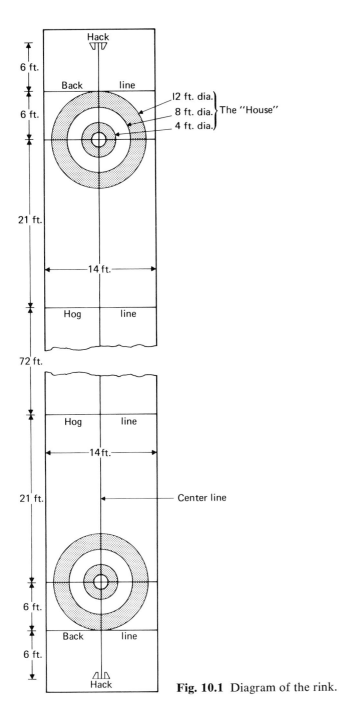

Fig. 10.1 Diagram of the rink.

this system of scoring, only one team can score in each end. Since each team delivers eight rocks in an end, the maximum score is 8. Actually this score is rarer than a hole-in-one in golf. At the other extreme, it is possible for neither team to score, a situation called a blank end. After the designated number of ends, if the teams are tied, an extra end is played to determine the winner. To win, a team must have a higher cumulative score than the opponent.

The success of a team is dependent on the unified efforts of the four players: the skip's strategy and the ice given, the two sweepers' judgment of speed and knowledge of the ice, and the shooter's weight and direction to the broom. All four members of the team must work together to make each shot. It is this necessity of skill and esprit de corps that appeals to the majority of curlers and keeps bringing them back each year to compete in the "ageless" game.

THE CURLING HERITAGE

Curlers have inherited traditions, customs, and attitudes from Scotland for playing the game. Curling was played in the Lowlands and in Scotland in the early 1500s. The Lowlands, through the work of the Flemish painter Peter Brueghel (1525–1569), who created "Winter Landscape" and "Hunters in the Snow," and Scotland, through its engraved Sterling monumental rock (1511), both have claimed to be the original homeland of curling (Creelman 1950). Although the inception of curling remains unknown, Scotland is universally recognized as the country which developed the rules, standardized the rocks, prompted standards of etiquette, and perpetuated the traditions that are universally accepted as a part of the game of curling.

Curling was an integral part of the early Scottish life-style. Clergymen encouraged their parishioners to participate in this healthful pastime. They utilized the game of curling to instill Christian concepts and perpetuate high standards of conduct and play. Hence, in early curling societies swearing and overdrinking were prohibited and fines were imposed to ensure good conduct of players (Kerr 1890, 1901). Since parishes competed against each other for amusement, it was natural that such traditions as the awarding of medals, curling for charities, banquets, singing, toasting, broomstacking (drinking), toasting, and storytelling evolved to become an essential part of the game (Howe 1950, p. 71).

Curling was used as an avenue to develop Scottish nationalism. As early as 1838 curling societies banded together to standardize rules and equipment and to unite into one organization called the Grand Caledonian Club which sponsored bonspiels between the northern and southern clubs of Scotland (Taylor 1887, p. 266). This parent organization received royal stature in 1843, the year after Queen Victoria and Prince Albert visited Scotland (Taylor

1887, p. 271). The Royal Caledonian Curling Society promulgated curling through Scotland and other lands. Scotsmen eulogized and perpetuated curling as a game valuable in providing healthful exercise and in developing mental alacrity. They credited it with developing religious values, a sense of humor, loyalty, brotherhood, amateurism, high standards of play, and a spirit of sociability (Howe 1968, p. 72).

Scotland has been known for breeding "rovers of the earth." The Scots were an influential force in the colonization of both Canada and the United States emigrating to the New World for religious, economic, and political reasons. Since curling was Scotland's national game, it was natural for a roving Scotsman to introduce the game wherever he found conditions suitable for it. Canada and the northern border states of the United States were ideally located for the game because of their cold weather, ample ponds and lakes, and Scotsmen who had the desire, the interest, and the skill to participate. Rocks were fashioned from indigenous material such as wood and granite. Although curling was believed to have been played earlier, it is officially documented that members of the Fraser Regiment (78th Highlanders), who fought under General Murray in 1760, melted down cannonballs for curling during their leisure time in the Franco-English War (Creelman 1950, p. 137). Interest grew in the vicinity of Quebec and The Royal Montreal Curling Club, which was founded in 1807, has the distinction of being the oldest curling club in North America (Munro 1902, p. 528). A second club, the Quebec City Curling Club, was founded in 1821. These clubs officially became affiliated with the Royal Caledonian Curling Society in Scotland (Munro 1902, p. 530).

In the United States, the first officially documented club was located at Orchard Lake, Michigan. Shipwrecked Scottish immigrants foraging the countryside for survival came upon Orchard Lake, liked the county and soil, and established themselves there. The Scotsmen found the winters in Orchard Lake ideal for curling and organized the Orchard Lake Curling Club in 1832 (Grand National Curling Club of America 1891, p. 36).

The Grand National Curling Club of America was formed in 1868 to unite United States curling clubs and to promote international curling (Grand National Curling Club of America 1891, p. 58). Although extensive international competition existed prior to this time, the patron, Robert Gordon, donated the Gordon International Medal in 1884 to be competed for annually, alternating between Montreal and the United States, under the direction of the Royal Caledonian Curling Club of Quebec (Hill 1967, p. 11). This medal is so highly valued that it is kept in a safety deposit box except during the four days of its competition. This is believed to be the oldest event in which United States and Canadian sports enthusiasts participate.

Scotland gave a royal heritage to curling, but Canada has achieved true dominance over it by developing the largest curling population in the world and by developing an improved scientific approach to the game. The Scottish game became Canadianized as Canadians standardized the use of the hack, developed a new form of sweeping, studied scientifically the concepts underlying the game, and developed the long slide (Howe 1968, p. 107). Canada became the foremost curling nation in the world and, through its dominance, influenced the Royal Caledonian Curling Society in Scotland to make several significant rule changes.

Since World War II, curling has gained in popularity. This is partially due to technological advances and sociological changes. Artificial ice enabled women and youth to participate in this sport where strength previously had been a prime factor. National championships became prevalent for men, women, the young and old, and mixed groups. Nationwide televising of Canadian bonspiels and world championships introduced thousands of people to the ancient game of curling.

Throughout the evolution of curling, the traditions and "spirit of curling" established by the Scotsmen have been retained. Curling etiquette is an integral part of the game. The unwritten rules are considered more important than the written rules by knowledgeable curlers. Participants are expected to adhere to concepts of sportsmanship and common courtesies that respect and give one's opposition the best opportunity to perform well. It is the goal of curlers to win but within the framework and within the spirit of the game.

APPAREL AND EQUIPMENT

Proper dress is a prerequisite for comfort and safety while curling. Although there is no standardized uniform for curling, women wear comfortable stretch-slacks or skirts, warm loose sweaters, light leather gloves, and curling shoes. Footwear should be warm, void of heels, with a smooth rubber composite sole to ensure satisfactory traction while moving. Women who slide in their delivery have a leather or Teflon insert affixed to the bottom of the ball of their sliding shoe.

Men wear comfortably fitting trousers, jackets, and sweaters. Curling shoes and sliders are also available for men. Rubbers are often worn over regular leather-bottomed shoes to ensure traction while moving. The rubber on the sliding foot is removed prior to shooting.

Curlers are responsible for providing themselves with curling brooms. These may be purchased at sporting-goods stores or curling clubs. A large assortment of manufactured curling brooms is available, so the curler may select the weight and composition which fulfills individual needs.

FACTORS THAT AFFECT SHOOTING

Ice conditions. The path a stone takes is governed by the ice. Water when frozen creates unique individualized ice crystals. It is the diverse arrangement of ice crystals which makes each sheet of ice different and challenging. It is virtually impossible to make a stone go down the ice straight, for somewhere along its path the rock will turn one way or the other because of some unevenness in the surface. Ice conditions are not "true" but have irregularities within the rink causing rocks to move slower, faster, fall off to a slide, or bend.

The ice surface will change daily because of variations in temperature and the care or the use it gets. It is necessary to clean the ice and to pebble (lightly sprinkle warm water on the ice) from hack to hack to prepare the ice for shooting. Without pebbling, rocks would have a tendency to consistently go through the house. The ice conditions fluctuate as a game progresses. A pebbled rink is slower at the beginning of the game, but becomes faster as play progresses. A rock has a tendency to curl or fall off more often as the pebble wears off. Players watch the ice for these irregularities and adjust their shots and vary their sweeping patterns accordingly. Quite often there is a large distance between the point of aim or target and the place where the rock eventually settles.

The in- and out-turn. A rock thrown with a straight handle will be affected by any irregularity in the ice. To gain control over ice irregularities and to get the rock to its destination, spin is important. A rock which rotates in a clockwise direction is called an in-turn; a rock which spins in a counterclockwise direction is called an out-turn. Three to five complete revolutions are desired as a rock travels its path from the hack to its destination. The in- and out-turns are used for every shot made in a game. Curlers should be adept at both.

Basic shots. A novice curler should practice the two basic shots: the draw shot and take-out. The draw shot should be the first shot learned. A draw shot is thrown with either an in- or out-turn and ends up in the house. The take-out shot, the basic defensive shot, is also thrown with either an in- or out-turn, but is a fast, hard-powered rock which knocks the opponent's stone out of play. Other shots, such as a guard, a bump-up or raise, a wick and roll are offshoots of the two basic shots. They require less weight than the take-out and more weight than the draw. The guard shot uses a lighter weight than the draw.

Shots are made through understanding the relationship of the turns and the curve or path that the rock will take, when different weights or forces are applied to it. Figure 10.2 shows the turn-weight curve.

Note that in the illustration the same target or point of aim is given for each turn and that the rock is released from the hack. A heavier thrown rock curls less while a rock thrown with a "light" weight tends to curve more, especially as it approaches its destination. Friction is overcome by the rock's outer

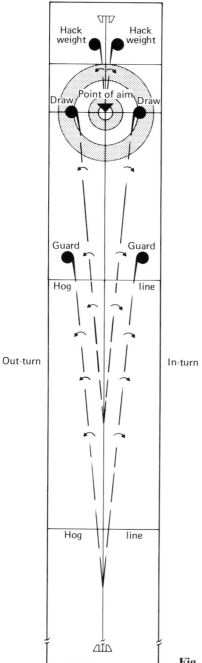

Fig. 10.2 Turn-weight chart.

edges as a rock moves slowly down a path. There is time for the rock's outer edges to adhere to the ice surface which permits the rock to curl extensively as it approaches its destination.

In the slide delivery the rock is released prior to the hog line. The rationale for sliding is to release the rock nearer to its destination thus leaving less time for the rock to curve. Curlers with a longer slide guide the rock over many ice irregularities, near the hack, which normally would adversely affect the rock's path. A rock released nearer to the target would have fewer ice flaws to overcome; hence, many skips prefer to have their shooters use a slide delivery for accuracy of shots.

ELEMENTS OF SHOOTING

A delivery should be smooth, rhythmical, coordinated, and apparently effortless. For discussion, the delivery will be divided into four parts:

1. Windup which includes the preparatory set, hand position for imparting spin, stance, and backswing;
2. Summation of force, which includes the backswing, foot-rock placement on the ice, and the forward thrust of the leg coming out of the hack into the slide;
3. Crucial instant, imparting spin, or the releasing of the rock on the ice toward the target;
4. Follow-through which includes the continuation of the slide and the extension of the body and arm toward the target after the rock has been released.

Windup. Curling is a game of concentration. A curler establishes a preparatory set for shooting by forming a routine of habits which puts him into the proper frame of mind for the task at hand. Figure 10.3 shows the preparatory position. Minor deviations occur, but most curlers use their brooms to clean the sole of the rock and the ice where the rock is to be delivered, settle themselves comfortably in the hack, visualize the rock's path from the point of aim or target to its destination, and kinesthetically feel the force needed to make the shot.

One's stance and backswing affect the total execution of the shot. The proper stance should align rock, shooter, and target. Good posture establishes the balance needed for executing a proper swing.

The ball of the right foot is placed against the back of the hack while the left foot takes a comfortable position beside and slightly in front of the right foot. The knees are bent lowering the body weight over the right foot,

Fig. 10.3 Preparatory position.

giving the appearance of sitting on the heel of the right foot. The broom should be held in the shooter's left hand with the wide surface of the broom straw resting on the ice. This provides balance. The body should be squared with the target or broom handle of the skip. Squaring the shoulders should bring the hips and knees in line with the target. Rock alignment is adjusted to the right or the left of the tee line with the curved handle of the rock pointing straight ahead. The rock handle should be firmly gripped with the thumb on one side and the fingertips cradling the rock. After the hand firmly grips the rock, the hand and arm turn jointly into position which will impart the spin. If an in-turn is desired, the rock is turned to the 11:30 o'clock position; if an out-turn is desired, the rock is turned to the 1:00 o'clock position. The hand, wrist, and elbow are locked into position so that no lateral movement occurs throughout the swing.

The rock is pressed forward toward the target for a short distance, then drawn back on the ice, the arm extended in a locked position; the right leg in the hack lifts the legs and hip to provide the backswing; the left hip and foot rotate outward at a 45° angle to counteract the 42.5-pound weight of the rock and provide equilibrium (Fig. 10.4).

Summation of force. At the top of the backswing there is a slight hesitation, when the rock momentarily stops, hanging like a pendulum, until it overcomes the exerted force to start the downward arc or the forward swing. The rock's weight reacts to the force of gravity to change the direction of the swing. Momentum is gained by the rock on its downward path. The curler

Fig. 10.4 Counterbalance position.

holds back the body weight to permit the rock to swing through naturally—the rock leading the body. The left leg that was balancing the body slides forward on the ice to support the body weight almost simultaneously with the forward swing of the rock. The weight is transferred from the right to the left leg, the left leg becomes the supporting leg, while the right leg thrusts forward to provide additional power to the shot (Fig. 10.5).

Hence we see the summation of force as a combination of the rock's backswing and leg thrust from the hack. Most curlers can control a shorter backswing with a firm leg thrust better than they can a longer backswing and forward thrust.

The shooter throughout the slide has a three-point balance (Fig. 10.6). Weight should be distributed on the broom, the left leg, and the trailing right

Fig. 10.5 Weight shift.

Fig. 10.6 Distribution of body weight. Front view and side view.

leg. No weight should be on the rock. The rock should be extended out in front of the left foot, the broom extended and on the ice at shoulder level, and the left foot under the chest, with the broom firmly locked in the armpit of the shooter. The trailing leg and foot should be extended to act somewhat as a rudder.

Crucial instant. The point of the release of the rock depends on the force applied and the length of slide of the shooter. There are two theories as to when the rock should be released. Some curlers release the rock at the same point every time, varying the weight with the backswing. Other curlers maintain the same backswing and leg thrust and release the rock at various points depending on the shot to be made. With this theory a take-out rock is released sooner, whereas in a draw shot the curler would slide farther toward the target and release the rock later. The writer advocates the use of the latter method for beginners. The crucial instant is the most important phase of the total delivery because the line of direction has been established by the backswing and forward swing, the force has been imparted to the rock, and what remains is the release of the hand grip for the rock to be on its way. It is during the crucial instant that spin is imparted to the rock by lowering the hand and shoulder closer to the ice and opening the hand toward the target. The in-turn starting at the 11:30 o'clock position is open so that it progresses toward the 12:00 o'clock position; while the out-turn starting at 1:00 o'clock is open toward the 12:00 o'clock position. When the rock is released, the shot is basically finished.

The follow-through. The follow-through, or the completion of the slide, does not affect the shot proper. The rock is already progressing toward its target. The value of the follow-through comes in analyzing whether the rock was released properly during the crucial instant. It becomes a guide in determining whether the backswing and forward swing were in the correct line of direction and whether the rock was released on target. By analyzing the follow-through, corrections can be made to facilitate the most important phase of the total swing, the crucial instant.

Analysis of the follow-through reveals these potential errors:

☐ Placing one's body weight on rock—hanging onto rock at release.

☐ Pushing the rock on release.

☐ Bending the arm at the elbow, to impart spin, usually caused by turning the handle and arm in the backswing.

☐ Body position askew after release, due to uneven thrust or body balance. Foot turned outward on slide.

☐ Coming up to a standing upright position immediately after release throwing the shot off and causing the rock to veer right with the in-turn, left with the out-turn.

☐ Foot beside the rock rather than behind it placing the rock off target laterally.

☐ Hand following through toward the ceiling, flipping the rock off to the side.

Practice of the parallel swing and slide, using the in- and out-turns for draw and take-out shots, is needed to develop balance and rhythm, line of direction, and weight. Cues that might help to establish a rhythm are: push rock slightly forward, bring rock back, lift with the legs, swing through and slide. Push forward, lift, swing, slide, release, slide. It takes time and practice to develop the feel of the swing—to keep one's head up and one's eye on the target during the balancing of the rock's weight and to slide out from the hack in this unusual position. As a curler gains confidence in the two basic shots, he should practice the variation of shots falling in-between the guard and the take-out shots.

SWEEPING

Sweeping is the physically strenuous part of curling. A recent study by Quinney (1973, p. 20) indicated that sweeping places a heavy load on the cardiovascular system in general, and the heart in particular. Bowers and Farrell (1976, p. 38) classified sweeping as a moderately strenuous activity for in a two-hour play period a sweeper expends 1000 calories. When ice is properly prepared and pebbled, it is the number of times the broom hits the ice plus the burnishing of the ice that determines sweeping efficiency (Meyer and Werlich 1965, p. 22). Strong sweepers, according to Meyer and Werlich (1965, p. 23), will add 15 or 16 feet to the distance a rock will travel depending on ice conditions. Powerful sweeping:

☐ Creates a vacuum in front of the stone and lessens the friction so that the rock travels farther;

☐ Changes the line of the rock's path;

☐ Cleans dirt particles and straw from the rock's path;

☐ Keeps the players warm and relaxed;

☐ Psychologically keeps the player's attention on the game and maintains team unity with each shot.

There are two methods of sweeping, the Scottish or eastern and the Canadian or western style. Different techniques and specialized brooms are required for each of these methods of sweeping. Both styles of sweeping are considered equally effective when properly executed. The Canadian or western-style broom has a short handle approximately 26 inches in length with straws about 20 inches long. The Scottish or eastern-style broom has a longer handle almost five feet in length inserted into a small platform which contains the bristles. These straws are about two inches long.

Canadian-style sweeping. The body position in Canadian-style sweeping is at a 90° angle, the upper trunk bent over at the waist with the knees slightly bent. The sweeper closest to the rock stands with feet slightly in back and to the side of the rock, bending forward at the waist and sweeping in front of the rock. The back is straight and the side on which a curler sweeps is determined by the manner of holding the broom. A person who places the left hand near the top of the broom handle and the right hand near the middle of the broom will sweep on the right side of the rock. A person would sweep on the opposite side if the hands were reversed. It is permissible for the lower hand to grip the handle with either a regular grip, palm and fingertips pointed down toward the ice, or a reverse grip with palm and fingertips facing up. The broom is angled with the top of the handle located near the sweeper's shoulders and with the straws facing the target in such a position that the sweeper has a clear view of the rocks or obstacles in the stone's path. The lower hand acts as a fulcrum with the power or whip coming from the upper arm movement. The lower hand should be relaxed with the fingers lightly gripping the broom. The footwork is like a dance that syncopates the drumbeat as it moves back and forth. The back foot pushes forward, while the front foot slides. As the right foot leads, the broom whips forward and back repeating the forward and back motion as the left foot draws up to the right foot. This whole process has four counts or beats. Power for sweeping comes through the legs and upper arms.

The strongest sweeper should be nearest the rock. Two curlers can sweep on the same side of the rock or on opposite sides without getting in each other's way if each has the proper technique. Common errors in sweeping are:

☐ Standing upright

☐ Using too much lower arm and wrist

☐ Permitting the elbows to stick out away from the body

☐ Standing sideways to the path of the rock rather than at a 45° angle

☐ Holding one's breath.

Developing a synchronized sweeping pattern is both a skill and an art worthy of practice.

Fig. 10.7 Two curlers sweeping.

As sweepers gain experience they learn to conserve their energy by sweeping lightly at the beginning of the rock's path and adding more power as the rock nears the end of its journey.

The push broom. The user of a push broom may assume a more upright position, the body position almost facing the house. The broom never leaves the ice, which is considered advantageous because it permits no space of ice to be omitted in front of the rock. The broom is pushed back and forth in front of the rock's path. One error, committed by the unknowing sweeper, is to push forward and backward in line with the rock's path rather than across the ice in front of the rock. In tournament play a sweeper could be called for illegal sweeping. As the rock slows down, one's body weight is used to apply additional pressure to the broom. Sweeping is a topic of discussion, for curlers who sweep well know they can help the rock get to its destination.

STRATEGY

Type of Game

In curling there are as many types of strategies as there are skips. A skip's strategy falls within a continuum between the original dead draw game and knock-out or take-out game.

The dead draw game used the gentleman's approach, attempting to keep most or all of the stones in play, yet scoring by nudging the opponent's rocks gently to the outer rings or by going through ports. It was a game that featured wicks, raises, and other shots made with draw weight. The skip was the predominant player ruling the rink with an "iron hand" telling them when to sweep, what shots were to be played, and taking sole responsibility for the strategy. Fluke shots were common and upset the intended strategy.

The take-out or knock-out game features a fast game with few rocks ending up in play. It is at the other end of the continuum where fast-thrown "runners" are common, and scores are kept to a minimum. Theoretically, if a perfect game is played, the team winning the toss of the coin and the handles for shooting last would win the game by a score of one to nothing. Conceivably, the defensive team making every shot would knock out its opponent's rocks, letting its own rock roll out too, to "blank" (no score) each end. The skip then would draw into the house with the last shot on the last end to score one point. Accuracy is a prime requisite of the knock-out game, with pressure being placed on every shot. Each player must shoot a better percentage than his opponent for one missed shot puts added pressure on the next player.

Most skips play a combination game drawing elements from the dead draw game and the take-out game. Unlike heavy runners, take-out shots are just heavy enough to push an opponent's rock out of the scoring area yet leave the team's own rock in play. There are not as many stones in and around the house as in the dead draw weight game, but there are enough stones in play so that wicks and raise shots are used.

Factors Affecting Strategy

The style of the game and the strategy employed are dependent on such factors as ice conditions, the skill level of each member of a team, the curling experience of each member of a team, the score of the game, the number of ends to be played, the skill level of the opposition, the style of play used by the opposition, and the skip's skill and experience in calling a game. The skip formulates strategy by assessing the various combinations of factors. Strategy becomes a decision-making process using the available information at hand, attempting to assess the present situation and projecting the acquired information into the building of each "head." The skip attempts to outmaneuver the opposition, anticipating the shots and strategy the opposing skip will use. The skip must have a sound memory for the shots previously played on various sections of the ice and store this information away for future use. A stone going in one direction will not react in the same way as a stone moving in the other direction on the same section of ice. The skip must bear this in mind and adapt the strategy accordingly. The ice will change during the game and the skip must also take this into account when planning the attack.

Principles of Strategy

The strategy for each game depends on the previously discussed factors necessitating decision making for the individual game. One's strategy must change as the situations change during the game's progress. However, there are some general principles that may be used as guides in planning the overall strategy. These principles were gathered and summarized from the writings of curling champions such as Ken Watson, Ernie Richardson, H. E. Weyman, Joyce McKee, and by talking with other curlers.

1. During the first two or three ends less ice is required for shots until the pebble wears off. As the game progresses, the amount of ice required for a comparable shot will increase.
2. Ice speeds up or becomes faster after the pebble wears off. The outside ice of the rink is usually slower than the center ice, and requires more weight when shooting.
3. The team with the handles should spread the rocks to the outside rings keeping the center open for the last shot. Conversely, the team without the handles should put a rock on the front center ice, establishing a position to score.

4. Rocks should be scattered on the rink. Rocks near the front are strategically better situated than rocks near the back rings. Rocks located in the back rings can be drawn down to, providing backing for the opposition. Rocks located on side ice are generally more difficult to hit than those situated on center ice.

5. A second shot rock strategically placed on the opposite side of the house provides a better offensive attack than throwing up a guard. It is difficult to place a guard in such a way that a shooter cannot curl around it by using either an in- or out-turn. Putting a second rock in the house puts one's opponents on the defensive.

6. It is sound practice for the skip to give the lead both an in- and out-turn during the first few ends. This shows the skip and his teammates how the turns act on a particular sheet of ice.

7. The standing score is a factor in determining if the strategy of a game is satisfactory. If a team is winning, all things being equal, it is a sign that the strategy is good. If a team is behind, an attempt should be made to switch to a different strategy.

8. A fairly long guard is better than a short one because an opponent may be able to take out both the guard and shot rock.

9. An attempt should be made to get a big "end" early in the game. Occasionally a gamble should be made for there are times when a safe shot will score one point while a risky shot may result in four or five points. If a team is winning, and a safe shot could assure scoring, a gamble should not be taken. If a team is losing, chances have to be taken.

10. If a team is ahead and there are only a few ends left to play, an attempt should be made to knock out the opponents' rocks so their scoring potential will be low.

11. It is desirable at times to blank an end (no score), rather than to count one point. At times, maintaining the handles or last shot is considered an advantage. This practice works on the theory that a team can set up a better scoring situation on the next end if the skip retains the last shot.

12. If the opponents have three or four rocks in the house, at times it is best to settle for second shot rather than attempt to outcount them. This decision depends on the difficulty of the shot.

13. On the last end, the team which is ahead has a choice of throwing the rocks through the house or filling up the front of the rink with rocks. If the score is close, it is best to keep an open house attempting to hit out all of the opponent's rocks.

14. A team should fight discouragement even if it is losing. A game is not won until the last rock is thrown.

These are basic principles intended as an introductory guide to show the nature of curling strategy. As individuals become involved in playing the game, increasingly complex principles will be added to these basic guides that will enlarge and enhance their repertoires of curling knowledge and make the game more interesting and challenging.

TERMINOLOGY

American Curling Foundation An organization established by United States curlers in 1957 to disseminate curling information and lend curling rocks to new curling clubs.

Blank end An end that is scoreless; may be an intentional play by the skip shooting the last rock to retain his advantage in the succeeding end.

Bonspiel A series of competitions made up of a number of individual events, in which each event declares a winner.

Brier championship The foremost national men's Canadian championship tournament, founded in 1927.

Broomstacking The curlers' traditional practice of putting their brooms away and drinking together after the game.

Button Area enclosing the central ring, commonly called the tee.

Canadian Ladies' Curling Association (CLCA) Unifying national association for Canadian women's provincial associations.

Channelstanes Rocks found in beds of streams and rivers used in early Scottish games for curling.

Counter A stone that is in scoring position.

Curling (knuting, coiting, quoiting) Curling is a game played on pebbled ice by two opposing teams, each team composed of four players. A missile or rock is projected or thrown by one player, using either an out-turn or an in-turn, toward a target, called the house, a distance of 126 feet away. The ice in the rock's path may be swept, with special brooms, by the shooter's teammates to facilitate the rock's progress toward the desired location. Each player throws two rocks, alternating with his opponents. The team which comes closest to the tee, or the centermost ring in the house, scores. One team may score as many as eight points in an end, if all its rocks are closer to the tee than those of its opponents. The number of ends to be played is determined prior to the starting of the game.

Dead draw game Also known as the gentleman's game. Based upon strategic use of the draw shot. This strategy keeps most of the rocks in play.

Dominion Curling Association (DCA) Unifying national organization for Canadian provincial curling associations.

Draw The distance between the skip's broom, and the final resting place of the stone.

Draw shot A shot that attempts to locate the rock in the house, near the tee.

Fall A portion of the ice surface whose effect on a delivered rock is contrary to what might normally be expected.

Freeze A stone that comes to rest touching another stone so that the other stone is behind the played stone.

Give ice The placing of the broom by the skip as an indication of aim for the curler in the hack.

Guard Any stone that blocks the path to another.

Grand National Curling Club of America Association founded by United States curling clubs in 1867 to unite curlers and to promote the game. It is the oldest curling association in the United States.

Hack Foothold at either end of the ice from which a player delivers his stone.

Heavy A stone that is delivered with more than desired weight.

Heavy ice Drug ice. Ice that requires a stone to be thrown with more than normal weight to reach the house.

Hog line Line 105 feet away from hack and past which a stone must come to rest in order to remain in play.

House Synonymous with head, circles, or rings. The scoring area located at each end of the rink, composed of four concentric rings—1, 4, 8, and 12 feet in diameter toward which the stones are to be played.

Off the broom A stone delivered along the imaginary line connecting the skip's broom to the position of the stone at rest.

Out-turn A stone to which a spin is imparted by turning the hand away from the body. Thus an out-turn for a right-handed curler rotates counter-clockwise; for a left-handed curler, clockwise.

Pebble A spray of warm water which freezes on contact with the ice to form a "blistered" playing surface.

Port An opening between two rocks sufficiently wide to allow a stone to pass through.

Raise The action of bumping a stone from one position to another position closer to the tee.

Rink 1. The building where curling is played. 2. The boundaries and specifications of markings for playing the game on one sheet of ice. 3. A team composed of four players.

Roaring game Another term for curling. Curling gets this name from the sound of the rock as it traverses its course and also from the shouts of encouragement given by the skip to the members of his rink.

Rock Stone.

Royal Caledonian Curling Club (RCCC) Mother association of curling clubs and associations the world over. Founded in 1838 as the Grand Caledonian Curling Club and honored with the title "Royal" in 1843.

Scotch Cup Competition Competition among curling countries of the world. Founded in 1959; terminated in 1967.

Second Player on a side who delivers the second pair of rocks.

Sheet A rink. Area of ice on which the game is played.

Silver Broom Competition World curling competition sponsored by Air Canada; founded in 1968.

Slide Follow-through on delivery.

Swingy ice Ice which causes a rock to pull in one direction more than is normally expected.

Take-out A stone delivered with sufficient momentum to remove another stone from play, when the latter is hit by the delivered stone.

Take-out game Game based upon the strategy of knocking rocks out of the scoring area.

Third The vice-skip. The player on a team who delivers the third pair of stones.

United States Men's Curling Association (USMCA) Unifying national curling organization for United States curling clubs. Founded in 1958.

United States Women's Curling Association (USWCA) Unifying curling organization for United States women's clubs. Founded in 1947.

Weight The amount of momentum imparted to a stone in delivery.

Wide A stone delivered outside of the imaginary line connecting the stone at rest and the broom, and the imaginary line connecting the stone at rest and the final desired position.

World competition International competition among all curling countries of the world.

REFERENCES

Backstrom, A. G. 1964. The legend of Bob Dunbar. *North American Curling News* **20** (December): 22–23.

Boreham, H. B. 1964. The brier—the never-before-told story of how it all began. *The Curler* **1** (March): 10–11.

Bowers, R. W., and P. A. Farrell 1976. How much does curling cost in calories? *The Physician and Sportsmedicine* **4** (January): 37–39.

Brown, R. 1830. *Memorabilia curliana Mabenensia.* Dumfries: John Sinclair; Edinburgh: Henry Constable; Glasgow: Atkinson; Ayr: John Dick.

Creelman, W. A. 1950. *Curling past and present.* Includes H. E. Weyman, An analysis of the art of curling. Toronto: McClelland and Stewart.

Curtis, D. 1959. *Curling . . . fun for everyone!* Willmette, Ill.: Dar Curtis.

Grand National Curling Club of America, Annual for 1880–1881 **9**, 1882. New York: L. D. and J. A. Robertson Steam.

———, *100th Anniversary Annual for 1867–1967* **38**, 1967. New York: Grand National Curling Club.

———, *Annual for 1890–1891* **19**, 1891. New York: Robertson's Thistle Print.

Grant, J. G. 1914. *The complete curler.* London: Adam and Charles Black.

Hill, L. T. 1967. Grand national marks 100th anniversary. *North American Curling News* **22** (January): 8–14.

Howe, R. A. 1968. *The development of curling in the United States.* Doctoral dissertation. Indiana University.

Kerr, J. 1904. *Curling in Canada and the United States.* Toronto: The Toronto News.

——— 1890. *History of curling.* Edinburgh: David Douglas.

Marshall, M. H. 1924. *The Scottish curlers in Canada and the United States: a record of their tour in 1922–23.* Edinburgh: T. and A. Constable at the University Press.

Meyer, W., and R. Werlich 1965. Sweep . . . your rink needs you. *The Curler* **2** (March): 22–23.

Mobbs, A. N., and F. McDermott 1929. *Curling in Switzerland.* London: Arrowsmith.

Munro, J. 1902. Curling in Canada. *Canadian Magazine* **18** (April): 527–534.

Northwestern Curling Association of America, First Annual 1893. St. Paul, Minn.: Railroader Printing House.

Quinney, A. 1973. How strenuous is curling? *The Curler* **10** (Winter): 20–21.

Richardson, E., J. McKee, and D. Maxwell 1963. *Curling.* New York: David McKay.

11
Fencing

Maxwell R. Garret, Mary F. Heinecke, and A. John Geraci

Fencing developed as a result of the very necessary historical need for young men to learn to defend themselves with a sword. The three modern fencing weapons, the foil, the épée or dueling sword, and saber (Fig. 11.1, a, b, and

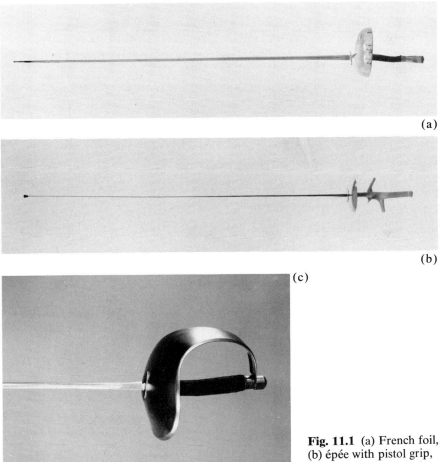

(a)

(b)

(c)

Fig. 11.1 (a) French foil, (b) épée with pistol grip, and (c) saber. Photos by A. John Geraci.

c, respectively), were each taught to emphasize certain skills necessary for offense and defense in serious sword fighting. The foil served to teach basic fundamentals, the épée emphasized the accurate thrust with the point, and the saber emphasized cutting and slashing, thrusting and defense of the entire body. Rules of fencing with each weapon have been developed to compensate for the fact that the battle is only simulated and to allow for an orderly sequence of attack and defense.

In foil the valid target includes the torso and the groin area. It excludes the arms, legs, the mask, and the bib of the mask. A point is scored when the point of the weapon hits the target in a manner that would create a puncture wound if the weapon were not blunted. (See Fig. 11.1a.)

In épée a point is also scored only by a thrust, but the valid target includes the entire body (Fig. 11.2).

In saber, points are scored both by cutting and thrusting. The target is limited to the area above the waist, including the arms and head (Fig. 11.3).

In foil and saber, certain rules of right-of-way have been established. Basically these rules say that a man who is attacked must defend himself by parrying the attack before making his own offensive action. Thus, if one fencer launches an attack and the other fencer, instead of parrying, merely

Fig. 11.2 Foil running attack by fencer on left. Fencer on right has made a four-parry and is executing a riposte with a coupe (cutover). Photo by A. John Geraci.

Fig. 11.3 Saber fencer on the left lunges for his opponent's head, while fencer on the right parries in preparation for counterattack. In background are scoring lights which indicate bout score. Photo by A. John Geraci.

extends his weapon or cuts into the attack, the attacking fencer will win the point even though both fencers scored valid hits at the same time, because the attacking fencer has the right-of-way. On the other hand, if the defender parries the attack successfully, the right-of-way passes to him and he may make a riposte or counterattack and the original attacker must then defend himself. It is the function of the director to determine which fencer has the right-of-way throughout the course of the exchange.

In épée, rules of right-of-way do not apply and the fencer who touches his opponent first wins the point.

Competition is conducted on a rectangular mat (strip, piste) as shown in Fig. 11.4.

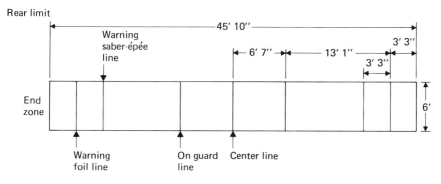

Fig. 11.4 Outline of fencing strip (piste).

Because of the great speed of movement, electrical devices have been developed in foil and épée to record the touches (Fig. 11.5). Foil fencers wear a metallic vest (lamé) which completely covers the valid target. The fencer's weapon is attached to a body cord which runs down his sword arm and is connected at the other end to a cord attached to a reel at the end of the fencing strip. The reel is in turn connected to a scoring machine. The scoring machine records a touch on valid target by flashing a colored light and a touch on invalid target by flashing a white light. If a foil fencer touches invalid target first and his point then penetrates to valid target, both a white and colored light will flash. No score is awarded in such circumstances since the invalid touch was scored first and nullifies the subsequent valid touch. If the fencer's point touches valid target first and then invalid target, only the colored light will flash and a touch is awarded since the initial action arrived on proper target. In foil fencing, you will observe that frequently both colored and/or white lights will go on indicating that both fencers have been touched. The scoring machine is geared to record all touches scored by both fencers within approximately one-fifth of a second of one another. It does not necessarily follow, however, that because one fencer touches his opponent a fraction of a second ahead of his opponent, he will win the point. When lights are burning, indicating that both fencers have been touched, it is incumbent upon the director to determine who had the right-of-way and won the point.

In épée, the entire body is valid target, and the scoring machine shows only whether a touch is scored since there is no invalid target. There is no right-of-way and the first fencer to touch his opponent wins the point. However, if both fencers scored within one-twenty-fifth of a second of one another, the machine will record a double touch and a point is awarded against both fencers.

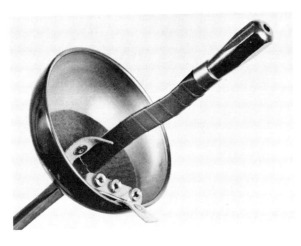

Fig. 11.5 Epée weapon showing electrical connection for body cord. Photo by A. John Geraci.

The electrical fencing strip is neutralized so that if the point of the weapon hits the floor, it will not register on the machine.

Electrical scoring devices have not been adopted for the saber as yet. Therefore, four judges, referred to as the "jury," and a director are used. There are two judges assigned to watch each fencer for touches scored against him. It is the function of the judges to determine whether a cut or thrust has been made on valid target. It is the principal function of the director to determine right-of-way, but he may also vote as to validity. The director has one and one-half votes and each judge has one vote.

In all weapons, a bout consists of five points except in women's foil where the bout consists of four points. In all men's events, there is a six-minute limit to a bout (five minutes in women's foil), but time is counted only while the fencers are engaged in actual combat and not during the deliberations of the director. Points are recorded against a fencer so that the fencer with the lowest score is winning the bout.

Since many of the basic fencing moves are not common to other activities, learning to fence requires patience. Instruction can be given individually by a fencing master or in an organized group. Basic courses in the fundamentals of fencing are, on the average, twenty hours in length and attempt to teach well a few basic skills enabling the beginner to experience some success in bouting at the conclusion of the course. The syllabus for such a course emphasizes conditioning, footwork, handwork, coordination of hand and feet, a small number of offensive and defensive maneuvers, and bout procedures and practices.

If used well, such physical attributes as long legs with explosive power, height, and long arms can be an advantage. However, because timing, a sense of distance, agility, experience, and the ability to outmaneuver an opponent are important factors in fencing, an individual's body build and age are generally not limiting factors. Research has attempted to determine whether there are distinct personality traits characteristic of the champion level fencer. Findings among female fencers seem to indicate that only the personality trait of dominance distinguishes among achievement levels.

The movements in fencing are lightning fast and top performance requires a fine correlation and coordination of footwork and action of the weapon hand and arm. In major tournaments a fencer today has to develop maximum physical fitness in order to maintain superiority over his opponents, and also the capacity to perform well over a long period of time without diminished efficiency. This phase of motor fitness must emphasize activities developing endurance, agility, flexibility, balance, power, and strength.

The Amateur Fencers League of America is the official governing body for amateur fencing in the United States and is so recognized by the Federation International d'Escrime, the United States Olympic Committee, and the Amateur Athletic Union. The AFLA cooperates with the National Collegiate

Athletic Association, the Intercollegiate Women's Fencing Association and other intercollegiate groups, and the National Fencing Coaches' Association of America in promoting the growth of fencing and in establishing and carrying out the rules of the sport.

The National Fencing Coaches' Association of America is the professional organization which includes many of the fencing coaches in the country. This organization attempts to elevate the standards of teaching and coaching, and is the first coaches' association to have developed an accreditation program leading to the awarding of a Master's Certificate to its members.

Fencing is frequently referred to as a physical game of chess, and in every bout each fencer draws deeply upon experience to find the strategy with which to outmaneuver his or her opponent.

REFERENCES

Amateur Fencers League of America. American Fencing Magazine, AFLA, 249 Eton Place, Westfield, New Jersey 07090.

————. Fencing rules–1970 edition. (Authorized translation of the FIE rules from the French by C-L. de Beaumont.) AFLA: 249 Eton Place, Westfield, New Jersey 07090.

Bower, M., and T. Mori 1966. *Fencing*. Dubuque, Iowa: William C. Brown.

Castello, H., and J. Castello 1962. *Fencing*. New York: Ronald.

Crosnier, R. 1961. *Fencing with the electric foil*. New York: A. S. Barnes.

———— 1951. *Fencing with foil*. London: Faber and Faber.

Deladrier, C. 1948. *Modern fencing*. Annapolis: United States Naval Institute.

The Division for Girls' and Women's Sports. *Bowling-fencing*. Washington, D.C.: AAHPER. Published biannually.

Garret, M., and M. Heinecke 1971. *Fencing*. Boston: Allyn and Bacon.

Garret, M. R. 1960. *Fencing instructor's guide*. Chicago: The Athletic Institute.

———— 1959. *How to improve your fencing*. Chicago: The Athletic Institute.

Lukovich, I. 1971. *Electric foil fencing*. Budapest: Corvina Press. Distributed by Castello Combative Sports Co., 836 Broadway, New York 10003.

Moody, D. L., and B. J. Hoepner 1972. *Modern foil fencing: fun and fundamentals*. Oakland, Calif.: B and D Publications.

Nadi, A. 1943. *On fencing*. New York: G. P. Putnam.

Pallfy-Alpar, J. 1967. *Sword and masque*. Philadelphia: F. A. Davis Co.

Simonian, C. 1968. *Fencing fundamentals*. Columbus, Ohio: Charles E. Merrill.

Williams, J., B. J. Hoepner, D. L. Moody, and B. C. Ogilvie 1970. Personality traits of champion level female fencers, *Res. Quart.* **41**, 3:446–453.

Wyrick, W. 1971. *Foil fencing*. Philadelphia: W. B. Saunders.

12
Field Hockey

Jenepher P. Shillingford and Ethel G. Encke

DEFINITION AND ORIGIN

Field hockey is an exciting game played throughout the world by both men and women. The game is much like soccer in arrangement and involves eleven players on a side. The object of the game is to hit the ball into the opposition's goal, a four-yard-wide structure. Players use slightly varying types of curved sticks and a hard ball, the size of a baseball. The goalkeepers wear protective padding on the legs and feet. The game progresses on the ground primarily, but lofted strokes are also permitted provided they are not dangerous.

The origin of field hockey is uncertain but the game may have derived from a game called "hurley" which was being played in Ireland as far back as 1272 B.C. On the other hand, it seems equally likely that the stick game of the ancient Persians was subsequently acquired by the Greeks and handed on to the Romans who in turn brought the game to the British Isles with their invasion (Hickey 1970).

> A sculpture in bas-relief discovered in 1922 which formed part of a Greek wall built nearly 2500 years ago does show six youths in action and two in particular taking part in a "bully" bearing a remarkable resemblance to that of our starting technique today.

Field hockey may possibly be the oldest game played with a ball and stick. Throughout much of its existence the men's game has centered in India and Pakistan, while the women's game has been best exemplified in Great Britain.

WOMEN'S FIELD HOCKEY

Women's field hockey was initiated in the United States in 1901 by a dynamic young Englishwoman named Constance Applebee. The game was first played as a result of her endeavors as a clinician at Wellesley, Mt. Holyoke, Smith, Radcliffe, and Bryn Mawr colleges where she chaired the physical education departments for many years. No other individual has been such a strong single contributing force over the first 50 years of field hockey. Even after reaching

Fig. 12.1 Field hockey is an outdoor game in which the object is to hit the ball through the opponents' goal. Courtesy of Luther College.

the age of 100, Miss Applebee remained deeply concerned about field hockey in both her native England and the United States.

Motivated by her energy, many dedicated American women joined together to form the United States Field Hockey Association in 1922. Today it continues to administer to the game of women's field hockey. From a single hockey club formed in Poughkeepsie, New York, in 1901, the association has grown to include 275 clubs and colleges.

The USFHA is a member of the International Federation of Women's Field Hockey, an organization of 22 member nations. This organization meets every four years for a conference and competition. Unlike the Olympics, in which representation is limited to 16 teams in an elimination type of competition, the conference games are played with every team meeting six other nations and with no championship awarded. Simultaneously, meetings are held with delegates from each member nation to discuss rules, constitution, and national problems. All countries operate under one Code of Rules.

MEN'S FIELD HOCKEY

Field hockey for men is included in the Olympics as a team event. Until the 1972 Olympics, India and Pakistan dominated post-World War II competition. However, in 1972 the Pakistan team was upset by a well-prepared West German team 1–0. The West German team went on to win the Gold Medal. Field hockey in the United States has grown slowly, perhaps because of the competition for time and space during the fall season. As a result, the men's national field hockey teams have often been selected from small groups of individuals. The sport is rapidly becoming more popular and concentrated; well-directed efforts are being made to work with the gifted high school and college boy. Men's field hockey is under the auspices of the Field Hockey Association of America working with the United States Olympic Committee for Field Hockey.

THE HOCKEY GAME DIMENSIONS

Hockey is an outdoor game played for the most part in the fall of the year. A team consists of eleven players: five linesmen or forwards, three halfbacks, two backs, and a goalkeeper (formation generally played but not compulsory).

The game consists of two halves of 35 minutes each for college and club players and 20 to 25 minutes for younger groups or high school players.

A game is controlled by two qualified officials (usually rated). The game is played on a rectangular field 60 yards by 100 yards and is marked as follows: (a) two dotted 25 yard lines parallel to the end lines, (b) a center line, (c) a striking semicircle at each end (radius—16 yards), (d) marks on sidelines five yards from and parallel to the goal lines, (e) dotted lines five yards inside of and parallel to the sidelines, and (f) goal line markings five and ten yards on either side of the goal, parallel to sidelines. There are goal posts at either end of the field midway between the sidelines and on the goal lines. A goal post is composed of two perpendicular posts four yards apart and joined together by a horizontal crossbar seven feet from the ground. Nets are firmly attached to the posts, crossbars, and ground behind the goal. See Fig. 12.2.

The ball is white leather, with a circumference not less than $8\frac{13}{16}$ inches and not more than $9\frac{1}{4}$ inches. Each player plays with a right-handed hockey stick (left-handed sticks are illegal). The stick, made of hard wood, has a flat face on its left side. The weight should not exceed 23 ounces with lengths of 35, 36, or 37 inches. There must be no sharp edges or splinters, but the blade may be plastic laminated.

BEGINNING THE GAME

The game is started by a bully, one player of each team bullying in the center of the field. Center bully is also used after each goal and halftime. To bully, the two opposing center forwards stand facing the sidelines with the ball on the ground between them and their goal lines on their right. Three times, they alternately tap the ground with the blades of their sticks and strike the face of their opponent's stick, after which each tries to obtain possession of the ball and pass it to a teammate. Players' terminology is "ground, sticks, ground, sticks, ground, sticks, and hit." A goal is scored when the whole ball passes entirely over the goal line under the bar, provided the ball is hit or

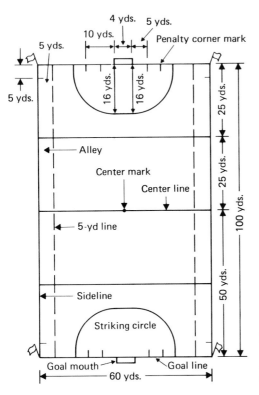

Fig. 12.2 Hockey field diagrams (a) from NAGWS *Field Hockey–Lacrosse Guide and* (b) Olympic standards.

glanced off the stick of an attacker within the striking circle. The team scoring the greater number of goals is the winner.

POSITION PLAY

The ball is passed by players to each other with the objective of traveling the length of the field and scoring a goal. The forward linesmen develop skill in passing the ball to their teammates, thereby moving into the striking circle for scoring purposes. The halfbacks back up the line playing offensively and defensively to keep the attack rolling. The fullbacks not only defend the goal, hitting the ball away from the striking circle, but offensively initiate the passing attack to linesmen or halfbacks. The fullbacks take the 15-yard free hit when an end line violation by an opponent occurs. The goalie within her area defends the goal, kicking or hitting the ball away from the goal and directing it to her offense.

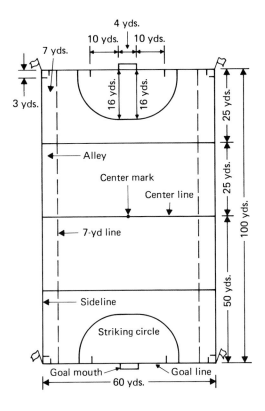

Fig. 12.3 The goalie within her area defends the goal, kicking or hitting the ball away. Courtesy of Southern Connecticut State College.

Hockey Rules

A player shall not:

1. Raise any part of stick above one's shoulder when playing.
2. Play the ball with the rounded side of stick.
3. Undercut the ball; hit blindly into an opponent or play the ball in such a way as to cause it to rise dangerously.
4. Strike, hit, hook, hold, or interfere in any way with opponent's stick.
5. Hit or pass the ball between her feet.
6. Stop the ball on the ground or in the air with any part of the body, except the hand. If the ball be caught, it shall be released into play immediately. The foot or leg may not be used to support the stick in order to resist an opponent.
7. Pick up, kick, throw, or carry the ball or propel it in any manner or direction, except with the stick, save as otherwise mentioned in specific rules.
8. Trip, shove, push, charge, strike at, or in any way personally handle her opponent.
9. Obstruct an opponent by rough or dangerous play.

Penalties are:

1. Outside the circles—a free hit to the opposing team on the spot where the breach occurred.
2. Inside the circles—for any breach by the attacking team a free hit to the defending team from any spot within the circle; for any breach by the defending team, a penalty corner or a penalty bully.
3. Inside or outside the circles—in the event of two players being simultaneously at fault, a bully is given on the spot where the breach of the rule occurred.
4. For rough, dangerous play or misconduct—in addition to awarding the appropriate penalty, the umpire may also warn the offending player or suspend her from further participation in the game.

Line violations

1. If the offense hits the ball over the end line, the opposing fullback receives a free 15-yard line hit.
2. If the defense hits the ball over the end line, a corner hit is awarded the attacking team. The *corner hit* is taken from the end line five yards from

the end or side line. If the ball is hit over the end line deliberately by the defense, a *short corner hit* is awarded the attacking team ten yards from the goal post.

3. When a player hits the ball over the sideline, the opposing team is awarded a roll in—taken from outside the sideline. The roll in may not be bounced or thrown in but must touch the ground in the field of play within one yard.

A player must always stay *onside*. When there are fewer than three defensive players between the offensive team and the goal, the team with the ball must remain behind the ball.

When a willful foul is committed by a defensive player inside the striking circle, a penalty bully may be awarded. A penalty bully is placed by the offender and one of the backs of the defending team on a spot five yards in front of the goal line. If the goalkeeper is in the bully, she may not remove her pads. All other players must be behind the 25-yard line and may not cross it until the penalty is completed. If a goal is scored, the game is resumed with a center bully; if not, it is resumed with a 25-yard line bully.

The game holds a strong place in the women's world and continues to gain popularity among the men. Its assets include expert stickwork, the many strategies of the game, and the constant fluid running necessary for good play.

SKILLS

As a player becomes more skilled, she enjoys the game more fully. The joy of effort and team play can never be underestimated. Skills to be developed are the dribble, push pass, flick, scoop, drive, lunge, circular tackle, dodge,

Fig. 12.4 Field hockey requires expert stickwork. Courtesy of Old Dominion University.

and free hit. Teamwork, fielding, shooting goals, speed, defensive and offensive tactics add excitement to the game.

Description of Skills

Dribble Moving the ball forward with a series of controlled taps while running.

Drive Passing the ball to a teammate or shooting for a goal.

Push pass Short pass, usually rolls, used in a situation where motion of stick is limited, or there is not time to execute a backswing. Right hand pushes the ball, left hand keeps top of stick ahead of ball.

Flick Similar to the push pass except that the ball is lifted off the ground as it leaves the blade. Effective when passing to a marked teammate.

Scoop Used from a dribble position, playing ball in front of and slightly to the right of the forward foot. Toe of blade is under the ball. Ball rises. Used to make a dodge, short pass, or shot to goal.

Dodge A player executes a dodge when she possesses the ball and wants to control it to progress forward and score a goal. Right and left dodges are used as well as a triangular pass.

Tackling A player tackles to gain possession of the ball by taking it from an opponent. In straight tackle the offensive player moves forward to meet her opponent—stick-to-stick; a circular tackle is used when the defensive player is on the left of the offensive player and they are running in the same direction.

Left-hand lunge When the defensive player is on the offensive player's stick or right side, facing her, the left-hand lunge is used.

Jab A one-handed spoiling stroke, a jab at the ball to get it away from an opponent.

REFERENCES

Barnes, M. J. 1969. *Field hockey; the coach and the player*. Boston: Allyn and Bacon.

Division for Girls and Women's Sports Guide 1972. *Field hockey–lacrosse*. AAHPER, Washington, D.C.

50th Anniversary Commemorative Program 1972, J. P. Shillingford (ed.). Philadelphia; USFHA.

Hickey, M. 1970. *Hockey for women*. London: Kaye and Ward.

Quadrennial Report 1961–1965. Asa S. Bushnell (sec.). USOC.

Stanley, D. K., and I. F. Waglow 1966. *Physical education activities handbook*. Boston: Allyn and Bacon.

13
Flag Football

Edward T. Dunn

The game of flag football is a variation of the game of tackle football which began in the colleges of this country around the middle of the 19th century. The first game of intercollegiate football was played between Rutgers and Princeton University in 1869.

It was only natural that boys and young men would seek to devise a game similar to tackle football which could be played with less equipment and training while still providing reasonable safety for the player. Touch football was the first variation adapted. Flag football evolved from touch football due to the need for objectivity in regard to the spot where the ball carrier was stopped. In touch football it is sometimes difficult to determine whether the man is actually touched. In flag football the presence of the flag in the defender's hand makes it official that the ball carrier was stopped at that point.

NATURE OF THE ACTIVITY

The game is most popular in the fall because of its similarity to the game of tackle football which has its regular season at that time. The scoring is the same with six points for a touchdown, three for a field goal, two for a safety, and either two or one for a try after a touchdown. It embodies nearly all of the fundamentals of the traditional game of American football with the exception of the hard contact of blocking, tackling, and forceful ball carrying. A great majority of the movement skills such as running, jumping, pivoting, and changing directions are basic parts of the game. The ball-handling skills of center snap procedures, hand-offs, fakes, pitch-outs, and passes are very essential parts of flag football. The entire kicking game, which involves place kicking and punting, is utilized.

It is safe to say that girls may enjoy the game of flag football with no greater chance of injury than in many other women's sports.

RULES OF THE GAME

Recommended Field Area

Regular football field lined every ten yards and with in-bounds markers for spotting the ball laterally when it is downed closer to the sideline than these points, or goes out of bounds. Goal posts should be placed ten yards deeper than goal line, on end zone line.

Team

a) Five to eleven players shall constitute a team with seven recommended.

b) A team captain shall be appointed for each game.

Offense

a) Number of men in line and backfield shall be decided by competing teams.

b) Blocking

   1. Blocking shall be from waist to shoulder area only.

   2. The blocks shall be stand-up chest and forearm blocks with blocker's hands in contact with his chest.

   3. There shall be no leaving of feet to block.

   4. Block may be used as screen only, with no forceful extension of the body into the contact.

   5. Penalty for infraction—15 yards from point of foul.

Defense

Defensive players are restricted in the use of their hands to the body and shoulders of offensive blockers. Penalty—loss of 15 yards from point of foul.

Equipment of Players

Sneakers or rubber-soled shoes recommended. Contrasting colors for teams optional.

Ball

Regulation (official) or junior size for junior high or elementary age teams.

Substitutions

a) Unlimited number of substitutions permitted.

b) A player may return to the game at any time.

Time

Optional: four 10- to 15-minute periods. Each team shall be allowed one time-out per period.

Kickoff

a) Normally made at the 40-yard line.

b) Kickoff spot governed by length of field.

Yardage and Downs

Team must advance ball 10 yards in four consecutive downs. Failure to do so results in loss of ball.

Note: This can be varied in many ways depending upon the length of the field. Sometimes each team is given a certain number of downs to score and must turn the ball over to the opponent after the downs are expended.

Forward Pass

May be thrown from any point behind line of scrimmage. This rule is sometimes adapted to allow a forward pass anywhere on field before flag is pulled. In this case if the pass is incomplete, the ball is dead at the spot from which the pass is thrown.

Eligible Pass Receivers

All players are eligible to catch passes.

Eligible Ball Carriers from Scrimmage

Ends and backs are eligible.

Player Is Down

a) Player is considered down when opponent has pulled flag and holds it above his head. Ball is dead at this point.

b) Tackling is prohibited (15-yard penalty).

c) Diving off feet for flag is prohibited (15-yard penalty).

Opportunity for Free Ball

A member of either team may recover a fumble, but may not leave feet to dive for ball, or shove opponent in order to get the ball.

Kicking

a) Running into kicker is not allowed at any time (penalty—15 yards and loss of ball). Both offensive and defensive teams must hold their positions until the kick has been made.

b) A two-inch kicking tee may be used for kick-offs, field goals, or place-kicks for the extra point after touchdown.

Forward Progress of Ball

At the end of a play, the ball shall be placed directly below the spot where it is carried when flag is pulled.

Example: If a player has the ball over the goal line and opponent pulls flag before the goal line, it is a touchdown.

Off-Side

A player, except the center, is off-side when any part of his body is over the line of scrimmage at the time the ball is snapped.

Flags

a) Made of heavy material—24″ long, 4″ wide.

b) No tying of flags permitted. Penalty—loss of ball.

c) 16″ of flag must be showing.

d) Jerseys must be worn inside the pants.

Officials

a) The referee shall be in complete charge of the game.

b) Only the two team captains shall be authorized to discuss decisions.

c) If there is a question as to interpretation of the rules, *only the captains and the coaches* shall be allowed to discuss it with the referee.

Deportment of Players

The deportment of players on the bench and on the playing field is the responsibility of the coach.

Scoring

a) Touchdown scores six points.

b) Field goal scores three points.

c) Safety scores two points.

d) Point after touchdown scores two points by passing or running, and one point when kicking by placekick or dropkick.

Penalties

a) Offside—5 yards

b) Tackling—15 yards

c) Illegal use of hands (defense)—15 yards

d) Illegal blocking on offense—15 yards

e) Running into kicker—15 yards

f) Repeated roughness—expulsion from game

g) Diving off feet for flag—15 yards

h) Use of straight-arm or holding flag by ball carrier—15 yards

The rules above, together with interscholastic football rules, shall govern flag football. Restrictions can be placed on the type of defense to be used to provide more scoring.

TERMINOLOGY

Back Player who lines up one yard or more behind the line of scrimmage.

Bootleg A fake handoff and a keep, usually by the quarterback.

Center Man who snaps the ball at start of play.

Contain Turning in the ball carrier on a sweep.

Conversion Play after touchdown—one point for a field goal, two points for a run or pass across the goal line.

Dropback pass Pass in which quarterback sprints back fast to position for throwing.

End Offensive player who lines up on end of line of scrimmage.

Field goal Placekick or dropkick of ball from scrimmage, over the crossbar.

Flood pass Pass play in which several receivers go to one area of field.

Free ball Ball still in play.

Handoff Exchange of ball from one player to another.

I-formation Formation in which backs line up in straight line.

In-bounds markers Spot where ball is placed for next play, approximately 18 yards from sidelines, whenever it is stopped in play nearer the sidelines or out of bounds.

Jet A fast-hitting, pitch-out play to the outside.

Long-arm motion Body mechanics of a long pass.

Man-to-man coverage Pass defense in which men cover specific opponents.

Mirrored offense Plays which can be run the same right and left.

Open-hand fake Fake in which ball carrier's open hand is placed in teammate's midsection, while ball is held with opposite hand on hip or in stomach.

Option play A play in which the ball carrier has the choice of running or passing (either a forward or lateral pass).

Pitchout Tossing a ball laterally or back to a teammate behind the line of scrimmage.

Pro-formation A formation with one man set out wide to either side of offensive set.

Pursuit Running after the ball carrier.

Regular football Tackle football.

Reverse Play that starts one way and, after a handoff, goes the other.

Ride fake Fake in which ball is placed on teammate's midsection and held there for a short time while he is running.

Safety Defensive team traps offense behind own goal after offense gave impetus to place ball in that area.

Screening Placing body between defensive men and ball carrier.

Shortarm action Quick bent-arm action for short pass.

Shotgun double wing formation A formation having two wingbacks and a quarterback who is not in contact with the center.

Shotgun formation A formation without a quarterback in contact with the center.

Square A pass route in which receiver turns 90° in or out.

Streak A pass route in which the receiver tries to outrun the defender.

Tackle football Official game of American football played on school, college, and professional levels.

Tee A holder from which the ball can be place-kicked.

Touch football Forerunner to flag football, in which the ball carrier is declared stopped at the place he is touched.

Touchdown Offensive team advances ball across opponent's goal.

Three-point stance Player in starting position with weight on the balls of the feet and with the fingertips of one hand on the ground.

Two-point stance Player in starting position with weight on balls of feet and with hands resting on knees.

Winged-T formation A popular offensive formation with the quarterback under the center and a wingback on the right or left end of the line.

Throwback pass Ball thrown back across the field after a back has run to opposite side.

Zone coverage Pass defense where men cover assigned areas of the field.

FUNDAMENTALS AND SKILLS

The primary fundamentals in flag football are skills involving stance, movement, ball handling, passing, pass receiving, kicking, kick receiving, screening, defensive pursuit, and flag pulling.

Stance

A two- or three-point stance is recommended depending upon whether a fast start, either forward or laterally, is desired. A three-point stance is better for a fast straight ahead start, whereas a two-point stance is better for lateral moves. The quarterback who is taking a handoff from the center will take a two-point stance. The center will take a stance with his hands on the ball and his head up, if the center to quarterback handoff is employed. He will normally look back between his legs on the snap to a deepback, the kicker, or holder on kick formations.

Movement Fundamentals

Running

In starting, the player should emphasize a good body lean during the first few steps. A vigorous arm action should parallel the leg action. The toes and knees should be pointed straight ahead. A high knee action is important once speed is gained to facilitate a good length of stride. When the main concern

Fig. 13.1 Stance: (a) 2-point, (b) 3-point.

(a)　　(b)

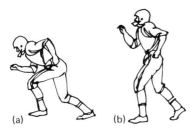

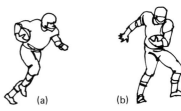

Fig. 13.2 Running: (a) speed form, (b) balance form for quickness and change of direction.

Fig. 13.3 Changing direction: (a) crossover step, (b) sidestep.

is quickness, balance, and sudden change of direction, the body should be more upright and the stride must be much shorter.

Changing directions

Two primary techniques used to avoid a defensive man are the sidestep and the crossover step. In both of these techniques, the player should shorten his stride to a degree before execution of the move. He then must plant one foot and drive the other leg either across the front of the supporting leg or off to the opposite side. It is also helpful to use a head-and-shoulder fake in the opposite direction just prior to the foot action.

Pass-Receiver Patterns

Hook

Any receiver can run this pattern. He should break out of his stance in a glide for two to four steps. He follows this with a sprint straight down field. When he sees the defensive man turn his side or back on him to cover him deep, he should plant his foot and turn back toward the line of scrimmage. He must have a good wide base in his foot position, and his knees must be bent to help him move immediately for the ball in any direction. If the ball is thrown above the waist, it should be caught with the fingers facing up, and if it is below the waist, fingers should be facing down.

Square-out or square-in

The square-out starts with a two- to four-yard glide which is followed by an explosion into a sprint. Once the defensive man commits himself to cover deep by turning and sprinting, the receiver will plant his inside foot at the required distance and cut 90° toward the sideline. The square-in is executed with the same technique except the receiver breaks in toward the middle of the field.

Streak

This is a "straight-down-the-field" pattern in which the receiver uses a change of pace to get behind the defender. He will normally catch the ball over his inside shoulder.

Square-out and streak

The receiver fakes a square-out at the normal distance for this pattern and then explodes into a sprint pattern.

Flag

The flag cut is very similar to the square-out except the receiver will break deeper for a spot on the sideline. He will normally take the ball over his outside shoulder.

Post

The post pattern is similar to the flag pattern except it is run to the inside of the field. The receiver breaks in the direction of the goalpost. He should normally catch the ball over his inside shoulder.

Cross

When running this pattern, the receiver should cut across the field to the inside. He will gain a distance of five to twenty yards from the line of scrimmage, according to prior agreement with the passer.

Flare

This is normally used by a slot or a wingback. He should break quickly into the flat area at a depth of five to eight yards deep and catch the ball over his outside shoulder. By making the cut more rounded instead of a square-out, the receiver is able to get out to a wider area more quickly.

Swing

The swing pattern is run by a back from behind the line of scrimmage. He should belly back deeper behind the line of scrimmage as he swings out toward the sideline. He will then catch the pass over his inside shoulder as he turns upfield.

Look-in

This is normally run by a receiver stationed on the line of scrimmage as the ball is snapped. The receiver takes two or three steps straight downfield, and then turns quickly to the inside for the ball. He must be ready for the ball as soon as he looks to the inside.

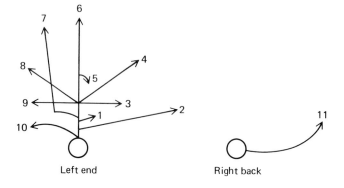

Fig. 13.4 Pass patterns: (1) look-in, (2) cross, (3) square-in, (4) post, (5) hook, (6) streak, (7) square-out and streak, (8) flag, (9) square-out, (10) flare, and (11) swing.

Ball-handling Skills

Center to quarterback ball exchange

Center

The center stance, except for the hands, is the same as a normal three-point stance. He will grip the ball with his strong hand on the forward part of the ball. The grip is the same as a forward passer's grip. His opposite hand should rest on the back and opposite side of the ball. The strong hand lifts the ball into the hands of the quarterback. There should be a slight counterclockwise turn of the ball as it is brought up in order to make it fit properly into the hands of the quarterback.

Quarterback

The quarterback should stand fairly erect, with his hands in the crotch of the center. His shoulders should be parallel to the line of scrimmage and his eyes should look straight downfield. He can best operate in a variety of movements from a parallel stance. His shoulders should be over the center's hips. His arms should be straight and his hands should be in position to receive the ball. To accommodate the ball better, the right hand should be rotated slightly in a clockwise direction. The quarterback should bring the ball immediately to his midsection once he receives it from the center.

Center exchange with holder, kicker, or deep back

The deep snap is made with the center looking back, between his legs. He should grip the ball with his strong hand in the same manner used by a forward passer. His opposite hand rests as a guide on the back portion of the ball. The passback is really thrown as an upside down forward pass. The ball must be extended out far enough in the starting position so only the head and hands of the center are over the ball. This puts the center in compliance with the rules.

Holder for placekick

The holder takes a position on one knee about five to seven yards from the ball. The holder's arms and hands are then extended toward the center. As soon as the ball is caught, it is placed on a tee with one hand remaining on the top in order to support it until it is kicked.

Backfield ball exchange

Handoff man. The handoff man should focus his eyes on the receiver's belt line and place the ball in that area with both hands. In order to minimize the chance for a fumble he should place it well across toward the far hip area. Once the ball is accepted by the receiver, the hands are relaxed and removed.

Receiver. The receiver of the handoff should look where he is running and not at the ball. His near arm is held high across the area of the upper chest. The palm of the hand should be facing down. The far arm is laid across the belt with the elbow resting in front of the far hip and the palm of the hand facing up. The upper arm should close down on the ball as the receiver feels the ball placed in his midsection.

Backfield faking

The ball is not actually exchanged, but the intent of the offense is to confuse the defense in its ability to diagnose whether it is being exchanged or not. The two types of fakes which can be used are the open-hand fake, and ride fake. In the open-hand fake, the ball is held in the belly or on the hip of the man in possession, while his other hand is placed in the midsection of the faking back. In the ride fake, the ball is actually put into the midsection of the faking back and held there for a certain amount of time, depending upon the type of play being used.

Passing

Grip

The ball is gripped with the pads of the fingers with the little and ring finger

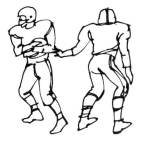

Fig. 13.5 The center to quarterback exchange.

Fig. 13.6 The handoff.

Fig. 13.7 Grip.

165

on the laces. the rest of the fingers are held off the laces toward the backside of the ball.

Short-arm action

The short-arm passing action is used on short passes. The passer takes a short step toward his target with the foot opposite the passing hand. The ball is thrown with a quick overhand snap throw, similar to a catcher's peg in baseball. The ball is thrown on a line, with very little trajectory, in order to get the ball quickly to an open man.

Long-arm action

This is a more powerful pass used on a long pass. The passer may use two steps before releasing the pass. The arm action is a much longer one to give more power to the throw. The ball is arched up much higher to allow for the natural trajectory of the ball on a long pass.

Pass receiving

Catching the ball

The pass receiver should watch the ball all the way into his hands, as the human tendency is to be disconcerted by opponents, or other distractions. The receiver should also try to keep his hands relaxed when the ball is being caught.

Kicking

Punting

The punter should assume a comfortable stance ready to move right, left or forward. The kicking foot should be forward slightly and there should be a six-inch lateral spread of the feet. The arms and fingers are extended at belt level. The punter should move into or in front of ball as it comes to him. He should take a short step with kicking foot for drive and balance and then a long step with opposite foot and kick. The ball should be stretched out full arm's length in front of kicking foot and the forward point of the ball turned down and in, to correspond with slant of the instep. The kicking leg should

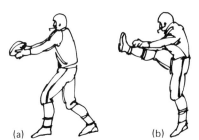

Fig. 13.8 Punting: (a) approach, (b) punt.

(a)   (b)

swing through with toe depressed and knee locking as contact with the ball is made.

Placekicking (conventional style)

The kicker takes a stride stance with kicking foot slightly in advance. His arms are swinging loosely at his side and his knees are bent slightly. His eyes are on the tee, with peripheral vision watching the holder for a clue as to when the ball will be snapped. As he observes the ball being brought to the tee, he starts his movement forward with a short step with his kicking foot for drive and balance. He then takes a longer stride with the opposite foot and places it about one to three inches behind the ball, and about four inches to the side of it. The kicking leg swings straight through with the contact point of the toe just below the middle of the ball. The head is down throughout with the eyes on the ball.

Placekicking (soccer style)

The kicker takes a similar stance to the conventional style, except he is off to the side of the directional line about a yard. The number and length of the steps are the same as the conventional style except the kicker is moving in to the ball from a side angle of about 45°. In the soccer-style kick, the kicking leg is swung in more of a circular motion, and the toe is kept depressed, with the ball kicked by the inside portion of the instep.

Kick receiving

Punt or placekick receiving

The receiver should sprint fast and get set under the ball. As he gains experience, he may stay slightly deeper than the ball and take it on the run. The receiver's elbows should be about six inches apart and fairly close to belt. The hands are about four inches apart at chin level, with the fingers pointing upward. He should stay relaxed. The ball should be caught in the hands and guided into the body as a trap or backstop for the ball.

Offensive screening

Side screen

The side screen is used primarily on running plays. In this type of screen the offensive player steps quickly to the side of the defensive man where the ball is going. He may not make any forceful aggressive move into the defensive man and may or may not be allowed to use a moving screen depending on the decision of the rule makers.

Front screen

The front screen is used primarily in protecting the passer. In this screen the offensive blocker moves in front of the defensive man and keeps between him and the passer. Again he cannot make any forceful aggressive moves into the defensive man but may be allowed to shift his screen in order to maintain a frontal position.

Defensive pursuit

Screen release
The defensive player is required to run around the screener to get to the ball carrier. He can use his hands on his opponent's body, with the exception of the head area, but cannot do it in a forceful manner other than warding off his opponent. He cannot hold at any time.

Pass defense
The regular interscholastic football rules shall govern offensive and defensive pass interference.

Flag pulling

The basic fundamentals of flag pulling are quite obvious. It is considered best, in the concern for safety, not to allow the defensive man to dive off his feet for the flag. Initially the defensive man should make sure he gets close enough to reach the flag. Normally he should use short choppy steps and keep a fairly erect trunk for proper balance. It is advisable to keep his eyes on the midsection or hips of his opponent as he has a little less chance of being faked than he would if he watched his opponent's head and shoulders. Once he gains a close position to the ball carrier, he should focus his attention on the flag and snatch it, with an upward or sideward arm motion.

TEAM PLAY

Because of the flexibility permitted in the number of players comprising a team, it is difficult to prescribe a set offense or defense as the most appropriate one for all teams. Each team should make adujstments according to the number of players they are using, and the strengths and weaknesses of their personnel. The basic offensive formations that can be utilized are the Pro T, the Pro Double Wing, the Pro I, and various Shotgun sets. The defense can be a zone coverage type on passes with a reasonable number of players assigned to rush the passer, or a man-to-man defense applied to each eligible receiver with the remaining man rushing. On running plays certain men can be assigned to contain the ball carrier with everyone else pursuing the flag.

On offense the running and passing game should be reasonably well balanced, but this will depend to a large degree on the talent of the players on the team. If fast elusive backs are available, a definite running threat can be established. If the team has a skilled passer and good receivers, it can develop a highly effective passing attack.

Considerable emphasis should be placed on the punting game. If a deepback offense is used from time to time on runs and passes, it may be wise to use the quick kick from scrimmage on any down when it is not expected. Otherwise the deep kick should be used from scrimmage with proper coverage of the kick. The defense should develop plans for the returning of kicks. Team play for the offensive and defensive phases of the field goal and kickoff must also be prepared.

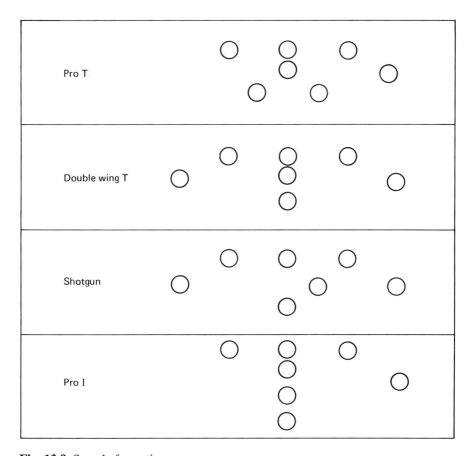

Fig. 13.9 Sample formations.

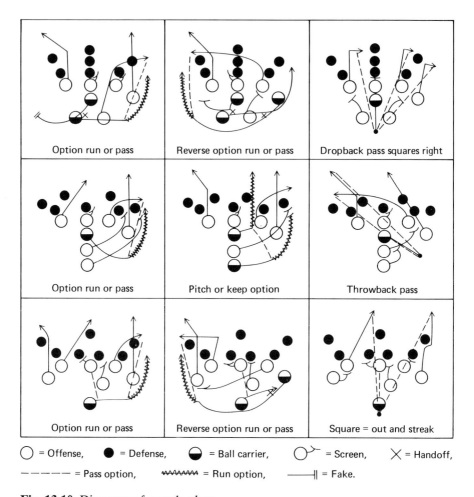

Option run or pass	Reverse option run or pass	Dropback pass squares right
Option run or pass	Pitch or keep option	Throwback pass
Option run or pass	Reverse option run or pass	Square = out and streak

◯ = Offense,　● = Defense,　◓ = Ball carrier,　◯ʳ = Screen,　✕ = Handoff,

– – – – – = Pass option,　〰〰〰 = Run option,　——⊣ = Fake.

Fig. 13.10 Diagrams of sample plays.

REFERENCES

The rules of the game of flag football presented in this paper are taken mainly from those used in the Public School System of Springfield, Massachusetts. They were developed by Russell Peterson, Director of Athletics at the time of their formation.

Dunn, E. T. 1970. *Springfield College football defense.* Bennington, Vt.: Broad Brook Press.

———— 1970. *Springfield College football offense.* Bennington, Vt.: Broad Brook Press.

Football, the naval aviation physical training manual 1943. United States Naval Institute.

14
Flickerball

Armond H. Seidler

INTRODUCTION

The game of flickerball developed as the answer to a question. Two University of Illinois professors of physical education attended an NFL professional football game at Wrigley Field in Chicago in the 1948 season. The two, Harold E. "Hek" Kenny and Armond H. Seidler, spent the three-hour trip returning to Champaign discussing the differences between college and professional football. The professionals had demonstrated superb passing and receiving. Most college and high school players of that time were relatively poor in ball-handling skills.

It occurred to them that the ball-handling skills of college and high school basketball players were high, and consequently they attempted to ascertain why such a discrepancy existed. They concluded that the leadup games for basketball and baseball were basketball and baseball, and that players in both were given innumerable opportunities to handle the ball, so that those with the potential to develop such skills did so, and made the high school and college teams.

The leadup game for football was touch or flag football, in which only a small number of players have a chance to throw a forward pass, or attempt to catch one. Frequently the owner of the ball is the team passer, and his best friend is the principal receiver. This means that some of the players, often those with the greatest potential as passers and receivers, are deprived of the opportunities to handle the ball, and as a result, they fail to develop ball-handling skills.

In the discussion that followed, the two tried to visualize a game played with a football, which would be fun to play and which would give all players many opportunities to catch and throw the ball, so that those with the greatest potential would become excellent receivers and passers. By the time the two colleagues reached home they were in basic agreement about the fundamental principles of the game.

The game of flickerball was named after the "flea-flicker" pass in football, always one of the most spectacular plays in the game. It was first taught as an activity course in the basic instructional program in physical education at the University of Illinois in the fall of 1949, and immediately became a fixture in the service program. It was very popular with boys and later be-

171

came a basic part of the girls' physical education curriculum. A number of exhibitions, such as a demonstration before the Illinois High School Coaches Football Clinic, and a half-time game between the halves of an Illinois–Indiana basketball game tended to spread the word about this new game, and many schools became interested. It is estimated that flickerball is played in as many as ten thousand schools in the United States, as an instructional unit, intramural or recreational sport, or as a varsity sport. Many football teams play flickerball as part of the training or conditioning for the sport.

Flickerball has enjoyed a steady development in the past two decades and it is anticipated that the game will continue to grow in popularity in the future.

THE GAME

Flickerball is a noncontact game played indoors or outdoors, using the ball-handling skills of football.

The game may be played indoors on a basketball court, the goals being equipped with a special bracket which enables them to be easily mounted on the regular basketball backboards.

The fact that the goals are convertible, and that the game may be played either indoors or outdoors is, of course, a tremendous advantage to the coach or physical education teacher, who will be able to use the game in any or all seasons of the year. The goals may be used to full advantage and their dual service will go a long way to justify their expense.

The flickerball goal is a board with a rounded rectangular hole in it through which the ball is passed. This board is mounted in such a manner that the center of the target hole is nine feet above the ground and equidistant between the two sidelines.

Flickerball is played with a football and the object of the game is to advance the ball by passing to a position from which a goal may be attempted. Any player on either team is allowed to handle the ball at any time. The ball may be advanced toward the goal only by means of passing. The player in control of the ball is not allowed to advance toward the goal while in possession of the ball. However, the ball may be carried laterally or backward. No contact is allowed in this game and with refinement the game is an extremely fluid sport in which lightning passes, sudden starts and stops, and rather close man-to-man play predominate. With experienced participants playing, all players have countless oppportunities to pass and receive the football and are constantly attempting to successfully execute these skills. Conversely, when on defense a player will be attempting to cover the opponent as well as play the ball.

One of the novel features of this game is the fact that any attempted goal results in loss of possession of the ball. The rules of this game are so designed that the goals are situated out of bounds with the specific intent of forcing the shooting team to throw the ball out of bounds and thus lose possession. After a successful or an unsuccessful goal attempt the defensive team puts the ball in play by throwing the ball in bounds from behind its own end line. This plan was deliberately introduced in order to place a premium on working for a good shot at the goal. The fact that any shot, successful or otherwise, causes loss of the ball for the shooting team forces the offensive team to work for better scoring opportunities and almost eliminates wild or haphazard shooting.

Another interesting feature of the game is the fact that a loose ball which remains on the playing field is a free ball which may be played by any player. This provision promotes fluidity of action and places a premium on quick reaction and alertness.

Penalty shots, or free throws, are awarded when a player is fouled. The offended player receives a free throw after which, successful or not, the free-throwing team is given possession of the ball out of bounds at the midline. The purpose of this provision is to hold fouls to a minimum.

Most players, including varsity football stars who have played this game, are extremely enthusiastic. They enjoy playing the game and think its possibilities as a developer of ball-handling skills in football are tremendous. Flickerball may develop into a fine spectator game as well as a player sport and it is conceivable that at some future time this game may emerge as an interscholastic sport in its own right.

Flickerball has many other advantages in the physical education and athletic programs. As a new game, it offers an opportunity to add variety to the sports program. Also, it can greatly increase the use of present indoor and outdoor facilities. Thus, flickerball should be a welcome addition to the programs of schools with limited play areas.

Most of the football field lines may also be used for flickerball. As the goals in the game of flickerball are 15 feet off the football field they may be permanently erected without interfering with its normal use.

This game is a boon to camps, public playgrounds, and parks. Since flickerball is a noncontact sport, it may be played safely with a minimum of supervision, and the injuries occurring are few in number. The fact that the game is not rough should help to overcome common parental objections.

One of the great advantages of the game of flickerball is that, like basketball, it may be played by a larger or smaller number of boys than prescribed in the rules. In congested situations, two games of half-court flickerball may be played at the same time. Variations of the game may be played by a small number of individuals, e.g., spot shooting or flickerball golf.

The game may be played outdoors in any type of weather, if the participants so desire, by players using a rubber football as a substitute for the regulation leather ball.

RULES FOR FLICKERBALL
Court Layout

Indoor dimensions. Indoors, flickerball shall be played on any regulation basketball court. The goal shall be mounted on the basketball backboard with the bottom of the hole eight feet from the floor. In the indoor game, a line shall be drawn parallel to the face of the goal, from sideline to sideline at a distance of 15 feet in front of the goal. This area shall be designated as the "no-score area."

Outdoor dimensions. The outdoor flickerball field shall be rectangular in shape, its length being 53⅓ yards, its width, 30 yards. Each goal shall be set five yards back of the end line, equidistant between the sidelines, and parallel to the end line. The bottom of the hole in the flickerball board shall be eight feet above the ground. A free throw line, six feet long, will be placed 30 feet in front of each end line, directly in front of the goal. (It is suggested that game fields be laid out across the width of a practice football field —as many as three flickerball fields may be laid across a regulation football field.)

The Number of Players

Outdoor game. The outdoor game shall be played by two teams each consisting of seven players. The players are not identified with a particular position on the field (such as, right forward or center forward). Definite positioning can be accomplished, however, in the many styles of offense and defense which may be employed in the game.

Indoor game. The indoor game shall be played by two teams, consisting of five players on each team.

A. General Rules

A.1. No one is permitted to advance toward the goal while ball is in his control. Player with ball in his control may move only in a lateral or backward direction.

a) If player gains control of ball while advancing toward goal he will be allowed a maximum of one and one-half steps in which to stop his advance, or to swerve to a lateral direction. (If player receives ball as he is on right foot, he may advance, place left foot, and will not be considered traveling until he again steps on the right foot). Note: In circumstances where players are playing with uncleated shoes or on slick surface, officials are advised to interpret this rule so that a player

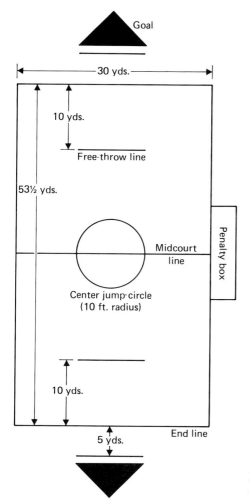

Fig. 14.1 Official playing field or court.

making obvious attempts to stop will not be considered traveling even though he exceeds the step and a half limitation.

b) If player is called for traveling (i.e., illegally advancing with ball in his control), referee will immediately blow whistle. Offending player must place ball on ground in order that nearest opponent can immediately put ball into play.

A.2. The following are situations in which the ball is whistled dead:

a) Player called for traveling. (A.1.b)

b) Personal foul. (C.1)

175

c) Technical foul. (C.2)

d) Ball goes out of bounds. (A.3)

e) Incomplete forward pass (incomplete through no interference on part of defensive player). (A.6.a)

f) Signaling of time-out or end of playing time. (E.1)

g) Violation of out-of-bounds rules. (A.12)

h) Violation of five-second rule (Ten-Second Rule). (A.11)

A.3. When ball goes out of bounds, an opponent of the player who last touched ball in bounds will be given possession at that point, out of bounds.

A.4. All attempted shots for score must be thrown with one-hand, overhand forward pass. Push shot will not count as a goal.

A.5. No player is allowed to retain possession of ball more than five seconds. Penalty—loss of ball on spot of infraction.

A.6. Incomplete passes.

a) If offensive team attempts a forward pass which is incomplete through no interference on the part of a defensive player (i.e., if attempted pass is poorly aimed, or receiver muffs the ball), whistle will be blown and possession of the ball will be given immediately to the nearest player of the defensive team, who will put the ball in play as soon as he is able, from the spot on which he gets control of the ball. (Ball may be put in play on playing field if that is where defensive player picks up ball.)
Out-of-bounds rules *apply* when ball is put in play on playing field.

(1) A ball whistled dead on the field of play remains dead until it is picked up by player entitled to put it in play. Opponents must be three feet away from player putting ball in play until moment ball is actually put in play by being picked up off ground by player.

(2) Any intentional handling of the ball by offense after whistle before ball is put in play by the defense is a technical foul.

b) If a forward pass is incomplete because a defensive player is the cause of the incompletion (i.e., defensive player bats ball out of hands of passer or receiver, or out of air), the ball remains a free ball and may be played by either team, unless it rolls out of bounds, in which case out-of-bounds rule applies.

c) Any incomplete *lateral* pass which remains on the field of play is a free ball and may be played by any player. (This applies to any lateral throw in from out of bounds.)

A.7. Any fumbled ball which remains on the field of play is a free ball which may be played by any player.

A.8. In the indoor game, play may take place in the "no-score area" but all goal shots must emanate from outside this area. Any goal shots attempted from this area shall be considered dead and no scores made from this area will be allowed. Penalty for shot from this area—loss of ball, score not counted.

A.9. In the outdoor game, since the goals are erected five yards behind the end line, and are therefore out of bounds, all balls will be dead as they cross the end line, whether try for goal is successful or not. In either case, possession of ball is given to the defending team behind its own end line.

A.10. In cases where the receiver of pass is bound by the rules to receive it within a certain area, he must gain definite control of ball within that area (i.e., if player received ball while off ground, both feet must land within area).

A.11. In putting ball in play in backcourt, following rules will apply:

a) A team putting ball in play in backcourt area at any time will be given 10 seconds in which to advance ball into front court (Scoring area). Penalty for failure to advance ball within 10 seconds is loss of ball at spot of infraction.

b) After ball has advanced past half-court line into the front-court area offensive team must continue to play ball in this area until a shot at the goal is attempted or until ball is lost to defense. Penalty for offensive team passing or carrying ball into backcourt area after ball has been advanced into front-court area, is loss of ball at point of infraction.

A.12. In passing ball in from out of bounds these rules apply:

a) When ball is out of bounds in front court, player must throw ball in with lateral pass.

b) When ball is out of bounds in backcourt, player must throw in anywhere in backcourt.

c) "Out-of-bounds" rules apply when ball is put in play on field after incomplete forward pass, or any other dead-ball situation.

A.13. When a team is given possession of the ball out of bounds it will be given five seconds in which to put the ball in play. Penalty for violation is loss of ball at approximate spot ball went out.

B. Scoring

B.1. Goal is scored by firing ball into hole, or striking the face of the board. A goal shot which enters the hole in the board and strikes the net scores *three* points. A goal shot which hits the face of the board but does not enter the hole scores *one* point.

B.2. Any attempt on part of defensive player to goal tend in dead-ball area (i.e., deliberately bat out attempted goal) shall result in award of three-point goal to shooting team.

B.3. a) An attempted shot which is blocked by a defensive player and remains on the field of play is a free ball and may be played by any player.

b) An attempted shot which is blocked by a defensive player and rolls out of bounds will be given to the defensive team out of bounds, at the approximate point that the ball went out. Since any shot which can be blocked is considered a poor shot, the intent of this rule is to penalize the shooter with loss of ball.

B.4. A free throw attempt which enters the hole in the board and strikes the net scores three points. A free throw attempt which strikes the *face* of the board but does not enter the hole scores one point. After free throw, possession of ball is given to defensive team behind end line.

C. Fouls

C.1. Personal fouls occur when any player causes personal contact with his opponent. Player committing personal foul must leave game and cannot return to the field of play until any field goal (three points or one point) is scored by either team. Player must remain in penalty box on sidelines until such time as he returns to play. He may not be substituted for while in the penalty box.

a) For personal foul—offended team will be given possession of the ball on the spot of the infraction and will put the ball in play as soon as offending player leaves field. Out-of-bounds rules apply.

b) If a player is fouled in the act of shooting an attempted goal shot, a personal foul will be charged to the offending player, the goal shot will be given free throw at the goal.

c) Four personal fouls disqualify a player.

C.2. Technical Foul—general penalty—one free throw. The following are technical fouls:

a) Diving on a loose ball.

b) Intentionally kicking ball.

Any foul construed by the official to be flagrant or any act of unsports-manlike conduct will be ruled a technical foul and handled as follows:

a) Indoor rules—fouled player gets a free shot at goal from center jump circle. Ball is dead and after shot, successful or otherwise, fouled team is given possession of ball out of bounds at center line. Thrower may not cross free throw line until after ball is dead. Offending player is ejected from game as in Rule C.1.

b) Outdoor rules—in the outdoor game a free throw is attempted from behind a free throw mark. After free throw, successful or other-wise, fouled team is given possession of the ball out of bounds at a point parallel to the free throw mark. Thrower may not cross free throw line until after ball is dead. Offending player is ejected from game as in Rule C.1. **Note:** In case of unsportsmanlike conduct, any member of offended team may attempt free throw.

D. Substitutions

D.1. Substitutions may be made any time ball is dead.

D.2. Any number of players may be substituted during a time-out period.

D.3. Any player out of play because of a penalty may not be substituted for until he reenters play.

E. Timing

E.1. Game will be two 20-minute halves. Time is out whenever ball is dead. Each team is allowed three 2-minute time-outs per half. Each extra time-out is a technical foul. Any player may shoot.

F. Jump Balls

F.1. Each half is started with a center jump.

F.2. Center jump consists of a ball tossed up between two centers, ends pointing toward goals. Player first obtaining ball after center jump must pass ball laterally. Player other than jumper must touch ball before jumper may again handle the ball in all jump-ball situations.

F.3. Players other than jumpers must remain outside imaginary circle with 10-foot diameter until ball is batted.

F.4. Jump-ball on spot will be used to settle all held-ball situations. Player receiving tap in jump-ball situations must throw laterally.

G. Equipment

G.1. A regulation leather or rubber football will be the official ball.

G.2. The goal shall be 4′ × 5′ rectangle, with a 2′ × 3′ rounded rectangular hole in it. The goal shall be mounted in such a manner that its surface is at right angles to the sidelines of the court, and the height of the lower edge of the rectangular hole shall be exactly eight feet from the floor.

H. Elastic Powers

H.1. The officials shall decide any question not specifically covered in the rules.

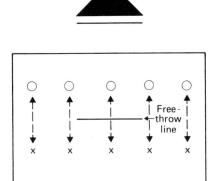

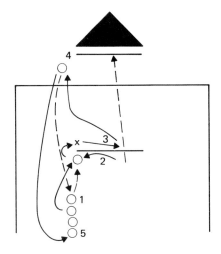

Fig. 14.2 Stationary straight line passing drill. Players practice throwing back and forth to each other from stationary position to stationary target concentrating on form and accuracy in passing.

Fig. 14.3 Shooting drill. No. 1 passes to No. 2 who attempts to evade defensive man (No. 3) to attempt shot at goal. After attempted shot, the ball is rebounded by No. 4 and passed to man in No. 1 position in line. Players rotate as indicated in diagram, 1 to 2 position, 2 to 3 position, 3 to 4 position, 4 to 5 position, 5 advances in line to No. 1 position. Scoring is same as in regulation game with each individual player keeping his own score. First player to reach specified number of points wins game. Five-second rule is observed during drill. To add interest, two or more lines may work this drill on same goal, all individuals competing with each other.

180

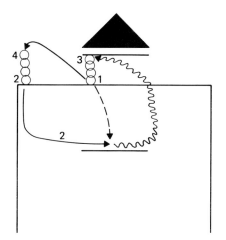

= Path of player with ball
= Path of player
= Path of ball

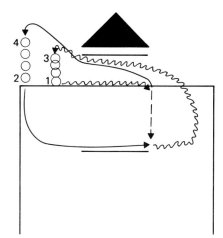

= Path of player with ball
= Path of player
= Path of ball

Fig. 14.4 Passing drill. Passer in stationary position passing to moving target. No. 1 passes to No. 2 who cuts across field in front of No. 1 about 8 to 10 yards out. After receiving pass, No. 2 goes to end of passing line behind No. 3. Each man in passing line has ball. No. 1 moves into receiving line behind No. 4.

Fig. 14.5 Passing drill. No. 1 runs from front of passing line laterally about 10 or 12 yards stops, sets and passes to No. 2 who has cut across in front of passer about 8 to 10 yards out. No. 1 moves to No. 4 position in receiver line and receiver No. 2 moves to end of passing line.

Fundamental Skills

The fundamental skills in flickerball are passing the football, catching the ball, running pass receiver routes, and playing man-to-man defense. Teaching techniques would include instruction in holding, throwing, and catching the football, with drills to develop these skills. Strategies would be covered in terms of offensive and defensive patterns of movement and drills designed to practice such maneuvers.

After the player understands the rules and the nature of the game, skills are best developed by actually playing the game.

Equipment

The only equipment required for flickerball is a regulation football, and two flickerball goals. Each goal normally has a net which covers the hole and is suspended by snap hooks from a rod or bar. In the event that indoor play is planned, an adaptor bracket (see Fig. 14.7) is required.

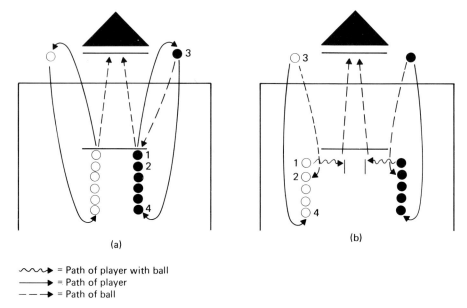

= Path of player with ball
= Path of player
= Path of ball

Fig. 14.6 The "21" game. (a) Two teams of 5 to 10 players on a team. No. 1 player throws at goal from position behind free-throw line. No. 3 rebounds the attempted shot and returns ball to No. 2 player who has moved into position on the free-throw line. No. 3 moves to position occupied by No. 4 who has advanced in line and No. 1 replaces No. 3 as rebounder after attempted shot. Scoring is the same as in regulation flickerball, three points for hole shots and one point for backboard shot. Teams call out cumulative score as each goal is made. First team to reach 21 points wins. (b) A variation of "21" game can be played in which thrower must run from his position to spot at center of field.

Information about Flickerball

Informal studies conducted at several different times disclosed some very interesting information about the game of flickerball. For example, in a regulation game, each player handles the ball about 82 times. That is, the player has the opportunity, in a single game, to attempt 82 pass receptions, and to make 82 passes. If the player is in a class, or on a team which plays often, he literally has thousands of opportunities to catch and throw the football in a competitive situation. Assuming that players have been properly taught fundamentals, those with good potential can and should develop a high degree of skill.

Another study was conducted in which players were equipped with pedometers during play. On the average, each player ran, in short sprints, a little more than a mile and seven-eighths in a regulation game. Participation in flickerball develops a high level of cardiovascular fitness.

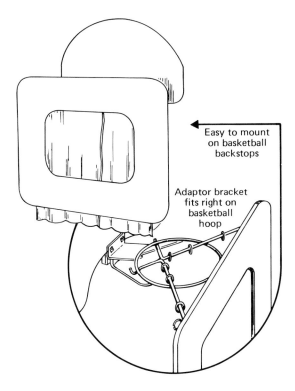

Easy to mount
on basketball
backstops

Adaptor bracket
fits right on
basketball
hoop

Fig. 14.7 Flickerball goal
and procedure for mounting
it on basket.

Questionnaires given to students over a period of several years asked them to compare flickerball and touch or flag football in terms of enjoyment. Better than 95 percent of those answering the questionnaire indicated that they preferred to play flickerball.

One of the interesting features of the game of flickerball is the fact that the goal seems deceptively easy to hit. A ball thrown into the hole must strike a target which, for practical purposes, is less than four square feet in size. This takes into consideration the fact that the $2' \times 3'$ hole has rounded corners and that the football is nine inches wide. A ball which misses the hole, but strikes the face of the board is hitting a target which is less than 19 square feet in area. This may seem like a large target but if one visualizes the target in a football pass play, it can be seen that a six-foot-tall receiver can reach a ball ten feet off the ground, his reach is six feet wide, and he can maneuver to catch the ball, so that in effect he represents a target of at least one hundred square feet, or more.

Articles on flickerball have appeared in *Southern Coach and Athlete, Parade Magazine, The Journal of Physical Education and Recreation,* and *The Journal of the National Recreation Association.*

15
Floor Hockey*
Roland Hess

Hockey has tremendous potential for improving the physical fitness of young people. Unfortunately, most schools and small colleges cannot afford ice hockey facilities. However, floor hockey is an exciting alternative to ice hockey which can be played on any gym floor with a minimum cost for equipment. The game is modified to compensate for the reduced size of the playing area and, since no protective equipment is worn except by the goalkeeper, body contact is not allowed.

Floor hockey is a popular physical education activity from elementary school through college. The original floor hockey equipment was made of flexible plastic and was used primarily by elementary and junior high schools. Recently, larger and more rigid equipment—especially the wooden stick with the nonmarking plastic blade—has made this activity available to senior high and college levels.

Floor hockey contributes greatly to students' physical fitness, neuromuscular skill, character development, and interpretive development.

The sport promotes cardiovascular development through interval training. Unlike ice hockey, there is no "coasting" in floor hockey; leg movement is continuous and the fast action calls for maximum effort of the player during his rotation period on the floor. Rotation intervals are set according to the age group involved and the number of players on each team. The effort put forth in floor hockey is much the same as that in the 220 or 440 dash, but with the added motivation of playing in a team situation with the possibility of scoring at any moment.

In floor hockey the skating aspect of the game is absent, and the neuromuscular development involved in stick handling receives maximum attention. Development of a fast moving attack with coordinated passing and goal-shooting techniques presents a challenge.

Interpretive development refers to the ability to "read" the play as it is happening and make the correct choice in terms of positional play and the fundamental skills of the activity.

The fast action in floor hockey creates emotionally charged situations that can contribute positively to the maturation of youth when properly

*   Reprinted by permission from *JOPER* **45,** 6 (September), 1974.

handled. Within the framework of elation over success or the frustration associated with error, the teacher can guide the development of wholesome social and emotional qualities in the participants' personalities.

Floor hockey rules published by equipment manufacturers are usually quite general and intended for the elementary grades. The following information pertains to the advanced version of the game as it has been developed at Hanover College. The game is taught, coached, and played almost the same as regular ice hockey. Those who want to start a floor hockey program should get the official scholastic and college ice hockey rules and a book on ice hockey coaching.

FLOOR HOCKEY GUIDELINES FOR SENIOR HIGH SCHOOL AND COLLEGE PROGRAMS

Playing Area

Any gymnasium floor (basketball size) is sufficient. Side and end walls are an important part of the playing area as far as passing and continuous play are concerned. If the gymnasium walls are not adjacent to the playing area, as in a large field house, portable barriers can be erected using 20 foot lengths of 2″ × 6″ lumber. The folding type gym mats make excellent side barriers when they are in the folded position and laid end to end.

The Team

A team consists of six players: one goalkeeper, one center forward, two wing forwards, and two defensemen. Although players are free to play anywhere on the floor, play is more coordinated if each player restricts himself to his basic position on offense and defense. Substitutes may enter a game at any time.

Equipment

Wooden sticks with replaceable plastic blades can be purchased from most sporting goods stores. Keep at least one dozen extra blades on hand, since they will break when players accidentally step on them during a game.

Hollow plastic pucks are too light for adequate play with this age group. A hollow rubber puck weighing approximately two ounces is heavy enough to give good performance and still be safe for play. A regulation ice hockey puck weighs six ounces.

The goals—4′ high × 6′ wide—can be made by a shop class or maintenance department from 2″ × 2″ lumber and wire mesh or regular netting material. Rubber pads should be attached under the goals to prevent scratching the floor.

The goalkeeper's equipment can be improvised by using girls' field hockey goal pads or baseball catcher's leg guards, a softball chest protector, and a softball first baseman's glove. The goalkeeper's stick hand can be protected by any type of leather glove; however, for adequate safety, the purchase of two pairs of regulation "youth" hockey gloves is recommended. Elbow pads are optional.

Regulation hockey masks can be purchased; however, a softball mask works very well with an extra head strap attached as low as possible. The extra snap is necessary to hold the mask tight against the face on quick turns and diving saves.

Shin guards for the offensive and defensive players are not really necessary, but girls' field hockey shin guards are light and functional. Certain types of soccer shin guards may also be used.

Penalties

The first rule in floor hockey is *no body checking.* Any body contact judged by the referee as being more than incidental must be immediately penalized if the game is to be kept under control. A body checking foul is called "roughing" in floor hockey and carries a 2-minute penalty, unless it is a flagrant act, for which a 5-minute penalty is assessed and the player may be expelled from the game. When a 5-minute penalty is assessed, the player cannot play for that length of time, but the team has to play shorthanded for only two minutes.

All ice hockey penalties, such as hooking, tripping, slashing, etc., are enforced. The most common penalty called when beginners play is "high sticking." They tend to lift the stick during the follow-through rather than rolling their wrist and keeping the stick below waist level.

The Game

The NCAA Ice Hockey Rules and Regulations are used in floor hockey, with the following exceptions:

1. There are 3 periods of 10 minutes each with no less than a 2-minute rest between periods.

2. Since the length of a gym floor is generally 90 to 100 feet, which is about one-half a regulation hockey rink, it is not practical to have neutral zones or to enforce the offside pass rule. The floor is divided into an attacking zone and a defensive zone by the center line. No goal may be scored from behind the center line. The blue lines used in ice hockey are also eliminated.

3. The "offside" rule in floor hockey is somewhat like the offside rule in soccer—you must have at least one defender plus the goalie between you and the goal until your team gains possession of the puck; then you are free to move into any part of the attacking zone.

4. The two defensemen *must* play on or near the center line when their team is attacking the opponent's goal. This is an important rule because it keeps the play limited to one-half of the floor at a time and allows the defending team to attempt a fast break when they steal or intercept the puck. If the defensemen were allowed to play tandem or to stand back near the goal, this would (1) virtually eliminate any fast break style of play; (2) make the offside rule practically useless; (3) limit the physical fitness aspect to some extent because players would tend to stay in their attacking or defending zones and wait for a pass; and (4) encourage long passes which are generally intercepted, and thus turn the game into a hit and chase affair, rather than a controlled short passing game with good positional play.

5. When two players running side by side are chasing a puck near a wall, the defensive man *must* slow down and assume a guarding position, thus allowing the attacking player to gain possession of the puck but making it difficult for him to pass or advance. This is a necessary rule in order to prevent players from colliding with the wall in an attempt to get to the puck first. If a collision occurs, the defensive man is penalized 2 minutes for "boarding."

6. During long intervals of continuous running, some players tend to forget their basic positions and play becomes disorganized. The following rules have been designed to provide a momentary break in the action so both teams may reorganize and continue play in a coordinated manner.

a) When a shot is taken at the goal and the goalkeeper catches it with his glove, play is stopped. The goalkeeper's team is given possession of the puck behind the goal, where they attempt a breakout play. The other team quickly sets up a defense to try to regain control of the puck. When a breakout play is attempted, no defensive player may enter the area behind the goal or cross the icing line with his body or stick until the offensive team has made two free passes behind the line or has passed, dribbled, or fumbled the puck over the line.

b) If a shot is stopped by the goalkeeper's body or pads as it passes under him or rebounds from his body, stick, or pads, or is fumbled and dropped during an attempted catch—thus causing him to cover up the puck with his glove or body—the whistle is blown, and play is stopped. The puck is put in play with a face-off at the nearest face-off mark. If the goalkeeper does not cover up the puck but hits it away with his stick or glove, then play is continued.

General Playing Techniques

It is essential to stress the importance of keeping the hands spread on the stick and to carry it low in readiness to receive a pass or to defend against an opponent's shot. A flicking motion with the wrist is the correct way to pass and shoot the puck, not a wide sweeping swing with the hands close together as in golf.

A retreating 2-1-2 zone defense is the basic defense used in floor hockey; however, if the opposing team is having success with a quick fast break, some teams prefer to fall back quickly when they lose possession of the puck and set up their defense near the center line.

During a breakout play by the opponents, a 2-2-1 zone press can be an effective defense.

The fast break offense is executed the same as in basketball, with the first pass going to the sideline, then advancing down floor to the centerman who passes to a cutting wingman.

Most basketball offenses used against a 2-1-2 zone defense can be adapted for use in floor hockey.

Floor hockey is a dynamic game that sells itself to girls and boys in elementary school, high school, or college. Your main problem will be trying to find enough time for all to play as often as they would like to.

16
Football, American
Bill Richerson

ORIGIN AND DEVELOPMENT

Historians recall a form of football being played in China as far back as 300 B.C. The Greeks later played a game called Harpaston which permitted running and was played on a rectangular field with sidelines, goal lines, and a center line. The Romans adopted the Greek game and later introduced it to the British Isles (Davis 1911).

Football in England through the early 19th century was a kicking game and players were not allowed to advance the ball by running or throwing. In 1823, William Ellis, an English schoolboy, playing in a highly contested game and with time running out, chose to break the traditional pattern and run with the ball, thereby providing the impetus for the development of an exciting new game called rugby (Danzig 1956).

Both games continued to grow in popularity and in 1862 advocates of the kicking game organized the London Football Association and adopted rules prohibiting running with the ball. This game became known as association football or soccer. Some years later, proponents of the running game established the Rugby Football Union which gave rugby full-fledged status and allowed it to maintain its identity (Davis 1911).

A form of football became a popular pastime among other countries as well. The Irish, seeking refuge from the day's labor, embraced their own style of play characteristic of their life-style. The game, called Gaelic football, was popular in Dublin during the early 1500s and allowed the ball to be advanced by any and all means. Canada and Australia also adopted their own style of play through the years. Canadian football is more rugged in nature and aligns closely with American football and rugby, while the Australian game emphasizes the art of kicking with no tackling, line plunging, or forward passing allowed (Menke 1975).

The origin of American football can be traced to 11th-century England where it evolved from association football (soccer) and rugby (Menke 1953). From 1800–1873, the game was introduced to America and patterned after English soccer. Although there is evidence of football being played by English settlers and by secondary schools and colleges in the early 1800s, the first intercollegiate contest played in America was between Princeton and Rutgers in 1869 (Danzig 1956). Prior to that year, football at the college level consisted of interclass competition. In 1874, rugby rules were initiated for a game between Harvard and McGill Universities (Stagg 1927). Both players and spectators reacted favorably to the rugby concept of running with the ball, and colleges began employing the Rugby Union rules to govern the style of play.

In 1880, two important rule changes occurred: (1) a scrimmage line was established in lieu of the rugby scrum; and (2) the number of participants was limited to eleven. A scrimmage line designated team possession and allowed for preconceived strategy while reducing the number of players made the deployment of personnel a highly prized tactical maneuver (*Spaulding's Official Football Guide* 1927).

Offensive formations varied significantly during this period with different combinations of linemen and backs being utilized for maximum effectiveness. Yale presented the formation which has stood the test of time, employing seven linemen and four backs. Although team possession prevailed, the rules did not require a team to relinquish possession except by a score or fumble. Safeties were not considered and a team pressed against its own goal line merely had to touch the ball behind its goal and resume play, without penalty, from the 25-yard line. Controversies arose over various rule interpretations which eventually led to rules penalizing the safety and regulating ball possession. A team was given three downs to make five yards or it had to give up possession from the succeeding spot (Davis 1911).

In 1888, running interference and tackling below the waist as far down

Fig. 16.1 Tackling below the waist is an integral part of football. Courtesy of Springfield College.

as the knees was approved, and blocking with extended arms was prohibited (Weyland 1955). This caused offensive tactics to change from a wide open type game with spread formations to tight formations and brought about the first uniform formation which was similar to the present "T" formation. The advent of tight formations marked the beginning of mass momentum football where the flying wedge, V trick, plough, and other such tactics came into prominence. The injuries inflicted with this type of play, however, placed the future of the game in jeopardy (Danzig 1956).

Public opinion to abolish football ran high, effecting several rule changes to preserve the game. In 1906, the rules committee legalized the forward pass, established a neutral zone to separate teams at the line of scrimmage, increased the distance to be gained in three downs from five to ten yards, and required six men to be on the line of scrimmage at the snap of the ball (Danzig 1956). The forward pass added a new dimension to the game and created a milestone in the development of offensive and defensive strategy. Through the years football has changed from brawn to brain with scientific innovations continuing to make the game more and more appealing to both players and spectators.

RULES

The following is adapted from *Official Football Rules* 1972. Football is played on a rectangular field 360 by 160 feet. Dimensions and markings are specified in Fig. 16.2. Goal lines are 300 feet apart with goalposts 30 feet back of each goal line (high school and college) and centrally placed between the sidelines. Each goal consists of two 20-foot uprights with a connecting horizontal crossbar, the top edge of which is 10 feet above the ground and 23'4" long.

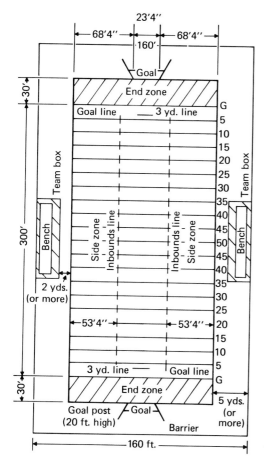

Fig. 16.2 Football field from Official Football Rules. In professional football the goalposts are on the goal lines instead of the end lines and inbound lines are 70' 9" from the sidelines.

The ball shall have a four-panel leather or composition cover encompassing a rubber bladder. Its weight shall be 14–15 ounces and it shall be inflated to a pressure of 12½–13½ pounds. The long axis shall be 11–11¼ inches; the long circumference, 28–28½ inches; and the short circumference 21–21¼ inches.

Playing time for a game shall consist of 60 minutes (48 for high schools) divided into four quarters of equal time. There is a one-minute intermission between the first and second and the third and fourth quarters to change goals and a 15–30 minute halftime intermission. Playing time is not extended to resolve a tie at the end of the fourth quarter.

Each team is made up of eleven offensive and eleven defensive players who are designated by position. Figure 16.3 depicts a typical offensive formation and the recommended numbering of players (numbers 1–99 are permitted in college and professional football) (*Official Football Rules* 1972).

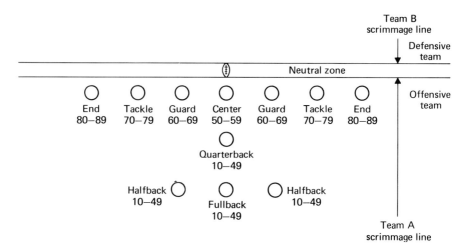

Fig. 16.3 Distribution of offensive personnel by position and number.

The scrimmage line for each team is a vertical plane parallel with the goal lines and passing through the point of the ball nearest its own goal line, and the neutral zone encompasses the space between the two scrimmage lines.

Defensively, players are commonly referred to as down linemen (guards, tackles, and ends), linebackers, and secondary with run and pass responsibilities given priority by position. Specific nomenclature is commensurate with deployment of personnel. Figure 16.4 indicates a popular alignment by position.

Free substitution prevails at all levels of competition when the ball is dead between downs. A substitute is not permitted, however, to enter and withdraw during the same dead ball period except after a touchdown.

Prior to starting time, the referee, in the presence of team captains, shall toss a coin which carries certain options. The winning team can kick off, receive, or choose a goal to defend. Before the second half, the opposing team is given the same options.

T — Tackle
E — End
S — Strong linebacker
M — Middle linebacker
W — Weak linebacker
LC — Left corner
SS — Strong safety
FS — Free safety
RC — Right corner

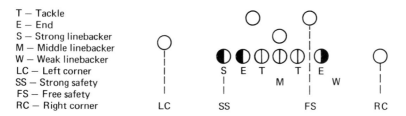

Fig. 16.4 Defensive alignment by position.

Play begins with a kickoff (drop- or placekick) from the kicking team's 40-yard line. Once the ball has traveled ten yards, it is free and belongs to the team recovering it. The team in possession after the kick is given a series of four downs to advance the ball ten yards (line to gain). A new series is established each time the ball is advanced beyond the line to gain, or team possession changes.

The ball may be advanced by running, passing, or kicking and the object of the game is to outscore the opponent. Points are scored in any of four ways: (1) touchdown, six points; (2) field goal, three points; (3) safety, two points; and (4) conversion after touchdown, one or two points. A forfeited game is scored 1–0. If the offended team is ahead, however, the official score stands.

SKILLS AND STRATEGY

Skills relevant to playing football include variations of running, catching, blocking, tackling, kicking, and centering. The physical qualities consistent with good performance are size, speed, strength, endurance, agility, and ruggedness. As these physical qualities tend to become equal, certain psychological characteristics appear to influence performance.

Offensive strategy is dictated by personnel and predicated on a sound running, passing, and kicking game. Regardless of formation, the running game is developed around an inside, off tackle, and outside attack (Fig. 16.5).

Running plays are grouped into series to lend continuity to the offensive design, and various blocking schemes are devised to provide blocking angles and to exploit certain defensive alignments and techniques. A feasible approach to an inside attack (series) might include the following considerations: (1) the blocking pattern to be employed, (2) coordinating line and backfield action, and (3) an understanding of the strategy behind each play.

The inside attack is based on a combination of straight, fold, trap, and isolation blocking. Straight and fold blocking should be coordinated and designed to apply pressure at the point of attack. Against the even defense (no man over the center on the line of scrimmage), should the middle linebacker (M) react quickly to straight blocking and prove difficult to block (Fig.

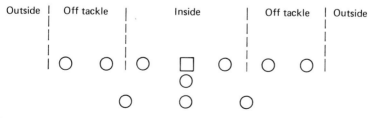

Fig. 16.5 Offensive areas of attack.

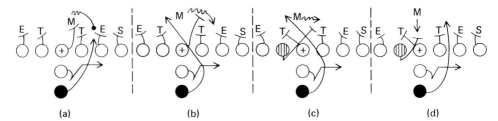

Fig. 16.6 (a) Straight blocking, (b) straight blocking with cut technique. (c) fold blocking with cut technique, and (d) combination straight/fold blocking. E = End, T = Tackle, M = Middle linebacker, and S = Safety.

16.6a), cut or fold blocking techniques (Figs. 16.6 b, c, and d) might enhance one's chances for success. If M reacts favorably to the fold block by stepping up into the hole, a combination straight/fold blocking technique to influence M's reaction might prove to be a viable alternative.

Trap blocking this area should include both quick and counter blocking schemes as the defense might react more judiciously to one than the other (Figs. 16.7 a and b). Isolation blocking could be utilized against the odd defense (man over the center on the line of scrimmage) with different blocking combinations, to improve offensive effectiveness (Figs. 16.7 c and d).

Different blocking schemes are designed for different defensive alignments with similar strategic maneuvers being applied to both the off tackle and outside areas. Whatever the tactical approach may be, one is assured that the opponent is not lying dormant and so "the perennial chess game goes on."

The passing game is paramount to a balanced offense and requires long hours of practice to develop the rhythm and timing essential for success. The fundamental ingredients of a passing attack include the passer, receiver, and protection. A thorough knowledge of pass coverage is also critical to success.

The working principles that evolve tend to exploit weaknesses in both

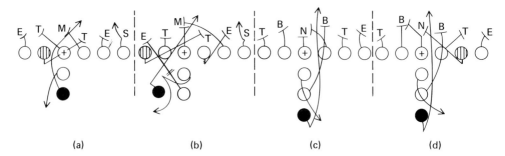

Fig. 16.7 (a) Quick trap blocking, (b) counter trap blocking, and (c) and (d) isolation blocking. N = Noseman, a defensive position who plays over Center of opposing team, and B = Backs.

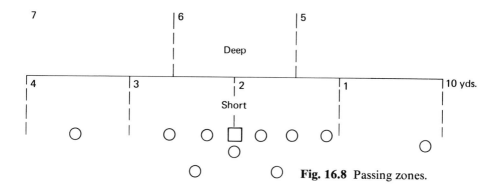

Fig. 16.8 Passing zones.

personnel and coverage. Passing zones are divided into seven areas, four short and three deep (Fig. 16.8). Failure to provide personnel to cover these seven areas renders the defense vulnerable and subject to probing by offensive strategists.

The kicking game is another avenue of concern to the practitioner. A sound kicking game not only assures good field position and provides additional scoring potential but also affords the spectator the opportunity to witness one of football's most exciting and dramatic plays—the successful kickoff or punt return.

Defensive theory is based on controlling the perimeter by assigning areas of responsibility to the running, passing, and kicking game. Specific defensive gaps or running lanes are lettered and assigned to linemen and linebackers, while defensive backs are responsible for supporting the outer perimeter (Fig. 16.9). Pass responsibilities are shared by both linebackers and backs and correspond to the seven passing zones illustrated in Fig. 16.8.

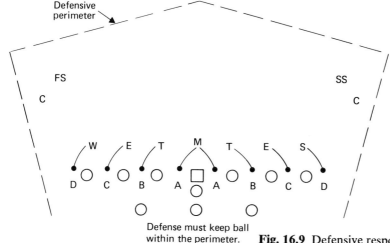

Defense must keep ball within the perimeter. **Fig. 16.9** Defensive responsibilities.

Although football has seen many changes in rules, strategy, and techniques, it continues to appeal to spectators and to challenge the minds of those dedicated to the pursuit of excellence.

REFERENCES

Danzig, A. 1956. *The history of American football.* Englewood Cliffs, N.J.: Prentice-Hall.

Davis, P. H. 1911. *Football: the American intercollegiate game.* New York: Scribner.

Menke, F. G. 1975. *Encyclopedia of sports.* New and rev. ed., New York: A. S. Barnes.

Official football rules 1972. Elgin, Ill.: National Federation of State High School Associations.

Spaulding's official football guide 1927. New York: American Sports Publishing Company.

Stagg, A. A. 1927. *Touchdown.* New York: Longmans, Green.

Weyland, A. M. 1955. *The saga of American football.* New York: Macmillan.

17
Gator Ball*

D. K. Stanley and Irving F. Waglow

The game of gator ball was first introduced at Seabreeze High School at Daytona Beach, Florida, in the fall of 1930.

D. K. Stanley, then a coach and physical education teacher, was confronted with the problem of having in one class large numbers of heterogeneously grouped students, grades seven through twelve, for whom was provided only one area about the size of a small football field. The game was evolved from some field games to which were added several basketball situations. As

---

* Reprinted by permission from D. K. Stanley, I. F. Waglow, R. Alexander, and others, *Activities Handbook for Men and Women* (3rd ed.). Boston: Allyn and Bacon, 1973. T. M. Scott assisted with the preparation of "Gator Ball" for publication.

the skills of individuals increased and playing areas became available, refinements were introduced. The game as now played at the University of Florida and many of the Florida public schools is the product of the original "mass" participation sport.

The general playing regulations are that the ball can, under certain conditions, be kicked, carried, or batted in any direction within the playing area. The goals are the modified soccer type and the ball can be thrown, kicked, or headed through the goal.

The most attractive features of the game are: It provides that varying numbers of small and large, fast and slow, skilled and unskilled alike can play together. While the game can be rough, this kind of participation is of the individual's own choosing. The ball moves enough so that everyone, at one time or another, can kick, punch, "swipe at," or run with the ball.

THE GAME

The game of gator ball is a team game combining the skills of soccer, touch football, and basketball, which has grown in popularity with students and teachers of physical education.

The skills and game situations presented by this activity fulfill the requisites of a team game designed to promote physical conditioning, as well as to provide for a high degree of competitive effort.

Playing area. The playing area is a rectangle 80 yards long and 40 yards wide, with lines drawn across the field every 20 yards, dividing it into four equal areas. (Fig. 17.1)

A circle with a 10-yard radius is located in the center of the field. The

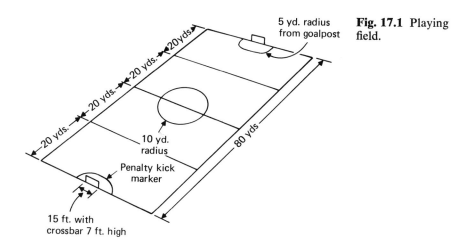

5 yd. radius
from goalpost

Fig. 17.1 Playing field.

20 yds.
20 yds.
20 yds.
20 yds.
20 yds.
80 yds
10 yd. radius
Penalty kick marker
15 ft. with crossbar 7 ft. high

goals on each end line are constructed of two uprights, 15 feet apart, with a crossbar 7 feet high. From each end of the goal, an arc with a 5-yard radius is drawn from the end line to a point directly in front of the goalposts. The tops of these two arcs are then joined by a straight line running parallel with the end line. Thus, the goal restraining arc is a minimum distance of 5 yards from any part of the goal.

Equipment. One soccer ball.

Players. A team is composed of from five to nine players.

Time element. The game is played in two 20-minute halves with a five-minute rest between halves. Each team is allowed two three-minute time-outs during which the clock continues to run. No time-outs are allowed during the final three minutes of play except to remove an injured player.

Kickoff. The ball is put in play at the beginning of each half and after each goal by a placekick from the middle of the center circle. When one team puts the ball in play at the start of the game, the other team shall put it in play at the start of the second half. On the kickoff, all players must be in their own half of the field and nonkicking team players must stay out of the center circle (Fig. 17.2). The kicker may stand anywhere in the center circle and kick the ball in any direction to put it in play—to the opponents or to his teammates; he may not play the ball again until it is touched by another player.

After each goal, the team scored upon has the option of putting the ball in play with a placekick or of allowing their opponents to do so.

As soon as initial contact is made with the ball, all players may cross the center line or restraining circle and play anywhere on the field.

Fly ball. A fly ball is defined as a ball in the air that has not touched the ground since touching a player. As soon as the ball becomes a fly ball, it should be played with the hands. When a fly ball is caught, it may be passed, run with, or kicked. When a player catches a fly ball and does not take more than one step, he must be defended against as a basketball player. That is, he may not be touched or overguarded and must not move the pivot foot. He may drop the ball to the ground and play it with his feet, but may not play it again with his hands until another player has caused it to become a fly ball. Ground or air dribbling with the hand is not allowed at any time.

Running. A player in possession of the ball may run with it at any time. If a player is tagged after taking more than one step with the ball in his possession, a free kick is awarded the opponent's team at the point where the tag is made. To avoid being tagged, a runner may drop the ball to the ground and play it with his feet, or pass it, or punt it.

198

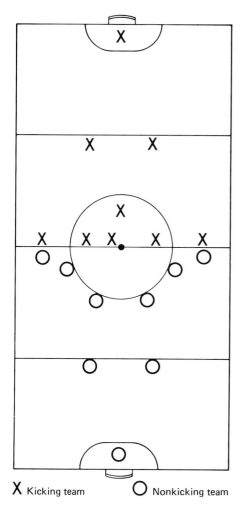

X Kicking team   **O** Nonkicking team   **Fig. 17.2** Starting lineup.

Scoring. A team scores one point each time the ball legally passes completely over the opponent's end line between the uprights and under the crossbar in any of the following ways:

1. Kicked through the goal from any point on the field outside the goal restraining arc.

2. Thrown through the goal from any point on the field outside the goal restraining arc.

3. Penalty kick—the ball is kicked from a point two yards outside the goal restraining arc. The goalkeeper must stand one yard in front of the goal and must be the only player between the kicker and the goal. This kick

is awarded only as the result of committing a flagrant personal foul or for unsportsmanlike conduct.

Fouls. The following constitute fouls:

1. Holding, pushing, tripping, hacking, striking, or violently charging.
2. Touching a ground ball with the hands.
3. Kicking a fly ball.
4. Playing a ball again on a kickoff, throw-in, free kick, or penalty kick before it has been touched by another player.
5. Making a dangerous kick, either by kicking into an opponent, or raising the foot dangerously in attempting to kick the ball.
6. Kicking a ball while inside the goal restraining arc.

Free kicks. Fouls are penalized by awarding the opposing team a free kick at the point where the foul occurred, except for fouls that involve a penalty kick. A free kick is also awarded a team when one of its players tags an opponent who has taken more than one step with the ball in his possession. (**Note:** A modification of this rule may be applied if players deliberately tag the man who is in possession of the ball and who has not taken more than one step, and the tagging player wishes to provoke a free kick situation instead of allowing the man to pass the ball with his hands. Then the defensive players must stand not less than five yards away and allow the man in possession of the ball an opportunity to pass the ball or kick it, whichever he wishes.) On a free kick, all players of the opposing team must be at least five yards from the ball at the time it is kicked. In order to score from a free kick, the ball must touch another player before going across the goal line; i.e., a goal may not be scored directly from a free kick but must be touched by another player first.

Out-of-bounds ball. When a ball crosses a field boundary (other than to score a legal goal) it is put in play by a throw-in at the point where it crossed the line by an opponent of the player who last touched the ball before it went out. But if the attacking team has the ball out of bounds over the end line, the ball may be put in play only by a throw-in from the nearest corner. Any member of a team may throw the ball in and he may use one or both hands to do so.

Held ball. A held ball occurs when two opposing players (1) cause the ball to go out of bounds, (2) gain possession of a fly ball, or (3) foul each other simultaneously. When any of these occurs, the ball is put in play by the team defending the nearer goal; one man takes the ball out-of-bounds at the nearer sideline and throws it in.

Goalkeeper. One player on each team is designated as goalkeeper. The goalkeeper may play anywhere on the field. However, when he is in the 20-yard zone nearest his goal, he has the privilege of playing ground balls with his hands. When the goalkeeper assumes possession of the ball within the goal restraining arc, he is given five seconds to move the ball out of the arc by throwing, hitting, kicking, or carrying the ball. If he should take longer, the ball is awarded the opposing team out of bounds at the nearer sideline.

Players of the attacking team must not cross the goal restraining arc under any circumstance.

RULES

Rules governing the game of gator ball are not inclusive and reference must be made to specific rules governing each of the three activities included in the game. For example, when the ball is on the ground, being played with the feet, no player can touch it with his hands or arms, as indicated in the rules governing soccer. When the ball is deflected into the air and caught with the hands, the player in possession may choose not to take more than one step. This situation comes under the rules governing basketball, and defending players must not touch the player in possession of the ball. If a person chooses to run with the ball, the rules of touch football apply and he may be tagged.

Officiating, conduct of the game, and interpretation of governing rules are for the sole purpose of providing for the safety and active participation of all the players.

SKILLS

There are three principal skills that need emphasis in learning and teaching the game of gator ball. Individual and team skills are closely interrelated and are most easily learned with the members of the group working together.

1. Lifting the ball into the air with the foot. This is a skill almost unique to the game of gator ball, and it requires practice for persons not used to playing the ball with the feet. The ball is deflected into the air most easily by contacting it with the toe while the foot moves sharply forward and upward. If the ball is not moving, or is moving slowly, flexing the foot quickly and making the movement mostly upward will result in the ball being raised off the ground. It is advisable to create a fly ball situation whenever possible so that players may run with the ball or pass it with their hands, and thus be more sure of advancing the ball.

2. Throwing and catching a fly ball with the hands. This is a relatively easily acquired skill because of the early experience most children have in

throwing and catching balls. In the game of gator ball, the runs are usually short and the ball is carried in two hands. For this reason, most catches and throws are made with two hands. The exception is one-handed throws that are made in an attempt to score.

The two-handed chest throw is made with fingers spread, hands behind the ball. The arms are extended forward at shoulder level, the wrists extending quickly as the ball is released. In any two-handed throw, the important thing is to extend the arms and hands toward the target and be moving toward the target if possible.

Of the one-handed throws, the most commonly used is the sidearm throw. Except in rare instances the throw to score is made by a player who is running rapidly toward or parallel to the goal line. It is worthwhile, then, to become skilled in throwing one-handed from a variety of running positions.

Skill in catching the ball is increased by letting the hands "give" with the ball, i.e., moving the hands in the same direction in which the ball is moving. The hands and the front of the body may be used to trap the ball and thus be more sure of retaining possession.

One of the best ways of advancing the ball is to run with it until an opposing player is about to tag, then throw it to a teammate. Team coordination is required in advancing the ball, in covering certain areas of the field offensively, and in being free to receive a throw when a teammate is about to be tagged.

3. Advancing and maintaining possession of the ball by kicking it with the feet. Skill must be developed in kicking the ball just hard enough to keep it ahead when running. (1) Short steps are used. (2) Best control is maintained by kicks made with the inside of the foot. This is done by turning the toe outward as the foot approaches contact with the ball. (3) Care must be taken not to overrun the ball. (4) Kicking too hard often means losing possession of the ball by advancing it far downfield. (5) Kicking on the ground to a teammate is often accomplished by turning the toe inward and contacting the ball with the outside of the foot to move it sidewards.

STRATEGY

Strategy, or concerted team effort, in the game of gator ball depends primarily upon both offensive and defensive coverage of all four areas of the field. The goalkeeper is a key player in the overall defensive setup. Some goalkeepers are aggressive, playing outside or around the goal restraining arc, keeping the ball from getting near the goal. Others stay right in the goal, depending upon quick reflexes and agility to deflect the ball out of the goal, or catch the ball before it enters the goal.

Common strategy calls for two players to act as guards, never leaving the 20-yard zone nearest their own goal. This prevents, in some measure, the possibility of a quick goal occurring as the ball changes possession around the middle of the field. In case one of the guards catches a fly ball and elects to run with it, another designated player on his team should drop back into the guard zone to take his place.

Very few situations occur in which teammates have a chance to work out offensive team strategy. Indeed, the basic design and rules are such that players of all skill levels and abilities should enjoy playing this game. The very nature of the game precludes the possibility of a few highly skilled players taking possession of the ball and not allowing players of less ability to actually play the ball.

DRILLS

Inasmuch as gator ball involves skills of three different games, drills designed to develop the more important skills are described:

1. Throwing and catching the ball while running (Fig. 17.3).
   1) Three men start on the same line. The middle man has the ball.
   2) Two side men advance.
   3) Ball is thrown to one advancing man (dotted line). Man throwing the ball runs behind the man to whom he throws the ball and continues to advance downfield (solid line).
   4) Repeat throw-and-run procedure, making sure that the man who throws the ball runs behind the man to whom he throws the ball and continues to advance downfield.

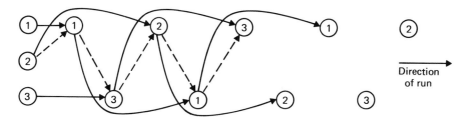

Fig. 17.3 Drill 1.

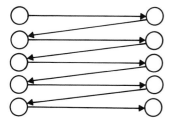

Fig. 17.4 Drill 2.

2. Lifting the ball into the air with the foot (Fig. 17.4).

    1) Form two lines of not more than five players each, facing each other, as indicated in diagram.

    2) End man on one line places the ball on the ground in front of him.

    3) After placing the toe of the kicking foot directly behind and in contact with the ball, he lifts it into the air to the man in the opposite line as indicated.

    4) As each man catches the ball with his hands, he places it on the ground and repeats the procedure.

    5) When the ball reaches the end man in the group, the direction of the ball is reversed.

3. Advancing the ball on the ground by a series of short kicks (Fig. 17.5).

    1) Two single-file rows of men face each other at a distance of at least 30 yards. In line with them are two obstacles (X) that are 10 yards apart and 10 yards from the first player in each line.

    2) The first man in one line places the ball on the ground in front of him. He begins by advancing the ball toward the first object, using a series of short kicks. He must move the ball around the first object on one side and around the second object on the other side. He continues kicking the ball until it approaches the line of men opposite him (solid line).

    3) When the first man in the opposite line takes possession of the ball, the man finishing the drill moves to the end of the line of men (dotted line).

    4) The procedure is repeated as many times as possible in the time allotted for this drill.

    5) Emphasis is on control of the ball with the feet, negotiating the course in the least possible time.

4. Throwing the ball through the goal (Fig. 17.6).

    1) Divide players at each goal into two equal groups—defensive and offensive.

    2) Place one defending player in front of goal as a goalkeeper (X).

    3) The offensive group stands on the field with the first man at least 10 yards from the goal restraining arc and to one side of the center of the field (O).

Fig. 17.5 Drill 3.

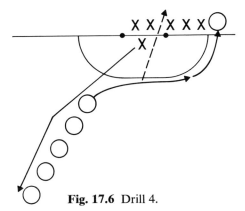

Fig. 17.6 Drill 4.

4) The first offensive man advances toward the goal with the ball in his hands. He attempts to score by throwing the ball through the goal but is careful not to enter the goal restraining arc. The defending goalkeeper attempts to prevent the goal from being scored by catching or deflecting the ball.

5) As each man throws for score, he goes to the end of the line of defensive men behind the goal.

6) After each man defends the goal once, he goes to the end of the line of offensive men.

7) When each man has completed the cycle two or three times, the line of men on the field moves to the opposite side, and advances toward the goal at the opposite angle.

5. Kicking the ball through the goal (Fig. 17.6).

1) Players in position of drill 4.

2) Same procedure except that offensive man attempts to score by advancing the ball on the ground and kicking it through the goal.

18
Golf

Dorothy F. Deach

HISTORY

The Royal and Ancient Club of St. Andrews, Scotland, founded in 1754, has become the recognized seat of authority for all aspects of the ancient game of golf. It was from this club that the 18-hole round originated. There is some evidence that Holland and the Low countries were the first home of the game of golf, although the game we know today originated in Scotland. It became so popular in Scotland that government decrees prohibited the play not only because it was so time consuming but also because archery, as a major defensive weapon, was being neglected.

Golf, as a sport for women, has been accepted since the time of Mary Queen of Scots who was an enthusiastic participant. It was during her reign after 1542 that the famous St. Andrews course was founded (Menke 1963, pp. 446–447). Playing privileges at private courses have been granted to women in the United States since early in the 20th century. John G. Reid, a Scotsman, is credited with introducing the game in the United States in 1885 and with establishing in 1888 one of the first golf clubs, St. Andrews of Yonkers. The annual membership fee was five dollars. In 1893 the Chicago Golf Club opened the first 18-hole golf course in the United States. From this time on there was a rapid increase of private clubs, mass production of equipment, the establishment of public courses, instruction in schools and clubs. All of these have combined to make golf a sport of the masses. In 1894 the United States Golf Association was founded and has continued to be the official ruling body for amateurs in the United States.

The golf course at the Royal and Ancient Club of St. Andrews consisted of 22 holes. The terms "out" on the first half of the course and "in" on the second half meant that players played the first 11 from the clubhouse out to the end of a small peninsula and the next 11 in on the return. Later, the plan of the course was changed making a total of 18 holes. This set the standard for other courses.

EQUIPMENT

The equipment for the game has been constantly improved. The first balls were made of leather and stuffed with feathers, but the introduction of the gum of the gutta-percha tree made possible balls which were cheaper and more resilient. Players discovered that balls with nicks and grooves went farther, so before long dimples were made on the surface to influence the trajectory of the flight. Now that tubular steel shafts are mass produced, players may purchase matched sets or as many clubs as they want and know that the clubs will be balanced and have similar characteristics. The design of the club head also has been changed markedly so more distance and accurate direction can be achieved. The fourteen clubs permitted by the USGA for a match are in two groups: woods and irons, each numbered so that the player selects the one most suited to distance required and the lay of the land.

Besides the clubs, equipment needed consists of a bag, balls and tees. Some may also want a golf glove and a golf cart. A beginner will have an adequate set with two woods (driver and spoon), four irons (3, 5, 7, and 9) and a putter. Clothing may be informal and comfortable. Skirts or Bermuda shorts for the ladies and slacks or Bermuda shorts for the men are the usual costume. PGA male tour players are required to wear slacks.

SCORING

The game of golf provides a continuous challenge even to the most highly skilled. The mental and physical discipline required to cope with the constantly changing situations during the play necessitates careful analysis and attention to strategy. The course is generally divided into eighteen units or "holes." A numerical value of par is assigned to each hole which consists of teeing ground, fairway, hazards, putting green, and cup with its flagstick. The cumulative score for a round of golf at par depends on each course, but is generally about 71 or 72. The player attempts to equal or better par for each hole; that is, to play each designated hole in the fewest number of strokes. It is important for each player to understand the design of each of the woods and irons and to know his or her own capabilities as to his or her playing distance with each club. The surface condition of the ball and its compression rating also will be determining factors in the trajectory and distance achieved.

ETIQUETTE

The code of etiquette involves the player's behavior on the course and the play of the game itself. Observation of the tenets of etiquette will contribute much to the enjoyment of the game by all concerned. The official rules of golf as approved by the United States Golf Association and the Royal and Ancient Golf Club of St. Andrews, Scotland are accepted as worldwide rules. Every possible situation related to competition, player status, organization and game circumstances are covered. Competition may be either match play or stroke play. In the former, the winner is determined by number of holes won, lost or halved and in stroke play it is by the total strokes scored. For a breach of the rules in stroke play, unless otherwise provided, two strokes are assessed, while in match play the penalty is the loss of the hole. Players should always consult the rule book if there is any uncertainty about the rules in a specific situation.

BASIC STROKES

The execution of the basic strokes depends upon the grip, stance, and swing. Most golfers seem to prefer the overlapping grip (Fig. 18.1). The little finger of the lower hand overlaps the index finger of the upper hand. The grip should be firm but there should be freedom of movement in the wrists. For the stance, the relationship of the feet to the flight line usually takes one of three forms: the parallel or square stance, the open stance, and the closed stance. There are advantages to each but there are apt to be greater deviations from the flight line with the open and closed stances than with the parallel stance. In the execution or swing, the hands play a vital role in directing the work of the club head. The upper hand controls the movement of the club head and the lower hand provides the power. The movement of the entire body should be coordinated with that of the hands so that the proper

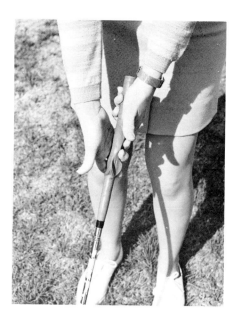

Fig. 18.1 Most golfers prefer the overlapping grip.

Fig. 18.2 Practice in addressing the ball is important.

Fig. 18.3 The use of artificial teaching devices is advocated by many.

movement results. Basic strokes include the drive, chip shot, pitch shot, and putt. The putting stroke is differentiated from the drive, pitch, and chip shot in that the putter travels low to the ground and does not describe an arc. The putter has only a very slight loft to the face of the club. A primary ingredient of all play is how well the golfer can analyze the conditions of the course, and adapt the appropriate strokes to those situations.

MAJOR COMPETITIVE EVENTS

U.S. National Amateur Championship. Amateurs who have handicaps of not more than three strokes may enter. Eligibility for the championship proper is limited to 150 players (Scharff 1973, pp. 36–37).

U.S. National Open Championship. Professional and amateurs with handicaps not exceeding two strokes are eligible for the championship proper (Sharff 1973, pp. 31–32).

USGA Women's Amateur Championship. This competition began with 15 women playing in 1895. The entries are open to women amateur golfers who have handicaps of not more than five strokes (Scharff 1973, 40–41).

U.S. Women's Open Championship. Formerly sponsored by the Women's Professional Golfer's Association and the Ladies PGA, USGA permits entries from both professionals and amateurs with handicaps of not more than five strokes (Scharff 1973, pp. 45–46).

National Collegiate Athletic Association (NCAA) Championship. Played more than any other championship, this was started in 1897 and has been held every year except three (1900, 1917, and 1918). An "All American" collegiate team was started in 1965 (Scharff 1973, pp. 85–86).

Women's National Intercollegiate Championship. Started in 1941, this play has continued to be an outstanding event for college women (Scharff 1973, p. 87.)

The vast interest created in professional and amateur golf by the wide television coverage of exciting players participating in countless tournaments has stimulated play at every age level. The junior tournaments and an increasing opportunity for collegiate golfers, together with instruction in public schools, colleges and private clubs contribute to an expansion of golf as a true lifetime sport.

REFERENCES

Bruce, B., and E. Davies 1962. *Beginning golf*. Belmont, Calif.: Wadsworth.

Chui, E. F. 1969. *Golf*. Pacific Palisades, Calif.: Goodyear.

Grimsley, W. 1966. *Golf: its history, people, and events*. Englewood Cliffs, N.J.: Prentice-Hall.

Menke, F. G. 1963. *Encyclopedia of sports*. New York: A. S. Barnes.

Scharff, R. (ed.) 1973. *Golf magazine's encyclopedia of golf*. New York: Harper & Row.

Vannier, M., and H. B. Poindexter 1968. *Individual and team sports for girls and women*. Philadelphia: W. B. Saunders, pp. 155–196.

Wind, H. W. 1948. *The story of American golf*. New York: Farrar, Straus.

19
Gymnastics

Two articles were needed to do justice to the complex sport of gymnastics. Lyle Welser defines terms, explains the various kinds of gymnastics and lists well-known teachers and coaches of this activity. He follows by explaining the qualities necessary to be a good gymnast.

R. Kireilis, J. Cobb, and H. Segrest describe in considerable detail the performance of the various gymnastic stunts and the techniques both with and without equipment. Rules are summarized and a terminology list is included. The two articles complement each other and provide a thorough exposition of the sport. RBF

General Gymnastics

Lyle Welser

DEFINITION AND SCOPE

Definitively the term gymnastics has many interpretations and ramifications. Diligent scholars who have gone back to its antiquity agree that the concept of gymnastics has not been uniform. They establish that educational gymnastics as well as medical gymnastics were already known to the Greeks. Fundamentally, Orbasius of Pergamon (A.D. 326–403) reduced such to two definitions: one that every intensified movement is gymnastic exercise and second that in each exercise there is the idea of active volition, which is an all-inclusive concept. On this basis one might include all exercises of the more vigorous type, to the lighter type involving the smaller muscles, e.g., finger exercises of the pianist or violinist, or facial gymnastics of the actor. Even mental gymnastics engaging the brain in mathematical or theoretical problems might be included.

In the Greco-Roman life of the middle ages, a boy's physical education began at the age of 14 with vigorous sports and exercises as mentioned in the "Mirror of Knights" as seven, namely: (1) Riding with rapid mounting and dismounting; (2) swimming and diving; (3) shooting with the bow and crossbow; (4) climbing on ropes and ladders; (5) fencing, wrestling, pushing stones, and jumping; (6) dancing, and (7) tournaments. Medical gymnastics included all healthful and health-furthering exercises. Acrobatics by professionals was for entertainment. Preceding the written accounts, gymnastics could be theoretically traced back to the prehistorical ages when humans survived by their ability to run, jump, climb, leap, vault, swing on tree limbs and vines, and do battle with whatever means were at hand. Certainly to be surefooted and well coordinated were basic essentials.

While there are places where overlapping occurs in aims and objectives, the whole subject of gymnastics might be broken down into the following categories:

Survival. As applied in the prehistorical era.

Military. As used in the early Greco-Roman military training and later revived by Frederick Ludwig Jahn (1778–1952).

Educational. As interpreted during the Renaissance and the rediscovery of Greek and Roman literature and when educational theory tried to achieve the aim of a classical education to produce a person of vigor and wisdom or to bring to the highest perfection the three elements of person: body, mind and soul. Also as used as an integral part of our modern day schools.

Medical. As including all exercises, curative, rehabilitative, developmental, corrective, therapeutic and preventive.

Exhibitional. As displayed by the professional or amateur performer or by the teacher for instructional purposes.

Recreational. As a release from nervous tensions by providing an escape from the monotonous humdrum of everyday living. Dancing to music might well fit into this category.

Competitive. As a natural outgrowth of a long history of elevating its merits in spite of some claims to the contrary. Men like Jahn, known as the "Father of Gymnastics," established the patterns of much of modern competition. The Federation of International Gymnastics (FIG) is the governing body.

SCHOOL GYMNASTICS

In the early part of the 20th century, much emphasis was placed on the formal type of gymnastics which included the use of lighter equipment such as dumbbells, wands, and Indian clubs. Free hand (no equipment) exercises,

Fig. 19.1 Many teachers consider ground tumbling basic to all forms of gymnastics. Courtesy of *JOPER.*

marching tactics, and folk dancing were also considered part of the educational program and some of these activities were set to music. Ground tumbling (single and combination with two or more) and work on the heavier apparatus, vaulting boxes, climbing ropes and poles, overhead traveling ladders and rings, were a part of school gymnastics. Pyramid building (with and without apparatus) and hand-to-hand balancing were also included. Many coaches and instructors consider ground tumbling basic to all forms of gymnastics. It is thought to be valuable in orienting the body while gyrating on the apparatus or in space. Present are the merits of challenge with the varied combinations of leaps, springs, somersaults and twists. It has appeal to many adults as well as youngsters even down to the early ages of three and four. Tumbling is a forerunner to fancy diving and work on the trampoline. Such carryover values can extend into later years. Tumbling in any form enables the performer to become acquainted first-hand with the laws of mechanics and gravity. Force, amounts of force, centrifugal and centripetal force, direction and timing of force, the laws of leverage and mechanical advantage, and principles of balance are all part of the knowledge so essential to success in the more intricate forms of gymnastics. It is reasonable to believe that such training has educational and social implications which can be applied to daily life.

On the secondary level, many phases of gymnastics might well have a place in the physical education program. On the college level, varied skills associated with the circus world (sphere and wire walking, balancing, juggling, unicycling, trapeze work, etc.) may challenge the more adept. At the secondary and college level, the international competitive events can be learned and put to use in intercollegiate or intramural competition. Such events are: free exercise, side and long horse, parallel bars, still rings, and horizontal bar.

COMPETITIVE GYMNASTICS

Competitive gymnastics in America for both men and women is growing steadily. More and more high schools and colleges are involved every year and there are more and more championship events conducted as the popularity of competitive gymnastics continues to soar. Accounting for some of this growth are the gymnastics clinics conducted annually for pupils and judges all over the country. These clinics are usually carried on by dedicated leaders in order to bring about a better understanding on the part of the public and educators. In judging competitive gymnastics, the aesthetic or cultural factors account for approximately 50 percent of the score. The other 50 percent is based on the degree of difficulty and a combination of grace, poise, and the beauty of the human form in smooth exacting movement which rounds out the total performance. To measure the arts by some scientific method has always been a difficult task and this is no less true in competitive gymnastics. The fine technicalities of performance are constantly being studied by FIG. Efforts are continually being made to improve the sport. Scoring has become extremely complicated and needs the simplification which would improve its validity and reliability. America is gradually proving its prowess in gymnastics.

As one reviews the whole conglomerate of gymnastic activities, it can be concluded, in part at least, that much of this work has in it the building blocks of physical fitness as outlined by Cureton, namely: strength, balance,

Fig. 19.2 Competitive gymnastics for both men and women is growing steadily. Courtesy of Nissen.

flexibility, power, agility and endurance. The last item (cardiovascular endurance), however, may be significantly lacking in most gymnastic work as compared with other forms of exercise, e.g., running and swimming. A good gymnast will find that muscular endurance is quite essential and is partially dependent on cardiovascular endurance.

Educational and philosophical interpretations will determine the scope of any gymnastic program to the extent of the equipment and teaching staff provided. In no case should the quality of such be underestimated in importance. A well-trained teacher with good equipment will go a long way in determining the achievement and safety of the students. A good instructor will know the best procedures and will know how to "spot" with personal physical assists or how to use safety belts (hand-held or rigged). Since "gravity never sleeps," both pupil and teacher must employ teamwork in guarding against injury. All equipment should be periodically inspected for safety. Sufficient insurance covering all concerned is essential in a program and negligence is inexcusable. The initial cost of good gymnastic equipment is high, but it may be the least expensive in the long run as it will serve for many years.

THERAPEUTIC GYMNASTICS

As we take a brief look at some of the individuals who have made outstanding contributions in helping shape the destinies of this activity, reference should be made to Allan J. Ryan's review of Dr. Joseph Ludwig's "A Medical History of Gymnastics" in *Ciba Symposia,* March–April, 1949. Summarily we might note Oribasius, 326–403, for original definitions; Galen and Avicenna for the concept that gymnastics are healthful and health furthering; Asclepiades, 128–68 B.C., for use of gymnastics in connection with massage and dietetics; Petrarch, 1304–1374, for using natural therapy exercises instead of medical remedies which poison the body; Vittorino Da Felter, 1378–1446, who made gymnastics obligatory in his educational program; Cardinal Piccolomini, 1404–1464, who sought to precede spiritual education with physical education; Barbaro Francesco, 1395–1440, who recommended exercise for young women and parents; Battista Alberti Leon, 1404–1472, who recommended exercise in early infancy; Duke Philbert of Savoy (as prepared by Philephus, a peripatetic teacher) who allowed two hours for gymnastics and games; Maffeus Vegius, 1407–1458, for recognition of two types of exercise: recreational and body strengthening; Juan Luis Vives, 1492–1540, who guarded against overfatigue and indicated that exercise should stimulate intellectual power; Hieronymous Mercurialis, 1530–1606, for his principles of medical gymnastics and for laying the groundwork for all books on gymnastics of the next centuries; Saint Archange Tuccaro, 1535, for his 53 varieties of jumping and his belief that strong exercise aids the body to expel excrements and to calm all sorts of humors; Ambroise Pare, 1510–1590, for

considering gymnastics as a part of general hygiene and useful after frac-
tures; Joseph Duchesne, 1544, for his overall belief in physiological benefits;
Laurent Joubert, 1529–1583, who considered physicians capable of prescribing gymnastics; Sanctorius Sanctorius, 1561–1636, who through physiology gave gymnastics a scientific basis; Jean Canappe, 1546, for increasing
interest in human and animal movement; Claude Perrault, 1680, for *Mechanics of Animals*; Girolamo Cardano, 1501–1576, who recommended light
exercise for pregnant women; Diderot and D'Alembert in the great "Encyclopedia" prescribed the use of different exercises to achieve different purposes;
Nicolas Andry, 1658–1774, who introduced the term "orthopedics" and who
was noted for preventing and correcting deformities of children; Joseph Tis-
sot, 1756–1826, for *Medical and Surgical Gymnastics;* Giuseppe Nenci, 1776,
for his work in avoiding stagnation of the blood; Peter Henry Ling, 1776–
1839, for his medical gymnastics, and Frederick Ludwig Jahn as aforementioned.

MODERN TEACHERS AND AUTHORITIES

Great names in the field of more modern educators would be such as Skar-
strom, Staley, McKenzie, McCurdy, Thulin, Zwarg, and Cureton for their
scientific treatises. Other names of great men and women who have contributed to the American scene would fill a book. The National Association
for College Gymnastic Coaches lists those who are on the Honor Roll as:
Max Younger '54 Dec.; Dr. Hartley Price '55 Ret.; Roy E. Moore '56 Dec.;
Dr. Leslie J. Judd '57 Ret.; Dr. Leopold Zwarg '58 Ret.; Gustav Heineman
'59 Dec.; Charlie Graves '60 Ret.; Louis Mang '61 Dec.; Dr. Ralph Piper
'62 Dec.; Erwin Volze '63 Dec.; Henry J. Smidl '64 Ret.; Gustav I. Kern '65
Ret.; Cecil Hollingsworth '66 Ret.; Alfred Bergman '67 Ret.; Lyle Welser
'68 Ret.; William Matthei '69 Ret.; Charles A. Pease '70; Rene Kern '71.

QUALITIES OF SUCCESSFUL GYMNASTS

The Japanese have perhaps made the most rapid progress in international
competition. The Japanese are very astute and determined, relatively small
in stature, with less weight and lighter bones, but with ideal proportions to
do gymnastics. The mechanical advantage of shorter levers along with great
strength per body weight would seem to be to their advantage. Since the
shoulders are the axes around which the body rotates or from which body
levers are held, a high center of gravity is a decided advantage. This would
indicate a well-developed pair of shoulders. Certainly back and abdominal
strength is an asset. The legs should be straight for reasons of aesthetics and
developed sufficiently for delivering the required force in events such as
vaulting and tumbling. It might be of interest to note that a gymnast in performing a double backward somersault will approach and sometimes surpass

the world high jump record; thus a combination of forces plus good leg development are of great significance. Forearm or grip strength cannot be overlooked since a gymnast in performing a giant swing around a horizontal bar will experience a centrifugal force ranging from 750 to 1000 pounds, depending on the weight of the performer and the rate of gyration (Bunn 1959, p. 286).

Flexibility with accompanying good musculature and resilience resulting from stretching (different from flexibility as a weakness due to flaccid muscles) and training, play enormous roles in successful gymnastic performance. The gymnast must be able to bend easily and gracefully forward, backward and sideward into many positions not normally assumed, e.g., back bends, side and regular leg splits. Shoulders, as well as hands and feet, must be flexible. Flexibility will facilitate and assure the continuous graceful streamlining of the body and the resultant good posture. A flexible body that can bend without wasting energy and overcome the resistance of antagonistic muscles will make for more efficient movement, greater agility, and a more attractive posture.

A high degree of balance can be critical in the static positions as well as in the dynamic movements. It must be such as to endure the many disorienting gyrations and changes of acceleration and momentum, even those resulting from movement such as a double somersault with twisting dismount and a landing executed with perfect balance and good form. Here a slight error in balance or direction could result in serious injury or loss of points because of an uncontrolled landing. The balance beam as an event in women's gymnastics points up the fine sense of balance necessary to do acrobatics on this apparatus which is only four inches wide. These acrobatics include such skills as forward and backward rolls, walkovers forward and backward, and handsprings and cartwheels coupled with various balances.

Fig. 19.3 A high degree of balance can be critical in the static positions as well as in dynamic movements. Courtesy of Southern Connecticut State College.

The average routine in men's gymnastics will include approximately a dozen varied movements and require considerable muscular endurance. Cardiovascular endurance is also needed as any taxing routine will cause the performer to breathe most vigorously. A well-conditioned gymnast will be able to offset the accumulation of fatigue products. Running and swimming, which tax the circulatory system even more than does gymnastics, are a way of supplementing one's training.

Considering strength singly as a basic component, a gymnast must be very strong so he can execute the presses and levers and gyrations. In each case he is handling his body weight with great precision and at all times he is expected to do the most difficult without any outward expression of strain. Many gymnasts agree that training with weights interspaced with regular workouts develops strength, and each has his own idea of the optimum method of procedure. Basically strength is enhanced by maximum exertion along with proper rest and nourishment. This could come about by lifting heavy weights a few times and/or by lifting lighter weights with more repetitions. In all cases where muscles are expected to perform with strength or power, a warming up procedure is essential to avoid tearing or other injury. One of the best treatises is a paper, *The science of training and seasoning of muscles, tendons, and ligaments,* by T. K. Cureton.

Besides the basic factors of strength, power, balance, agility, flexibility, and endurance along with the characteristics of a well-proportioned, ideal physique are a couple of psychological factors. Love of the activity is a prime

Fig. 19.4 To excel and to surpass competitively is to know the reward and the "joy of effort." Courtesy of California State College at Fullerton.

requisite. A gymnast who is fascinated and captivated by all the varied challenges will find it within himself to obey the rules of good training and he will discipline his body and mind in order to achieve peak success. To excel and to surpass competitively is to know the reward and the "joy of effort."

REFERENCES

General

Baley, J. A. 1965. *Gymnastics in the schools.* Boston: Allyn and Bacon.

Bunn, J. W. 1959. *Principles of coaching.* Englewood Cliffs, N.J.: Prentice-Hall.

George, G. S. (ed.), 1969. *The magic of gymnastics.* Compiled for the 84th Anniversary Convention of the American Association for Health, Physical Education and Recreation, Boston, 1969. Washington, D.C.: AAHPER.

Loken, N. C., and R. J. Willoughby 1967. *Complete book of gymnastics.* (2nd ed.) Englewood Cliffs, N.J.: Prentice-Hall.

Price, H. D. *et al.* 1964. *Gymnastics and tumbling.* (3rd ed.) Annapolis, Md.: United States Naval Institute.

West, W. D. 1942. *The gymnast's manual.* Englewood Cliffs, N.J.: Prentice-Hall.

Zwarg, L. F. 1930. *A study of the history, uses, and values of apparatus in physical education.* Philadelphia: Westbrook.

Tumbling and Trampolining

Griswold, L. V. 1970. *Trampoline tumbling today.* (2nd rev. ed.) South Brunswick: A. S. Barnes.

LaDue, F., and J. Norman 1954. *This is trampolining.* Cedar Rapids, Iowa: Nissen Trampoline Co.

LaPorte, W. R., and A. G. Renner 1944. *The tumbler's manual.* Englewood Cliffs, N.J.: Prentice-Hall.

Cross References

Burton, W. 1971. *The sportsman's encyclopedia.* New York: Grosset and Dunlap, Oppenheimer's Publishers, pp. 245–271 on gymnastics and tumbling.

Colliers Encyclopedia **11,** 1969, pp. 550–52.

Compton's Pictured Encyclopedia **6,** 1967.

Encyclopedia Americana **13,** p. 587.

Encyclopaedia Britannica **10,** 1970, p. 1058.

Encyclopedia International **8,** New York: Stratford Press, 1970, p. 242.

Menke, F. 1969. *The encyclopedia of sports* (4th ed.) New York: A. S. Barnes, pp. 473–482.

Pratt, J. L., and J. Benagh 1964. *The official encyclopedia of sports*. New York: Franklin Watts.

Webster's New World Dictionary and Thesaurus of the American Language, 1968, p. 625.

World Book Encyclopedia 8-G, Chicago: Field Enterprises Educational Corporation, 1970, p. 431.

RULES

Gymnastics rules are now more or less standardized as set forth by FIG and any adaptations are usually of a minor nature to suit the individual situation such as college, high school, and YMCA.

Available from the United States Federation of Gymnastics, USGF Press, P.O. Box 4699, Tucson, Ariz. 85717:

FIG Code of Points for Men (Official International Rule Book)

FIG Code of Points for Women (Official International Rule Book)

Gymnastics: Basic Instruction*

Ramon W. Kireilis, John W. Cobb, and Herman B. Segrest

Gymnastics offers a challenge to the participant and is a fine spectator sport. In addition to these reasons for the popularity of the activity, gymnastics is becoming a great aid in upgrading the fitness level of the American youth.

HISTORY

The exact origin of gymnastics as a form of exercise and physical training is unknown. Most authorities on gymnastics, however, believe that China was the first country to develop activities of a gymnastic nature. China had two systems of exercise: one for young men for war, and the other for everyone to use in healing diseases. Thus, the Chinese can be credited with the earliest use of any type of apparatus for corrective and remedial exercises.

It was in ancient Greece, nevertheless, that great emphasis was placed upon gymnastic activities. In Greece, records have been found which give tangible proof that the art of gymnastics was practiced as early as 2100–2000 B.C. The development of the body was fundamental to Grecian supremacy.

---

* Reprinted by permission. R. W. Kireilis, J. W. Cobb, Jr., H. B. Segrest, *Handbook of Physical Activities for Men*. Philadelphia: F. A. Davis, 1969.

The Greeks gave us the name "gymnastics," which, literally translated, means "the naked art."

As the Roman Empire came to power, the rulers recognized the need for gymnastics and introduced it into their military program. Their goal was military rather than educational in nature. The educational influence of gymnastics on the people was slight since they regarded it as nothing but popular amusement.

During the early period of Christianity, the art of gymnastics and all other physical exercises disappeared among the common people. They led a life of strict self-denial and practiced only spiritual or intellectual discipline. Throughout the Middle Ages, only the knights and warriors engaged in organized exercises or gymnastics.

It was not until the 18th century that physical exercise and gymnastics were revived. The efforts of Johann Basedow, Johann Guts Muths, Gerhard Vieth, and Johann Pestalozzi initiated modern gymnastics.

Johann Basedow was the first teacher to organize gymnastics and include it in the schools as a part of the regular program. Basedow's idea that gymnastics contributed toward the general education of the child was promoted by Johann Guts Muths, who wrote the first book on gymnastics, *Gymnastics for Youth.*

Due to his inventions of the horizontal bar, side horse, and parallel bars, Frederick Jahn, a German, has become known as the "Father of Gymnastics." Jahn impaired his program in Germany by trying to educate children with adults' gymnastics. However, this program was enthusiastically received by the youth of Germany and soon spread to other European countries. Gymnastics is still a very popular sport in the physical education programs throughout Europe today.

Franz Nachtegall (1777–1847), the father of Danish gymnastics, devoted his whole life to the development of gymnastics in the schools. He is known for his establishment of the first recorded school of gymnastics teachers. In 1804 Nachtegall was asked by Frederick VI to build a national program of gymnastics for Denmark. The Military Gymnastic Institute was organized in 1804. Due to the popularity of this program, physical education was made compulsory in all public schools in Denmark in 1814. In 1842 Germany and Sweden also began their compulsory physical education programs in the public schools.

In Denmark, Ling (1776–1839) succeeded Nachtegall and added intensive studies of anatomy and physiology to the program. He believed in the therapeutic and corrective values of formal gymnastic activities.

The introduction of gymnastics into the United States came with the immigration of Germans to this country in the early 19th century. Charles Bech, Charles Follen, and Francis Lieber were the pioneers of gymnastics in the United States. These men were disciples of Jahn and introduced the

Jahn type of gymnastics and established gymnasiums at Round Hill School, Northampton, Massachusetts, at Harvard University, and in Boston. Turnvereins (gymnastics clubs) were established in many of our large cities when a great number of German immigrants had settled in that locality. The turnverein has furnished, and continues to furnish, the important early training for many of our best gymnasts who compete on intercollegiate teams and represent the United States in international competition. In 1866 the Turners established a normal college for the training of teachers and, through their efforts, introduced physical education into the schools.

The YMCA, with fully equipped gymnasiums and trained instructors in most of its organizations, has also made a significant contribution to the growth and development of gymnastics in the United States.

After World War I, the trend in physical education was toward the recreational type of activity and away from the gymnastic type. But World War II reemphasized the need for a more strenuous conditioning program for American youth. As a result, gymnastics became a part of postwar physical education programs throughout the country.

The history of the trampoline is given separately and apart from that of gymnastics. It is believed that a French acrobat named Du Trampoline, who was a circus flying trapeze performer of the Middle Ages, invented the trampoline. He first conceived the idea of doing tumbling stunts on the safety nets suspended below the high trapeze acts. The size of these nets was reduced, and such stunts as flips, turns, and twists were performed upon the nets.

The trampoline was introduced into the United States in 1939 by George Nissen. It was not, however, until the outbreak of World War II that the idea of trampoline tumbling as suitable only for professional acrobat or tumbler was really disproved. Today many schools offer trampolining in their physical education program.

SKILLS

Gymnastic skills begin with elementary tumbling and balancing, and progress into the more advanced skills demonstrated on the various apparatus such as parallel bars, side horse, vaulting buck, still rings, flying rings, high horizontal bar, and the trampoline.

It is believed that elementary tumbling provides the basis of stunts and knowledge helpful for all other gymnastic events. Therefore, the explanation of skills, techniques, and fundamentals will begin with tumbling.

Tumbling

A padded mat is all that is required. The mat is generally 2 inches thick and may be of several different sizes: 5 x 10 feet, 5 x 30 feet, etc. For the more difficult stunts, it is recommended that a safety belt be used until the student has developed sufficient skill and confidence to execute the stunt without this protection.

Forward roll (Fig. 19.5). Start from a squatting position at the end of the mat with the hands on the mat and the knees between the arms. To start the forward roll, rock forward on hands until off balance. When off balance, push off by extending thighs and legs, and tuck chin to your chest. When the push-off is complete, flex thighs and legs. Roll forward on neck and shoulders. When the weight leaves the hands, grab the shins and pull yourself up to your feet.

Fig. 19.5 Forward roll.

Backward roll (Fig. 19.6). Start from a squatting position as described in the forward roll except with the back to the length of the mat. Push off with hands to a sitting position, using hands to break the fall. Quickly move the hands upward over the shoulders with fingers pointing to the rear. When hands come into contact with the mat, push hard until the feel roll under, and then stand up. (More advanced students may start from a standing position.)

Fig. 19.6 Backward roll.

Shoulder roll (Fig. 19.7). Start from a standing position at the end of the mat. For a shoulder roll to the right, extend the right arm at shoulder height and hold the left arm close to the side with the forearm parallel to the floor. Roll the right shoulder toward the mat, letting the right forearm and elbow take some of the body weight momentarily. Continue the roll onto the right shoulder and upper portion of the back, bending the knees in toward the stomach. Roll onto the left knee and leg; then take up the weight on them. The momentum will carry one onto the right foot and left leg, and then to the feet in a standing position. If shoulder rolls are to be done in series, alternate shoulders and stay in a straight line as much as possible.

Fig. 19.7 Shoulder roll.

Dive and roll (Fig. 19.8). Using a short run, dive toward the mat, breaking the fall with the hands and arms. Duck the head and put the chin on the chest, lowering the neck and shoulders to the mat. Move into forward roll, holding the tuck position until the balance position on the feet is gained.

Fig. 19.8 Dive and roll.

Combined forward and backward roll. Start from a standing position with one foot crossed in front of the other. Do a forward roll. Come out of the forward roll into the squatting position, make a fast turn, and go into the backward roll. If the right foot is crossed in front of the left foot, turn to the left, and if the left foot is crossed in front of the right foot, turn right.

Hand balance in squat position (Fig. 19.9). From a squat position, move forward by pushing with the toes until the weight is supported by the hands. The knees rest on the upper arm above the elbow with the feet off the mat. Keep the head up and the toes pointed. To control the balance if falling forward, press hard on the fingertips and raise the head. If falling backward, lower the head slightly and pull the shoulders forward.

Fig. 19.9 Hand balance in squat position.

The head stand (Fig. 19.10). Start from a squatting position with the hands pointed forward, a shoulder width apart. Place the forehead on the mat 10 to 12 inches from the hands to form a triangular base. Place one foot close to the hand with the knee bent. Place the other foot back with the knee straight. Raise the hips high above the head, straighten the leg upward slowly, and push off with the bent leg. Arch the back and hold the balance with the weight distributed equally on the hands and forehead.

Fig. 19.10 The head stand.

Forearm balance. Start with the forearms on the mat with the palms down. The elbows should be slightly behind the shoulder. Keep the head up and move the feet as close as possible to the elbows. Kick up one leg and then the other to a point directly over the head with the back well arched, head up, and the weight of the body supported by the forearms and hands. To control the balance if falling forward, press hard on the fingertips, raise the head, and shift the shoulders slightly back away from the hands. If falling backwards, dig in with the fingertips and pull the shoulders slightly forward over the hands.

The handstand. The starting position is a modified sprinter's stance with hands a shoulder width apart on the mat. Grip the mat with the hands and fingers. Place one foot close to the hands and the other foot back with the leg extended. Kick up with the back leg and then push off with the other leg. Near the balance point, bring the feet together. Arch the back, keep the head up, and hold the balance.

Hand walking (Fig. 19.11). Use a one-foot take-off and kick up into an over-balanced handstand position. Keep the head up and, when overbalanced, walk on the hands to keep up with the overbalanced hips and legs.

Fig. 19.11 Hand walking.

The cartwheel. Start from a standing position with the feet spread comfortably and the arms over the head. Lean to the left or right and place the leading hand on the mat about two feet from the leading foot. Continue the sideward throw and bring the trailing leg and hand upward rapidly to pass over the head. When the trailing leg and hand touch the mat, push off hard with the foot still on the mat and bring both legs up and over the head, keeping them spread apart. Hold the arms, legs, and body as straight as possible. Keeping the momentum of the sideward throw going, let the leading leg touch the mat. As the trailing leg swings down, push off with the hand still on the mat and return to a spread standing position.

Snap-up. Start from a lying-down position. Roll back and place the hands well over the shoulders. The weight of the body should be on the hands and shoulders. Take advantage of the natural rebound of the body and kick the legs vigorously upward and forward at a 45° angle, arch the back, and push hard with the hands and head. Bring the feet under the body with the knees bent to land. Land with feet spread, head up, and arms in front of the body.

Headspring (Fig. 19.12). Walk into a pike position with the forehead and hands placed on a rolled mat. Push off with the feet and swing the legs up over the head, outward and downward. At the same time, push hard with the hands. As the feet hit the mat, flex the knees and come to a standing position. Once the stunt is mastered on the rolled mat, gradually unroll the mat until you are doing the headspring on a flat mat.

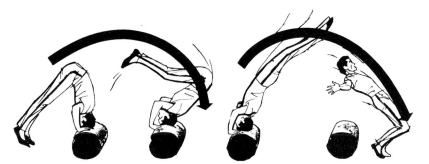

Fig. 19.12 Headspring.

Bent-arm handspring (Fig. 19.13). Use a short run with a skip on the last step. Flex at the hips and throw the arms down, placing the hands near the take-off foot. Kick the back leg up as the hands are going down. Push with the arms as the legs snap over the head. Arch the back well and bring the legs back under to land with a quick hip snap.

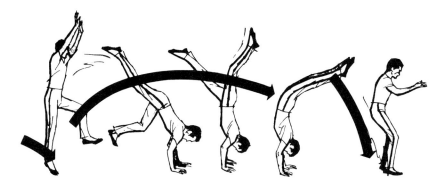

Fig. 19.13 Bent-arm handspring.

Straight-arm handspring (Fig. 19.14). Start with a short run and use a skip on the last step. By flexing at the hips, bring the hands down close to the take-off foot. Kick the back leg up vigorously as the hands are going down. Keep the elbows straight and look straight ahead. As the legs snap over into the arch position, push hard with the shoulders. Land by bending at the knees, not the hips.

Back somersault. Start from a standing position with the back to the length

Fig. 19.14 Straight-arm handspring.

of the mat. Use a good spotter or a safety belt. Swing the arms upward for lift and spring upward. Jump for height with both feet. Pull the knees to the chest quickly, keeping the trunk erect. Tip the head backward as the feet are leaving the mat. Hold the tuck until the feet are nearing the mat and keep the eyes open. Land by flexing the knees.

Rope climb. From a standing start, using both hands and feet, climb the 20-foot rope within 15 seconds or less. Descend slowly; a rapid descent will burn.

Rope climb in competitive gymnastics is a hand-over-hand climbing against time. Do not use the legs or feet. The contestant sits on the mat, grasping the rope with the hands. The legs are spread, fully extended, and astraddle the rope. Watches are started when the first pull is exerted, and stopped when the climber rings the tambourine, a plywood disk 24 inches in diameter through which the rope passes. The tambourine is fastened to the rope at a height of 20 feet.

Parallel Bars

Basic Positions

Jump to cross-rest position (Fig. 19.15). Start at the end of the two bars, place the hands on the inner top sides of the bars, and jump upward and forward. Keep the arms extended and support the weight of the body by the hands.

Jump to cross upper arm hang. Use a short run and take off from both feet with the body in a slight forward-lean position. Jump high enough to carry the shoulders above the bars. Swing the hands upward and forward until they come to rest on the top of the bars. The weight is supported by the

Fig. 19.15 Jump to cross-rest position.

hands until the forward motion stops, and then is supported by the upper arms.

Stunts

Swing from shoulders (Fig. 19.16). Start from a cross-rest position. Swing from the shoulders backward and forward. Lean slightly forward when swinging backward and slightly backward when swinging forward. Keep the body arched, the head up, and the toes pointed.

Dips. From a cross-rest position, drop to a bent-arm position and push back to the cross-rest position.

Walk the length of bar. Start from a cross-rest position with back arched, the toes pointed, and the elbows locked. Walk the length of the bars with short steps. Shift the weight from side to side. This exercise may also be done from a bent-arm position.

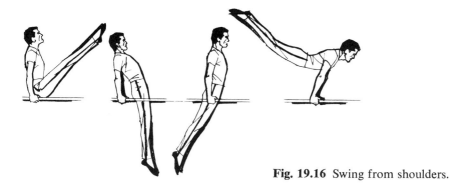

Fig. 19.16 Swing from shoulders.

229

Dip swing from straddle seat to straddle seat. Stand facing the end of the bars; jump forward and upward to a momentary straight-arm position support. Swing the legs forward and straddle both bars. Spread the legs wide, point the toes downward, and keep the knees straight. Reach well forward and grasp the bars in front of the thighs. Bend the elbows and lie flat on top of the bars, bring the feet and legs together, and kick the legs backward as high as possible. Swing the legs through the bars, and at the height of the forward swing, straddle the bars in front of the hands. Push up with the arms and assume the straddle-seat position.

Forward roll from a straddle-seat position. Start from a cross-rest position and swing to the straddle-seat position. Place the hands on the bars in front of the thighs and start to roll forward. Spread the elbows, complete the forward roll, and return to the straddle-seat position. Place the hands under the buttocks, with the arms along the bars, to assist the body in completing the forward roll to the straddle-seat position.

Flank vault. Start with a shoulder swing. At the end of the forward swing, push hard with the left or right hand. At the height of the swing, turn the body sideways and lean on the support arm. Swing the body up without bending at the waist. Keep the head up and the back arched as the body and legs move over the bar. Land with the knees flexed and the back to the bar.

Single-leg cut-off. Start from a cross-rest position at the end of the bars, and swing either the right or left leg up over the bar. Push off backward with the hands, carrying the leg over and outside, landing on both feet.

Double-leg cut-off (Fig. 19.17). Start from a cross-rest position at the end of the bars, swing both legs up over the bars, push off backward with the hands, carrying the legs over and outside the bars and landing on both feet.

Fig. 19.17 Double-leg cut-off.

Side Horse

This piece of apparatus consists of a leather-covered, cylindrical body approximately 5 feet long and about 15 inches in diameter. There are two curved hand grips (pommels) mounted on top of the horse. The height of the horse is adjustable.

Most of the vaults and stunts explained here for the side horse may be adapted to the vaulting box, buck, long horse, and vaulting bar.

Squat vault (Fig. 19.18). This vault may be done with or without a running start. Take off from both feet, forward and upward, with the hands grasping the pommels. To clear the horse, bring the feet and legs forward between the pommels with the knees tucked to the chest. Push with the hands and extend the legs on the dismount. Land with the knees slightly flexed and the arms extended to the side. Assume a standing position.

Fig. 19.18 Squat vault.

Straddle vault. Stand facing the horse, grasping the pommels firmly. Jump upward and forward and, as the body begins to clear the horse, spread the legs as wide as possible. Keep the head up, point the toes, and push with the hands. On the dismount, release the hands and fling the arms sideward and upward. Land with the feet together in a straight standing position, facing forward, knees slightly flexed, arms extended sideward and upward.

Fig. 19.19 Front vault.

Front vault (Fig. 19.19). Stand facing the horse, grasping the pommels firmly. Jump upward and forward so the weight of the body rests on the hands, and swing the body to the right or left over the horse with the body facing downward. The body is arched and makes a quarter turn to either right or left from the starting point, with the hand still grasping the pommel.

Flank vault. Stand facing the horse and jump forward, grasping the pommels, with the shoulders directly above the supporting hands. Throw the feet and legs sideward and upward to the right. To clear the horse, release the right hand, leaning to the left so that the left shoulder is directly above the supporting left hand. Keep the body and legs straight, feet together and high above the horse. Face forward with the left side of the body facing downward toward the horse. As the feet and legs swing downward toward the mat, release the left hand, landing in a standing position with the back to the horse.

Headspring. Use a two-foot take-off. Spring up, lifting the legs and hips as the head is placed on the horse between the pommels. Place the hands on the pommels. As the hips and legs move over the head, arch the back and continue until you are balanced forward. Push hard with the arms and drop to a landing in a standing position with the back to the horse. This stunt should be spotted closely with two spotters.

Handspring. Use a two-foot take-off. Place the hands on the pommels and spring up forcefully, lifting the hips and legs over the head. Arch the back and flex the arms slightly. As the legs and hips pass over the head, kick outward with the legs and push with the arms. Land in a standing position with the legs flexed. This stunt should be spotted closely with two spotters.

Half circle. The starting position is a front support. Swing either leg over the side of the horse and across the pommel. As you start the leg swing, release the pommel with the same hand as the swinging leg (right leg and right hand). Shift your weight away from the swinging leg to the supporting arm (right leg and left arm). Swing from the shoulders. As the leg crosses the pommel and the front of the horse, regrasp the pommel and assume a support with both legs straight.

Full circle (Fig. 19.20). Start from a front support. Swing either leg over the side of the horse and across the pommel, the right leg in a full circle to left. Shift the weight away from the swinging leg to the supporting left arm. After the regrasp, shift the weight away from the swinging leg to the supporting right arm. Swing the right leg back over the horse and regrasp the left pommel. Reassume front support. Strive for rhythm in the leg swing and regrasps.

Fig. 19.20 The full circle.

Travel. Jump to a support position on the neck of the horse. Swing the right leg in a half circle to the left. Then swing the left leg in a half circle to the right, coming to the outside of the left leg. As you complete the second half circle by the left leg, bring the right leg in a half circle to the right. During this move, the right hand is moved from the neck to the right pommel along with the left hand. Swing the left leg to the left in a half circle and move the left hand to the left pommel. This position places you in front support at the saddle of the horse. Repeat the movements and continue to travel the length of the horse.

Rear-vault dismount (Fig. 19.21). Start from a back support at the saddle of the horse. Feint in the opposite direction from your intended vault and then swing both legs over the horse. Keep the hips low, the legs high and straight, the supporting arm straight, and the back of the legs and body to the horse. As you clear the horse, release the pommel with the support hand, turn inward toward the horse, and regrasp the pommel that was first released at the start of the leg swing. Land in a controlled semicrouch with the hand still grasping the pommel.

Fig. 19.21 Rear-vault dismount.

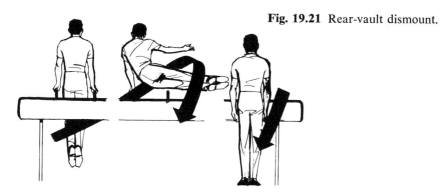

Flank circle. From a front support with the hands on the pommels, swing at the shoulders and swing the legs up over the horse and into the back-support position. Continue through the back-support position, swinging the legs over the horse and returning to the front-support position. Legs and arms must be kept straight throughout the circle movements.

Still Rings

Chins. From the front position, pull up until the chin is level with the bottom of the rings, keeping the rings close to the chest. This should be repeated several times.

Inverted hang. From the front-hang position, move the head backward, and with a tucking movement, raise the knees and legs to a position between the arm and the rings. From this key position, then extend the legs and body straight up between the rings, bringing the body into a vertical position with the floor. Keep the body arched, the head back, the legs and feet together, and the arms fully extended.

Skin the cat. From the front-hang position, chin slightly and bring the legs between the arms as in starting the inverted hang. Continue on through the arms so that the legs rotate backward and downward as far as possible for the feet. Pull the legs back through the arms. Repeat as many times as possible without releasing the hold on the rings.

Dislocate. Starting in a kip position (inverted hang with legs and feet extended parallel to the gymnasium floor), quickly kick the legs upward and backward, keeping the head moving back. As the legs drop floorward, turn the arms outward and pull up with the arms to take up the shock of the dislocate.

Kip. Starting in a kip position as described in the dislocate maneuver, kick the legs upward and outward. As the legs move downward, pull very forcefully with the arms to raise the hips to the rings, with the rings to the back. Keep the body arched at the completion of the stunt.

Muscle-up. Starting from the front position with the hands in an overgrip on the rings, pull up quickly with the arms and lean forward to obtain a good push-up position. As you pull upward, keep the elbows close together and the legs flexed slightly. As the legs move backward on the pull, raise the elbows and press to a straight-arm support. The head is up and back, the legs straight with the toes together and pointed, and the body arched. Keep the rings to your back.

Shoulder balance. Use a kip or muscle-up to raise yourself to a straight-arm support. From this position, tuck closely and roll your shoulders into the rings. Balance yourself with the elbows against the rings, and from this position extend the legs upward. As the legs straighten upward, keep the body arched, the head up and back, and the feet together and pointed. Hold the balance. To dismount, reverse the procedure or roll backward.

Double-leg cut-off. From the front-hang position, spread the legs and swing them upward over the head. Do not release the rings until the feet are over the head. Continue the swing, keeping the head back, eyes open, shoulders back, and legs spread outside of the rings. As the feet pass over the head, release the rings and land on the ball of the foot in a semi-crouch position.

High Horizontal Bar

Chinning. Grip the bar with a forward grip at shoulder width and start this exercise from a dead hang. The legs should be kept extended throughout the chinning, with the head forward. Pull up with the arms until the chin clears the bar each time. Do not swing the body.

Muscle-up. Grip the bar with a forward grip and start this exercise from a dead hang. Pull yourself up to a front-rest position with the hips against the bar. In the front-rest position, the head should be back, chin in, back slightly arched, arms straight, shoulders just ahead of hands, legs straight, and toes pointed. A slight kick helps in the pull-up action if it is coordinated with the pull or muscle-up by each arm.

Swing and dismount. Take a chinning position, and do a chin-up. After the chin, kick the feet up, out, and down, and extend the arms on the forward swing. As the body comes perpendicular to the bar on the back swing, begin pulling up toward the bar and dismount at the height of the back swing. Land with the body straight, slightly bending the knees.

The underswing dismount. This dismount takes place on the front of the swing. To begin this swing, jump forward and grasp the bar. As the feet and legs swing forward, bend the hips and bring the feet up to the bar, while at the same time pulling up with the arms. You will start the dismount just as you reach the vertical-hang position that precedes the forward half of the swing. To do this, bring the legs together, flex the elbows and pull upward, arch the back slightly, shoot the feet outward and upward at a 60-degree angle. Release the bar just as the feet are shot outward. The arms and body should be completely extended before the downward and backward swing begins. Hold the arch momentarily, drop the feet to the mat, and land in a controlled vertical position.

Kip. Grab the bar with the regular grip and start by building up a medium-high swing. At the midpoint of the swing (hanging straight down from the bar), thrust the chest and hips forward so that the body is extended into an extreme arch. Follow through, and maintain this arch until the forward swing is complete. Then, as the hips start the return swing, bring the insteps into the bar. Snap the legs up, out, and down, pulling down on the bar with straight arms. The last snap is the kip. Keep the shoulders forced well forward.

The single-knee swing-up. Grab the bar with the regular grip and obtain a swing. On the forward swing, bend the hips and bring the feet and legs forward and upward toward the bar. At the height of the forward swing, bring one leg between the arms and over the bar. Swing the free straight leg out and downward in a forceful movement, bend the arms and pull from the shoulders, throw the head forward, and come to the rest position on top of the bar.

Single-knee circle (backward). Use the single-knee swing-up to get into the starting position on top of the bar. From this stationary position, extend the right leg back, keep the left knee hooked to the bar, then throw the head and shoulders back on the downswing. As the body reaches under the bar, bring the right thigh close to the bar, bending the arms at the top of the swing. Repeat the procedure for consecutive spins.

Single-knee circle (forward). Grab the bar with the regular grip and use the single-knee swing-up to get into the starting position on top of the bar. Lengthen on top of the bar, fall forward, outward, and downward away from the bar. As you fall outward, hook the bent leg on the bar and keep the thigh of the straight leg against the bar. Swing under and upward in a smooth circle, shift the hips over the bar as you complete the circle, tighten the grip, and stop in the starting rest position. Repeat the procedure for consecutive spins.

Forward hip circle. Assume a reverse grip on the bar. Pull up to a front-rest position, thighs touching the bars, and throw the legs slightly upward and off the bar. As the legs come down and forward to start the circling of the bar, throw the head and shoulders backward. The lower stomach region sticks to the bar at all times, making a complete circle. Finish with a front-rest position and repeat the stunt.

Skin the cat. Take a forward grip on the bar. Chin slightly and swing the legs up and through the arms; allow the legs to pass through and drop as far as possible. Pull the legs back through and drop down as far as possible. Pull the legs back through the arms.

Flying Rings

Elementary Positions

Front hang. This position is attained by standing beneath the apparatus and reaching upward, grasping the rings by a forward, upward motion of the hands. This is the initial starting position. The swing is generally obtained by a push from a fellow gymnast.

Kip position (Fig. 19.22). Pull up on the rings and swing the legs forward and upward so that the feet are above the head and between the two rings and the body is in a pike position.

Advanced Positions

Dismount forward. While swinging forward, bring the legs up slightly in a partial sitting position, then quickly extend them, release the rings, and land on both feet.

Dismount backward. While swinging backward, pull up on the rings, bring the body vertical to the floor, and then release the rings to drop straight to the floor, landing on both feet.

Bird's nest. Roll into the kip position on the end of the front swing, place the insteps in the rings, and push backward with the feet so the body faces the floor. Keep the head up and the body arched.

Inverted hang (Fig. 19.23). On the front swing, pull the legs up into position between and parallel to the straps, so the body is in a position vertical to the floor. Look at the toes and keep the arms fully extended.

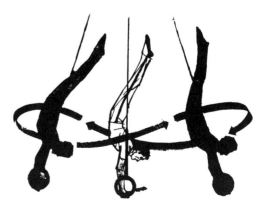

Fig. 19.22 Elementary kip position.

Fig. 19.23 Inverted hang.

Kip position on back, stretch on front swing. On the backward swing, pull up into the kip position, extend the legs upward and outward on the front swing, and swing from the shoulders.

Trampoline

The straight bounce. Start with the feet about shoulder width apart in the middle of the bed of the trampoline. The knees will be bent slightly when landing and straightened out upon the take-offs. Keep the head level, but look at the bed approximately six feet forward of the foot contact area. The arm should be thrown upward and outward, and should travel in front of and to the side of the body, which is kept straight while in the air with only a slight bend at the trunk, legs straight, toes pointed, and feet together. The feet will spread back to shoulder width upon contact with the bed of the trampoline. The beginner should use a low, controlled bounce and gradually add height as he gains more control. To stop, bend the knees.

The seat drop (Fig. 19.24). Start by lifting the knees straight up and extending the legs forward as you drop toward the bed of the trampoline. Land in a sitting position at the spot where the feet left the bed at the start of the stunt. Legs should be together and extended so that the backs of the legs are in contact with the bed. The trunk should be leaning slightly backward with the hands on the bed just to the rear of the hips. The arms are slightly bent and the fingers pointed forward. As the lift begins, raise the arms as in a normal bounce and return to a standing position.

Fig. 19.24 The seat drop.

The knee drop (Fig. 19.25). Bend the knees in the air and extend the feet to the rear. The body must stay directly above the knees throughout the stunt.

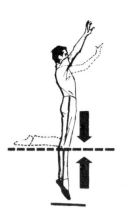

Fig. 19.25 The knee drop.

Fig. 19.26 The back drop.

Land on the bed in a kneeling position with knees, shins, and insteps contacting the bed. The arms should be slightly to the front with elbows bent and thumbs up. Let the trampoline throw you back up to your feet. Do not attempt to bounce up off the knees.

The back drop (Fig. 19.26). Start with a straight bounce from the spot. Land on the back just behind the spot. As you bounce up, lift the knees, letting them bend slightly. At the same time rotate backward on a lateral axis through the hips and drop toward the bed, where you should land in a supine position with the legs together and extended almost straight. The leg and stomach muscles should be tight to prevent the legs from sagging into the stomach or bed of the trampoline. The arms are in front, elbows flared, and thumbs up. As the bed pitches you upward, raise the arms as in the normal bounce and reassume a standing position. The head does not touch the bed at any time during the stunt.

The front drop (Fig. 19.27). As you bounce up, bend the knees slightly and extend the feet backward. At the same time rotate forward through the hips (lateral axis) and drop to the bed. *Do not dive.* Your stomach should land on the area occupied by the feet at the start of the stunt. As you land in the prone position, the arms should be extended slightly forward, elbows flexed, forearms and palms on the bed, head up, and the muscles of the arms tensed. Points in contact with the bed should be the palms, forearms, abdomen, thighs, and toes. Ride the bounce up and push with the hands as you start off the bed. Lift the arms upward, bring the feet under the body, and land in a standing position.

Fig. 19.27 The front drop.

Cradle (Fig. 19.28). This is a short name for a back drop one-half twist to a back drop. Start by doing a back drop, and as you bounce up, work for height. As the arms come up and forward, kick up and forward with the legs. With the extra height, you will continue onward beyond the vertical position and start to fall into a front drop. When this happens, turn the head and arms to the left (or right) so as to execute a one-half twist. The completion of the twist will permit you to land in a back-drop position, and to bounce up on the feet again.

Fig. 19.28 Cradle.

The blutch (half turntable) (Fig. 19.29). Start from a front-drop position, and as you are starting to be lifted by the bed of the trampoline, tuck into a semi-pike position and turn around 180 degrees. As the body rotates in the horizontal plane, the trunk should stay level, with the chest, abdomen, and front of the legs facing the bed. After completing the one-half turntable, open the tuck and drop into a front drop. From the front drop, ride up into a standing position.

Swivel hips (Fig. 19.30). This is a seat drop one-half twist to a seat drop. Start by landing in a good seat-drop position, and as you begin to ride up off the bed, push hard with your hands, then reach forward and upward for a power take-off and at the same time drive the legs straight under you. As the

Fig. 19.29 The blutch (half turntable).

legs come directly under the body, turn the head and arms to the right to start the one-half twist. Lead with the head on the turn. As the legs swing under and past the body, the twist should be completed. Next, flex the hips into a seat-drop position. Ride up into a standing position.

Fig. 19.30 Swivel hips.

Front drop with a half twist to back drop (Fig. 19.31). Start by landing in a good front-drop position, and as you begin to ride up off the bed, go into a pike position. After clearing the bed, throw the arm across the body with the hand passing within a few inches of the knees. The shoulders and upper body will follow as the twist is executed. When the twist is completed, drop into a back-drop position. Ride the bed up into a standing position.

The front flip. On the take-off bounce, the arms should lift up rapidly to hold the height of the bounce, and to provide for a higher bounce. Lean slightly forward and throw downward with the head, arms, and shoulders. The chin should come to the chest on the throw action. As you feel the feet pass overhead and start to move downward, pull the head back slightly to stop the flip. The feet will drop to the bed and you will be in a standing posi-

Fig. 19.31 Front drop with a half twist to back drop.

tion. The feet should be shoulder width apart, and your arms should be held slightly forward of the chest in a flexed position.

The back flip. Execute a good power take-off by lifting forcefully with the arms to achieve moderate bounce height, and to hold the height longer. After leaving the bed, lean back slightly and throw the head and arms upward and backward. When starting the action of the flip, bring the knees toward the chest in a semitucked position. Use the arms to follow through with the initial throw for the flip. Do not grasp the knees. As the feet pass overhead, keep them spread and the knees flexed for the landing. Land on the bed in a standing position with the feet spread shoulder width apart, knees flexed, and arms held at chest height in a flexed position. Master the stunt in a safety belt first.

RULES

The rules that have been written for gymnastics pertain to the conducting of gymnastics meets, which are divided into dual meets and conference meets. These rules are written by both the NCAA and AAU. High Schools use the NCAA or AAU rules, or some modification. The collegiate gymnastic meets use the National Collegiate Athletic Association rules (1969). These are as follows:

1. There shall be a maximum of ten men on a team.
2. The events shall include: free exercise, trampoline, rope climb, side horse, horizontal bar, parallel bars, long horse (in the Olympic year and for all-around championship only), flying rings, tumbling, and all-around. This order of events is for one session of dual meets.
3. Three men from each team may enter each event. Any one team member may enter as many events as the coach feels is necessary.

4. Each gymnast shall perform an optional routine, for which three judges shall score him on the basis of 100 points. The 100 points is divided as follows: 50 points for difficulty of the exercise and 50 points for form and continuity. A total of 300 points is possible (100 from each judge).

5. Places in each event shall be determined by the accumulated score by the three judges.

6. Team points will be awarded for each event with first place awarded six points; second place awarded four points; third place awarded three points; fourth place awarded two points; and fifth place awarded one point.

7. The team that accumulates the highest number of points on the basis of Rule 6, above, shall be the winner of the meet.

SAFETY RULES

Safety in gymnastics is largely a matter of common sense and good judgment. Experience has taught, however, that the following hints will aid in ensuring the participants against injury.

☐ Keep your mind on what you are doing; do nothing to distract others; no "horseplay."

☐ Do not use defective apparatus.

☐ Activities should not be presented without having proper and adequate mats placed under all apparatus and around the edges. These mats should be cut out to fit around irregular metal bases, which are dangerous in case of a fall.

☐ Tumbling mats should be at least doubled, and in some cases tripled in order to cushion the shock of rolls, falls, and other movements. They should be snug-locked together when used in series.

☐ Be sure, when you practice a stunt, that it is within your capabilities.

☐ Master the fundamentals, and follow the progressive order of learning the required stunts.

☐ Safety belts should always be used in exercises and stunts in which there is an element of danger. A net should be used under all apparatus high in the air, such as flying rings and the high bar.

☐ Handguards and gymnastic chalk should always be available, not only for hand protection, but also to help maintain a good grip in the performance of bar exercises.

☐ Make sure that the apparatus is set up properly.

☐ Adequate space should be arranged between all pieces of apparatus.

☐ No distractions should be present in the activity area.

☐ The matter of spotting or assisting is highly important and should be studied and carefully planned for in all exercise groups.

☐ Do not be foolhardy.

☐ Do not jest with a performer until he has dismounted.

☐ Never change your mind in the middle of a stunt.

☐ If something happens that the performer cannot control, he should:
   a. Relax and give with the fall.
   b. Keep the palms down when falling, and the fingers forward and together.
   c. Follow through with the stunt and not tense up.
   d. Make maximum use of rolling motion.

☐ Care must be exercised when raising or lowering horizontal bars to be sure that they are properly locked and that all floor supports are in place.

☐ Use four spotters or guards, one at each end and one at each side, for the trampoline.

☐ All beginners should learn to "kill" their spring by flexing the knees immediately upon landing on the canvas to prevent an uncontrolled bounce off the trampoline.

☐ Never jump from the canvas of the trampoline to the floor.

☐ Spectators should be kept at a safe distance from all apparatus activities at all times. Street-clad experimenters should not be allowed either on the mats or on the trampoline. Proper exercise dress is important.

☐ Proper warm-up is always indicated before starting difficult exercises. Preconditioning is important. Injuries to joints, muscles, ligaments, and organs occur most frequently when persons have not been preconditioned for strenuous performance.

TERMINOLOGY

Abduction A movement of any member away from the median line or, in the case of the fingers, away from the median line of the hand.

Adduction A movement of any member toward or across the median line.

Arabesque A one-foot balance with one leg raised backward with arms placed in various positions.

Bridge The position of lying on the mat using the head and legs to raise the body from the floor.

Check To halt or slow the body revolutions when performing on a trampoline.

Circumduction A movement of the trunk or any extremity in which the part farthest from the center of motion describes a circle. The term is used interchangeably with circle.

Croup Space between the right pommel and right end.

Dip A maneuver performed on the end of the parallel bars by lowering and raising the body by arm strength alone.

Dolly A small low platform on rollers used for moving bulky or heavy objects.

Exercise on parallel bars Terms remain constant as applied from the start.

Extension Reverse of flexion.

Fan A stunt on the parallel bars which starts with a swinging pirouette but finishes with a half turn away from the bar.

Far end Opposite end of approach.

Flexion Applied only to extremities. A moving of a whole part of the extremity in the direction in which it can be most closely approximated. Full flexion means flexed to the fullest extent. Half flexion is a partial flexion.

Gainer A back flip in which the performer lands ahead of the take-off spot.

Jackknife A position with the legs straight and the hips flexed.

Left pommel Neck pommel.

Lunger A strong leather or webbing belt to circle the body of a gymnast, with ropes attached to its sides by swivels.

Near end End of approach.

Near side Side of approach.

Neck Space between the left pommel and left end. Parallel bars are designated right and left corresponding to the side of the body.

Pommels Raised handles on horses.

Right pommel Croup pommel.

Saddle Space between pommels.

Shinny To climb.

Spotter Guard assisting the performer to prevent injury.

Tinsica A front handspring with a cartwheel action, one hand being ahead of the other.

Vault A leap, jump, or spring in which the hands assist the performer to clear an obstacle.

Whip A vigorous powerful drive with a part of the body, usually the legs, to get sufficient force to execute a stunt.

TEST QUESTIONS ON GYMNASTICS

If the answer is True, circle the T; if the answer is False, circle the F.

T   F   1. Elementary tumbling provides the basis of stunts and knowledge helpful for all other gymnastic events.

T   F   2. In the forward roll, when the weight leaves the hands, the person grabs his shins and pulls himself up to his feet.

T   F   3. The tinsica is a front handspring with a cartwheel action, one hand being ahead of the other.

T   F   4. The near side is the end of the approach.

T   F   5. A jackknife is a position with the legs straight, the hips flexed.

T   F   6. A pommel is a vigorous powerful drive with a part of the body, usually the legs, to get sufficient force to execute a stunt.

T   F   7. The far end is the opposite end of the approach.

T   F   8. Five men from each team may enter each event.

T   F   9. Gymnastics rules are written by both the NCAA and AAU.

T   F   10. There is no progressive order of learning in gymnastics.

Discussion

☐ Explain the difference between abduction and adduction.

☐ Describe a fan.

☐ Define a vault.

☐ Explain the headspring.

☐ List the stunts.

REFERENCES

Kireilis, R. W., and H. E. Buchanan 1959. *Elementary tumbling manual*. Lubbock, Tex.: Mimeo-Steno Service.

Ladue, F., and J. Norman 1954. *This is trampolining*. Cedar Rapids, Iowa: Nissen Trampoline Company.

Means, L. E., and H. K. Jack 1965. *Physical education activities, sports, and games*. Los Angeles: University of Southern California.

Seaton, D., I. A. Clayton, H. C. Leibee, and L. Messersmith 1959. *Physical education handbook*. Englewood Cliffs, N.J.: Prentice-Hall.

Segrest, H. B. 1962. *Syllabus for the required physical education program*. College Station, Tex.: Texas A & M College.

Stanley, D. K., and I. F. Waglow 1962. *Physical education activities handbook*. Boston: Allyn and Bacon.

Vavra, G. 1956. *Gymnastics, Colorado University handbook*. Boulder, Colo.

20
Handball
Emery W. Seymour

EARLY BEGINNINGS

The start of basketball is credited to the invention of the game in 1891 by James Naismith; and the contest between Rutgers and Princeton universities in 1869 marks the beginning of intercollegiate American football. However, the game of handball has existed for a vastly longer period of time than has either of the games above. The precise date when it began is uncertain. In his review of the history of handball, Phillips (1940) found references to a version of handball in Homer's *Odyssey* and stated that handball similar to the present game was played during the Middle Ages in the countries of France, Italy, and Spain. Historical research provides evidence that ball games were a part of Chinese activity during this time and that ancient Indian tribes in Mexico also engaged in ball games at the time of the Middle Ages. A number of volleying activities utilizing striking objects other than the hand are believed to be outgrowths of handball. The similarities in technique and strategy between the game of handball and racket sports of today are numerous and obvious.

As is true with most games and sport activities, handball has experienced many changes and modifications throughout the history of the game. As originally played, it utilized a hard ball quite similar in construction to a baseball with a cork center and horsehide cover. Today, all play involves the smaller and faster handball made of rubber. Courts have undergone numerous changes in dimensions and in construction. While handball has been characterized as

247

primarily a participant sport, the relatively recent use of glass for surfaces other than the front wall has enabled handball enthusiasts to derive additional pleasure from watching outstanding performers. For many years, handball was referred to by the French as "palm play" because no covering of any sort was worn over the hand. Modern rules not only permit the wearing of gloves but make them compulsory and prescribe glove specifications in detail. Despite its name, handball at one time could be played with the feet as well as with the hands and the Irish handball rules still permit this. As reported by O'Connell (1964), John Ryan of Wexford, Ireland, owed much of his considerable success to his ability to make maximum use of his kicking skill in combination with the rest of his game.

Mention of Ireland is appropriate since there is a full agreement that, regardless of where or when handball was first played, handball in the United States was introduced by Irish immigrants about 1840. The better performers throughout the remainder of the 19th century were likely to be Irish and it was they who were instrumental in popularizing the game. Authorities agree that the "father of handball in the United States" was Philip Casey who built the first handball court in America in the 1880s and was one of the early outstanding players (O'Connell 1964, Tyson 1971). "Casey's Court" differed markedly from the ones now in use with longer, wider and higher dimensions than the present ones.

DEVELOPMENT IN THE UNITED STATES

Until the past quarter-century, two organizations served to spread interest and participation in handball. Beginning with its first championship in 1919, the Amateur Athletic Union (AAU) launched a continuous affiliation with the game. Six years later, the YMCA held its first national championship. The first set of rules corresponding to the present game was formulated by the YMCA. For many years the official rules were revised and published by the AAU. Another organization dedicated to handball, the United States Handball Association, came into existence in 1951. For a time, the different organizations which sponsored handball tournaments had their own sets of rules with some small differences among them. A major development leading to standardization of the game occurred in 1959. At that time, the AAU, YMCA, USHA, and JWB (National Jewish Welfare Board) agreed upon a single set of Unified Handball Playing Rules.

It is not possible to estimate with any degree of accuracy the number of people now playing handball. Since "Casey's Court," courts have been built by YMCAs, YMHAs, athletic clubs, community centers, and colleges and universities. Improvised courts can be observed in many high schools and elsewhere throughout numerous communities. Along the East Coast and particularly in the New York City area, courts for one-wall handball can be noted in profusion. Truly a "Lifetime Sport," handball has its National Masters Single championship for which players must be over forty years old, its National Juniors Tournament restricted to players under nineteen years of age and various other championships unrestricted by age limits. Once considered a game to be played by males only, handball is now enjoyed by a great many girls and women as indicated by O'Connell's (1969) observation of the appreciable numbers of women entering city handball tournaments sponsored by the New York City Recreation Department. Certainly it is a game in which a relatively small number of persons have developed amazing ability and have participated in championship tournaments where their performances have thrilled increasingly larger numbers of spectators. More significantly, however, handball has attracted in much larger numbers men and women who respond eagerly to the pleasure of activity, the challenge of competition and the beneficial exercise provided by the game.

THE GAME

One cannot properly speak of the game of handball since there are two official versions, each of which has its adherents. They are designated as four-wall and one-wall handball with the different courts calling for rule differences and bringing into play strategical variations. Four-wall handball is perhaps the game most widely played and the one to which most frequent reference is made. With the 1959 rules standardization, a single set of dimensions was agreed upon whereby courts must be 20 feet wide, 20 feet high, and 40 feet long with a back wall 12 feet high. For official tournaments, courts of these dimensions only are acceptable. At the same time, it has frequently been necessary to adjust to available space and courts may not coincide exactly with all the official dimensions. The official rules are still followed and satisfaction from participation is reduced only slightly, if at all, because of the variations.

Once play has been initiated, the entire court is utilized and only a few floor markings are required. These mark off a *service area* which is bounded to the rear by a *short line* which is parallel to the front and back walls and equidistant from both. Five feet in front of the short line and parallel to it is the *service line*. At the start of play, the server must be within this area throughout the serve and the receiver must stand at least five feet to the rear of the short line while the ball is being served. The only other markings are used for doubles play when the partner of the server must stand within one of the two *service boxes*. These are spaces within the service area bounded by the side wall and a line eighteen inches from and parallel to the side wall with front and back sides provided by the service and short lines, respectively.

As stated earlier, the official game is played by either two players (singles) or four players (doubles) and is similar to other volleying games where players (singles) or teams (doubles) alternately play the shots. A regu-

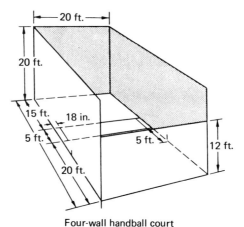

Four-wall handball court

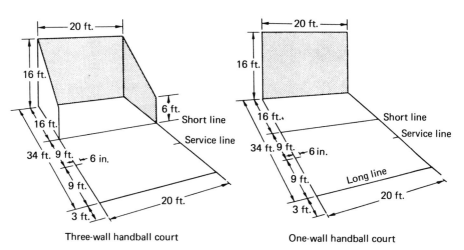

Three-wall handball court   One-wall handball court

Fig. 20.1 Handball court dimensions and markings. From D. R. Casady, *Sports Activities for Men,* New York: Macmillan, 1974, p. 272.

lation game is over when one player or team has scored 21 points, with only the serving side able to score. A match is complete when one side has won two games.

To begin play, the server drops the ball to the floor and strikes it on the first bounce as it rebounds from the floor. To be a legal serve, the ball must go directly to the front wall before it touches the floor or any other wall. Failure to hit the front wall first is an immediate loss of serve. Beyond hitting the front wall first, a legal serve requires that the rebound go beyond the short line before hitting the floor; further, the rebound must strike the floor before hitting the back wall or ceiling. Lastly, the served ball may not hit more than one side wall before hitting the floor. These latter violations where the ball hits the front wall first are termed *shorts* and two shorts on a point result in a loss of serve.

Once the ball has been legally put in play, the receiving side may play it off the front wall before it touches the floor and must play it before it touches the floor more than once. A legal return is any shot which hits the front wall before hitting the floor with side walls and ceiling often being contacted by the ball before it hits the front wall. Failure by the receiving side to make a legal return results in a point for the serving player or team. Failure of the serving side to make a legal return produces a *hand-out*. In singles, this means that the opponent then becomes the server. In doubles, except for the beginning of a game, both players on a team have a turn at serving so that two hand outs cause a *side-out* and the serve goes to the other team. At the very beginning of a game, the side which has the initial serve is entitled to only one hand out.

After the ball has been legally served, play continues until such time as a team or player fails to make a legal return. As mentioned earlier, this normally produces either a point or a hand-out. In some instances, though, a player may not have a fair chance to return the ball because of obstruction or interference by an opponent. At other times, a return may fail to reach the front wall because it has hit an opponent before hitting the floor. Where this is unintentional interference by the opponent, it is designated a *hinder* and the point is replayed. Occasionally, court conditions may be such that a live ball goes over the back wall, hits an obstruction on a side wall, or in some other way as established by local rules becomes a dead ball. As with the ball which hits an opponent before hitting the floor or reaching the front wall, this is a dead ball hinder and the point is replayed. Where a match is refereed, the referee is expected to call hinders. Most games do not have a referee and decisions on hinders are arrived at by the players. It is common practice for the offending player to call a hinder against himself or for a player to ask an opponent whether he was hindered. In some instances, the player who is interfered with will indicate that he was obstructed and will request a hinder.

A less frequent violation is the *avoidable* or *intentional hinder*. As implied, interference with the opponent is purposely committed in order to prevent a legal return. The consequence of such a hinder is a hand-out if the violator is on the serving side or a point for the opponent where the latter is serving. The referee is responsible for calling the avoidable hinder. Because fair play and sportsmanship are so much a part of the game of handball, the intentional hinder has no place in a player's "game plan." Every effort should be made to see that the opponent has a fair chance to make the best possible play. Beyond that, if there is any question as to whether one has obstructed an opponent, he should offer him the opportunity to request a hinder.

SKILLS AND TECHNIQUES

There are many skills involved in hitting a handball effectively. Good body mechanics are essential if one is to play the game properly. Because the entire court is in play, one must be ready to make shots from virtually every spot on the floor. Most beginning players and a number of experienced players find difficulty in returns which force them to their "weak side." Just as tennis, squash, or badminton players normally turn their bodies and play a backhand shot, handball players are obliged to turn, but rather than using a backhand, to use the nondominant hand. For the beginner, this is often frustrating until some degree of mastery is attained. Unless one learns to use both hands, one will never become even reasonably proficient at the game. While few persons reach the stage where they are equally effective with either hand, diligent practice can produce considerable improvement in the ability to use the nondominant hand. One of the mistakes many beginners make is to try to play all shots with the dominant hand or "run around a shot." Not only does this frequently place one in an awkward position for effective stroking but it also makes it extremely difficult to cover the entire court for subsequent returns.

In connection with this, footwork is vitally important in handball. The statement, "Hit with your feet," is often misunderstood. Its implication is that one should endeavor whenever possible to be in the best position to make a strong and accurate shot. In general, this involves having the body facing a side wall with the feet roughly parallel to the front and back walls. The player then moves toward the front wall in a series of sliding steps, drawing the striking arm back and with the eyes constantly on the ball. The closer to the floor the ball is when contacted by the hand, the greater the probability of hitting a ball low against the front wall with correspondingly increased difficulty for the opponent to reach the ball before it has hit the floor more than once. Expert players endeavor whenever possible to play the ball at a height between the knee and ankle following the general principle of "the lower, the better." The manner in which the gloved hand contacts the ball is subject to a number of variations and dependent on the skill of the performer. The standard technique is one wherein the hand is slightly cupped, the fingers are together, and the wrist is loose. Contact with the ball is made at the base of the fingers with the body then turning toward the front wall in a follow-through motion which puts the player in position to move to any place on the court from which he may be required to make his next shot. Other techniques include the use of the heel of the hand and the "punch" ball which employs the fist rather than the cupped hand. Particularly when in a defensive position, beginning players often hit with the heel of the hand when using the weak hand since it produces considerably greater force. Advanced players make considerable use of the "punch" ball because of the force imparted at impact although it is a much more difficult shot to control.

TACTICS AND STRATEGY

Success in handball is determined by the extent to which the opposition is unable to make a legal return. Accordingly, if serving, one tries to serve in such a way that the receiver fails to play the ball until it has struck the floor more than once (an *ace*), is unable to get the ball to the front wall on the fly, or makes a weak legal return which permits the serving side to "put the ball away" where it can't be reached. There are various types of serve and a player should learn a number of these so that he can vary the speed of the serve and the location to which it will be hit. Once the ball has been put into play and legally returned, a player strives to play it so that his opponent cannot get to it in time or cannot return the ball with force and direction. The ability so to place a shot that the opponent is forced off balance and out of position is an integral part of the game and frequently leads to a return whereby a *kill shot* may be the outcome. A kill shot is one which strikes the front wall or a combination of front wall and a side wall so low off the floor that the ball has little or no rebound from the floor and the opponent cannot get to it in time to make a legal return. The ace and the kill shot in handball correspond to the "big serve" and "overhead kill" in tennis. They bring an abrupt end to play. At the same time, because the kill shot is played so low, one runs greater risk of hitting the floor before reaching the front wall and losing a point or a serve. Thus, players also try to maneuver opponents out of position so they can *pass* them or prevent them from reaching a shot. Accordingly, a good player will place the ball in various parts of the court so that his opponent will have trouble getting to the ball. The ability to deliver both kill and passing shots is necessary for one who hopes to become a proficient handball player and it is enjoyable to watch two good handball players or teams placing their shots in such a manner as to force a weak return and a subsequent "putting away" of the ball.

Mention has been made of the fact that handball may be played as a singles or a doubles game. In singles, the player knows that he must play every other shot. In doubles, on the other hand, the two partners must work closely with one another. As a team, they alternate with the other team in playing shots but the determination as to which partner is to play the shot and the manner in which partners seek to cover the entire playing area are items of major consequence relative to their success. The usual alignment is to have a right and left side player where the one on the left plays the majority of the shots. The right side or "up" player protects against passing shots down the right side and attempts to return "near kills" in the front of

Fig. 20.2 The ability to combine individual talent into effective doubles play comes only after a great deal of experience and adjustment of the partners to one another. United States Army photo.

the court. In general, balls which can be played by either partner are taken by the left side player. Usually, one player acts as captain to indicate which one should play a shot where there may be uncertainty. In similar fashion, there are many instances where a player may be obliged to move from his normal position in order to make a shot. The other player may then move over to the vacated part of the court to provide coverage. A call of "switch" is then employed to ensure that each player knows where his partner will be. The ability to combine individual talent into effective doubles play comes only after a great deal of experience and adjustment to one another. There have been many excellent doubles teams in the history of the game. Perhaps the greatest of these was that of Phil Collins and Johnny Sloan who won five consecutive National AAU Doubles Championships during the years 1956–1960.

GAME VARIATIONS

Much of what has been written to this point about four-wall handball may be applied to one-wall handball as well. The one-wall court uses a 20-foot-wide court and wall which is the same as for four-wall; however, the height of the wall is only 16 feet and the length of the court is 34 feet. Because there are no side or back walls, it is necessary that there be at least three feet of free space at the open end of the court and at least six feet beyond each of the side lines. The back edge of the court is bounded by a *long line*. A *short line* runs across the width of the court at a distance 16 feet from the wall. A *service zone* is indicated in front by the short line and to the rear by *service markers* which are lines at least six inches long parallel to the short line and nine feet to the rear of it. There is one of these on either side which begins at the side line, extends toward the center by way of an imaginary extension to the other service marker and forms a *service line*. The legal *receiving zone* is within the floor area to the rear of the short line with the receiver stationed behind the service line. Once the ball has been legally put in play, the entire floor area constitutes the playing zone. Beyond the fact that balls hitting the floor must do so before passing the long line and the side lines, the major difference between the one-wall and the four-wall rules is that the hinder rule is markedly different. What is designated as a *legal block* occurs in instances where an opponent who has played the shot is completely stationary either in front or to the side of the player attempting the next shot. Obstruction from the rear remains a hinder. Because of the absence of side and back walls, one must get to all balls before or immediately after they hit the floor and cannot play them after they rebound from a wall which is common in the four-wall game.

Both four-wall and one-wall handball are official games which have specifically designated court dimensions and rules. There are instances where two- or three-wall handball is played and the lack of uniformity of dimensions, location of walls, and rules variations are frequently attributable to the fact that the court may have been formed as an accommodation to existent facilities. In a two-wall game, it is usual for the other wall to be a back wall. Occasionally, the game is played with a front wall and a side wall. Similarly, the most common arrangement for the three-wall game is to have a front wall, two side walls and a long line at the rear. The official dimensions are the same as those for four-wall handball and playing rules are the same except for balls passing over the long line where one-wall rules prevail. A more recent (1959) version of the three-wall game is one which employs a front wall, back wall, and one side wall in what is entitled a three-wall jai-alai type of court. This is played in accordance with four-wall rules except for the open side where one-wall rules are in effect. With this court it is possible to retain most of the various back wall shots which are an important part of the four-wall game.

Official handball is restricted not only to the four-wall and one-wall games but also to two (singles) or four (doubles) players. There is a form of handball which, while in no way official, is an enjoyable game when there are three people available for play. Known as "cutthroat," it is a combination of singles and doubles with each of the three players earning his own score. The server plays against the other two players until a hand-out following which one of them becomes server. Because of its "two against one" nature, the game is a strenuous one and points are more difficult to come by than in either singles or doubles. In some instances, another version of three player handball may be played wherein the best player may play an entire game or match against the other two. Unless there is a vast difference in ability, this offers a virtually insurmountable challenge for the one who plays alone and the previously mentioned "cutthroat" game probably represents a better way for three-person participation.

EQUIPMENT

In an earlier discussion, mention was made of gloves. Apart from them, some type of gymnasium shoes such as those worn for basketball is needed. The normal uniform includes a light-weight shirt and shorts although many players frequently wear sweatsuits when not engaged in tournament play. For the latter, the official rules prescribe an entirely white uniform which permits the black handball to be as visible as possible to the participants.

RESOURCES

For those who are interested in a deeper insight into the skills and strategies connected with handball, a number of excellent sources are available. The following are some which are recommended:

Haber, P. 1970. *Inside handball.* Chicago: Reilly and Lee.

Nelson, R. C., and H. S. Berger 1971. *Handball.* Englewood Cliffs, N.J.: Prentice-Hall.

O'Connell, C. 1964. *Handball illustrated.* New York: Ronald Co.

Phillips, B. E. 1957. *Handball: its play and management.* New York: Ronald.

Tyson, P. 1971. *Handball.* Pacific Palisades, Calif.: Goodyear.

Yessis, M. 1972. *Handball.* (2nd ed.) Dubuque, Iowa: Wm. C. Brown.

Another reference which many handball enthusiasts enjoy is *Ace Handball Magazine* which is the official publication of the United States Handball Association. Interesting articles on handball personalities, results of various tournaments and announcements of forthcoming events are among the contents of this periodical.

RESEARCH

A review of research conducted at various collegiate institutions shows that considerable attention has been devoted to formulation of handball tests and to analysis of the techniques employed in the game. Among studies of the past ten years, the following deserve mention:

Davies, D. B. 1971. A comparative study of the whole and part methods of teaching handball to beginning students. Doctoral dissertation, University of Oregon.

Jacobson, M. 1967. A comparative study of the differences between four-wall and one-wall handball. Master's thesis, Springfield College.

Millonzi, F. C. 1972. The development and validation of a handball skill test. Master's thesis, University of Wisconsin at LaCrosse.

Moxley, D. E. 1973. Analysis and comparison of game strategy used by class A and intermediate four-wall handball players during singles and doubles competition. Master's thesis, Washington State University.

Sattler, T. P. 1973. The development of an instrument to measure handball ability of beginning level players in a physical education class. Doctoral dissertation, Oklahoma State University.

Tyson, K. W. 1970. A handball skill test for college men. Master's thesis, University of Texas at Austin.

Yeo, D. G. 1968. The relationship of reaction time, performance time and handball velocity to success in handball. Master's thesis, Springfield College.

TEAM HANDBALL

Because team handball (also designated as eleven-a-side handball, handball for seven, and handball for five) is discussed on pages 537–543 within this volume, only passing reference to it is made here. Although they share the name *handball,* the two games are completely different and each has separate playing courts, rules, and participant appeal.

REFERENCES

O'Connell, C. 1964. *Handball illustrated.* New York: Ronald.

Phillips, B. E. 1940. *Fundamental handball.* New York: A. S. Barnes.

Tyson, P. 1971. *Handball.* Pacific Palisades, Calif.: Goodyear.

21
Horseshoes

Daniel L. Canada

HISTORY

The origin of horseshoe pitching is uncertain. Some historians claim that horseshoe pitching originated at least two centuries before the Christian Era. It is known that horseshoe pitching was practiced by Roman soldiers as a form of recreation. Initially the horseshoes were thrown for distance, whereas later they were thrown for accuracy. Eventually ground stakes were used as targets.

The game was introduced to America by British soldiers during the American Revolutionary War. It was not uncommon to find both British and American soldiers pitching horseshoes for recreation. This was a desirable game in that equipment was readily available, it was fun, and led to improved hand-eye coordination.

THE GAME

The game is played by throwing, or pitching, horseshoes at stakes set apart in the ground. Points are scored by the player whose shoes lie closer to the stake. The object of the game is to throw "ringers."

COURT

Two 1″ diameter steel stakes are set 30′ apart for women and 40′ apart for men. Stakes are extended 14″ above ground which is of a clay substance 6″ deep and contained in a 6′ square wooden box.

EQUIPMENT

Four regulation steel horseshoes each weighing 2½ pounds. A shoe measures 7½″ long and 7″ wide having an opening of 3½″ between the caulks at the toes.

RULES

Either singles or doubles may be played.

☐ Choice of pitch at the beginning of the game is decided by the toss of a coin. In successive games the loser will have first pitch.

☐ A game is divided into two innings. The pitching of two shoes by each side constitutes an inning.

☐ A "ringer" is declared when a shoe encircles the stake so that a straight line can be drawn between the toes of the shoe without touching the stake. A "leaner" is declared when a shoe is in an upright position and is supported by leaning against the stake.

☐ In doubles or team play the shoes are pitched from one box to the other by alternate partners.

SCORING

☐ Game score is either 21 or 50 points, with 50 points being common.

☐ A shoe must be within 6″ of the stake to score. Closest shoe to stake scores one point. One ringer counts three points. Two shoes closer than any shoe of the opponent's scores two points. One shoe closer and a ringer of same player scores four points. Side with two ringers for opponent's one, scores three points. All equals count as a tie and no points are scored. When each side has a ringer, the next closest shoe scores one point if within 6″ of the stake. A leaning shoe has no value over one touching the stake.

TECHNIQUES

Until the 20th century, horseshoes were pitched in a single straightforward manner. In 1920 George May of Akron, Ohio, developed a technique of pitching horseshoes in which he controlled the spin of the shoe and thereby consistently threw ringers. With the single straightforward method, one or two ringers a game might be expected. By imparting a spin in the throw, ringers could be thrown with great consistency.

☐ The shoe should be held with fingers rather than palm of hand.

☐ The shoe should be thrown with caulks down.

☐ Players should throw in such a manner that the shoe slowly spins in the air and lands with the open side toward the stake.

☐ It is important to release the shoe quickly.

ASSOCIATION

The National Horseshoe Pitchers Association of America is located at 431 Polk Street, Gary, Indiana 46402. This association was founded in 1914.

REFERENCES

Harbin, E. O. 1968. *The fun encyclopedia.* New York: Abingdon.

Horseshoes 1952. In Louis E. Means and Harold K. Jack (eds.), *Physical education activities, sports, and games.* Dubuque, Iowa: Wm. C. Brown.

Menke, F. G. 1972. Horseshoe and quoit pitching. *Colliers Encyclopedia* **20**: 711–712. New York: Crowell-Collier Education Corp.

Menke, F. G. 1947. *The new encyclopedia of sports.* New York: A. S. Barnes.

Sportcraft official rules, Bergenfield, N.J.: General Sportcraft.

Van der Smissen, B., and H. Knierin 1964. *Recreational sports and games.* Minneapolis: Burgess.

22
Ice Hockey

Dick Bertrand

DEFINITION

hock·ey (hok·e), *n.,* a game in which opposing sides seek with clubs curved at one end to drive a disc into their opponent's goal. 2. the club so used (hockey stick). (Derived from *hock,* stick with hook at end, variation of hook)

HISTORY AND BACKGROUND

Skating probably dates back to the first time that people put runners on their feet to glide on ice. There is evidence that this occurred some 2000 years ago.

Undoubtedly, the game of hockey has gained some of its character from a game called "bandi," played in the Scandinavian countries for the past two or three hundred years. The game as we know it today drew its name from the French word *Hocquet,* and originated in Canada between 1783 and 1855 through, by and large, the ingenuity of the British imperial troops stationed in Canada at that time. There is clear documentary evidence of the game taking form by 1855. In the beginning hockey drew the attention of servicemen, university students, businessmen, and politicians; hence, hockey had the necessary support to get the game well and truly established.

There are many claims as to where, when, and by whom the first games were played; however, the general consensus is that the game was officially launched in Halifax and Kingston about 1855. By 1879, games were being played with regular rules; British field hockey and soccer rules played a major part in providing the basis for the early rules adopted. It appears that two McGill University students (Robertson and Smith) get the recognition for producing the first effective set of rules for hockey. By 1893, Lord Stanley presented the Stanley Cup to encourage amateur competition and urged members of parliament to assist. In 1910, the Ontario Hockey Association (OHA) was formed through the initiative and urging of Sir Arthur Stanley, third son of Lord Stanley.

Although the game developed rapidly, it was not until between the two World Wars that the game really flourished. During this period, it became apparent there were two types of hockey to be played in Canada—hockey "for play," but also hockey "for pay." From 1927 to the present time, professional hockey has flourished, but amateur hockey maintained pace only until the post-World War II period. At this time, amateur hockey began to lose ground for many reasons—lack of boys playing due to war, lack of leadership since hockey men were more urgently needed elsewhere, inroads by the professionals, distractions such as cars, TV, and drive-in theaters, and a lack of qualified coaches and adequate facilities.

The game graduated from natural to artificial ice; from outdoor to indoor rinks; from strap-to-your-boots, double-runner aluminum or wooden or rock skates to the single steel blade and leather (or plastic) boot. Furthermore, it went from skimpy equipment to maximum protection equipment; from hockey being played only in certain areas like Canada to areas all over the United States and world in the last decade; and from fun, amateur hockey to highly paid professional hockey!

AN ICE HOCKEY RINK OR SURFACE— WHERE THE GAME IS PLAYED

Ice hockey is played on an ice surface known as a rink (Fig. 22.1).

The rink. Dimensions for an ice surface range anywhere from 165 to 205 feet long by 85 feet wide. The rink is surrounded by smooth boards made of wood or plastic which are anywhere from 42 inches to 48 inches high.

Ice lines or markings. The ice surface is divided into three zones—defending, in which one team's goal is located; neutral; and attacking, in which the opposing goal is located. The area between the two goals is divided by blue lines 12 inches in width, 60 feet out from the goal lines extending across the rink, parallel with the goal lines and vertically up the side of the boards.

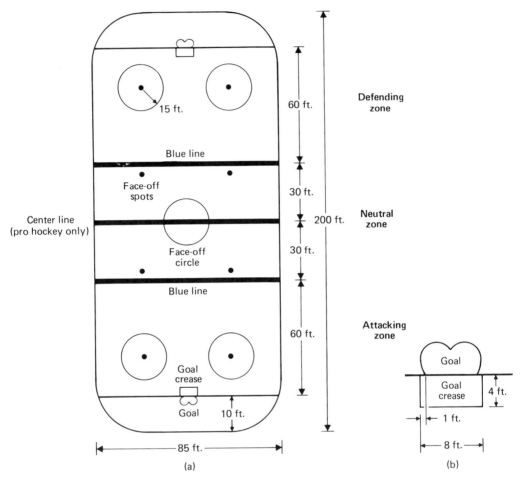

Fig. 22.1 (a) Ice hockey rink dimensions and (b) detail of goal and goal crease.

There is also a center red line 12 inches in width, extending across the rink parallel with the two goal lines and vertically up the side of the boards. This center line divides the ice surface in half.

The object of the game of ice hockey is to put the puck or disc into the goal or net. The goal or net is located 10 or 15 feet from each end of the rink. It is also in the center of a red line two inches wide, drawn across the width of the ice and vertically up the sideboards. This red line is called a goal line. The nets or goals are stationary. The goalposts rise four feet above the ice surface and six feet apart from post to post. A white net is draped over the frame to stop the disc or puck when it enters and to prevent it from bouncing out. The goal frame is usually painted red. In front of each goal is a goal

THE TEAMS

crease which is a red line, two inches in width, extending one foot from the outside of each goal post and four feet in length and two inches in width, drawn at right angles to the goal line and each line farthest from the goal joined by another line two inches in width.

To the right and left of each goal in each end are red "face-off" circles and spots. The face-off spots are two feet in diameter and the circles anywhere from 15 feet to 24 feet in diameter from the center of the face-off spots.

At exactly center ice, there is a circular blue spot one foot in diameter; a blue circle two inches in width of anywhere from 15 feet to 24 feet in diameter is drawn from the center of the spot. Two red face-off spots, two feet in diameter, are marked in the ice in the neutral ice zone, five feet from each blue line and a uniform distance from the adjacent boards.

Along the sides—usually on the same side and in the neutral zone—are players' benches and a penalty box.

THE TEAMS

Each team consists of from 17 to 20 players, made up of two goaltenders, four or five defensemen, and three or four forward lines (Fig. 22.2). There are three players to a forward line, made up of a centerman and a right winger and left winger. There are six players on the ice at a time: a goalie, a right and left defenseman, right and left wingers, and a centerman.

To distinguish between the teams, one team usually wears light jerseys and the other team, dark jerseys. On the back of each player's jersey there is

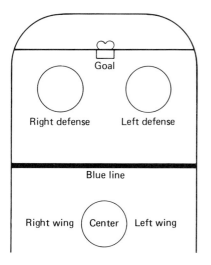

Fig. 22.2 The teams.

a distinguishing number approximately ten inches high. Most players also have their names on the backs of their jerseys.

EQUIPMENT

Hockey players wear a lot of protective equipment because of the speed of the game and the body contact involved. Forwards and defensemen use helmets, shoulder pads, elbow pads, protective cup and supporters, pants, shin guards, and skates, gloves, ankle guards, suspenders, a sweater, stockings, and—naturally, a stick! (See Figs. 22.3, 22.4, 22.5 and 22.6(a), (b) and (c).)

A goaltender uses a mask, shoulder and arm pads, chest protector, elbow pads, slightly larger pants, stick glove, catching glove, leg pads and special skates, a larger-than-average stick, garter belt, suspenders, protective cup and supporter.

In order to play the game of ice hockey, one must be able to skate and to handle a stick properly. Some of the things to look for in a skate are proper fit, leather, lacing, support, blade and toe quality. Some of the things you should be able to do when skating is to quick-start from a stopped position, frontwards and backwards and sideways; have a long, graceful stride; know when to two-foot stop, one-foot stop, go backwards, cut, turn and crossover.

Fig. 22.3 A forward or defenseman.

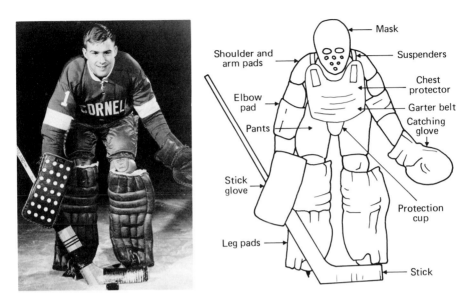

Fig. 22.4 A goalie.

Fig. 22.5 A forward or defenseman's skate.

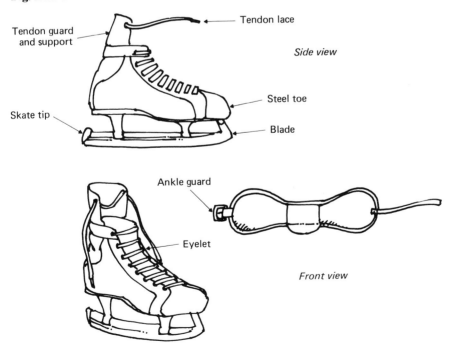

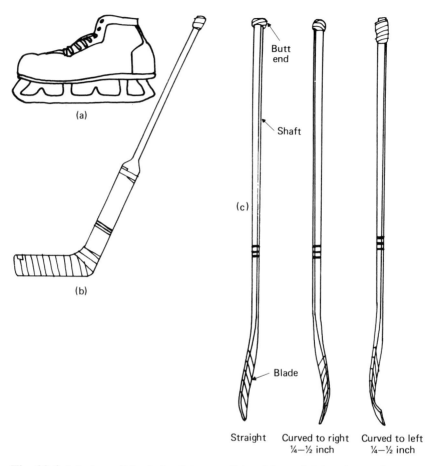

Fig. 22.6 (a) A goalie's skate, (b) a goalie's stick, and (c) a forward or defenseman's sticks.

Proper use of a hockey stick in the game of ice hockey is essential for face-offs, giving and taking a pass, and shooting. Selecting a stick is important. Next to the skates, it is probably the most important piece of equipment. There are many different types of sticks to choose from: the straight stick, or stick curved to the right, or stick curved to the left. Sticks may be curved no more than ½ inch. The most common stick used is the stick curved approximately ¼ inch.

Sticks must be of correct "lie" and length. If the stick comes up to somewhere between the neck and chin, with the skates on, it is of proper length. (If it comes up to the nose with shoes on, it is of proper length.) The lie of a stick may fall in the 4–7 range, which is indicated by a number on the handle of the stick.

Taping the stick with black or white tape may also prevent your stick from breaking. It's wise to tape at least half of the blade of the stick.

The puck. A puck is usually made of vulcanized rubber, one inch thick, three inches in diameter, and between five and one-half and six ounces in weight.

THE GAME

Ice hockey usually has three 20-minute stop-time (or free-running) periods. This will vary depending upon age classification. "Stop time" means that every time a referee or linesman blows the whistle because of an infraction for a face-off, the timekeeper stops the clock. "Running-time" means the clock does not stop for any reason outside of perhaps an injury or unusual delay in the progress of the game.

Each period begins with a face-off at center ice in the face-off circle. Players facing off stand facing each other and the opponents' end. Each player must be on his side of the red line running through the face-off spot. No player other than the player taking the face-off is allowed to enter the face-off circle or be within 15 feet of the players facing off. This applies to all face-offs in any circle.

The object of the game is to put the puck into the net or goal past the goaltender by shooting the puck with the stick. The puck has to be completely across the goal line. Should any part of the puck simply be touching the goal line, then it is not a goal. The puck cannot be kicked in. The puck shot, however, by a player, and bouncing off any part of the player's body counts as a goal. The person last shooting or touching the puck before it goes into the goal or net is credited with what is called a goal and is given one point. The last two players on the team of the scoring player who passed the puck to the scoring player get "assists," and also one point. There is one point for a goal and one point for each assist, with only the goal showing on the scoreboard.

Players, after a face-off, try to set up offensively and defensively to score a goal and to prevent a goal being scored, respectively. By means of set, practiced plays, forechecking, backchecking, break-outs, systems, patterns, and game plans, offenses and defenses are set up in many, many ways to make the game competitive, fluid, and action-packed.

Player substitutions may be made when there is a break in the play, as when the referee or linesman blows the whistle to signify stoppage of play for a face-off. Substitutions may also be made while play is in progress. The player coming off the ice must be at his bench and out of the play before the substituting player enters play on the ice.

THE FUNDAMENTALS

Skating. If you can't ice skate, you can't play ice hockey. Ice skating is the single most important fundamental in hockey. Skating is not hard to learn. It's like everything else you do. With practice and hard work you get better.

With proper fitting ice skates, well sharpened, the fundamentals can be mastered. To start from a stopped position frontwards, feet should be shoulder-width apart, knees slightly bent, body bent slightly forward. Turn one foot slightly to the side, press the toe of the skate firmly into the ice and shove off, landing on the other foot. Continue this procedure, increasing the length of the stride if possible. It is very important to have proper arm and leg rhythm. Arms should be swinging, but not too high. Legs should be slightly bent, with the lower half and the upper half of the leg approximately 90° to each other.

To stop going frontward, using both feet, turn the body to one side, bend knees slightly, bring feet slightly together, dig the outside edge of one skate and the inside edge of the other skate into the ice, forming an angle with the body and the ice.

To start from a stopped position backwards, feet should be shoulder-width apart, knees slightly bent, head up, and backside down. In other words, the body should be in a half-sitting position. Turn the skate slightly inward and shove off, bringing the foot around, forming an arc; then the other foot, forming another arc, while at the same time working the knees, shoving off harder and harder each time, forming larger arcs and swinging the hips slightly.

To stop going backward, turn both feet outwards, forming a V or backward snowplow. Bend the knees, bend the body slightly forward, and come to a halt. Once skaters have mastered skating straight backwards, with cutting, turning and cross-over practice they will be able to maneuver and steer their skates in many directions.

Crossing over and lateral movements are preliminaries to the all-important cuts and turns. In order to master skating, one must be able to cross over, cut and turn. Practice crossing over by standing on the blue, red, or goal lines. With head up and with or without a hockey stick, body erect, bring one leg up high with the knee almost touching the chest, cross it over the other leg, moving sideways along the lines, one leg crossing over the other. Repeat this back and forth along the lines for as long as it takes to get the feel of crossing over, right and left, and moving sideways. Cutting and turning require practice. Good skaters must know how to cut and to turn. Once they have a feel for crossing over, right and left, they should use the whole rink, then half the rink, then a third of the rink, to simply skate around and around clockwise and counterclockwise, paying attention to cuts and turns. Then they should change the pattern of their skating from going around and around to figure eights.

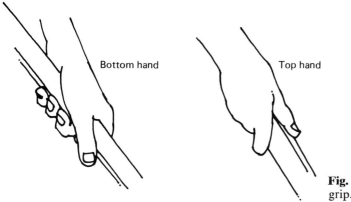

Fig. 22.7 Stickhandling grip.

Stickhandling. Stickhandling is the art of keeping possession and control of the puck. Before one can stickhandle, it is important to know how to hold the stick. (See Figs. 22.7 and 22.8.)

The top hand is the left hand for a right-handed shot, and the right hand for a left-handed shot. Place the top hand flush with the end of the shaft or butt end, with fingers tightly gripping the stick with the thumb on the side of the stick shaft. (A butt end is a handle, made of black or white tape found at the end of the shaft of the stick for easier gripping with the top hand.)

The other hand has the fingers on the shaft with the thumb on the side

Fig. 22.8 Stickhandling.

of the shaft approximately half-way down the shaft. The elbow of the hand on the lower part of the shaft of the stick should be straight.

To stickhandle, the blade of the stick is flat on the ice, not too far in front, feet shoulder-width apart, knees slightly bent, and the back comfortable. The stick is now rotated from side to side in a sweeping motion forming a semicircle. The sweeps extend no farther than between the shoulder blades. The head is kept up.

PASSING AND RECEIVING

To give a forehand pass, simply cup the stick over the puck, from ⅓ to ½ the distance down the blade, with head up and looking at your target, in a nice, easy motion, slide the puck along the ice toward the target. Don't slap the puck. Have a low follow-through to keep the puck low. The higher the follow-through, the higher the puck is going to go. The backhand pass is simply the reverse of the forehand pass.

To receive a forehand pass, have the stick on the ice at an angle to the path of the puck, relax the arms, and grip the stick firmly with two hands. As the puck hits the stick, let the blade give to cushion the impact, whether a hard or soft pass. Receiving a backhand pass is the reverse of receiving the forehand pass. (See Fig. 22.9.)

The forehand sweep pass. For the forehand sweep pass, the puck is placed in the middle of the stick, the stick-blade flat on the ice and cupped slightly over the puck. Look at the target and pass the puck, transfering the weight from rear to front foot. Pass, following through in a straight line, towards the target, keeping the stick low in order to keep the puck low. The puck should have a spin when the follow-through is finished, due to wrist and

Fig. 22.9 Passing and receiving.

tape action. The *backhand sweep pass* is made the same way as the fore-hand sweep pass except that it is the reverse of the forehand sweep pass. (See Fig. 22.10.)

Shooting. In order to be able to shoot the puck properly and to score a goal on the goaltender, which is the name of the game, the stick must be of proper length, lie, curve, and flexibility. (See Figs. 22.11 and 22.12.)

An important factor in taking a shot is proper *weight transfer* from the rear foot to the front foot. Grip is also important. It must be firm with the thumb over the *shaft*. The speed of the shot depends upon weight transfer and grip. The height of the shot depends upon the *follow-through*. Following through means sweeping the stick close or high to the ice after the shot is taken. A low follow-through and rolling the wrists slightly equal a low shot. A high follow-through and rolling the wrists more equal a higher shot.

Fig. 22.10 Forehand pass.

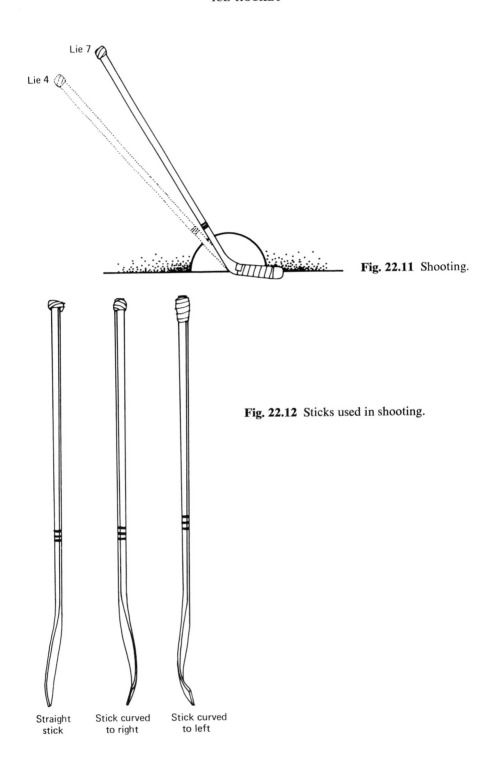

Lie 7

Lie 4

Fig. 22.11 Shooting.

Fig. 22.12 Sticks used in shooting.

Straight
stick

Stick curved
to right

Stick curved
to left

Players look at target for all shots except the slap shot. On the slap shot, they look at the puck.

SOME SHOTS

The forehand wrist shot. This shot is taken by sweeping the stick along the ice, breaking, rolling or snapping the wrists. Weight is transferred from the back leg to the front leg while the puck is being swept along the ice in front of the player. The weight of the body is over the puck and the puck is released when it reaches the front skate. Players have a firm grip and try to look at their target. This shot is the most accurate yet the least used in hockey. (See Fig. 22.13.)

The backhand wrist shot. This shot (Fig. 22.14) is simply the reverse of the forehand wrist shot. This is another shot which is effective and accurate but not used much. It is perhaps the hardest shot for a goaltender to stop because it is deceptive, since the player's body is between the puck and the opposing player, or the goaltender himself. Players should try to shoot the puck from the side of their bodies and not from out front.

The slap shot. This is the most widely used shot (Fig. 22.15). Beginners use it all the time without knowing it! They slap or bang away at the puck because they haven't as yet learned proper skate balance and coordination,

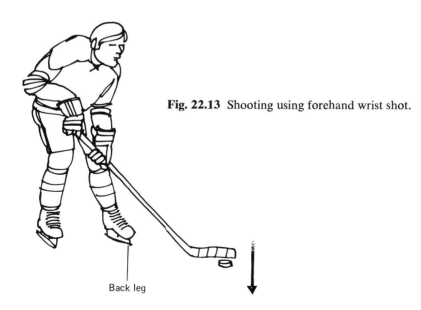

Fig. 22.13 Shooting using forehand wrist shot.

Back leg

Back leg

Fig. 22.14 Shooting using backhand wrist shot.

weight transfer, or wrist, arm, or head action. This shot is also the most inaccurate. It should be the last shot learned.

For this shot, players look at the *puck* and not at their target. Their legs are spread apart slightly under the distance used for the other shots. Players drop their bottom hands from 5 to 8 inches, and grip the stick *very* firmly—this is very important. They can have a high, medium, or low swing at the puck. This depends on their style and how much time they've got to get the shot away. Players hit the ice with the stick approximately three inches behind the puck, which should be between the skates. The entire force of the body moves into the shot as the body weight transfers from back to front. Once again, the lower the follow-through, the lower the shot. The shot is usually taken from the middle of the blade.

Breakaways, tip-ins, deflections, rebounds. These terms represent some of the unusual goal scoring opportunities that sometimes present themselves. Naturally, they give goaltenders nightmares, but also defensemen and forwards who may or may not be doing their jobs.

On a *breakaway,* players should shoot rather than "deke." The shot they take depends upon the amount of time they have and the shot they are best at.

A *tip-in* usually results when any shot is taken in the offensive zone inside the blue line. A player is positioned in front of or off to the side of the net, and the stick is on the ice. The player tips the puck into the net from the shot, or a short or long pass is taken towards the goal and a

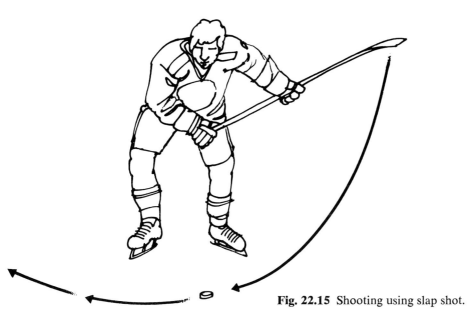

Fig. 22.15 Shooting using slap shot.

player is there with the stick and tips it in. Or, on a passing situation between two or three players, the last pass made is so close to the net it is tipped in off the stick. (These are just a few tip-in situations.)

A *deflection* occurs when any shot is taken and the puck is deflected by a player's stick below the waist or skate or any part of the player's body, whether it be a player on the same team or an opponent. *Important! A puck may not be kicked into the net with the skate.*

A *rebound* usually occurs after a shot is taken at the goalie or comes rebounding at an angle off the boards. The goaltender doesn't control the save with pad or stick, and it comes out in front of the net. Many, many goals are scored from rebounds. Many, many more *would* be scored by players from Mite to Pro if in shooting they kept their eyes on the puck all the time, but especially after a shot is taken.

CHECKING

Since hockey is a body contact sport, being able to give and to take a body check is not only a very essential part of the game, it also is the hardest fundamental of the game to learn. To effectively body check, one must own some of the following characteristics: courage, determination, heart, speed and agility, to name a few! Along with balance, poise, strength, timing and anticipation.

Some of the more common body checks given include the following.

Shoulder check. To administer this check (Fig. 22.16), the shoulder is aimed at the opponent's chest and the check is made with the shoulder side of the body. The body is kept fairly low, knees bent, and feet shoulder-width apart for balance. The skates dig into the ice. The top part of the body is bent forward, the head is up, no more than two strides are taken, and the shoulder is aimed at the opponent's chest and, as the check is given, the player pushes upward and inward, driving the side of his body into the opponent. This check is most effective when a player has his head down and the key to when he should make his move occurs when he is a stick-length from his opponent.

Hip check. This check (Fig. 22.17) is best dished out when a player is skating along the boards. Once again, defensemen seem to use this check more than anybody else. However, it can be thrown anywhere on the ice. *Timing* is probably the biggest variable when dealing with this check. If a player misses his opponent, he may take himself right out of the play and give the other team the added-man advantage.

As the check indicates, the player tries to drive his hip into the opponent's body, preferably in the leg, hip, or stomach region. So the player is skating backwards, head up, knees bent, stick in poke-checking position, other arm up for protection. Now the player turns or swings right or left on the inside skate (skate nearest boards), keeping low, and pushes hard off the other skate, directing his hip into the opponent's body.

Players should practice the shoulder check drills and the hip check similarly. However, they must remember they cannot hip check the boards

Fig. 22.16 Shoulder check.

Fig. 22.17 Hip check.

or hip check a dummy. They can practice with a fellow player by having the teammate skate down the ice, with or without a puck. The player tries to keep the teammate between himself and the boards while practicing the hip check.

Board check. This check (Fig. 22.18) is the simplest and one that's used the most as it involves the least body contact. It is very effective because it ties up an opponent. This check also involves taking an opponent into the boards with the arms and body. The player pushes at the opponent with the arms and moves his whole body into the opponent, thus taking him into the boards. The player can have one or two hands on the stick, keeping the stick low. Two hands on the stick give more power, but may throw the player off balance.

One way for a player to practice the board check is to have a teammate come down the boards with or without the puck. The player tries to keep his teammate between him and the boards. At the right moment, the player forces the teammate into the boards with his arm (or arms), stick and body. The player should take no more than two strides, keeping the stick waist- or stomach-high.

In making all of the body checks, players must not look at the puck. Instead they look at the opponent's waist, stomach, or shoulder. A thinking hockey player coming down on a defenseman will attempt to head-, shoulder-, or leg-fake him, but cannot make a waist or stomach fake. Therefore, players should not be faked out once their timing is down.

The most common check given is the board check, which is naturally

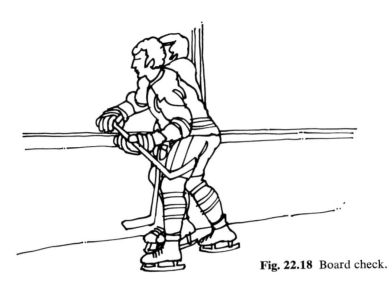

Fig. 22.18 Board check.

given along the boards. The next most common check is the shoulder check, which is given almost anywhere but especially in front of the net and in the offensive and defensive mid-ice areas. The hip check is usually given along the boards but can be thrown anywhere on the ice—and usually is!

A rule on body checks is to "never play the puck when you can play the man."

When the player is forechecking, which means going after the puck in the offensive zone in any way that he can, using the stick and/or the body, he can press the opposing team using a few systems, depending upon what his coach wants:

One-man forechecking system. Here, the first man into the offensive zone goes after the man or puck and tries to tie him up with stick or body, or both.

Two-man forechecking system. Here, the first man goes for the man, the next man in goes for the puck.

No-man-in forechecking system. Here, nobody goes after the man or puck until the offensive team makes a move or play.

FACE-OFFS

A big variable in maintaining a successful offense is to win face-offs (Fig. 22.19). Face-offs are important. Losing a crucial face-off can make the difference between saving and scoring a goal or winning and losing a game. Usually, the centermen take all face-offs. The job of a centerman is to get

Backhand sweep

Fig. 22.19 Face-offs.

Forehand sweep

the puck or the face-off and should he not be able to do this, then he must keep his body between his opponent and the puck so that someone else may be able to.

Every player on the ice should be able to take face-offs. Some common face-off maneuvers include trying to draw the puck to the backhand side and the forehand side.

The strongest side to draw to is the backhand. A big clue in taking face-offs is to watch the referee's hand. Timing, concentration, and position of skates are very important variables in taking face-offs.

The face-off man is also like a quarterback on a football team in that he lines his team up and waits for them to be in position.

RULES

Some of the more basic rules are that there are six players (including the goalie) on the ice at a time, when a team is at full strength. A team may be penalized often, in which case the penalized player goes to the penalty box or is ejected from the game, depending on the type of penalty. However, a team can have no fewer than four players (including the goaltender) on the ice, regardless of how many penalties a team has.

Offsides—Two-line Pass

The ice surface is broken down into three major zones for a reason. Whether in professional hockey, where the red line is used, or in hockey other than professional, where the red line is *not* used, no two-line pass (not counting the red goal line) can be made from one player to another. If such a pass is made, the player receiving the two-line pass is *offside* and a linesman will blow his whistle signaling such. (See Fig. 22.20.)

Offsides—Player Preceding Puck

Another offside call will result if a team on offense or attack has a player who precedes the puck over the attacking blue line with two feet. A player may straddle the blue line, which means having one foot on the blue line and the other over the blue line, and not be offside. The position of the skates, not of the stick, determines the offside. Most whistles for stoppages of play in the game of ice hockey are because of offsides. (See Fig. 22.21.)

Icing—Using the Red Line

Icing occurs using the center red line when the puck is shot from the defensive zone over the red center line into the offensive zone over the red goal line and not touched by anyone including the goalie. (See Fig. 22.22.)

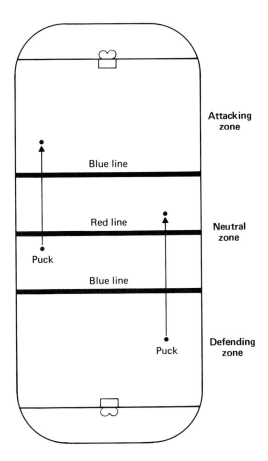

Fig. 22.20 Offsides—2-line pass.

Icing—Not Using the Red Line

Icing occurs, *not* using the center red line, when the puck is shot from the defensive zone from inside the defensive blue line over the offensive blue line and red goal lines and is not touched by anyone including the goalie. Should the goalie at any time touch the puck before or after it goes over the red goal line and it is not automatic icing, it is *not* icing. (See Fig. 22.23.)

Some leagues have the automatic icing rule, which means that as soon as the puck crosses the red goal line on an icing call, the referee blows the whistle. Other leagues use the rule that a player must touch the puck first on an icing call before the referee blows the whistle. Remember, if a player is onside (that is, in his defensive zone at the time of the icing) and he beats the defending player to the puck, it is *not* icing, and he is *not* offside.

A whistle results on an icing call and the linesman or referee will face-off the puck in the zone of the player shooting the puck into the offensive zone from the defensive zone.

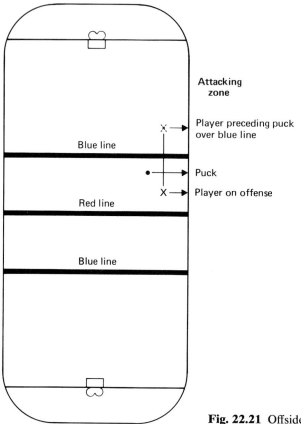

Attacking
zone

Player preceding puck
over blue line

Blue line

Puck

Player on offense

Red line

Blue line

Fig. 22.21 Offsides—player preceding puck.

Icing will not be called, usually, if the puck touches a defensive player before reaching the goal line, but goes over the goal line; if an onside attacking player touches the puck; if a team is shorthanded due to a penalty; if the goalie touches the puck; if a defending player has an opportunity to intercept the puck before it crosses the goal line.

OFFICIALS

The game of ice hockey is controlled by officials on the ice. In hockey other than professional, there are two referees on the ice—one referee who is in charge, and an assistant referee. In professional hockey, there are three officials; one referee who has an orange band on each arm and who is in charge, and two linesmen who mainly look after the offsides, icing calls, and breaking up fights.

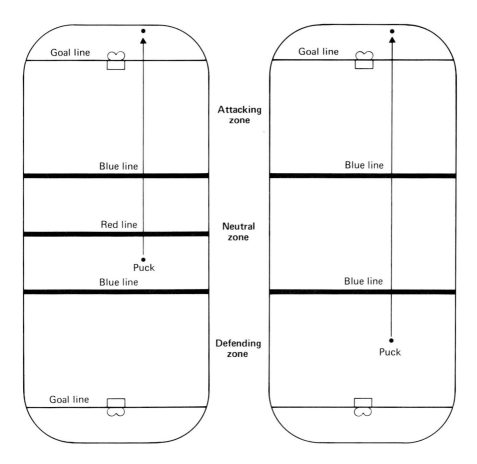

Fig. 22.22 Icing using the red line.　　**Fig. 22.23** Icing not using the red line.

The primary job of the referee in professional hockey is to call penalties. In hockey other than professional, both referees call penalties.

Other minor officials include two goal judges located in an enclosed area behind each goal, a penalty timekeeper who sits in the penalty box, a timekeeper who runs the clock, and an announcer, who usually sits beside the timekeeper, and a scorer.

PENALTIES

Since hockey is the fastest game around, involves the use of a potentially dangerous weapon, a stick, and is a body contact sport, there's a lot of room for misuse of legs, arms, hands, sticks, skates—you name it. Anyone misusing the rules of the game with those parts of the body and equipment just mentioned is subject to a penalty.

Penalties are broken down into several categories. Let's start with the most serious penalties that affect the individual and team the most.

The game misconduct or match penalty. This penalty in professional hockey not only means "out" for the game but also has a fine attached to it. This penalty in hockey other than professional means out for that particular game, and the next game. In professional hockey a player can get a match penalty for such things as being third man into a fight, roughing or shoving the referee, verbally abusing the referee, refusing to get into the penalty box or to follow the direction of the referee, to name a few situations. In nonprofessional hockey a player can get a game misconduct for such things as fighting, extensive physical violence with stick or body, physically or verbally abusing the referee, refusing to get into the penalty box or to follow directions of the referee, to name a few.

Misconduct penalty. This is a ten-minute penalty. A teammate is permitted to replace the player serving a ten-minute misconduct penalty. One can get a misconduct for abusive language directed to the referee from on the ice or bench, or refusing to follow the directions of a referee after a penalty or at any other time during a game or deliberate injury. A *major* penalty is for five minutes. It's usually given for such things as (in pro hockey) fighting; (in nonprofessional hockey) spearing, attempting to injure, drawing blood, and other excessive misuses of the stick and body.

Minor penalties. There are many minor penalties. Some of these are:

Boarding penalty
This penalty is given usually when a player is taken into the boards very hard and unnecessarily, and a charging or cross-check cannot be called.

Charging penalty
This penalty usually has two minutes attached to it but five minutes can be given for this infraction, depending on the severity of the charge. A gauge for the referee is if more than two steps are taken when a player runs or steps into an opponent.

Cross-checking penalty
This can also be for five minutes if an injury occurs. This penalty involves checking an opponent with both hands on the stick, usually above the waist, and administered by shoving at a distance of from an arm's length to half an arm's length out against the upper part of the opponent's body.

A delay of game penalty

This has no referee signal. It is usually given for such things as pulling the puck into or under the body, holding it when it is possible to play it, or holding the puck up against the boards when there's nobody around, or if the goaltender holds the puck when he can put it into play or he shoots the puck into the crowd to unnecessarily stop play.

Elbowing

Getting the elbow into an opponent's body—usually anywhere in the upper part of the body. Here, as well, if injury is caused, a five-minute major can be called.

High-sticking

If the stick is carried or involved in an above-the-shoulders skirmish, a high-sticking penalty will be called.

Holding

This penalty is given when a player holds an opponent with hands or stick or in any other way impedes his progress.

Hooking

Here, the stick is used as a hook and a player's progress impeded. The player can be hooked under the arm or pulled down with the stick on any part of the body.

Interference

An interference penalty results when a player interferes with another by getting in his way or grabbing him or touching him in any way when he doesn't have the puck.

Kneeing

This penalty involves using the knee to check an opponent.

Leaving the player's bench

There's no signal for this. A major penalty is called when a player leaves his bench to enter a mix-up, fight, or skirmish of any kind when he has no business doing that.

A penalty shot

This occurs when such things as tripping a man from behind, who may be in on a clear-cut breakaway or any player other than the goalie falling on the puck in the goal crease, or closing the hand over the puck in the goal crease, or throwing the stick at a player's stick who has the puck and may or may not be in on a breakaway.

Roughing penalty

There's a thin line between roughing and fighting. Roughing can be called for a lot of shoving, jostling, or wrestling. The moment a punch is thrown, it becomes a fight and is given a five-minute major penalty.

Slashing

This penalty is given for slashing an opponent with the stick on his stick or any part of the body.

Tripping

This penalty is given if a player trips another with stick, knee, foot, hand, causing him to fall.

When a team has a minor penalty or penalties and certain major penalties, it is forced to play one or two men short. Certain basic things must be done in playing one or two men short. This is called "killing penalties."

OFFENSIVE OR ATTACKING TEAM PLAY

Offensive team play (Fig. 22.24) means having control of the puck and getting into good scoring positions and scoring goals in the attacking offensive zone.

Offensively, players must play positional hockey; that is, right wingers and defensemen play in their lanes and areas, left wingers and defensemen play in their lanes and areas, centers in their lanes, and goaltenders in the goals. As the offense becomes more sophisticated, each position is interchangeable with all players backing one another up. However, the same pattern is always adhered to which is to have someone in the right lane and right defense area, left wing and left defense lane and area, centers at center, and goaltender in the goal.

Players must maintain their positions and move the puck around so as to create goal-scoring opportunities and goals in the attacking or offensive area. A successful offensive attack is one that tries to force the defense out of position so as to get into position for at least a shot at the goalie. An offense will employ such things as a 1 on 0, which is one man against the goalie; a 1 on 1, which is one player against another; 2 on 1, which is two players against one; 2 on 2, which is two players against two; 3 on 2, which is three players against two, and so on. Offensive teams try to create 2 on 1s more than anything else.

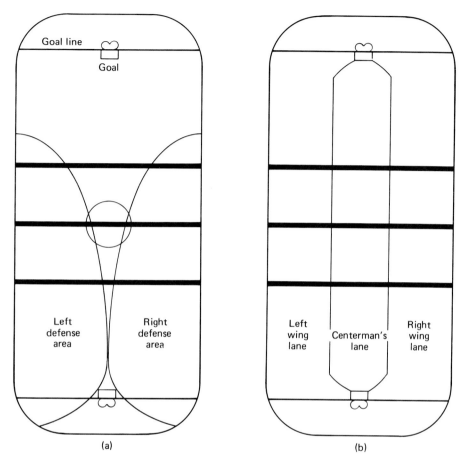

Fig. 22.24 Offensive team play: (a) defensemen and areas and (b) forwards and lanes.

DEFENSIVE TEAM PLAY

Defensive team play (Fig. 22.25) means *not* having control of the puck and getting into position so as to *stop* goal scoring opportunities and goals in the defensive zone. Defensively, as well as offensively, players must play positional hockey; that is, every player playing his lane or area. As with the offense, once the defense becomes sophisticated enough, each lane or area becomes interchangeable amongst the players. However, each lane and area has a defensive player or players in it.

Defensive players maintain their positions and attempt to take the puck away from the offense or to create bad scoring opportunities and goals

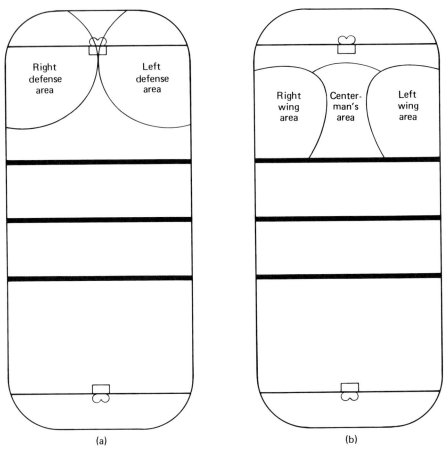

Fig. 22.25 Defensive team play: (a) defensemen and (b) forwards.

in the defensive zone. A successful defense is one that tries to force the offense to give up the puck by not getting forced out of position by any of the tactics and plays employed by the offense in their 1 on 0s, 1 on 1s, 2 on 1s, 2 on 2s, 3 on 2s, and so on.

When nobody has the puck it is a "loose" puck, and each team races for it. Until a team player comes up with the puck, everyone should be defense-minded.

TERMINOLOGY

Attacking zone That zone in which the opponent's goal cage is located.

Backchecking The act of skating back toward one's own goal and covering opposing players so that they cannot gain an advantageous position.

Body check To hit an opponent with the body in order to take him out of a play or block his progress.

Breakaway A player skating in on a goaltender with only the goalie opposing to beat.

Butt end The end of the shaft of the stick opposite the blade. A butt end is usually fashioned to the liking of a player for a better grip, with black or white tape.

Charging An illegal act of taking two or more steps or strides before checking an opponent, which calls for a minor penalty.

Checking The attempt to cover an opponent to prevent him from gaining a better position.

Cross-check An illegal act of hitting an opponent with hands on the stick, no part of the stick on the ice; calls for a minor penalty.

Cross-over The act of bringing one leg over the other in skating to effectively cut and turn.

Cutting A turning maneuver in skating.

Defenseman A player who normally plays in front of the goal he defends when the puck is in his defensive zone.

Defensive zone Area between the blue line and the end boards in which the team's own goal cage is located.

Deke A deceptive move to fake an opponent out of position.

Elbowing An illegal act of hitting an opponent with the elbow (usually in the face), which calls for a minor penalty.

Face-off The dropping of the puck between the sticks of two opponents to start or resume play. Face-off is to hockey what jump ball is to basketball.

Fighting To engage in fisticuffs, which calls for a major penalty.

Forechecking The act of checking opponents in their defensive zone to prevent them from getting a play started.

Forwards The three men on a forward line.

Goal That which a goaltender protects and at which opposing teams shoot pucks at in order to score.

Goal crease The $4' \times 8'$ area immediately in front of the goal, marked by a 2-inch red line.

Goal line A 2-inch red line extended across the rink forming the forward edge of the goal crease.

High sticking An act of playing or carrying the stick above shoulder level. It is illegal and calls for a penalty.

Holding An illegal act of using hands to hold an opponent or his stick. Calls for a minor penalty.

Hooking An illegal act of using the blade of the stick to grab an opponent from behind and calls for a minor penalty.

Icing The act of shooting the puck from the defensive zone the length of the ice over the opponent's goal line (the red line running across the front of his net).

Interference An illegal act of interfering or having contact with an opponent who is not in possession of the puck and calls for a minor penalty.

Major penalty A five-minute penalty. (This is in a regulation 60-minute game.)

Match penalty Suspension for the balance of the game.

Minor penalty A two-minute penalty. (This is in a regulation 60-minute game.)

Misconduct penalty A ten-minute penalty against an individual. (His team does not play short-handed during this period.)

Neutral zone The center area between the defensive and offensive zones (or between the blue lines).

Offsides Occur when the player precedes the puck in the attacking zone. This calls for stoppage of play and a face-off.

On-the-fly Changing (or substituting) players while play is still in progress.

Power play Usually used when the team has a man advantage and a team goes all out to score.

Protective dribble Keeping the body between the puck and the opponent.

Puck A vulcanized black rubber disk that is one inch in thickness, three inches in diameter, and weighs from 5½ to 6 ounces.

Rink The playing surface of ice.

Roughing An illegal act of engaging in a light punching or shoving about and calls for a minor penalty.

Scoring A goal is scored when the puck legally played crosses the red line entirely between the goal posts.

Side boards Boards placed around the rink.

Slashing An illegal act of swinging the stick at an opponent.

Spearing An illegal act of jabbing at an opponent with the stick as one would with a spear.

Stick lie The angle between the blade and shaft of a stick.

Stickhandling Keeping possession and control of the puck.

Wing A forward who lines up near center of rink, on one side of his center teammate.

REFERENCE

Hockey handbook. March 1969 Edition. The Canadian Amateur Hockey Leadership Institute National Clinic, MacDonald College, Ste. Anne de Bellevue, Provence de Quebec.

23
Lacrosse

*Carole L. Mushier and Carolyn E. Baker's article provides a succinct intro-
duction to the game of lacrosse. They touch on its origin and development,
describe the nature of the game and the equipment, and define the commonly used terms. They also describe the performance of the basic fundamentals. Their article is essentially from the women's viewpoint. Al Pisano also
touches on the history, equipment and basic rules but goes into considerably
more detail as to the execution of fundamentals and the strategy of the
game. Team offense and defense are described in some detail and offensive
and defensive team play explained. RBF*

Women's Lacrosse
Carole L. Mushier and Carolyn E. Baker

ORIGIN AND DEVELOPMENT

Lacrosse is a team sport owing its origin to the Northern American Indian.
The Indian game, called baggataway, pitted tribe against tribe over great
distances and was a rough version of today's lacrosse. Modification of the
sport was initiated in 1705 by a Frenchman who observed Indians playing
in Quebec, and changed the name to lacrosse because of the similarity of
the stick to the French crozier. French Canadians adopted lacrosse and it
became the national sport of Canada in 1867. Canadian and Indian teams
took the sport to England where the English adopted it in 1876. Sometime
later English women adopted a modified version and subsequently introduced women's lacrosse in the United States. In 1931, the United States
Women's Lacrosse Association (USWLA) was formed as the national governing organization. Three years later the United States began international
competition, promoting further growth and higher standards of play. Exchange tours of national teams occur periodically. The USWLA remains as
the national governing organization with rules developed in conjunction with
the National Association for Girls and Women's Sport of the American

Alliance for Health, Physical Education and Recreation. There is no international governing body.

THE GAME AND EQUIPMENT

Women's lacrosse is played by teams of 12 players each. Players throw and catch a hard rubber ball with a stick and attempt to score by shooting the ball into the opponent's goal. Endurance and conditioning are essential as each half is 25 minutes long with no time-outs. Substitution is permitted only in case of injury. The field is 130–140 yards long and 50 yards wide with goals placed 90–110 yards apart. Natural boundaries and the play of the game determine out-of-bounds as there are no definite boundary lines. A center circle with a radius of 10 yards is drawn midway between the two goals. Each goal cage is surrounded by a circle with an 8½ foot radius called the goal crease.

All handling of the ball by players other than the goalkeeper must be done with the lacrosse stick, often called a "crosse." The stick is made of wood and is strung with leather thongs, catgut, or nylon. The stick may not exceed four feet in length nor 20 ounces in weight. It cannot be wider than nine inches at its widest point and no metal of any kind is permitted on the crosse.

The lacrosse ball is hard rubber with a solid center and is usually white in color. Its circumference is 7¾ to 8 inches and weight is 4½–5¼ ounces.

Goalkeepers wear special protective equipment. Leg guards protect the lower leg and thigh. A lacrosse chest protector covers the upper thigh and entire trunk. Lacrosse masks provide protection for the face and head.

The lacrosse goal is six feet high and six feet wide. Netting is attached to the posts and crossbar and secured to the ground six feet behind the center of the goal line.

THE RULES

In general, the rules of women's lacrosse are designed to control the actions of the players so as to provide for the safety of the participants and maintain an open and free-flowing game. Body contact of any kind is illegal. Players may not use their crosses in uncontrolled or dangerous checks. The rules prohibit checking the stick into the face of the player and over the shoulder of an opponent. A player may not protect her stick by holding it to one side while fending off opponents with her free arm. The use of natural boundaries such as trees, bleachers, and fences is a part of the freedom of the game. Officials' judgment determines when a ball is out of bounds. The player closest to the ball gains possession of the ball. Whenever the whistle is blown on the field, except after a successful goal, all players must stand in their position at the time of the whistle. Maintaining position on the field is, therefore, a very important element of the game.

BASIC SKILLS

The basic skills of the game include throwing, catching, cradling, picking up, dodging, body checking, shooting, goalkeeping, crosse-checking, turning, and the draw.

The Grip

The top or throwing hand should grip the crosse at the collar or top of the handle with the open head of the crosse facing the player. The V formed by the thumb and first finger parallels the V of the head of the stick; the palm of the hand faces away from the player. The bottom hand grips the butt or end of the stick in a similar manner, the V of the hand in line with the V of the head of the stick.

The Cradle

The primary purpose of the cradle is to keep the ball in the stick while running. It also provides a means of control when catching, passing, picking up, and dodging. The primary principle in the cradle is the centrifugal force generated by a controlled swinging action. The stick is held 20–30° from the vertical toward the top hand side. The top arm is extended upward in a comfortable position with the forearm parallel to the stick and the head of the stick close to the head of the player. The bottom hand is at waist height or higher and close to the body. As the stick is moved to the top hand side of the body, the top wrist rotates outward, the bottom wrist inward to the side of the body. At this point, the open face of the stick is away from the player. The stick then moves with a rhythmical swing to the opposite side. The top wrist wraps the stick around close to the player's head. The bottom wrist rotates outward with the forearm approximately parallel to the ground. The bottom elbow remains in front of the body, the forearm and wrist pivoting around the elbow. The cradling action is timed to the speed of the run. With each step, the stick is cradled to the side of that step. As speed increases, the cradling action becomes smaller.

Pick Up

Although lacrosse is basically an aerial game, the ball will be on the ground quite often in the beginning stages of skill development. The ball may be in a stationary position or rolling toward or away from a player at various angles. The primary objective of the pick up is to execute it as quickly as possible so as to avoid opponents. With a stationary ball or a ball rolling away from the player, the stick should be held in a low position directly behind the ball. The stick is on the side of the bottom hand as the player, on the run, approaches the ball. As the opposite foot reaches the ball, the knees bend, permitting the player to slide the stick under the ball. As soon as the ball enters the stick, the player accelerates, pushing down with her bottom hand to start the head of the stick toward an upright position. At the same time, the player begins the cradle using as few cradles as possible until the stick is in the normal cradling position. When the ball is moving toward the player, the head of the stick is held low and the butt of the stick is up so the stick forms an angle with the ground. The faster the speed of the ball, the greater the angle with the ground. The player advances to meet the ball, giving backward to absorb the impact as the ball enters the stick. As the give occurs, the cradle begins and the normal cradling position is regained.

The Catch

The player should be able to catch the ball at any point or angle within the reach of her stick. The stick is extended toward the ball permitting the ball to run down the face of the stick if possible. Depending on the speed of the ball, the stick gives in the direction the ball is traveling before the cradle. The first cradle is across the body and is firm and more definite than subsequent cradles. The stick wraps around the ball after it has entered the stick.

Fig. 23.1 The "catch" and the "over-arm throw" are basic fundamentals of lacrosse. Courtesy of *JOPER*.

Overarm Throw

The overarm throw is the basic pass and shot in the game. While the top hand action is similar to that of throwing a fly ball in softball, there are differences that can interfere in the performance from one skill to the other. In preparation for the throw, the stick is cradled to the top-hand side with the top hand rotating slightly under the stick. The pass is initiated with a lift of the bottom hand, pointing the butt end of the stick in the direction of the throw. The top arm extends up and forward, while the bottom hand pulls the stick toward the throwing arm. The height of the follow-through determines the height of the throw. The force of the wrist snap of the top hand and the amount of pull of the bottom hand will determine the speed and distance. This pass can be executed to the left or right with appropriate twisting of the upper body.

Underarm Throw

The underarm throw can be used as a pass or shot for goal. It is not as accurate or direct as the overarm throw, but it does allow an easy pass to the top-hand side of the player. The player cradles to her bottom-hand side. The head of the stick makes a circular arc around, down, and out in the direction of the pass. As the head of the stick drops, the bottom hand raises the butt of the stick until the stick approximates a vertical position with the head toward the ground. The top hand then pulls the stick in the direction of the pass. The circular action must be continuous from the time the head of the stick is dropped until the ball is released.

Body Checking

Body checking occurs when a player is between an opponent with the ball and her goal. Body checking is a method of slowing the player, forcing her off her intended path, or forcing her to pass while maintaining a position to crosse-check.

The body checker extends her stick toward the oncoming player in possession of the ball and begins to move backward in the same direction. The oncoming player is forced to slow down, veer away, pass, or attempt to dodge the body checker. In any of the first three conditions, the body checker has been successful. If the attacking player attempts to dodge or get past the body checker, the body checker continues to place her body in the path of her opponent and rotates her hips in the direction of the dodge. The body checker runs with her opponent, always attempting to force her off her intended path. Should the opponent be within stick distance, the body checker attempts to crosse-check and dislodge the ball from her opponent's stick throughout the body check and dodge.

The Dodge

A dodge is an attempt by the player with the ball to elude an opponent who is between her and the goal. The player should approach her opponent at top speed without giving any indication of the direction of her dodge. When she is approximately a stick's length away from her opponent, she accelerates and pulls her stick to one side away from her opponent and attempts to go around her. Preceding the pull of the stick for the dodge, the player may feint a pull to the opposite side to deceive the opponent. As the stick is pulled to one side, the dodger continues to cradle using a smaller action than in the normal full cradle. The dodger should attempt to force her opponent to commit herself to one side and then dodge to the opposite side.

Pivot Turn

The pivot turn is used by players in possession of the ball when they have received the ball while moving in a direction opposite from their intended direction. The turn is executed as soon as the ball is controlled in the stick. If the right foot is forward, the turn will be made to the left; if the left foot is forward, the turn will be made to the right. The forward foot is planted firmly and the stick is firmly cradled to the same side in preparation for the turn. The forward foot pushes off shifting the weight toward the rear foot and the player pivots on both feet. As the pivot occurs, the stick is cradled over the head in one action and the player then immediately accelerates and cradles in the new direction.

Shooting

Shooting for goal is, basically, accurate passing. Some typical shots for goal are the long bounce shot, close overarm shot, and close underarm shot.

The bounce shot can be used at any distance. However, it is particularly effective when the shooter is 15–20 yards away from the goal. The ball is released with a hard overarm throw action, directing it out and down so that it bounces just inside the crease. The ball will hit the ground in front of the goalkeeper and rebound into the goal. The close overarm shot is a placement of the ball past the goalkeeper at any height or angle. This shot is most effective after the goalkeeper has been forced to move and the ball is directed into the resulting space. The close underarm shot is often used when the shooter is crossing in front of goal with her top-hand side closest to the goal. The ball may be directed along the ground or into a space. Advanced players develop other shots for specific situations.

Crosse-checking

Crosse-checking is an attempt to dislodge the ball from an opponent's stick with a controlled hit or series of taps with the stick. This is done without body contact and must be a controlled move that is not dangerous to the opponent. The top hand provides the force and control of the stick. Players may check the stick of an opponent whenever the ball is in the stick.

The Draw

A draw is used to begin each half of the game and following each goal. Each of the two opposing centers stands with one foot toeing the center line with her cross between the ball and the goal she is defending. The sticks are held about chest level, parallel to the center line. On the signal by the umpire, the players draw their sticks up and away from one another attempting to put the ball in the air in the direction of their respective left attack wings. The top hand must be firm, with the shoulder in line with the hand.

Goalkeeping

The goalkeeper positions herself in front of the goal line within the crease so as to be between the shooter and the goal. She should move with short, quick side steps to maintain this position. She must be ready to move in any direction and use her stick to catch the ball at any point or angle. The goalkeeper's body should be behind her stick on each catch, when possible, should she miss or deflect the ball with her stick. She may use her hand or any part of her body to prevent the ball from entering the goal. After securing the ball in her stick, the goalkeeper then clears the ball to one of her teammates down field.

GENERAL STRATEGY

Each team consists of twelve players positioned up and down the field. The team in possession of the ball is on offense; the team without the ball is on defense. Each team attempts to score as many goals as possible while preventing the opposing team from scoring.

The 12 players begin the game as shown in Fig. 23.2. Each offensive player has a defensive player who marks her in a basic player-to-player defense. While the rules do not prohibit a player from moving to any point on the field, the players maintain relative areas so as to adequately cover the field and move the ball from one end to the other. Offensive patterns create spaces into which players may cut to receive the ball. The first and third homes tend to pull to the same side of the field to create spaces in the middle of the field. The second home pulls in the opposite direction. Ideally, two or three players are cutting in various directions to give the player with the ball many options for her pass. In general, attack wings and center receive the ball to the homes for a shot on goal. While the attack can pass, catch, run and shoot even when their opponents are marking, offensive strategy attempts to get a free player

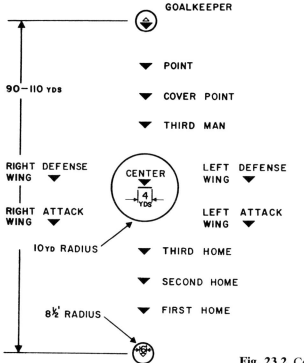

Fig. 23.2 Center draw.

advancing the ball. If there is a free attack, the defense must interchange their positions so as to pick up the free player.

REFERENCES

Boyd, M. 1971. *Lacrosse, playing and coaching.* (Rev. ed.) London: Nicholas Kay.

Delano, A. L. 1970. *Lacrosse for girls and women.* Dubuque: Wm. C. Brown.

DGWS. *Field hockey—lacrosse guide.* Washington, D.C.: AAHPER. Published every two years.

Lewis, B. J. 1970. *Play lacrosse the easy way.* London: Candium.

Mushier, C. L. 1973. *Team sports for girls and women.* Dubuque: Wm. C. Brown.

Poindexter, H. B., and C. L. Mushier, 1973. *Coaching competitive team sports for girls and women.* Philadelphia: W. B. Saunders.

Men's Lacrosse

Al Pisano

HISTORY

The game of lacrosse was originated by the North American Indians. It began as a ceremonial contest between different tribes with the outcome often having a significant effect on tribal policy. As a "war game" it was often used to settle major conflicts and establish tribal boundaries.

The Indians played this violent and skillful game over a limitless area, and at times each team consisted of a thousand or more young braves. The first stick used was not more than a yard long and had a circular laced head of about three inches in diameter. The ball was about the size of a golf ball, constructed of leather stuffed with hair.

Each tribe had its own name for the sport. The Iroquois called it Tehontshikaheks, but the name most frequently used in reference to the historical Indian game is Baggataway, from the Ojibwa dialect. The sport took on its present title when the first French explorers in North America saw the bloody contest and noted that the stick used resembled a bishop's cross, "La Crozier." In recent times, the name has been simplified to lacrosse.

White men first started playing the game in Canada, where rules were developed which made lacrosse more organized and less brutal. Interest in the game spread rapidly to England and the United States. Several clubs were established throughout the East and Midwest but the most vigorous growth occurred in the Baltimore area and parts of New York State and New England.

With the advent of intercollegiate lacrosse programs, the game took its greatest strides in development. Harvard, Yale, and Princeton played the first championship games in the late 1800s. As other colleges began to field teams, leagues and conferences were formed. In 1926, the United States Intercollegiate Lacrosse Association was established and, in conjunction with the NCAA, is now the governing body of the sport in this country.

With the more recent expansion of lacrosse into the interscholastic programs, the United States Lacrosse Coaches Association was organized. This group includes all those with interest in the game and has been particularly active in its promotion.

The most significant event in the present-day development of lacrosse was the establishment by the NCAA of an Eight Team National Championship Tournament. This tournament, the first of which was held at the close of the season in 1971, has had a tremendous impact on the recognition of lacrosse as a national sport.

THE GAME

A game of lacrosse is played by two teams consisting of ten players each; three attackmen, three midfielders, three defensemen, and a goalkeeper. It is played on a rectangular field with a goal at each end.

The purpose of each team is to score by causing the ball to enter the goal of its opponent and to prevent the other team from gaining possession of the ball and scoring. When the ball is in play, it may be carried, thrown, batted with the crosse, rolled or kicked in any direction, but may not be touched by the hands except by the goalkeeper subject to the restrictions laid down by the official rules.

The regulation playing time of a lacrosse game is 60 minutes, divided into four periods of 15 minutes each; if at the end of regulation time the score is tied, play continues for two four-minute overtime periods. If the score is still tied at the end of the second overtime period, sudden-death play begins, and the game ends upon the scoring of the next goal.

Lacrosse is very similar in strategy to the team games of basketball, hockey, and soccer. The ball moves up and down the field with each team making rapid transitions between offense and defense. The running and bodily contact make it very physical, and although this aspect may vary in degree with styles of play, it is an essential phase of the game. A high level of teamwork is necessary on both offense and defense and the coordination of ball and player movement is essential for success in either area.

Stickhandling ability is the unique aspect of the game. Individual stickwork is often the "great equalizer" and enables the smaller player to compete on equal terms with a larger and stronger opponent. The ball-control skills of stick protection, passing, catching, scooping, dodging, and shooting all enable a player to contribute to his team's offensive success. The basic defensive skills of footwork, body position, stickchecking, and body checking provide the foundation for sound team defense.

Because the offside rule designates the number of players which each team must have in the offensive and defensive halves of the field at all times, the game is limited to a six-man offense and a seven-man defense (including goalkeeper). On offense, the individual skills are used in various combinations in order to execute dodging, cutting, and passing patterns that will result in an effective shot on the goal.

The six players in the defensive unit cover their men in a manner very similar to defensive players in basketball. When an offensive player is in possession of the ball, the defensive man uses his stick and body in such a way as to prevent a dodge, a pass, or an effective shot. He attempts to dislodge the ball from his opponent's stick by striking (checking) it with his stick. When the defensive player's man is not in possession of the ball, he drops off and plays in a position that will enable him to help his defensive teammates or return to his man if the ball is passed to him.

Along with the two major parts of the game, team offense and team defense, there are several other integral parts of the total team strategy. These include: the face-off at the start of each period and after each score, a fast-break offense and defense, a clearing pattern to move the ball out of the defensive half of the field, a riding system that prevents the opposition from clearing the ball out of their defensive zone, an extra-man offense and an extra-man defense to be used when one or more men are out of the game in a penalty situation, and the play of the goalkeeper, which in some aspects is different from the responsibilities of the other nine players on the field.

EQUIPMENT

The general equipment used in a game of lacrosse includes: (1) a pair of goals, each consisting of two vertical posts six feet apart attached to a rigid top crossbar six feet from the ground, (2) a set of two pyramid-shaped cord nets, each attached to a goal and fastened on the ground to a point seven feet in back of the goal line, and (3) a hard rubber ball of white or orange color with a circumference of eight inches and a weight of five ounces which, when dropped from a height of six feet upon a hardwood floor, must bounce between 43 and 51 inches.

The personal equipment used by a player in a lacrosse game includes: (1) a lacrosse stick, which varies in size by position. The conventional model was historically constructed of wood with a cord, rawhide, or catgut pocket stringing. In recent years, the wood stick has given way to a more modern version which has a molded plastic head, a nylon mesh pocket, and a lightweight aluminum handle, (2) a protective headgear with a face mask and attached chin pad, (3) a pair of padded gloves similar to those used in ice hockey, (4) a pair of lacrosse arm pads, designed to protect the forearms, elbows, and upper arms, (5) a pair of lightweight shoulder pads also similar to those used in ice hockey, and (6) a football-style jersey, basketball-style shorts, and cleated or molded-sole shoes.

The goalkeeper uses equipment specific to his position. It consists of: (1) a stick with a larger head which can measure up to twelve inches in width, (2) a chest protector similar to, but smaller than, that used by a baseball catcher, (3) a headgear equipped with a longer, more protective face mask, (4) elbow pads, and (5) warmups or sweat pants.

PLAYING RULES

The official rules of lacrosse are governed by the United States Intercollegiate Lacrosse Association and the United States Lacrosse Coaches Association in conjunction with the National Collegiate Athletic Association. The following are basic playing rules as extracted from the Official, Collegiate-Scholastic Lacrosse Guide published annually by the NCAA.

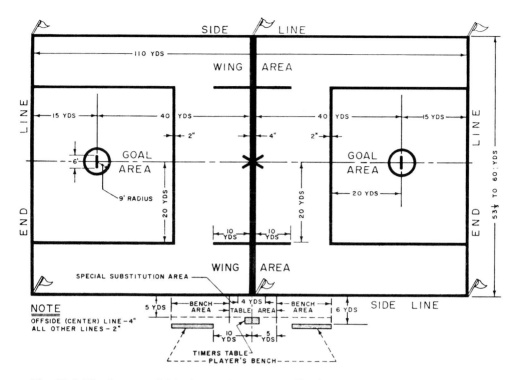

Fig. 23.3 The lacrosse field of play. From the *Official Lacrosse Guide* 1975.

The playing field. The lacrosse playing field is a rectangular field, 110 yards long and 53⅓–60 yards wide. The goals are centered 80 yards apart and 15 yards from each end line. The center line is marked through the center of the field perpendicular to the sidelines (Figure 23.3).

Teams and substitutions. Ten players make up a full team and they are designated as; goalkeeper (1), close defense (3), midfield (3), and close attack (3). There is no limit to the number of substitutes a team may have for each position. Substitutions may be made when play has been suspended by the officials, for a man in the penalty box, or from a special substitution area when the ball is in play.

Officials. The game is controlled by two officials, a referee and an umpire.

Length of game: The regulation playing time of a lacrosse game is 60 minutes, divided into four periods of 15 minutes each.

Face-off. Play starts at the beginning of each period and after each goal by two players facing-the-ball at the center of the field. When the ball is being faced at center, each team must confine the goalkeeper and three other players in the defense goal area, three players in the attack goal area, and one player in each of the wing areas. When the whistle sounds to start play, the wing area players are released but the goal area players must remain confined until possession is obtained, the ball goes out of bounds, or the ball crosses either goal area line.

Loose ball–out of bounds. When a loose ball goes out of bounds, the ball is awarded to a player on the team opposite to that of the player who last touched it. However, when a loose ball goes out of bounds as a result of a shot or deflected shot at the goal, it is awarded to the team which had one of its players nearest to the ball when it went out of bounds.

Goal scored. A goal is scored when a loose ball passes completely through the imaginary plane formed by the rear edges of the goal line, the goalposts, and the crossbar. A goal counts one point.

Offside. A team is considered offside when it has fewer than three men in its attack half of the field or fewer than four men in its defensive half of the field.

Goalkeeper privileges. Within his own goal crease area, the designated goalkeeper may stop or block the ball in any manner with his stick or body and he or any member of his team may receive a pass while in the crease. No opposing player can interfere with the goalkeeper while he is within the crease area and any player in possession of the ball cannot remain in the crease for longer than four seconds.

Personal fouls. Personal fouls include: body checking from the rear, swinging the stick with deliberate viciousness, tripping, unnecessary roughness, unsportsmanlike conduct, and the use of an illegal stick. The penalty for a personal foul is suspension from the game for one to three minutes depending on the severity of the violation.

Expulsion fouls. The act of deliberately striking anyone associated with the game: player, coach, or official, with the hand, stick, ball, or otherwise, is an expulsion foul. A player is also expelled from the game if and when he commits his fifth personal foul. The expulsion penalty is suspension for the remainder of the game.

Technical fouls. Technical fouls are those of the less serious kind in the game. They include: interference, illegal screening, holding, pushing, touching the ball with the hand, withholding the ball from play, illegal substitution, illegal procedure, stalling, and offsides. The penalty for a technical foul is suspension for 30 seconds, if the offending team is not in possession of the ball, or loss-of-ball, if the offending team has possession.

Slow whistle technique. The slow whistle technique is an aspect of penalty enforcement in a lacrosse game that is unique. If a defensive player commits a foul against an offensive player who has possession of the ball and is in the offensive half of the field, the official drops a red signal flag and withholds his whistle until the scoring play has been completed.

OFFENSIVE FUNDAMENTALS

Holding the stick. When a player begins to learn to "handle" a stick, he must start out with the proper grip. If he is a right-hander, he holds the handle of the stick parallel to the ground with the left hand at the butt-end and the palm facing down. The right hand is placed a comfortable, shoulder-width distance from the left with the palm facing up. The stick should always be held in a relaxed fashion avoiding a rigid or clutching type grip that will impede fluid stickwork.

Cradling. Once the ball is placed in the pocket of the stick, the player must use what is termed a "cradling" motion to maintain possession while he is moving and attempting to keep the ball in a position that will enable him to perform the necessary stick skills. In bringing the stick to the proper cradling position, the right elbow is flexed so that the right hand is elevated to a position about six inches in front of the right shoulder. At the same time, the left elbow is also flexed and the left hand moves to a position at the waistline. At this point, the grip of the right hand changes and the handle of the stick rests in a diagonal position across the palm with the fingers held in a fashion very similar to that used when gripping a tennis racket or golf club. From this position, the cradling motion is accomplished by a partial extension-flexion of the right elbow and a curling type flexion-extension of the right wrist. The left hand maintains a somewhat stationary position at the belt line and the left wrist flexes and extends in conjunction with the movement of the right arm. This basic arm and wrist motion causes the head of the stick to rock in an arc-shaped path from side to front and employs the physical laws of centripetal and centrifugal force, keeping the ball in a stationary position in the pocket of the stick.

Stick protection. Once the proper cradling motion is accomplished and the player is able to control the ball, he must then learn to protect the stick from an opponent's check. With practice, the player will learn to adjust his cradling position and use his head and body to "hide" the stick from his defensive opponent. During play, stick protection is accomplished not only by effective

Fig. 23.4 Holding the stick while running. Courtesy of *JOPER*.

cradling and use of the body but also through constant movement by the offensive player.

Throwing. In teaching a beginner the proper throwing motion, it should be pointed out that the body position and movements are very similar to those used in throwing a baseball. For a right-handed player, the left side is turned toward the target and the left foot steps in that direction as the right hand begins the throwing action.

In preparation for throwing with the stick, the ball should be placed in the pocket with the right hand in a position slightly behind the right shoulder and the left hand in front of the abdomen. The throw is accomplished by pushing the right hand forward toward the target as the left hand pulls slightly and guides the butt-end of the stick to a position under the upper part of the right arm. The body is used by shifting the weight from the right side to the left as the step with the left foot is taken.

As the player improves in stickwork skills, he will learn to throw the ball from various positions and in different ways. To be an accomplished passer, one must throw with both the right and left hand and master the overhead, side arm, underhand, and backhand passes.

Catching. Catching is not a difficult lacrosse skill to learn but does involve a degree of eye-hand coordination and a sense of being able to "feel" the ball enter the pocket of the stick. There are two basic ways to catch the lacrosse ball. The first is by opening the head of the stick to the ball as it approaches and then giving with the impact as it enters the pocket. The second is to open the head of the stick in the same way, but then use a short, quick cradling motion as the ball enters the pocket. In using either of these methods, the player should immediately protect his stick and begin his cradle as soon as the catch is made.

Scooping. Picking the loose ball up off the ground is a very essential fundamental of the game of lacrosse. Most successful coaches spend a great portion of the fundamental drill period in each practice session working on various scooping drills. In many lacrosse games, the ball spends more time on the ground than it does in a team's possession, so the players with superior scooping ability give their team a decided advantage.

In order to effectively pick a loose ball up off the ground, the player should hold the stick in the normal manner with the right hand closer to the throat for better control. As he approaches the ball, the player flexes his knees and bends at the waist with the stick held to the side of his body and nearly parallel to the ground. He then places the top edge of the head of the stick on the ground about two inches in front of the ball and while running through it, he scoops up the ball with a shovel-like motion. As the player picks the ball off the ground, he should immediately begin his cradling motion and bring the stick to a protected position.

Eventually, the player must learn to scoop with either hand and use his body to ward off an opponent challenging him for possession of the loose ball.

Dodging. A dodge is a technique with which a player in possession of the ball outmaneuvers or evades an opponent in order to protect the ball, move it up the field, or create a scoring opportunity. It is an essential offensive skill that must be learned and practiced by all members of the team.

There are four basic dodges: the change of pace, the change of direction, the face dodge, and the roll dodge.

The *change-of-pace dodge* is executed by drawing the defensive player away from the goal, normally to one side of the field, starting to run at half speed and then by using a quick change of pace, running by him. This dodge is often used by midfielders in the common "sweep play" from out front.

The *change-of-direction dodge* is similar to the change-of-pace dodge but is used to take advantage of a player's quickness rather than speed. In this move, the defensive player is drawn to a position away from the goal where the offensive man has the option to move either way and still have a shooting angle on the goal. He then drives the defender one way, changes direction quickly, and accelerates in the opposite direction for a shot or pass.

The *face dodge* is best used against a defensive player who is moving at the man with the ball and is committing his stick in an attempt to check the stick of the offensive player. The dodge is executed by faking a shot or pass over the shoulder of the defensive man and quickly crossing the stick from the right side to the left, while at the same time rolling the shoulder and stepping across with the right foot. When executed properly, the offensive man eludes the defender, decreases his distance to the opponent's goal, and is in a position to pass or shoot.

The *roll dodge* can be used from almost any position and is executed by driving hard on the defensive opponent in one direction in an attempt to get him to overcommit his body and stick. Once this is accomplished, the offensive player plants his inside foot and pivots quickly in the opposite direction forcing his free leg toward the goal. As the roll is being executed, the offensive player must remember to protect his stick until he gets into a position for a shot or pass.

Shooting. Effective shooting skill is the refinement of the passing technique with added emphasis on accuracy, power, and quickness of release. This fundamental is often overlooked by coaches and many take for granted the player's shooting ability, considering it a natural skill derived from passing. The basics of shooting must be taught and drilled as a stickwork fundamental.

For the beginner, accuracy should be the number one concern. The *three-quarter arm bounce shot* is the most natural and the easiest to control. The player should start out by using this shot in various stationary positions from 15 to 20 yards in front of the goal. When a high degree of consistency is achieved from a stationary position, he should then work on the same shot while running across the face of the goal at a similar distance. As the player becomes more skilled in all areas of stickwork, he will then be capable of adjusting his shooting technique. Although accuracy must still be the main concern, the player should learn to shoot hard, high and low on the goal, from various positions on the field, and with either hand.

Along with the physical skills involved, the strategy of shooting plays an important part in scoring ability. The good shooter learns to consider the following factors and adjusts his shots accordingly: (1) the field conditions, (2) his shooting angle on the goal, and (3) the goalie's position and weakness. He also develops the ability to shoot around the goalie when in close and use a teammate's screen on the goalie when shooting from the outside.

DEFENSIVE FUNDAMENTALS

Stance and body position. When introducing defensive fundamentals to the beginning player, the first step must be to have the player learn to assume the proper stance and align himself with his opponent in such a manner that will enable him to react, move, and adjust to the maneuvers of the offensive man.

In the *basic defensive stance,* the feet are spread a comfortable distance, slightly less than shoulder-width apart. The knees are flexed to an angle of about 120° and the back is straight. The body weight is distributed equally on both feet. The defensive player stands facing his opponent at a stick's length distance, slightly favoring his stick side. He grips his own stick in the normal way and holds it in an upright manner so the head of it is in line with that of his opponent's. The defensive player should not change hands if his opponent switches his stick from right to left, but instead, simply draw the top hand toward him and pass the head of the stick across his body to the opposite side, maintaining a stick-on-stick position. He should keep both hands in front of his body to facilitate a fluid movement of the stick on any change of direction.

Footwork. The ability to move the feet quickly is probably the single most important factor in defensive ability. There are three basic types of foot movement: the shuffle, running hip-to-hip, and the drop-step.

The *shuffle* is used when the offensive player is moving at a slow to moderate speed attempting to feed or to set up the defensive man for a dodge. In executing the shuffle, the defensive player assumes a balanced stance in a stick-on-stick position. As the offensive player starts to move, the defensive man takes a quick lateral step with the lead foot in the same direction. The trailing foot follows quickly along the same line as the defender keeps his shoulders and hips parallel to the offensive player's path. He continues this shuffling action and attempts to stay slightly ahead of his opponent as he moves.

At times, the offensive player will accelerate to a full running pace and make it physically impossible for the defender to keep up with him using the shuffle. At this point, the defender must turn his hips and shoulders and run *hip-to-hip* while maintaining the stick-on-stick position. Once the offensive man slows to a moderate pace, the defender can return to the shuffle.

Changing direction while shuffling is not difficult. It involves a quick reaction and a planting of the lead foot to drive off it and start the shuffle in the opposite direction. Since changing direction when running hip-to-hip involves a complete 180° turn of the shoulders and hips, it necessitates not only a quick reaction but a coordinated *drop-step*. The drop-step is accomplished by planting the outside foot and pivoting back to the inside on a turn slightly greater than 180°. This enables the defender to give ground on the opponent's change of direction and resume the hip-to-hip running in the opposite direction.

Stick checks. For the defensive player to be effective, he must use his stick as a tool to prevent the opponent from feeding, dodging, or shooting. With practice and experience, he will also develop the ability to take the ball away from his opponent and add to his team's offensive opportunities. To accomplish these goals, each player must begin by learning the basic stick checks: the poke, the chop, the slap, and the block.

The *poke check* is executed by the defender dropping the handle of his stick to a horizontal position, with its head in the vicinity of the offensive player's bottom hand. He then uses a cue-stick type motion, allowing the handle of his stick to slide through the top hand as he propels it with the bottom hand, and thrusts its head at the butt-end or handle of his opponent's stick.

The initial stick position for the *chop check* is the same as is used for the poke. The chop is executed by using the top hand to draw the head of the stick on a horizontal plane away from the opponent to about a 12-inch distance. A quick hard return of the head attempting to strike the handle of the crosse is used in an effort to dislodge the ball from the stick.

In using the *slap check* the defensive player uses the top hand to lift the head of the stick and, as the name implies, slap down on his opponent's butt hand. This check is particularly effective against a feeder.

The *block check* is used in an attempt to block the opponent's pass or shot. Anticipating the throwing motion, the defender tries to match the face of the offensive player's stick with his own.

In using any of these basic checks, the defensive player must always concentrate on maintaining a balanced position and avoid lunging or stepping at his opponent.

THE FACE-OFF

The *face-off* or *center draw* is the method by which the ball is put into play at the beginning of each period and after each score. The two opposing players who face are normally midfielders. Each stands on the same side of the centerline as the goal his team is defending. Holding their sticks with right hands at the throat and left hands at the butt end, the players place them on the ground along the centerline with the backside of the heads facing one another and the walls resting on the ground approximately one inch apart. Both hands must remain in contact with the ground until the whistle sounds to start play.

In assuming the proper body position, the facing players place their feet a little less than shoulder-width apart with the right foot as close to the right hand as possible and the left foot about ten inches from the handle of the stick. The knees and back are bent so the body is in a crouched position. Each player leans to the head of his stick with his weight up on the balls of his feet.

The ball is placed between, in the center, and resting on the reverse surfaces of the walls of each stick. At this time, the players focus their attention on the ball and watch it throughout the face-off. Once the official sounds his whistle to start play, there are various maneuvers the face-off players may use in an attempt to gain possession of the ball, the most basic being the *step-clamp*.

In executing the step-clamp, the player steps with the right foot toward the ball while driving off the left leg. Simultaneously, he clamps the head of his stick over the ball by rotating it downward, lifting his left hand, and moving the butt-end of his stick toward his body. In making this move the player must stay low and move quickly and aggressively. As these initial moves are made, he must concentrate on getting the center of his body over the ball and pivoting on his right foot as he rotates back into his opponent. From this position, he can either scoop the ball up immediately or push it out with his stick or foot to a more advantageous location.

FAST BREAK (4 against 3)

When a player gains possession of the ball in his defensive half of the field and breaks into the offensive zone ahead of any of his opponents, he establishes a 4 against 3 fast break. In order to take advantage of the extra man in this situation, the three close attackmen must move to an established formation as the break-man moves toward the attack goal area.

A basic fast-break setup is the conventional right-handed box formation. To execute this pattern, the three attackmen drop toward the face of the goal as soon as they see the break begin to develop. The two wing attackmen position themselves on either side of the goal even with its face and about five to seven yards out. The point attackman takes a position to the left side of the approaching break-man and about three yards inside the attack goal area at a slightly greater distance to the side of the goal than the left wing attackman. As the break-man approaches, he runs to the same relative position as the point attackman on the opposite side. In doing this, he completes the box formation (Fig. 23.5).

In executing the play options, the break-man continues carrying the ball in toward the goal until a defender attempts to play him. Once this occurs, he passes off to the point attackman and delays until the next pass is made. When the point attackman receives the ball from the break-man, he reacts to the slide of the remaining two defenders and executes one of the following

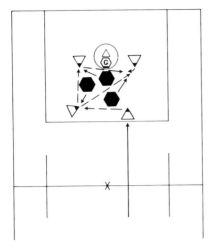

Fig. 23.5 The fast-break box formation.

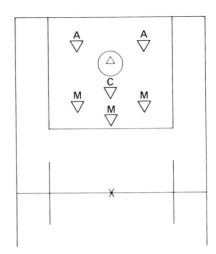

Fig. 23.6 The 2–1–3 offensive formation.

options: (1) he passes to the wing attackman on the same side, (2) he throws across the cage to the wing attackman on the opposite side, (3) he makes a return pass to the break-man, or (4) he evades the defender sliding to him and shoots at the goal.

TEAM OFFENSE

Once a team brings the ball into its offensive zone and an all-even situation is established, it is essential to set up some type of offensive pattern. Using a predetermined formation, the offensive players can execute dodging and feeding plays that will result in effective shots on goal.

The most common offensive formation in use is the 2–1–3. This formation places two attackmen behind the goal, one attackman in front of the crease, and three midfielders in a semicircle out in front of the goal (Fig. 23.6).

In using this formation, specific responsibilities are assigned to the players in each position. The wing attackmen behind the cage can dodge and shoot individually, work two-man plays, feed the crease attackman or a cutting midfielder, and back up the end line on shots from out front. The crease attackman makes cuts to the man with the ball for a feed, sets a pick for cutters, screens the goalie on outside shots, and attempts to recover or bat loose balls into the goal. The three midfielders make single cuts to the ball for a feed, work dodges, sweeps, or two and three man plays for shots, and back up the midfield area to recover stray feeds from attackman behind the goal.

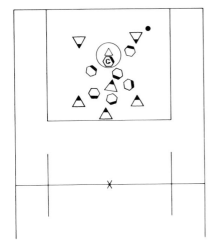 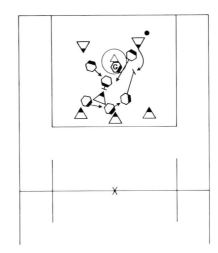

Fig. 23.7 Defensive alignment against a 2–1–3.

Fig. 23.8 The defensive slide.

Along with the individual player responsibilities of any formation, unit plays can be developed to add to a team's offensive effectiveness.

TEAM DEFENSE

There are several types of team defense, the most common being the *helping man-to-man*. As the name implies, this is a man-on-man system with zone tendencies. The foundation of the helping man-to-man defense is based on sound individual play, communication, and team reaction.

In this defensive system, the man playing on the ball uses an aggressive man-on-man technique. The other defensive players in the perimeter play off their men in a position that will enable them to help out if the man playing the ball gets beaten by a dodge or a drive to the goal. In assuming an offball position, each player turns his body so that he can see his man and the man with the ball at all times. He must also be certain that he can get back to his man at the same time that a pass could reach him (Fig. 23.7).

Constant communication is essential. The goalkeeper must keep the man playing the ball informed of his position by calling to him, while the adjacent defenders let him know that they have him "backed up" on either side.

If the defender playing the ball is beaten, an adjacent defender slides from his position to cover the man with the ball and the remaining defensive players adjust their positions toward the ball, leaving the farthest offensive player uncovered (Fig. 23.8).

313

CLEARING

The *clear* is used to move the ball from the defensive half of the field into the offensive half, while the opposition exerts individual or zone pressure in an attempt to regain possession. Using the goalkeeper in the clearing play gives a team a man advantage in its defensive zone. When starting to advance the ball upfield, the goalie and the three close defensemen normally work against the three riding attackmen. In establishing an effective pattern, this clearing unit attempts to isolate one riding player and take advantage of a two-on-one situation to easily move the ball into its offensive zone.

The *four-back formation* is one of the more popular clearing patterns. In executing the basic clear from this pattern, the goalkeeper starts the ball upfield and draws one of the attackmen to him. He then passes to the open defenseman on the overloaded side of the field. This defenseman then draws the next rider and passes the ball to the outside defenseman who in turn runs the ball into the offensive zone (Fig. 23.9).

Because the opponents may attempt to use various maneuvers to prevent a successful clear, the clearing players must always be prepared to make adjustments to the basic clearing play. These adjustments may include: (1) passing the ball directly upfield to an uncovered midfielder or attackman, (2) running the ball over the center line, or (3) redirecting the ball back to the goalkeeper and up the weak side of the field.

RIDING

The *ride* is the means by which a team attempts to prevent the opponent from successfully moving the ball from its defensive half of the field into its offensive zone. If the riding team can break the clear and recover the ball quickly, it can often take advantage of the clearing players' spread positions and get a close-in shot on goal.

The most basic and safest type of ride is one in which the three attackmen use a rotation or zone principle to cover the goalkeeper and the three clearing defensemen, while the riding midfielders and defensemen play their men, man-for-man. The objective of this type of ride is to force the four clearing players to make several passes, increasing their chances of throwing the ball away. The clearers must also be concerned about a violation of the offside rule as they approach the centerline and indecision at that point may enable the riders to pressure them into losing the ball (Fig. 23.10).

EXTRA-MAN OFFENSE

An extra-man offensive situation in lacrosse is similar to the power play in ice hockey. It occurs when a team is in violation of the rules and a penalty is enforced by the official. The penalty time can range from 30 seconds to three

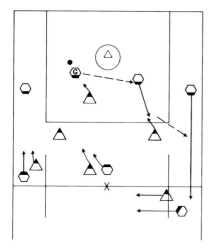

Fig. 23.9 The basic four-back clear.

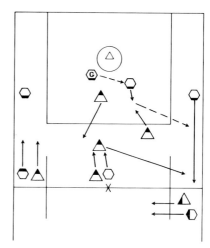

Fig. 23.10 The attack rotation ride.

minutes, depending on the severity of the infraction. A penalty situation may involve the suspension from the game of one or more players.

In the most common penalty situation, the offensive team has a one-man advantage and a six-on-five scoring opportunity. The strategy employed in developing an effective extra-man play is to make every man in the unit a potential scorer and have the ball passed more rapidly than the five defenders can move to cover it.

A popular extra-man offensive formation is the 1–3–2. In this pattern, one player is positioned behind the goal to feed, back up the goal on shots from out front, and sneak around the crease for a feed from one of his team-mates. The crease attackman plays his normal position assuming his crease responsibilities. Two players position themselves in the wing areas, even with the crease attackman and about seven yards out to each side of the goal. The remaining two players take up positions at the midfield 15–18 yards out and slightly inside the wingmen (Fig. 23.11).

In using the 1–3–2 formation, the ball is passed around the perimeter rapidly with each player observing the movement of the defensive unit. Passes may be made through seams in the defense, over the top, or to a teammate cutting into an open area away from the ball. As each player receives a pass, he looks for an opportunity to shoot before he passes the ball on to a team-mate.

EXTRA-MAN DEFENSE

In order to combat the opponents' extra-man offensive play, a team must have an efficient *extra-man defense*. There are several types of systems in use and the most basic is the five-point zone.

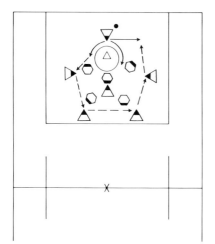

Fig. 23.11 The 1–3–2 extra-man offense.

As the name implies, the *five-point zone defense* places five defenders in specific zones in front of the goal. The areas covered are those most vulnerable to scoring opportunities and include: the area in front of the crease, the wing areas on either side of the goal, and the two large midfield areas. These zones overlap one another and each player favors the area of his zone closest to the ball. The defenders play with their sticks in a raised position while facing the ball. They attempt to knock down passes, block shots, and gang check any offensive player attempting to receive a feed in the crease area (Figs. 23.12 and 23.13).

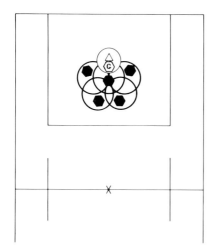

Fig. 23.12 Extra-man defensive zones.

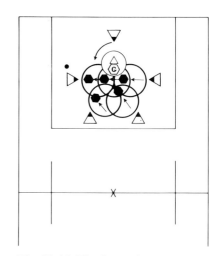

Fig. 23.13 The five-point zone.

THE GOALKEEPER

The goalkeeper is the defensive unit's key player. He is the "last line of defense" and his responsibilities include: (1) stopping the ball from entering the goal, (2) directing and controlling his teammates when the ball enters their defensive area, and (3) exercising leadership in the clearing and riding situations.

The characteristics of a good goalkeeper are agility, courage, mental alertness, quickness of reaction, stickwork, and speed. Size is also a valuable asset.

Body position. In assuming the proper stance, the goalie spreads his feet to about shoulder width. His knees are flexed with his weight distributed equally upon both feet. His body is bent slightly at the waist. His eyes must be on the ball at all times. When the player with the ball is out in front of the cage, the goalie operates on a curved path that extends from one goal upright to the other. As the ball moves, the goalie follows this path with short shuffling steps keeping himself in direct line with the ball and the center of the goal. When the ball is even with the plane of the goalface, the goalie is tight on the corresponding upright. When it is directly out front, the goalie is positioned at the apex of the arc (Fig. 23.14). The purpose of having the goalkeeper move on this arc-shaped path is to cut down on the offensive player's shooting angle and minimize the open areas of the goal.

With the ball in a position behind the cage, the goalkeeper turns, favoring the ball side. He then moves on a line parallel to the goal plane, as the ball changes position behind (Fig. 23.15). If the player with the ball moves around the crease and toward the front of the goal, the goalie must move tight to the corresponding upright and anticipate following the arc if the ball con-

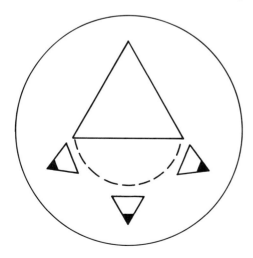

Fig. 23.14 Goalie position when the ball is in front of the goal.

Fig. 23.15 Goalie position when the ball is behind the goal.

tinues out front. If a pass is made from behind the cage to the front, the goalie turns with the flight of the ball, never taking his eyes off it, and readjusts his position accordingly.

Stick position. If the ball is out 15 or more yards in front of the goal, the goalie should carry his stick at a waist-high position. His hands should be ten to twelve inches apart with his elbows in front of his body. This position enables him to move his stick freely in a plane about six inches in front of his body. As the ball approaches the goal, the goalie gradually raises the stick to a position in front of and alongside his head to protect against high shots.

When the player with the ball is behind the cage in a feeding position, the goalie holds his stick higher than usual in an attempt to knock down or intercept passes. As a feed is made or as the attackman moves around the goal, the stick is drawn down to the normal position alongside the head.

Playing the shot. When playing a high shot, the goalie must step at the ball with the closest foot. At the same time, he must concentrate on getting his body directly behind the ball and keeping the face of his stick open as he quickly moves it into position for the stop.

In recovering a bounce shot, he must also step into the oncoming ball. As he takes this step and leads with his body, he simultaneously follows with his stick in a sweeping motion opening its head to the shot and collecting the ball with an inverted cradling action.

If the goalie's vision is screened by an offensive opponent on the crease, he should step slightly to the side of the screen in order to see the ball. When it is shot, he should then step immediately toward the feet of the screening player, even though he cannot see the ball.

Communication. The goalie is the defensive quarterback and must keep his defenders informed of the position of the ball and constantly remind them of their responsibilities. He uses the following vocabulary:

- ☐ "The ball is left front, center front, right behind, etc."
- ☐ "Pick-up, who's got the ball!"
- ☐ "Who's got him backed right-left!"
- ☐ "Drop in—you're out too far!"
- ☐ "Square up!" (When defender on the ball is not in line with the ball and goal.)
- ☐ "Hold!" (Defender is close enough—don't let him penetrate any farther with the ball.)
- ☐ "Check!" (Check all sticks on the crease, a feed has been made.)
- ☐ "Slide!" (A defender has been beaten on a dodge, the entire defense must shift into the ball.)

TERMINOLOGY

All even The situation where both teams are at full strength, no players are in the penalty box.

Assist A pass from one player to his teammate who in turn scores without having to dodge or evade an opponent.

Attack A unit of three players charged with controlling the offense, and generally restricted to the offensive half of the field.

Backing up The situation where a defensive player is in a position to help out a teammate who is playing the man with the ball.

Body check The use of a legal body block on an opponent in possession of the ball or within five yards of a free ball.

Centerline An extra heavy (2 in.) white line marked through the center of the field perpendicular to the sidelines.

Check To strike an opponent's stick in order to dislodge the ball, or to prevent his passing, shooting, or receiving the ball.

Clear A pattern used by a team in moving the ball from their defensive half of the field to their offensive half of the field.

Crease A circle marked around the goal with a radius of nine feet.

Crosse-check An illegal stickcheck, when a player thrusts that part of the handle of his stick held between the hands at his opponent.

Defense A unit of three players charged with covering the three opposing attackmen, and generally restricted to the defensive half of the field.

Dodge A maneuver used by a player to evade his opponent and maintain control of the ball.

End line The out-of-bounds line at each end of the field.

Evener A player returning to the field from the penalty box after penalty time has elapsed and the sides become all even.

Extra-man defense A system used to prevent the opponents from scoring when a defensive player is out of the game on a penalty.

Extra-man offense A pattern used by an offensive unit in attempting to score when the opponents have one or more men out of the game on a penalty.

Face-off The center draw. The means by which the ball is put into play before each period and after each score.

Fast break The situation where a player gains possession of the ball and breaks ahead of the opposition into the offensive area of the field creating a one or more man advantage.

Feeder A player who makes a pass to a teammate in position to score.

Flip off The situation where an offensive player, who is being double-teamed as he moves into position for a shot, quickly passes off to the adjacent teammate who was left unguarded.

Goal A goal is scored when a loose ball passes from the front, completely through the imaginary plane formed by the rear edges of the goal line and the goalposts.

Goal areas Areas marked at each end of the field, centered on the goals, 40 yards in width and 35 yards from the end lines.

Goalie The designated player who assumes the position in front of the goal and inside the crease attempting to prevent shots from entering the goal.

Midfield A unit of three players who move up and down the entire field and play both offense and defense.

Offsides A violation of the rules when a team has less than three players in the defensive half of the field.

Penalty box Two seats for each team on each side of the timer's table.

Personal fouls Rules' violations: illegal body checking, slashing, crosse-checking, tripping, unnecessary roughness, unsportsmanlike conduct or the use of an illegal stick. Penalty time from one to three minutes.

Pick A maneuver in which an offensive player positions himself motionless in the path of a defensive player to prevent him from staying with his man on a cut or a drive for the goal.

Ride A team maneuver used to prevent the opposition from moving the ball out of their defensive half of the field.

Save The goalie stopping or deflecting with any part of his body or stick a ball which, if it had not been stopped or deflected, would have resulted in a score.

Screening A maneuver by the offensive players to obstruct the goalie's vision when a shot is taken.

Shot The throwing of the ball toward the goal in an attempt to score.

Slash The action of a player swinging his stick at an opponent's with deliberate viciousness or reckless abandon. An illegal check.

Stalling An illegal team maneuver designed to hold the ball in the offensive or defensive half of the field to protect a lead.

Switch A two-man defensive maneuver used when one defensive player runs into an offensive pick and both men are forced into switching offensive opponents.

Technical foul Any violation of the Official Rules that is not specifically defined as a personal or expulsion foul. The penalty is either a 30-second suspension or loss of possession of the ball.

Wing areas Designated areas between the sidelines and two parallel lines, 10 yards in length which are 20 yards from the center of the field and bisecting the centerline.

REFERENCES

Evans, G. H., III, and R. E. Anderson 1966. *Lacrosse fundamentals.* New York: A. S. Barnes.

Morrill, W. K. 1951. *Lacrosse.* New York: A. S. Barnes.

National Collegiate Athletic Association. *The official lacrosse guide.* Shawnee Mission, Kan.: NCAA Publishing Service. Published periodically.

Stanwick, T. 1940. *Lacrosse.* New York: A. S. Barnes.

Weyand, A. M., and M. R. Roberts 1965. *The lacrosse story.* Baltimore: H. and A. Herman.

24

The Sport of Luge

Fred Hushla

THE ORIGIN OF LUGE

Luge or "Rodel" as it is called in most European countries is a modern competitive sled racing sport, whose origins go back many years. The term "luge" is French for the word "toboggan," and primarily defines the present day sled that is used on *Naturbahns* and ice tracks.

The sport of luge originated in the mountainous regions of Europe and has spread to many other countries. Since earliest times, sleds have been used as vehicles to move materials or for transportation. In certain areas of the world they are still used as such. They were also used as recreational devices so it is only natural that competition developed between sled riders on snowy or icy hills and roads. From this probable beginning developed the sport of luge as we know it. Many of the early contests were held on natural terrain. Aside from marking out the area, the entire objective was to traverse this course as rapidly as possible. Obstacles were considered and used to test the riders' skill. Even now this type of natural track racing is popular in many areas of Europe.

Switzerland is credited with the first recorded international contest. This event occurred on February 12, 1883, on the road between Wolfgang and Klosters. Twenty-one lugers from eight nations competed on a course measuring four kilometers. The race ended with a tie between Robertson of Australia and Minsche of Switzerland with the time of nine minutes and fifteen seconds. From that first race, bobsledding, skeleton or cresta racing and luge racing or tobogganing have evolved.

MODERN LUGE

Luge racing has developed very quickly. The first riders used sleds which were similar to the present day European child's sled. At the first European luge championships held in Reichenburg, Germany in 1914, many different types of sleds were used: those with runners on their edges to make a sharp gliding surface; those with flat runners; some which were maneuvered by the rider touching the track with steel-gloved hands, and others that were steered with a 3.5 meter long stick which was used as a rudder. These last sleds were most common in Norway and Switzerland, and were used by the Norwegians until

1962 when they were ruled out of competition by the International Federation of Luge (FIL).

During the 1930s a great change came when the first flexible sled was designed and constructed. This was the beginning of successful luge sleds. Steering possibilities became as great as with the bobsled, and, since there were no mechanical parts, all steering was performed by the rider's body.

In 1954, in Athens, Greece, luge took its first important step forward when it was included in the Olympic program in place of skeleton (cresta) riding, which had been on the 1948 program. The first world luge championship took place in Oslo, Norway, in 1955 with 52 competitors from eight countries.

The year 1957 was also an important one for luge which, until then, had just been the "T" in FIBT (Fédération Internationale de Bobsledding et de Tobogganing). Its own International Federation was formed . . . Fédération Internationale de Luge de Course (FIL). This meant a great deal to the development of the sport. In 1961, again in Athens, the International Olympic Committee accepted a proposal stating that luge would be included in the Winter Olympic Program as follows: 4 men (single), 2 two-seater (men), and 3 women (single) per country. These races were included in the Olympic Games at Innsbruck, Austria, in 1964, at Grenoble, France, in 1968, and at Sapporo, Japan, in 1972 and again in Innsbruck in 1976.

Another phase in the conduct of the sport competition occurred in Innsbruck, Austria, where the 1976 Winter Olympic Games were held. For the first time the track was designed for both bobsled and luge competitions. Prior to this, both sports had separate installations.

Today, luge races involving international or national competition are conducted on artificial or refrigerated tracks. The ice track or the *Kunsteisrodelbahn* is a course built specially for sled racing. The construction lines of the bends are calculated during the summer and built up with earth, wood, reinforced cement, or stone. An artificial course consists of straight stretches and curves.

The refrigerated track or *Kunsteisrodelbahn* is an innovation. A refrigerated track has the required straight stretch and curves completely built with cement forms over piping through which cold liquid (ammonia) is pumped. This makes possible the covering of the entire track with an even layer of artificial ice. Because of this smooth surface, the lugers do not have to contend with bumps or rough areas that might impede their performance. Changing the temperature of the cold liquid makes it possible for the ice to be soft or hard. The harder the ice, the faster the speed of the luger.

Several refrigerated ice tracks are now in use. The first was built at Konigssee, Bavaria, in the late 1960s, followed by the ice course at Oberhof, East Germany, and the track constructed at Innsbruck for the 1976 Olympic Games.

Besides the sophisticated artificial or refrigerated ice track, there are many other types of courses open to the beginner as well as the expert. These are called *Naturbahns* or natural tracks. This could be any forest path, downhill course, or winter road that has been prepared for luge racing. Some of the curves can be built up with straw bales or snow. These tracks are usually prepared in consideration of terrain and other local conditions. With this type of track, competitions can be built in nearly every area that has sufficient snow.

LUGE REQUIREMENTS

To test the ability and expertise of the luger, the regulation ice course has to meet certain requirements. The course can be 1000 to 2000 meters in length, the width from 1.35 to 1.50 meters and the rate of descent between 9 and 12 percent. Various curves must be included: a left curve (a bend curving to the left), a right curve (a bend curving to the right), a hairpin curve (a bend having an outer angle of 140° to 180°), an S-curve (two bends following each other and curving in different directions), a labryinth (several bends following each other and curving in different directions) and a finish curve with an out run (upward inclined area to slow down the sled at the finish). Most tracks usually have 14 to 16 curves. A curve as related to luge has three elements:

- ☐ The entrance-passage from the straight stretch to the arc.
- ☐ The arc or curve.
- ☐ The exit-passage from the arc to the straight stretch.

Next, the sled itself (see Fig. 24.1a, b, and c) has from its basic beginning evolved into a very precise sport sled. There are three sizes of sleds, 1, 1½ and 2. These sleds vary slightly in length according to size, approximately 51″ to 59″, and have a maximum weight of 22 kilograms. A double (2-man) sled has a maximum weight of 24 kilograms. Besides these, there are 12 kilogram training sleds for juniors and some of a smaller size weighing only 8 kilograms.

The sleds are made of either wood or combinations of wood, steel, and fiberglass. The runners are of laminated wood, usually ash, and have steel runners attached to them. These steels are angled, thus having a sharp edge for a gliding surface. The grinding of the runners differs, depending on ice surface conditions. The steels can be changed from one side to the other to gain a more even surface on the snow on natural tracks. The sled is narrower at the front, about 13″, and on each runner's fore end a strap is attached, which is used for steering. The entire sled is flexible which makes it maneuverable. The sled's track width is 45 cm, the height is 20 cm, and the length 140–150 cm.

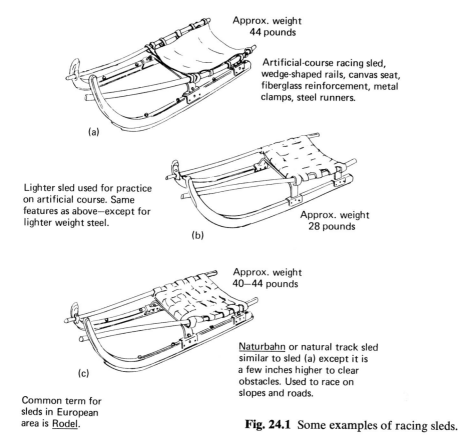

Approx. weight
44 pounds

Artificial-course racing sled, wedge-shaped rails, canvas seat, fiberglass reinforcement, metal clamps, steel runners.

(a)

Lighter sled used for practice on artificial course. Same features as above—except for lighter weight steel.

(b)

Approx. weight
28 pounds

Approx. weight
40—44 pounds

Naturbahn or natural track sled similar to sled (a) except it is a few inches higher to clear obstacles. Used to race on slopes and roads.

(c)

Common term for sleds in European area is Rodel.

Fig. 24.1 Some examples of racing sleds.

Runners are usually prepared by grinding with the aid of different implements: files, whetstone, sandpaper, steel wool, grinding paste and polishes. Waxes are used on the runners. These are similar to those used by downhill skiers.

A good deal of handwork is involved in preparing these runners. The outside edge is beveled to a ⅛″ radius for safety requirements, as the sharp edge could dig in and cause an upset while skidding. Each sled has to be customized for the individual rider. A balance point has to be determined. To do this, a sled with the luger in his competitive gear, lying in a prone position on the sled, is balanced on a broomstick handle or a similar rounded dowel. The balance point is marked. For a start the inside edge of the steel runner is kept sharp to about 6″ forward of the mark and to about 12″ behind the mark. This could vary as the luger becomes more expert. The rest of the gliding edge is beveled to about 1/16″ starting from the front of the sled and gradually tapering to a sharp edge. This is also done from the

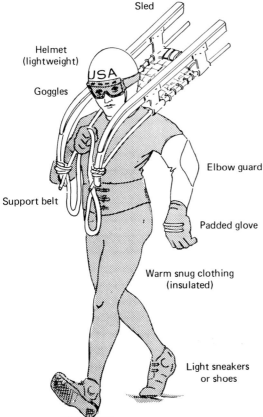

Sled

Helmet
(lightweight)

Goggles

Support belt

Elbow guard

Padded glove

Warm snug clothing
(insulated)

Light sneakers
or shoes

Fig. 24.2 The luger and his gear.

back of the sled. The sharp edge remaining has an influence on the riding efficiency of the sled. Runners have to be checked to determine if they are parallel and also for bowing in the steel runner. Usually, the preparation of a sled will involve anywhere from 4 to 8 hours. After each day's run, additional work is required to check and remove even the slightest scratch or chip—making the runner mirror smooth.

The luge rider's equipment includes, besides the sled, a tight-fitting windproof racing suit, light basketball-type shoes, kidney belt, elbow guards, goggles, back-ribbed gloves. A helmet is mandatory (see Fig. 24.2).

Having all this equipment, the rider has to develop a technique for riding the luge. Various approaches for the beginner luger are favored by different instructors. Basically, the luger lies on his back on the luge sled. One hand grasps the reins or straps attached to the runners. The other hand has a grip on the stabilizer bar. The legs should be stretched out and pressed firmly on the runners from the outside.

The rider performs three basic actions in steering the sled:

1. Lifts up the forward section of the inner runner with the strap causing the rear section of the runner to brake slightly.
2. Presses inward on the forepart of the outside runner so that it cuts into the surface.
3. Applies pressure of the shoulder on to the runner in the direction that the luger wishes to go.

Each of these actions causes the sled to turn slightly. It is the luger's option to find the right combination of these actions for each occasion.

To turn left, the right leg is pressed against the right runner and at the same time the weight of the body is applied over the left runner as the left runner's fore edge is lifted slightly with the strap. On straight stretches, air resistance is minimized by the luger's maintaining a flat profile.

Together with the training exercises, the luger should maintain a rigorous physical program to develop good stomach, neck, and leg muscles. In fact, nearly every part of the body has a direct influence on the luger's ability and expertise on the track.

Competitions in luge racing are usually covered by FIL Rules and Regulations. Before the regular final race runs are made, the registered athletes are required to make 4 or 5 systematic training runs. This involves making one run from each of several specified points of the track—starting at a lower level and finally running the full course. This is to acquaint the athletes with the ice track before the race. This also gives the jury (judges) an opportunity to determine if the luger is capable of negotiating the course safely. After these runs, the regular race events are held. Four runs are usually held, three in daylight and one under night conditions. If weather or track conditions become unfavorable, these runs can be cut down to three at the discretion of race officials at a meeting of the team leaders. Total fastest accumulated race run times determine the winner and placers in the event.

Race officials will usually allow any reasonable number of athletes from each club or organization to enter the systematic training runs. However only four men and four women from each organization can enter the regular singles race competition. For doubles (two-man) competition only two teams from each organization can usually compete in the race. During the Olympic Games each country is allowed three men and three women in the singles, and two teams in the doubles.

Officials at these competitions are assigned various tasks. The meet director, the track technician or the supervisor has to maintain vigilance over the course conditions. Three men act as a jury (judges) to observe and make decisions involving athletes and the conduct of the competition. Safety is stressed throughout and observers are stationed at various points along the course to clear it for each run.

At the completion of each run the sleds and athletes are weighed separately. Single sleds cannot exceed 22 kilograms and doubles sleds cannot be more than 24 kilograms. Overweight readings will suspend the luger from the competition. The sled runners are also checked at the start of the race with a heat sensing device. Heated runners can give faster runs. The readings must be within 3° of the registered outdoor temperature. An innovation was voted in during 1975. This involves the wearing of the weights. Since it is known that a heavier person, on most courses, has the advantage, the FIL has devised a method of shortening this advantage. A weight of 209 lbs for men and 187 lbs for women is used as a basis. Men and women over this basic weight can compete without any restrictions except for the addition of 8.8 lbs of competitive clothing. Anyone under the basic weight can add 50 percent of their weight difference, but not to exceed 22 lbs for men and 17.6 lbs for women. To this 8.8 lbs of competitive equipment can be added. Thus, body weight plus 50 percent of weight difference plus competitive clothing equals competitive weight. These weights are calculated at a weigh-in of the lugers before the race events. A calculated list is then in the hands of the judges weighing the athletes after each run.

Since the weight rule is comparatively new, there are many variations as to where to place the weights on the body. Actually, the weights should be located close to the balance center of the sled and preferably in back of the luger. However, a luger has to be conditioned to make this weight addition, as it could disturb his normal riding ability.

The rules and regulations above can be changed or simplified for local competition in various areas. Emphasis is on conducting sled races whenever and however possible. Only in this way can the sport of luge grow.

The past number of years the sport has gained impetus under the direction of the USOC (United States Olympic Committee) development programs. Anyone desiring to become involved in any phase of the sport can contact the USOC in New York City or the National AAU office in Indianapolis, Indiana, for details.

25
Quoits

Daniel L. Canada

HISTORY

As with the origin of horseshoes, the origin of quoit pitching is uncertain. It is possible that quoits, as well as horseshoes, may also trace their lineage back to the ancient Greek sport of discus throwing. Quoits, as we know it today, was very popular in England and played by nobility, as well as by commoners. The English brought the game to American shores. Although today horseshoes is more popular in the United States, there once was a time when quoits was its rival.

THE GAME

The game is played by throwing rings, or quoits, at stakes set apart in the ground. Points are scored according to accuracy.

COURT

The playing court is somewhat similar to the one used in pitching horseshoes. Two stakes are set 54' apart. The stakes extend 6" above the surface and are perpendicular to the surface. Stakes are 1" in diameter and are made of steel, wood, or hard plastic. Steel stakes are used with outdoor quoits and are driven into the level ground. When indoor quoits are used, the stakes may be supported by a one-inch wooden base.

EQUIPMENT

Outdoor quoits are iron rings. Indoor quoits are generally made of rope; however, rubber is also frequently used to make quoits. Traditional regulation outdoor iron quoits are circular in shape, flat on the bottom, and have a rounded surface on the top. The total diameter is 9" with the hole in the center being 4" in diameter. Iron quoits are also made similar in shape to rope quoits. Rope quoits are made of material ¾" in diameter with the finished product being a ring with a diameter of 6".

RULES

Either singles or doubles may be played. In doubles, the partners of a team are located opposite each other, one at each end of the court. Players remain at their respective end of the court and do not rotate in any manner. Players pitch four quoits alternately. The losing players have the option of being first for the next turn.

The game is scored in the following manner.

- ☐ One point for the closest ring
- ☐ Two points for two rings closer than any of the opponent's
- ☐ Three for a "ringer"
- ☐ Two points for a "leaner"
- ☐ Equals tie and no points are awarded

It should be noted that a player's quoits do not count if:

- ☐ One distracts one's opponent.
- ☐ One moves the rings before the inning is completed.
- ☐ One steps over the foul line when tossing the ring.

TECHNIQUE

- ☐ The quoit is held with fingers and thumb.
- ☐ The player should release the quoit slowly and follow through.
- ☐ The player should aim for the top of the stake so that when the quoit strikes it, the trailing edge will make contact about one inch down the stake.

ASSOCIATIONS

The National Horseshoe Pitchers Association of America is located at 341 Polk Street, Gary, Indiana 46402. This association was founded in 1914.

SOURCES OF EQUIPMENT

Demco-Gray Company
207 East Sixth Street
Dayton, Ohio   45402

Flaghouse, Inc.
18W 18th Street
New York, New York   10011

General Sportcraft Co.
33 New Bridge Road
Bergenfield, New Jersey   07621

Select Service and Supply Co., Inc.
180 Allen Road N.E.
Atlanta, Georgia   30328

U.S. Games, Inc.
1393 Cypress Avenue
Box E.G. 874
Melbourne, Florida   32935

REFERENCES

Harbin, E. O. 1968. *The fun encyclopedia,* New York: The Abingdon Press.

Menke, F. G. 1972. Horseshoe and quoit pitching. *Colliers Encyclopedia* **20:** 711–712. New York: Crowell-Collier Education Corp.

Pitching, propelling, and special game skills 1958. In R. J. Donnelly *et al.* (eds.) *Active games and contests.* New York: Ronald.

Quoits. 1937. In Jesse H. Bancroft (ed.), *Games.* New York: Macmillan.

Van der Smissen, B., and H. Knierin 1964. *Recreational sports and games.* Minneapolis: Burgess.

26
Racquetball
Philip E. Allsen

HISTORY

In the early 1930s Earl Riskey, of the University of Michigan, observed tennis players practicing their shots in a handball court. He decided that one could play a game similar to handball that would also include the skills of tennis. He first used solid wooden paddles that were approximately seventeen inches long and a soft rubber ball. The rules of the game were the same as those of handball.

During World War II, paddleball was adopted as an activity in the United States Armed Forces Conditioning Program that was conducted at the University of Michigan. Many of the men who trained in this program introduced it to other parts of the country and it soon spread in popularity. In 1952 the National Paddleball Association was formed and Earl Riskey, the originator of the game of paddleball, was elected president. The first national paddleball tournament was conducted in 1961.

As the game spread through the YMCAs and other recreational centers, different types of equipment came to be used. In addition to the solid wooden paddle, strung-type rackets were manufactured and used by an increasing number of players. Also many types of balls of various weights and colors began to be used.

Joe Sobek, a former tennis and squash professional, became acquainted with the game of paddleball which was played with a solid wooden racket, in 1949 while he was a member of the Greenwich, Connecticut, YMCA. He felt that a strung racket would impart more speed to the ball and also give a player more control and so he designed and had manufactured such a racket. This new concept was enthusiastically received by the members of the Greenwich YMCA and an eager group of local players developed. As the players moved to the other parts of the country, they introduced the game to others and more interest was generated. It was during these years that tournaments were held at the Greenwich YMCA and were known as the Paddle-Rackets Championships.

For the next ten years Sobek promoted the game through the YMCAs and the sport spread nationwide. During this time the game was known by various names such as "paddle-rackets," "paddle-tennis," and "paddleball." Also many different types of balls were experimented with in an attempt to develop one that would be the most satisfactory.

In 1969 a group of interested players decided to hold a national tournament and organize into a group to give stability to the new sport that was being played by so many participants. At the organizational meetings that were conducted in St. Louis on April 26, 1969, those that attended voted to select a name that would give a good description of the game. The name selected was "racquetball" and the International Racquetball Association was organized at this time. It was suggested that "racquet" and "racquetball" (rather than racket and racketball) be used as names for the equipment and the game, respectively.

Since that time, thousands of people have started playing the game. It requires a minimum of relatively inexpensive equipment. The basic skills can be learned quickly and the game can be played by both men and women of all ages.

Racquetball is a fast moving game requiring the use of nearly all parts of the body and is rated an excellent conditioning activity. In our sedentary types of life there is a need for an activity to stimulate the body and to serve as a release from daily tension. Racquetball certainly meets these needs.

NATURE OF THE GAME

Racquetball may be played by two players (singles) or four players (doubles). The objective is to win each serve or volley by returning the ball so the opponent will be unable to keep the ball in play.

To start the game, the server stands within the service zone and, after letting the ball bounce once, strikes the ball so that it rebounds off the front wall. The ball must land behind the short line to be in play. The server is given two attempts on the serve. If the first serve is not legal, the server is given another serve. The opponent must then return the ball in such a manner that it will hit the front wall before it strikes the floor. Play continues until either the server or receiving side is unable to return the ball legally. This play action is known as a "volley." The only person who can score is the server. The server failing to return the ball loses the serve. The opponent now becomes the server and the previous server, the receiver. A complete game ends when one side scores 21 points.

In doubles, each player is allowed to serve before a loss of team serve occurs, except in the case of the initial serve. Either player on the doubles team may return the ball. A match continues until one side or the other wins two games.

PLAYING COURT

Figure 26.1 contains the dimensions of the four-, three-, and one-wall courts. The dimensions of the three-wall court are the same as those of the one-wall

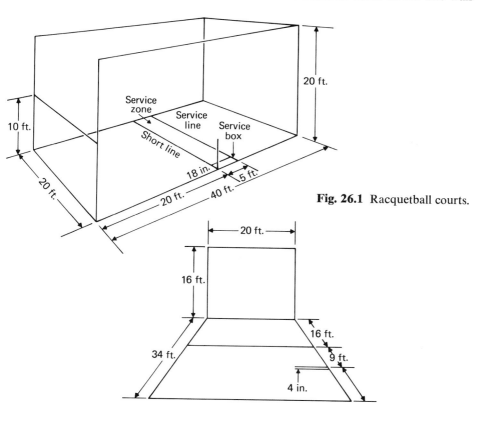

Fig. 26.1 Racquetball courts.

333

court. However, it has two sidewalls extending from the top of the front wall back along either sideline and slanting downward to a height of six feet at the short line, at which they end.

EQUIPMENT

The racquet that is used must conform to the following rule specifications. It can have a maximum head length of 11″ and a width of 9″. The handle may not be longer than 7″ and the total length and width of the racquet may not exceed a total of 27″. The strings of the racquet can be catgut, nylon, metal, or monofilament. Attached to the racquet handle must be a thong which is required to be wrapped on the player's wrist. This is a protective device to keep the racquet from flying out of a wet hand and striking another player.

The official ball, adopted by the United States Racquetball Association, is the green Seamco 559 racquetball. Other balls are also acceptable if they meet the official specifications. The ball must be 2.25″ in diameter, weigh approximately 1.40 oz., and bounce to a height of 68–72″ when dropped from a one-hundred inch height at a temperature of 76°F.

The rules state that all parts of the uniform, consisting of a shirt, shorts, and socks, shall be clean and either white or brightly colored. In tournament play only the club insignia, name of club, name of racquetball organization, name of tournament, or name of sponsor may be on the uniform. Players may not play without shirts.

BASIC PLAYING RULES

A complete copy of the official rules of racquetball can be obtained from the United States Racquetball Association, 401 Dempster Street, Skokie, Illinois 60076.

I. Serve

A) Order—The player or side winning the toss becomes the first server and starts the first game, and the third game, if any.

B) Start—Games are started from any place in the service zone. No part of either foot may be extended beyond either line of the service zone. Stepping on the line, but not beyond it, is permitted. The server must remain in the service zone until the served ball passes the short line. Violations are called "foot faults."

C) Manner—A serve is commenced by bouncing the ball to the floor in the service zone, and on the first bounce the ball is

Fig. 26.2 Ready for the serve.

struck by the server's racquet so that it hits the front wall and on the rebound hits the floor back of the short line, either with or without touching one of the sidewalls.

D) Serve in doubles—At the beginning of each game in doubles, each side shall inform the referee of the order of service, which shall be followed throughout the game.

E) Defective Services—Defective serves are of three types resulting in penalties as follows:

1. *Dead-ball serve.* A dead-ball serve results in no penalty and the server is given another serve without cancelling a prior illegal serve.

2. *Fault serve.* Two fault serves results in a handout. The following are examples of fault serves.

   a) Foot faults—When a server leaves the service zone before the served ball passes the short line or when the server's partner leaves the service box before the served ball passes the short line.

   b) Short serve—Any served ball that first hits the front wall and on the rebound hits the floor in front of the back edge of the short line either with or without touching one sidewall.

   c) Two-side serve—Any ball served that first hits the front wall and on the rebound hits the two sidewalls before touching the floor.

   d) Ceiling serve—Any served ball that touches the ceiling

335

after hitting the front wall either with or without touching one sidewall.

   e) Long serve—Any served ball that first hits the front wall and rebounds to the back wall before touching the floor.

   f) Out-of-court serve—Any ball going out of the court on the serve.

3. *Out serves*. Any one of the following serves results in a hand-out.

   a) Bounces—Bouncing the ball more than three times while in the service zone before striking the ball. The ball may not be bounced anywhere but on the floor within the service zone.

   b) Missed ball—Any attempt to strike the ball on the first bounce that results in a total miss or in the ball touching any part of the server's body other than his racquet.

   c) Nonfront serve—Any served ball that strikes the server's partner, or the ceiling, floor or sidewall before striking the front wall.

   d) Touched serve—Any served ball that on the rebound from the front wall touches the server, or touches the server's partner while any part of his body is out of the service box, or the server's partner intentionally catches the served ball on the fly.

   e) Out-of-order serve—In doubles, this occurs when either partner serves out of order.

   f) Crotch serve—If the served ball hits the crotch in the front wall it is considered the same as hitting the floor and is an out. A crotch serve in the back wall is good and is in play.

F) Return of serve

1. *Receiving position*. The receiver or receivers must stand at least 5 feet in back of the short line and cannot return the ball until it passes the short line. Any infraction results in a point for the server.

2. *Legal return*. After the ball is legally served, one of the players on the receiving side must strike the ball with his racquet either on the fly or after the first bounce and before the ball touches the floor the second time; the receiver must return the ball to the front wall either directly or after touching one or both sidewalls, the back wall or the ceiling, or any combination of those surfaces. A returned ball may not touch the floor before touching the front wall. It is legal to return the ball by striking the ball into the back wall first, then hitting the front wall on the fly or after hitting the sidewall or ceiling.

G) Volleys—Each legal return after the serve is called a volley. Play during volleys shall be according to the following rules:

1. *One or both hands.* Only the head of the racquet may be used at any time to return the ball. The ball must be hit with the racquet in one or both hands. Switching hands to hit the ball is out. The use of any portion of the body to strike the ball is out.

2. *One touch.* In attempting returns, the ball may be touched only once by one player on the returning side. In doubles both partners may swing at, but only one may hit, the ball.

3. *Return attempts.* In singles if a player swings at but misses the ball in play, the player may repeat his attempts to return the ball until it touches the floor the second time. In doubles if one player swings at but misses the ball, both he and his partner may make further attempts to return the ball until it touches the floor the second time.

4. *Hinders.* In singles or doubles, if a player swings at but misses the ball in play, and in his, or his partner's attempt again to play the ball there is an unintentional interference by an opponent it shall be a hinder.

5. *Out-of-court ball.* Any ball returned to the front wall which on the rebound or on the first bounce goes into the gallery or through any opening in a sidewall shall be declared dead and the serve replayed.

6. *No return.* Any ball not returned to the front wall, but which caroms off a player's racquet into the gallery or into any opening in a sidewall either with or without touching the ceiling, side or back wall, shall be an out or point against the players failing to make the return.

7. *Dry ball.* During the game and particularly on service every effort should be made to keep the ball dry. Deliberately wetting it shall result in an out.

8. *Broken ball.* If there is any suspicion that a ball has broken on the serve or during a volley, play shall continue until the end of the volley. The players will then examine the ball and, if it is defective or broken, a new ball shall be put into play and the point replayed.

9. *Play stoppage.* If a player loses a shoe or other equipment, or foreign objects enter the court, or any other outside interference occurs, play should be stopped and the point replayed. If a player loses control of his racquet, time should be called after the point has been decided, providing the racquet does not strike an opponent or interfere with ensuing play.

10. *Between games.* A five-minute rest period is allowed between the first and second games and a ten-minute rest period between the second and third games.

11. *During game.* During a game a player may request a "time-out" but it must not exceed 30 seconds. No more than three "time-outs" shall be taken in a game.

PLAYING SKILLS

The skills in racquetball are fairly simple to learn and this is one of the reasons why it is such a popular activity. All of the instructions will be given for right-handed players. Accuracy depends upon a combination of good footwork, balance, keeping the eye on the ball, good arm action, and correct follow-through.

There are three fundamental strokes in the game of racquetball. They are the forehand drive, backhand drive, and the serve. Once a player has mastered these three strokes, he can play with reasonable skill.

Forehand Drive

The forehand drive is a very natural stroke and, in its simplest form, is accomplished by drawing the racquet back until it points towards the back wall, then drawing it forward to meet the ball waist high. To be able to swing the racquet back and then forward to meet the ball, a player first of all needs to know how to grip the racquet.

The recommended grip is known as a Continental grip and will allow the player to hit both the forehand drive and backhand drive using the same grip. This helps the player to save time during a game by not having to change grips to hit different strokes.

This grip is accomplished by placing the hand out as if shaking hands and then placing the racquet in the hand so that the racquet head is perpendicular to the floor. The first segment of the index finger will be against the back of the racquet handle. The fingers should be spread slightly and the V formed by the thumb and index finger will be on top of the left edge of the handle.

In racquetball the ready position is assumed prior to hitting any stroke. This is a position facing the front wall with the knees bent to give balance and the racquet held in the middle of the body waist high. This position allows the player to go either to his right or left with equal facility.

In the forehand, as the ball approaches, the player turns his body to the right. The left shoulder will point toward the front wall and the left foot will be approximately at a 45° angle toward the front wall. A line drawn from the left to the right foot would be approximately parallel with the right wall. As the ball approaches, the racquet is brought back and then swung forward. The player should attempt to hit the ball when it is about knee or thigh high. As the racquet hits the ball, the body weight should move forward from the back foot toward the ball and the weight is transferred to the front foot. A good follow-through with the racquet should be made to impart speed and control to the ball.

Backhand Drive

In the backhand drive, the right arm is drawn across to the left side. The grip used for the forehand can also be used for the backhand with a slight adjustment. The V formed by the thumb and the hand should be to the left of the center of the handle. The fingers are fairly close together to increase the power of the stroke.

The stance for the backhand is the exact opposite for the forehand drive. As the ball approaches, the body pivots to the left, with the right shoulder facing the front wall. The knees should be slightly bent for good balance. As in the forehand drive, the ball should be hit knee or thigh high, but the player should hit the ball about twelve to eighteen inches nearer to the front wall than the right hip and as the ball is hit, the body weight should transfer from the back to the front foot.

Serve

The serve is very important as every point begins with the serve. Beginners should spend enough time in practicing their serve to develop both speed and accuracy. The two serves most commonly used are the power serve and the lob serve. The grip for the serve is the same as that utilized in the forehand drive.

In taking a position to serve, the body is approximately parallel to the right wall with the knees slightly bent. The ball is dropped in front of the body and toward the right sideline. As the ball hits the floor and bounces upward, the backswing must be coordinated with the shifting of the weight and the swing of the racquet.

The power serve is hit with a great deal of speed and the player attempts to keep the ball low and away from his opponent. A variation of the power serve is the short-angle serve in which the serve rebounds from the front wall to the sidewall opposite the serve at such an angle that the ball lands behind the short line. This type of serve can be made with a higher trajectory so that the ball rebounds to the back wall and corner behind the server.

A lob serve is a ball that is hit so that it has a high rebound. The serve should be placed as high and as close to the wall and back corner as possible, so that in attempting to return it to the front wall, the opponent has difficulty in making a full swing at the ball.

PLAYING STRATEGY

Many beginning racquetball players have the false impression that the only way to beat an opponent is to hit the ball hard all of the time. Good headwork is important when striving to become an accomplished player. The following hints are presented to assist a beginner who is trying to improve:

☐ Always work for good court position. The best spot is near the center of the court and about six to eight feet back of the short line. A player should always remember that the front court is the attacking area. The back court is the defensive area.

☐ Be aware of your opponent's position. Use a variety of shots to keep him off balance.

☐ Strive to plan ahead and, through a series of preliminary shots, set up the winning shot.

☐ Be alert for low hit balls or corner kill shots.

☐ When in doubt on what shot to use, always keep the ball in play rather than hitting a low percentage shot.

☐ Remember to keep eyes on the ball. A player must keep his eyes on the ball or watch the ball into the center of the racquet in order to hit the ball at exactly the right moment to generate speed, placement and direction.

INDIVIDUAL PRACTICE

Racquetball is a game in which a player can practice many of the shots individually without a partner. Following are some drills that will help to speed up player development.

☐ Practice hitting the ball to the front wall at various angles and receiving the rebounds.

☐ Practice serving and study angles that the ball rebounds.

☐ A ball hit low on the wall is difficult to return. Practice this type of shot with both the forehand and backhand drives.

REFERENCES

Allsen, P., and A. Witbeck 1972. *Racquetball and paddleball.* Dubuque, Iowa: Wm. C. Brown.

Hammer, H. 1974. *Paddleball: how to play the game.* New York: Grosset and Dunlap.

Kosare, A., R. G. Trambeau, and E. Riskey 1967. *Beginning paddleball.* Belmont, Calif.: Wadsworth.

Wickstrom, R., and C. Carson 1972. *Racquetball and paddleball: fundamentals.* Columbus, Ohio: Charles E. Merrill.

27
Rowing
Peter H. Raymond

HISTORY

The sleek eight-man shell churning to the finish line with precise unity has its origin in the trireme which, though slower, raced to a more significant goal in the battle of Salamis of 480 B.C. Classicists suggest that early oarsmen slid fore and aft on cushions suspended from their waists using their legs as the modern oarsmen do (Hale 1973, p. 24). However, this idea was lost until early in the 19th century when a crew of Englishmen raced in the rain on slippery bench seats and rediscovered the use of their legs in rowing. No subsequent modification has been as important as the moving seat or "slide," though the outrigger, or "rigger," introduced about 1850 (Gardner 1974, p. 39), narrowed and lightened the shell and consequently increased its speed.

England was responsible for the nurturing of rowing and to this day maintains two of the oldest and most honored regattas, the Royal Henley Regatta held in early July, and the Boat Race, an annual four-mile race between Oxford and Cambridge which brings London crowding to the banks of the Thames.

In the United States, rowing is proud of the first intercollegiate sporting event in the nation, a race between Harvard and Yale in 1825 which became institutionalized as an early June, four-mile race in New London, Connecticut. However, professional rowing had long been one of the nation's most popular sports, as witnessed by the crowd of 30,000 that boated on New York waters in 1825 to witness the *American Star*'s victory over *Sudden Death,* a British crew (Gardner 1974, p. 40). Professional rowing entertained the American public through the midcentury until the 1878 Hop Bitters Scandal in which Edward Hanlan of Canada and Charles "Pop" Courtney were unable to race for a $6000 prize due to the bisection by saw of Mr. Courtney's shell (Mendenhall 1975, p. 28). The National Association of Amateur Oarsmen (NAAO), founded in 1872, finally protected the sport from such questionable activities, but the damage was done; to this day the United States public is only mildly attentive to the sport in which only the coaches are paid.

A Sport of Amateurs

Rowing's amateurism is not unique to the United States; the Federation Internationale des Societées d'Aviron (FISA), the international governing body of the sport, conducts clinics and regattas attended by representatives from all European, most Eastern Bloc nations, and nearly half of the American countries. Rowing is also well established in nations formerly under British rule, notably Australia, Canada, and New Zealand, but the Germans boast the greatest number of participants and the greatest success internationally. For many, rowing is as much a social sport as it is an intense activity for serious athletes, with gatherings in the boathouse after a friendly race.

The majority of United States participants are in either collegiate or scholastic programs, though the ratio of rowing colleges to clubs is nearly balanced. The national concentrations of rowing are in Boston, Seattle, and Philadelphia; the latter's East River Drive features a section of road, Boathouse Row, where buildings in an architectural style peculiar to boathouses, with boat bays below and ballrooms above, hold shells of all vintages. Nearly every rivered city at one time had a boathouse and its crew; many such clubs have survived the period of collegiate growth, prompting new clubs and academically founded programs at the rate of 5 to 10 a year, and adding to the estimated 6000 to 8000 oarsmen and oarswomen competing today.

Once considered an elitist sport transplanted from England where gentlemen and working class professionals were kept separate, rowing has happily lost its pretensions, though the general limitation of the sport to college students has unintentionally precluded the greater public from rowing. Consequently, what public opinion there is tends to be unwarranted; the apparent grace of the crew and its relative distance from spectators disguise the physical stress of the race, one of the most intense demands of energy among middle distance sports.

Despite the public's relative unfamiliarity with rowing, a few regattas capture public attention, such as the Intercollegiate Rowing Association regatta, which is raced on Syracuse's Lake Onandaga in early June, is televised, and fills the park along the lake shores. Similarly, the Eastern and Western Sprint Rowing Championships, determining regional collegiate rankings for the nation, flood the host cities with rowing buffs.

On the international level, the rowing events at the Olympics involve more participants than any other sport except track and field, and are televised throughout Europe.

Competition begins in mid-adolescence, since boatbuilders are rarely asked to design craft to a child's scale. There is competition at all levels for rowers of all ages; it is even possible for a child to cox an Olympic crew, then grow to compete at the junior and intermediate levels before moving on to elite or international regattas; a child might even compete in the rapidly expanding veteran's or "masters" level which groups older rowers by age and provides them the opportunity for international regattas.

There is only one division by size in rowing, that between heavyweight and lightweight crews. The latter requires international competitors to average 154 lbs. (70 kg.) as a crew (155 lbs. in United States rules), with no individual over 159 lbs. (72.5 kg., but 160 lbs. in the United States). The heavyweight class oarsmen can range from 6', 170 lbs. to 6'6", 235 lbs. Lightweight competition, while not yet an Olympic sport, is growing throughout the rowing nations, and will most likely gain equal status by 1984 if the Olympic Games are willing to expand.

Women's rowing began with a surge in the late 1960s. This is reflected by the inclusion of women's events in the 1976 Olympics.

Spring is the college racing season, though a number of less formal regattas known as "head" regattas (after the "Head of The River" in London) take place in the fall. The Head of the Charles (Cambridge), the Head of the Schuykill (Philadelphia), and the Head of the Harbor (Los Angeles) bring as many as 1500 college and club rowers together to race over three- to four-mile courses for time.

The highest level of rowing takes place during the latter part of the summer for the elite men's, women's and junior crews. National championships are held in the summer as well; in the United States, these may be hosted by any community with the facilities and personnel to meet the requirements of the regatta. Recent sites have been Camden, N.J., Philadelphia, and Orchard Beach, N.Y. Clubs have depended largely upon scholastic and collegiate rowers for their peak summer activity which is aimed at national regattas, though numerous other races are held through the summer. The NAAO sanctions these regattas and provides licensed officials for them, as part of its promotion of rowing.

MODERN TRENDS

Modern trends in rowing reflect a growing base among high schools and newer colleges; the NAAO has responded to this growth by hiring a National Technical Advisor, Allen P. Rosenberg, of Rochester, N.Y., Olympic coach of the 1964 and 1976 United States eight-oared shells, to provide clinics and guidance to the rowing community.

In the late 1960s, world rowing technique changed as a result of the successful West German crews of 1960–1968, coached by Karl Adam of Ratzeburg, West Germany. By the early 1970s, the transition in United States crews from the 1920s style, made world famous by creator Hiram Conibear of the University of Washington, was completed, though not without some confusion. The primary United States innovator was Harry Parker of Harvard University, whose crews and oarsmen have dominated the college and United States international ranks of the 1960s and 1970s.

Rowing physiology, studied extensively in the Germanys and the Eastern Bloc countries, expanded in the United States under Dr. Frederick Hagerman of Ohio University, who tested each elite men's team beginning in 1967. His research appears regularly in the *Oarsman,* the official publication of the NAAO.

The selection process for the international teams, formerly chosen through a trials method, changed following the lead of the astonishingly successful New Zealand crews (Fig. 27.1). In 1972 the United States first chose its eight and four-with-cox by inviting individuals from all over the country to compete for a seat in one of the crews; earlier the colleges and clubs competed against each other as intact crews for the chance to represent the nation in international competition. In 1976, six of the United States crews were selected by this "camp" method.

THE SPORT

There are eight kinds of racing shells in rowing and, depending on the regatta in which they are used, may be categorized by gender, weight, age, competence, and experience. A rower can use either a sweep oar or two sculls; the sweep boats are the eight (always with a coxswain), the coxed and coxless four, and the coxed and coxless pair. The sculling boats, the single, double, and quadruple scull, are all coxless with the exception of the woman's quad. The most common event in United States rowing is the eight.

The oarsman sits facing the stern with his feet secured within shoes attached to the shell (Fig. 27.2); as a sweep oarsman, he grasps one oar, while as a sculler he holds one in each hand; moving sternward on a rolling seat, he reaches out to place his oar in the water. When the oar is anchored, he presses his legs out of their compressed state, transferring this pressure through his back and arms to the oar handle, and brings the handle toward the bow and his body, at which point he removes the oar from the water and begins a new cycle.

FISA sets the men's distance at 2000 meters, or nearly 1.42 miles, with the juniors' at 1500m and the women's at 1000m, though the latter may change to 1500m.

At a FISA regatta, there must be six straight and parallel lanes with one

Fig. 27.1 The New Zealand Eight training for the Olympic Games. Courtesy of *Oarsman.*

Fig. 27.2 View of the interior of the shell showing shoes attached to the shell.

returning lane, each at least 12.5m (41') wide; the depth must be uniform and at least three meters (9.8'), and the length must allow 250m beyond the finish line. The course must be separated into lanes by buoys placed every 20m and arranged horizontally, floating from underwater cables running the length of the course. There must be no moving water, no bridges, or prevailing crosswinds.

Such demanding specifications cannot be met by any course in the United States, but for the 1968, 1972, and 1976 Olympics and the 1975 world championships in England, the host countries built perfect rowing basins at Xochimilco, Mexico; Oberschleissheim, West Germany; Ile de Notre Dame, Montreal, Canada; and Nottingham, England, respectively. Most courses in the United States lie on rivers and lakes, many with bends and bridges or without protection from the wind, tide, or current.

A system of heats and repechages (from French *repêcher,* "to fish again") allows losers of preliminary heats to qualify for the semifinals by rowing and placing first or second (depending upon the number of entries) in a second race; the first two or three finishes in the semifinals qualify for the grand finals, held after a race for places 7–12 called the petit finals. (French is the international language of rowing; all crews are addressed by the officials at the start in French, so that the starting commands are "Etes-vous prêts?

Partez!") The regatta is held over six days, allowing rest after the repechages and the semifinals.

Although oarsmen disdain the imbalanced responsibility of positions in other sports, there is an unequal division of labor in rowing. The coxswain, selected for his lightness, ability to steer, and racing wiles, manipulates the rudder with cables, informs the crew of its position along the course and relative to other crews, and calls encouragement as well as tactical moves during the race. The stroke, or most sternward oarsman, is responsible for the crew's pace or strokes per minute; in many respects he is the leader, though not necessarily in strength, for his fluidity and sharpness directly affect his responding teammates; it is also he who must both maintain the necessary pace and raise it for the sprint. The other seats are not differentiated, though general tendencies in all crews suggest that the most aggressive oarsman, if he is not the stroke, sits immediately behind the stroke; the most powerful members (and perhaps the least technically able) are located in the middle of the boat, while the lighter and quickest oarsmen sit toward the bow.

In the coxless boats, except for the rudderless double, any oarsman may be the steersman, though he is most often the bow or stroke; a rower steers by swiveling a special shoe, to the toe of which are attached cables leading through pulleys to the rudder. In unbuoyed courses, he must continually pivot in his seat to check his course, while on a FISA or buoyed course, he may steer off either the buoys in the water or the overhead lane markers suspended by cable.

Because oarsmen, unlike racers in other sports, are looking behind them, it is important psychologically to lead; this explains the racing start, a series of quick strokes followed by a flat-out sprint for about a minute, after which the crew settles to its racing pace, which varies from crew to crew and from event to event. Generally, the greater the load per rower (such as the coxed pair), the lower the rating, so that while eights may settle to 37–39 strokes per minute (spm), the pair with cox is likely to row 32 spm. Headwinds usually force stroke rates down as well.

Tactics during the race are limited to ten- or twenty-stroke drives calculated to unnerve opponents at their most vulnerable moments; the rating may or may not rise during such a drive, but most often it remains constant, since changes in stroke may spoil the swing of a crew or cost too dearly in energy. Races usually end with a sprint for the last minute or more, during which the stroke rises with an increase in power as the crew seeks its greatest possible speed.

There are numerous elements affecting a crew's performance, among which are the following: the unity of the members throughout the rowing cycle, especially in application of power, which decreases the resistance felt by each rower; the "keel," or balance; and the ability of each member to take and release the water on time without "catching a crab." The coxswain's steering can also affect the crew not only in the distance they row but also in the loss of balance from a sudden rudder application. Another obvious factor in performance is the interdependence of the members; a crew with seven men pulling is significantly heavier than one with eight pulling; a four or a pair will go offkeel or offcourse if one member lightens his pressure in the drive.

Despite the best efforts of planners and regatta committees, races occasionally become meaningless due to unfair wind conditions or current. The wind has affected the significance of Olympic and world championship races, and countless regattas of lesser stature. It is a variable the oarsmen must accept, though in extreme cases, regattas can be postponed.

Rules of racing center about fouling, i.e., invading the water of opponent crews, protests about the same, false starts, and late arrivals to the starting line. Rowing is fortunate in that most regattas never require the interference of the referee, especially at higher levels.

TERMINOLOGY

Many of the following terms are illustrated in Figs. 27.2 and 27.3.

Blade 1 Oar. 2 The wide, cupped area of the oar that provides resistance to the water.

Button The adjustable collar determining the fulcrum on the oar.

Catch Oar's entrance into water.

Catching a crab Failure of rower to extract oar from water while under way, resulting in blade's swinging astern and hitting rower with handle.

Double scull Two rowers with two sculls each, rudderless. Shell length: approx. 33'. Times for world champions: Men's: 6:30, Women's: 3:24.

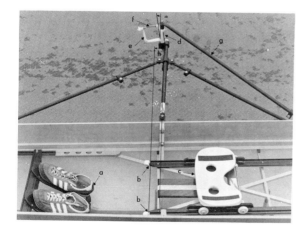

Fig. 27.3 Nomenclature: (a) adjustable stretchers, (b) tracks, (c) slide, seat, (d) pin, (e) oarlock, (f) keeper, gate, (g) backbrace, (h) distance between the pin and seat at catch, or "work through pin," and (α) arc of pitch.

Drive 1 Portion of rowing cycle with oar in the water. 2 Time while oar is stressed.

Feather While the oar is out of the water, it is twisted so the blade lies parallel to the water to offer the least possible wind resistance and greatest possible clearance over waves.

Finish Last part of drive before the release.

Four with cox Four rowers with one sweep each. Shell length: approx. 46'. Times for world champions: Men's: 6:24, Women's: 3.29.

Four without cox Shell length: approx. 43'. Time for world champion: Men's: 6:19 (No women's events).

Gig A stable, broad-beamed single for novices.

Inboard Part of oar from the button to the end of the oar handle.

Inside Extremities of rower nearest his rigger, as inside hand, leg, etc.

Knife To insert the oar into the water while it is only partially squared.

Miss water To catch at less than attained reach.

Outboard Part of oar from button to tip of blade.

Outside Rower's extremities furthest from rigger.

Pair with cox Two rowers with one sweep each. Shell length: approx. 37'. Time for world champion: Men's: 7:18. (No women's events).

Pair without cox Shell length: approx. 33'. Times for world champions: Men's: 6:50, Women's: 3:43.

Perpendicular Point in drive or recovery when the oar is perpendicular to the keel of the boat.

Pin Bolt holding oarlock to rigger.

Quad with cox Shell length: same as four with cox. Time for world champion: Women's: 3:20 (No men's events).

Quadruple scull Four rowers with two sculls each. Shell length: same as four without cox. Time for world champion: Men's: 6:02 (No women's events).

Reach Degree of extension of rower's shoulders and arms sternward before or at the catch.

Recovery Portion of rowing cycle when oar is out of the water.

Release Extraction of oar from water.

Scull 1 An oar for one-handed use, shorter (9′6″) than sweep, and lighter. 2 Single scull.

Sectional Eight-oared shell that can be unbolted into two or three sections for transportation.

Shell Any racing boat made for lightness, with or without ribs, of thin cedar or fiberglass skin.

Shoot the slide Incorrect connection between back and legs such that legs extend on the drive without appropriate bowward motion of the shoulders and oar handle.

Short Insufficient reach at the catch or early release.

Single scull Shell for one rower. Shell length: 27′. Times for world champions: Men's: 7:10, Women's: 3:46.

Sleeve Protective plastic or leather sheath around oar at button.

Slide 1 Carved, wheeled seat. 2 Tracks for seat.

Square Proper unfeathered attitude of blade in water.

Stretcher The shoe assembly anchored to the keel and gunwales, adjustable for leg length.

Fig. 27.4 Nomenclature for oar and positions: (a) blade, (b) buttons, (c) sleeve, (d) inside hand position, (e) outside hand position, (f) inboard, (g) outboard, and (h) spread.

Stroke 1 One cycle of the rowing motion. 2 Most sternward rower. 3 Rating, or strokes per minute.

Sweep Oar pulled with both hands. Length: 12′6″.

Tracks Guides for wheels of seat, adjustable.

Wash out To release while finishing, lifting water on the blade.

Wherry Same as **Gig.**

TECHNIQUE

Sweeps

The following stroke approximates the rowing style as performed by most United States crews in 1976.

One might choose to begin with the moment at which all flex leaves the oar while it is still buried before the release; the outside hand presses down on the handle and lifts the blade out of the water while the inside wrist twists backwards and down, feathering the oar (Fig. 27.5).

The outside hand's slight downward motion arcs away from the stomach, which it has just brushed, and moves out over the thighs, while the inside wrist, having completely feathered the oar, relaxes its grip on the handle without moving the fingertips so that the wrist is no longer flexed. In this position, the inside thumb and palm should lose effective contact with the handle (Fig. 27.6).

When the outside arm is nearly extended at a level just over the knees, and so that the feathered blade is about eight inches off the water, the upper body

Fig. 27.5 Just after release, oar feathered.

Fig. 27.6 Catch, oar squared and entering water, seat at full slide.

rocks forward from the hips to beyond the vertical; at this point the slide is drawn sternward by the bending legs. As the outside hand controls the oar handle past the midshins, it should be fully extended as the knees begin to rise on either side of it. The inside hand regains its flexed grip on the handle and begins to square the oar after the handle passes over the toes; by this time all forward body angle must be attained (the angle at which the middle of chest comes into contact with the inside leg at the catch is about proper body angle).

The seat is now halfway up the slide; from this moment, only two major motions occur: the seat comes to the stern stops, or the stern end of the tracks, while the extended outside arm lifts the handle on a diagonal toward the catch, placing the oar in the water. During the lifting motion, the inside hand has squared the oar so that the backs of both hands are parallel with the water; the oar should be held in the fingers, which form a hook rather then a clenching clamp (Fig. 27.6).

A common mistake in the last part of the recovery is to keep the inside arm straight as the oar traces an arc (pivoting in the oarlock). Approaching the catch, the inside arm should bend at the elbow enough to allow for the difference in reach as compared to the outside arm, so that the shoulders remain as comfortably facing astern as possible, and at the same level.

To change direction at the catch without hesitation, so that the blade is buried at just the moment the seat arrives at and leaves the stern stops, is one of the most challenging movements in sport. The momentum of the body on the recovery has to be overcome without slowing the seat as it approaches the catch, and the power application must be as instantaneous as possible. The legs press against the stretchers as the back and shoulders form an unyielding connection between the legs and oar; the back begins to lean bowward as the oar passes the perpendicular and the arms begin to bend at the

Fig. 27.7 Drive, pressure with legs and back, oar fully buried, arms still straight.

Fig. 27.8 Single scull, sculler resting with sculls feathered on water.

elbow just before the legs extend completely and the seat reaches the bow stops, for the arms are only connectors, and are third in effectiveness behind the legs and back (Fig. 27.7).

The spine continues to lean backward until it is some 20–25 degrees past vertical as the arms draw the handle into the sternal region, or lower. Throughout the entire stroke, the back of the outside hand should remain parallel to the water, and both hands should be in this position throughout the drive, with the fingers, and not the thumbs, securing the oar.

Posture of the spine, arms, and shoulders should be as natural as possible. At a normal racing cadence, the time through the water is about two-thirds the time on the recovery. The slide on the recovery should move at a constant rate and translate that speed into the drive without any slowdown or hesitation. The legs should be compressed at the catch so that the shins are vertical, and the stretchers should be set so that the greatest possible travel of the slide is used. That is, with the legs extended, the seat's wheels sit within an inch of the bowstops.

SCULLING

Sculling uses all principles of sweep rowing except that the legs need not be divided at the catch since the arms will go outside the knees; secondly, the sculls will overlap.

Holding the sculls must incorporate the best from the sweep's inside and outside hands. A scull must be feathered by dropping the wrist, but then the wrist must unflex as the scull handle is held gently in the finger and the thumb tip (Fig. 27.8).

There should be no palm contact with the scull handle on the recovery, and squaring must be done with fingers only.

The overlap demands positions of the wrist during the recovery described above. A sculling boat is rigged with one rigger slightly higher than the other for the overlap, and the upper hand normally precedes the lower on the recovery, though the hands may be in contact. Direct crossover of the hands is awkward and cramped, while no unsettling to the keel is caused by differing fore and aft speeds of the hands as long as they are held at the same level.

TECHNICAL PROBLEMS

Holding the Oar

Novices tend to grip the oar in the arc between their thumb and first finger; a line drawn through the first knuckle of the middle finger and the center of the wrist should be kept parallel to the keel in both hands except the inside hand at the finish when it is feathering. In other words, the oar must pivot within the outside hand so that the wrist tendons remain as straight as possible.

Lunging

If the rower does not have his body angle before his seat stops, and leans sternward just before the catch, *after* the seat stops, his body's momentum is translated to the hull rather than to his oar, which increases the natural variation in hull speed and the wetted surface, which in turn increases the drag at a geometric rate.

Back and Legs

The delicate balance between (1) extending the legs and (2) leaning back determines much of the effectiveness of an oarsman; the major drive of the rowing stroke is generated by the legs while the back works primarily as a static connector between the arms and legs. However, the backward lean does contribute, from the catch to the finish, some two feet of drive. The general feeling is that the legs must initiate the drive, and the back must lift through the legs' pressure.

Sky

This is the blade's rise while approaching the catch, a fault caused by the tendency of the hands to lower as the rower leans forward from the waist and finishes the slide.

TRAINING

Rowing demands one of the greatest levels of energy output (absolute maximal V_{0_2} 5750 ml/min) as a middle distance sport, lasting from 5½ minutes for world-class eights to 7½ minutes for the coxed pair. The balance of aerobic exercise to anaerobic is about three to one, (Hagerman *et al.* 1976), and therefore the majority of training for rowing is steady-state, i.e., lengthy workouts with up to an hour of constant effort (pulse rate near 120).

Oarsmen train on the water whenever possible, but in intemperate weather (hail or ice), or in the winter months when the waters freeze, they run on the flat or up stadium steps, row in indoor tanks which partially duplicate the feeling of rowing in a boat, swim, cross-country ski, cycle, or row on ergometers (devices which couple the rowing motion to a braked flywheel).

All college crews and some scholastic crews train nine months of the year for a 5–6 week season of weekend races, while serious elite competitors train the year around. The autumn is dedicated to steady-state rowing at a low stroke, improvement of technique, and less intense workouts than in the winter and spring. Winters are devoted to strength work and running; the spring's early steady-state emphasis makes room for the three-to-one ratio with anaerobic training in interval work which consists of bursts from 10 to 50 strokes and timed pieces over distances of 1,000 m or less.

Because strength is one of the three most important factors in a rower's potential, much effort is concentrated during the winter months on developing strength in the skeletal muscles through the use of both heavy weights with low repetitions and light weights with high repetitions. Favored exercises are the leg press or squat, the dead lift, the bench row, and the power clean, all of which address primary muscle groups in the rowing exercise.

RIGGING

The adjustment of the rigger and oarlock allows exact control over the "work," or resistance the oarsman faces in the stroke; it determines the length of his stroke and the behavior of the oar in the water (Rose 1972, pp. 26–27).

Rigging can refer either to the arrangement of riggers on a shell or the adjustment of the individual rigger. With respect to the former, the standard rigging alternates sides with bow on starboard and stroke on port. Sometimes, if the best stroke available rows starboard (few oarsman can row both sides), this pattern might be reversed.

German Rig

Because the entire starboard side in the standard rig is more bowward than the port, and because the more bowward side has a prying advantage at the catch which pushes the shell's bow away from that side, coaches will some-times rig the bow four (or bow pair in a four) in a standard fashion and the stern half in reverse, so that the numbers four and five (numbered from the bow in the United States and from the stern in Europe) are on the same side. This counteracts the sideward motion of the bow through the stroke.

In the *Italian rig,* the rigging is as described above, but in a four.

Height

This is the distance in height between the midpoint of the oar's resting place in the lock and the middle of the seat, usually 6–6½″, increased for rough water, larger oarsmen, and novices.

Pitch

This describes the attitude of the face of the blade when "square," in rela-tion to the vertical. The blade is twisted with the top edge aft of the bottom. European oars are built with four degrees pitch in the oar, with adjustable locks making up the additional 3 to 5 degrees for a total of 7 to 9; unadjust-able locks pitch 8 degrees and the oars must be without internal pitch. (See Fig. 27.3.)

Outboard Pitch. This is the attitude of the pin, which transfixes the back of the oarlock and around which the lock pivots. It is sometimes pitched 2 to 4 degrees outboard from the vertical to create oversquaring of the blade at the catch to counteract the downward motion of the blade; outboard pitch also diminishes the pitch at the finish, helping to keep the oar secure in the water when most rowers tend to wash out.

Work through the Pin. This is the distance the stern part of the seat rolls past the pin at the catch, usually 1–6″, with the greater examples in faster boats; to compensate for the difficulty in achieving early flex in the oar at high speeds, this increases the reach of the oar, allowing the power to achieve maximum flex in the blade before swinging into the most effective range, near the per-pendicular, of the oar's arc in the drive (Figs. 27.3 and 27.9).

Buttoning. Usually fixed about 44″ from the end of the handle, or with an in-board/outboard ratio of 1/2.43, the button, if moved toward the blade, light-ens the work for the rower for slow events or headwinds (Fig. 27.4).

Spread. Spread is the distance, about 32″, between the pin and the keel, ad-justed like the button to ease work, or like the pin (fore and aft) to increase or decrease the length of the drive. For scullers, *span* replaces spread; this is the distance between pins, usually 61″ with 35″ inboard on 9′9″ sculls (Fig. 27.4).

EQUIPMENT

There are virtually no regulations in rowing concerning equipment; while coxswains must not weigh less than 110 pounds in FISA competition, shells may be as light as the team can afford. The shells of The Boat Race in the 1920s were built to endure only one race, and sometimes failed even in that, for they were constructed with a minimum of struts, ribs, and skin. The average shell today is more hardy because the expense of the hand-crafted shells (about $6000 for an American eight) is too great for just one race, except perhaps an Olympic regatta.

Most shells are strutted with oak, braced with aluminum or stainless steel, and hulled with cedar; the year 1972 saw the first fiberglass shell in the Olympics, used by the West Germans. Fiberglass boats are now common in the United States since their upkeep is less than that of wooden shells.

In the early days of boatbuilding when cedar from the Pacific Northwest was plentiful, shell skins were often made from one plank shaved into two pieces which formed mirror images down the keel; this maintained balance in pressure as the wood aged, dried, or swelled with moisture. It is now impossi-

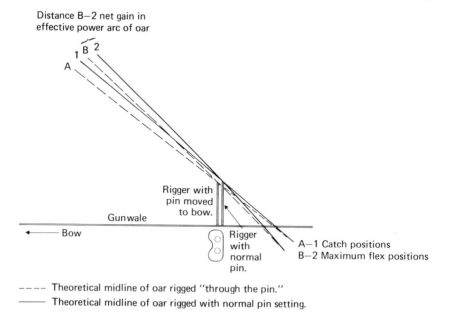

Fig. 27.9 Moving pin toward the bow achieves earlier flex in the oar, increasing effective arc of the oar.

ble to find one flawless piece large enough for an entire craft, and even singles are made from numerous pieces.

Oars are hollow in the shaft, constructed with laminated strips of woods differing in tensile and compression strength, a process which creates light-weight strength in flex and torque. Oars differ in length, weight, size and shape of shaft and blade, reflecting the whims of coaches and designers. Fiberglass oars appeared on the market in 1973 without great reception, but were refined for use by the British eight for the 1976 Olympics.

A list of the prominent boatmakers is found in the Appendix.

TEACHING ROWING

No certification system evaluates United States rowing coaches because there are perhaps only 20 full-salaried positions in the nation. Most coaches come directly from the oarsmen's ranks and are hired on the basis of their availability, rowing experience, and willingness to coach for nominal remuneration.

The best boat for learning to row is the single, in which novices quickly understand (1) the dynamics of controlling the shell's balance with the handles and not by leaning and (2) the effects of poor bladework upon the progress of the shell. Most oarsmen, however, learn in barges; these 16-seat affairs, built for stability and without regard to speed, place two rows of eight men side by side.

Instruction begins with proper placement of the hands. Because feathering is a skill of major difficulty, it is not taught for a number of outings, so that beginners may familiarize themselves with the motion of the oar and its reaction to the water.

In the beginning strokes are rowed one at a time, and then for increasing repetitions. After two to three weeks, there is sufficient competence for outings in the less valued shells.

Drills teach the finer points of rowing by breaking the stroke at various points so that the rower may concentrate on his body and oar positions. Rowing with one hand, rowing with squared blades, and varying the stroke, the pressure, and the speed of the slide all have specific values in learning to row. For novices, drills, and for warmups, eights and fours often row with only half the crew to stabilize the boat.

PHYSIOLOGICAL PROFILE

Testing of the three national United States teams between 1972 and 1974 (Hagerman *et al.* 1975, p. 36) revealed the following average profile determined from a six-minute effort on a Gamut Rowing Ergometer with 5½ lbs resistance.

Age 22	Weight 194 lbs
Height 6′ 3″	% body fat 11.5%
Maximal power output	0.500
Maximal heart rate	186 beats/min
Maximal pulmonary ventilation	193 liters/min
Absolute max V_{O_2}	5750 ml/min
Relative max V_{O_2}	65 ml/kg/min
Maximal net O_2 debt	17500 ml
Maximal ventilation equivalent	27 liters
Max lactate concentration	170 % mg
Mechanical efficiency	21%

Rowing is unusual in that it places almost equal emphasis on the total power and endurance of skeletal muscles, cardiovascular conditioning, and coordination. As a team sport in which no individuals appear to excel in victory, and in which the coach is superfluous during competition, rowing offers a unique relationship between the stroke and the others of the crew. This is most clearly seen in the results of rowing at high altitude such as in the Mexico 1968 Olympics, where at the altitude of 7700 feet, many oarsmen were driven by their strokes beyond their capacity to perform and lost consciousness. The fact that, in other sports, loss of consciousness befell only those athletes who were drugged, ill, or overheated demonstrates that an oarsman is forced by his teammates to continue whereas, if he were rowing alone, he would not.

From another physiological point of view, rowing differs from most middle-distance sports in the early oxygen debt incurred at the start; the psychological value of leading and seeing the opponent must be weighed against the physiological stress and inefficiency of carrying an oxygen debt throughout the performance.

SUMMARY

Some colorful traditions in rowing are the exchange or betting of racing shirts in United States college crews, the dunking of the victorious coxswain by his teammates, and the pomp of christening a new shell. Rowers remain loyal to their sport for its camaraderie; for its education through challenges; for the lake or river setting in which the elements are reflected; and for the rare moment when a shell seems to come alive beneath a crew and grows light with speed and grace through the water. Great experiences in the sport are as likely to occur during practice one lovely evening as in the intensity of a memorable race; it is a sport enjoyed as much for the training as for the racing.

APPENDIX

E. Ayling and Sons, Ltd.
Embankment, London S.W. 15
England

F. Collar, Oar, Scull, and
Mast Specialist
c/o Hart Perry
Kent School
Kent, Connecticut 06757

Donoratico
c/o Allen Rosenberg
415 Cobbs Hill Drive
Rochester, N.Y. 14610

Kaschper Racing Shells, Ltd.
P.O. Box 40
Lucan, Ontario
Canada

Martin Marin Company
Box 2510 Pepperell Road
Kittery Point, Maine 03905

Helmut Schoenbrod
North Main Street
Georgetown, Connecticut 06829

A. H. Baker (Derby), Ltd.
45 Hill Top Breadsall
Derby, England

Croker Oars
108 Bowden St./Meadowbank
2114 Sydney, Australia

Fiji Sculls
L.S.A. Perry
235 Indian Creek Road
Philadelphia, Pa. 19151

Wilhelm Karlisch Shells and
Persch Rowing Shells
c/o Dietrich Rose
756 Hill Road
Philadelphia, Pa. 19128

Geo. Pocock Racing Shells, Inc.
P.O. Box 111 University Station
Seattle, Washington 98105

Alfred Stampfli
Bootswerst 8038 Zurich
Seestrasse 489, Schweitz

REFERENCES

Gardener, J. 1974. The early days of rowing sport. *Oarsman* **6,** 5 (November–December).

Hagerman, F. *et al.,* 1976. Report of sports medicine committee to the NAAO annual meeting. Alexandria, Va., (January).

Hale, J. 1973. Cushion and oar, part II. *Oarsman* **5,** 3 (July–August).

——— *et al.,* 1975. A summary of physiological stress at the United States national rowing camp. *Oarsman* **7,** 2 (May–June).

Mendenhall, T. C. 1975. Rowing's isms: amateur and professional. *Oarsman* **7,** 4 (September–October).

Rose, D. 1972. The rigging of sweep boats. *Oarsman* **4,** 2 (May).

28
Rugby
A. Martin Underwood

RUGBY UNION FOOTBALL

Origins

Among the many recreative activities pursued by the human race, the various kicking and passing games are as numerous as the tribes and traditions which have allowed them to evolve. Historical evidence indicates that the present day game of Rugby Union Football—from now on referred to as rugby—has developed quite naturally from the primitive skirmishes played with warriors' heads—dead, of course—stones, wooden balls, objects made out of metal, and animal bladders. In many cases the "ball" was too heavy to be kicked and, therefore, had to be handled, although many early games were a combination of kicking and passing.

Two codes of football—the "dribbling" code and the "handling" code—inevitably emerged but both can claim to have the same ancient antecedents. From these ancient beginnings the reader will observe that it was necessary to impose limitations upon the barbaric freedom of early games in order that the contest be more appropriate for a civilized society.

A history of the Han Dynasty (207 B.C.–A.D. 220) mentions the two forms of *"Tsu Chu"*—kickball (Green 1953, p. 5). In one form, players took turns in an attempt to kick the ball through a target, while the other form encouraged clever dribbling antics using head, stomach, back, chest, and feet. Japan's *"Kemari"* (Green 1953, p. 6) has been played for fourteen centuries. In this game eight players ceremoniously kick the ball to each other in a fourteen metre square which has a tree in each corner. Both of these games appear rather gentlemanly and are not an indication of the civility in which all games were played.

Part of the military fitness training of the Roman legions in England during the 4th century was a game called *"Harpastum"* (Owen 1955, p. 16). A small, hard, round ball was passed from hand to hand between players who were attempting to cross their opponent's line with the ball. Tackling—around the neck mainly—was part of the game. Other variations of Harpastum required the ball to be thrown through targets at each end of the playing area and often the game was played indoors.

Another possible parent of rugby is *"La Soule"* (Owen 1955, p. 17) which was a free-for-all contest originating in Normandy. It had much in common with the intervillage melees which later passed for football in England. One such melee was the game of hurling (Moss 1962, p. 84) dating back to the Bronze Age. It was particularly popular in Cornwall, England, where village met village or village met country. A wooden corkball was carried by players between goals often four miles apart. The outcome of these games was a combination of unarmed combat and all-in wrestling with an unlimited number of players. The trail of broken bodies failed to deter the rabid enthusiasts and these games of 'mob' football—as they were known—became traditional Shrove Tuesday celebrations.

The description by Richard Carew (1970, p. 22) of "Hurling over Country" written in 1602 is worth repeating:

> Two or three parishes agreed to hurl against two or three other parishes— number of players unlimited. 'That company which could catch or carry it [the ball] by force or slight [strategem] to the place assigned gaineth the victory.' The hurlers 'take their way over hilles, dales, hedges, ditches, yea and thorow bushes, briars, mires, plashes and rivers whatsoever, so you shall sometimes see twenty or thirty lie tugging together in the water, scrambling and scratching for the ball!

This description embraces all the dimensions of early football which may have lasted from a few minutes to a few days, involved up to five hundred players, and occupied limited or unlimited space in which to achieve its objectives.

Another Roman game was camp ball (Moss 1962, p. 58) which had similar objectives to hurling. The ball was a stuffed animal bladder—sometimes stuffed with dried peas—and whole villages condemned themselves to periods of insanity in an effort to transport the ball to a goal some miles away. The inevitable barbarism took place, and often innocent bystanders were hauled into fearful skirmishes.

Medieval football rightly earned its evil reputation and was condemned by every serious-minded citizen, by the church, and was even declared illegal by Parliament. Kings and queens enacted laws against the game which had become violent to the point of brutality. Sir Thomas Elyot (Punchard 1928, p. 4) speaks of football in 1531 as being:

> ... nothing but beastly fury and extreme violence whereof proceedeth hurte and consequently rancour and malice do remayne with thym that be wounded, whereof it is to be put in perpetual silence.

Edward II, Edward III, Richard II, Henry VIII, and Elizabeth I all condemned the game. They wanted it prohibited on account of the "decadence of archery" (Titley and McWhurter 1970, p. 20), the standards of which had to be maintained for military reasons.

Most of these early games were associated with a local privilege or celebration, e.g., the granting of a charter. Unfortunately they progressed to being an excuse for rowdyism and the original cause of the celebration was forgotten. This culminated in a total ban upon street football in England and it is still to this day illegal to play football on the Kings Highway. Many a boy must have wondered why it is considered a crime to play with a ball in the street and how the offense originated.

The broad spectrum of "football" is now clear, in particular the traumatic variations of ball-handling games. The hurly burly of Harpastum with its variations of running with the ball, tackling and scrummages, now has its derivates in Rugby Union, Rugby League, American and Canadian Football. Hurling, la soule and camp ball differed somewhat but have the "carrying" similarity and obviously influenced the emergence of the purer version of rugby which began to develop rapidly in the 19th century.

THE DEVELOPMENT OF RUGBY FROM PRIMEVAL ORIGINS

Who Started It All?

Unquestionably the debate of the century could concern itself solely with the topic concerning a gentleman called William Webb Ellis, and whether he was responsible for the modern version of rugby. The debate commences.

With the increase in prosperity and power of England at the start of the 19th century, an expansion in secondary education became of prime importance. The new fashionable "public" (fee-paying) schools began to develop rapidly and their curriculum was influenced by the great reformer of the 1830s, Dr. Thomas Arnold, Headmaster of Rugby Public School, England. Organized games grew rapidly and "were regarded as a powerful force in the education of the sons of middle and upper classes" (McIntosh 1968, p. 11). The educated students of the public schools took their newly found games traditions with them to the Universities of Oxford and Cambridge and the base for the development of rugby was established.

It is significant that Rugby School should be at the center of the controversy. A tablet set in the wall of Rugby Close summarizes and oversimplifies a report made by the Old Rugbeian Society in 1896. The account is a second-hand version of an old boy of the school, Mathew Bloxham, who left the school five years before it was supposed to have occurred (Arlot et al. 1975, p. 882).

THIS STONE
COMMEMORATES THE EXPLOIT OF
WILLIAM WEBB ELLIS
WHO WITH A FINE DISREGARD FOR THE RULES OF FOOTBALL
AS PLAYED IN HIS TIME
FIRST TOOK THE BALL IN HIS ARMS AND RAN WITH IT
THUS ORIGINATING THE DISTINCTIVE FEATURE OF
THE RUGBY GAME
A.D. 1823

Neither of the earliest historians of the game, Shearman (1885) and Marshall (1892), recalled Ellis's name and a contemporary of Ellis, T. Harris, described him as a person "inclined to take unfair advantages at football." From historical evidence it is not impertinent to suggest that Ellis was not the first to run with the ball. Indeed a description of the game will help the reader to appreciate that the manner of playing differed very little from medieval football!

The object of the game was to score goals by kicking the ball over the bar of the goalposts by any means except a punt (Reyburn 1975, p. 14). In order to attempt the kick, the attacking team had to make a touchdown—touch the ball down on the ground—over the opponents' goal line and this then qualified them for "a try" at goal. This is the origin of the word "try." Spectators would shout "a try"—meaning a try for goal—when the ball had been touched down. Only goals counted in the final score, and could also be scored by dropkicks and placekicks from behind the mark made by a fair catch—explained later. The ball was "dribbled" more than "handled." Picking the ball up and running forward with it was expressly forbidden and so progress to make a "touchdown" had to be made with the feet. Catching the ball "on the full" and immediately kicking it was allowed. If you didn't have time to kick the ball, then you could retreat toward your own goal line while your opponents were forbidden to cross the mark where you made the fair catch. However, should you be caught while catching the ball, or when picking it up, a "scrimmage" would be formed around the player holding the ball. At this point the game portrayed some of the early barbaric customs and unruly traits which brought football into disrepute. "Hacking"—kicking of shins while running, "hacking over"—kicking shins in a scrimmage, "scragging"—throttling, and tripping were all popular (Cross 1971). Sometimes 300 boys would be playing the game on a large field. When most of these converged on one person, the chances of the ball emerging were slight and so kicking players out of the way seemed a logical tactic. The laws, however, catered for these delays by saying: "All matches are drawn after five days or after three days if no goal has been kicked!"

Innovation was obviously necessary, and perhaps William Webb Ellis was one of many who possessed an instinctive desire to change the laws. Unfortunately his act of rebelliousness was not approved of and not immediately accepted. Hughes—author of *Tom Brown's Schooldays*—explained that when he went to Rugby School in 1834, 11 years after Ellis, running with the ball, while not absolutely forbidden, would have been almost suicidal. Indeed he goes on further to suggest that the practice became popular only in 1838 after a sixth-former, Jem Mackie, "fleet of foot and brawny of shoulder," continually ran with the ball.

The arguments will continue to exist forever, and perhaps it is only fair to mention that there is a general acceptance that William Webb Ellis was the first to stimulate the concept, that running forward with the ball could be a worthy innovation. As all innovations take time to come to fruition, and traditions die hard, it is hardly surprising that some ten years later other people are credited with the same "invention."

The Next Stage

The public schools continued to develop "football" and the style very much reflected the facilities at their disposal. In the cloisters at Charterhouse, for example, "dribbling" on the flagged pavement was much safer than "handling." At Rugby School a wide-open grass area lent itself to handling the ball and "collaring" by opponents (Reyburn 1975, p. 13). Other variations in the laws were inevitable so all discrepancies and disputes were resolved by the captains of the day. Fortunately a great deal of confusion was eliminated when Rugby School published the *Laws of Football as Played at Rugby School* in 1846. These were not a description of the game but contained a number of significant points:

- ☐ Players could run with the ball as long as they didn't pick it up from the ground.
- ☐ Only the player holding the ball could be held.
- ☐ Players holding the ball carrier must not hack.
- ☐ No hacking with the heel and then only below the knee.

The Two Codes Separate

The two broad categories of football were still difficult to reconcile: the "dribbling" game as played at Eton, Harrow, Westminster and Charterhouse Public Schools, and the "handling" game of rugby at Marlborough and Cheltenham. Etonians were so incensed that Rugbeians kept picking up the ball, mauling and hacking each other, that at a meeting in Cambridge in 1846—which was dominated by Etonians—the Cambridge Rules were formulated. Adherents of both codes continued to play together but in 1863 the division between association football (soccer) and rugby football became clear. The Football Association was formed in 1863 and as a national body grew from strength to strength. In the same year a conference of eleven London Clubs and Schools accepted the handling code with all its misgivings. The policy, however, was rejected by the London club of Blackheath who enjoyed the "handling" code but objected to hacking. The most significant step came in 1866 when there was a private agreement between Blackheath and Richmond to abolish hacking. The motives for such a decision were probably provoked by forced cancellations of fixtures between the clubs because so many players had been lamed by hacking. Other accounts suggest a Richmond player had died in a practice match.

Blackheath and Richmond featured greatly in the further development of the "handling" code and invited clubs "who profess to play the Rugby

Game" to join them "in forming a code to be generally adopted." At this meeting on January 26, 1871, twenty-one clubs were represented and the Rugby Football Union (RFU) was formed, eight years after the formation of the Football Association (FA).

Fifty-nine laws of the game were drafted in the same year and, as expected, significant changes were made in the Cambridge Rules. Hacking was completely forbidden, and players could pick up the ball from the ground. When mauls occurred, players were allowed to push forward but still the interminable delays occurred before the ball emerged. Twenty players per team appeared to be the norm, but the heavy forwards dominated most of the games by being involved in the mauls. The ball occasionally emerged to give the rest of the players some running and passing backwards involvement.

SUMMARY

An interesting picture emerges when trying to establish the history of rugby football. The contradictions and diffuseness of information frustrate the researcher who requires precise analysis. Consolation may be sought after reading the main conclusions of a special subcommittee of the Old Rugbeians which was set up "to enquire into the origins of Rugby Football" (Titley and McWhirter 1970, p. 27).

☐ In 1820, the form of football in vogue at Rugby was something more closely associated with association football than what is known as rugby football today.

☐ That at some date between 1820 and 1830 the innovation of running with the ball was introduced.

☐ That this was in all probability done in the latter half of 1823 by Mr. W. Ellis, who is credited by Mr. Bloxham with the invention and whose "unfair practices" were (according to Mr. Harris) the subject of general remark at the time.

To be more precise would be pure conjecture, but many other features are certain. The early history of the game belongs exclusively to England. It was developed at Rugby School and then logically continued at the universities of Oxford and Cambridge. The sophistications and refinements were pioneered by Blackheath and Richmond until the formation of the RFU which published the first generally accepted code of laws.

THE GREAT SCHISM

The RFU from the outset has insisted that the game should be an amateur one. "There is a fierce, almost obsessive opposition to any hint of professionalism" (Cross 1971).

After the formation of the RFU in 1871, the game made steady progress. Unfortunately towards the end of the 1880s an inevitable storm developed which challenged the concept of professionalism. The RFU became aware of the rumors that certain clubs in the North of England were offering financial inducements to talented players to join them. This was sufficient to provoke them into passing a resolution forbidding players to make a profit from the game, although this was not the motive behind the players' acceptance of money. In order to play the game, many players lost a whole shift at work and were therefore financially worse off. The Northern Clubs tried to persuade the RFU to accept the proposal "that players be allowed compensation for bona fide loss of time" but an amendment won the day. It was moved that "this meeting, believing that the above principle is contrary to the true interest of the game and its spirit, declines to sanction the same." The amendment was carried by 282 votes to 136.

Many Northern Clubs immediately withdrew from the RFU and in 1895 the Northern RFU was formed. In 1922 the name was changed to the Rugby Football League. As a result of this split, Rugby Union in England was adversely affected by loss of revenue, support, and a host of talented players. Consequently they succeeded in winning only 13 out of 48 international matches over the following 15 years.

The separation still exists today. Rugby League "scouts" make inviting financial offers to outstanding Rugby Union players and the practice is frowned upon. Players who play Rugby League are still banned from returning to the clubhouses where they were once active Rugby Union members. Perhaps the future will see a softening of this viewpoint and social integration will be accepted.

Both amateurs and professionals play Rugby League and in the north of England there are approximately 700 amateur clubs and 30 professional clubs. No players are full-time professionals, all have a variety of occupations, but the professionals obviously receive additional payment for playing, above "bona fide expenses."

Some Playing Variations

Rugby League teams have only 13 players, 6 forwards and 7 backs. Several law differences also allow the game to be much more open and attractive (National Westminster Bank 1974):

- ☐ Scrums take the place of lineouts.
- ☐ The ball can only go direct to touch from a penalty. In all other cases it has to bounce first.
- ☐ When tackled a player has to get up and "play" the ball in a two-man scrum formed with the player who has tackled him.

☐ All goals, whether penalty, dropped, or converted, count as two points and the try counts three points.

The variations in the rules have been dictated by the need to make the game spectacular as its survival depends on the support it receives at the turnstiles.

Rugby League soon spread in popularity to New Zealand, and in Australia it has ousted Rugby Union as the most popular winter sport. In 1935 France adopted the code and tours are now regularly conducted throughout these four major playing countries. It will be interesting to see how the rest of the world decides which code to adopt, although Rugby Union certainly has the strongest hold at present.

International Development (Rugby Union)

England's recovery after "The Great Schism" centered around the building of Twickenham which is now the home of the RFU. In 1907, Mr. W. Williams purchased a 10¼ acre "cabbage patch" which has now sprung into an area of more than 30 acres. As the headquarters of the RFU the name "Twickenham" has become a household word in the English language. All rugby players have a secret ambition to tread the turf at Twickenham and few can resist the social revelry which occurs on the day of an international match.

Other countries, of course, continued with parallel developments. Rugby was introduced to Scotland in 1855 at Edinburgh Academy and one year later the first Irish Club at Dublin University was formed. It is said to be the second oldest club in the world. Guy's Hospital, England, is the oldest. Wales developed rather more slowly but by 1876 the six major clubs of Newport, Neath, Swansea, Cardiff, Aberavon, and Llanelli had been formed. Since then the Welsh have made such a close technical study of the game, and generated so much enthusiasm, that it is understandable why they are now the world's masters. The spread of the game overseas is due in no small way to the "hwyl" of the rugby-worshipping Welshmen.

New Zealand

Rugby was first played in New Zealand in 1870 (McCarthy 1968, p. 11). The Wellington Club was formed by 1871, and with the same fervor as the Welsh they were soon to become very formidable opponents. The game is also a religion and is always frontpage news. Players are idolized with the same enthusiasm as pop stars. They have a passion for competition even down to the school level where over 90,000 schoolboys play on Saturday mornings. The children are carefully graded into size and ability and every team down to the most junior level has a coach. There are something like 200,000 people out of a population of 2¾ millions engaged in rugby each

Saturday in New Zealand, which is more than twice the number involved in the British Isles (Thomas 1970, p. 14). Perhaps the world is indebted to the way in which they have taught and developed the skill of rucking to a level beyond most teams' wildest dreams.

South Africa

The only other country to claim an equal share of the world domination would be South Africa. The first rugby played was in 1862, but the Hamilton Club of 1872 was the first official club to be formed. The successful part of their history has been founded upon the tradition of playing very heavy, highly skilled forwards whose scrummaging power pulverized all opposition (South African Rugby Board 1964, p. 9). The backs play a supporting role and even though not a spectacular game of rugby it is highly efficient and successful.

Australia

Although Australia has not achieved the rugby prestige enjoyed by New Zealand and South Africa, they started playing early. The Southern RFU was founded in 1875 and by 1882 International Tours to New Zealand had begun. The main reason why Australian Rugby Union hasn't developed as much as in other countries is because it has to compete with Australian Rules Football and Rugby League. However, a recent resurgence of effort now makes them a strong rugby-playing nation. Their passion for victory and undoubted dedication to the cause will ensure that progress is maintained.

Fiji

The game has been played in Fiji since 1880 and undoubtedly they are the most exciting players to emerge in this century. The Fijian Rugby Union was formed in 1913 and now rugby is the chief winter sport with over 600 clubs participating. Their colorful and spectacular play has attracted record crowds and great respect is shown for their innovation, flair, and spontaneity of action which has injected a new air of excitement into the game.

Japan

The Japanese Rugby Union was formed in 1926 but the game was first started in 1897. The game was originally confined to schools and universities—Meizi, Keio, and Waseda—but now there are well over a thousand clubs in existence. In 1930 Japan made its first tour to Canada and recorded five wins and a draw in six matches. They rely on high fitness levels and quick thinking, and at present the game is undergoing rapid expansion and the future looks promising.

Canada

Immigrants from Britain influenced the development of the game in Canada and by 1882 the game was established in Ontario. The vast distance between the East and West Coasts has hampered the development of the game and little rugby is played in the central provinces. There is also an inactive gap in the middle of the season because of the severity of Canadian winters. However, schools are finding it economically advantageous to adopt Rugby Football rather than Canadian Football. Over the past ten years great technical progress has been made and with more children playing the game, Canada can look forward to competing successfully with overseas opposition within the next decade.

The United States

Early history of football is somewhat confused between rugby and soccer. There is some evidence to indicate that McGill University, Montreal, played Harvard in 1874 and in the following year Harvard played Yale. Other colleges played the game but began to modify the rules so much that the game became very different. Indeed, it could be argued that the American Football game is more akin to the game played at Rugby School in 1823 than the modern version of Rugby Union.

Maximum popularity for rugby is found in California where the university teams have aspired to great heights considering the amenities available to them. In the 1930s, New York became affiliated with the RFU in London and the future looked good. Unfortunately, even the further impetus of visiting teams hasn't stirred the Americans into seriously considering a game where they could surely compete successfully at world level. However, pockets of enthusiasts are growing each year and, with overseas coaches to help plus the need to play "less expensive" games in schools, the game may yet achieve the popularity it deserves.

Argentina

By 1880 rugby was being played by British residents, and by 1899 the Argentina Rugby Union was founded. The game developed on a keenly organized competitive basis and many clubs have financial security as they form part of multisports clubs which are in full use throughout the year.

France

British businessmen took the game to France as early as 1877. They now play an exhilarating fast open game which makes them formidable opposition for anyone. The Sports Athletic Union of France (founded in 1887) looked after the interest of early French rugby players, but in 1919 the Fédération

Francaise de Rugby (FFR) took over at the helm and still remains there today. Bleak years existed between 1931 and 1946 when the fierce competitiveness of their game led to violent occurrences and hints of professionalism. Fixtures were cancelled between France and Britain but now happily they have been restored and their speed, dexterity and mercurial opportunism can be witnessed by all enthusiasts of the game.

RUGBY WORLDWIDE

It now appears that the world has accepted Rugby Union Football as a major recreation for a large number of people. It has great advantages for schools where costs are minimal. The fitness demands are high, it encourages flair, and all individuals are allowed to play spontaneously as well as contributing to total team strategy. Few games offer more physical and social benefits and the proof of its modern popularity can be seen in the list of countries which in 1971 went to the RFU Centenary Conference at Cambridge (Titley and McWhirter 1970, p. 215).

Africa:	Liberia, Morocco, South Africa, Zambia
America:	(North and Central) Barbados, Bermuda, Canada, Jamaica, Trinidad and Tobago, United States (South) Argentina, Brazil, Chile
Asia:	Ceylon, China (Taiwan), Hong Kong, India, Japan, Kuwait, Malaysia, Pakistan, Singapore, South Korea
Australasia:	Australia, New Zealand
Europe:	Belgium, Czechoslovakia, Denmark, France, Ireland, Italy, Netherlands, Poland, Portugal, Romania, Scotland, Spain, Sweden, Wales, West Germany, Yugoslavia
Oceania:	Fiji, Tonga, Hawaii (U.S.)

Team Composition and Scoring Values from 1871

After 1871 the game continued to develop according to the 59 Laws written by the RFU. Twenty players were accepted as the maximum per team although by 1875, 15 had been accepted as the norm. This is composed of ten forwards, two halfbacks and three fullbacks. By 1880 the pattern had changed to nine forwards, three three-quarter backs, two halfbacks and one fullback. A more fluent style of rugby had already emerged and it is interesting to see how closely the positions are akin to present day formations.

At this stage no points were given for tries—only the conversion counted. However, by 1876 it was agreed that if no goals were scored, then the majority of tries would count giving added impetus for players to run with the ball. By 1880 heeling the ball from the scrum had developed which gave further opportunity for the backs to show their attacking skills.

Since 1880 there have been many changes in scoring values. The most recent changes were in 1971 when the values were agreed upon as follows:

Four points for a try

Six points for a goal from a try (try discounted)

Three points for every other goal.

Other law changes were significant at the time but perhaps these seven have influenced the game more than any others:

1896   The referee has sole control of the game.

1913   The ball on entering the scrum must pass a player of each team if it is to be fair.

1958   Unintentional knock-ons (ball projected forward) from a kick are not penalized if the ball is caught before it touches the ground. This law creates fewer stoppages.

1958   The ball need not be played with the foot after a tackle, which aids continuity.

1965   Back divisions must keep ten yards back from the line of their forwards at a lineout. This gives more time and space to develop attacking ploys.

1968   The "Australian Dispensation Law." No kicking directly to touch between the 25-yard lines. The ball must bounce before going into touch and the backs are thus encouraged to run with the ball and not kick defensively.

1972   The knock-on from a pass is penalized only if it is intentional or the ball comes into contact with the ground. Again this prevents many stoppages of play, and encourages continuity.

It is significant to see that the major law changes over the years have been particularly designed to create a game which contains fewer stoppages, more time and space for ploys and, as a consequence, a much better spectator spectacle.

THE MODERN GAME

There are now 27 Laws of the game which can be obtained from any National Rugby Football Union. The following is a simple description of the game containing some of the essential elements required to make up the game of Rugby Union Football.

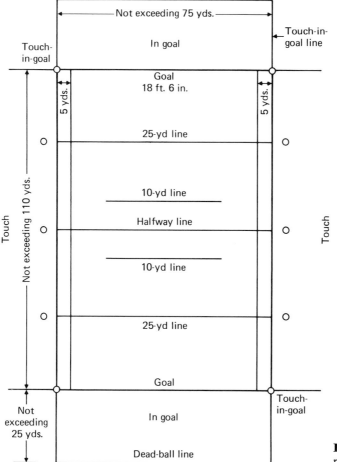

Fig. 28.1 The rugby playing area.

Players. Each team consists of fifteen players: 8 forwards, 2 halfbacks, 4 three-quarter backs and one fullback.

Unique peculiarity. Rugby is a team game involving passing the ball from the hands of one player to the next. In contrast to all other games, all passes must be made in a backward direction; i.e., passes must be made in a direction along or behind an imaginary line which runs through the ball and parallel with the goal lines at the end of the field of play.

As a result of this unique factor, it means that all the other 14 players are continually attempting to disperse themselves behind the man with the ball. Players in front of the ball are technically offside and will be punished if they try to interfere with play while in this offside position.

Object of the game

1. To score tries—four points
2. To score goals by kicking:
   a) from tries—six points
   b) from penalties—three points
   c) from "fair catches"—three points
   d) by dropkicking—three points

Scoring tries—four points. A try is scored when the ball is grounded in the "in goal" area by exerting a downward pressure on the ball with the hands or with any part of the body from the waist to the neck.

Basic tactical approach to scoring tries. The game is very simple, but confusing because of frequent law infringements, and lack of skill on the part of the players.

At the kickoff, each team assembles in its own half of the field. The team kicking off must propel the ball at least 10 yards forward in the direction of the opponents' goal line. They then chase after it in an attempt to tackle from the back or the side the man who catches the ball, and regain possession at B. The player receiving this kick is aware of the opponents' pressure and chooses either to (1) run with it, (2) pass it to a teammate, (3) kick it, or (4) take the tackle and form a maul—described later. *It must be remembered that blocking, tripping, and obstructing are barred from rugby and only the ball carrier may be tackled.*

1. Theoretically, on receiving the ball, a player could run right through the opposition and score a great individual try. Such happenings are rare, but not unknown.
2. Usually the team in possession of the ball develops a series of passing movements aimed at breaking the opposition's defense and a member of the team scoring a try. Providing all passes are backward, the ball not knocked-on, no one infringes the law, the skill level high enough to pass while under opponents' pressure, and the fitness to enable support players to be with the ball carrier, then a try will result.
3. When receiving possession of the ball the player could choose to kick it. He can either do this defensively and put the ball into touch—over the sideline—or he could kick offensively where his team would hope to regain possession. In the first instance, a lineout would form, and in the second instance a ruck or maul would form—described later.
4. If he decides to "take the tackle," then a ruck or maul would form around him where it is hoped that his team could maintain possession of the ball.

Scoring goals by kicking

a) *From tries—six points* (*try discounted if goal successful*). After a try has been scored, an attempt is made to "convert" the try by kicking the ball over the bar of the goalposts, either with a dropkick or by placing the ball on the ground and kicking it from there. The kick is taken from any point on a line, perpendicular to the goal line from a point where the try was scored. It is therefore always an advantage to score a try close to the goalposts.

b) *From penalties—three points.* If the law is infringed then the nonoffending team can choose to attempt to kick the ball over the crossbar from the point of infringement or from along a line parallel to the touch lines from which the infringement took place.

c) *From fair catches—three points.* If a player receives a ball, before it has bounced from an opponent's kick, knock-on or throw forward, he can turn it to his advantage. Usually the fair catch is made on catching an opponent's kick when opponents are bearing down upon the catcher. If, at the point of receiving the ball, (player is stationary, has both feet on the ground, catches the ball clearly) he exclaims "Mark" then he is awarded a free kick. From this kick it is possible to score a goal worth three points.

d) *Dropped goals—three points.* Any player, from any point on the field of play can elect to dropkick the ball over the bar of his opponents' goal. A dropkick is made after the ball has been dropped by the kicker and is immediately kicked by him as it rebounds off the ground.

Scoring records. Some schools have achieved scores of over 150 points in a game, and the first team to score over 1000 points in a season was St. Luke's College, Exeter, England, (1953–1954).

Everything sounds very simple so far, but because of the lack of technical expertise, other features of the game emerge.

The scrum contains a minimum of three forwards all in the front row, but more usually all eight forwards are linked together in three rows. It is a major "restart" feature of the game. Figure 28.2 shows the players getting in position for the scrum.

There are several occasions when a referee will call for a scrum but the two main ones relate to forward passes and knock-ons. The eight forwards from each team interlock in such a way that it resembles a human crab with 32 legs.

One player, called a scrum-half, is responsible for putting the ball into the scrum as fairly as possible. The hooker of each team waits for the ball to come into the scrum and then attempts to hook the ball back with his foot and channel it through the feet of the scrum. Meanwhile the rest of the backs are lined up in an attacking position and ready to receive the ball from the scrum-half who picks the ball up when it emerges from the

Fig. 28.2 The scrum. Photo by Katherine Purcell and Michael Bird.

scrum. The scrummage is a contest of strength and technique, and is considered to be the platform on which most teams base their success. There are usually over 30 scrums in a game but the lower the skill level, the more scrums there will be.

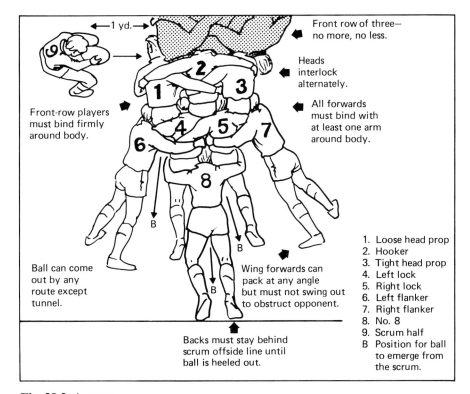

← 1 yd. →

Front row of three— no more, no less.

Heads interlock alternately.

Front-row players must bind firmly around body.

All forwards must bind with at least one arm around body.

Ball can come out by any route except tunnel.

Wing forwards can pack at any angle but must not swing out to obstruct opponent.

1. Loose head prop
2. Hooker
3. Tight head prop
4. Left lock
5. Right lock
6. Left flanker
7. Right flanker
8. No. 8
9. Scrum half
B. Position for ball to emerge from the scrum.

Backs must stay behind scrum offside line until ball is heeled out.

Fig. 28.3 A scrum.

Fig. 28.4 The line out. Courtesy of *JOPER.*

The lineout contains a minimum of two people and a maximum of eight. On many occasions a player will find himself in a position where he feels that the best tactical play at that moment would be to kick the ball into touch, off the field of play. The eight forwards from each team line up parallel to each other and two feet apart. They stand opposite to where the ball went out, and five meters into the field of play. They must also be one meter away from their own man in front of them.

The team not responsible for kicking the ball into touch now throws the ball high and down the midline of the two sets of forwards. A prearranged signal would tell the "thrower-in" which player to throw to. Some players from each team jump for the ball and attempt to get it to their scrum-half who is waiting to pass the ball to the backs who are lined up 10 yards away and poised for attack.

There is nothing so open to criticism as the lineout and referees could find enough faults to penalize someone every time. Dannie Craven (1952, p. 46) called this phase of the game "the illegal child of Rugby" because so much illegal interference occurs between the two opposing lines of forwards.

Ruck–ball on the floor; and maul–ball in the hands. Probably the most difficult phases of the game to refine and perfect are the ruck and maul. Players are obviously tackled before they have a chance to release the ball and there are techniques by which teams can ensure continued possession. New Zealand has taught the world that this phase of the game is not a haphazard wrestling match, but an aspect of the game which, when technically correct, can not only produce fluent exciting rugby, but can lead to many scoring opportunities.

When a man is held or tackled, a flurry of players should be in support who bind around the ball carrier, or step over the man on the ground, and attempt to shield this person until the ball can be gathered. The players drive

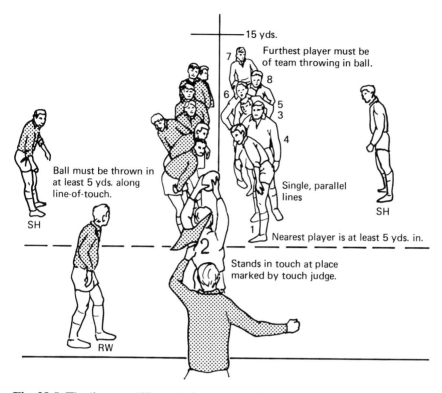

15 yds.

7 Furthest player must be of team throwing in ball.

8

6

5
3

4

Ball must be thrown in at least 5 yds. along line-of-touch.

Single, parallel lines

SH

SH

1 Nearest player is at least 5 yds. in.

2 Stands in touch at place marked by touch judge.

RW

Fig. 28.5 The line out. SH stands for scrum half.

Fig. 28.6 Player may be tackled before the release of the ball. Courtesy of *JOPER*.

into the opposition linked together almost creating a running scrum, and with any luck, by "smuggling" the ball through sets of hands, or by driving right over the man on the ground, the ball will merge. It must be remembered that when a player is tackled he must release the ball. For the definition of the tackle read the Laws of the game published annually (International Rugby Football Board) or books by Derek Robinson (1975). There are many occasions when the ruck and maul develop and teams are advised to develop the fitness and technique of both of them if they want their game to show improvement.

Supportive detail. Rugby is played for 40 minutes each way (80 minutes). Players remain on the field at halftime and traditionally suck orange sections and drink the trainer's bottle of water! No protective padding is allowed except for gum shields and scrum caps although under special circumstances the referee may allow some shoulder padding if a player is returning to the game after injury.

If players are injured, two substitutes are allowed, but these can play only if a medical practitioner certifies the injured player shouldn't continue.

Some further technical considerations. The skills of rugby can be categorized under four main headings: handling, contact, kicking, and running. The best players possess a number of these skills to a high degree, but specialist skills are required for each position and the coach should be continually looking for a correct balance of skills. Each team will need specialists to cover the following skills: goal kicking, hooking, lineout jumping, scrum-half techniques, and propping. It would be fair to say that backs are more interchangeable among themselves than forwards, who require particular body strengths for the positions in the scrum. The modern game, however, does expect the forwards to perform with the same agility as the backs even though they are considerably bigger. On the other hand, the optimistic coach would be looking for backs who were physically as strong as forwards but with twice the speed!

Not only must the teacher and coach consider the individual skills, but he has to develop the collective skills of groups of players. These are the "unit" skills and are clearly defined as follows: (1) scrum, (2) lineout, (3) ruck and maul, and (4) back play.

The primary object of the first three unit skills is to obtain good quick possession of the ball in order that the back units can launch attacks. However, each unit is not restricted to this pattern of play and is encouraged to develop its own attacking varieties. For instance, if the ball is channeled to the back of the scrum by the hooker, the man in the middle of the back row could pick up the ball, run with it, and start a series of passing movements either with the backs, or with his own forwards who are running in support.

Infinite possibilities of back-row players launching attacks are possible and, indeed, essential if the team wishes to develop a balanced attacking strategy.

Similarly in the lineout, the ball could be thrown to a player at the back of the lineout. He then passes the ball to his own forwards who are running from the front of the lineout, looping around him and then heading for the opponents' goal line—known as a peel.

In both of the attacking ploys above from scrum and lineout, a ruck or maul would probably form as the defending side would obviously be trying to prevent the play from succeeding. A well-organized rucking unit would be able to keep possession of the ball and quickly distribute the ball to the back unit who would use their flair, imagination, and skill to out-maneuver the opposition, and score. This, however, is pure optimism because play is likely to break down again and so another ruck or maul would form. The team that is extremely fit and can keep regaining possession from the broken play occurrences by good ruck and maul techniques will surely score a multitude of points.

Ploys. There are many occasions when the forwards decide to get the ball to the backs and allow them to initiate the attacks. There are various ploys and each is mainly designed to involve the strengths of the unit, e.g., you may have a very fast wingman who would be wasted if the ball never reached his hands, or a fullback whose flair for entering the back line to create "overlaps" is excellent. Each individual has his own contribution to make either as a good defender, or good attacker, or both, but as in all ploys, more than one man is involved and the following is an explanation of some of the most popular combined skills.

1) *The scissors or switch.* The direction of attack is changed when one player receives the ball from another in his team who is moving in a different direction.

2) *The loop or run around.* After passing the ball to another player, the passer runs around the back of this player and receives a return pass on the other side.

3) *The miss-out.* A player with the ball doesn't pass to the man next to him, but to the one beyond.

4) *The extra man.* The modern game very effectively uses the ploy of encouraging the fullback to run into the back line to create a numerical supremacy of players over the opposition back line. The "blind" sidewing— the wing who finds the direction of play moving *away* from him—can also be used effectively in the same way.

5) *Strategic kicking.* There are areas of the field which are not closely

marked by defenders. Carefully placed kicks into these areas can cause considerable discomfort to the opponents. Aimless kicking which doesn't enable the kicking team to regain possession is a feature of a great deal of rugby. The two kicks used in the run are usually the punt, in the air—or the grubber, along the ground.

6) *Counterattack*. This is a positive thinking attitude by the whole team whereby the defenders turn defense into attack by reorganizing themselves quickly when under pressure. It often occurs after the aimless kicking as mentioned above.

It is essential for the back unit to remember in all of these ploys that they attempt to get the ball in front of their own forwards. Until they have done this, they are losing ground by virtue of their alignment behind the forwards.

Mistakes should be eliminated; otherwise good possession from the forwards is an embarrassment. In fact New Zealand for years relied on the opposition to make mistakes before they were in front of their forwards (Jarden 1950). It meant that *they* could go *forward* into the ensuing ruck or maul even though they had lost possession. As they were particularly adept at this skill and usually obtained possession, it seems ironic to think that it may be an advantage to let the opposition have the ball, especially if they were prone to making mistakes!

Perhaps it is sufficient to say that everyone is an individual on the field of play and is allowed to run, kick, and pass the ball at his own free will. There isn't an obsession for ploys although the modern game does demand great discipline, thought, and effort in order to eliminate the wealth of mistakes prevalent in the past.

Training, Teaching, and Coaching

The fitness demands for rugby are great. Many forwards will run over three miles during an 80-minute game, and much of this is at submaximal speed for over 50 yards. Because rugby is an amateur game, few clubs are lucky enough to get the whole team training twice a week. Therefore, fitness is very much the responsibility of the individual. However, many players have an inability to motivate themselves to train alone, and so the standards of fitness in many clubs are appallingly low.

Most of the training sessions consist of simple warm-up exercises, some ball-handling skills but the bulk of the time is spent on perfecting the unit skills and team skills applicable to team strategy. Unfortunately there are rarely enough players to practice against and much of the work is done through unopposed or semiopposed rugby. It isn't satisfactory but inevitable in an amateur game in which the performers play for a variety of reasons.

All the training has to be done during the evenings and, as only a limited number of clubs have floodlights, a vast majority of teams trains under the dim reflection of street lights, moonlight, or even car headlights if an important game is imminent. Perhaps in some instances we haven't moved far from the conditions at the end of the 19th century. Watkins (1925, p. 6) writes:

> We were enthusiasts in those days—as long as we could get our boot to it we would kick it, and there were many vacant spots in and around the cities and their adjoining suburbs where we could indulge our bent to its full. *I have even known lads who played by moonlight and, when there was no moon, who placed lighted candles on the posts of the fences surrounding the ground.* Most times they could only tell where the ball was by the rush of the players in a certain direction. That, by the way, is an indication of the enthusiasm for the game when we were boys.

Over the past decade, the teaching and coaching of rugby has considerably improved, particularly in the British Isles. The RFU has recognized the value of coaching and as a result the world is now looking to them for guidance. Wales in particular is near the pinnacle of perfection and produces a very efficient brand of rugby pleasing to both player and spectator.

At school level, more thought is given to the variables of progression, physique, and psychological problems (Underwood *et al.* 1973, p. 37). Should children of different sizes be introduced to the full game of rugby with one ball between thirty players and all laws allowed? It seems incredible that anyone should do this, but it happens to a degree in many areas. Enjoyment is a result of success and sensitive teaching is a sound ideal and so far, these goals are being realized. All over the country, young boys from the age of seven upwards are engaged in "minirugby" on Sunday mornings. This is a nine-a-side game played across half of the field (Rugby Football Union 1975, p. 22).

> It is simple, yet exciting; you don't have to be an expert to organize it: yet it covers every position on the field in a full-size game. It develops the skills of running, handling, and tackling while it teaches the basis of fifteen-a-side rugby. Above all, boys like it.

Minirugby is not to be confused with seven-a-side rugby which is a very popular end-of-season game. Of seven players, three are forwards, and the remaining four are backs. It is a very strenuous game, played for 7 to 10 minutes each way under knockout tournament conditions.

Every session bears the motto, "activity, enjoyment, and purpose" (Advisory Panel of the RFU 1965, p. 1) and undoubtedly the skill levels of all players from school to international 15s have considerably improved.

A Deviation from the Serious Norm

Perhaps it is pertinent at this stage to mention the sociological phenomena which surround rugby football. Seventy-five percent of rugby is played for social pleasure, rather than for the "glory of winning." Rugby players are notorious for their love of alcoholic beverage and all the fringe benefits which they believe are associated with playing such a masculine game. It is not surprising therefore to find expensive clubhouses built purely for social refuge on the side of a rugby field which is occupied by cows and sheep for the greater part of the week. Many coarse rugby grounds "are near a river, stream or canal or open sewer (is it because the ground is so water-logged as to be unfit for anything else?)" (Green 1960) Changing accommodation can be found in mangers, showers can be nonexistent, and spectators often number one man and his dog. In the event of injury, many an unsuspecting toilet door has to be ripped off to substitute for a stretcher, while specialist treatment for injury is usually a cold sponge wrapped around the neck after being immersed in muddy water! Rugby is a truly amateur game, essentially for the player and not the spectator, although we must be fair to the more serious-minded clubs who have considerably professionalized the standards necessary to acquire top level success. Played with fitness, flair, and fortitude, there can be few games more exciting to play in and watch.

TERMINOLOGY*

Accidental offside This occurs when a player holding the ball accidentally runs into a player on his team. The obstructing player must be in front of the man with the ball. Unlike other offside offenses, this results in a scrum-down.

Back row The last or hindmost line in the scrum, made up of the two wing-forwards and the number 8.

Backs A collective name for the players who stand behind the scrum. Generally they are lighter in weight than the forwards and are good ball handlers and speedy.

Binding The method by which the forwards take hold of each other in order to form a tight and solid unit.

Blind side The narrow side of the play. That is the area of the field of play which is closest to the sideline.

Centers These players can also be termed inside or outside centers or left

---

* Prepared by M. Bird.

and right, purely a matter of personal preference. They may be likened to the halfbacks in American football.

Conversion Kicking the ball between the uprights of the goalposts from a penalty, a dropkick or the kick taken as the result of a try.

Cross kick Usually employed as a tactic when the opposition is concentrated towards one sideline. Kicking the ball high across the field towards the opposite sideline or the center of the field facilitates an effective change in the direction of attack.

Drop out This occurs from the 25-yard line and is the method of restarting play after the ball has gone dead (out of play) behind the defending side's goal line. A dropkick is employed in executing this play.

Dropkick This occurs when the ball is purposely kicked on the half-volley. That is immediately it has bounced on the ground after being released from the hands.

Dummy A fake move, employed to confuse or mislead the opposition.

Fair catch (mark) When the ball is caught, the heel of one foot is dug into the ground and the player calls "mark." All of these actions are done simultaneously. This allows a free kick for touch in an effort to relieve pressure by the defensive team.

Five-yard scrum Taken five yards out from the goal line when a defending player carries the ball over his own goal line and touches it down.

Flankers (wing-forwards or break aways) Players in the forwards who lie on the edge of the scrum, in the back row.

Fly-half (outside half, half-back, standoff back) Similar to the American football quarterback. Generally the link man and tactician of the team.

Forward pass A ball that is thrown laterally which travels in front or forward of the passer. This will result in a scrum down, the ball going to the other side to be put in.

Forwards (scrum, pack) The "engine room" of every side. They may be likened to the front line in football. Generally heavy and extremely strong players whose function is to supply the ball to the backs via the scrum half.

Front row These are players who make up the first line of the scrum, namely the two props and the hooker who stands between them.

Gain line An imaginary line beyond which territory is gained. This line runs from the original source of play such as a scrum or ruck.

Gary-Owen (up and under) A kick which is hoisted very high into the defending side's territory. The height of the kick enables the offensive side to get under the ball as it lands or is caught.

Goal This is a try, worth four points, plus a conversion, which, if successfully executed, is worth an additional two points. Thus a goal may be worth six points.

Good ball Possession by well-timed feeding of the ball to the scrum half by the forwards.

Grounded ball Occurs when the ball has downward pressure exerted on it behind the goal line by either a defending or attacking player. In the case of a defending player it may result in a five-yard scrum or a dropout, depending on who moved the ball over the line in the first place. If an attacking player grounds the ball, a try is awarded.

Grub kick A tactical kick often used in wet conditions. The ball is kicked along the ground. The ball's shape and the slippery ground make it difficult to field.

Head (against the head, with the head) When the ball is put into the scrum and the head of one's own prop forward is closer to the ball it is said to be *"put in with the head."* If the prop's head is concealed by his opponent's head, it is said to be *"put in against your head."*

Heel When the ball is in a scrum or a ruck it cannot be played with the hands. It must be moved out with the feet and especially the heel of the shoe.

Hooker In a set scrum the hooker is the player who strikes for the ball with his foot and attempts to hook it back so that it may be heeled.

In goal area That area behind the try or goal line where a try may be scored.

Knock-on Occurs when a ball is fumbled, projected forward, and dropped on the ground. This can be from a pass, a kick, or letting the ball slip from the player's grasp.

Line-out The forwards gather in two straight lines at right angles to the touch line and facilitate the throwing of the ball back into play.

Lock (second row) These two titles have been regularly used interchangeably over the past five years. However, "second row" is the more accurate as the number 8 is often termed the lock as well. The second row forwards bind the front row forwards together into a scrum.

Loose The ball is running free and there is a ruck or maul or any play where the referee has not organized it.

Loose head The prop forward whose head is on the outside of his opponents and who is on the left-hand side of his front row.

Loose scrum There is, or rather should not be, any such thing. All scrums should be tightly formed and this is a falsely used term. Loose scrum means a scrum which has formed as a consequence of play rather than one which has been organized by the referee.

Mark *See* **Fair catch.**

No-side This signifies the end of the game. The referee will blow his whistle when the ball becomes dead after the full period of time has elapsed. No-side cannot be signaled until there is a breakdown in play.

Number 8 The middle man in the back row of the scrum. At one time he was also termed the lock, because he supposedly "locked" the rest of the forwards together.

Open side That area of the field which is greater from the source or point of play.

Pass Made with the hands in a lateral direction and which does not travel forward (toward the goal defended by the opponents).

Peel A continuous follow-up of players (forwards) running round the back of their own line in a close handling or passing move.

Penalty An award of a free kick due to an infringement of the rules. The kick may be at goal, into touch, or a tapped kick into the kicker's hands to initiate a running and passing play.

Props The two forwards who support the hooker in the front row of the scrum.

Push over try When the ball is held in the back row of the scrum at a player's feet and the scrum pushes the opposition over their own line. The number 8 on achieving this position will then usually break from the scrum and touch the ball down for a try. Alternatively he may heel the ball out for his scrum half to score. The number 8 must not play the ball with his hands while he is still in physical contact with the scrum.

Put in The action of putting the ball into the tunnel of the scrum.

Ruck Occurs when the players gather round the ball which is on the floor (ground) and attempt to heel it back after a player has been tackled and has released the ball.

REFERENCES

Advisory Panel of the RFU (England). *A guide for coaches* 1965. London: Rugby Football Union. (Pamphlet 8.)

Arlott, J. *et al.* 1975. *The Oxford companion to sports and games.* London, New York, Toronto: Oxford University Press, p. 882.

Carew, R. 1970. Survey of Cornwall (1602). In U. A. Titley and R. McWhirter, *Centenary history of the Rugby Football Union.* London: Rugby Football Union.

Craven, D. 1952. *Danie Craven on rugby.* Cape Town: R. Beerman.

Cross, J. 1971. *Rugby.* London: Jackdaw.

Elyot, T. 1531. Boke named the governour. In F. N. Punchard 1928, *Survivals of folk football.* College of Physical Education, Dunfermline, Scotland.

Green, G. 1953. *The history of the football association.* London: Naldreth.

Green, M. 1960. *The art of coarse rugby.* London: Hutchinson.

International Rugby Football Board. *The laws of the game of rugby football with instructions and notes on the laws.* (Published annually.) Rugby Football Union.

Jarden, R. 1950. *Rugby on attack.* Christchurch, N.Z.: Whitcombe and Tombs.

Jones, J. R. 1958. *The encyclopaedia of rugby football,* London: Robert Hale, p. 127.

McCarthy, W. 1968. *Haka! The all blacks story.* London: Pelham Books.

McIntosh, P. C. 1968. *Physical education in England since 1800.* London: G. Bell.

Moss, P. 1962. *Sports and pastimes through the ages.* London, Toronto, Wellington, Sydney: George G. Harrap.

National Westminster Bank 1974. *Rugby league.* London: Training and Education Associates.

Owen, O. L. 1955. *The history of the Rugby Football Union.* London: Playfair Books.

Reyburn, R. 1975. *The men in white.* London: Pelham Books, p. 14.

Robinson, D. 1975. *Rugby—success starts here.* London: Rugby Football Union.

Rugby Football Union 1975. *Coaching scheme 1975–1976.* Rugby Football Union.

South African Rugby Board 1964. *Rugby in South Africa.* Cape Town: Johnson B. Neville, p. 9.

Thomas, J. B. G. 1970. The lions' den–New Zealand. In *Rugby world.* London: I.P.C. Specialist and Professional Press, (November), p. 14.

Titley, U. A., and R. McWhirter, 1970. *Centenary history of the Rugby Football Union.* Rugby Football Union.

Underwood, A. M. *et al.* 1973. *Better rugby.* London: Rugby Football Union.

Watkins, L. T. 1925. *The triumphant tour of the all blacks in England, Ireland, and Wales.* Wellington, N.Z.: L. T. Watkins.

29
Shuffleboard

Daniel L. Canada

HISTORY

Shuffleboard has been played for centuries. Although the game of shuffleboard may be successfully traced back to ancient Persia, it first became popular during the 15th century in England. Shuffleboard was played in the United States for a brief period during the 19th century, when it was a fad. In 1913, in Daytona, Florida, many people began to play shuffleboard and its popularity soon spread to the other 47 states. It also found favor as a shipboard recreational activity. Originally, the game was not standardized and had several different names. For example, the game was once called "shovel penny."

In 1931, the National Shuffleboard Association was organized for the purpose of establishing uniform rules of play and standardizing the court. With the founding of this organization, the game was well on its way toward its present acceptance. Currently, nearly ten million persons play the game both in the United States and abroad. The game is still very popular in Florida, with many tournaments taking place annually.

THE GAME

The game is played by pushing flat disks toward target diagrams at both ends of a narrow court. The pushing device is a long stick with a head designed to fit the disks.

THE COURT

The official court measures 52' in length and 6' in width. It shall be marked as indicated in the court diagram (Fig. 29.1). Minimum width of lines shall be ¾ inch and maximum width shall be 1½ inches. The playing surface shall be concrete or terrazzo, preferably concrete.

EQUIPMENT

Equipment consists of disks and cues. There are four red disks and four black disks. The disks shall be made of composition, not less than $\frac{9}{16}$ of an inch and not more than one inch in thickness and six inches in diameter. Disk

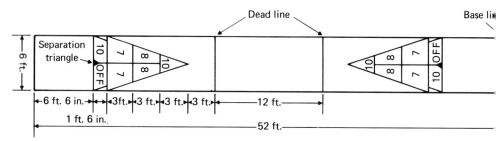

Fig. 29.1 Shuffleboard court.

Fig. 29.2 Shuffleboard cues. Cues range in length from 48 to 75″ and may be made of wood, aluminum, or fiberglass.

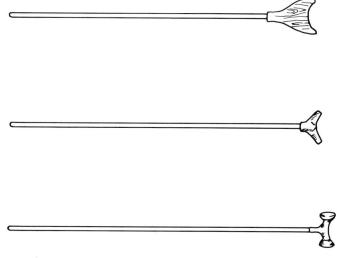

weight shall be between 11½ ounces and 15 ounces. Cues used to propel the disks shall not exceed 6 feet, 3 inches in length (Fig. 29.2).

Note: Since disk sets will differ in weight due to varying degrees of wear, it is not advisable to mix disks from different sets.

RULES

1. To determine color choice, opposing players (one from each side) shoot a disk to the far dead line. The player whose disk is nearer to the line has choice of color. If the second disk touches or moves the first disk, the color choice goes to the opponent.

2. To start a game, the red disk is shot first. Play alternates—red, then black, until all eight disks are shot. Red shall always be played from the right side of head of court and left side of foot of court.

3. A game is considered to be 50, 75, or 100 points. All national tournaments are two out of three 75-point games.

4. The second game is started by the black at the head of the court. The third game is started by red at the head of the court.

5. Players shall place their four disks within and not touching lines of their respective half of 10-off area. *Penalty five points off.*

6. Players shall not step on or over the baseline of court, except to gather and place their discs. *Penalty five points off.*

7. Interference: Players shall not stand in the way of, or have the cue in the way of an opponent, or interfere in any manner with an opponent who is executing a play. Also, players must not talk or make remarks to distract or disconcert opponents' play. *Penalty five points off.*

8. A disk, or disks, returning or remaining on the playing area of the court after having struck any object outside the playing area shall be removed before further play. It is called a dead disk. If a dead disk moves or displaces a live disk, that half round shall be played over.

9. A disk which stops in the area between the farthest dead line and the starting area is dead, and shall be removed before further play. If disk is touching farthest dead line, it is in play.

10. A disk is also considered dead if it hits a foreign object and it should be removed from the playing area.

11. A disk which stops fewer than eight inches beyond the farthest baseline shall be removed.

12. In singles, after all disks are played, constituting a half round, the players walk to the opposite end of the court and start play with the color lead changing.

13. In doubles, the color lead does not change until both ends have played.

Persons wishing additional rulings as to officials, appeals, substitutes, and interpretations for tournament play, may write the National Shuffleboard Association.

SCORING

Scoring diagram—one 10-point area; two 8-point areas; two 7-point areas; one 10-off area. (See Fig. 29.1.)

After both players have shot their four disks, score all disks on the diagram within and *not* touching lines; separation triangle in 10-off area, not included.

When judging disk in relation to lines, the player or official shall sight directly down.

A mounted disk, or disk resting on top of another disk, sometimes occurs when excessive shooting force is used. Each disk shall be judged separately according to regulation scoring rules.

If a tie results at the end of a game in singles, one round of play should decide a tie. Two complete rounds should be played to decide a tie in doubles.

TECHNIQUE

1. The cue should be held at the end lightly but firmly to prevent wavering during shot. Free pendulum motion should be used.

2. A player should take a long step forward keeping cue in constant contact with the disk and floor during the stroke.

3. A player should always follow through on shots.

4. One should practice to determine the speed with which one can shoot most accurately and effectively.

ASSOCIATIONS

The National Shuffleboard Association is located at 10418 NE 2nd Avenue, Miami, Florida 33138. This association was founded in 1931.

Since the popular reception of the game, several modified versions of shuffleboard have developed. For information on indoor shuffleboard, the American Shuffleboard Leagues should be contacted. They are located at 533 Third Street, Union City, New Jersey 07807. This association was founded in 1949.

REFERENCES

Harbin, E. O. 1968. *The fun encyclopedia,* New York: Abingdon.

Haslam, C. S. 1955. *How-to book of shufflleboard,* St. Petersburg, Fla.: Great Outdoors Association.

Menke, F. G. 1947. *The new encyclopedia of sports.* New York: A. S. Barnes.

———— 1972. Shuffleboard. *Colliers Encyclopedia,* **12:** 288, Crowell-Collier Education Corp.

Seaton, D. C. *et al.* 1965. *Physical education handbook.* (4th ed.) Englewood Cliffs, N.J.: Prentice-Hall.

Van der Smissen, B., and H. Knierin 1964. *Recreational sports and games.* Minneapolis: Burgess.

Van Hagen, W., G. Dexter, and J. F. Williams 1951. *Physical education in the elementary school.* Sacramento: California State Printing Office.

30
Skiing

Because there are so many kinds of skiing, even when limited to snow, two articles were solicited on this subject. Richard W. Bowers summarizes the history and describes the equipment needed in a general way. He touches on teaching methods and describes basic techniques carefully. He then provides some general information on ski programs in schools and colleges.

Patrick O'Shea writes on cross-country and wilderness skiing. He explains what is meant by Nordic skiing and discusses equipment and its upkeep. He writes about basic instruction in the various skills as well as methods of learning them. The clothing needed under various circumstances is also covered in detail. The skills needed for safe skiing and living on the trails are carefully outlined. RBF

Skiing: Basic Instruction
Richard W. Bowers

HISTORY

It is well documented that some form of skiing was practiced at least 2500 years ago. In the Djugarden Museum in Stockholm, there is a pair of skis on display estimated to be 4000 years old. There are other remnants of early skis that have been unearthed in the bogs of Sweden, Finland, and Norway. The earliest written accounts of skiing are recorded in the *Sagas* of the Norse Vikings. Among their various icons, the Vikings had a god and goddess of

Fig. 30.1 Ski jumping is for the expert. However, the recreational and sporting value of skiing is also now recognized. Courtesy of *JOPER*.

skiing. Skada (or Odurrdis) was the goddess of skiing while Uller was known as the god of skiing and of winter.

Early on, skiing was purely utilitarian, being a means of transportation. It was what we would classify today as Nordic or cross-country skiing. From about A.D. 1200 onward, skiing became prominent in a military sense. Finally, the recreational and sporting value of skiing came to the forefront in the early 1800s. Downhill, or Alpine, skiing became popular and has proliferated. An excellent history of skiing appears in *Ski Magazine's Encyclopedia of Skiing*.

Since the introduction of the rope tow in the 1930s, skiing has grown from a little known activity for the hardy to a popular winter recreation enjoyed by millions of enthusiasts. Skiing has become so popular that instructional programs have developed even within schools and universities that are conspicuous for their lack of mountainous or hilly terrain. One doesn't need a large hill to learn the rudiments of the activity.

EQUIPMENT

When one decides to become involved in skiing one also commits oneself to an initial investment for equipment and clothing. Eventually, one will need boots, skis, safety bindings, poles, goggles, gloves, ski sweater, turtleneck shirt, thermal underwear, thermal socks, ski jacket, and cap. Other items include warm-up pants, which can be used in lieu of regular ski pants, and a lightweight wind shirt or jacket.

Although this list appears to be formidable, it is possible to gradually acquire all of the essentials. Most ski experts agree that the key purchase is a good pair of boots. Next in order of importance is the package of skis, safety bindings, and poles. Because there is a wide range of prices it is rec-

Fig. 30.2 When one decides to become involved in skiing, consideration must be given to the right kind of equipment. Courtesy of Washington State University.

ommended that beginning and intermediate skiers purchase equipment in the middle price range.

Next in purchasing priorities would be thermal underwear and gloves. From this point on, the skier's personal tastes and desires should be the guideline as to what to purchase. It may take the new skier two, three, or four ski seasons before becoming completely outfitted. Most ski shops are very helpful in working with new skiers and are well known for their honesty, sincerity, and enthusiasm.

TEACHING METHODS

At the risk of oversimplification, two currently popular teaching methods will be described. The first of these is the American Ski Method (ASM) as championed by the Professional Ski Instructors Association (PSIA). The American Ski Method can be described as a progression of correct ski forms. As a student learns and accomplishes certain basic skills he then moves on to a more complex skill, until reaching the goal of skiing parallel.

The GLM (Graduated Length Method) approach is the second major teaching technique and is growing rapidly in popularity. Cliff Taylor is generally recognized as the innovator of GLM. Although there have been some offshoots of the Taylor GLM system, the primary concept is to start a novice skier on short skis (skis that are three feet in length). After a period of adjustment the novice then progresses to four-foot skis, five-foot skis and finally to normal length skis. The advantage of GLM is that from the first lesson, the skier is skiing parallel.

Regardless of the teaching technique to which a novice is exposed, a reasonable goal is to be able to ski down a hill, continuously turning, traversing, and adapting to both the subtle and sudden changes in terrain. This is an objective that can be accomplished in a relatively short period of time. With recent advances in teaching technique, it is now possible for any person with "normal" coordination, strength, and endurance to learn to ski.

The PSIA emphasizes several basic principles in its approach to skiing. The more important of the principles are listed and briefly described below.

☐ *Natural position.* Within the limitations imposed by the concept of finished forms, body segments should be maintained in good anatomical alignment. There should be no undue muscular strain except that which is imposed by the dynamics of skiing.

☐ *Total motion* implies a smooth, rhythmic motion throughout the execution of a ski maneuver. Any ski motion is a constant series of minor adjustments to maintain smoothness and continuity. In the learning process, elements of a maneuver are taught individually and eventually put together in achieving total motion.

☐ *Unweighting* is a process wherein the pressure (or friction) between the skis and the snow is reduced momentarily.

Up-unweighting is characterized by a quick forward-upward extension of the body. The moment of unweighting occurs as the body reaches its maximum extension.

Down-unweighting occurs with a rapid lowering of the center of gravity. The speed of the lowering will determine how much unweighting occurs.

☐ *Axial motion* simply refers to the movement of the body around its central vertical axis. Axial motion can be used to imply either a turning force or a position change. Counterrotation as an axial motion was at one time a very important element in the American Ski Technique. It is still present but emphasized to a much lesser extent.

☐ *Edge control* is determined by the lateral movement of the lower leg. It is the relationship of the edges and bottom of the ski to the slope. Most skiing is performed on the ski edges.

☐ *Weight transfer* means exactly what it implies, a shifting of weight from one ski to another or from one edge of a ski to the other edge. Weight transfer is valuable in the context of turning and balance.

Elements of the American Ski Method

When first introduced in the 1950s the ASM (then called the American Ski Technique) was a very regimented approach to learning the fundamentals of skiing. Regardless of the discomfort to, and natural abilities of, the skier, he or she had to achieve a prescribed finished form. Much to the credit of the PSIA the trend today is to incorporate a more flexible approach to instruction and to utilize, to a much greater extent, the natural abilities of the skier.

The following is a description of the progressions of the ASM. They are presented here in the order which is generally used by ski schools. Colleges universities, and high schools can readily adapt the elements of ASM to their own situations. The reader must keep in mind that the descriptions which follow are very abbreviated and for more detailed information should consult the references.

Class A: Walking, straight running, gliding wedge, and wedge turns.

Class B: Basic christy, traverse I, and sideslip I.

Class C: Mileage (distance), straight running-traverse II, sideslip II, and wedge christy.

Class D: Wedge christy and wide track christy.

Class E: Christy with preturn, short-swing, wedeln, and step-christies.

Class F: Review and refining of Class E, moguls, deep snow.

Straight running position. The skis are parallel to one another and flat on the snow. The skier's weight is evenly distributed on both skis. The body assumes a position of forward lean. The arms are placed so that the hands are about waist high, with the elbows bent. The tips of the ski poles are about one foot off the ground.

This position is used by novices to descend slopes with very small incline and to become oriented to ski equipment. The skier should focus attention forward, relax, and enjoy the ride.

Gliding wedge. This was formerly called the snowplow position. The gliding wedge is the skier's first exposure to skiing on the edges of the skis. For the beginning skier, the gliding wedge is an excellent way to control speed and to stop. The intermediate and advanced skier will also occasionally use the gliding wedge when skiing slowly.

By the very nature of the position of the skis (a V position) the gliding wedge is a braking maneuver. The tails of the skis are positioned away from the center line and the tips are placed about 4 to 6 inches apart. The skis are resting on the snow on their inside edges. The skier's weight should be distributed equally on each ski and the skier maintains control by keeping the tips of the skis about four to six inches apart and the tails spread as previously indicated. The ankles, knees, and hips are flexed slightly and pressure should be felt on the front surface of the ankles.

Speed is controlled by either allowing the tails to come closer together (to go faster) or "sitting" and driving the tails wider (to slow down or stop).

Wedge Turn

This is probably the most critical point in a novice skier's career. The concept of weight shift is introduced at this point.

As novice skiers are descending a small slope in a controlled wedge and desire to make a turn to the left they apply pressure to the *right* ski by transferring the body weight to that side. (Professional ski instructors frown upon the use of "left" or "right" ski, but it gets the point across to a novice skier.)

At the completion of this maneuver skiers have two options: (1) to initiate a turn to the right by "weighting" the left ski, angulating, and counterrotating (rotating back) the left shoulder, or (2) simply bring the center of gravity back to the center between the two skis. This second option will result in a turning motion until the tips of the skis are again moving along the fallline (straight down the slope.) When several wedge turns are executed in succession, they are said to be linked.

Basic christy. Any kind of christy maneuver is a sliding turn. From a wedge-turning position, the skier pivots the inside (or uphill) ski toward the outside (or downhill) ski. Once the skis have been brought together, inertia will create a skid or slide. As the slide develops, the skier should sink by pressing the knees toward the tips of the skis. This will have the effect of increasing edge control.

Traverse position. Traverse position is used when going across (traversing) a slope. The uphill knee, hip, and shoulder are slightly ahead of the downhill counterparts. The same is true for the uphill ski and foot. There is slightly more weight on the downhill ski (the uphill edge). The steeper the slope, the more weight there is on the downhill ski.

The skier is skiing on the uphill edges of both skis with the skis slightly apart. As the skier gains balance and control, the skis will be brought closer together. Angulation, partially determined by the steepness of the hill, dictates edge control.

Fig. 30.3 The traverse position is used when going across a slope. Courtesy of *JOPER*.

Again, as with the straight running position, the ankles, knees, and hips are slightly flexed. The uphill arm is slightly in advance of the downhill arm. However, to get the proper feel for arm and hand position, skiers should feel as though they were carrying a food tray across the slope. The closer the traverse comes to following the fall-line, the faster the skiers will go.

Forward sideslip. Forward sideslipping serves at least two important functions for novice skiers: (1) it allows them to get out of difficult situations on steep terrain and (2) it enables them to further refine the basic christy.

From the traverse position, sideslipping is initiated by a slight upmotion and a decrease in angulation. This combination of movements decreases the angle between the ski bottoms and the snow. As the angle is decreased the skier sideslips faster.

An excellent description of sideslipping technique is offered in *Skiing Simplified* (Pfeiffer 1970).

Wedge christy. The wedge christy is a more dynamic and exciting form of the basic christy. It can be executed under a variety of conditions of both terrain and speed.

While in a traverse, the skier wedges the skis. Wedging in this circumstance serves two purposes: (1) to change the edges; (2) to place the outside (uphill) ski into a position where it will respond to a weight transfer. The skier is now in a position to shift the weight to the outside ski in much the same manner as when executing a wedge turn. The skis will slide or skid through the turn. Most of the skier's weight is on the outside or turning ski.

The wedge christy is now taught in place of the stem turn. The major differences between the wedge christy and stem turn are (1) there are at least three alternatives into gaining the wedge position and (2) when the wedge christy is completed, the skis are merely brought to a parallel position as opposed to a "closed" position in the stem turn. The wedge christy is the transition into advanced skiing.

Downstem christy. When practicing the skills of wedge christy and wide track christy turns in Class D, the downstem christy maneuver will emerge. The downstem motion with the inside (or downhill) ski stemmed (slide away from the outside ski) provides a "checking" action. A checking action allows for a quick weight transfer to the outside ski. The downstem motion also can be used as a braking maneuver in an emergency.

Christy with preturn. A lead-up skill to this particular christy is a "hockey" stop where both skis are pivoted energetically with the body facing the direction of the slide. The body is lowered by knee and ankle flexion to increase edging and force the stop. This may be called a stop christy. The preturn is executed by releasing the edges before stopping. With the use of the ski poles the body will "unwind" and both skis should pivot toward the fall-line. As the skis pivot, the maneuver is completed with a christy. Short swing and wedeln will follow in the teaching progression.

Moguls and deep snow. The skier who progresses to Class F is an accomplished skier interested in refining skills, learning how to ski moguls and to ski deep snow (powder) when the opportunity arises.

There are numerous additional skills and modifications of the skills described above available to challenge the skier. New maneuvers and techniques are continually being introduced via articles in magazines that cater to the skiing enthusiast.

SKI PROGRAMS IN SCHOOLS AND UNIVERSITIES

With modern technology and innovations, ski classes as part of a physical education curriculum are now feasible in schools and universities that previously could not provide such offerings. Modern transportation systems, artificial snow surfaces, man-made snow, and modern, easily adjustable ski equipment make class offerings available and attractive.

The potential for developing small areas for beginning instruction is great. An illustration of what can be done and how to overcome problems of construction and maintenance of such a facility by a university is presented by Gazette (1973, pp. 89–92). If it is not feasible to actually install a small ski area, an alternative is to ski on mats or some other artificial surface. Gorton, Jenkins, and Risser (1968, p. 100) present such an alternative. Another very popular approach is to work out arrangements with a local ski area. Usually, ski areas are most cooperative and provide attractive packages for lift tickets, lessons, and equipment. Transportation can be arranged by the schools and universities. Some universities transport students as far as 90 miles for classes.

Skiing has become one of the most enthusiastically accepted recreational activities in our country today. Students who have the opportunity to learn skiing are most enthusiastic. From an instructor's point of view, it is easy to see progress among class members. In a program that includes a grouping of four to seven lessons, a novice can progress to Class C or Class D skills. Ski instruction can be provided by qualified staff members or by members of the ski school staff at local ski areas.

REFERENCES

Abraham, H. 1972. *American ski method.* PSIA Technical Committee, Vail, Colorado.

Broten, G. A., and G. R. Twardokens 1970. Skiing is creditable. *JOHPER* **41**, 9 (November–December): 31–33.

Fig. 30.4 Skiing has become one of the most acceptable recreational activities in our country today. Courtesy of *JOPER*.

Gazette, C. P. 1969. Constructing skiing facilities. *JOHPER* **40,** 2 (February).

Gorton, L., W. Jenkins, and J. Risser 1968. Skiing without snow. *JOHPER* **39, 8** (October).

Greene, M. 1970. Skis and boots for everyone. *JOHPER* **41,** 9 (November–December): 34.

Iselin, F., and A. C. Spectorsky 1965. *Invitation to modern skiing.* New York: Simon and Schuster.

Lund, M. 1970. *Ski GLM.* New York: Dial.

Pfeiffer, D. J. 1970. *Skiing simplified.* New York: Grosset.

Robinson, G. R. 1974. *Skiing: conditioning and technique.* Palo Alto, Calif.: National Press.

Scharf, R., (ed.) 1970. *Ski magazine's encyclopedia of skiing.* New York: Harper & Row.

Ski. Universal Publishing and Distributing, 235 East 45th St., New York 10017.

Skiing. Subscription Services Office, P.O. Box 1098, Flushing, New York 11325.

Nordic Skiing

Patrick O'Shea

Nordic skiing (cross-country skiing) is by tradition the most common form of skiing in the Scandinavian countries—Finland, Norway, and Sweden. The major difference between Nordic skiing and Alpine (downhill skiing) is that skis used in the former are thinner and lighter. Boots are much lighter and are fastened to simple toe pieces and the heel is completely free to lift off the ski. Nordic equipment and technique permit you to ski uphill, downhill, on the flat—or just about anywhere that your skill level allows. The realm of Nordic touring includes open flat terrain, woods, gentle hills to steep mountain glaciers, and even city parks. Anywhere there is snow, Nordic touring skis can be used.

HISTORY

The history of Nordic skiing can be traced far back into antiquity. Stone Age rock carvings four thousand years old found in arctic Norway depict Norsemen traveling and hunting on primitive skis. In 1521 the Swedes gained their freedom from the Danes when the great Swedish patriot Gastavus Vasa skied from Salen to Mora in order to lead his countrymen in battle against Christian II of Denmark. The Swedes now commemorate his achievement each year when they hold their famed Vasaloppet ski race. The race follows the route taken by Vasa—85 kilometers (53 miles) in length. Over 8000 skiers from around the world participate annually.

In the arctic part of Scandinavia which most of the year is a stern and frozen wilderness, skiing is still the primary means of travel for the nomadic Laplanders. As their ancestors did for hundreds of years before them, the Lapps still use skis in their migration across the arctic circle and in tending their reindeer herds.

Nordic skiing was brought to North America in the mid-1800s by Scandinavian settlers. One of the early skiing pioneers was the famous "Snowshoe Thompson" from Telemark, Norway. Skis were called snowshoes until about 1900. In the 1850s Thompson skied with the mail over the Sierras from Placerville, California, to Carson City, Nevada. In 1857 a United States postage stamp was issued to celebrate him, and his exploits are still commemorated today by an annual cross-country ski race over his route.

Today, in the Scandinavian countries the most popular wintertime recreational activity is Nordic touring. In Finland alone there are over 4000 cross-country ski races each year. Many of these races include orienteering (land navigation with map and compass) as part of their competition.

The popular growth of Nordic skiing as a form of general recreation in the United States and Canada began in the upper New England states in the mid-1960s. In the following decade it quickly spread westward through the Rockies and on to the Cascades of Oregon and Washington. The rapid growth of Nordic skiing may be attributed to a number of factors. First, the extremely high cost of downhill skiing equipment and lift tickets far exceeds the recreational benefits to be derived. Too, extremely crowded conditions including long lift lines and rush hour traffic on the slopes generated general dissatisfaction with Alpine skiing. People were also becoming more interested in the natural wintertime environment, in being physically fit, and in the sport of Nordic skiing.

Nordic skiing added a new dimension to the activities of the backpacker and mountain climber. They were now able to enjoy the wilderness and mountains on a year-round basis.

Nordic skiing provides people with an alternative to the crowded conditions of downhill skiing. Nordic skiing has the potential to release the free spirit that exists in all people who seek a lasting experience with the white wilderness of winter.

Anyone from four to a hundred-and-four can participate in Nordic touring. It fits well into most physical education programs (where there is snow, of course) for it builds upon what students are already capable of— walking. Once students master the basic level stride, there is nothing to prevent them from taking off on an all-day cross-country tour. When combined with orienteering, Nordic touring offers a very challenging educational experience.

EQUIPMENT

In the past few years some major technical advances have been made in the design and manufacturing of Nordic skis and boots. The best advice a beginner can follow regarding equipment is to rent or borrow it until enough knowledge has been gained to permit an intelligent purchase of skis, poles, and boots. The best approach is to become familiar with the current literature and then to consult several experts.

Nordic ski tourers may not be so concerned about speed but the proper performance of their equipment is important to them; therefore, it is helpful for tourers to know what to look for. There are four types of Nordic skiing— *light touring, general touring, mountain touring,* and *cross-country racing.* Each type of equipment in a touring category is designed for a specific technique and terrain. A brief description of each category is as follows:

Light touring. The vast majority of Nordic skiers are day skiers, making this the most popular type of ski touring today. This category offers the largest selection of lightweight ski touring equipment. The skis are designed for lightness plus ease in moving across the snow. They are adaptable to a broad range of snow conditions and terrain. The skis are 50 to 52 mm. wide. Most models are available with hickory soles and lignostone edges. Lignostone edges are made of compressed, resin-impregnated beechwood, and offer a very hard edge for durability. Some models are available with synthetic bases which do not require treatment with pine tar. Best results are obtained with a toe binding. The boots are ankle height and combine light weight and flexibility.

General touring. The skis used for general touring are well adapted to winter backpacking over varied terrain and to deep, untracked snow in high mountainous areas. The skis are fairly wide and offer a good deal of stability. They are 55 to 77 mm. wide, moderately heavy, and strong for their weight. Models are available with a full hickory sole or hickory sole with lignostone edges and synthetic bases. For safety a cable binding is preferred in general touring. General touring boots should cover the ankle and give substantial support.

Mountain touring. The skis used in mountain touring are designed for rugged terrain and steep, icy slopes. They are used for winter mountaineering and backpacking in areas where long runs with a heavy pack through varying snow conditions are common. Mountain touring gear opens new vistas for winter travel in the mountains. The skis are the widest and heaviest of all the Nordic types and are equipped with metal edges. The bindings used are a strong cable type. Mountaineering boots which will give maximum support are recommended.

Cross-country racing. The skis used in this category are the narrowest and lightest of all the Nordic type skis. They are classified as either training racers or competition skis. Training racers are heavier, stronger, and are used by citizen class racers or expert tourers in moderate conditions. Competition skis are very lightweight, utilizing air channels, balsa wood or foam in their internal construction. These skis are designed for competitive racing on a prepared track. Pin bindings are always used. The boots are very lightweight, low cut, and flexible.

Ski Selection

Basically there are two types of ski bottom: wood and synthetic.

Wood. This is the traditional ski. Hardwood bottoms with lignostone edges are the most rugged. Wood bottoms require both a base treatment of pine tar and waxing. Waxholding ability is achieved by a laminated wood construction.

Nordic skis may use as many as 32 individual laminations in a builtup construction. Spruce is almost universally used for the midsection, while birch, hickory, and oak are used for the side and top laminations. Birch holds wax better and is lighter while hickory and lignostone make the most durable wood Nordic skis. Individuals using wood skis must learn how to wax. Waxing is one of the challenges of the sport for true purists.

Synthetic bottom skis. Nordic skis with synthetic bottoms come in various types, some of which require waxing and others which do not. Synthetic bottoms, usually of plastic (P-tex) and/or resins, are found on wood skis or on synthetic (usually fiberglass) skis. A P-Tex base ski is more durable than black plastic or wood bases of traditional skis. Nicks and scratches are easily repaired with a P-Tex candle.

The no-wax skis can be broken down into two types. One has mohair or some synthetic, usually fuzzy, material laid in strips into the bottom of the ski. This material helps in climbing steep hills and provides grip on the flats to stride out in the classic cross-country style. The other no-wax bottom ski has a pattern of steps or fish-scale which assists in climbing and holding on the flat as the mohair strips do. While these skis provide a definite advantage on uphill running, they are very slow on the downhill run and striding on the flat.

There is little doubt that the traditional wood ski will soon be a thing of the past. Competitors set the trend that tourists follow and today in international competition there is not a racer of note using the old wood ski.

The fiberglass are faster, lighter, and incredibly durable. One pair should last a tourer a lifetime.

Bindings

The three pin binding is the most commonly used touring binding. It is simple in design, lightweight, foolproof in operation, easy to install and virtually maintenance free.

In recent years manufacturers of bindings have adopted what is called the Nordic Norm. This is a standardization of angles, widths, heights, and pin

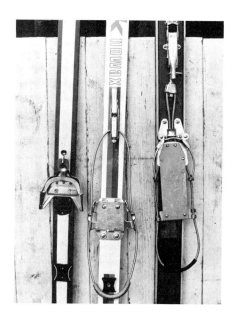

Fig. 30.5 Nordic bindings—(left) the three pin binding for general touring and racing, (middle and right) cable bindings which hold the heel down on downhill runs, (right) Selvritta binding for ski mountaineering. All photos in this article courtesy of Patrick O'Shea.

placement on bindings, and similar standardization of widths and hole placement on boots. This standardization allows one to interchange boots and bindings which meet Nordic Norm specifications.

Cable bindings are more valuable in ski mountaineering than touring bindings. The principle purpose of the cable binding is to hold the heel down to give more control on a downhill run. The cable binding frequently used by ski mountaineers is the Silvretta. Its main features are the ability to accommodate a mountaineering boot, give good forward flex, and provide an effective safety release. Good heel-to-toe flexibility is necessary for enjoyable touring.

Boots

While it is possible to ski fairly well on any ski you may buy, a pair of ill-fitting, poorly designed boots will make a tour of even one mile a miserable experience. The Nordic Norm makes most pin-binding boots compatible with different bindings. Good touring boots must have the heel-to-toe flexibility and lateral rigidity necessary for good skiing.

For the racer and tourer wanting to be more than a "shuffler," a boot must be flexible under the ball of the foot and the toes since this is the point from which the main thrust of the diagonal stride comes.

While a boot must have longitudinal flexibility it must be laterally or torsionally rigid. A torsionally rigid boot keeps the skier's weight directly over the ski during the gliding phase of the diagonal stride and on downhill runs.

A leather sole has good torsional rigidity while a rubber sole flexes easily under the ball of the foot. Most Nordic boots now have synthetic or rubber molded soles which are lighter and more durable.

Fig. 30.6 Nordic touring boot and binding which permits the heel to lift off for the "kick and glide."

Poles

Selection of good quality Nordic poles is critical, for close to 30 percent of a skier's thrust in a diagonal stride comes from poling. The first consideration in pole selection is how to choose the right length pole for one's height. A well-fitting Nordic pole should reach from a person's armpit to the floor as one stands in street shoes (see Table 30.1). If one cannot find a pole precisely the right length it is better to choose one that is a little long.

Nordic ski poles are available in either tonkin cane (bamboo) or metal. A quality tonkin pole has good flexibility, will absorb a great deal of weight in a fall, take general wear and tear, and can be easily repaired (by taping) in case of minor cracks or breaks.

Metal shafts come in many grades, from low-grade aluminum alloy to

Table 30.1*

Sizing Chart for Cross-country Skis and Poles

Skier's height cm/ft in.	Skier's weight lbs	Ski size cm	Pole size cm	Pole size in.
90 3′		100		
100 3′3″		110		
110 3′7″		120		
115 3′9″		130	90	35″
125 4′1″		140	95	37″
130 4′3″		150	100	39″
135 4′5″		160	105	41″
140 4′7″		170	110	43″
145 4′9″	100	180	110–115	43–45″
155 5′1″	115	190	120	47″
160 5′3″	130	195	125	49″
165 5′5″	140	200	130	51″
170 5′7″	150	205	135	53″
175 5′9″	160–180	210	140	55″
180 5′11″	160–180	210	145	57″
185 6′1″	180–200	215	150	59″
190 6′3″		To	155	61″
195 6′5″	200+	220	160	63″

Ski length is determined by both weight and height. If a person is heavier or lighter than average, skis should be chosen one size longer or shorter, respectively.

Pole length is determined from the floor to midshoulder. Racers generally prefer longer poles. For mountain touring, poles may be somewhat shorter. For small children, poles are sometimes a nuisance and can be eliminated altogether.

*   Table courtesy of Recreational Equipment, Inc., Seattle, Washington.

Fig. 30.7 Correct ski length: stand with one arm raised up; ski tip should reach up to the wrist. Correct pole length: stand with arm outstretched; pole should fit into the armpit.

metals of a very high quality. The cheap metal poles are not resilient and are liable to break easily or bend out of shape permanently with the least pressure.

The more expensive metal poles are very durable, flexible, and extremely light. There are two classes of high-grade metal poles available: (1) those in a midrange suitable for general touring, touring racing, and mountaineering and (2) those designed for racing. In ski mountaineering, metal poles should always be used.

For general touring, the standard 4¼″ diameter plastic basket is sufficient. If one skis in the wilds with powder up to the kneecaps a wider basket is preferable. Baskets on metal poles are usually smaller (3¼″ diameter) and canted, since the poles are used mainly for track skiing and weight is a consideration.

The tip of a Nordic pole is bent forward so that it will easily extract from the snow as the skier starts to bring the pole forward while poling. Tonkin touring poles have only the tip curved forward, while more expensive poles will be canted forward from the basket on down, the tip also curved forward. The more exaggerated cant helps in release while racing or touring on a prepared track.

TECHNIQUE OF NORDIC SKIING

The fundamental techniques of Nordic skiing are not difficult to learn. If one can walk, one can cross-country ski. This may sound rather simplistic but it is true.

Basic instruction begins by checking to see that the skis and poles are of the right length and are being worn properly. The left and right skis must be on the appropriate feet (since each ski binding, like a shoe, is made to fit either a left foot or right foot). Proper pole position is obtained by placing the hands, palms facing away from the body, up through the dangling pole straps and grasping the pole handles lightly, over the straps, and exerting a downward pressure. The final check is to see that the skis are properly waxed for grip and glide on the snow, or that the skis are the no-wax type.

The basic diagonal stride. The basic diagonal stride in its simplest form is a rhythmic shuffle of the feet with the forward knee slightly bent and swinging the arms alternately while planting the pole. The arms should swing as if walking at a brisk pace. If one is relaxed, one will find that as one steps forward with the right foot the left hand swings forward. On the skis, the right pole should be planted in the snow and used to give a starting push as the right foot and left hand come forward. The Scandinavians often practice without poles to master the arm–leg coordination. This diagonal stride is the basis of all Nordic touring and cross-country technique.

Kick and glide. To acquire the true feeling of the diagonal stride, one must change from a slow shuffling forward movement into a more dynamic stride,

Fig. 30.8 Proper way to hold a pole: put hand in from beneath and grasp the straps and handgrip.

Fig. 30.9 The diagonal stride, the basis of all Nordic skiing. Poling is coordinated with the kick and glide movement of the legs.

into a *kick* and *glide* movement. The kick is really a push off the ground with a vigorous extension of the leg and a forward drive of the opposite hand. The other ski starts gliding forward as a result of this push or kick. Now, the next step is to smoothly transfer the body weight onto the gliding ski. At the moment the push is finished, the entire body weight should be on the forward, gliding ski. The gliding thus described is much like ice skating.

In the kick and glide the body is bent slightly at the waist and there is no vertical lifting of the body. Poling must be coordinated with the kick and glide.

The kick and glide is best mastered by practicing on flat terrain. Working for full extension of the driving leg, one should concentrate on relaxing the poling hand as it passes the body. The pole should be planted slanting backward at the same level as the kicking foot to get the strongest push. And most important, one must concentrate extra hard on driving the whole weight forward on the gliding ski.

Kick turn. The kick turn is a method of reversing direction 180° when in a standing position. It is used on both flat and steep terrain. To execute the kick turn to the left one must move the left foot and ski slightly to the rear. The left ski is then swung forward to a vertical position and the heel placed in the snow, approximately even with the right ski tip. From this vertical position the left ski is allowed to swing away from the body, keeping the heel in place, and rotated 180° until it is parallel with the right ski. The right ski is lifted and rotated around to the new position, parallel with the left ski. On a steep slope, the skis are placed horizontally across the slope and edged into the slope. Both ski poles are initially placed in the snow above the skis and the downhill ski is turned first.

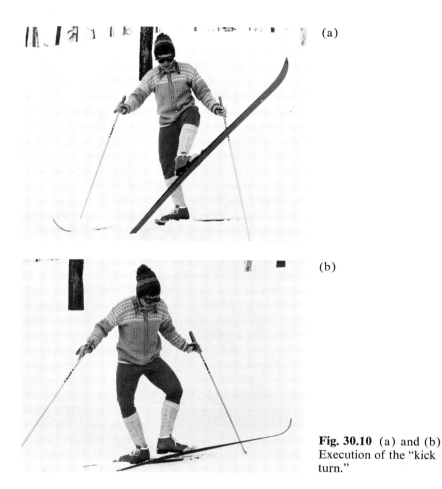

(a)

(b)

Fig. 30.10 (a) and (b) Execution of the "kick turn."

Hill Climbing

Hill climbing can be hard work and the ease with which a skier can climb a hill will depend upon its steepness, the type of wax being used, and the level of physical fitness. At a certain steepness, depending on the snow and wax, you will begin to have difficulty gripping. This problem is overcome by slapping the skis down hard onto the snow instead of shuffling them upon the surface, and keeping your knees and ankles well bent so that your weight rests on the whole ski and not just on the tails. If you are rather proficient with the diagonal stride, try skiing up the slope instead of just shuffling up, by shortening your strides into a kind of bouncy, aggressive dogtrot. Whichever method you may use, when the point is reached at which your skis no longer grip, the following methods may be used.

Sidestep. The sidestep is an effective method of climbing a short, steep slope and where space is confined, it may be the only practical means of ascending slopes. The skis are placed horizontally across the slope and then walked up one at a time, as though climbing a staircase sideways. To prevent slipping sideways, the uphill edges of both skis are forced into the snow by pushing both knees forward and toward the slope. One should avoid leaning into the slope. Initially, the weight of the body is placed on the lower ski. The uphill ski is lifted up the slope and the body weight placed upon it. The upper ski pole is moved at the same time and placed above and alongside this ski. The lower ski is then moved up as close as possible to the uphill ski, while the skier is supported by a push on the lower pole. This pole is then brought up and placed alongside the lower ski. One cycle of the sidestep is now completed.

Uphill traverse. This method of climbing is used when the slope becomes too steep for going straight uphill. Traversing means moving on a diagonal across the slope, either diagonally up, or diagonally down. Although a traverse generally involves a zigzag route, it will often be the least tiring method of ascending. One must track back and forth up the slope in a series of zigzags, choosing an angle of ascent that seems comfortable or practical. The zigs are linked to the zags by a stepped turn, on the uphill side, if the slope is not too steep; or, on steeper slopes, by a proper kick turn facing downhill.

Herringbone. The herringbone is used to climb short, moderate, or steep slopes. It provides a quicker ascent than the sidestep. However, it is very tiring and should be used only for relatively short ascents. In using the herringbone, the body is faced uphill with the skis spread to form a wide V. The

Fig. 30.11 Sidestepping, an effective method of climbing a short, steep slope.

Fig. 30.12 Herringbone technique for a quick ascent up a short, steep slope.

skis are edged sharply inward, to prevent backslip, by bending the knees forward and inward. The first step is made by placing the weight on one ski, raising the other slightly above the snow and moving it forward and upward. This ski is then placed in the snow, edged inward, and the body weight transferred to it. The other ski is then moved in the same manner and placed slightly ahead. At the same time, the ski poles are used in the same manner as the sidestep, except they are alternately placed to the rear of the body and to the outside of each ski to act as a brace and to aid in the climb.

Downhill Running

Skiing downhill on a pair of Nordic skis can be an exhilarating experience, but one must be careful not to accelerate so rapidly as to go out of control. It is wise to start out with a small hill which provides a good run-out where one can glide to a stop. For downhill running, the following position should be assumed: slightly crouched, wide stance, skis about as wide as the hips; ankles, knees and hips loosely flexed; weight distributed evenly over the flat of the feet, or slightly more toward the heel; and hands widespread for lateral balance. One should stay relaxed and loose, feeling where the balance really is, and enjoy the sensation of free movement down the hill.

Controlling movements in untracked snow on a downhill run is marginal on Nordic skis. In deep powder snow one must sit back on the heels and let the snow build up in front. This will slow one's pace and keep speed under control. Mastering the step turn and the snowplow turn is useful for safe downhill running.

Step turn. Before turning, the skier should lead with the ski which corresponds to the direction of the turn, i.e., right ski ahead when turning to the

Fig. 30.13 Snowplow, an effective method for slowing down, stopping, and turning.

right. In turning to the right the weight is placed upon the left ski, which is then edged to the right. The unweighted right ski is raised and placed on the snow in the new direction. The weight is transferred to this ski by moving the body in the new direction while pushing off from the left ski. The unweighted ski is then lifted off the snow, and placed parallel to the right ski to complete the turn. Complete transfer of body weight is essential, and the movements must be made smoothly and simultaneously. The higher the speed, the more the center of gravity is lowered by bending the knees and ankles. This adds stability and aids in keeping up with the turn. The steps can be continued as long as the skier is in forward motion and until the desired direction is obtained.

Snowplow. The snowplow is efficient for slowing down, stopping, and turning. It is especially useful when carrying a heavy pack. In the snowplow maneuver, the skis are held in a wedge position. To assume a snowplow position, both heels are pushed outward evenly, keeping the ski tips even and close together, forcing the skis to form a wide V. The body weight is evenly distributed on both skis. The knees are bent well forward in the direction of the ski tips, causing the skis to be edged slightly inward. Continuous outward heel pressure is applied on the skis. At the same time, the upper part of the body and the ski poles are held as in the straight downhill running position.

Snowplow turn. In executing a snowplow turn to the *left* while snowplowing directly down a slope, the body weight is transferred smoothly onto and over the right ski (note that this ski is already pointed to the left) by a rotation of the body to the right and by a pronounced bend of the right knee to slip all body weight onto the right ski. This transfer of body weight initiates the

Fig. 30.14 Telemark position. For straight running downhill, over bumpy ground, or where sliding conditions are unpredictable.

turning action. As the turn progresses, the body is not allowed to rotate beyond the new direction of travel. The left knee is kept well bent with this ski flat and unweighted throughout the turn. When the turn is completed, the body weight is either placed evenly on both skis to continue in a snowplow or gradually transferred to the left ski to start a turn to the right.

Double poling. On a slight downhill run, it is often more convenient to push off the top with both poles than to stride off using diagonal poling. To double pole, one simply brings both poles forward—instead of one as in the diagonal —both hands nearly in front of the nose, and pushes off with both simultaneously. After the push, the arms will be extended to the rear momentarily and the upper body will be in a forward position before resuming the stride.

Lastly, while one is learning and practicing Nordic skiing one should remember to enjoy the white wilderness of winter. For Nordic skiing is really a means to this end.

WAXING OF SKIS

One of the technical challenges of Nordic skiing is waxing. The ability to ski uphill, downhill, or on the flat without slipping backward every time the skier pushes off into a glide is made possible by waxing. Without waxing (or the mohair or fish-scale bottoms of no-wax skis) Nordic skiing would be exhausting work or, in most situations, impossible.

It is difficult to explain why a waxed ski will both grip and glide. Snow is viscoelastic, in that it has some properties of both viscous fluids and elastic solids. Snow density, crystal type, and temperature determine the exact properties and thus the way the snow will react to force.

A microscopic view of a snow surface shows many irregularities varying in direction, size, stiffness, and spacing. A microscopic view of a waxed ski on the snow shows that these irregularities penetrate the wax. The way they penetrate determines how the ski acts on the snow surface. When a ski is waxed correctly for touring, the small microscopic particles of the snow surface penetrate the wax just enough to allow a good grip with a motionless, weighted ski. But as soon as the ski moves forward, the same irregularities in the snow cannot penetrate the wax. Thus the wax both grips and glides. A correctly waxed ski glides as long as it is in motion. When the motion stops, the ski must be unweighted before it can glide again.

An incorrectly waxed ski may be waxed either "too hard" or "too soft." If the wax is too hard for the snow involved, the ski will only glide and slip both when weighted and unweighted. If the wax is too soft, snow particles can penetrate too far into the wax and remain there: the skis will glide poorly, collect snow, and ice up. The whole secret of waxing lies in the ability to judge snow conditions and properly apply the wax.

Base preparation. Wood bottom skis must be waterproofed before waxing. Wood absorbs water easily; wet skis can and will ice up, and wax will not hold on water or ice. To prevent the wood from soaking up moisture and icing, and to give adhesion to the wax, the bottoms must be impregnated with a pine tar preparation.

Before applying the tar, the skis are cleaned of old wax by using a blow torch and a rag. Propane is not affected by low temperatures as is butane and is the recommended fuel.

One type of tar preparation can be applied without heat. Another type is brushed or wiped on with a rag in a thin film and then heated into the ski using a blow torch. The torch is run over the surface until the tar begins to bubble and dry. The torch must move continuously to avoid singeing or burning the wood. The torch must be followed with a rag to remove excess tar while it is hot. The results should be a dry, chocolate-brown base. No single treatment will last the life of a pair of skis. The bottoms must be treated whenever bare wood shows. Best waxing results are obtained by letting the tar dry overnight.

Base waxes. Base waxes, binders with excellent wax-holding ability but little protecting ability, may be applied to synthetic bottom or wood bottom skis which have been treated with a base preparation. The application of base wax (or base klister) is an intermediate step that can be left out unless the snow conditions are very granular.

Running waxes. There are four main types of wax: hard wax and soft wax for all dry snow, klister wax for transition, or borderline, conditions, and klisters for wet and icy conditions. Hard waxes, in the color scheme of most of the manufacturers, are green and blue, with blue softer than green. Soft waxes are purple and red. The lower the snow temperature and the drier the snow, the harder the wax to be used—and vice versa. Under ambivalent conditions, with dry snow changing to wet, often a gooey yellow klister wax is required. Yellow klister wax is a stopgap between a wax and a klister.

Klister is a Norwegian word meaning "sticky stuff." It is essential on ice, crust, corn snow, slush, and sometimes wet powder. Whereas wax and klister wax are ironed on, klister is warmed in the tube and then dabbed on and spread out in a thin layer with a putty knife or the palm of the hand.

Basic Rules of Waxing

☐ All waxes must be applied to a clean, dry base-prepared or permanent-base surface, or over the dry surface of a harder wax.

☐ Several thin layers of wax are better than a single thick layer. More layers give more "kick" while fewer layers give more glide.

☐ The entire running surface of the ski should be waxed. It is common to wax the length of the ski hard for glide, and a two-foot strip under the foot for better grip.

☐ Hard waxes, green and blue, should be used for powder snow below freezing.

☐ Temperatures around freezing present the greatest waxing problems. Here soft waxes are used, purple and red and klister wax. Klisters, blue and red, are used both above and below freezing, under conditions where the snow has changed radically from its original state to become ice, crust, corn snow, wet powder, or slush.

☐ Waxing is best done at room temperature. Outside, a waxing iron or cork is generally used to smooth out the wax.

☐ A hard wax should not be put on over a soft wax. If the skis are clogging with snow the soft wax or klister must be scraped off with a knife. If clogging persists, or under conditions of wet, falling snow, silver downhill wax is the only thing that works.

☐ Judging which wax is correct is a matter of matching one set of conditions (wax) against another (snow). The simplest guide to judging snow type is to squeeze a handful of snow in a gloved hand. If the snow does not clump at all and can be blown out of the hand, it is dry. If it just clumps and some particles can be blown away, it is transition. If it clumps into a snowball, it is wet. Measuring the temperature of the snow with a waxing thermometer is also an excellent method of determining which wax to use.

☐ Snow conditions vary from one section of the country to another. Normally, higher elevations are colder, northern exposures are colder, and conditions vary from one time of the day to another. When skiing from bright sunshine into shady areas one finds different conditions.

☐ It is virtually impossible to wax correctly for all conditions. This holds true even for experts.

TOURING

Nordic touring offers a variety of opportunities to get close to the beauty of our wintertime environment. Ski tours, from the one-day tour to multiday tours, can be planned. The extent to which individuals can get involved in cross-country skiing will depend upon skiing ability, level of fitness, and knowledge of cold weather survival skills. For a backpacker or mountain climber the transition from summer camping to winter camping is quite easy. Survival in all seasons of the year begins with a firm understanding of the term "hypothermia." More commonly referred to as exposure, hypothermia is the most immediate threat to every skier's survival whether on a single-day outing or a multiday tour.

Hypothermia

By definition hypothermia means a lowering of body temperature due to a loss of body heat at a rate faster than it can be produced. Below freezing temperatures are not a necessary precondition for hypothermia. Exposure to wet, cold and windy conditions is the most common situation leading to hypothermia. Physical exhaustion and insufficient food intake are contributing factors.

In hypothermia, as the core body temperature falls from the normal 98.6°F, various body processes are slowed. Circulation of the blood is retarded, movements become sluggish, coordination is reduced, and judgment becomes impaired. With further cooling, unconsciousness results. If the body core temperature drops below 80°F, there is increased risk of disorganized heart action or heart stoppage which results in sudden death.

Treatment of hypothermia involves rewarming the body evenly and without delay, but not so rapidly as to further disorganize body functions such as circulation. A hypothermia victim should be immediately protected by all available dry clothing or a sleeping bag and then be moved to a warm enclosure. Out in the white wilderness of winter this may mean a snow cave or igloo. Warm liquids may be given gradually to a conscious person. High, quick energy carbohydrate foods such as candy and honey should be fed but not forced down. *Alcohol must never be used in the rewarming process* as it can drive the cold blood from the surface vessels to the body's inner core, thus reducing core temperature.

Defense against hypothermia consists of taking the proper steps to prevent rapid and uncontrolled loss of body heat. To a great extent guarding against hypothermia is having a basic understanding of the methods by which body heat is lost and the "layer principle of clothing" for skiing.

Methods of body heat loss. Body heat is lost to the environment through the processes of conduction, radiation, and convection. Conduction is the heat exchange between objects at different temperatures that are in contact with one another. The amount of heat transferred by conduction is proportionate to the temperature difference between the body and the surrounding air. The colder the air, the greater the conduction. Heat loss through conduction is a problem when carrying a metal ice axe or sitting on cold rocks and snow.

Radiation is the transfer of body heat to the surrounding environment. The head is the most critical area in heat loss by radiation. At 40°F, 50 percent of the body heat is lost through the head and at 5°F, close to 75 percent. Every skier must remember that when the feet get cold it is time to put on the hat.

Convection is the most important consideration in keeping warm, and wind is the most significant factor here. The human body warms a thin layer of surrounding air by conduction and radiation. However, if the air is being removed by wind convection currents as rapidly as it is warmed up, a high thermal gradient and rate of body heat loss will result. (See Table 30.2.)

Clothing

The primary purpose of clothing is to assist the body in maintaining thermal equilibrium. Proper clothing, correctly worn, will help the body to adjust to all climatic conditions. In cold weather the clothing does this by holding in the body heat, thereby insulating the body against the outside air. (See Table

Table 30.2

Windchill Chart

Cooling power of wind expressed as "Equivalent Chill Temperature"

Wind speed (mph)	Actual air temp °F—							
	40	30	20	10	0	−10	−20	−30
5	35	25	15	−5	−5	−15	−25	−35
10	30	15	5	−10	−20	−35	−45	−60
15	25	10	−5	−20	−30	−45	−60	−70
20	20	5	−10	−25	−35	−50	−65	−80
25	15	0	−15	−30	−45	−60	−75	−90
30	10	0	−20	−30	−50	−65	−80	−95
35	10	−5	−20	−35	−50	−65	−80	−100
40	10	−5	−20	−35	−55	−70	−85	−100

Table 30.3

Insulation Thickness Required at Various Temperatures

Effective Temperature	Sleeping	Light work	Heavy work
40°F	1.5"	0.8"	0.20"
20°F	2.0"	1.0"	0.27"
0°F	2.5"	1.3"	0.35"
−20°F	3.0"	1.6"	0.40"
−40°F	3.5"	1.9"	0.48"
−60°F	4.0"	2.1"	0.52"

30.3.) The problem of protection becomes acute in wet and near freezing temperatures. If clothing should become wet it must be removed as soon as possible. When cross-country skiing, it is as imperative to remove and adjust clothing to prevent excessive overheating as it is to add clothing to prevent heat loss. To do this requires implementation of the layer principle of clothing.

Layer principle of clothing. The layer principle of dressing for cross-country skiing involves wearing 3 to 5 layers of light garments rather than 1 or 2 heavy ones. This system permits clothing to be shed or donned as the demands for body heat decrease or increase. Skiing fast or with a fairly heavy pack creates unique clothing problems in this regard. While skiing, considerable body heat is being generated and unless this heat can escape it will collect as condensation on the inner garments and may freeze when the skier stops. Light garments that "breathe" must be worn to allow excess body heat to escape. Correct layers of clothing for skiing, from the skin side out, are fishnet underwear, a cotton T-shirt, a light wool shirt or sweater, and a lightweight nylon wind parka or anorak. The parka must not be waterproof but water repellent to allow condensation to escape.

Back Country Touring

In recent years many Pacific Northwest backpackers and climbers—especially Oregonians—have discovered the exhilarated feeling found only in wilderness skiing. The Sierra Club Totebook of Wilderness Skiing describes it as, "not one homogeneous sport, but rather a whole variety of feelings, of excursions, of movements; plodding under giant packs; gliding through forest. It may last for days or weeks at a time."

What is so attractive and appealing about wilderness skiing? Primarily, it offers an escape from the artificial existence and comforts of contemporary urban life. An 8-hour-a-day sedentary desk job may be a necessary factor in making the wheels of industry turn but it does little for intellectual and physical stimulation. A wilderness ski trip of three or four days helps the body and mind become attuned to nature. Upon returning to civilization one is better able to cope with the demands of everyday living. Wilderness skiing is a challenge to one's physical readiness. Survival is an important consideration in wilderness skiing and the aerobically fit skier will be able to withstand extreme changes in temperature for long periods of time. This higher tolerance for extreme thermal variations can be attributed to greater cardiovascular and muscular efficiency. Physical fitness is the best insurance one can have in the event of an accident or other emergency in the back country.

In planning a multiday ski tour into the back country, total pack weight becomes a crucial factor. Weight to the very ounce must be considered in the selection of clothing, food, sleeping bag, tent, sleeping pad, pack stove, cookware, plastic eating utensils, snow shovel, ski waxing kit, extra ski tips, cables, flashlight, and camera. Total pack weight will be about 40–50 pounds. To tote all this gear a frameless tour pack is recommended. A tour pack is more stable than the frame type when cross-country skiing.

Through experience overall pack weight can be somewhat reduced. It is almost impossible to reduce the weight of food and stove. Clothing and sleeping bags offer a few options to reduce weight. They must be light, compressible, and strong. Packing an ultralight down sleeping bag meets this criterion. For snow camping, however, where the chances of getting wet are high, a foam or synthetic fiber-filled bag is often desirable. Down filler when wet offers little protection against the cold. Whatever the type of sleeping bag it should provide warmth to $-15°F$. Functional clothing for an extended bivouac in the backcountry consists of fishnet underwear, which ventilates and insulates the body; two T-shirts; one light and one heavy wool sweater; heavy wool pants or ski warm-ups to wear over light ski touring knickers made of elastic stretch fabric; two pairs of light socks and two pairs of heavy wool long socks which rise above the knee to avoid the common "knicker gap" of cold skin; wool hat; two pairs of wool mittens with shells of heavy waterproof nylon; wind parka; rain poncho; down jacket or vest; and down boots—optional but great for keeping the feet warm while sitting around in a cold tent, snow cave, or igloo.

Low light Nordic touring shoes are definitely not recommended for wilderness skiing. They are not adequate to keep the feet warm. A heavy mountaineering boot is preferred. Heavier boots will protect the feet from frostbite in the event one has to walk instead of ski out of the wilderness. Expedition overboots are also an asset, as they slip on over the ski boots, keeping the feet warm and dry while a snow camp is set up. High-cut boot gaiters, too, can do the job of keeping the snow out of the boots especially when one is skiing through deep powder snow.

A rain poncho is an important item to include in one's pack. In addition to providing protection from rain, it can function as ground cover or as a roof over a slit trench shelter.

The greatest reduction in pack weight can be achieved through the elimination of the tent. With sufficient snow depth—three feet or more—and a little experience working with snow, one can learn to build a slit trench, snow cave, or igloo for shelter.

A slit trench is an emergency type shelter requiring about 15 minutes to construct. All that is necessary is a light mountaineering snow shovel to dig a trench deep enough to provide protection from the wind. The trench roof is made by laying your skis and poles across the top and then covering them with a poncho or plastic ground cover. Snow must be piled along the edges of the poncho to keep it from blowing off. On clear nights there is no real need for a roof. Sleeping in the open provides a spectacular view of the winter heavens.

Snow caves and igloos offer a tremendous advantage over tent shelters. They are roomier, quieter, dryer and give 100 percent protection in a blizzard. In 1912, the great arctic explorer Stefansson pointed out that it could be as much as $10°$ warmer inside an igloo than outside. When it was $50°F$ below zero outside, the temperature in the entranceway was $-40°F$, $0°$ at the doorway, $20°F$ at the floor (bed) level, $40°F$ above at shoulder height, and as high as $60°F$ above near the ceiling. A tribute to the efficiency of the igloo is the fact that Eskimos raise their families in them.

Construction of a snow cave or igloo requires a snow saw, snow shovel, and rain pants or equivalent. Protection of the hands is particularly important and rubber gloves with wool inner gloves will do the job.

Digging a snow cave is less complicated than constructing an igloo. A roomy cave for two or three skiers requires about 2 hours to dig while building an igloo takes 3 hours. Both types of shelters are used as permanent base camps during extended wilderness trips. Details with regard to construction of snow caves or igloos can be found in most winter survival manuals.

Everyone using a snow cave or igloo must be aware of the threat of carbon monoxide poisoning, one of the primary causes of death in the wilderness. Cooking inside a sealed cave consumes gallons of oxygen. When the oxygen level inside the cave falls below a critical point, the stove begins to produce carbon monoxide. With no warning and no respiratory distress, the individual feels drowsy, falls asleep and dies.

Cross ventilation is established by placing an exhaust vent high in the cave roof and leaving the entrance partially open. The vent hole must be checked every two or three hours to ensure that it has not become clogged by snow or by icing.

Maximum safety is the first consideration on a wilderness ski trip. It is important to have a minimum of three in a party. If something should happen to one member, the other two can handle almost any situation.

When white wilderness skiing, great care must be taken to protect the eyes from ultraviolet radiation. Snow reflects 75 percent of the incident ultraviolet radiation. Total ultraviolet radiation may increase on an overcast day when the hazard is unapparent to the skier. Exposing the eyes to ultraviolet radiation from the sun results in snowblindness. There is no warning that the eyes are being overexposed. Symptoms develop 8–12 hours after exposure. The eyes then feel like they are full of sand. Sunglasses that filter out 90 percent of the ultraviolet light and blackout reflected light should be selected.

Skill in using a map and compass is essential for anyone venturing into the white wilderness of winter. There are few marked ski trails in the back country and it does not take long for blowing snow to cover a track. Skiers must know what the magnetic declination is for the area, have skill in taking back bearings and cross-bearings, and be able to convert from a quadrant to an azimuth bearing. The latter is important because United States Forest Service signs give a compass bearing in the quadrant scale.

In the final analysis, proper clothing, good equipment, and a map and compass do not guarantee survival; however, common sense does. Common sense permits a natural adjustment to the white wilderness of winter.

REFERENCES

Baldwin, E. R. 1973. *The cross-country skiing handbook.* New York: Scribner's.

Brady, M. M. 1971. *Nordic touring and cross-country skiing.* (Second edition.) Oslo, Norway: Gunna A. Nielson.

Caldwell, J. 1968. *The cross-country ski book.* Brattleboro, Vt.: Stephen Green Press.

Chickering, R., (ed.) 1972. *Cross-country skiing.* New Canaan, Ct.: Toby.

Discover cross-country skiing 1974. Mountain View, Calif.: World Publications.
Flores, L., and A. Steck 1972. *Wilderness skiing.* San Francisco: Sierra Club.

Lathrop, T. 1973. *Hypothermia: killer of the unprepared.* Portland, Ore.: Mazamas.

Washburn, B. 1974. *Frostbite.* Boston: Museum of Science.

31
Soccer

P. S. Fardy's article explains the nature of soccer, describes the field, and outlines the position of the players. Defensive and offensive organization as well as tactics and strategy are briefly discussed. The fundamental skills of soccer and methods of teaching them are explained.

In an article now over 40 years old, Mildred Vanderhoof has described skills tests which are as useful today as when they were first written. This article provides an added dimension to the entire discussion of soccer. RBF

Soccer: Basic Instruction
Paul S. Fardy

Soccer, one of the world's most popular sports, is also particularly attractive as a physical education activity. It is a game that:

☐ requires quick thinking and individual initiative, yet is dependent upon a cooperative team effort,

☐ provides vigorous physical activity, while relatively free from serious injury,

☐ is inexpensive and can be incorporated easily into the physical education curriculum at any level,

☐ can be enjoyed thoroughly by all regardless of their age, sex, or size,

☐ by eliminating hand and arm usage, provides an exciting challenge that is uniquely in contrast to most other American sports,

☐ is easily learned and understood, even at the elementary level.

This article provides the potential teacher and/or participant the ingredients of a basic instruction soccer program. Special attention has been given to developing guidelines that will enhance the teaching of soccer, with particular reference to age, sex, group size, and facility considerations.

THE GAME

A soccer game consists of two teams attempting to propel a ball through a goal with any part of the body except the hands or arms, but usually with the feet or head. Each team consists of eleven players although for teaching purposes this number can be modified. A large field can accommodate additional players. If field space is limited a reduction in the team size might well enhance overall play. As few as five or six can make up a team on a very small field or in a gymnasium, as in indoor soccer. Reducing the number of players permits each player added time with the ball, and consequently leads to more rapid skill development.

PLAYING FIELD

A regulation collegiate soccer field is illustrated in Fig. 31.1. For basic instruction purposes, however, it is advisable to modify the field size according to participant sex and age. For every three to five years less than college age, the width should be reduced by about ten yards and the length by approximately twenty yards. These dimensions should be further decreased five to ten percent for females. Reducing the height and width of the goal for females and younger male participants should also be considered.

EQUIPMENT

Little equipment is needed to play soccer. Weather permitting, shorts, a light shirt, and gym shoes are sufficient. Soccer shoes enhance the caliber of play, particularly on slippery surfaces, but they are expensive and certainly are not needed at the beginning level. Inexpensive soccer shoes might be suggested for college players. Leather balls should be used as they are much easier to control and create less physical discomfort than less expensive rubber balls. An ideal teaching situation would provide one ball for every two participants; one for every five or six can suffice but fewer than this number limits teaching effectiveness.

The size of the ball should be adapted to the sex and age of the members of the class. A smaller and lighter ball will enable younger players to raise the level of their play and assure increased enjoyment. The use of a lighter ball, i.e., a volleyball, when introducing heading will minimize the possibility of discomfort to the beginner. The disadvantage of this practice is that prolonged usage can result in learning bad techniques.

POSITIONING

Positioning in soccer, as in other team sports, can assume a variety of alignments. The most common of these are the 2-3-3-2, 3-2-2-3, 4-2-4, and 4-3-3 formations.

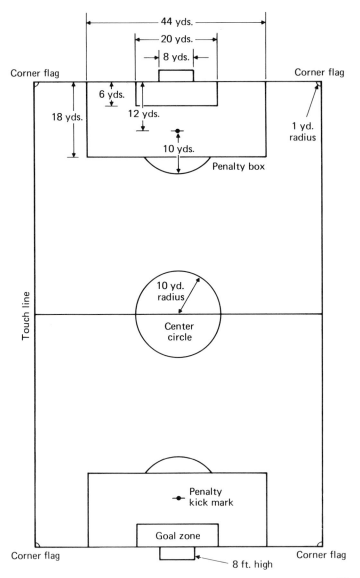

Fig. 31.1 Regulation collegiate soccer field.

Length — 110 yds. min. to 120 yds. max.
Width — 65 yds. min. to 75 yds. max.

Of these, the simplest for beginners to learn are the 2-3-3-2 and 3-2-2-3 formations which provide for easier coverage of the center of the field where the ball is most frequently played. Additional formations can be introduced as the caliber of play improves. *It is very important,* regardless of the forma-

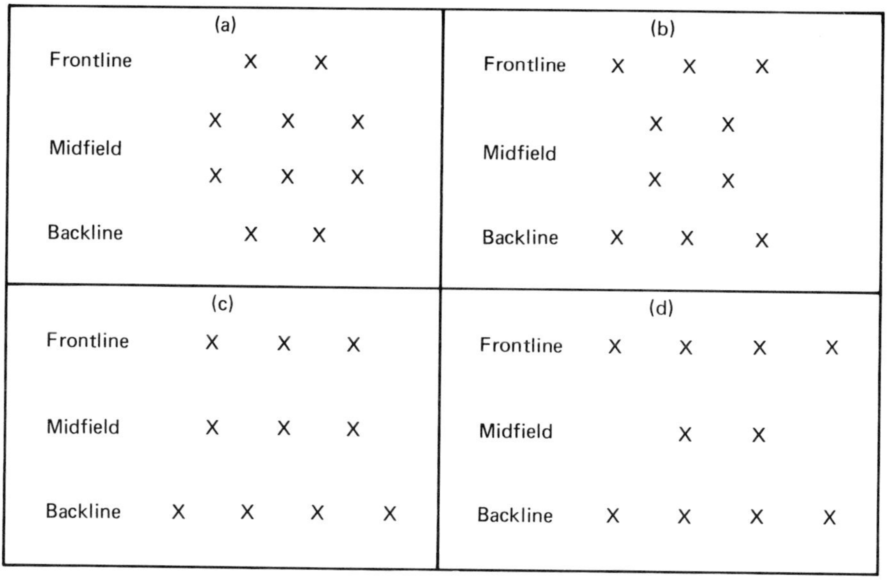

(a)				(b)			
Frontline	X	X		Frontline	X	X	X
Midfield	X X X			Midfield	X X		
	X X X				X X		
Backline	X	X		Backline	X	X	X
(c)				(d)			
Frontline	X	X	X	Frontline	X	X	X X
Midfield	X	X	X	Midfield	X	X	
Backline	X X X X			Backline	X	X	X X

Fig. 31.2 Soccer formations: (a) 2-3-3-2, (b) 3-2-2-3, (c) 3-3-4, and (d) 4-2-4.

tion selected, *that all players have an opportunity to try each position.* The opportunity to specialize at a given position should be made available later. It is sometimes advantageous at the elementary level to divide the field initially into halves or thirds and restrict the movement of certain positions within these zones. As soon as the concept of positioning is learned, however, it is important that these restrictions be removed.

Team positioning is most easily taught to beginning players as "lines of play." Within the prescribed alignment, it is essential to emphasize that *all players have both offensive and defensive responsibilities.*

Front line players (forwards). The primary responsibility of the forwards is to score goals. Most of the scoring will probably come from the center positions since these players have a better shooting angle. The attack, however, should develop from the outside positions. In general, these should be the most skillful players.

Middle line players (halfbacks). These players are responsible for covering the field's center. Since this requires covering more field space than other positions, halfbacks must possess a high level of stamina. Offensively their prime function is to set up scoring opportunities by clever passing to the forward line. Occasionally, however, they should also attempt to score goals, thereby keeping the defense off balance. The primary defensive responsibility of the halfback line is to check the opposite midfield players.

Back line players (fullbacks). The main responsibility of the fullbacks is to prevent the scoring of goals. Therefore, they must be aggressive, sure tacklers, with quick reactions and sufficient speed to check the opposing forwards.

Goalkeeper. The goalkeeper is the last line of defense and assumes the responsibility for directing the coverage in this area of the field. This is the only player permitted to use the hands and obviously is concerned mainly with preventing the ball from going into the goal. A good goalie must possess sure hands, sound judgment, and must not hesitate, if necessary, to make an aggressive charge out from the goal in pursuit of the ball. The goalkeeper can also assist the offense by kicking and throwing the ball with distance and accuracy.

OFFENSIVE STRATEGY

When offensive strategy is first introduced, several items should be stressed. These include:

- ☐ maintaining correct positioning at all times,
- ☐ moving the ball by passing not dribbling,
- ☐ continuously changing the play from one side of the field to the other,
- ☐ not concentrating the ball in the middle of the field,
- ☐ shooting when the opportunity presents itself.

The simplest approach to teaching these concepts and at the same time emphasizing proper positioning is to incorporate a flexible *zone play*. The field is divided so that each player is responsible for an area. Switching positions is permissible, and should be encouraged as long as the respective field positions are "loosely" covered. In addition, a long passing attack should be employed initially since this requires less skill. As the skill level improves, a short passing or combination short–long passing strategy can be introduced.

DEFENSIVE STRATEGY

The concept of defensive alignment is much easier to teach to beginners. The simplest approach is to teach *one-on-one coverage,* emphasizing that each player assume a defensive position between the goal and the player being defended. The resulting formation, therefore, will be the same as the opposition's offensive alignment.

Whether discussing offensive or defensive strategy, however, it is important to stress the effectiveness of being able to change quickly from one to the other. The success of both offensive and defensive play will be enhanced by this ability.

FUNDAMENTALS

The key to successful teaching of fundamentals is *simplification*. This is especially true in soccer where the basic skills are very different from those of other more familiar activities. It is also advantageous to introduce only those fundamentals essential to basic play, and to teach more advanced skills at a later date. The following fundamentals are those which should be taught initially:

Passing Skills

The skills of passing usually are performed with the feet or head. Whichever techniques are being taught it is important to stress that the ball must be moved with purpose at all times, and that random kicking or heading should be avoided.

1. Inside of the foot pass. The supporting foot is placed alongside the ball pointing in the direction of the intended pass while the kicking foot is turned outward. The body is positioned well over the ball and contact is made on the inner ankle bone. The ball is usually contacted slightly above center thereby creating an overspin to keep the ball on the ground and rolling true. Eye contact is maintained throughout the kick and follow through. The inside of the foot pass is the most accurate and most frequently utilized passing technique. It can also be employed successfully for shooting from short distances where accuracy is more important than power (Fig. 31.3).

2. Instep of the foot pass. The kicking approach is either from an angle or straight on. In either case the supporting foot is placed alongside the ball, again pointing in the direction of the intended pass. The ball is contacted

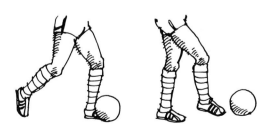

Fig. 31.3 Inside of the foot pass.

Fig. 31.4 Instep of the foot pass.   **Fig. 31.5** Outside of the foot pass.

midway up the laces with the kicking action originating at the hip, followed by the appropriate knee action. The kicking foot must remain extended throughout the contact and follow through. The instep of the foot pass is probably the most widely used soccer skill. It is the most powerful method of kicking, making it effective for both passing and shooting (Fig. 31.4).

3. Outside of the foot pass. This passing technique is primarily used for the short "flick" pass to the outside. By turning the foot inward and slightly downward, however, it may be used similar to the instep kick. A more advanced skill using the outside of the foot is to kick the ball slightly inside of center causing an outspin and a deceptive slicing action (Fig. 31.5).

Since passing success is dependent, in part, on supporting foot placement, the kicker must envision where the foot will be in relation to the ball at the moment of contact. Consequently, a ball rolling away from the kicker requires placement of the supporting foot slightly ahead of the ball so that by the time of contact it will have rolled to the correct kicking position.

The direction and height of the pass are influenced by a number of factors; for example, a high kick requires more backward body lean, position of the supporting foot farther behind the ball, less extension in the kicking foot, and a lower point of foot contact on the ball. Obviously, when teaching kicking, it is important to indicate that these factors should be modified according to the desired objective, i.e., short, hard pass along the ground; high, lofty pass across the field, etc. Remember, however, that since the ball is most effectively played with the feet, *it is usually advantageous to keep the pass low or on the ground.*

4. Heading. Heading is another passing skill. When performed correctly, it is both an accurate and powerful means of moving the ball. Proper execution

Fig. 31.6 Heading the ball.

Fig. 31.7 Sole of the foot trap.

necessitates watching the ball throughout its flight, positioning oneself under the ball, moving the head and trunk in the direction of the intended pass, and making contact at the top of the forehead. If done correctly, it seldom causes any discomfort to the header. It should be stressed again that in general the ball is directed toward the ground (Fig. 31.6).

Trapping Techniques

Trapping is a means of bringing a moving ball under control and includes two basic techniques.

1. "Kill" trap, i.e., sole of the foot trap. This method of trapping has the effect of instantly stopping the ball's movement. This is accomplished by pinning the ball between the ground and the particular body part, usually the sole of the foot, inside of the foot, or shins. A ball that is bouncing or in flight must be timed so that it is stopped just as it contacts the ground (Fig. 31.7).

2. Cushion trap, i.e., chest trap. The cushion trap usually involves the use of the inner thigh, abdomen, or chest, and has the effect of absorbing the ball's impact by giving with the ball at the moment of contact (Fig. 31.8).

(a)

(b)

Fig. 31.8 Chest trap (a) of low ball, (b) of high ball.

Dribbling

The skill of dribbling should purposely be taught following that of passing. It should also be made clear that *the ball can be moved more effectively by passing than by dribbling*. Dribbling, therefore, should be introduced as a means to set up a pass or shot. Monopolizing the ball by dribbling rather than passing is ineffective and permits the defense added time to get back into position.

In order to control the ball, it must be played close to the feet. Of course, there are situations when the ball may be pushed farther ahead, as long as control is maintained. The inside and outside of both feet should be utilized, thus permitting the flexibility of movement in several directions. Changes of speed as well as quick starting and stopping should also be taught.

Tackling

Tackling is a means of using the feet to take the ball from the opponent. In general, the tackler approaches from the front or side at an angle that forces the opponent away from the goal and into a position that will facilitate the ensuing tackle. A slight feint by the tackler might also prove useful in achieving this end. The skill is performed by blocking and lifting the ball, usually with the inside of the foot. The appropriate moment for the tackle is just as the ball leaves the opponent's foot. The timing must be precise and includes moving to the ball as quickly as possible without being faked. The tackler must also be aggressive so as to ensure gaining possession following the initial contact. Nullifying the opponent's effectiveness by forcing a bad pass can also be a successful outcome of aggressive tackling (Fig. 31.9).

Throw-in

The objective of the throw-in is to put the ball into play from out of bounds over the touch line. The thrower's feet must be positioned on or behind the

Fig. 31.9 Tackling.

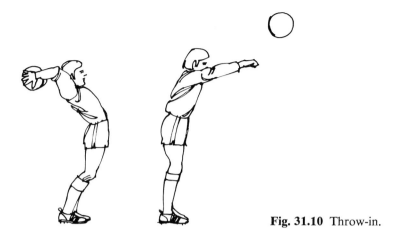

Fig. 31.10 Throw-in.

line and the ball must be delivered from overhead equally with both hands. The feet must remain on the ground until the ball is in play.

The throw-in may be performed from either a standing position or running approach. The running approach is utilized when greater distance is desired. A long throw-in to an area in front of the goal can be a dangerous offensive ploy (Fig. 31.10).

TEACHING DRILLS

New skill and strategy concepts should be described and broken down in easy to follow drills. It is a mistake to make the drill more complicated than the skill, thus diverting attention from that which is being taught. Learning is more effective when the activity is enjoyed. A brief introduction and familiarization with the fundamentals should quickly lead to competitive play.

Initial orientation to the essentials should be approximately one hour in duration. This includes time for introducing passing, dribbling, trapping, tackling, the throw-in, and a brief orientation to offensive positioning. Often drill time can be more effectively utilized by combining skills, i.e., inside of the foot pass and sole of the foot trap. More advanced skills, strategies, and situational plays, i.e., corner kicks, penalty kicks, etc., should be incorporated into the class later in the course. These are guidelines only and should be used accordingly. Modifications to best fit the needs of a particular situation should be the rule and not the exception.

LEAD-UP ACTIVITIES

There are a number of lead-up games for introducing soccer, particularly at the elementary level. These activities are simply organized and provide considerable enjoyment as well as the opportunity for the practice of fundamentals. Such games include:

1. Line soccer. Two lines of players face each other 10 to 20 yards apart standing side by side at arms or double arms distance. Each player is assigned a number so that both lines possess the same numbers. A ball is rolled between the lines and one or more numbers are called. Those players run to the center and attempt to kick the ball through the opposition's line. The players remaining in line serve as goalkeepers and can use their hands. A ball kicked over the head of the line players doesn't count.

2. Kickball. The game is played as softball except that the pitcher rolls a soccer ball and the batter kicks it and runs the bases.

3. Keep away. A circle is formed with one or more players in the center. The object is to keep the ball away from these center players through continuous passing. Those forming the circle may or may not use their hands according to the desired objectives.

4. Relays. A variety of relays can be devised to incorporate such fundamentals as passing, dribbling, and trapping.

SUMMARY

- ☐ Equipment and facilities should be adapted according to participant age and sex.
- ☐ Offensive positioning can be taught most easily as flexible zone play.
- ☐ Defensive alignment should stress one-to-one coverage with the correct position between the person being defensed and the goal.
- ☐ Participants should be familiarized with essential fundamentals, including kicking, heading, dribbling, trapping, tackling, and the throw-in, and then quickly introduced to competitive game play.
- ☐ Drills should be simplified. Complex drills divert attention from that which is being practiced.

REFERENCES

AAHPER soccer-speedball guide. AAHPER, Washington, D.C. (Published every other year).

Csandi, A. 1965. *Soccer.* (2 vol.) Budapest, Hungary: Corvina.

Fardy, P. S., and E. R. Anderson 1970. Care and prevention of soccer injuries, *Athl. J.* **5:** 24.

Fardy, P. S. 1969. The effects of soccer training and detraining upon selected cardiac and metabolic measures. *Res. Quart.* **40:** 502.

———— 1968. Conditioning and avoiding fatigue in soccer. *Athl. J.* **48:** 50.

Menke, F. G. 1963. *The encyclopedia of sports.* New York: A. S. Barnes.

Moore, A. C., and M. R. Schmid 1965. *Soccer anthology.* Published by authors.

National soccer coaches association of America, soccer journal. D. Yonker (ed.). Philadelphia (quarterly publication).

The official national collegiate athletic association soccer guide. Phoenix, Ariz.: College Athletics Publishing Service. (Yearly publication).

Schmid, I. R., J. McKeon, and M. Schmid 1968. *Skills and strategies of successful soccer.* Englewood Cliffs, N.J.: Prentice-Hall.

Soccer News. Milton Miller (ed.). New Rochelle, N.Y.: Soccer Publications. (Monthly publication of *International and United States Soccer News*).

Wade, A. 1967. *Soccer: guide to training and coaching.* New York: Funk and Wagnalls.

Soccer Skill Tests*

Mildred Vanderhoof

Skill tests have two important functions, namely: (1) they give the teacher and the student an accurate comparison of one student's ability with another, (2) they are objective measures of the improvement made during the season. To be of most value the tests should be given at the beginning, and again at the end, of the season to stimulate the students to improve their skill and to provide a record which may be compared with the one taken at the beginning of the season.

The soccer season is here. Try these tests with your group and see if they are usable.

The Dribble

a) **Purpose.** A time and accuracy test showing ability to maintain control of the ball while advancing and dodging obstacles.

b) **Preliminary arrangements.** Three Indian clubs or similar objects placed at 8-yd intervals, the first club measuring 9 yds from the starting line. The distance from the starting line to the third club is 25 yds.

---

*   Reprinted by permission from *JOHPER* **3,** 8, (October), 1932.

c) Procedure. Before commencing, the soccer ball should be placed on the starting line in front of the clubs. On a signal from the timekeeper, dribble the ball to the right of the first club, to the left of the second, and around to the right of the third. Without stopping, dribble the ball straight back across the starting line. The dribbling may start either to the right or left of the first club.

d) Scoring. The best time out of three trials is recorded. If a foul occurs, the time is not taken. The individual dribbling in the least amount of time receives 10 points; others are graded in accordance, deducting 2 percent for every second over best record.

e) Fouls. 1. Passing a club without going around it. 2. Knocking over a club. 3. Kicking the ball back instead of dribbling.

Trapping

a) Purpose. An accuracy test for stopping and gaining control of the ball.

b) Preliminary arrangement. Two parallel lines drawn 6 yds apart.

c) Procedure. The player stands on one line facing the official who is on the opposite line with the ball. The ball is thrown about waist high toward the player, who attempts to trap the ball by using any legal trap such as the one foot, ankle, or double knee stop. The ball is thrown five times to the player. When trapping the ball, one foot must remain behind the line.

d) Scoring. Two points are scored for each successful legal stop. If a foul is made, no points are to be given for that trial. Highest possible score for trapping—ten points.

e) Fouls. 1 Stopping ball illegally. 2 Crossing the 6-yd line with more than one foot.

Foot

Ankle

Knee

The Throw-in

a) Purpose. An accuracy test for placing the ball at various distances with the legal overhead throw.

b) Preliminary arrangements. Place three baseball bags in a straight line 3 yds from the touch line and 2 yds apart—measurements are taken from center of bases. The bases are 3 yds, 5 yds, and 7 yds, respectively, from the throw line.

c) Procedure. Standing on the touch line, five overhead throw-ins are taken. The object of the test is to hit the bags. Points increase with the distance. A legal overhead throw must be taken: 1 Feet on or behind the touch line. 2 Part of both feet remaining on the ground. 3 Ball thrown with two hands over head. 4 Facing field of play.

d) Scoring. Ball hitting the first base scores one-half point. Ball hitting the second base scores one point. Ball hitting the third base scores two points. The score of the five trials is recorded. Highest possible score is ten points.

e) Fouls. Illegal throw-in does not score.

The Placekick

a) Purpose. An accuracy test for goal kicking.

b) Preliminary arrangements. Be sure the penalty kick mark is 12 yds from the end line in front of the goal.

c) Procedure. The ball is placed on the penalty kick mark and kicked toward the goal. No guarding of the goal is essential. The object is to kick the ball between the goalposts underneath the crossbar. Only one kick for each trial is allowed. Five trials constitute the test.

d) Scoring. If the ball enters the goal mouth on the fly, two points are awarded; on the bounce, one point is awarded; on the roll, one-half point is awarded. No points will be given if the goal is not made. Record total number of points made on the five kicks.

e) Fouls. 1 Kicking the ball from any spot other than the 12-yd penalty kick mark. 2 Kicking the ball when it is not stationary. 3 Kicking the ball more than once on a trial.

The Drop Ball

a) Purpose. A test for securing distance on the kick, especially when the ball is in the air.

b) Preliminary arrangements. A space at least 50 yds long is marked at 5-yd intervals. The distance from the starting line to the first line is 10 yds, others are all 5 yds apart.

c) Procedure. Standing on or behind the starting line, the ball is thrown straight up into the air, and after allowing it to bounce on the ground to knee height, it is kicked. Measurement is taken from the spot where the ball first touches the ground after the kick. Three kicks are taken. Record the best out of the three trials.

d) Scoring. The scoring will follow the plan below. If the ball lands between: 1–10 yds, one point is awarded; 10–15 yds, two points are awarded; 15–20 yds, three points are awarded; 20–25 yds, four points are awarded; 25–30 yds, five points are awarded; 30–35 yds, six points are awarded; 35–40 yds, seven points are awarded; 40–45 yds, eight points are awarded; 45–50 yds, nine points are awarded; 50 yds or over ten points are awarded. Any ball bouncing on the 50-yd line or beyond receives ten points, which is the maximum score. If a foul is made, no points are given for that trial.

e) Fouls. 1 Failing to kick the ball on the first bounce. 2 Kicking the ball before it has reached the ground. 3 Not facing field of play.

Volleying

a) Purpose. A test for measuring the distance a player can propel the ball before it strikes the ground. This test consists of the use of just the forehead, shoulder, hip, and knee.

b) Preliminary arrangements. A space at least 10 yds in length is marked out at one yd intervals for 10 yds distance; a line being 5 yds from the starting line.

c) Procedure. The ball is thrown rather high by the official who stands on the 5-yd line facing the starting line. The player volleys the ball straight ahead by using the hip, knee, shoulder, or forehead. The record is taken from the spot where the ball first hits the ground. Three trials are allowed. The player must be behind the line at the end of the volleying.

d) Scoring. The best record out of the three volleys is recorded. If the ball lands between: 1–5 yds, one point is awarded; 5–6 yds, five points are awarded; 6–7 yds, six points are awarded; 7–8 yds, seven points are awarded; 8–9 yds, eight points are awarded; 9–10 yds, nine points are awarded; 10 yds or beyond, ten points are awarded. A player volleying the ball 10 yds or beyond receives ten points. No points are given for a trial if a foul occurs.

e) Fouls. 1 Illegal volley. 2 Crossing the starting line during the trials at volleying.

The Throw-down

a) Purpose. To test speed and ability of securing the ball legally from the opponent.

b) Preliminary arrangements. A six-yd circle divided in half.

c) Procedure. Two opponents of about equal ability stand in opposite halves of the circle facing each other. The ball is dropped between the two players by the official. The object of the test is to kick the ball out of the opponents' half of the circle without involving personal contact. Each couple has five throw-downs. Individual record of the test is kept by the official.

d) Scoring. Two points are awarded to the winner of each successful play. The throw-down is repeated five times. The highest possible score is 10 points. If a foul occurs, the point is given to the opponent who was fouled against. If a double foul occurs, no points are awarded.

e) Fouls. Not abiding by official soccer rules.

Tackling

a) Purpose. To test ability and skill of intercepting and gaining possession of the ball when maintained by opponent.

b) Preliminary arrangements. Two parallel lines 15 yds apart.

c) Procedure. Two players stand opposite each other, 15 yds apart, on the two lines. The player who is not being tested, player A, has the ball. On a signal from the official, both players advance toward each other. Player A dribbles the ball straight ahead. Player B attempts to make a legal tackle and on securing it, takes the ball ahead past the 15-yd line. The inside or outside of the foot may be used for tackling. Do not kick the ball into the opponent or too far away so that possession of it cannot be maintained.

d) Scoring. Each successful legal tackle counts two points. Five tries are allowed. No points are given to Player B: 1 If failure to make the tackle within the 15-yd area; 2 If a foul occurs.

e) Fouls. If the tackle is not legal according to the official soccer rules.

The Corner Kick

a) Purpose. To test skill and accuracy in placing the ball when awarded a corner kick.

b) Preliminary arrangements. Mark a 6-yd square on the field directly in front of the goal posts. Be sure the corners of the field are clearly marked.

c) Procedure. The ball is placed within one yard of either corner and kicked. The object of the test is for the ball to land within designated area (6 yd square).

d) Scoring. The best two scores out of five are recorded. If ball lands directly in the 6-yd square, five points are awarded. If from the corner kick the ball touches in any way the designated area other than by a fly, two points shall be awarded. No points are given: 1 If a foul occurs; 2 If the ball does not touch 6-yd square. Highest possible score is ten points.

e) Fouls. Violating soccer rules on the corner kick.

The Goalkeeper's Test

a) Purpose. To test on the knowledge and skills used by the goalkeeper in order to prevent goals from scoring.

b) Preliminary arrangements. Be sure that the penalty area is clearly marked. Draw a semicircle 15 yds from the goalposts, the 6-yd line in front of the poles being straight.

c) Procedure. The goalkeeper who is being tested stands near the goal. Several other people arrange themselves behind the 15-yd circle and pass the soccer ball among themselves until someone, without advancing inward, decides to kick for a goal. The goalkeeper has five attempts to stop the ball from going between the goalposts, at which time she may use all her privileges. Record number of successful stops.

d) Scoring. Each successful legal stop scores two points. Highest possible score, ten points. If the goalkeeper fouls, no point is given for that trial.

e) Fouls. Breaking goalkeeper's privileges.

Points	10	9	8	7	6	5	4	3	2	1	0
Dribbling					●						
Trapping			●								
Throw-in							●				
Placekick						●					
Drop ball			●								
Volleying					●						
Throw-down					●						
Tackling			●								
Corner kick									●		
Goalkeeper's test			●								

A graph readily shows the pupil and the teacher the things that need special attention and practice. The maximum score for the Skill Test is 100 points. There are ten events each counting ten points.

If a pupil is high in practically all tests, she is good material for the first class team and should be encouraged to come out and enjoy the game of soccer. If a pupil is low in the majority of the tests, then extra practice and time should be given her.

The position for which the individual is best suited may readily be seen by the graph picture. If her score is high in trapping, kicking for distance, and tackling, but low in place kicks, corner kicks, and dribbling, she will probably be best suited in a back position rather than one on the forward line, and vice versa.

32
Softball

Because the game of softball is played almost equally by both sexes, two authors, a man and a woman, were invited to write about it. Peter W. Everett discusses the origin of the game, its development, and the governing bodies involved. He also presents a detailed description of the field. Finally, he summarizes the place of softball in American society.

Irene Shea outlines the rules of softball and then discusses the teaching and learning of the basic fundamentals. Game strategy and softball terminology are also presented. RBF

Men's Softball

Peter W. Everett

ORIGIN

The present-day game of softball had its beginning in 1887 as an indoor imitation of baseball. The first game occurred Thanksgiving day at a gymnasium in Chicago in which a group of men started playing a ball game with a broomstick and a boxing glove. Since the game was enjoyed by all participants, Mr. George W. Hancock of the Farragut Boat Club agreed to develop some rules along with a ball and bat that would not damage the gymnasium. The resulting game was called "indoor baseball" and the players used a soft, 16" in circumference ball with a slim bat.

The indoor game soon became very popular but the lack of adequate facilities and the desire for a game that could be played by all age groups and both sexes stimulated the development of a variation that could be played outdoors. The outdoor game has been credited to Lewis Rober of the Minneapolis Fire Department in 1895.

DEVELOPMENT

Popularity of the game increased rapidly as well as the number of variations when different cities inaugurated the outdoor game. Various names for the game included recreation ball, twilight ball, lightning baseball, diamond ball, army ball, navy ball, pumpkin ball, indoor-outdoor, mush ball, kitten ball, and softball. The balls used were mainly 17" in circumference, but balls of 16, 14, 13, and 12" in circumference were also used. The bats varied in length, weight, and diameter. The distance between bases varied from 30 to 60', and the distance from pitcher to batter from 30 to 45'. The rules for many of these variations stipulated ten players on a team instead of nine with the tenth player assuming a roaming position or one behind second base in a short field position—thus the name "short fielder."

GOVERNING BODIES

Playground leaders in Minneapolis, St. Paul, and Chicago did much to promote the game at the turn of the century. In 1908 the National Amateur

Playground Ball Association of the United States was formed in Chicago. It soon developed an official handbook with rules and plans for intercity play that was printed by the American Sports Publishing Company. The rules in this handbook are very similar to present-day rules. In spite of these accomplishments, the NAPBA never became an effective body for promoting softball.

The International Joint Rules Committee on Softball is the present governing body of softball in the world. It consists of representatives from the following: National Recreation and Parks Association, Amateur Softball Association, American Association for Health, Physical Education and Recreation, Young Men's Christian Association, Division of Girls' and Women's Sports, National Industrial Recreation Association, and International Softball Federation. This committee standardizes the rules wherever the game is played, recommends changes as they are needed, and works to secure standard and satisfactory equipment from manufacturers. The forerunner of this group was the Playground Baseball Committee appointed by Joseph Lee of the National Recreation Association in 1923 to standardize the outdoor game. This committee, after much deliberation, agreed on one set of rules, published them, developed a campaign that promoted the game and in 1932 selected the name "softball" for the game. The committee was expanded in 1933 and called the Joint Rules Committee on Softball. It was further expanded in representation and jurisdiction in 1936 to its present name and composition.

The Amateur Softball Association of America (ASA) was organized in 1932 and has become the governing body for promotion and control of organized softball competition in the United States. It is affiliated with the Amateur Athletic Union, National Recreation and Parks Association, United States Olympic Committee, and the National Industrial Recreation Association. From its inception there has been a tremendous growth in team memberships. At present there are approximately 42,000 adult teams, 18,000 junior (age 12–18 years) softball teams, and 17,000 umpires registered with the ASA. The organization is one of the largest and fastest growing amateur sports associations in America sponsoring a program that is nongovernmental, nonpartisan, nonprofit and which accepts all who qualify as amateurs regardless of sex, color, creed, or national origin. There are nine area vice-presidents, approximately one hundred state and metropolitan commissioners, and some 2500 district and deputy commissioners working diligently as a governing body to regulate competition and to ensure fairness and equal opportunity to all who participate under their jurisdiction.

THE GAME

Early emphasis, rules, and organization were concerned with fast-pitch softball. Pitching became one of the most important aspects of topflight teams as the speed with which pitchers throw the softball compares with that of baseball pitchers. Since the softball pitcher is much closer, the batter has more difficulty hitting the ball. This has led to low-scoring games and a challenge between pitcher and batter.

Slow-pitch softball, which requires the pitcher to put an arch of three to ten feet on the ball, places emphasis on hitting and defensive play. With increased popularity it has developed a sophistication and encourages the development of players who can hit home runs. This decreases defensive play, one of the game's major attributes, and has led to the use of a "restricted flight" ball and the moving of the outfield fence farther from home plate.

Softball continues to be similar to baseball in the fundamentals of throwing, catching, fielding, and batting. Pitching and several rules concerning field dimensions and equipment are different. A regulation game in baseball lasts nine innings; in softball, it lasts seven innings. Both baseball and fast-pitch use nine players while the regular and sixteen-inch slow-pitch games use ten. Bunting is permitted in baseball and fast-pitch but not in the slow-pitch games. Other differences are:

- ☐ Distance to outfield fence: baseball—a minimum unobstructed radius of 250′ or more needed from home plate between the foul lines, recommended to be 320′ or more along the foul lines and 400′ or more to center field; fast-pitch—the unobstructed radius needed is 225′; slow-pitch—the distance is 275′; sixteen-inch slow-pitch—the distance is 250′ for men and 200′ for women.

- ☐ Distance between bases: Baseball—90′; fast- and slow-pitch—60′ (see Fig. 32.1); sixteen-inch slow pitch—55′ for men and 50′ for women.

- ☐ Distance from home plate to pitcher's plate: baseball—60′, 6″; fast- and slow-pitch—46′ for men and 40′ for women; sixteen-inch slow-pitch—38′ for both men and women.

- ☐ Ball circumference: baseball—9 to 9¼″; fast- and slow-pitch—11⅞ to 12⅛″; sixteen-inch slow-pitch—15¾ to 16¼ inches.

- ☐ Ball weight: baseball—5 to 5¼ oz; fast- and slow-pitch—6¼ to 7 oz; sixteen-inch slow-pitch—9 to 10 oz.

- ☐ Bat size: baseball—not more than 42″ in length nor more than 2¾″ in diameter at largest part; fast-, slow- and sixteen-inch slow-pitch—not more than 34″ in length nor more than 2¼″ in diameter at largest part with a 10″ safety grip of cork, tape, or composition material required.

- ☐ Pitching: baseball—overhand or sidearm; fast-pitch—underhand motion with wrist closer to body than elbow at release; slow-pitch—underhand motion at moderate speed with a 3 to 10′ arc above pitching hand at release point; sixteen-inch slow-pitch—underhand motion at slow speed.

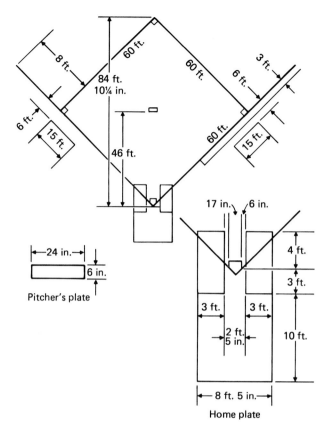

Fig. 32.1 Official dimensions of softball diamond.

☐ Stealing bases: baseball—permitted when ball in is play; fast-pitch—permitted after ball leaves pitcher's hand but runner must be in contact with base occupied at that time; slow-pitch and sixteen-inch slow-pitch—no stealing. Runner cannot leave occupied base until ball is batted.

HALL OF FAME

A National Softball Hall of Fame was established in 1957 at Oklahoma City, Oklahoma, for outstanding softball players. The honorees selected between 1957 and 1972 were players from men's and women's fast-pitch teams. This procedure was expanded in 1973 to include players who had participated in men's slow-pitch softball. In order to be nominated, players must be retired from active play for at least three years and, to be considered by the selection committee, must fulfill other stringent requirements.

POPULARITY

It is estimated that over 25,000,000 adults and youngsters annually play some form of competitive or recreational softball. The competitive aspect of softball was present from the very beginning as teams challenged a cross-town rival or the team in the next town. Almost immediately after its inception, the ASA organized national championships. In adult play, men's and women's fast-pitch softball have had national tournaments since 1933. National tournaments started in 1954 for Men's Open Slow Pitch, in 1957 for Industrial Slow Pitch, in 1962 for Women's Slow Pitch, and in 1964 for Sixteen-inch Slow Pitch.

The Junior Softball Program has grown from a membership of 50,000 boys in 1961 to approximately 300,000 at present. Competition is in both fast-pitch and slow-pitch play. National championship play started for the 13 to 15 year-old age group in 1973.

The recreational aspect involves many participants both as players and as spectators. The fact that the game can be played with a minimum of equipment in a reasonably small area contributes greatly to its being played in a variety of places and on a variety of occasions. The keen competition between teams, the advent of lighted parks, the brief time span of a game (approximately one hour), and the variety of age groups participating have brought millions to the ball parks to watch their favorite team or person play. The game of softball has truly become one of America's favorite sports for the player and spectator alike.

REFERENCES

Encyclopaedia Britannica **20,** 1972. Chicago: Encyclopaedia Britannica, Inc.

Everett, P. W. 1954. *Instructional materials for teaching sport skills in the required physical education program in a large university.* Unpublished doctoral dissertation. Iowa City, Iowa: University of Iowa.

Mitchell, E. D. *et al.,* 1936. *Sports for recreation and how to play them.* New York: A. S. Barnes.

Noren, A. T. 1966. *Softball with official rules.* (3d ed., Revised Printing.) New York: Ronald.

Softball: official rule book and guide 1973. Oklahoma City: ASA.

World book encyclopedia **18,** 1972. Chicago: Field Enterprises Educational Corp.

Women's Softball

Irene Shea

More individuals participate in softball than in any other team sport in the United States. Over 26 million adults and youngsters play some form of competitive or recreational softball annually. It is also widely played throughout the world. In fact, 47 countries are presently members of the International Softball Federation.

The Amateur Softball Association (ASA) provides the organization and leadership for most of the softball played in the United States. The ASA provides competition for girls, boys, men, and women. It sanctions leagues and tournaments for fast-pitch, slow-pitch, and medium-pitch softball.

The game of softball is the direct descendant of baseball. A game of indoor baseball was originated in 1887 by George W. Hancock in Chicago. It was originally played with a broom as a bat and a boxing glove ball. The game attracted many followers as Hancock devised rules and provided a large softball and a small-headed bat. Variations of the game were played under the names of mush ball, pumpkin ball, and kitten ball. Recreation groups moved the sport outdoors under the title of playground ball. It grew in popularity for both men and women. Softball was officially adopted in 1933 after the first national tournament in Chicago.

THE GAME

The game of softball is played by two opposing teams on a diamond-shaped field (see below). The teams perform throwing, batting, catching, and running skills throughout a regulation game of 7 innings. Both teams play offense and

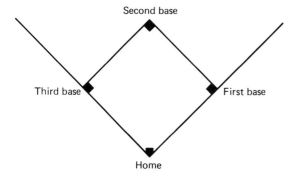

Fig. 32.2 A close play at home is always exciting. Courtesy of Southern Connecticut State College.

defense in each inning. Each team consists of nine players (fast-pitch) or ten players (slow-pitch) who alternate turns at bat and in the field. The team at bat remains in the offensive (batting) position until the defending (fielding) team successfully gets three of the offensive players out.

The defending players have specific positions to play when on defense. They are catcher, pitcher, first, second and third base, shortstop, left field, center field and right field. In the game of slow pitch, there is an extra outfielder. Each position is primarily responsible for covering a specific area of the field. (See Fig. 32.3 for the responsibilities.)

The game begins with one team in fielding position and the other team

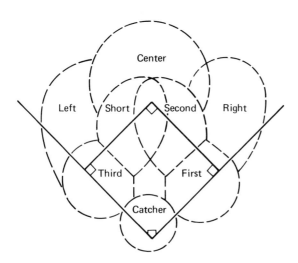

Fig. 32.3 Areas of responsibility.

batting one at a time. The pitcher delivers the ball toward the batting area with an underhand motion. The batter attempts to hit the pitched ball with the bat so that the ball travels into fair territory. The batter's objective is to hit the ball and at least get to first base without a defensive player catching the hit ball before it touches the ground or before the ball gets to first base.

When the ball is hit foul (and is not caught), the batter may remain at bat. If the batter is successful in hitting the ball into fair territory, she attempts to run to first, second, third, and home to score a run. Baserunners do not need to run all the bases at once, but may stop safely at any of the first three bases and await a teammate's hit to move them to the next base. The defensive team tries to tag the baserunner with the ball as she is running between bases or to get the ball to a base ahead of the base runner in order to force her out. The objective of the game is to score more runs than the opposing team.

SIMPLIFIED RULES

An official game consists of seven innings. A full seven innings do not have to be played if the team second at bat has more runs in six and one-half innings. A game tied at the end of seven innings shall continue until one team has more runs at the end of a complete inning or until the team second at bat has scored more runs. Each team may have substitutes. Once a player is removed, she may not reenter the game as a player.

The following simplified rules cover the most frequent situations:

Strike:

1. A batter swings at a pitched ball and misses.
2. A pitched ball is delivered over home plate between the top of the knees and the armpits of the batter.
3. A fly ball goes foul and is not caught, and the batter has fewer than two strikes.
4. A batter with fewer than two strikes is hit by her own batted ball inside the batter's box.

Ball:

1. A pitched ball that does not go over home plate within the strike zone and is not swung at by the batter.
2. An illegally pitched ball.

Fair Ball:

1. A ball that lands and stays within the lines from home to first and home to third.

2. A ball that lands in fair territory within the lines extended beyond first and third base along the borders of the outfield.

Foul Ball:

1. A ball that comes to rest, having not been touched by a defensive player, outside the lines from home to first and home to third.

2. A ball that touches outside the lines from home to first and from home to third.

Batter Out:

1. The third strike is caught by the catcher.

2. The batter bunts foul after two strikes.

3. A foul ball is caught before it touches the ground.

Baserunner Out:

1. The ball reaches first base before the runner reaches the base.

2. A batted fly ball is caught.

3. The runner interferes with a fielder trying to field a ball.

4. A runner passes another baserunner.

5. The runner leaves the base before the ball leaves the pitcher's hand.

6. The runner is hit by a batted ball before it is touched or passes a fielder.

FACILITIES AND EQUIPMENT

Field. The field area should be level and unobstructed with a radius of at least 200′ from home plate between the foul lines. The infield diamond has 60′ baselines with a pitching distance of 40′ (46′ for men). The basic layout of the diamond is indicated in Fig. 32.4.

Balls and bats. The official softball must be between 11⅞ and 12⅛″ in circumference. It may weigh between 6 and 6¾ oz. The exterior is cowhide smoothly seamed with concealed stitches. The rubber-covered balls are ideal for play on damp ground. The official bats are either solid hardwood or the more popular aluminum. They vary in length and weight but should be marked "official softball."

Gloves and mitts. A protective hand-covering for catching and fielding the ball is recommended for all defensive players. Only the catcher and the first basewoman are allowed to wear mitts (gloves without separate fingers). The fingered gloves are worn by all the other fielders.

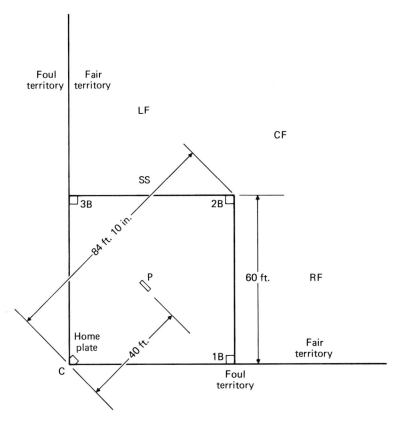

Fig. 32.4 Basic layout: C = Catcher, P = Pitcher, 1B = first base, 2B = second base, 3B = third base, SS = shortstop, LF = left field, CF = center field, and RF = right field.

BASIC SKILLS

Throwing. The overhand throw is used by the defensive players during the game situations. The player takes the ball in the throwing hand back behind the head about ear level. The elbow of the throwing hand points away from the body with the upper arm parallel to the ground. The opposite shoulder is pointed in the direction that the throw will be made. The player executes the throw by stepping with the foot opposite the throwing hand in the direction that the throw will be made. While the step is being made, the hand with the ball is brought forward by rotating the shoulders and hips toward the direction of the throw (Fig. 32.5).

Catching. The body position when making a catch depends on both the height and speed of the ball and the throw the fielder wants to make. Generally

Fig. 32.5 As the throw is made, the player should step forward with the foot opposite the throwing hand. Courtesy of Luther College.

both hands should be used to catch the ball. As the ball hits the glove or mitt, the fingers squeeze and the other hand closes over the top so that the ball will not come out of the glove or mitt. The free hand is also ready to take the ball out of the glove or mitt to make a throw. The hands and arms "give" with the impact of the ball, cushioning the catch.

Fielding ground balls. All of the defensive players except the catcher must be concerned with fielding a ground ball. The fielder's ready position while waiting for a ball to be hit is with the weight distributed evenly and comfortably on both feet which are approximately shoulder-width apart. From this position the fielder can be ready to move quickly in any direction. The key points in fielding a ground ball are to watch the ball, keep relaxed, and stay low on the ball. The glove should also be kept low. It is easier to come up on a ground ball than to go down. The fielder should try to get in front of the ball by keeping it in line with the center of her body. The ball is fielded with both hands out in front, loose and relaxed. After fielding the ground ball the ball should be taken back into the throwing position in one continuous motion and delivered to the appropriate target.

The following are some drills that can be used to improve a player's skill in fielding ground balls:

☐ *Agility* While in the low crouched position with the arm hanging relaxed, another player rolls a ball to the left. The player must sidestep and retrieve the ball in the center of her stance. In one continuous motion, the ball should be fielded, taken out of the glove, and thrown underhand back to the other player. The ball is then rolled to the right and this continues with the player remaining in the low crouched position at all times.

☐ *Ground balls* Hit ground balls at a player. The speed of the hit balls as well as the direction should be varied.

☐ *Two ball* Hit a ground ball at a player. The ball is fielded and returned quickly to a catcher as the batter is hitting a second ball. The process continues with both balls in play.

Fielding fly balls. Whenever possible fielders should catch the ball with two hands. This will enable the fielder to have the throwing hand on the ball as soon as it is caught. The fielder should try to catch the fly ball in front of her body at eye level. The ball should be kept slightly to the side of the throwing hand whenever possible, with the body in the throwing position.

The following two drills will help the player improve her skill in fielding fly balls:

☐ *Catching fly balls* The fly balls should be hit to the left, right, in front of, and behind the fielder. The height and distance should be varied.

☐ *Footwork drill* The player faces the coach who tosses a ball over the player's head to the right or left. The player must turn and go back to catch the fly ball.

Hitting. One of the most difficult skills to execute successfully in softball is hitting. Batters attempt to hit balls moving toward them at varying speeds, often breaking in different directions. Hitting the ball properly is dependent to a large extent on the ability to time the contact of the bat with the ball. In order to make solid contact, the batter must coordinate the movements of the shoulders, arms, hips, wrists and hands in a smoothly blended and perfectly timed act.

The placement of the batter's hands on the bat is dependent upon her ability to control the bat during the swing. Some batters will place their hands down at the end of the bat while others will "choke up" for more control. The hands should be together so that they will function as a single unit during the swing. The grip should be extremely firm, especially during the actual swing.

The exact place in the batter's box where the batter assumes the ready position varies with the individual. Most batters stand with their front foot slightly closer to the plate (closed stance). Other batters stand with both feet the same distance from home plate (square stance) or with their front feet farther away from the plate (open stance). No matter which particular stance the batter assumes, the important movement is that the step with the front foot should be into the pitch or toward the pitcher. The back foot should be well planted. The batter's weight should be slightly forward on the balls of the feet and evenly distributed over both feet.

The batter's head should be kept as still as possible during the actual swing. The batter must be careful not to lunge at the ball. If this does occur, the body weight will be too far forward and the batter's power will be diminished.

The movement of the batter's hips during the swing is extremely important to the amount of power generated. As she strides with the front foot, her hips remain square to the pitcher. In fact, during the stride, the hips are being "cocked" and released at completion of the stride. The release is a pivot around the axis of the body. The hips must clear the way for every other part of the swing to follow naturally.

The length of the stride will vary among individual batters. The batter must be careful not to overstride because from this position the hips are locked and unable to pivot around the axis of the body. This reduces power. A common fault among batters when striding is called "stepping in the bucket" or "bailing out." Depending somewhat on the exact spot where the ball crosses the plate, the batter's stride is generally away from the perpendicular line drawn from the pitching plate to home plate. By stepping away from this line the batter immediately opens up her hips. Thus, there is nothing to pivot and no power is generated.

The batter should keep her eye on the ball until contact is made. Eye contact should be maintained with very little head movement during the swing. This can be accomplished by concentrating on watching the ball from the pitcher's hand into the catcher's mitt and by tucking the chin in toward the front shoulder throughout the actual swing.

Many batters in a game situation will try to hit to the opposite field. To execute this requires a slight change in the stance and stride. The stance is moved a little farther from the plate. The stride is slightly more into the pitch or toward the plate. The swing is more of push or punch at the ball with the hands ahead of the bat. The ball is contacted directly over the plate rather than at the normal point of contact out in front of the plate. A ball on the outside of the plate is the easiest to hit to the opposite field.

□ *Batting practice* Hitting sessions should be purposeful and meaningful. The prime concern would be to make good contact with a level, well-timed swing. Getting the hitters' timing sharp should be the basic purpose of any batting practice. This would be the time to work on any flaws in the hitting swing.

□ *Pepper* This can help players educate themselves to do certain things. It can be a help to the hitter who is having trouble holding her body back.

The hitter would take a short stride and go at hitting the ball the same as she would during batting practice. The hitter can learn to guide the ball, hit the ball where she wants to, and even practice swinging slightly down on high pitches. In addition to developing eye and hand coordination, pepper games can develop much needed bat control.

☐ *Batting tee* The batting tee can be a valuable training aid in developing the swing and snap at the ball. The batting tee can be placed anywhere in relationship to the plate so the hitter can work on her weakness or strength from there. It can be effective in pointing out to the player that she has to hit the inside pitch out in front of the plate more. Conversely, when the ball is on the outside part of the plate, it can prove to the hitter that she can wait a little longer and hit the ball straightaway or to the opposite field.

Bunting. In the fast-pitch game, the execution of bunts can play a vital role in the team's offensive strategy. The bunt can be used to advance a runner or as an element of surprise by a batter.

There are two stances that have become popular for bunting, Both stances bring the batter's hip and shoulders around square to the pitcher. The first stance is the square method whereby the batter shifts her feet around in a squared position toward the pitcher. The second stance is assumed by the batter by merely pivoting her feet toward the pitcher. This pivot is achieved by pivoting on the heel of the front foot (so that the toe is pointing toward the pitcher) and on the ball of the back foot.

The bunter, while in the squared around position, should be in a slight crouched position being sure the bat has the plate well covered. The arms should be held parallel to the ground, chest high, and covering the plate. The top hand should slide up close to the trademark of the bat. The bat should be gripped lightly with the upper hand, keeping the fingers underneath and the thumb on top. The bunter should let the ball come to the bat and "give" slightly with the bat on contact.

The bat should be held at the top of the strike zone. This is to prevent pop-ups by keeping the bat on top of the ball at contact. The direction in which the ball is bunted depends on the angle of the bat at contact.

The key rule in executing the sacrifice bunt is for the batter to get the ball on the ground and advance the runner. The batter attempts to bunt the ball only if the pitch is a strike.

The batter should not square around toward the pitcher until the very last instant. A right-handed batter should take one stride backward with her left foot. As this movement is made, the weight should be shifted to the right foot. However, once the feet are set, the weight should be shifted again to the left foot. A left-handed batter has an advantage in bunting for a base hit, since she is a full step closer to first base. She should step toward the pitcher with her left foot. When contact is made for the bunt, the weight is on the right foot, with the left foot trailing slightly, ready to cross over the right toward first base.

After a fake bunt has been used to draw the infielders in, the batter should swing or slap at the ball. The swing is a short one in a downward direction. Batters should step with the front foot toward the ball as they swing.

Sliding. Sliding into a base can mean the difference between being out or safe. A good baserunner must be able to slide on either her left or right side. Sliding is really controlled falling. The runner simply drops to the ground according to the slide desired, and the momentum of the run does the rest.

Timing is essential for a good slide. The slide must not start too soon or too late, and the slider should keep relaxed when hitting the ground. Once the runner decides to slide, she must go through with it.

The bent-leg slide is the most popular and easiest to become proficient at. It also enables the base runner to spring up quickly, ready to run if the ball goes through.

The following are coaching hints in learning the bent-leg slide:

☐ Start to slide at least 10′ from the base.

☐ Take off from either leg and bend it under.

☐ Slide on the calf of the bent leg (bottom leg).

☐ Stay low to the ground as the slide is started.

☐ Throw the head back as the slide is started.

☐ Tag the base with the top leg.

The hook slide is used by a runner to avoid being tagged by an infielder. It should be done to both sides away from the tag of the infielder. When the runner does a hook slide, she should execute a bent-leg slide toward an aiming point that is about a foot to two feet to either side of the base. As she slides toward this aiming point the top leg should reach back for the base and remain in contact with it as the slider finishes the slide to the side of the base.

The following progression can be used to learn the bent-leg slide:

☐ Assume the correct position for the bent-leg slide while on the ground. You should have the bottom leg bent under you. The body should be slightly turned to the same side as the bent leg so that the upper thigh of that side will be in contact with the ground. The upper part of the body should be leaning back with the arms free of contact with the ground.

☐ Walk in a circle and, on a signal, drop to the ground into the correct sliding position.

Fig. 32.6 A softball pitcher delivers the throw with an underhand motion. Courtesy of University of Nebraska at Omaha.

☐ Increase the speed of the walk in order to begin to slide slighlty along the ground.

☐ Run and slide at increasing speeds until you are able to slide while running at top speed.

Pitching. The pitcher stands on the pitching plate squarely, facing the batter with the ball held in both hands. The ball is taken backward in an arc from a downward motion of the arm. The body rotates as the arm is taken back. While delivering the ball, the pitcher may take one step only. This step must be toward the batter and taken as the delivery is made. The ball must be delivered with an underhand motion, the release and follow-through forward, beyond the straight line of the body. On the follow-through, the right foot moves parallel with the left in a side stride position. Power is generated from a full arm swing, elbow extension, wrist snap, and body rotation.

STRATEGY

Offensive strategy. This is dependent on batting and base-running skills of the players combined to make a team contribution.

☐ The order of batting is one of the moves a team plans. Generally, the leadoff batter is one who can get on base; the second, a fair hitter and bunter; third, a consistent hitter; fourth, the strongest and longest hitter, who can advance baserunners. The weakest hitters should be at the end of the batting order.

☐ Bunts and sacrifice flies serve to advance players to scoring position, but both usually result in an out for the hitter. The sacrifice bunt is used when runners are on first or first and second and there are fewer than two outs.

☐ A batter should run as fast as possible for first base, touching it and over-running it along the right field line. If it is possible to advance more than one base on the hit, the batter moves into foul territory before reaching first base and turn toward second base.

☐ On fly balls, other than with two outs, runners advance a safe distance toward the next base so they can return to their original bases if the ball is caught, or be ready to advance if the ball is dropped. When a fly ball is hit deep and the runner has time to advance after the ball is caught, she may hold near the base, touch, and then advance.

Defensive strategy. The defensive team depends upon the individual skills and player cooperation.

☐ If possible, **put out** the runner who is closest to home plate.

☐ Make the third out at the nearest and surest base.

☐ Normal playing position is assumed when there are no baserunners and a shift to the fielder's right is made for a right-handed batter and to the left for a left-handed batter.

☐ To cover a **bunt**, the pitcher, third, and first basewomen move in to field the ball as the second basewoman moves to cover first and the short-stop covers second.

TERMINOLOGY

Appeal play A play upon which an umpire cannot make a decision until re-quested by a player. The appeal must be made before the pitcher's next de-livery.

Assist A credit awarded each player who handles the ball in a series of plays which results in a baserunner being put out.

Base on balls A walk. The batter is allowed to take a position as a base-runner on first base when four balls are called before the batter hits, strikes out, or is put out.

Battery The pitcher and the catcher.

Double A two-base hit.

Double play A defensive play that results in two outs.

Error A misplay on a ball which the scorer rules as avoidable.

Fielder's choice An option which a fielder has in playing a ball in which she may retire the baserunner rather than the batter.

Hot corner Third base.

Infield fly A fly to the infield which is caught or, in the opinion of the umpire, could easily be caught by an infielder. It is ruled only when there are runners at first and second with fewer than two outs.

Inning One of seven sections of the game in which teams alternate offensive and defensive turns. Three outs for each side constitute an inning.

Interference The act of hindering a batter by a defensive player; or an act of fielding that is hindered by a baserunner so that the defensive player cannot make a play on a hit ball.

No hitter A game in which one team is not able to get a safe hit.

Sacrifice A bunt, fly, or hit intended to advance the baserunner. It results in an out for the batter.

Single One-base hit.

Squeeze play Bringing a player home from third base on a bunt.

Stolen base A surprise advance to a base closer to scoring position made by a baserunner. It must be done as soon as the ball leaves the pitcher's hand.

Triple A three-base hit.

33
Speedball
JoAnne Thorpe

INTRODUCTION

The game of speedball was created in 1921 by Elmer D. Mitchell at the University of Michigan, Ann Arbor. Originally it was developed to fill a need for a fall sport in the men's intramural program (Meyer and Swarz 1965, pp. 312–336). Currently the game is played much more extensively by girls than by boys, as is evident by the fact that the National Association for Girls and Women in Sport (NAGWS) is the recognized rules-making body.

Although speedball was originally designed for the intramural program, it now is an important activity in most instructional programs at all levels, and is also being played to some extent at an interscholastic level (Blackman 1974–1976, pp. 84–85).

The game is complex, demands many skills, and brings the total body into play. From this standpoint, it is ideal as an educational tool. Few, if any, other games require the dexterity of the feet and hands that speedball does. In basketball, for example, the feet merely support the body so that the hands can be used to score and/or defend. In soccer, almost total use of the feet is required whereas in speedball the game demands alternating but independent skill in all parts of the upper and lower extremities, and scoring can be accomplished by either. It is a totally demanding game.

The game of speedball has an intellectual dimension that some games do not have. The participant is required to think constantly and to make decisions about the appropriate method of playing the ball—sometimes with the feet and sometimes with the hands. Much depends upon choosing the method which is most effective.

THE GAME

The game is played by two teams of 11 players each. The field is 60×100 yd. Figure 33.1 is a diagram depicting field markings and player positions at the beginning of the game.

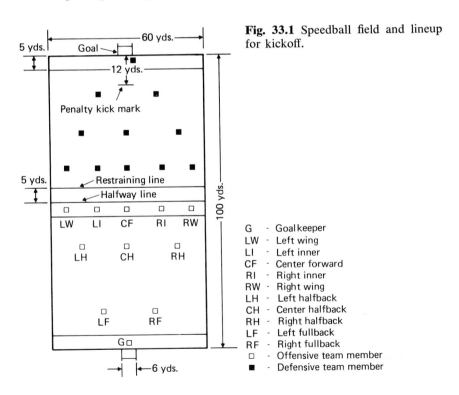

Fig. 33.1 Speedball field and lineup for kickoff.

G - Goalkeeper
LW - Left wing
LI - Left inner
CF - Center forward
RI - Right inner
RW - Right wing
LH - Left halfback
CH - Center halfback
RH - Right halfback
LF - Left fullback
RF - Right fullback
□ - Offensive team member
■ - Defensive team member

The game is begun by a kickoff. From that point on, the ball must be played either as an aerial or a ground ball. When the ball is on the ground, even though it may bounce from the ground into the air, it is nevertheless a ground ball. Only when the ball has been legally converted into an aerial ball may it be played as an aerial ball. Play of ground balls resembles soccer while play of aerial balls resembles basketball. The game involves the constant shifting back and forth between ground and aerial play.

A game consists of four 8-minute quarters with two minutes rest between quarters and a ten-minute rest between halves. Unlimited substitution is allowed, the time for which is 30 seconds. A team is allowed to play with fewer than 11 players but, if reduced to fewer than 9, must forfeit.

TERMINOLOGY

Aerial ball A ball that has come from a kick or conversion and is eligible to be played in the air.

Attacking team The offensive team which is attempting to score.

Block A method of intercepting the ball which is described under the term "blocking the ball." This applies predominantly to ground balls. An aerial ball once blocked becomes a ground ball.

Body block A technique of using one's body to shield the ball by placing the body between the ball and the opponent.

Center The technique of centering is used by the outside forwards to place the ball in a position for the inside forwards to score. Usually the wing is the player who centers the ball to the inners or center forward.

Conversion A means of changing a ground ball to an aerial ball. The various methods include allowing the ball to roll up the foot or leg, then catching it, lifting the ball from the ground with the foot, and volleying the ball with the foot and catching it before it touches the ground.

Defending team The team which is attempting to prevent the attacking team from scoring and at the same time gain possession of the ball.

Direct free kick A free kick from which a goal may be scored.

Dodge A method of evading an opponent by using deception to fake one way and move another.

Double foul Fouls committed simultaneously by members of both teams.

Draw The tactic which consists of tempting the defense to come to the ball. Implied in the draw is waiting until the defense comes, then passing off.

Dropkick A ball which is dropped and kicked just as it rebounds from the ground.

Fouls Fouls include the individual fouls of blocking, charging, pushing, tagging, hacking, holding, tripping, handling the ball, traveling with the ball, holding the ball, unnecessary roughness, threatening the eyes, delaying the game, and others specified in the current rule book. Also included are the team fouls of taking too many time-outs, having too many players on the field, and making an illegal substitution.

Free kick A placekick which is awarded for a foul when the ball is being played as a ground ball. Free kicks may be direct or indirect.

Free throw An unguarded throw which is awarded for a foul when the ball is being played as an aerial ball.

Ground ball A ball that has not been converted to an aerial ball and is either on the ground or bouncing on the ground.

Indirect free kick A free kick from which a goal may not be scored.

Own goal The goal which a team is defending.

Pass A method of moving the ball from one teammate to another while attempting to retain possession of the ball. The "inside of the instep" or "outside of the foot" are the two methods most commonly used for passing ground balls. Passing as in basketball is used for aerial balls. Passes should be placed well ahead of a player who is running.

Placekick Two styles of kicks are currently used—the soccer style and the football style. The soccer style involves a side approach to the ball and an instep contact. The football style involves getting the toe under the ball and using a straight approach. In both types the player taking the kick runs toward the stationary ball and kicks it into the air.

Tackle The tackle is a means of taking the ball away from an opponent when it is being played on the ground. Types of tackles include the front tackle, side tackle, hook tackle, and split tackle.

Toss-up A jump ball which is awarded to two opponents.

Trap The ball may be stopped by using the sole of the foot, the inner side of the calf of the leg, the knee(s), or the fronts of the legs.

Volley The ball may be intercepted in the air (volleyed) by using the knee, shoulder, head, hip, or foot.

TACTICS AND STRATEGY

Markings. Marking is the form of defense (or guarding) which is used in speedball. It involves covering in the following manner.

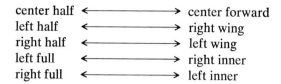

Interchange. Interchange is a technique utilized by the offense to pick up a pass and involves an exchange of positions usually between forwards. It may involve a fullback crossing over to cover for the other fullback; however, when the defense interchanges, it is usually termed "covering."

Rushing. When there is an attempt for a field goal or even the possibility for one, the forwards should rush. This means that everyone on the forward line should converge on the goal in an attempt to force the ball through.

Out-of-bounds plays. A throw-in, kick-in, punt, dropkick, or placekick may be used in various situations. The most recent rule book should be consulted for the specific rules.

Toss-up. For either aerial or ground balls involving double fouls or tie situations, a toss-up is used to resume play.

Penalty kick. A penalty kick is awarded the attacking team when the defending team fouls within its own penalty area or behind its own goal line. A dropkick must be used and in order to score, the ball must travel over the crossbar.

Kickoff. Play begins with a kickoff. This consists of placing the ball on the halfway line in the exact center of the field. The center forward of the team entitled to the ball utilizes either a pass or a placekick to put the ball in play. (The most recent rule book lists the various conditions which are required on the kickoff and the various penalties imposed for failure to follow the rules.)

Scoring

Scoring is computed as follows:

Field goal—two points   Penalty kick—one point
Touchdown—two points   Dropkick—three points

A field goal is scored when any player causes the ball to pass off the foot under the crossbar and between the goalposts. A touchdown is scored when an attacking player who is outside of the penalty area and within the field of play completes a pass to a teammate who is beyond the goal line. A penalty kick is scored when the attacking team sends the ball over the crossbar from a dropkick as described under **penalty kick.** A dropkick is scored when a player who has legally caught the ball properly executes a dropkick which goes over the crossbar and between the uprights of the goalposts or their imaginary extensions. (The current rule book should be consulted for specific requirements and penalties for the dropkick.)

ETIQUETTE AND ETHICS

It is customary to inform the umpire when a known foul is committed or a ball is sent out-of-bounds. It is also an act of good sportsmanship to assist the opponents and/or the umpire in retrieving balls from out of bounds or in placing balls for free kicks as expeditiously as possible.

EQUIPMENT

Traditional equipment includes canvas shoes with rubber cleats, shorts, a long-sleeved jersey, and shin guards (if one wishes). Shin guards help to prevent intimidation; however, some players tend to kick more than usual when shin guards are worn. Official equipment includes the ball which is an official soccer ball, pinnies, and the goalposts. Goalposts are six yards apart with a crossbar eight feet high and uprights twenty feet high.

ANALYSIS

Apparently biomechanical analyses in speedball per se are not available to date. One thorough analysis of the soccer placekick is relevant, however. Glassow and Mortimer (1964–1966) compared the soccer and football styles of placekicking and found that longer distances are usually obtained through the soccer style. Greater height is probably obtained through the football style as a result of using a straight approach and getting the toe under the ball. The longer distance of the soccer style is probably attributable to greater pelvic rotation resulting from a diagonal approach to the ball and placing the supporting foot beside rather than behind the ball.

SUMMARY

Speedball is a game involving total use of the body—both lower and upper extremities. Probably no other game requires so much large muscle and fine muscle coordination. It makes very strenuous physical and mental demands of the players. The game is especially suitable in a program of physical education because of the many variables and decision-making opportunities. The opportunity for all-round development is inherent in the game itself when properly played.

REFERENCES

Bailey, C. J., and F. L. Teller 1970. *Soccer.* Philadelphia: W. B. Saunders.

Blackman, C. 1974–1976. Interscholastic speedball. *Soccer-speedball-flag football guide.* National Association for Girls and Women in Sport. Washington, D.C.: AAHPER.

Callaghan, J. 1969. *Soccer.* Pacific Palisades, Calif.: Goodyear.

Glassow, R. B., and E. M. Mortimer 1964–1966. Analysis of kicking. *Soccer-speedball guide.* NAGWS. Washington, D.C., pp. 11–16.

Meyer, M. H., and M. M. Swarz 1965. *Team sports for girls and women.* Philadelphia: W. B. Saunders.

Mott, J. A. 1972. *Soccer and speedball for women.* Dubuque: Wm. C. Brown.

NAGWS 1976. *Soccer-speedball flag football guide,* 1976–78. Washington, D.C.: AAHPER.

Nelson, R. L. 1966. *Soccer.* Dubuque: Wm. C. Brown.

Schmid, I. R. 1967. *Beginning soccer.* Belmont, Calif.: Wadsworth.

FILMS

The Athletic Institute films on soccer are most current. Athletic Institute, 805 Merchandise Mart, Chicago, Ill. 60654.

The references recommended have lists of films showing game play primarily in soccer but appropriate for speedball.

34
Sports in Camping*
Gerald P. Burns

The dynamic role of sports and games in organized camping is of sufficient importance to educators to warrant continued observation and evaluation. The theory of active play as derived from games and sports is much the same everywhere. While the theory or purpose may be the same, the values gained

---

* Reprinted by permission from *JOHPER* **20,** 5 (May), 1949. Original title: The Role of Sports and Games in Organized Camping.

from athletic activity vary under different environmental conditions. Every teacher, coach, and camp director is aware of his responsibility in bringing his class, team, or camp ever closer to the main goal of education—making better citizens for tomorrow. The goal is universal, but the methods are peculiar to the setting in which they operate.

THE CAMP SITUATION

The usual camp closely approaches the "ideal" situation in athletics, including sports, games, and physical education activities, because of the uniqueness of camping. Obviously, the closer a program approaches the ideal, the greater are its values to the participants. Modifying factors enter into the sports programs of the majority of camps which invariably react beneficially for the athlete.

For example, players function under less pressure, less crowded facilities are available, maximum opportunity exists for individual coaching and guidance, fewer safety hazards are present, and the scheduling of games and practice sessions is regulated for the good of the camper. The educational implications of camping are clearly evident in the sports program of the better camps.

EDUCATIONAL IMPLICATIONS

In the present day and age there exists marked diversity of educational practice and philosophy. This is as true in recreation and camping as in formal education. But certain principles remain constant in the face of conflicting theories, however. Five of these principles of training apply to athletics in camp. They are comprehensiveness, intensiveness, continuity, individuality, and purposefulness. In playing its proper role in the general camp program—making maximum contribution to overall growth and development of participants—the sports program is aided by these five implications. While one or two of these are found under other environmental conditions, it is left to the camp to supply all five at the same time.

The first implication, that of *comprehensiveness,* indicates that the wide scope of the activities available in the usual camp makes a rich variety of games and a balanced athletic program immediately available. The second, *intensiveness,* implies that living under close, favorable conditions with the counselor (teacher) makes for ease in learning. A third principle, that of *continuity,* reflects the educational values inherent in the full schedule of the camper. The *individualized,* or fourth, implication points up the individually designed program and personnel guidance available to each participant due to the low counselor-camper ratio (teacher load). Finally, the fifth principle or implication is that of *purposefulness,* or the direct meaning that the camper is able to immediately see, feel, and understand in the camp sports and other related phases of the camp program.

IMPORTANCE OF SPORTS IN CAMP

There is no contesting the fact that athletics, in one form or another, are important to all educational and recreational programs. Being an important facet of education and a major phase of recreation, *a priori* reasoning validates the close relationship of sports to the camping program. The values accruing from efficiently planned and conducted games programs in the *usual settings* are well known; the additional values to be gained from the same program in the *camp setting* are seldom understood.

As the educational implications or principles in the above paragraphs point out, the camp offers a unique environment for the best in teaching and coaching, especially on the beginner's level. Moreover, the large-muscle activity that characterizes sports and games is a necessity in many camps where the remainder of an otherwise well balanced program may concern itself with sedentary activities. The few camps which frown on athletics as an important part of the program are those which need it most, due to the tendency of such camps to emphasize nature lore, hobby crafts, music, dramatics, photography, and other excellent but less active pursuits.

This is not a plea for the erection of indoor facilities and vast city-type playfields. The best in camping occurs outdoors—in the water, on the trails, in the woods, and on the playfields.

The argument that athletics should be omitted from the camp program "because the boys and girls indulge in such activities at home" is also educationally unsound. The wise teacher does not sever all connecting bonds in a sequence, but rather, seeks to build relationships and interrelated values.

EFFECTIVE INTEGRATION

Athletics may be most effectively integrated with the camp program by carefully studying all the factors involved and developing a relationship between this and other phases of the total program. Efficient camp directors exhibit excellent overall programs because of their shrewd insight into the promising character of the various components of the program. Unlike other phases of education, the heavy hand of tradition has not fallen upon camping. Freedom from traditional fixations, open-mindedness, and a scientific approach permit great variations and flexibility in the activity schedule of the usual camp.

The amount of time allocated to athletics varies from almost zero to nearly one hundred percent. The method of integration, the relationship to other activities, and the amount of time allocated sports and games vary with the camp. Some of the variables which must be carefully studied and certain of the factors involved in developing relationships are as follows: equipment facilities; climate; staff; number, age, skill, and desires of campers; specialty, objectives, or philosophy of the camp; etc.

The director or person designing the program and integrating athletics must have considerable knowledge and wisdom in three major areas. Listing the three in their order of importance, he must understand *children,* know *camping,* and be familiar with *athletics.* It is not sufficient that we simply add new activities to the existing program, but rather that we observe the necessity for careful integration, perhaps to the extent of completely reorganizing the program as a whole in relation to guiding principles.

LEADERSHIP IN CAMP SPORTS

Dynamic, effective, and creative leadership is as essential to the sports program in camp as it is to any other phase of camp activity. The person or persons selected to handle this portion of the total program must be skilled in both camping and athletics. In the larger camps, where several staff members are concerned with the games program, it is imperative that the department head be well versed in all phases of camping (as well as athletics) in order that he may most effectively integrate athletics with the other activities in camp. His assistants need not have extensive training and experience in camping, but must add to their required skill in sports coaching the spirit, method, and "approach" of the camp. In the final analysis, the most important prerequisite for success in handling the camp athletic program, or any of its many facets, is an understanding of, and love for, children. It is not athletics or camping that we are chiefly concerned with but *children.*

Most camps sponsoring any sort of land-sports program employ an "athletic counselor." In considering the role of athletics in camping it would be a mistake to omit a brief analysis of the type of leader obtained for this job. Like the program itself, the type of leadership secured varies greatly. Some camps desire "name" players and college stars. Other camps select young men and women trained in physical education and/or recreation. Very frequently the latter are employed as coaches or physical education instructors during the academic year and find camp work a pleasing environmental change during July and August. The most important single ingredient in camping from the standpoint of administration is not the food or the weather, not the facilities or the equipment, but always the leadership.

THE PROGRAM

That popular cliché of the day, "it varies with the type of camp," must again be invoked. For the purpose of this resume, the broadest possible definition of athletics is used. Just as the Olympic Games feature all types of athletics, so too, the connotation of recreational athletics used for the camps of America must be all-inclusive. When athletics and physical education are mentioned in certain quarters only a handful of the more highly organized physical activities are envisioned; i.e., baseball, boxing, football, calisthenics, etc. The full gamut of athletics available in the different camps ranges from riding to riflery, from winter sports to water sports, from individual contests to mass games. There are few forms of athletics that cannot be participated in at camp. There are many forms of athletics that can *best* be participated in at camp; i.e., woodland games, nature contests, mountain climbing, etc. We rather like the broad definition given the word "athlete" in Webster's *New International,* to wit: "Anyone trained or fit to contest in exercises requiring physical agility, stamina, and, often, strength."

There is little value in listing the dozens of games most suitable to camps, simply because their value varies from camp to camp. Rather, let us set up five catagories in which the camp director and the athletic counselor may readily find the desired sports activities: games of low organization, games of high organization, woodland games, water games, and miscellaneous athletic activities.

Obviously, the sports program in a camp must consist of those activities that contribute most to the goals and philosophy of the particular camp. Limitations and modifications will be invoked in every camp due to the many variables listed earlier such as facilities, equipment, leadership, etc. If the athletic activities fail to contribute to the overall aims of the camp, they should be changed or discarded for other activities.

35

Squash

Marigold A. Edwards

HISTORICAL DEVELOPMENT

Squash, more properly squash racquets, should not be confused with squash tennis or with squash's progenitor, hard racquets. Squash evolved as a form of racquets using a small India-rubber ball which struck the walls with a mushy sound—hence the name. (The modern ball is harder.) Precisely how the game evolved is not known. It was played at Harrow as early as 1850, and Dickens's Mr. Pickwick saw it, or something like it, being played against the walls of the Fleet Street prison. British men's clubs began to build private courts in the 1890s. At about the same time, play began along the eastern seaboard of North America, especially in Philadelphia. Now all fifty states have courts and the game is growing in the West and South, but pockets of squash activity exist only sporadically across the continent most often in men's clubs and universities. Development of commercial squash centers and courts in connection with other racquet facilities is leading to rapid expansion of the game.

In the meantime, the game spread from Britain to her colonies, and the parts of the world in which modern squash is strongest are former British colonies and countries of the United Kingdom—Australia, Egypt, New Zealand, India, Pakistan, and South Africa. In the last decade, the game has spread rapidly in Mexico—half a dozen courts have multiplied into more than 1500. And Japanese entrepreneurs are discussing court building in the thousands. There is a worldwide squash boom.

It is impossible to do justice in a short space to the many famous players who have made the game what it is today. From Pakistan have come the Khans, led by the peerless Hashim Khan, who dominated world squash for many years; many of the family, including Hashim, are now in the United States as club professionals. And his son, Sharif, has continued to dominate play in North America for the past eight years. Egypt has produced Amir Bay and Dardir Ali El-Bakaray, probably the number one coach in the world, who brought Egypt's players to world class before revolutionizing the game in Australia. In turn, Australia has been producing world-class players.

Unfortunately for American players, and for present and prospective international competition, squash grew up in the United States with court dimensions and with standards for the ball that differ from those of the game as played in England and now in other parts of the world.

For details of differences between the two games, as well as for other fine points that cannot be covered in this brief account, the interested reader should consult the sources in the references. The description in the chapter is of American squash.

EQUIPMENT AND FACILITIES

Squash is a racquet-and-ball game played within a rectangular, walled court, all four walls being used in play. The ideal court is built of wood, sometimes with a rear wall of glass for spectators' convenience; sometimes composition or cement is used. The court is white; the marking lines are red. The door is in the back wall and must close flush with the wall's surface.

The dimensions of a singles court for American squash are indicated in Fig. 35.1. Dimensions were standardized in 1931; odd-sized courts still exist.

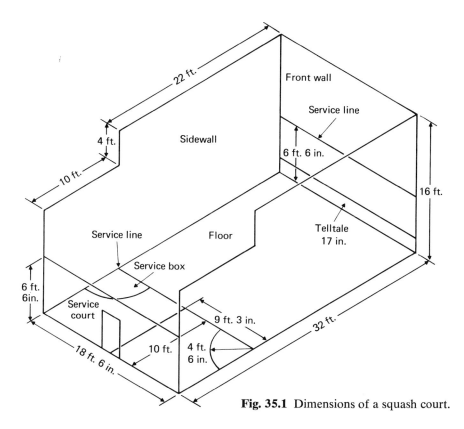

Fig. 35.1 Dimensions of a squash court.

Double courts are larger. Consult the USSRA playing rules if necessary. Court plans, criteria for construction materials and methods, and cost estimates are available from the USSRA.

The racquet, finer and lighter than a tennis racquet but of equal length (27″ maximum), has a small circular head 9″ across, strung with catgut or synthetics; metal is authorized only in the shaft, and all-wood racquets remain the popular choice. (Frames are not guaranteed against breakage, as clearly stated on the shaft, since the effort to play a wall ball can result in a crack or clean break on the first swing.)

The hard but hollow rubber ball of golfball size, which often travels at the speed of a baseball pitcher's fastball (120 mph and up), leaves its black marks on the walls and sometimes on the players. Doubles requires a livelier ball. (See USSRA ball specifications.)

THE PLAY

The object of the game is to accumulate points. A point is won by hitting a legal shot—serve or subsequent return—which the opponent cannot legally

Fig. 35.2 Squash is a racquet-and-ball game played in a rectangular box. Courtesy of the United States Squash-Racquets Association.

return. Both server and receiver can score any given point (in contrast to the British game, in which only the server can score).

The players spin a racquet for first serve. The server must keep at least one foot within the service box until the serve is struck. A legal serve must hit the front wall first, above the service line, and hit the floor first in the opponent's service court; it may, however, hit any other wall or walls before the floor, and the receiver may return it before it strikes the floor.

The server who hits an illegal serve, or fault, serves again; a second consecutive illegal serve, or double fault, costs a point and gives the opponent the serve.

After a legal serve, the floor service lines and boxes no longer matter to the play.

A legal return must be hit before the ball strikes the floor twice; it may be hit before the ball strikes the floor at all. It must hit the front wall, between the telltale and the 16' top line, before it hits the floor once; it may, however, hit other walls in any number or succession before and after hitting the front wall.

Shots after the first return of service are subject to the same rules as the first return. The first player to hit a shot which the opponent cannot legally return wins a point.

A server who wins a point moves to the alternate service box and serves again. The receiver who wins a point becomes a server.

A player hit by his own ball loses the point. A player hit by his opponent's ball (1) loses the point if the ball was headed for the front wall; (2) wins the point if the ball would not have reached the front wall. If the ball would have hit a sidewall, the point must be replayed. If a player interferes with his opponent, or holds back a stroke to avoid hitting his opponent,

Fig. 35.3 Good length strokes force the opponent off the coveted T and into the corners. Courtesy of the United States Squash-Racquets Association.

a "let" is called and the point must be replayed. In formal matches, a referee decides such issues.

Since both players share the same playing area, courtesy to the opponent is a primary responsibility of each, even at the risk of tactical disadvantage.

The first player to score 15 points wins the game. When a game is tied at 13–13, however, the player losing the tying point "sets" the game's winning score at 15, 16, or 18 points. If a game is tied at 14–14 without having been tied at 13–13, the loser of the tying point sets the game at 15 or 17. A match is three out of five games.

(For such complications as the management of service in doubles and the differences between the American and British games, consult the sources listed in the references.)

SKILLS OF THE GAME

Since the fundamental elements of squash—stroking, footwork, variety of shots, strategy, and conditioning—are standard, the reader is referred to any book on technique. Strokes made all with a single grip, the tennis Continental, are generally most efficient. They should be made in a vertical rather than horizontal plane and often with the racquet face slightly open to impart varying amounts of backspin to the ball.

One can play a good game with two basic strokes: cross-court shots and alleys or rails (close and parallel to the sidewalls). The effectiveness of both depends upon length; the ball should not rebound off the back wall. Correct length on these two strokes is the essence of basic squash. Both force the

Fig. 35.4 When the opponent is behind, hit short. Courtesy of the United States Squash-Racquets Association.

opponent off the coveted T—the waiting position at the intersection of the floor service lines—and into the back corners. Shots requiring more finesse and played off more than one wall are refinements to be practiced after the basic game is well established.

Squash strategy in its simplest form, as in any racquet sport, is to put the ball where the opponent is not. When the opponent is in front, hit past him; when he's behind, hit short.

Hashim Khan, the first and greatest of the fantastic Khans, writes in his delightful book (1967):

> Forty-five years I have racquet in hand, and what I learn goes in one page. *Keep eye on ball. Move quick to T. Stay in crouch. Take big step. Keep ball far away from opponent. Have many different shots ready so opponent does not know what you do next. Do not relax because you play good shot. Maybe opponent retrieves that ball; better you get ready for next stroke. Soon as can, find out where opponent has idea to send ball, then quick take position for return shot. Have reason for every stroke you make.* You can put these ideas in your head in a few minutes, yes. Now, you learn to make these ideas belong to you, you remember them in court, never you need anything more, they give you good games all your life!

The great Egyptian coach, Dardir, in stating, "The player of world class will have finishing shots to go with his sound basic game," leaves no doubt as to the sequence of mastery for both strokes and strategy.

DOMESTIC ORGANIZATION

There are approximately a half-million players in the United States in city, state, and regional associations each with its schedule of tournaments at A,

B, and/or C levels of play. Men and women have independent associations. The men's U.S. Squash-Racquets Association sponsors National Singles and Doubles with age categories and team championships for amateur members, and the North American Open which includes professionals. It also sponsors the Lapham (singles) and Grant (doubles) Cups. The latter are technically open to the world but, because of differences between the British and American games, are reduced to the traditional United States–Canada confrontation. The recent rapid growth led the USSRA to establish a permanent office with a full-time paid Executive Director: 211 Ford Road; Bala Cynwyd, Pa. 19004. The United States Women's SRA organized in 1933, sanctions about 25 singles and doubles tournaments and the interdistrict Howe Cup team matches annually. Contact may be made through the USSRA office.

Both associations conduct teaching/coaching seminars and clinics. For the first time, the 1976 National Singles in Philadelphia were held for men and women at the same time. Bancroft Sporting Goods Company sponsored the 1976 North American Open Singles with prize money and the 1976 National Women's Singles. They have agreed to sponsor an International Invitational Women's event with prize money to be held in New York City in 1977 and the South or West after that.

Also functioning are men's and women's intercollegiate associations and an association for professionals, most of whom are teaching in clubs (information through USSRA office).

The USSRA official yearbook covers the various national championships; the USWSRA and the Canadian, Mexican, Professional and Intercollegiate SRAs; regional reports, tournament schedules; club and member lists; committees and historical data. Court, racquet and ball specifications, rules booklet and interpretations and two 15-minute films, including one instructional, may be obtained from the previous address.

INTERNATIONAL ORGANIZATION

The International Squash Raquets Federation has existed since 1967, and world competitions (in the British game) have been played in alternate years since then; Australia and now Pakistan have dominated play. Hopes for American success and aspirations for the inclusion of squash among Olympic sports are uncertain and depend upon some future standardization by making compromises between the American and British games.

VALUES

Squash is increasing in popularity and gives promise of continuing to do so. The rudiments are easily picked up by any beginner, especially one who knows anything about tennis, badminton, or handball. Squash is also more fun for the beginner than many other games: the beginner seldom hits the ball out of bounds and doesn't have to chase it far. The game can be played year round, unaffected by weather, and usually costs the city dweller less time and travel than golf or tennis.

A typical period of play is 30–45 minutes of vigorous activity with an energy expenditure as high as 650-plus calories per hour. The game is therefore excellent for weight control and for stimulation of the cardiorespiratory system. For the busy executive or professional person, squash is a quick and adequate exercise after eight hours behind a desk.

The beginner can enjoy the game almost immediately and need not suffer the discouragement of near-total failure that often accompanies one's first experience of golf or tennis. Even the beginner can appreciate the light and shade of squash rallies that mix hard drives, soft drops, and lobs for a cat-and-mouse effect. This is where the fun is.

REFERENCES

American Association for Health, Physical Education, and Recreation, Division for Girls' and Women's Sports. *Tennis-badminton-squash guide* 1972–1974, 1974–1976, and 1976–1978. By the Association, Washington, D.C. 20036.

Barnaby, J. M. 1961. *Squash racquets in brief*. South Lincoln, Mass.: Available from the author by mail.

Dardir, and G. Gilmour 1971. *Dardir on squash*. Auckland, N. Z.: Holly Press.

Khan, H., with R. E. Randall 1967. *Squash racquets: The Khan game*. Detroit: State University Press.

Palmer, M. (ed.) 1975. *World of squash*. London: Queen Anne Press.

Rowland, J. 1976. *Squash basics*. Lawrence, Mass.: Two Continents Publishing Company (Methuen Sports Basics Books series).

Sports illustrated book of squash 1963. Philadelphia and New York: J. P. Lippincott.

Truby, J. O., Jr. 1975. *The science and strategy of squash*. New York: Scribners.

Varner, M., and N. B. Bramall 1967. *Squash racquets*. Dubuque: Wm. C. Brown.

Wood, P. 1972. *The book of squash*. New York: Van Nostrand.

36
Swimming

Because of the diverse nature of activities which fall under the label of swimming, six authors were selected to make contributions. Robert K. Stallman presented an historical summary with illustrations which portrayed the development of teaching techniques and the equipment used. He concluded with a paragraph entitled, "Where are we now?" G. E. Darda wrote an exhaustive presentation on the teaching and learning of competitive diving.

This discussion of swimming includes two brief papers by T. K. Cureton, one on Water Safety *and the other on* Survival Aquatics. *Bernard E. Empleton has described the fundamentals of skin and scuba diving as well as safety precautions and first-aid techniques.*

M. G. Sholtis explains the term Swimnastics *and discusses it under the headings of Origin and Development, Objectives, Equipment and Supplies, Teaching Hints, and Swimming for the Handicapped. Finally, Joanne L. Smith presents her article on the origin and place of* Synchronized Swimming.

The water sport enthusiast will also wish to consult Chapter 44, "Water Polo." RBF

Basic Swimming Instruction
Robert K. Stallman

INTRODUCTION

Perhaps more has been written about swimming than about any other sport. The number of volumes published in the English language alone since the mid-1800s is staggering. These were preceded by several historically notable works, dating back to the 16th century. Archeological artifacts provide much evidence of artistic works depicting swimmers at play or in combat (Sinclair and Henry 1893; Thomas 1893).

The British, with their 19th-century flair for sport and for organizing everything and anything, can be credited with launching the proliferation of swimming literature that began in the 1830s and continues today. The Japanese had the first national association for swimming in 1603. The National Swimming Association of England was formed in 1837. Australia held the first major swimming championships in 1846 (Oppenheim 1970). Thenceforth, swimming clubs flourished in Britain and Australia, soon spreading to Europe and North America. These clubs promoted competition and teaching.

Many countries where swimming is popular today have a rich historical literature in the art. Noteworthy examples are Japan, Germany, France, and Hungary.

The purpose of this chapter is to briefly outline the evolution of teaching methods, to discuss where we appear to be today regarding teaching methods, and to offer a selection of references most useful in understanding teaching and learning and in understanding the physiopsychological rationale for the position of our contemporary leaders in the teaching of swimming.

AGENCIES AND PROGRAMS

The Japanese national governing body for swimming was formed to promote the teaching of swimming in the schools. The Royal Lifesaving Society of England was founded in 1891 and quickly spread over the British Commonwealth.

The Surf Lifesaving Associations of Australia, New Zealand, and South Africa were formed in the early 1900s and are famous today for their progress in surf lifesaving and water safety.

The International YMCA became involved in aquatics in 1909 and has played a major leadership role ever since.

In 1914 the American Red Cross accepted a proposal to launch a national water safety program. They began with training lifesavers, training and certifying teachers, and promoting local learn-to-swim campaigns.

Dozens of youth organizations the world over foster swimming instruction, train their own leaders, and support award systems. The Boy Scouts, Girl Scouts, or Girl Guides of many nations are a few examples.

Most of the agencies mentioned in preceding paragraphs have developed their own award systems, teaching methods and teacher training programs. Virtually anywhere in the world with accessible water, a child can earn a badge or crest for learning to swim.

These facts have pertinence in that they led naturally to the evolution of mass methods of teaching. Such programs by their very nature required certain assumptions and led to hundreds of useful innovations. It is also true, however, that humans learn differently. Mass teaching sometimes overshadows the intricacies of learning and the advancement of our knowledge of the learning process may have been impeded.

Such agencies as mentioned in the preceding paragraphs have today many more similarities than differences. Conscientious teachers who succeed in avoiding dogmatic devotion to any one system can borrow from each, developing their own workable approach, thus humanizing rather than regimenting.

The development of the Council for National Cooperation in Aquatics in the United States is significant. The gathering of any and all interested persons and agencies who have aquatic interests under one umbrella has promoted communication and broken down many barriers between agencies. The council has produced several outstanding publications in recent years and the proceedings of their meetings contain many relevant and sophisticated papers (Council for National Cooperation in Aquatics).

The Canadian Council for Cooperation in Aquatics has recently launched a similarly ambitious program. The historic first joint meeting of these two umbrella organizations was held in Quebec City in November, 1972.

What Is a Beginner?

If one were to examine the methods, curricula, examinations, and awards of the multitude of aquatic agencies, a pattern would emerge. There is considerable agreement as to the definition of a successful candidate for a beginner's award. Virtually everyone agrees that self-sufficiency in deep water is the most important criterion. Obviously, details regarding strokes and distances swum or time afloat vary somewhat. It is almost universally agreed that to be safely self-sufficient the graduating beginner can:

☐ Swim a stroke on the front

☐ Swim a stroke on the back

☐ Roll over from front to back and vice versa

☐ Change direction while on front or back

☐ Enter deep water headfirst or feetfirst and regain a horizontal position to begin swimming

☐ Rest motionlessly or nearly motionlessly with minimum energy expenditure

One of the most thorough and perhaps first sophisticated analysis of test items was that by T. K. Cureton, *Standards for Testing Beginning Swimming,* 1939.

Statistical analysis of dozens of test items administered to hundreds of pupils identified skills of confidence, support, and propulsion as being of paramount importance. Such skills had much greater predictive value of eventual success than land drills and isolated, unrelated skills. The most predictive items were those which combined several skills of confidence, support, and propulsion.

The Evolution of Method

The earliest attempts at divining the right magic to teach swimming are quite comical by today's standards (Sinclair and Henry 1893). The learner was

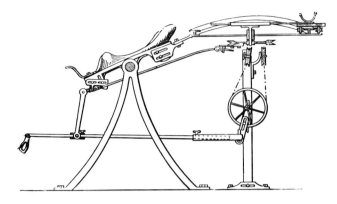

Fig. 36.1 Machine to teach swimming. From Sinclair and Henry, 1893, *Swimming*, London: Longmans, Green, p. 44.

sometimes strapped into a machine (Fig. 36.1), forced through certain movements, and supposedly emerged possessing a finished stroke. No less comical were the intricate land drills promoted as being the means to a finished stroke (Thomas 1893). Schools with no access to the water were fond of teaching drills in the classroom or gymnasium and assumed that they had accomplished their purpose without testing the product.

Numerous ways of supporting the learner by various suspension devices were popular until the 1920s or 1930s (Fig. 36.2). The most popular seems to have been the pole and belt system. One person stood on a deck, dock, or boat holding a pole from which hung a belt which supported the person in the water.

A similar rig suspended from overhead pulleys is described by Sinclair and Henry (Fig. 36.3). This writer has seen such pulley systems in modern

Fig. 36.2 One of the many suspension devices tested in the early 20th century. From Thomas, 1904, *Swimming,* London: Sampson Low, Marston, p. 397.

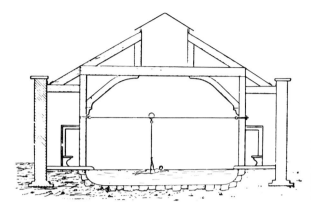

Fig. 36.3 Overhead pulley system. From Sinclair and Henry, 1893, *Swimming,* London: Longmans, Green, p. 45.

pools in Europe as recently as 1970. Indeed, they may have limited use in some unique situation.

A third technique involved simply tying the learner to a rope and hauling him toward the "professor."

A host of appurtenances was devised to support or propel the body. The list is endless and the literature is full of humorous illustrations. The most useful, however, are still in use today. Swim fins or flippers of some kind and mitts or hand paddles (Fig. 36.4) were depicted early in the literature (Sinclair and Henry 1893).

A more modern advocate of fins was the great Robert J. H. Kiphuth (1950). Recently Krizan has reported great success in launching beginners with fins and mask.

Hand paddles have, of course, recently been popularized again by Flip Darr and several of his protégés. Those in popular use now are not unlike the one illustrated in Fig. 36.4b.

The argument over the use of flotation devices has only recently subsided. Advice against them appears frequently in the pre-1900 literature. However, George Corsan, a pioneer of mass teaching methods, strongly advocated their worth in attaining correct body position. Cureton (1946) also argued in their favor as long as care was taken not to allow overdependence. Discreet use of such devices can be of considerable use when introduced at the right time. Overdependence, however, can postpone the attainment of self-sufficiency.

Charles E. Silvia has developed a large program for children making extensive use of an egg-shaped float and belt. Much research on human variability in buoyancy and factors related to swimming success provides the rationale for mechanically supplementing buoyancy and floating angle.

Mass Teaching Methods

Mass teaching methods began to appear just after the turn of the century. Pioneers in teaching methods were motivated by a rising number of tragedies

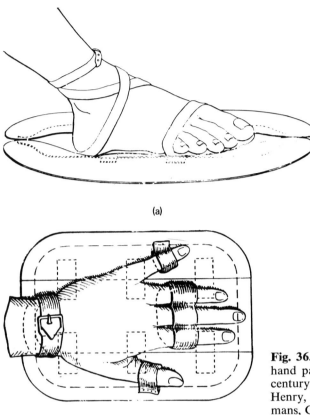

(a)

(b)

Fig. 36.4 (a) Flipper and (b) hand paddle used in the 19th century. From Sinclair and Henry, 1893, London: Longmans, Green, pp. 32 and 40, respectively.

in occupational and recreational activities. Naturally an evangelistic fervor gripped such pioneers as Wilbur Longfellow and George Corsan and countless others in Europe and Australia. There followed an era of the barnstorming evangelist who came into town for the local learn-to-swim campaign one day and was on the road the next.

This era supplied today's teachers of swimming an infinite number of progressions, patterns, aids, and philosophies. During World Wars I and II the military was forced to waterproof thousands of men quickly.

The "station method" or "assembly line" method was popularized by both barnstormers and the military and is in wide use today in local learn-to-swim campaigns (American National Red Cross 1963; Brown 1953).

Both the miiltary and such organizations as the Royal Lifesaving Society of Great Britain of the 1930s and 1940s made use of teaching by the numbers or by "penny numbers." Although such techniques have certain uses, they are far less popular today (United States Navy 1944).

Fig. 36.5 Mass teaching with flutterboards. From Brown, *Teaching progressions for the swimming instructor,* Silver Spring, Md.: R. L. Brown, p. 22.

The Brink system (Dr. B. Dean Brink) was very popular in the 1920s. It emphasized mind-pictures (the hungry duck, the jellyfish float) as a distraction from normal anxieties.

The Cubbon Confidence Method saw wide use during World War I. It consisted of six steps, one leading into the next. When learners achieve the appropriate degree of confidence at one level they pass on to the next (Cureton 1946).

George Corsan, L. de B. Handley, and others popularized "Easy Step" methods. Interestingly, Corsan did not believe in teaching the breaststroke and also was quoted as saying he could teach one hundred girls to do the back crawl in the same time required to teach one girl the front crawl.

Captain Fred Mills expanded and modified elements of these "cookbook" methods for use in camps of the Boy Scouts of America. Carrol Bryant incorporated many of these techniques into the programs of the American Red Cross.

Whether motor skills are learned more efficiently and completely when one breaks a movement down into its parts and practices them separately, or when one tries to perform the entire motor pattern in the early stages of learning, continues to be controversial. The readiness of the pupil, the complexity of the movement, and the quality of the teaching are factors which must be considered. In most instances the "whole-part-whole" method is most effective. In this way the pupil first becomes familiar with the total movement pattern and the situation in which it is used. Weaknesses in the learner's performances are then discovered, parts of the movement can be practiced individually, and the activity again practiced as a whole. This is expanded as follows by Smith (1971a and b).*

---

* The author has benefited extensively from the writings and advice of Dr. Murray F. R. Smith, University of Alberta, Edmonton Alberta, Canada. Dr. Smith's most recent papers as cited in the list of references are so pertinent as to be considered essential to the modern student of motor learning generally and to teachers of swimming specifically. His papers and his programs are an enlightening and rare example of bridging the "practice-theory gap."

Children are marvelous learners. Virtually all of them learn to talk very well using only their own bodily resources and calling on the natural (as opposed to professionally trained) help of those around them. Talking is surely the most complex skill one will ever be required to learn. We cannot *teach* it. Yet, thankfully, it can be readily *learned*. To extend the example, Margaret Mead writing of the Manus people of New Guinea points out that, "There is not a child of five who cannot swim well. A Manus child who couldn't swim would be as aberrant, as definitely subnormal as an American child of five who couldn't walk." Why is it then that learning to read, which certainly cannot be any more difficult than learning to talk, often results in so much frustration and in what we choose to call *reading problems?* And how can Manus children, with no instruction, outlearn children from the best programs where instruction is by professionals and facilities are the finest. It is difficult to avoid the conclusion that our efforts to *teach* often run counter to the way *learning* occurs.

Nowhere is this better illustrated than in the *part, whole* question which has been with us since the beginning. It is time to ignore the question at least and bury it if possible. One can understand the value of the distinction between part and whole learning in research. It opens the door to countless experiments, but the results of these studies have shed very little light on the problems faced by the overwhelming majority of physical educators who earn their livings teaching children in our schools.

Advanced Skills

Most programs and curricula of aquatic agencies provide a ladder of awards supposedly carrying the pupil through progressively more challenging and more comprehensive skills and activities. Some emphasize additional skills, e.g., new strokes, underwater techniques, treading and sculling and diving; some, innovative survival techniques such as drownproofing; some, water safety and life saving; some, distance swimming and fitness training; some, aquatic games and recreational activities; and some, aquatic and aesthetic and creative activities.

Any comprehensive program should surely cater to all of the areas of interest and outlets for human energy and satisfaction through movement in the aquatic medium.

Where Are We Now?

As Smith so clearly points out, progress in research in learning theory has had little impact over the years on practice in education (1971a). There seems to be a resistance to change and we as teachers fail to put to use available, well-established findings of research. There is a vast gap between the practice of *teaching* and the theory of *learning*.

If a single development in recent years can be identified as most important in the advancement of the teaching of motor skills (including swimming), it is a shift of emphasis from content to the learner. A more intimate knowledge of how people learn is of far greater importance than the number of ways we can devise to teach. More interaction with learners will give us greater insight into what motivates the learner, what arouses fear, what offers a challenge, how the learner receives and dispenses information. Smith says, "We are, after all, teachers of *children,* not teachers of activities."

Some additional comments to those previously cited regarding the part versus whole question are pertinent.

Though "whole" practice has been demonstrated to be superior to "part" practice, the important "whole" is usually not the element discussed in the literature or imposed by the teacher, but one having meaning to the learner (even if to no one else). Learners are the prime decision makers in determining what the bits and pieces are and the magnitude and succession of the pieces (meaningful "wholes"). In this way learners also control the rate of progress, selecting a rate suitable to their ability, promoting success and confidence and controlling increments of difficulty as if programmed. The teacher's role is primarily to enhance the quality of these efforts and to suggest alternative goals or ways of achieving goals. Generating an atmosphere of enthusiasm and creating situations which arouse curiosity and exploration are essential.

Implicit in the comments above is the idea that learners differ widely. Progress for each pupil, at an optimal rate for him or her and in a way meaningful to him or her (satisfying his or her own objectives) is impossible in large classes where all pupils follow rigid progressions laid down by the teacher. This does not mean that drill and whole class activities are not effective but only that they have limited effect and must be supplemented by much more individual teaching than is often available.

Excessive competition has also been demonstrated as being detrimental to learning. When anxiety is overwhelming, a child is too often destined to fail in a situation structured by the teacher.

Conscientious attempts to discover how the learners perceive advice from the teacher, how they evaluate their own progress, how they perceive their own efforts will give us insight into the scale used by learners to measure *their* progress toward *their* goals. Events can easily be structured which provide learners with instant feedback as to their progress. Traditionally teachers have been better at pointing out what is wrong than what is right.

Lastly, special attention must be paid to the relationship between teacher and pupil. Honest attempts at communication, genuine concern for the student as a person, consistency in treatment of the student, and preservation of the learner's self-respect are all essential.

Successful teachers will have an intimate knowledge of the physics and physiology of swimming made readily available to us by such writers and researchers as Councilman, Cureton, Faulkner, and Kinnear. They will have an intimate knowledge of the techniques of teaching given to us by Cureton, Brown, Corsan, Silvia, and such agencies as the YMCAs, the Royal Life-saving Societies, and the Red Cross Societies of many nations. Teachers will have an intimate knowledge of the nature of learning and the nature of the learner, provided for us by such researchers as Singer, Cratty, Bilodeau, Whiting, and Smith.

The greatest asset of teachers, however, will be a burning desire to treat each learner as an individual and to help him or her enjoy an active life-style, exploring the joys of healthful activity, of mastering new and challenging skills, and of expressing himself or herself in a very personal way through movement in the water.

REFERENCES

Amateur Swimming Association, Great Britain, *ASA handbook, swimming*. ASA of Great Britain.

American National Red Cross 1963. *Instructors manual, swimming and water safety*. Washington, D.C.: ANRC.

Brown, R. 1953. *Teaching progression for the swimming instructor*. Richard L. Brown.

Canadian Red Cross Society 1967. *Instructor's guide and reference*. Toronto: CRCS, Water Safety Division. (Reprint.)

Council for National Cooperation in Aquatics. *Proceedings*. Biannual Meetings, 1201 16th St., N.W. Washington, D.C. Published biennially.

Councilman, J. E. 1968. *The science of swimming*, Englewood Cliffs, N.J.: Prentice-Hall.

Cureton, T. K. 1946. *How to teach swimming and diving*. New York: Association Press.

———— 1939. *Standards for testing beginning swimming*. New York: Association Press.

Kiputh, R. J. H., and H. Burke 1950. *Basic swimming*. Yale University Press.

Lanoue, F. 1963. *Drownproofing*. Englewood Cliffs, N.J.: Prentice-Hall.

Oppenheim, F. 1970. *The history of swimming*. North Hollywood, Calif.: Swimming World Publications.

Royal Lifesaving Society of Canada 1970. (2nd ed.) *Canadian Lifesaving Manual*, Toronto: RLSS of Canada.

Silvia, C. E. 1970. *Manual and lesson plans: methods of teaching*. Springfield, Mass.: Charles E. Silvia.

Sinclair, A., and W. Henry 1893. *Swimming*. London: Longmans, Green.

Smith, M. 1971a. The psychological rationale for a new method of teaching swimming. *Proceedings*. Canadian Council for Cooperation in Aquatics.

———— 1971b. New approaches in teaching physical skills. *Proceedings, Canadian Association for Health, Physical Education and Recreation* (June).

Swimming technique. Swimming World Publications, Quarterly Journal of American Swimming Coaches Association, North Hollywood, Calif.

Thomas, R. 1904. *Swimming.* London: Sampson, Low, Marston.

United States Navy 1944. *Swimming.* Annapolis: Naval Aviation Physical Training Manual, United States Naval Institute.

The Instructional Aspect of Competitive Diving

G. E. Darda

INTRODUCTION

In any teaching, the essential prerequisite for the instructor is to possess knowledge of the subject and the ability to communicate this knowledge to the students. The first prerequisite can be satisfied easily. The fundamental purpose of this article is to provide this knowledge. The ability to communicate, however, defines the art of teaching, and this ability must be developed in some other way. The purpose of this article is to present the teaching cues and strategies which have proved successful in the teaching of diving skills. The diving skills are presented in a logical progression of increasing difficulty.

PREREQUISITE TO LEARNING DIVING

Before any younster is taught to dive, he or she should have some swimming skill. The ability to swim at least 25 yards unassisted is a good basis for the safe and successful introduction of diving instruction.

Age is not a strong factor in determining when to introduce a youngster to diving instruction. However, it is a strong factor in determining the rate of learning. Dick Kimball, former NCAA diving champion and current diving coach at the University of Michigan, began diving at the age of four. Ken Sitzberger, 1964 Olympic springboard diving champion, began taking diving lessons at the age of six.

A five-year-old child may be perfectly capable of learning the first dozen or so skills described below from the one-meter (low) springboard. However, it may be inadvisable for the instructor to encourage this youngster to attempt even the simple front dive from the three-meter (high) springboard for the following reasons. The forces acting on the human body upon entry into the water from the three-meter springboard are significantly greater than they are from the one-meter springboard. A five-year-old may not have developed enough natural strength to maintain correct body position upon entry from the higher level. Consequently, severe injuries such as pulled and strained shoulder or neck muscles could result.

It is the instructor's responsibility to make good judgments about the proper rate of progression. It is important at times to encourage children to overcome their "fear barriers" and move along to more difficult dives. All novice divers regardless of age experience natural fear barriers. Although novice divers may have a mental picture of a given dive, they have not had the kinesthetic experience of performing the dive. This unknown quality essentially defines the fear barrier, and fear barriers in diving are gradually broken down by successful experiences in the learning of new dives in an orderly, logical progression.

PROPER SEQUENCE OF BASIC DIVING

For the novice diver who possesses the minimum 25-yard swimming skill, the basic diving skills should be taught in the following order:

1. The kneeling dive from the side of the pool or pier.
2. The sitting dive from the side of the pool or pier.
3. The standing dive from the side of the pool, pier, and one-meter springboard.
4. The forward approach, hurdle step, and press.
5. The springing action of the diving board.
6. The plain forward dive with approach, hurdle step, and press.
7. The forward jackknife with approach, hurdle step, and press.
8. The forward swan dive with approach, hurdle step, and press.
9. The forward dive with one-half twist with approach, hurdle step, and press.
10. The backward press.
11. The backward fall-off dive.
12. The backward dive with press.
13. The inward dive with press.
14. The forward jackknife with half twist with approach, hurdle step, and press.
15. The forward somersault with approach, hurdle step, and press. (The forward one and one-half somersault with approach, hurdle step, and press.)

16. The backward somersault with press.
17. The reverse dive with approach, hurdle step, and press.
18. Twisting somersaults.
19. The forward somersault with one twist.
20. The backward somersault with one and one-half twist.

The first skill, the kneeling dive, will provide the youngster with the sensation of entering the water hands and head first for the very first time. Following this experience and after developing a well-executed standing front dive, the novice diver will go on to the proper use of the springboard and diving from it.

The Kneeling Dive

The diver kneels on one knee at the side of the pool or the pier. It is desirable to have a height of 6–18 inches between the pool deck and water level. However, if this is not possible, good, basic diving can still be taught. The diver is instructed to curl the toes of one foot over the edge of the pool. This is to help serve as traction and to aid in applying force during the act of executing this dive for the first time. The arms are aimed toward the point of entry with the hands clasped together and with the eyes focused on the point of entry which is some 12–16 inches from the edge of the pool. At a command from the instructor, the diver elevates the hips to raise the center of gravity. At the same time, the diver is instructed to lean forward while pointing the hands at the point of entry into the water. During this process, he or she drops the chin on the chest and leans forward, extending off the foot which is in contact with and curled over the side of the pool. Leaning forward causes gravity to act on the body while pushing off of the back leg ensures that the diver's legs will rise and that the diver will enter the water hands-and-headfirst. It may be necessary during the first few trials for the instructor to guide the diver by holding him or her at the hips to prevent the diver from landing on the stomach.

To review, the key factors in learning this dive are as follows:

☐ The elevation of the hips so that the diver can rise off one knee while simultaneously leaning forward.

☐ Keeping the head down with the chin tucked into the chest and the arms extended forward reaching to the point of entry.

By manually assisting the diver, the teacher can help prevent a belly flop. Depending upon the size of the youngster, it is also possible for the teacher to prevent a belly flop by lifting the back leg or the hips of the pupil. This dive should be initially practiced approximately six times so that the diver will become comfortable about entering the water hands-and-headfirst. Immediate success will further aid in the development of self-confidence as well as confidence in the instructor. On successive tries the diver should continue practicing the kneeling dive but gradually elevate the hips farther each time. Eventually the diver will learn a standing dive. The dive evolves from the kneeling dive to a stooping dive where both knees are off the deck of the pool, then to the bending dive where a diver has the knees only slightly flexed but is bending forward at the hips and, finally, to the standing dive.

A very important element in a successful hands-and-headfirst entry of the basic dive is that the diver keep the head down. This will prevent the diver from slapping his or her face upon entering the water in a too horizontal or flat position.

The Sitting Dive

If the diver is learning a dive for the first time at a beach equipped with a pier, the sitting dive, an alternative to the kneeling dive, can be learned. In this dive, the diver sits on the pier and, by reaching out in front to the point of entry, falls forward and rotates about the buttocks entering the water hands-and-headfirst. There are two disadvantages to the sitting dive. First, it is a little hard on the fabric of the bathing suit. Secondly, if the ledge or pier is not high enough (approximately 2 or 3 feet or more) it is difficult to get enough rotation to guarantee a hands-and-headfirst entry. Once the fundamental kneeling or sitting dive has been learned, a novice diver should progress to the standing dive.

The Standing Dive

The mechanics of the standing dive are similar to those of the kneeling dive. A great help in the early stages of the standing dive is to have the diver lift one leg backward while standing on the other leg and simultaneously leaning forward and bending at the hips. This aids in a forward rotation about the stationary foot and guarantees a hands-and-headfirst entry. The instructor can assist by lifting the raised leg as the diver pushes off the stationary foot thus preventing the diver from landing on the front of the thighs or shins upon entry. Again this dive should be practiced at least six times before attempting the next skill—the standing front dive from a two-footed takeoff.

While executing a standing front dive from the two-footed takeoff, several teaching cues are important: the diver should be told to push off the legs and drive the hips up. This ensures that the legs will rise above the head upon takeoff and to a degree guarantees a successful entry. Next, it is possible to have the novice diver attempt the standing dive from greater heights. Logically, the one-meter springboard (low board) would be the next height and, if the youngster is strong enough, it would even be desirable to encourage progress to the three-meter springboard. In essence the mechanics of the dive are exactly the same at all levels. However, youngsters who are not capable of holding their body position firm upon entry into the water should not be encouraged to attempt this dive from the three-meter springboard.

The Forward Approach, Hurdle Step, and Press

The successful execution of any forward dive involves the precise execution of the forward approach, hurdle step, and takeoff from the springboard. Since all of these skills are quite complex, it is beneficial to teach the forward approach and hurdle step on dry land. This can be done on the deck of the pool or even in a gymnasium. The young diver is taught to start by assuming the position of attention. Then the diver takes three steps which are slightly longer than normal walking steps followed by the hurdle step which is nothing more than a jump by pushing off one leg. The hurdle is simply a continuation of the approach and consists of a one-footed takeoff followed by landing on both feet simultaneously. This should be demonstrated by the instructor or a highly skilled diver and then imitated by the novice diver. If the diver is encouraged to practice the approach and hurdle several times on the deck of the pool before advancing to the springboard, the learning process will be significantly accelerated. Also, as the youngster learns a reasonably smooth approach on the deck, certain qualities which are characteristic of a good approach and hurdle can be emphasized by the instructor. The coaching cues should be as follows:

a) Walk erect—keep eyes focused on the point which represents the end of the springboard.

b) Swing the arms naturally. They may either be swung together in opposition to the legs or they may be swung as in the act of walking.

c) Get a very strong jump off the back leg during the hurdle. This jump should be vertical emphasizing pushing forcefully off the back leg.

d) Do not lean during the hurdle. The length of the hurdle, depending upon the size of the diver, should be at least two feet (for adult males, approximately three feet).

e) Lift the hurdle knee as you push off the back leg. Keep the thigh parallel to the deck and the lifted leg perpendicular to the deck.

f) In the hurdle, coordinate the arm swing with the lifting of the knee. As the knee is lifted, the arms are lifted over head. The arms and the hurdle knee work together in this movement.

To review, three actions occur almost simultaneously during the hurdle step.

☐ The diver drives off the back leg.

☐ The diver lifts the opposite knee.

☐ The diver reaches over head with the arms.

Both feet contact the board simultaneously upon landing on the end of the diving board.

g) Upon contact with the board, the arms should have been circled from a position over the head to slightly behind the hips.

All the factors above should be emphasized by the instructor while teaching the forward approach on dry land before advancing the youngster to the springboard. Many competitive divers, both veterans and newcomers, use dry land work to aid in the development of smoothness and consistency in the movement pattern of the forward approach. To ensure that the diver uses steps of consistent length, strips of adhesive tape can be placed on the deck or the springboard. The length of the diver's steps are in proportion to his or her height.

After the novice has learned a relatively consistent approach and has a general idea of the pattern of the steps in the hurdle, he or she is ready to advance to the springboard. The first lesson on the springboard is to have the diver measure the length of the approach and the hurdle step in order to know the starting point whenever preparing to execute a dive. This can be done by having the diver walk to the diving end of the board, turn around as if to execute a backward dive, place the heels flush up against the diving board edge, and then take the complete approach in the direction of the anchor end of the springboard. The spot at which the hurdle is completed determines the starting point. This point should be marked either with a pencil or a piece of tape. The youngster then turns around and from this point practices the forward approach and the hurdle. This should be practiced several times without entering the water. It might be necessary to adjust the length of the steps or hurdle if they were not measured correctly during the first attempt. This correction should be made before advancing to the next skill.

THE SPRINGING ACTION OF THE DIVING BOARD

Once the youngster is capable of executing the forward approach and the hurdle on the springboard, a feetfirst jump into the water can be added to this pattern. These forward feetfirst drills aid in the proper use of the springing action of the board and help to develop a good sense of rhythm. At this point, if a trampoline is available, its use should be introduced. This device serves as a valuable aid to learning many diving techniques. During the early stages of learning diving, the trampoline aids the youngster in learning the spring action of the diving board. Multiple bouncing on the trampoline can help the diver develop the proper sense of the springing action of the board so necessary to good diving.

It is essential that during the early phase of learning the approach, hurdle, and use of the springboard, the diver should not be overcoached. Analysis of the novice diver's weaknesses should be done in a very general fashion. Learning will occur more rapidly if the instructor avoids making many corrections on fine points. The primary objective during the early stages of teaching diving is to teach the basic fundamental patterns of movement. Confusing the diver with too much detail can result in a loss of self-confidence and a disinterest in the activity.

"Riding the board" is an expression frequently used to describe the interaction of the diver and the springboard to effect a smooth takeoff in which the diver uses the maximum energy of the board to obtain the greatest possible height. To ride the springboard properly, the diver must think of landing very softly on the end of the board in order to avoid stomping it. Although an analysis of slow-motion films shows that many of the great divers land nearly flat-footed, the process of a soft landing does require the diver to *think* of landing initially on the toes and balls of the feet and subsequently on the full surface of the foot. A good exercise for this skill is multiple bouncing on the end of the springboard. During the multiple bouncing drill, the diver's back should be held erect. The feet should be slightly apart and the arms should circle in reverse at shoulder level. These movements will aid in maintaining balance and help the diver bounce to the natural rhythm of the board. The youngster should not bounce too high but simply bounce in the natural rhythm of the springboard.

THE IMPORTANCE OF JUMPING INTO THE HURDLE STEP

Usually the beginning diver does not appreciate the importance of forcefully driving off the back leg during the jump into the hurdle step. A very good dry land exercise which significantly emphasizes the importance of this skill follows: A pole is laid on the floor from a bench or an elevation of approximately two feet so that the diver can practice hurdling over the pole at various heights. During this drill, the youngster gets a chance to concentrate on pushing off the back leg without having to worry about the other important mechanics of the hurdle.

This skill should be practiced several times, and the diver should be taught that the toes of the driving foot should clear the pole while the driving leg is straight. In other words, when the diver pushes off the back leg during the hurdle step, this leg is in full extension at the knee and hip joint as the toes pass over the pole. The diver should clear the bar at progressively higher and higher heights. The diver who has successfully cleared the bar at distances of 6 to 12 inches in height is ready to advance to learning new dives.

TYPES OF DIVES

The Plain Forward Dive

The plain forward dive is executed in much the same fashion as the standing front dive. It is simply a dive which incorporates the approach and the hurdle step. Springing from the board, the diver drives the hips up with some force and reaches for the water at a distance three to four feet in front of the board edge in preparation for the entry. Occasionally, this may be a difficult transition for a youngster who has just learned the standing front dive from the springboard. A good intermediate step is to walk out to the end of the board and dive in without the use of the hurdle step. This gives the novice the sense of transferring the momentum of the walk into the momentum of the dive.

The Forward Jackknife

Prior to attempting the jackknife for the first time, the youngster should be introduced to the fundamental exercise of "jumping the hips up." The diver stands at the base of the springboard, places the hands flat on the diving board surface, and while maintaining this hand position jumps the hips up while keeping the knees extended. This action very closely parallels that of the jackknife. A person who has practiced this exercise several times is then ready to move onto the springboard and attempt a jackknife. Care must be taken that the "hip-lifting" action occurs immediately upon takeoff from the springboard and that the diver does not have excess lean. The proper description from the instructor should be, "I want you to think of doing a vertical jump and immediately upon takeoff lift your hips and reach down with your arms, touching your toes." Excess lean during the execution of this dive will make it impossible for the diver to complete the touch of the toes prior to straightening and entering the water. After touching the toes, the diver should look at the point of entry while reaching for it with the hands. The entry point will be approximately three feet in front of the diving board edge. The common mistakes that the instructor will observe during the teaching of this dive are:

☐ Too much lean in the hurdle.

☐ Lifting the legs up too far in front of the body.

The first problem will make it impossible for the diver to complete the toe touch. The second problem will prevent the diver from having an adequate rotation and cause him or her to be short of the vertical upon entering the water.

The Forward Swan Dive

For many divers the forward swan dive (Fig. 36.6) is the most difficult to execute consistently well. However, the dive can be taught to the beginner without elaborating on the minute characteristics which make it so difficult. A very good dry land drill can be used to illustrate the important body position in this dive. Have the youngsters lie on their stomachs on the deck of the pool with their arms outstretched in a lateral T (swan) position. Then on command have them lift their legs off of the floor while keeping their knees straight and their toes pointed. While doing this, they also simultaneously lift the trunk, the head, and the shoulders off the ground. Although this maneuver introduces excessive arch, it does give the youngsters the feeling of pressing back the legs which is an important action (hyperextension of the hips) in the learning of the swan dive.

When the swan dive is executed from the diving board, the most common problem experienced is the flexing at the hips. This problem exists because the divers more than likely have just learned the jackknife, and the hip flexion, very essential to the jackknife, continues to be done as they attempt the "new" swan dive. Repetitions of the dry land exercise will help eliminate the flexing action at the start of the swan dive. The coach should emphasize the simultaneous placement of the arms in the T position coupled with the strong hyperextension of the thigh at the hip joint upon takeoff.

The Forward Dive with the Half Twist

Once divers have learned some type of swan dive they are ready to move on to

Fig. 36.6 For many divers the forward swan dive is the most difficult to execute consistently well. Courtesy of *JOPER*.

the forward dive with a half twist. This dive is rather complex and has given many competitive divers difficulty throughout their careers. However, for the recreational or beginning diver, the fundamental mechanics which initiate the twist are quite simple. The easiest way to teach this dive is to start with a dry land or deck exercise. The diver should point one arm at the floor and the other at the ceiling (or sky). Upon takeoff from the springboard, as the arms come through on the press, one arm should be pointed immediately at the water (point of entry) and the other arm directly overhead (sky or ceiling). This arm action, which is a simultaneous motion, occurs immediately upon takeoff from the springboard and serves to initiate the twist. The diver is encouraged not to think of turning the body or turning the head or forcing any type of twisting action. The eyes focus on the point of entry as the lower arm points toward it. To review, as the diver comes off of the springboard, one arm is pointed immediately toward the sky or ceiling while the other arm points directly at the water. Advanced techniques of executing the half twist are not the same as the learning techniques which are described here.

The Backward Press

Before a diver can adequately perform a backward dive or an inward dive (Fig. 36.7) incorporating the use of the backward takeoff, he or she must be taught how to use the springboard properly for the backward takeoff. Again, a dry land exercise should be incorporated. Most children and adults have a

Fig. 36.7 Before divers can adequately perform a backward dive, they must be taught how to use the springboard properly for the backward takeoff. Courtesy of Southern Connecticut State College.

basic understanding of a vertical jump. The action which is utilized in spring-board diving to depress the board in a backward spring dive is very much like a simple vertical jump. The diver bends at the knees and hips and then jumps off both feet simultaneously. The arm action during this sequence is somewhat unusual. First the arms lift laterally to a position slightly above the diver's shoulders. Then, as the diver bends at the hips and knees, the arms circle and press down slightly behind the body at the hips with a slight bend at the elbow joint. The arms continue to come through in front of the body as the diver springs off the legs and makes the jump. Again the instructor should keep the coaching cues simple. They should be:

☐ Rise up on the toes and lift the arms laterally to a point slightly above the shoulders.

☐ Bend at the hips and knees with the arms circling down slightly behind the hips.

☐ Jump as high as you can swinging the arms in front of the body overhead to a point of full reach (full shoulder extension).

These moves should be done in a smooth and fluid fashion. Once a diver learns to do this reasonably well on the deck of the pool, he or she can attempt a backward press on the springboard. Next comes the execution of the backward press followed by a foot-first entry into the water. The foot position on the board incorporates half the surface of the foot in contact with the diving board surface. That is, the entire ball of the foot and toes should be in contact with the springboard surface. The backward press and foot-first jump should be repeated several times before advancing to the next skill.

The Backward Fall-Off Dive

A fundamental dive which should be taught to novice divers is the fall-off dive. This particular skill does not incorporate the springing action of the board by use of the backward press. In this skill the diver stands backward on the springboard in preparation of a backward live. The arms are held overhead with the hands clasped and the head is rotated as far back as possible. While keeping the rest of the body very firm, the diver falls backward continuing to look for the water. By following these directions, exactly as they are given, the diver will successfully execute the backward fall-off dive. Gravity and friction do all of the work. During the fall-off dive the feet are in contact with the diving board as the diver falls and looks for the water. The hands and the head will enter the water first because gravity continues to act on these members as the feet remain in contact with the nonskid surface of the diving board. One of the major problems is that the diver has never had the sensation of entering the water backwards and will have a very strong tendency to change head position because of fear. Therefore, it is imperative for the instructor to provide some manual guidance during the early trials of this skill. The instructor should hold the diver at the hips and at the same time give instructions on the mechanics of the dive. As the diver begins to fall, the coach can assist by steering the diver into the water head-first. Assistance also can be given by lifting the legs of the diver to ensure that the headfirst entry will result. The typical beginner needs assistance only in one or two initial trials.

The Backward Dive with Press

The combination of the two previous skills define the backward spring dive. The mechanics are very similar to the backward fall-off dive except that they include the press of the springboard. The key points to remember during the first attempt of the backward spring dive are:

- ☐ Take a very strong bold press.
- ☐ Jump with as much force as possible reaching overhead.
- ☐ Put the head back during the ascent.

If this procedure is followed, the diver will probably execute the dive success-fully on the first attempt. The common mistakes include putting the head back too late, which will cause the diver to be short of the vertical upon entry. The other major mistake is the exact opposite of this; that is the swinging of the arms and head too soon upon takeoff, thereby initiating too much rota-tion. This will cause the diver to be significantly over (beyond the vertical) and land on the stomach. The instructor must advise and encourage the proper compensation in order that the correct entry be achieved.

The Inward Dive Pike

The inward dive appears, by the nature of its execution, to be a very danger-ous dive. However, if properly taught, it is nearly impossible for the diver to hit the diving board. The correct mechanics which prevent the diver from hitting the board are as follows: the arms reach up over the head and then press down in front of the diver toward the board as the diver jumps the hips up. As the arms come down, they are applying a force toward the board. The reaction to this force, following Newton's Third Law of Motion (action-reaction), is that the board acting through the diver's legs pushes the hips up and away from the springboard. The only way to incur an injury is if the diver leans into the board during the takeoff. In order to be doubly sure of safety, the instructor should have the diver stand on one corner of the diving board rather than in the center, then encourage a slight turning away from the board during the initial trials of the dive. The employment of this

Fig. 36.8 The inward dive appears, by the nature of its execution, to be a very dangerous dive. Courtesy of Ohio State University.

teaching technique, however, may introduce some bad habits and is not recommended after the first two or three trials.

The Forward Dive Pike and a Half Twist

Another dive is the forward dive with one half twist in the pike position. This is nothing more than a forward jackknife followed by a half twist upon entry. After the toe touch of the jackknife is completed, the diver points one arm directly at the point of entry while the other arm is brought across the pointing arm. The crossing arm action provides the necessary impetus to the half twist. The diver continues to sight the entry point during the jackknife and twist.

The Forward Somersault

The simplest way to learn the forward somersault is to attempt it on the trampoline. The proper teaching progression which can be accomplished in a matter of minutes for any youngster is as follows: first a diver learns to multiple bounce on a trampoline. Second, the diver is taught to stop the bounce, which is called checking. Third, the basic drops on the trampoline are learned. These include the knee drop, seat drop, front drop, and back drop. The knee drop, which is the easiest of the basic drops, should be learned first. After successful completion of the knee drop and repetitions of the knee drop to the feet and back again to the knees, the diver is then ready to learn what is called the knee drop front somersault. This is a very easy trick, and it takes more determination than skill to execute it successfully the first time. Immediately upon coming off the knees, the diver thrusts head and arms down as hard as possible toward the mat. This initiates the somersaulting motion.

The instructor should assist by spotting the diver during the first several attempts. This is done by manually guiding the novice's head around while standing on the frame of the trampoline. The instructor can keep one hand on the head of the diver so that when the somersault is initiated, the instructor's hand can simply follow the head and neck of the diver around. If the diver happens to be a youngster who changes his or her mind in the first trial or is a little bit stuck in the somersaulting action, the application of a small force behind the head will aid in completing the somersault. This spotting technique is very valuable in the prevention of a possible injury. Once the diver has successfully executed the knee drop front somersault several times, he or she can attempt the forward somersault from the standing position. Following a successful standing somersault on the trampoline the diver should advance to the springboard.

The standing somersault on the springboard is done exactly in the same manner as on the trampoline. Following the takeoff from the springboard, the diver immediately throws the head and arms down in front of the body while lifting the hips up. The key point for the unskilled diver is to make sure that the head is thrown forcefully down. The somersaulting action will then to a great degree take care of itself. After the somersault is learned, it should be repeated several times the first day so that the diver develops the necessary confidence. As the dive is practiced, the diver should then be taught to establish a good tight tuck position. During the learning phase of all dives most individuals who are new to diving will be more concerned with their personal safety and their survival than with body form and finesse.

The novice diver can next attempt the forward one-and-one-half somersault by simply starting the spin earlier and looking for the water prior to entry.

The Backward Somersault

The backward somersault can be learned in much the same fashion as the forward somersault. It can be learned either on the trampoline or on the springboard with equal ease. In order to learn this trick on the trampoline the instructor must employ the correct spotting techniques, namely, standing with one foot on the trampoline bed and the other foot on the frame of the trampoline. As the diver starts multiple bouncing, the coach should hold the diver at the waist of the diving suit. This can be done either by clasping the material of the suit or it can be done by wrapping a towel around the waist of the diver.

The somersaulting action in the backward somersault is initiated by throwing the arms and head backward as the legs are jumped up to the chest. The diver is instructed to attempt a backward somersault on the trampoline after three successive bounces. As the diver throws for the somersault, the coach lifts up on the towel in order to assist in the attainment of height. Meanwhile the coach lifts the diver's legs at the calves and pulls them over in the direction of the spin.

Perhaps the obvious advantage of learning to somersault on the trampoline is that the young diver will have the security of the instructor's immediate availability for assistance during the first few attempts. However, this particular dive can be learned just as easily from the springboard providing the diver is willing to *go through with the dive* as directed by the coach.

In summary, the coaching cues for the backward somersault as mentioned earlier are a strong jump from the backward press, followed by thrusting the arms and head backward while the knees are simultaneously brought up to the chest. The diver who makes an honest and strong effort to do these things will successfully execute the backward somersault during the first try. Any new dive should be practiced at least three times during the first practice period. This, of course, is to ensure that the diver will develop confidence so that during the subsequent practice sessions she or he will continue to do the dive with increased skill.

The Reverse Dive

Perhaps the most difficult dive for the novice to learn is the reverse dive. The feeling of jumping up and initiating a backward action toward the springboard will be extremely uncomfortable, and most novice divers are quite reluctant to try the reverse dive for the first time. However, a proper sequence can be employed in teaching this dive which makes it much easier for both the diver and the instructor.

It is strongly recommended that the trampoline be incorporated in the learning progression. First, the diver should be taught the fundamental back drop on the trampoline. This can be done by having the diver stand in the center of the trampoline and kick one leg very high as if in the act of kicking a football. While kicking the leg, the diver leans and falls backward and lands on the back on the soft bed of the trampoline. After repeating this several times, the diver is then ready to attempt the trick off both legs. This is done by jumping and bringing both legs to the chest while keeping the chin down and rotating to the backward landing position. Next, the diver can do the backward drop in the pike position. The diver jumps up, reaches overhead with the hands, brings the legs to the hands while keeping the knees straight, subsequently landing on the back. This skill should be executed several times and the diver should have a very consistent back drop on the trampoline before progressing to the reverse dive from the springboard.

The first reverse dive from the springboard should be executed in the simplest possible fashion, that is, the tuck position. Once the novice has learned the back drop on the trampoline, it is just a matter of incorporating that technique in the forward takeoff and, of course, instead of landing on the back in the water the diver continues to look overhead toward the water as the knees are brought up to the chest. This skill requires much more courage than talent during the first attempt.

It is possible to teach the reverse dive initially in the pike position to some beginners who seem to exhibit a great deal of coordination. Here the instructor should cue the diver to kick the legs up immediately upon takeoff to the hands which have set a target directly overhead. If the legs are kicked up soon enough, all that the diver has to do after the touch is to look for the water. The looking toward the water is a very natural reaction for most divers and will result in a successful entry into the water.

Learning Twisting Somersaults

Twisting somersaults appear to the layman to be the most difficult dives that youngsters can learn. An instructor who possesses the proper knowledge of the fundamental mechanics involved in twisting–somersaulting dives can teach these dives to relatively inexperienced divers. A twisting somersault incorporates a somersault action of either a forward somersault, backward somersault, reverse somersault, or inward somersault and a pirouette type action (which defines twisting). More precisely, a twist is the act of rotating around the longitudinal axis of the body. Before learning a twisting somersault the diver should learn how to somersault independently as described earlier. The diver should also learn how to twist independently.

Here again the trampoline serves as a wonderful learning device. After executing several multiple bounces on the trampoline, the diver should attempt a half twist. This is a very simple maneuver. This half twist is in fact a half pirouette or a half turn. After this, the diver should attempt a full turn (a full 360° pirouette). Eventually, the novice diver will be able to work up to a one-and-a-half or even a double twist from the standing position on the trampoline.

Actually, these skills can be learned in a matter of minutes. Next the diver should execute essentially the same skills, i.e., pirouettes from the springboard. These should be done incorporating the forward approach and hurdle step. The following groups of skills should be practiced: the forward jump with half twist, the forward jump with full twist, the forward jump with one-and-a-half twist, and the forward jump with double twist. Also, the backward jump with a half twist and the backward jump with the full twist should be learned. Once the diver has mastered the basic standing jumps as well as good somersaulting technique, both forward and backward, he or she can put the two skills together and learn the forward somersault with one twist and the backward somersault with one-and-a-half twists. Although these seem to be more advanced diving skills, they can be learned with relative ease if the progression above is followed.

The Forward Somersault with One Twist

The diver should have a very good forward somersault in the pike position before attempting the forward somersault with one twist. The first step is to execute the forward somersault pike with the arms held in a lateral or swan position during the entire somersaulting action. To review, the pike position is that body position in which the diver bends only at the hips with the knees straight and the toes pointed. After performing the forward somersault pike successfully, the next step is for the diver to incorporate a slight snap or straightening action of the body over the top of the somersault; that is, during the execution of the forward somersault pike, the diver immediately snaps out very rapidly holding the arms in a lateral position. The snap should occur at the early part of the somersaulting action, and it will provide enough impetus for the entire somersault to be completed prior to the entry.

This dive is appropriately named the snap somersault pike. Note that during the execution of the somersault and the snap somersault pike the arms are maintained in a lateral or swan position. This is done in order that they can be brought in to initiate the twist later on. The diver should be encouraged to play the entries on these front somersault pikes slightly short of the vertical because once the twist is added, the action of the twist will tend to carry the somersaulting action a little farther beyond the vertical.

The diver who has learned a good snap somersault will be ready to add the twist. The easiest way to learn this is to add the twist just prior to entering the water. It usually helps if the coach aids the youngster by calling when to add the twist. The teacher can observe that the diver is near vertical prior to entry. This is the point at which the twist should be introduced. The diver executes the forward snap somersault and just prior to the entry and upon command from the instructor, brings the arms in across the chest and pirouettes. This is done in much the same fashion as on the trampoline and is similar to the pirouettes of an ice skater. More than likely, the first try will not yield success in this particular dive. Usually a half twist results. This is a common problem in learning this particular dive. It usually is the result of the youngster's attempt to drop the head early in the twist in an effort to see the water. The youngster does this because of the uncomfortable feeling of twisting and somersaulting blindly. This very common error prevents the completion of the twist in many twisting dives. The diver must make an effort as the snap somersault is completed to keep the head *back* and the body straight (good layout position) during the twisting action. No pirouetting action can be successfully achieved unless the body is in a relatively straight or layout position with the arms high and with the head straight or slightly back. By encouraging proper head position, the instructor can help the diver achieve early success in learning twisting dives.

The Backward Somersault with One-and-one-half Twist

Here again the progression of learning the backward somersault with one-and-one-half twist is very similar to that of forward somersaulting with twists. The diver must be able to execute a backward somersault layout with relatively little difficulty. Once again it is desirable to play the angle of entry short of the vertical. On the backward somersault, the introduction of the twisting action has a tendency to carry the somersault somewhat beyond the vertical. After divers have executed a backward somersault layout (slightly short of vertical) to the satisfaction of themselves and their coaches, they are ready to attempt the twist.

In adding the twist, it is desirable to start the twisting action just prior to the entry into the water. In other words, the diver thinks only of the backward somersault layout. Just prior to entry, the coach should call to the diver to twist at which time the diver thrusts arms across chest in the preferred twisting direction and pirouettes. If the head is held in line or slightly back and if the diver maintains a layout position and emphasizes the twist action from the shoulders and the hips, he or she will be successful in executing the twist during the first trial. With successive trials eventually the backward somersault with one-and-one-half twists will be learned.

Note that during the learning phases there should be no discussion of how to stop the twists or of the diver's sensing spatial awareness. It is not important that divers know where they are in space. The twisting dives are essentially blind dives during the learning phase. After the diver becomes more experienced, he or she will be able to sight the water or possibly the wall or some other landmark at the completion of a single or multiple twisting somersault. During the early stages of learning, the sensations the diver experiences will be quite strange and one should be unconcerned with one's location in space throughout the twisting and somersaulting action.

The mechanics of twisting are fundamental to all twisting–somersaulting dives, whether they incorporate a full twist, one-and-one-half twists, double twists, two-and-one-half twists, or even triple twists. A diver who pirouettes in proper fashion can stop the twist by the simultaneous action of thrusting the arms from the body while bending at the hips. The simultaneous use of both of these actions is necessary in order to stop the twist appropriately. After successfully learning the correct twisting action, the diver should be taught to stop the twist by placing the arms in the swan position while simultaneously lifting up the legs into a slight pike position. This resembles the action of sitting in a chair with the arms in the swan position. When done correctly, this action enables the diver to stop the twisting action sharply.

This technique, however, is not taught until after the diver has learned to successfully complete the number of twists desired.

There are two general methods of utilizing the arms while initiating twists. These are the ice skater's twist as described earlier and the one arm behind the head the other arm across the chest technique. Both methods have been used successfully by skilled divers. The important teaching cue for arm position in twisting dives is to emphasize that the arms be placed across the chest and close to the body and that these forces are applied at approximately shoulder level.

SUMMARY

The rate at which youngsters should advance from one diving skill to the next will be determined by the instructor. Most classes in diving will include individuals who possess the complete range of athletic ability. It is therefore advisable that novice divers be encouraged to advance at their own learning rates. In dealing with young children, the progression of learning may be somewhat slower. Nevertheless, variable rates of progression among individuals in this group should also be practiced.

The station method of teaching diving has proven to be a successful tool for class organization. The class is divided into several smaller groups based on skill level. A specific basic skill is taught and practiced at each of the stations. The instructor must supervise and move from station to station while providing several minutes of instruction at each station during a given class period. The establishment of appropriate stations depends to a large degree on the facilities available.

It is most desirable to have a diving well separate from the swimming pool. Although many modern pools incorporate the separate diving well, many of the older pools do not. For purposes of safety, no swimming should be permitted in the diving area during instruction. The youngsters who are practicing the fundamental dives from the side of the pool should be a safe distance from the springboards in order to avoid a serious injury which could result from a collision.

REFERENCES

Batterman, C. A. 1959. Springboard diving. *Scholastic Coach* **29:** 44–45, (October).

———— 1968. *Techniques of springboard diving,* Cambridge: Mass.: The M.I.T. Press.

Billingsley, H. W. 1965. *Diving illustrated.* New York: Ronald.

Clothworth, R. D. 1962. *The young sportsman's guide to diving.* New York: Thomas Nelson.

Cole, E. S. 1960. *Diving and rebound tumbling.* Cedar Rapids, Iowa: A. S. Barnes.

Dawson, R. K. 1966. *Diving: for teacher and pupil.* London: Pelham Books.

Eaves, G. E. 1969. *Diving: the mechanics of springboard and firmboard techniques.* Cedar Rapids, Iowa: A. S. Barnes.

Fairbanks, A. R. 1963. *Teaching springboard diving.* Englewood Cliffs, N.J.: Prentice-Hall.

Groves, W. H. 1950. A mechanical analysis of diving. *Res. Quart.* **21:** 132–144, (May).

Harlan, B. D. 1963. *Diving.* New York: The Athletic Institute.

Harper, D. A. 1966. Physical principles in diving. *Athl. J.* **47:** 34, (November).

Havner, R. B. 1949. *The diver's manual.* San Francisco: Millwood Press.

Lanoue, F. K. 1940. Analysis of basic factors involved in fancy diving. *Res. Quart.* **11:** 102, (March).

Mills, E. T. 1968. Use of trampoline to condition divers. *Athl. J.* **48:** 68–69, (January).

Moriarity, P. N. 1959. *Springboard diving.* New York: Ronald.

O'Brien, R. F. 1967. *Springboard diving fundamentals,* Columbus, Ohio: Charles E. Merrill.

Peppe, M. F. 1956. Developing fancy skills. *AAHPER Journal* **27:** 58, (March).

Winter, F. W. 1965. "Mechanics of the tuck position in executing the forward three-and-one-half somersault." *Athl. J.* **45:** 19, (January).

Lifesaving and Water Safety Courses

Thomas K. Cureton, Jr.

Following the pioneer work of the Royal Humane Society (1774), the Massachusetts Humane Society (1786), and the United States Coast Guard Lifesaving Service (1871), the National YMCA entered the lifesaving field between 1885 and 1890. The United Volunteer Lifesaving Corps was organized in 1890. By 1911 lifesaving work was established at the International YMCA College (now Springfield College) at Springfield, Massachusetts. In 1914 the American Red Cross entered this field of instruction to train volunteer leaders, especially to serve in emergency flood water and war situations. More recently, many large city recreation departments and colleges and universities have established courses in this area, usually with the cooperation of the Red Cross or YMCA. Many teach both versions of the program. Some universities have scientific courses.

From 1924 the YMCA program went ahead strongly under Dr. John

Fig. 36.9 Water safety courses often utilize the pool deck for their instruction. Courtesy of SUNY at Buffalo.

Brown, Jr., Dr. Henry F. Kallenberg, and John W. Fuhrer. In 1937 Thomas K. Cureton, Jr. took the place of Dr. Kallenberg who retired. At this time the manual prepared by the committee above projected the first National YMCA Aquatic Conference at George Williams College Chicago. After 1928, Springfield College played a major role in graduate research studies supervised by Cureton in swimming, lifesaving, and water games; and studies on artificial resuscitation under P. V. Karpovich. Cureton and Silvia collaborated on new experimental programs in lifesaving and water safety, and firmly established a strong collegiate offering for credit in this area as part of the new National Aquatic Leadership Plan, of the American Association (now Alliance) for Health, Physical Education and Recreation, and the National YMCA. World War II brought forth many new problems of open water, boat and ship safety, types of new cold water equipment, and many new water safety devices. In 1943 Cureton published *Warfare Aquatics* with the help of the Navy and United States Coast Guard. The YMCA, the Red Cross and many colleges and universities conduct courses in what is now called aquatics, skin diving, and scuba. New and higher standards have developed and much new literature has appeared. It is covered as follows:

National Council of the YMCAs and the Association Press

A. *Student series:*
   It's fun to swim the Y's way, H. T. Friermood

B. *Professional series:*
Adventures in artificial respiration, Peter V. Karpovich
Camp waterfront programs and management, Richard H. Pohndorf
Fun in the water, Thomas K. Cureton, Jr.
Lifesaving and water safety today, Charles E. Silvia

C. *Operational manuals and booklets:*
The new science of skin and scuba diving, Bernard E. Empleton
The new YMCA aquatic notebook, (ed.) Harold T. Friermood
100 revised and new questions with confidential answers on YMCA life-saving and water safety
Skin and scuba diving training and leadership preparation, national standards for certification, H. T. Friermood

The address for all of the above materials is National Council of the YMCAs of North America, Association Press, 291 Broadway, New York 10007. Operating under the National Council of YMCAs of the United States of America, a comprehensive swimming, lifesaving and water safety, and recreational and competitive swimming program is carried out. Three principal levels of trained leadership are employed: Certified Aquatic Director, Certified Aquatic Instructor, and Certified Leader-Examiner. Some 1200 YMCAs and several hundred summer camps are involved. The program is regulated through a series of National Aquatic Conferences held every five years. Correspondence about materials should be with the Association Press. Technical information can be sought from the National Director for Health and Physical Education at the National Council Headquarters in New York, and also from the Chairman of the National Aquatic Committee.

American National Red Cross (18th. and E Sts., N.W., Washington, D.C. 20006)

Training course for water safety instructors, Washington, D.C.: (mimeographed), 1955, Part I, p. 9; 1964, Part II.

Ibid., Part II. 1964.

Instructor's outline, Washington, D.C.: (Swimmer Aide Orientation Course).

Instructor's manual water safety aide training course. (Undated, not copyrighted). p. 19.

Instructor's manual, survival swimming (mimeographed). Washington, D.C.: The American National Red Cross, 1952.

Swimming and water safety courses, instructor's manual, Washington, D.C.: The American National Red Cross, 1968.

Lifesaving, rescue and water safety, Garden City: Doubleday, 1974.

This foregoing book covers personal safety in the aquatic environment; safety and rescue equipment; nonswimming and equipment rescues; water rescues; defenses, releases, and escapes; searching for and rescuing a submerged victim; the job of lifeguard; small craft safety; ice safety and rescue; survival swimming in civilian emergencies; respiratory emergencies and artificial respiration; and emergency first aid.

Lifesaving and water safety, Garden City: Doubleday, August, 1969.

Swimming and water safety textbook, Washington, D.C.: The American National Red Cross, 1968. (2nd printing, 1st ed.)

Lifesaving and water safety courses, instructor's manual, Washington, D.C.: The American National Red Cross, 1968.

OTHER ORGANIZATIONS

Many other organizations teach lifesaving and water safety courses, e.g., the Boy Scouts and Girl Scouts of America, the Campfire Girls, the Boys Clubs of America. For information concerning their work in these areas, contact the individual organizations.

Council for National Cooperation in Aquatics (CNCA)

This council has headquarters with the American Alliance for Health, Physical Education, and Recreation, 1201 16th Street NW, Washington, D.C. 20036. This organization is most concerned with aquatic courses of all types as well as *professional* aquatic leadership in colleges and universities—quite in addition to the large *volunteer* organizations (YMCA and Red Cross). The CNCA has promoted a series of national conferences and has sponsored a new line of cooperative literature. Organizations are working well individually and are cooperating with each other. Differences are to be expected and probably no one program is entirely adequate to meet all situations, as open-water situations will always be different from indoor pool situations; and Army, Navy, Coast Guard, and Air Force will each have different problems. The United States Service Academies have all cooperated with the CNCA, but must deal in their own way with their unique problems.

Colleges and universities may be expected to delve into the history and the scientific problems much more fully than do volunteer youth groups. They will continuously project experimental work in the various laboratories. The technical literature is well covered in the *Swimming and Diving Bibliography* of the CNCA, published by the Association Press. This is an excellent source book for all types of aquatic literature.

Skin Diving and Scuba Diving

Bernard E. Empleton

DEFINITION AND SCOPE

Skin diving refers to diving beneath the surface of the water using fins, faceplate, and snorkel. Or, for that matter, a skin diver could dive without any equipment. A scuba diver on the other hand is one who dives with the help of self-contained underwater breathing apparatus. Thus the word *scuba* originates from the first letter in each of the words mentioned above. The scuba diver carries, in addition to the basic fins, faceplate, and snorkel, a tank or tanks of compressed air. This enables the diver to stay beneath the surface for a period of time relative to the depth of the dive and the energy output.

It is difficult to know the precise number of divers currently active in the United States. Estimates place the number of scuba divers at nearly two million and the number of skin divers at many times that figure.

During World War II the Frenchmen, Cousteau and Gagnon, invented a scuba which effectively launched the modern era of sports diving. Since the end of World War II the sport has burgeoned and the equipment has grown ever more sophisticated. Improved tanks, regulators, and gas mixtures have expanded the scope of diving enormously and the world of the sport diver is now considered to be that area encompassed by the hundred-foot level.

Early Origins

Great interest in the area beneath the sea is as old as human history. Indeed, crude diving bells date back as far as 300 B.C. Alexander the Great descended in some type of diving bell. Divers were used in several naval battles between the years 400 B.C. and A.D. 1795. Early snorkel use is mentioned by Pliny (A.D. 23–79) who wrote about military divers breathing through tubes which extended above the surface of the water. Apparatus of this type is practical only for very shallow use (about 12 inches).

The history of diving is nicely set out in the United States Navy Diving Manual (1970) and will not be treated in detail here.

Skin Diving

To avoid confusion between the terms "skin" and "scuba" diving, it is well to remember that the only air skin divers carry is that contained in their own lungs. This limits the time skin divers can spend below the surface. The absence of tension coupled with the ability to conserve energy will enable one to remain below for a longer period. A two-minute dive might be considered a long time down, although there are many instances of quiet bottom sitting up to four minutes or more.

Hyperventilation will increase the ability of the diver to remain below longer. Breath-holding skills are fine up to a point. The need to breathe is signaled by a carbon dioxide buildup. The carbon dioxide mechanism may be overridden by practice. Nature, however, will ultimately demand action. An overload of carbon dioxide may cause divers to blackout and breathe water into their lungs.

Skin divers' principal aids are faceplate, fins, and snorkel. In cold water they will need a protective suit which will require a weight belt to aid in the adjustment to neutral buoyancy.

The faceplate should be of shatterproof glass (not plastic) set in a soft rubber or neoprene housing that conforms to the face without leaking. The faceplate provides an air space for one to see through. Objects will appear about one-third larger underwater. Those with vision problems may secure a faceplate optically ground (at great expense) or mount a small jig to hold a pair of glasses minus the side pieces.

The *snorkel* is a small rubber or neoprene J-shaped tube about a foot long. This enables the diver to swim facedown in the water and observe below while breathing through the snorkel tube. A little practice with this can soon set one at ease and provide a great saving of energy. The human head weighs between 19 and 23 pounds. Holding it out of water requires the expenditure of a great deal of energy and results in a loss of the view below.

Fins should fit comfortably to the feet without friction. The rubber or neoprene should be soft with enough firmness in the fin to provide a good thrust. The larger the fin, the greater the energy to drive it.

The flutterkick in an easy, relaxed manner is a good method of propulsion. The dolphin kick is also useful though more difficult to master. Although one's speed underwater is limited to about one knot per hour, fins do greatly enhance the diver's motility.

It is not the intent here to provide an instruction manual. This is covered adequately in *The New Science of Skin and Scuba Diving* (CNCA 1973). There is no simple substitute for a good course of instruction in the art of skin diving. Mastery of this essential leads naturally to the more complex art of scuba diving. The pleasures of skin diving are many.

The protective suit. Diving in cold water whether with skin or scuba rig requires protective cover. The dry suit is designed to prevent any water from contacting the diver. Protective underwear is worn under the dry suit in very cold water. Dry suits are largely impractical as currently designed. Any inadvertent water entry can ruin the concept and cause great discomfort. The wet suit on the other hand is designed to be wet. Water is trapped in the tiny cells, of which there are many thousands. The suit is made of neoprene from ⅛ to ³⁄₁₆″ thick or ¼″ thick. Once the water enters the cells, it is warmed by body heat. The loss of heat thereafter is greatly lessened.

The trapped air in the cells of the suit makes it impossible to submerge without additional weight. This is provided in the form of either lead shot or preformed molded weights strung on a stout belt. The belt is held on by a quick safety release buckle or hitch.

Release of the belt in an emergency situation will allow the diver to surface far more easily. Failure to release the belt has, too frequently, resulted in casualty. In applying weights, neutral buoyancy is the desired end so that ease in ascent or descent is effected.

Scuba Diving

There are three types of scuba: the closed circuit, semiclosed circuit, and open-circuit scuba. The first two types, closed and semiclosed, are restricted for primary use by the military, or by highly skilled professionals. In closed-circuit scuba the breathing medium is recirculated and rebreathed. In open-circuit scuba, the air once breathed is exhaled into the water and not reused.

The most common type of scuba used today is the single-hose design. The two-hose design is still in use and preferred in some situations by the cognoscenti. It is advisable for the diver to train in the use of both single-hose and two-hose scuba.

Fig. 36.10 Instruction in the use of equipment has first priority. Courtesy of the University of Utah.

A full faceplate design scuba with the air being fed into the faceplate has special accommodation for the diver with dental plates. This, however, carries its own special problems of mask clearing.

The open-circuit, single-hose scuba, commonly used for sports diving, consists of a high-pressure air cylinder, a cylinder valve and a regulator valve to control the high-pressure air coming from the cylinder to the diver. A mask or mouthpiece is used for inhalation and a valve for exhalation.

The detail of operation will not be treated here, instead the elements of concern for the diver, a methodology for averting problems, and an emphasis on proper training will be presented.

When divers take a supply of air under water, they immediately incur the problems involved in the natural laws related to gas under pressure. An understanding of these laws is necessary for the comprehension of human tolerances in the submarine environment. To be fit for the sport, divers must have sound cardiovascular systems and be free of ear and sinus problems. They must be at ease in adapting to pressure variations as they go either down or up.

An air embolism is an air bubble in the vascular system which interferes with the circulation of blood. The treatment is prompt recompression. Often this treatment is not readily available. First aid involves artificial respiration if the victim is not breathing. Sometimes lowering the head and rocking between the head down and the horizontal position may relieve the bubble stoppage.

Decompression sickness is another common hazard for divers who do not pay proper attention to the dive tables and gas laws. Commonly known as the bends, decompression sickness is caused by an increased partial pressure of gas entering the diver's tissues and blood. When the diver rises toward the surface, pressure is reduced and the gas tends to form bubbles. When body tolerance is exceeded, there may be considerable pain. This happens especially in the joints. The standard Navy diving tables should be utilized to avoid decompression sickness. Other symptoms of bends are dizziness, paralysis, weakness, and often a numbness in the body. Loss of consciousness, blindness, or impairment of vision, and ringing in the ears are other symptoms of decompression sickness.

Safety. Learning to scuba dive is relatively easy. Because it is easy to learn may lull some learners into paying hasty and careless attention to the all-important laws of diving.

The fundamental skills of water sports are essential. One should be at ease in the water, skilled in the use of the various strokes, and free of physical problems that might endanger one under pressure. Good physical fitness is absolutely essential to deal with emergencies when they arise. Psychological adaptation is also very necessary. Some persons have trouble adjusting to the act of breathing while submerged.

In addition to knowing the various strokes, the diver should be skilled in the use of the basic equipment. Both full exposure to the theory of diving and the development of expertise in the performance of required skills are important.

Simple rules of diving include:

- ☐ Inspect equipment before diving.
- ☐ Do not dive if ill or otherwise indisposed.
- ☐ Dive with a buddy who is reliable.
- ☐ Don't overstay your time below.
- ☐ Carry a reliable timepiece in order to remain aware of the time limitations.

First aid. Much common first-aid lore will apply to diving. Such specialized maladies as bends and embolism will not respond to ordinary treatment. Accordingly, it is altogether necessary for the student diver to be exposed to the first-aid procedures that relate specifically to diving. A good course of instruction will include this information.

The Council for National Cooperation in Aquatics has published *The New Science of Skin and Scuba Diving* (1973). This text carries a full description of the necessary information related to diving. Careful study will provide the safety knowledge necessary to enjoy scuba diving—one of the greatest sports in one of our last frontiers.

The American National Standards Institute under the auspices of the Council for National Cooperation in Aquatics (CNCA) has sponsored the Z-86 project on underwater safety. This involves such matters as basic course content for diving instruction, air purity, accident reporting, boat carrier safety standards, and equipment performance standards.

THE ENVIRONMENT

Diving conditions vary widely from one location to another. Study the environment wherever you dive. Ask the local practitioners about local conditions. Study the flora and fauna in the various environments. Because of the broad differences in the many climates and geographical locations, it is well to study the broad spectrum of possibilities. This will make comprehension of local conditions simpler.

REFERENCES

The new science of skin and scuba diving 1973. New York: Association Press.

Gilbert, P. W. 1976. *Sharks and survival.* Lexington, Mass.: D. C. Heath.

Halstead, B. W. 1959. *Dangerous marine animals.* Cambridge, Md.: Cornell Maritime Press.

Lanphier, E. H., and H. Rahn. *Man, water, pressure.* State University of New York at Buffalo.

United States Navy diving manual. 1970. Washington, D.C.

Survival Aquatics

Thomas K. Cureton, Jr.

DIFFERENT CONDITIONS

During World War II the survival aquatics program was adapted to wartime needs. Survival aquatics was renamed warfare aquatics. It was soon seen that many situations developed which called for protective and rescue methods which went beyond the bounds of the standard lifesaving and water safety course. These included the open-water situation, debarkation in rough water and in clothes, sometimes initiated with jumping from the deck of a ship 20 to 40' above water. Improper use of equipment could result in an injury, such as a broken neck from carelessly placing a ring buoy over the head and jumping with it in this position. Oil on the water, or fire, made conditions very different from those in the indoor pool. Lifesaving carries were adapted to two-on-one, three-on-one, or four-on-one. Swimming with equipment was sometimes involved.

New Emphases

Emphasis was first placed on teaching all adults to swim at least 440 yards. Emphasis was also placed on helping others in the water and lifting and carrying others who had possible injuries. The use of various types of rescue apparatus: lifeboats, preservers, wet suits, and "dunking" drills were involved. Endurance was practiced with longer swims and longer carries; some struggling (water combat) was deliberately introduced as preparation for what might easily be encountered in a struggle for a beachhead, a boat or a rifle. Water jiujitsu was introduced. New strokes were taught for swimming through oil or flames, for "lookout" in rough water, for carrying a rifle or machine gun in the water. Obstacle courses in the water, "commando" tactics and group swimming were practiced, including long swims in formation. Capsize drills were practiced from various types of water craft (Buckley 1962, pp. 77–79).

Survival swimming for all types of swimmers emphasized aspects of swimming applied to simulated wartime conditions. It combined the usual lifesaving instruction with longer and harder exposure drills, with much emphasis on endurance and survival. Dodging machine gun fire with "pop-up swimming" and considerable underwater swimming, walking on the bottom, and serial porpoise dives were practiced. Some water polo, jiujitsu, and breath-holding drills were also involved. Swimming and wrestling in clothes, and defense against attack by blocks and parries were taught.

Some Practical Drills on Land, or Water

Carry equipment with a partner, or others (4s, 6s, 8s) canoe, boat, luggage, log, etc.

Jog-walk; repeat, repeat, etc. two miles minimum.

Run and jump into deep water, and then bob to a given destination.

Practice "pop-up" swimming, i.e., swim 10–20 feet underwater, then pop up for air; repeat, repeat.

Swim with head high for "lookout."

Tread water for endurance, five min or more, without hands.

Scull for endurance, five min or more, without use of feet.

Demonstrate three towing strokes (side, back, breast).

Practice parrying a swimmer who swims in to grapple with you; i.e., turn him aside with an arm-sweep, reverse and over-head throw, kickoff.

Defend for two mins against an attacker in the water, or on land.

Pick up and carry someone of your own size.

Working with a partner, carry a person with a simulated injury.

Show three ways of swimming under water (reach and pull, breaststroke, etc.).

Swim through rough water or against a current.

Swim with a rifle, or iron pipe.

Swim with a loaded pack.

Lift and carry a partner from shallow water, or lift from the pool and lift and carry.

Swim through an improvised obstacle course.

Tip over and then rescue the canoe or boat.

Swim in single file, as noiselessly as possible.

Swim in a column of 2s, and then 4s.

Take part in a dunking drill in which 20–30 or more work to dunk each other for five minutes.

Practice the "splash" stroke, used to splash away oil or flaming oil.

Practice a swim of 440 yards in clothes, without shoes. Carry shoes around neck or tied to belt.

Inflate and launch an inflatable boat, then get out and get in.

Swim one mile with a partner.

Practice rescues with ropes, buoys and poles, working squads of three or four.

Stay afloat for an hour, any way at all, in deep water (survival drill), using any combination of floating, sculling, treading, or swimming but without holding onto the side or any other person.

Sustain another individual for ten minutes and indicate how you could give artificial mouth-to-mouth respiration in the water if necessary.

Demonstrate your ability to swim in a wet suit in cold water.

Practice caring for ropes, buoys, oars, paddles, rubber boats, wet suits, canoes, or boats.

Practice water wrestling in two bouts, one on the defensive for two minutes and one on the attack for two minutes.

Practice breaking a body scissors hold with the opponent on your back.

Practice breaking a body scissors hold with the opponent on your front.

Practice conditioning drills, such as:

>Defend goal against one who tries to get through to touch it
>Hold the springboard against an attacker who tries to dislodge the defender
>Pole tug-of-war in the water
>Run through a defense line
>Horse and rider tug-of-war in shallow water
>Horse and rider race in shallow water
>Canoe tilting
>Log tussle
>Hold the dock

Practice three methods of resuscitation, including mouth-to-mouth, and either Neilsen arm-lift and press, or Silvester method.

Practice protection from the sun for four hours.

Demonstrate by simulation how a "cramp" in the calf may be broken.

Work 10–20 periods teaching others to swim.

REFERENCES

Buckley, R. W. 1962. *Survival swimming*. Council for National Cooperation in Aquatics 12th Annual Report.

Cureton, T. K., Jr. 1952. Survival aquatics. *JOHPER* **23:** 41–42, (June).

——— 1943. *Warfare aquatics*. Champaign, Ill.: Stipes, p. 170.

Higgins, J. M., A. R. Barr, and B. F. Grady 1962. The V-5 aquatic program. (3rd. ed.) Annapolis: V-5 Association of America. U.S. Naval Institute.

Kiputh, R. J. H. 1952. Survival aquatics for your community. *JOHPER* **23:** 52, (April).

Swimnastics

M. G. Sholtis

INTRODUCTION

The human body needs to recuperate from muscle fatigue, stress, and strain. During the past two years, health experts have come to realize that exercises and activities created especially for swimming areas can satisfy these needs while toning the muscles, strengthening the heart, improving circulation, and pacifying the spirit of people of all ages and conditions.

People have been using various forms of swimming as a recreational pastime for thousands of years. Recreational swimming activities maintain their interests, break monotony, offer relief from tension, and facilitate the mastery of fundamental skills. They also afford an opportunity for worthy use of increasing amounts of leisure time.

Swimnastics is the use of various conditioning programs designed to attain and maintain physical fitness through water activities while the body is submerged in water. Swimnastics is designed to encourage one to become involved in recreational water activities, so that he or she may reap better personal fitness rewards while having *fun!* Through the use of sound teaching principles, swimnastics can be enjoyed with benefit by young and old, healthy and infirm, and swimmers and nonswimmers.

There is a demand for qualified personnel to instigate, organize, administer, and evaluate swimnastics programs each year. Health, physical education, and recreation curricula can give students an opportunity to study the various techniques and methods employed in such programs.

ORIGIN AND DEVELOPMENT

The dictionary defines recreation as "refreshment after toil" or the "act of creating anew." Therefore, swimnastics must be as old as the bathtub. However, the first swimnastics programs were offered sometime later in YMCAs, YWCAs, hospitals and organizations with retirement facilities. Swimnastics is an outgrowth of physical therapy and hydrotherapy which offer temporary relief from discomfort and pain. For this reason, swimnastics is not only popular with all ages in municipal recreation but also very helpful to elderly participants and other special populations. Because of its many possibilities, swimnastics has a strong appeal to the college student and the general public. From an educational point of view, it affords an opportunity for creative experiences in an aquatic environment while facilitating the mastery of fundamental swimming skills.

Before choosing a swimnastic activity, sound teaching principles require that appropriate caution be exercised in the evaluation of games, contests, stunts, relays, and/or conditioning programs in terms of their suitability and benefit to the participants. Some factors that influence the suitability of recreational water activities are comfort of the participants—temperature of both air and water, age, ability, sex, number of participants, time allotment, water space, equipment required, swimmer interests and preferences, relationship to instructor, safety, physical and social benefits, and practicality.

Objectives

□ To develop an appreciation and understanding of swimnastics.

□ To instill self-assurance in performing fundamental skills while the body is submerged in water.

□ To help the student develop strength, stamina, and endurance through swimnastics activities.

□ To enhance coordination, flexibility, and agility.

□ To stimulate the student to maintain a maximum level of individual physical fitness throughout life.

□ To give the student the knowledge needed to discipline the body in water.

□ To help the student improve muscle tone and circulation.

□ To teach respect for the water and its effects on the human body.

□ To promote safety and fun in water-related activities.

□ To acquaint the student with innovative and creative aquatic experiences that will promote and develop methods of program presentation.

Types of Swimnastics

□ Water exercises—calisthenics, circuit training, individual, partner, group, routines, music, aquacises, and aquathenics.

□ Relays and races—individual and team competition.

□ Novelty games—individual, partner, group, novice, beginner, intermediate, swimmer, and lifesaving.

□ Sports—water-related and adapted games (water polo, basketball, volleyball, field hockey, etc.).

□ Drills—circle, diagonal, variations.

☐ Conditioning programs—for competitive teams, for senior citizens, isometrics.

☐ Special events—water carnivals, synchronized swimming, skill testing, combatives.

☐ Special population activities—handicapped, disabled, blind, elderly.

Equipment and Supplies

Swimnastics equipment and supplies are very inexpensive. Students will enjoy a scavenger hunt to locate items that will bring them many hours of fun. Have each student collect the following items to keep in a small plastic household bag filled with these "goodies":

small bag of balloons
plastic spoon
2 table tennis balls
6 adhesive bandage strips
5 pennies
smooth stone (hand size)
newspaper sheet

pair 40″ shoelaces
2 birthday candles
matches
2 plastic corks
whistle
rubber ball (hand size)
6 plastic straws

Most swimnastics activities require little or no additional expense. However, special event activities call for some additional items from the instructor:

2 water polo or playground balls
3 pieces of ½″ rope
4 batons
stone alphabet sets
homemade instruments (maracas, etc.)
panty hose
plastic drinking glasses
Frisbees®

Hula hoops
food items (bananas, apples, crackers)
tire tubes
hopscotch court
lifeline (usually installed in pool)
straw hats
whiffle bat
plastic jug containers

Teaching Hints

The instructor should:

☐ Emphasize activities which keep the *entire group* active.

☐ Make the membership of teams equal in number and ability to preserve the challenge of a competitive situation.

☐ Exercise judicious control over the participants.

☐ Be enthusiastic without dominating the group. The instructor's personality can help to make the game fun.

☐ Explain each game, stunt, or relay completely and clearly and then ask for questions. Rules should be simple and safe. They should be changed if they do not fit the situation or the facilities. A winner should always be announced.

☐ Be mindful of the factors which affect suitability and benefits of recreational water activities.

Teaching Hints at Skill Levels

☐ At the learn-to-swim level, especially with children, swimming should be an enjoyable activity. Where possible, everything should be a game or stunt. The instructor should ascertain the ability and interest of the group and provide activities which reinforce basic skills.

☐ At the junior level, a sense of accomplishment can be achieved by using skills and strokes already learned. Repetition will encourage mastery.

☐ At the intermediate and senior levels, good vigorous activities are excellent for conditioning. Relays and games with the element of competition should be used to alleviate boredom and monotony. Endurance and stamina can be increased at this level.

☐ At the end of the session, the instructor should assemble the group and explain why the activity was included. If the activity was competitive, a winner should be declared. The class should be dismissed under control. This is good safety practice!

SWIMMING FOR SPECIAL POPULATIONS

Swimming for the Handicapped

"If a person has a physical or mental problem, he is *disabled;* if a person cannot try and work to overcome this problem, he is *handicapped.*" This remark was made by Jeannette Kutash, a blind graduate student at Southern Connecticut State College. The values of a recreational swimming program for the retarded and physically handicapped are infinite. Persons who have learning difficulties and certain handicapping conditions are exposed to an improved learning environment; namely, the water. A handicapped person benefits from water, learning techniques that reach beyond academia. A newly found self-sufficiency and mobility in water create a greater independence and offer a purposeful outlet for energies. The development of a year-round form of enjoyable participation in water activities encourages mastery of swimming skills and promotes self-esteem through accomplishment.

Understanding the Handicapped

Before one can teach the handicapped to swim and enjoy the water, the instructor must have an understanding of the pupil as a *person.*

☐ The handicapped is a person first, and handicapped second

☐ This person has desires, urges, emotions, and drives

☐ The individual wants to be a contributing member of society—accepted and respected by others

☐ The individual does *not* want sympathy, but craves understanding

☐ Teaching and learning processes should be enjoyable and meaningful

☐ Handicapped individuals may also be educationally deprived and have limited attention spans. Abbreviated lessons with individual involvement will tend to increase the length of the attention span

Teaching the Handicapped

☐ The teaching approach should be *positive. WORK WITH THE ABILITY, NOT THE DISABILITY*

☐ The teaching approach should be one through which the instructor develops a good teacher-pupil relationship

☐ The instructor should make a determined effort to learn as much as possible about the student, so that the program can be planned to meet the student's specific needs

☐ Both the teaching and learning processes should be enjoyable and meaningful

☐ Instructors should encourage students to work to the limits of their capacity.

Values of Swimnastics for Special Populations

☐ Swimnastics is a recreational activity that can involve participants without competition

☐ Swimnastics movements are so diversified that most learners can experience success. As a result, satisfaction and confidence motivate them to attempt other activities

☐ Swimnastics teaches a variety of safety skills

☐ Overcoming fear of the water through swimnastics activities may enhance one's ability to overcome other fears

☐ Improved coordination developed through swimnastics may carry over into the normal activity of living

☐ Swimnastics activities can be adapted to the performance level of the individual

☐ Swimnastics is an outlet for tension and a means of social relaxation for all

"Mainstreaming" through Swimnastics Activities

Swimnastics offers an opportunity to incorporate members of special populations into regular classes and/or activities. Instructors can make numerous adaptations to game rules and equipment, so that disabled individuals are able to participate actively and constructively. It is vitally important that individuals be given the opportunity to share in the joy of discovery while having their personal needs for movement met.

TERMINOLOGY

Mainstreaming Incorporation of members of special populations into regular swimnastics activities.

Special event An activity designed for water carnivals and/or water demonstrations.

Special populations Those individuals who have learning difficulties and/or certain incapacitating conditions.

Swimnastics The study of various conditioning programs designed to attain and maintain physical fitness through activities performed in water.

SUMMARY

Any fun-filled activity that can be adapted to an aquatic environment has potential to become a swimnastics idea. Swimnastics activities help to maintain interest, to break monotony and, in general, offer relief from tension which may result from sustained effort. The mastery of swimming fundamentals is also facilitated. Swimnastics activities are easily incorporated into a regular swimming program at any level of instruction. They can be altered to meet the needs of special populations.

A swimnastics program is innovative and creative. It can be a valuable adjunct to fitness programs in schools and colleges, recreation departments, retirement facilities, camps, and youth-serving facilities such as YMCAs and YWCAs. The benefits, especially to the elderly and handicapped, are immeasurable.

Most important, swimnastics programs offer everyone an opportunity to enjoy recreational water activities and reap better personal fitness rewards.
Swimnastics is fun!!!

SAMPLE SWIMNASTICS ACTIVITIES*

Water Exercises—Routine

This is a warm-up series of exercises designed with the beginner in mind. Time allotment for each exercise: approximately 10 minutes.

---

* This section is excerpted from *Swimnastics Is Fun* by M. G. Sholtis, Connecticut State College, New Haven, Conn., 1975. Reprinted by permission of the American Alliance for Health, Physical Education and Recreation.

☐ Toe touch—(shallow water) students touch toes with hand in slow rhythm using rhythmic breathing

☐ Hand–toe touch—(back against wall in shallow water) students alternate toe raise to hand in slow motion, arms outstretched

☐ The cramp—(shallow water) students alternate knee pull to chest with hands clasped around leg

☐ Bend-straight-down—students alternate knee pull to chest, leg extension in horizontal position and slow lowering of leg

☐ 180-degree circle—students swing arms in low half-circle under water

☐ 360-degree circle—students swing arms in low full circle both under and above water

☐ Quarry pickup—students singly locate a rock on the pool bottom and use a walk to pick it up and return to side of pool

☐ Toy soldier—students single file, cross the pool using flutter kick and return using squat position, keeping back straight with hands on hips

☐ The kick—students singly return to the side of the pool by alternately "kicking legs" while jumping in shallow water

☐ The explosion—students swing arms in full circle and push off bottom using jump locomotor movement

☐ Variations—rearrange order of exercises; increase numbers of each exercise; use music; use relay formation to complete series

GAMES AND CONTESTS

Beginners

Electricity
Number of contestants: Any number
Equipment: None
Action: The players stand in shallow water and form a circle holding hands. The instructor squeezes the hand of his or her neighbor, who submerges and then passes the squeeze to the next player's hand, and so on, until back to the instructor. All are now submerged. The instructor starts the current again and when a player's hand is squeezed this time he or she stands back up.
Purpose: To teach water adjustment and breath control.

Toy sailboat race
Number of contestants: Any number
Equipment: Table tennis ball for each contestant; straws
Action: Players line up in the shallow water with a straw inserted into mouth. At the signal, "Go," each contestant tries to blow air through the straw,

forcing the "boat" (table tennis ball) to the other side of the pool. The first boat reaching the opposite side wins.

Purpose: To teach water adjustment and alleviate panic by blowing air out through straw while submerged in water.

Intermediate Swimmers

Flutterboard fight

Number of contestants: Any number
Equipment: Flutterboard
Action: The two teams line up at opposite edges of the pool. A flutterboard is placed in the center of the pool to float on the water. At the signal, the first players on each team go to the flutterboard, grasp it, and at the command, "Go," begin to flutter kick and try to bring the opponent to their home side. The player who is captured then becomes a member of the capturing team.
Purpose: To increase stamina and endurance; strengthen the flutter kick.

Couples germ tag

Number of contestants: Any even number
Equipment: None
Action: One couple is "it" and tries to tag other couples without breaking hands. If tagged, a couple joins the "it" couple and helps the "it" couple continue the pursuit. If any couple breaks hold, the tag does not count. Play continues until there is one untagged couple which becomes "it" for the next game.
Purpose: Fun and exercise!

Advanced Swimmers

Water punch ball

Number of contestants: 6–18
Equipment: Water polo ball
Action: A diamond is made in deep water by having flutterboards at each base. The team is treading water except for the catcher who rests against the edge of the pool. Batters stand in front of the catcher and attempt to punch the thrown ball. Batters who get a hit swim toward first base. The fielders try to catch batters off base by swimming toward them and tagging them out. The game is scored like baseball.
Purpose: To increase stamina and endurance; teach treading water skills.

Water basketball

Number of contestants: Any number
Equipment: Ball
Action: Water basketball is played just like regular basketball except for

dribbling. There are two teams; each divides into forwards and guards. The forwards try to make baskets or points while the guards try to stop and delay their opponents from scoring. The team with the most points wins. When played in shallow water, the dribbling is done upside down; that is, the ball is thrown up in the air for every step taken. When played in deep water, the ball is just carried along or passed from player to player. The game is played the width, not the length, of the pool.

Purpose: To increase stamina and endurance; to have fun; and to improve accuracy in throwing, catching, and dribbling while the body is submerged.

Special Populations

Blindman's swim
Number of contestants: Any number
Equipment: Whistle, blindfolds
Action: All swimmers are blindfolded except one, who is "it." "It" swims underwater with a whistle. Each time "it" surfaces, "it" must blow the whistle, and the others try to tag "it." The player who makes the tag becomes "it" and takes possession of the whistle.
Note: It is important to have all blind children wear blindfolds to attain a feeling of belongingness in the class.
Purpose: Fun-filled game for blind participants and others.

Red rover
Number of contestants: Any number
Equipment: None
Action: One contestant calls out to contestants, "Send (contestant's name) over." The person named tries to swim past the caller without being tagged. If a tag is made, the one who was tagged joins the caller and both "call" and endeavor to catch the next contestants. Contestants may surface dive and swim underwater to elude the caller. Those not tagged win the game.
Variations: Participants may wear blindfolds; participants may use an arm stroke only, or be limited to just a leg stroke. In shallow water, contestants may float or walk over.
Purpose: To familiarize players with each others' names.

Special Event Activities

Tight relay
Number of contestants: 8
Equipment: Two pairs of panty hose
Action: Two swimmers, one from each team, line up at the four corners of the pool. At the signal, swimmers 1 of each team put on a pair of panty hose, jump into the pool and swim to the opposite end of the pool. The panty

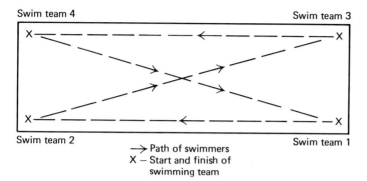

Swim team 4   Swim team 3

Swim team 2   Swim team 1

→ Path of swimmers
X – Start and finish of
swimming team

Fig. 36.11 Pathways of swimmers in the game of *Tight Relay*.

hose wearers then climb out of the pool, remove the hose and hand them to swimmers 2, who put on the panty hose, jump in and swim diagonally across the pool. Swimmers 3 and 4 follow the same procedure except that swimmers 3 swim the length of the pool and swimmers 4 swim diagonally across pool (see Fig. 36.11). This continues until each member has had a turn. The first team to finish wins.

Balloon bottom buster

Number of contestants: Any number

Equipment: Balloons for each contestant

Action: This game, adaptable to any level of skill, is composed of two teams. Half of each team is lined up on either side of the pool opposite one another. Each contestant has a balloon. The first contestant on each team enters the water by any method, swims to the opposite side of the pool and gets out onto the deck. The contestant then blows up the balloon and sits on it to break it. The signal for the next contestant to start is the bursting of the balloon. The winner is the first team which has popped all its balloons and is sitting in a straight line on deck.

Variations: Beginners may run along the bottom of the pool if necessary. For advanced swimmers (1) the race can take place at the deep end and/or go the length of the pool, (2) swimmers can be required to enter the water in a different manner from that of the teammates who preceded them, or (3) swimmers can be required to use a specific stroke.

REFERENCES

Cureton, T. K., Jr. 1949. *Fun in the water.* Association Press.

Hackett, L. C., and C. C. Lawrence 1975. *Water learning: a new adventure.* Palo Alto, Calif.: Peek Publications.

Sholtis, M. G. 1975. *Swimnastics is fun.* American Alliance for Health, Physical Education and Recreation, Washington, D.C.

Synchronized Swimming

Joanne L. Smith

Inherently, people desire activities which fulfill recreational needs, stimulate creativity, provide challenge, and ultimately enhance self-image. While speed swimming provided just such goal-fulfillment for many aquatic enthusiasts in the early 1900s, there were many who needed a different channel in which to direct their swimming abilities. Synchronized swimming has evolved as an aquatic activity that offers countless opportunities to recreate, improve physical conditioning, develop watermanship, and even to enrich interest in music and art.

Synchronized swimming is an activity in which one or more swimmers participate in a swimming composition which is organized to present a design or idea and which is executed in harmony with musical accompaniment. Synchronized swimming differs from regular swimming in that (1) modified strokes are used with a lower leg kick (to avoid splashing) and with the head held out of the water; (2) meaningful arm movements are added to regular strokes to portray a theme and also to create spectator appeal; (3) there is little or no splashing, unless desired for effect; (4) stunts, performed on or below the water surface, are executed to portray ideas through body movement; and (5) rhythmical accompaniment is used to support the quality, structure, and mood of a thematic composition.

The term "synchronized swimming" became part of aquatic vocabulary in 1934 as a result of the water show that took place at the Chicago World's

Fig. 36.12 Synchronized swimming is an activity in which swimmers participate in a composition which presents an idea and which is executed in harmony with the music. Courtesy of *JOPER.*

Fair. The name was originated by Norman Ross to describe the physical arrangement of Katherine Curtis's Modern Mermaids who were performing in the Lagoon Theatre. The swimmers were divided into two groups, one swimming on either side of a raised platform. Both groups moved at the same time, in the same way, and appeared to Ross to be doing "synchronized swimming."

The actual start of synchronized swimming is attributed to the contributions of Katherine Curtis at the University of Wisconsin in 1916. It started as a creative activity through her desire to perform diving stunts in the water instead of in the air. Her coach, an old vaudeville acrobat, encouraged the innovations. Later, while teaching at the University of Chicago, she used stunts in her swimming classes. Soon, thereafter, background music was added and synchronized body movements were developed. This was the start of "rhythmic swimming" of standard strokes to definite musical patterns. While in Chicago, Curtis organized coeducational swimming teams and began the first competitive synchronized swimming using rules similar to competitive diving.

The era from 1910–1933, prior to the innovation of synchronized swimming, involved participation in swimming activities such as stunting, pageantry, and group swimming formations with and without musical accompaniment. "Rhythmic swimming" or "water ballet," and water plays were being used for demonstrations and the idea of stunt competition had developed. People were turning to form and skill in swimming as alternatives to speed. Little technique was employed beyond standard strokes, basic somersaults, turns, and circles. Typical water productions were presentations with girls swimming in pretty patterns with flowers floating in the water.

The modern concept of synchronized swimming developed between 1934 and 1940, first as another name for rhythmic swimming, and gradually as a water composition which expressed an idea or design.

Acceptance of synchronized swimming as a competitive sport in the early 1940s led to a great increase in its popularity in the United States. Integration of movement with the accompaniment in contrast to using music just for a background or prop, became increasingly important. Synchronized swimming became an AAU (Amateur Athletic Union) national championship event in 1945, first including duet and team competition only and a few years later adding men's solo competition (1950) and then stunt competition (1958). With the intent of keeping synchronized swimming a sport, the AAU began stressing rigid specifications for all competition, which ultimately began limiting a swimmer's creative freedom.

For the purpose of promoting the growth of synchronized swimming in the creative and artistic directions on a noncompetitive basis, the International Academy of Aquatic Art (IAAA) was formed in 1955. Members of the organization were opposed to the AAU's emphasis on execution of difficult stunts and felt that synchronized swimming was more of an art form than a sport. "Aquatic art" explores the aquatic medium for "truly artistic self-expression" with the creative aspect being emphasized. The success of an aquatic art composition is based on its aesthetic appeal and thematic interpretation, with stunt execution considered as a means to an end, and not the actual goal itself. The IAAA conducts instructional and noncompetitive symposiums and festivals for men and women. AAU competition today is restricted to female participation.

The Association of Synchronized Swimming for College Women was formed in the mid-1950s with membership open to any college or university synchronized swimming club. Its aim is "to gain a more comprehensive understanding of the art of synchronized swimming by sharing ideas and information which will further its growth and development."

Synchronized swimming was first included in the Pan American Games in 1955 in Mexico City. Since that time, it has been voted in and out of the Games for various reasons, one being a lack of participating countries. Synchronized swimming has been promoted throughout the world in an effort to stimulate sufficient interest to lead to its inclusion in the Olympic Games. Thus far, synchronized swimming has only been demonstrated at the Olympic Games. Two reasons for reluctance to accept synchronized swimming into the Olympic and Pan American games are: (1) people question whether it has the status of a true sport and (2) some are adverse to including another judged event in international competition.

Synchronized swimming is an artistic and cultural addition to the physical aspect of education, providing opportunity for self-expression through many media: water skills, dance movements, art in costume design, and musical selection and interpretation. Participation in this aquatic activity aids in the

Fig. 36.13 The basic skills of synchronized swimming are useful in school, camp, recreation, and swimming club programs. Courtesy of Springfield College.

development of organic vigor and neuromuscular skill; it makes stringent demands on the swimmer for breath control, endurance, strength, body control, balance, precision of body movement, and rhythmic perception.

One of the most challenging and creative swimming activities involves the combining of synchronized movements and techniques into compositions (routines). Natagraphy, which is the art of creating synchronized swimming compositions, is similar to dance choreography in that movement qualities, pattern flow, and mood portrayal are vital elements of the creative process. The natagrapher, after selecting and analyzing a functional musical accompaniment, works with elements of space, time, and force to create a dynamic design which interprets a theme. Developing the deck work (those movements performed on the deck at the start of a routine prior to entry in the water), and working with color, design, and materials to create costumes further enrich the natagrapher's appreciation for music, dance, and art.

The basic skills of synchronized swimming are useful in school, camp, recreation, and swimming club programs. Synchronized swimming skills add interest and variety to a swimming program, while they prepare swimmers to be relaxed and to maneuver the body well in water, which enhances safety and self-reliance. Although age and ability affect performance levels attainable, the range of skills in synchronized swimming is sufficiently varied to permit all ages and levels of swimmers, both female and male, to participate.

A conditioning program for synchronized swimmers should include the development of muscular strength, muscular endurance, flexibility, and cardiorespiratory endurance. Emphasis is usually placed on forearm strength for sculling (a propulsive and supportive arm movement used for stroke and stunt execution); leg strength for powerful kicks; leg, shoulder girdle, and back flexibility (for ease in stunt execution and transitions); and sufficient cardiorespiratory endurance to execute a four- to six-minute routine of strenuous swimming skills. Training programs should include practice of standard strokes, sculling techniques and stunts, and work on rhythmic perception, grace, body control, and kinesthetic awareness.

Synchronized swimming clinics are offered throughout the United States to practice and demonstrate techniques, examine ideas for compositions and water shows, exchange ideas about exhibitions and competitions, and to train judges. Synchronized swimming has grown tremendously since its creation, as is evidenced by the 222 stunts now recognized in the AAU Official Rulebook in Synchronized Swimming. This activity is becoming increasingly popular in the United States, Canada, Japan, England, Holland, East and West Germany, South Africa and Denmark. If synchronized swimming is to be recognized as an international sport, the "creative" aspect, which is difficult to judge objectively, will probably have to be left to water shows and demonstrations and not brought into the competitive phase of the sport. The issue of whether synchronized swimming is actually a sport or an art form may never be resolved, since the strength, stamina, and skill proficiency it requires identify it as a sport, and the creative aspect of natagraphy identifies it as an art form. Its value in developing watermanship and providing an opportunity to employ aquatic skills other than for speed swimming makes it an activity that has educational value for everyone, regardless of age, sex, or swimming ability.

REFERENCES

Bean, D. P., editor-publisher 1972. *Synchro-Info.* Bimonthly synchronized swimming magazine **10,** 1, (February). Santa Ana, Calif.

Official rules for synchronized swimming 1973. Indianapolis, Ind.: Amateur Athletic Union of the United States.

Rackham, G. 1968. *Synchronized swimming.* London: Faber and Faber.

Stoerker, M. L. 1956. The origin and development of synchronized swimming in the United States. Unpublished master's thesis. The University of Wisconsin.

Vickers, B. J. 1965. *Teaching synchronized swimming.* N.J.: Prentice-Hall.

37
Table Tennis
Frank H. Fu

INTRODUCTION

Table tennis, also called ping pong, has had its ups and downs ever since it was first introduced in the 1890s. The improvement of equipment and facilities during the 1950s and 1960s has enabled the game to be played more competitively than ever before. With increasing exposure through television in the 1970s, table tennis was finally introduced to the public not only as a recreational game played in the basement but also as an extremely competitive sport which requires a high degree of skill and stamina. The "ping-pong diplomacy" during the Nixon Administration was the first step in the renewal of Chinese-American relations since the communist takeover of mainland China in 1949. Today, table tennis is still primarily a recreational game played by millions of people all over the world.

EARLY BEGINNINGS

Several versions have been presented to explain the origin of table tennis. One source claimed that it originated in New England, another source said it was in London, and yet another source claimed that it was in China. While there is no consensus as to the place of origin, all three sources agreed that table tennis was first introduced around 1890.

The name ping pong was derived from the two different sounds which were made by the ball on hitting the racket (ping) and the table (pong). In its rudimentary stage, the table was narrower, the net was higher, and the ball was softer. For these reasons, the game was highly disadvantageous to the offensive player.

In the beginning of the 20th century, ping pong reached the height of its popularity in Europe. However, just as quickly as it rose to fame, ping pong was forgotten. It was revived in 1920 in the European countries under a different name, "table tennis." In 1926, the International Table Tennis Federation (ITTF) was created in Berlin with more than 30 national associations as its members. The American Ping Pong Association was founded three years later and was followed by its rival organization, the United States Table Tennis Association (USTTA). The latter organization was allied with the international body in Europe and eventually became the representative body in America. World championships have been held annually since 1927 and biennially since 1957 under the ITTF. Besides winning the world titles, the European and Asian champions were the more prestigious. The game has flourished since the 1930s. Both the quality and quantity of competition have risen throughout the years. The game has now finally established itself as both a competitive and a spectator sport.

GENERAL DESCRIPTION

Playing Equipment

1. Table. The official table is 5′ wide, 9′ long, and 30″ high. The color of the table surface is usually dark green. The net is 6 to 6¾″ high and 6′ wide. It is placed at the middle of the width of the table where a white line ⅛″ wide divides the table into 2 courts. All other white lines on the table are ¾″ wide.

2. Racket. There is no rule with regard to the size and weight of the racket. However, it can only be one of the following five colors: dark red, dark green, dark brown, dark blue, and dark black. The surface of the racket cannot be shiny and where both sides of the racket are used, they must be the same color. In the case of a wooden racket, the finish of the surface cannot be shiny or waxy. If sponge or rubber is used, the thickness of the sponge or rubber is limited to 4 mm.

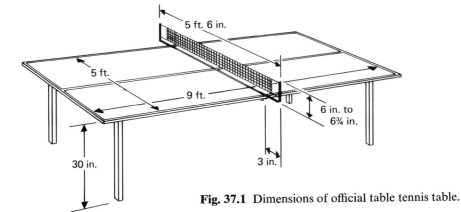

Fig. 37.1 Dimensions of official table tennis table.

3. Ball. The average weight of a ball is $\frac{1}{10}$ ounce, and it ranges from $4\frac{1}{2}''$ to $4\frac{3}{4}''$ in circumference. The elasticity coefficient of the ball is about 0.82 and its color must be white.

BASIC PLAYING

Singles and doubles are both played in table tennis. The play begins with the server tossing the ball vertically into the air from the open palm of the hand. The server cannot hide the ball or apply any kind of force to the ball other than striking it with the racket. After the ball is hit, it must bounce once on the server's side of the net, over the net, and onto the receiver's court. The receiver must return the ball by hitting it over the net after it has bounced once. Volleying is not allowed in any exchange. Points are scored for both server and receiver. Players alternate serving every five points. The player who is the first to score 21 points wins. If the score is tied at 20 points apiece, the game is extended. The service will then be alternated every point and the winner is the one who first gains a two-point lead.

For doubles, the rules are the same except that the service must be made from the right half of the server's court to the right half of the receiver's court. The server must hit the ball diagonally from the server's side of the court to the opposite side. The service is alternated between teams every five points and also between partners.

All balls hitting the net are playable except those during the service. Players are usually forbidden to wear brightly colored clothes such as orange or yellow T-shirts. For tournament play, it is recommended that the rules of the ITTF be followed.

COMMON FAULTS

☐ Hitting the ball inside the area of the court during the service.

☐ Hitting the ball more than once before the opponent hits it.

☐ Allowing the racket to touch or reach over the net.

☐ Applying spin or force to the ball with the hand, during the service.

☐ Touching the table with the free hand or with any part of the body.

☐ The ball hitting the net and going out.

☐ Moving before the server hits the ball.

☐ Leaning on the table.

☐ Being hit by the ball inside one's court.

☐ Volleying a ball when the ball is off the court.

☐ The ball hitting the net two or more times before it goes over to the other side.

☐ Serving or receiving out of order.

☐ Using an illegal racket.

☐ Hitting the ball with any part of the hand or body.

☐ The ball hitting the side of the table edge and not the upper edge (see Fig. 37.2).

☐ Hitting the ball inside the court or outside the sides of the table during the service (see Fig. 37.3).

TERMINOLOGY

Block A semivolley, a ball is hit and returned in the minimum amount of time possible.

Chop A stroke which creates an underspin on the ball. The racket is moved vertically downward during the stroke.

Flick A fast smash in which very little windup is involved.

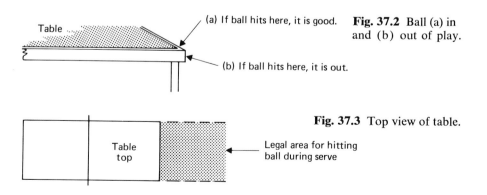

Table

(a) If ball hits here, it is good.

(b) If ball hits here, it is out.

Fig. 37.2 Ball (a) in and (b) out of play.

Table top

Fig. 37.3 Top view of table.

Legal area for hitting ball during serve

Kill A hard smash.

Lob A ball which is not hit hard but follows a high loop in its trajectory.

Net Occurs only during the service when the ball hits the net once and bounces over. The point is played over.

Penholder grip The grip in which the racket is held like a pen.

Push A semiblock stroke in which more force is involved and in which the ball is directed very carefully to the desired spot in the opponent's court.

Reflex The ability of the player to react quickly to hit the ball.

Shakehand grip or tennis grip The grip in which the racket is held as if shaking hands.

Topspin A stroke which creates an overspin on the ball. Topspin is usually used together with a lob.

Touch The ability to control the ball and place it.

Volley A stroke in which the ball is hit before it bounces on the table. This is not legal in table tennis.

Wood Occurs when the ball hits the *upper* edge of the table. The ball is good and still in play.

FUNDAMENTALS IN TEACHING TECHNIQUES

Grip

The two major grips in table tennis are the *penholder* and *shakehand* or tennis grips. However, there are many variations and the actual number of grips amounts to eight. Figure 37.4 illustrates the most common varieties.

Footwork

Proper footwork as well as transfer of force will facilitate the process of responding to the oncoming ball. The most common kinds of footwork are: *single step, change step, straddle step,* and *jump step*. Single step involves the movement of only one foot toward the ball; change step involves the repositioning of both feet; straddle step is a sideward movement of both feet; and jump step involves a leaping movement and a repositioning of both feet (Fig. 37.5).

Concentration

Although most movements in table tennis are conditioned reflexes, it is extremely important to be able to read the spin and force on the ball if one is to

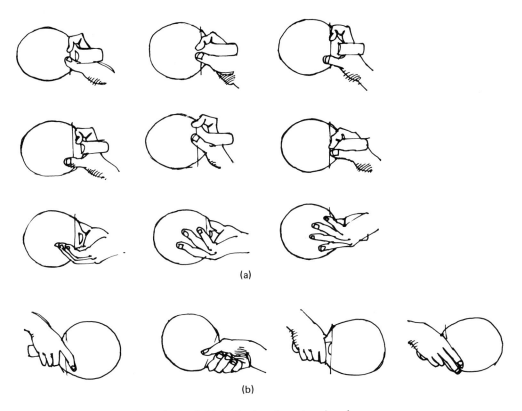

(a)

(b)

Fig. 37.4 (a) Penholder grips and (b) shake-hands or tennis grips.

react properly. A high degree of concentration is required, especially at a competitive level.

Serve

The serve is very important because it takes the initiative away from the opponent. Some research has shown that the server has a significantly higher chance to win the point than the receiver. The service provides a unique situation because the server has all the time necessary to put the ball into play and also can apply different amounts of force and spin on the ball (through hitting the ball and not throwing it).

Spin

The topspin is usually employed in a controlled game when the player waits for the opponent to make a mistake. A topspin ball will bounce lower but farther away from the table. On the other hand, a ball with underspin will

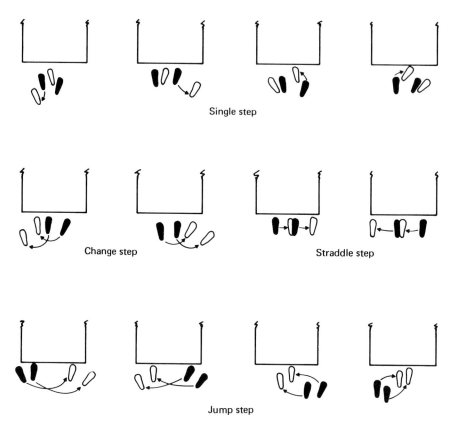

Fig. 37.5 Footwork.

bounce higher but drop nearer to the net. Underspin is usually applied during the chop—a defensive stroke. The sidespin is often used in conjunction with the topspin and the underspin. It serves to make the ball move sideways so that the opponent does not have a clear shot.

TACTICS AND STRATEGIES

There are three major strategies involved in table tennis, namely, offensive, defensive, and a combination of both. Very often, the strategy which can be applied depends on the ability of the player and the ability and strategy of the opponent. Psychology also plays a central role in planning strategy. Offensive strategy emphasizes the use of the service, push, smash, and topspin. Defensive strategy utilizes more chops, blocks, placement of shots, spin, and control. A combination of offensive and defensive strategies will emphasize a variety of strokes ranging from chop to topspin lob. The emphasis here is to control the game and wait for a kill. This is usually the more successful approach.

In doubles, the strategies are similar. Teamwork is, however, very important. The players must be familiar with each other's positions and movements. Common formations are front and back, figure 8, circular, and diagonal patterns.

REFERENCES

Carr, J. 1969. *Advanced table tennis.* New York: A. S. Barnes.

Chung, C. M. 1971. *Techniques of ping pong.* (In Chinese.) Hong Kong: Sun Ah.

Lam, S. S. 1971. *Table-tennis training.* (Translated from Japanese to Chinese.) Hong Kong: Shanghai.

Leach, J. 1971. *Table tennis for the seventies.* New York: A. S. Barnes.

Miles, D. 1968. *The game of table tennis.* Philadelphia and New York: J. B. Lippincott.

Neuberger, L. 1969. Table tennis. In F. G. Menke (ed.), *Encyclopedia of sports.* New York: A. S. Barnes.

Rowe, D. 1965. *Table tennis.* London: Stanley Paul.

Varner, M., and J. Harrison 1967. *Table tennis.* Dubuque, Iowa: Wm. C. Brown.

Yiu, C. 1971. *A practical approach to ping pong.* (In Chinese.) Hong Kong: L. Hing.

38
Team Handball
Richard Abrahamson

One of the newest permanent Olympic sports, *team handball,* is beginning to gain a foothold in physical education and intramural programs at the high school and college level. Although first introduced to the Olympic format in the Berlin, 1936 Olympic Games, team handball was not included on the schedule of events until 1972 in Munich.

BACKGROUND

Team handball was first developed in the early 1900s in Denmark as a form of indoor soccer. It differs from soccer in that players in playing the ball use their hands rather than their feet. As a result, a fast-action, hard-hitting team sport with the objective of throwing a leather ball (approx. 7" in diameter) past the defense and goalie into the goal has developed throughout Europe, Africa, the Far East, Central and South America and, more recently, the United States.

Handball in most every European country is second only to soccer in popularity and is played widely in well-developed leagues for all age groups of both men and women. In most European countries it shares the popularity that football, baseball, and basketball enjoy in the United States. Presently, there are over 60 countries with extensive handball programs for all age groups. It is a team sport of considerable significance throughout the world and contributes greatly to the fitness of more than three million participants involved actively in the game.

If it were possible to select a sport which is fundamental to the basic skills of the American athlete, team handball would probably be selected by physical educators as the sport most likely to include the majority of basic skills developed in our varied American system of sport. The fundamental skills of running, jumping, throwing, and catching practiced in the competitive atmosphere of football, basketball, baseball, track, and many other popular sports within our well-developed school athletic and physical education programs are all equally utilized in the new Olympic sport of team handball.

This fast-moving passing game has developed steadily since it was introduced on an organized level in 1959 by a group of European immigrants headed by the current president of the federation, Dr. Peter Buehning. Its early beginnings were in the New York–New Jersey area which continues to be the "hub" of handball in the United States. However, handball has now spread throughout the fifty states, partly due to the involvement of the Army and the initiation in 1970 of General Westmoreland's Army Champs Program. Army Champs was organized and supported by General Westmoreland to develop team handball in a major way within the military at the "grassroots" level. The game soon spread to every major Army installation in the United States, Europe, and the Far East, and as a result of the success of the program, handball has grown tremendously at the club level and within physical education programs at numerous schools across the country.

Normally played indoors on a hardwood surface, team handball is a fast-moving passing game with many similarities to soccer and basketball. The basic rules are quite simple, and one can learn to play the game in a short period of time. A game is started with a "throw-on" in which a team, which consists of six court players and one goalie, starts play by throwing the ball in from the half-court line. The six court players set up on perimeter approximately twenty feet in front of the goal on the six-meter line. The offensive team attacks the defense and goal by quickly passing the ball around the perimeter of the defense much as in the sport of water polo. Since a basic rule of the game states "the ball may be held for a maximum time of three seconds," a fast-moving, passing game develops. Another basic rule allows the offensive player to move not more than three steps while holding the ball. Dribbling the ball repeatedly with one hand when running, walking or standing is also permitted. The movement of the ball develops many one-on-one attack situations for the offensive player as in basketball. "Give and go," "back door" situations, and the popular "pick and roll" play, so evident in college and professional basketball, often develop. Offensive patterns similar to those employed in basketball are created to enable a player to take a clear shot at the goal past the defense. Defensively, a team concerns itself with body and arm checking to prevent the offense from taking a clear shot on goal. Considerable body contact is allowed although tackling and grabbing are prohibited. Upon an unsuccessful scoring attempt, the defense becomes the offensive team and advances the ball to the opposite end of the floor attacking the goal from a perimeter offensive pattern. During the transition from defense to offense, a fast-break offense frequently develops. Just as in basketball the fast break, when properly utilized, becomes a potent offensive weapon.

Team handball can be played in nearly all existing gymnasiums. Figure 38.1 illustrates the dimensions of a regulation handball playing court.

CONCEPT OF THE GAME

A game is started with a *throw-on,* taken from the center line. The offensive team throws the ball in play and attacks the defense set up on the six-meter line (19'8") from the goal. The area within the six-meter line is the goal area. At no time is a defensive player other than the goalie allowed in this area. An offensive player is allowed in the goal area only when attempting a shot on goal. The player must leave the ground outside the six-meter line and release the shot prior to landing in the goal area.

A goal is scored when a player has thrown the ball into the goal of the opposing team (Fig. 38.2). After a goal has been scored, the game is restarted with a throw-on from the center of the court by a player of the team against which the goal was scored.

The fast break becomes an important part of the game during the transition period of a lost possession either via a fumble, bad pass, or missed shot. The defense, upon recovery of the ball, usually attempts a controlled fast break trying to set up a good shot on goal before the offensive team can retreat to set up a defensive position.

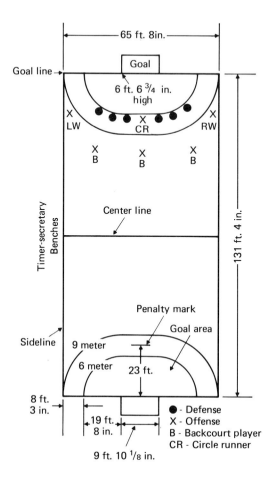

Fig. 38.1 Dimensions of a regulation team handball playing court and positions of players. LW and RW stand for left wing and right wing, respectively.

Fig. 38.2 A goal is scored by throwing the ball into the goal of the opposing team. Here the author of this chapter attempts a shot at the Munich Olympics. Courtesy of Richard Abrahamson.

The duration of a game is two equal periods of 30 minutes with an intermission of 10 minutes. Usually, however, the game time is cut back 10 or more minutes for women and junior players. Average scores per game range from 15 to 20 goals with one goal accounting for one point.

TERMINOLOGY

In order to better understand the concept of the game the basic terminology used in handball is described below.

Corner throw If the entire ball passes over the goal line outside the goal either in the air or on the ground, *having last touched a player on the defensive team,* a corner throw shall be awarded to the attacking team. The corner throw is taken by the offensive team from the corner of the court (where goal line and sideline meet) on the side of the goal where the ball went over the goal line. It involves merely throwing the ball in play and setting up play again.

Free throw Usually occurs between the six-meter and nine-meter lines on the court and is a free throw-in for the offensive team. If the defense causes a turnover of the ball via excessive body contact or at any time demonstrates excessive contact, a free throw is generally awarded the offensive team nearest the point of infraction on the nine-meter line.

Penalty throw Usually occurs for a serious infraction of the rules which destroys a clear chance of scoring a goal. A penalty throw is awarded for excessive body contact and after a defensive player intentionally enters the goal area for defensive advantage. A penalty throw is a free shot on goal except that it is taken from the seven-meter line with the goalie attempting to stop the goal.

Throw-in If the entire ball crosses the sideline on the ground or in the air, the play shall be restarted by a throw-in. The throw-in is from the spot where the ball went out of bounds and is made by a player of the team opposite the one which last touched the ball inbounds.

Throw-off A throw-off occurs if the ball passes over the goal line outside the goal, either in the air or on the ground, having last been touched by a player of the attacking team or the goalkeeper of the defending team in the goal area. The throw-off is taken by the goalkeeper from the goal area on to the court via a pass to a teammate now on the offensive.

Throw-on A throw-on starts a game and occurs at the center-court line after a score.

A BASIC OFFENSE

The universal offensive system used by top teams is the *3–3 system* (see Fig. 38.1). Three backcourt (BC) players are set up at approximately 15 meters from the goal with the best ball handler directly in front of the goal, and the other two backcourt players aligned on either side. The backcourt players are generally the most adept at ball handling and are the strongest and most accurate shooters. The remaining three court players comprise the wing positions, indicated in Fig. 38.1 as left wing (LW) and right wing (RW). The circle runner (CR), like the center in basketball, moves with the movement of the ball along the six-meter line and is always an inside threat to score when open.

Another popular offensive pattern is a *2–4 system* in which the center backcourt player goes inside to the six-meter line and becomes a circle runner. Thus, there would be two backcourt players and four players along the six-meter line—two wing players and two circle runners. This creates a much stronger inside threat to score.

Offensive plays are created from the 3–3 and 2–4 systems to allow for much movement, thus creating an opening and clear shot. Incorporated in a basic offense are numerous "pick and roll" and "back door" combinations so popular in basketball today. Continuity in the offense is of prime importance and, therefore, many offensive systems involve figure 8 patterns to allow maximum movement and yet retain court spread and position.

DEFENSIVE SYSTEMS

Defensively, there are three basic systems; first, as depicted in Fig. 38.1 is the *6–0 system* where all six defensive players are set up on the six-meter line. Second, the *5–1 system* utilizes five defensive players on the six-meter line and one player in the center at seven to eight meters to break up the continuity of the offensive system's backcourt. Third, the *4–2 system* utilizes four players on the six-meter line and two out front at eight meters to break up passing lanes. It is also recommended to defend against a strong outside shooting team.

The basic defensive stance is very similar to that in basketball with the player constantly moving with the flow of the offense and the ball. The defense shifts as a unit with the ball and attempts to prevent the offense from obtaining a clear shot on goal by using "body and hand" checks.

BASIC SKILLS

The skills involved in team handball are very natural to the American athlete. Quick passing and quick footwork both offensively and defensively are essential in handball. Speed is important in developing an effective fast break and strong and accurate shooting is a very important skill needed to excel as an offensive player. The ability to handle the ball well is needed if one is to become an expert player. These skills are quite basic and can be developed through a number of passing, shooting, and footwork drills.

STARTING A TEAM HANDBALL PROGRAM

Team handball programs have now been started in all 50 states. The vast majority of these programs has been highly successful and satisfactory for coaches and participants alike. The game of team handball is for men and women, boys and girls, and for all age levels.

The main reasons for the rather unusual and quick success of team handball are:

☐ Team handball is easy to learn. It uses "natural" athletic skills; running, jumping, throwing, and catching. Experience shows that most athletes possess these skills in an amount sufficient to play team handball in a very short time at a respectable and enjoyable level.

☐ Team handball is fun to play and exciting to watch. Players and spectators alike enjoy the fast, continuous play, the fast breaks, the body contact, and the goalie action. Once introduced to team handball, players and spectators tend to stay with it.

☐ A team handball program is inexpensive to start. A ball and a set of goals and nets are all that is needed. The game fits into existing gymnasiums and, even more important, it can also be played outdoors on grass. Team handball is not confined to a special season of the year, although fall, spring, and summer seem to be the best choice in order to avoid interference with basketball and football. The playing field can be easily established using masking tape indoors or chalk outdoors.

☐ Team handball can be played and enjoyed by all. There are regular National and World Championships for men and women and Olympic competition for men. This is a team sport well suited for women and girls and many schools and colleges are teaching and playing team handball in their women's physical education programs.

Those who wish to learn more about team handball or desire rules, books, or films on the subject should write the United States Team Handball Federation at 10 Nottingham Rd., Short Hills, N.J.   07078.

39
Team Sports
Philip K. Wilson

Team games and team sports have unquestionably become an important aspect of physical education. However, the acceptance of team sports as an integral part of physical education, recreation, and competitive athletics has not been a recent happening but has developed over the past 100 years. Prior to the mid-1800s, organized, or even nonorganized, team activities were rare. Before the turn of the 19th century, recreational and competitive physical activity involved one individual against another.

HISTORICAL BACKGROUND

The Greeks and Romans—800 B.C. to A.D. 500

The period prior to the birth of Christ found the Spartan Greeks, the Athenian Greeks, and the Romans emphasizing the development of the individual through individual activities. In some cases, to a greater or lesser degree, both the Greeks and the Romans placed primary emphasis on military training and games and physical activities of low organization such as running, leaping, swimming, hunting, wrestling, boxing, throwing, fencing, archery, and riding. During later days of the Roman Empire, the civilians ignored most forms of physical activity in favor of spectator sports such as festivals, circuses, and gladiatorial exhibitions. During this period, only professional soldiers participated in competitive physical activity. This was truly a period of mass "spectatoritis."

The Middle Ages and the Renaissance—500 to 1700

During the Middle Ages (A.D. 500 to 1300) the Huns, Goths, Norsemen, and other barbarians conquered, ravaged, and mingled with other European populations. While they brought hardiness and good health with them, art, culture, and education sank to their lowest level. Christianity, which began to flourish after its repression by the Greeks and Romans, brought with it *asceticism*. The emphasis on spiritual and intellectual development led to *scholasticism*. Both asceticism and scholasticism hindered the growth and development of true physical education.

With the Renaissance (1300–1700) came the rebirth of physical education. Interest in running, jumping, archery, wrestling, and boxing increased and hunting, fishing, ball games, and dancing emerged as popular activities.

Throughout the Renaissance the interest in physical activity grew for both the male and female, until such participation became almost universally accepted. Francis Bacon (1938, p. 27), in his *Advancement of Learning: The New Atlantis,* written in 1627, stated:

> As for games of recreation, I hold them to belong to civil life and education. And thus much of that particular human philosophy which concerns the body, which is but the tabernacle of the mind.

Rousseau (1909, p. 92), in *Emile,* claimed:

> In learning to think, we must therefore employ our members, our senses, our organs, all of which are the apparatus of our understanding. And to use them to the best advantage, the body which furnishes them must be sound and robust. Our reason is therefore so far from being independent of the body, that a good constitution renders mental operations easy and accurate.

Rousseau (1909, p. 93) further elaborates on the thoughts of others toward his philosophy of making the mind robust by hardening the muscles:

> The wise Locke, the excellent Rollin, the learned Fleury, the pedantic de Crouzas, so different in everything else, agree exactly on this point of abundant physical exercise for children. It is the wisest lesson they ever taught, but the one that is and always will be most neglected.

Throughout the Renaissance and the Age of Enlightenment, physical activity became an expected function of education centering around swimming, dancing, riding, wrestling, some ball playing, and general exercise.

The United States—1800 to 1850

Swedish and German gymnastics influenced early physical education in America. Until the early 1800s, most physical activity in the United States centered around existence and survival within the hostile environment. Physical activity was a part of the daily routine of the people. However, by the early or mid-1800s, the value of physical activity within the established educational structures became apparent, and this was the forerunner of team sports within the United States.

The United States—1850 to 1900

Team sports reached a pinnacle in the United States with the first game of intercollegiate football played on November 6, 1869, between Princeton and Rutgers. The period 1850 to 1900 saw the rise of many of the present-day popular team sports in the United States. Baseball was called the "national game" by 1870. Volleyball, a game invented in the United States, became prominent during this period. Tennis, though originating in England, became popular in the United States during the 1870s and 1880s. Basketball, another United States invention, became popular by 1900. The period of 1850 to 1900 signaled the arrival of many team sports and the open participation of women in physical activity. Women became extensively involved in basketball, as well as croquet, hiking, bicycling, tennis, archery, dancing, track and field, and gymnastics.

The United States—1900 to present

Except in times of war, team games and sports have held a high position of priority in physical education instruction since 1900. At the turn of the century, students began to demand recreational types of physical participation, in contrast with the then universally existent formal gymnastics. The "new physical education," as popularized by Thomas Wood, emphasized a games and sports approach. By 1920, through the efforts of Clark Hetherington, a student of Thomas Wood, "the new physical education" was firmly entrenched in the physical education curricula of the existent educational structures. Physical activities, of both the individual and team games nature, became a medium through which the values and goals of education were to be achieved. Sports and games were the most popular part of the programs. Through the 1930s, physical education in the schools became a victim of the depression and was eliminated from most curricula. Toward the latter part of the 1930s and the early 1940s, strength and endurance became the paramount goal of physical education instruction at the expense of team sports. However, with the end of World War II, team sports again were emphasized, mostly for recreational benefits. During the 1950s, with the findings of the Kraus-Weber Tests (Kraus and Hirschland 1953, pp. 17–19) and resulting ramifications, physical fitness again was emphasized. However, this renewed emphasis on physical fitness was not, as it was in the past, at the expense of team sports. To the present day, the relationship of physical fitness to participation in team sports has remained an important concept within physical education instruction and was supported by Presidents Kennedy, Johnson, and Nixon.

The establishment of team sports in the physical education curriculums of the 1970s has been a long time in development. The evolution of physical activity from Greek and Roman times to the present concept of modern day physical activity has truly been a magnificent and remarkable phenomenon. The question in modern day physical education programs now is, "What actually is the place and purpose of team sports?"

TEAM SPORTS AND PRESENT-DAY PHYSICAL EDUCATION

Current Status

Team sports have become an important part of present-day physical education. Team size varies from two-member teams to eleven-member teams.

Below is a representative list of team sports utilized in many present-day physical education curriculums:

Two Members	Four Members	Six Members	Ten Members
Badminton	Bowling	Ice hockey	Lacrosse
Canoeing	Badminton	Volleyball	Slow-pitch softball
Fencing	Handball	*Seven Members*	*Eleven Members*
Handball	Tennis	Water polo	Field hockey
Sailing	*Five Members*	*Eight Members*	Football
Squash	Basketball	Square dance	Soccer
Racquetball	Touch Football	*Nine Members*	Speedball
Tennis	(5–11)	Softball	

Participation Objectives, Physical Education, and Team Sports

The objectives of physical education instruction and resultant team sport participation are interwoven into the objectives and goals of the entire present-day physical education profession. However, controversy centers around what exactly are the objectives of physical education. There appear to be three established "camps" or "theories" when examining the objectives of physical education and, therefore, the desired end result of participation by the student in team sports.

One "camp" identifies organic development (physical fitness) and neuromuscular development (skill development) as the primary and sole objectives of physical education and completely rejects the claims of the opposite camp. The opposite camp claims personality development, a democratic way of life, creativity, social development, and similar related objectives as being primary objectives of physical education instruction, with organic and neuromuscular development being less important. The third group subscribes

Fig. 39.1 Soccer is a team sport popular throughout the world. Courtesy of Springfield College.

to a combination of the philosophies of the diametrically opposed camps and selects organic and neuromuscular development as being primary objectives, with personality, creativity, social development, and the democratic way of living being important secondary objectives. This moderate philosophy appears to be the most realistic, logical, and acceptable.

The individual team member must function organically and neuromuscularly as a team member. The efficiency of the team is partially indicative of the organic and neuromuscular efficiency of each individual team member. Weaknesses of individual team members, in terms of organic development and/or neuromuscular development, will have a disastrous effect upon the optimum success, or lack of success, of the team. The individual physical education teacher must therefore emphasize individual organic and neuromuscular development prior to emphasis of and expectations concerning organic and neuromuscular development of the team. Conversely, personality, socialization, creativity, democratic way of life, and related objectives will most advantageously be an outgrowth of actual team participation. These outcomes are not, however, automatic and must actually be cultivated. The physical education teacher and/or coach who considers such important secondary outcomes to be automatically attained is making a grave educational error.

Separation of physical education objectives and team sport participation objectives is an impossible task. The two are truly interwoven and complemented by one another. Those who attempt to separate physical education instruction and team sports participation are doing an injustice to the individual physical education students and team sport participants.

Fig. 39.2 Modern teaching methods in baseball include the use of videotapes and pitching machines. Courtesy of *JOPER*.

THE TEACHING OF TEAM SPORTS

Learning is certainly a complicated process, whether the task to be learned is of a mental, physical, or combination mental-physical nature, Though learning theories are equally complicated in nature, there appear to be two basic philosophies of those who profess to explain the mechanisms and manner in which an individual learns. One group of learning theorists are proponents of the Stimulus Response (S–R) Concept, or what is sometimes referred to as the Association Concept. A second philosophy of the theory of learning is categorized as the Gestalt Theory, often referred to as the field or cognitive theory.

The S–R (Association) Learning Theory

The stimulus-reponse theory has evolved from the cognitive theory, and is considered by many to be a more scientific approach to learning. The basic premise of the S–R theory is that the individual will "learn" and retain those experiences which are satisfying and are positively reinforced and, conversely, will not "learn" or retain those experiences which are not satisfying and are, therefore, negatively reinforced. The S–R theory, therefore, derives its name from the relationship of the stimulus to the response. Fundamentally, if the stimulus is favorably reinforced, it is assumed that the act is more likely to be "learned" and retained than if the stimulus is negatively reinforced. There are a number of "subtheories" within the broad philosophy of the S–R Concept. The Thorndike learning theory is categorized as "Connectionism," due to its strong emphasis upon the relationship between the stimulus and the response. Thorndike professed that a strong bond must be developed between the stimulus and the response, and the connections or bonds are developed through learning by the trial and error method. Thorndike (1872–1949), possibly the foremost of S–R theorists, is often remembered for his three Laws of Learning—the Laws of readiness, of exercise, and of effect. Guthrie's (1886–1959) "Contiguity Theory" also emphasizes the association between the stimulus and the response. In addition, however, Guthrie's theory states that what is retained is dependent upon the time span between the stimulus and the response. Guthrie felt that the response must be immediately after the stimulus for retention to occur. The "Reinforcement S–R Theory" of Hull (1884–1952) emphasizes the importance of the neural response, or reinforcement, which results in a drive, or a motivating or energizing factor, within the learner. Skinner's (1904) "Operant Conditioning Theory" emphasizes the situation and environment of the learner during the period of reinforcement to the stimulus. The Operant Conditioning Theory emphasizes that learners will be likely to learn, or repeat what they are actually doing during the period of reinforcement.

Of first importance to the physical education teacher or coach involved in the teaching of team sports by the stimulus-response theory is the relationship of the stimulus to the response. This theory emphasizes that, whether instructing the team member as an individual or instructing the team as a team, primary concern must be given to the relationship between the presented stimulus and the resulting response. Obviously, to create this relationship requires extensive prethought and planning regarding the presentation of skills to the individual team member or the entire team by the physical education teacher or coach.

Cognitive Theory (Gestalt or Field Theory)

Basic to the philosophy of the cognitive theorists is the assumption that the individual learns best when the learning situation is presented as an entire "happening" and not as a stimulus requiring a specific response. The Gestalt theorists feel that perception is based upon whole concepts, and not concepts which can be divided into stimuli and responses. Gestalt psychologists emphasize signs and symbols which, it is thought, lead the learner to the correct choice of solutions to the presented problem. To the Gestalt followers, stimuli and responses are nothing more than signs which are utilized for the solution of the presented problem. Though there are differences of opinion among the various cognitive theorists (Wertheimer, 1880–1943, Koffka, 1886–1941, Kohler, 1887, Tolman, 1886–1959, Lewin, 1890–1947), the basic premise that the individual learns concepts when they are presented as an entire situation, in contrast to the emphasis of stimuli and responses, is persistent throughout each of the cognitive theorist's individual philosophies.

SUMMARY

The Place of Team Sports in Physical Education Instruction

Team sports certainly hold a very prominent position within present-day physical education programs. Historically, one can trace the development of this emphasis from the Greek and Roman times through the Middle Ages, the Renaissance Period, the Naturalism Period, and in the United States beginning approximately 1850. Today, between 20 and 30 team sports, ranging from two-member teams to eleven-member teams, can be found in many physical education curricula. Examination of the objectives of physical education provides support to the involvement of physical education students in team sports. However, team sport involvement must not be at the expense of individual development of accepted objectives of physical education instruction. One must consider ultimately the purposes of physical education instruction in our present-day educational structure, select the most desirable method of instruction to suit those purposes, and dedicate oneself to the accomplishment of such objectives in each and every student. Upon such analysis, the place of team sports, and the method of instruction, will be properly established so as to most advantageously affect those of greatest consideration—the students in physical education classes on all educational levels.

REFERENCES

Bacon, F. 1938. *The advancement of learning and new Atlantis.* London: Oxford University Press.

Burgess, W. C. 1959. *The life of Thomas Dennison Wood, M.D., and his contributions to health, education, and physical education.* Ed.D. project. Columbia University.

Burr, H. S. 1960. *The neural basis of human behavior.* Springfield, Ill.: Charles C Thomas.

Durant, J. (ed.), 1956. *Yesterday in sports.* New York: A. S. Barnes.

Durant, J., and O. Bettman 1952. *Pictorial history of American sports.* New York: A. S. Barnes.

Hackensmith, C. W. 1966. *History of physical education.* New York: Harper & Row.

Kraus, H., and R. P. Hirschland 1953. Muscular fitness and health. *JOHPER* **24,** 10, (December).

Lee, M., and B. L. Bennett 1960. This is our heritage. *JOHPER* **31,** (April): 25–85.

Leonard, F. E. 1919. *Pioneers of modern physical training.* New York: Association Press.

Manchester, H. 1931. *Four centuries of sport in America, 1490–1890.* New York: Derrydale.

Means, L. E., and K. Jack 1965. *Physical education activities, sports and games.* Dubuque, Iowa: Wm. C. Brown.

Menke, F. E. 1963. *Encyclopedia of sports.* New York: A. S. Barnes.

Rainwater, C. A. 1922. *The play movement in the United States.* Chicago: University of Chicago Press.

——— 1972. *Res. Quart.* Special Issue. Skill Learning and Performance. *JOHPER* **43,** 3, (October).

Rousseau, J. J. 1909. *Emile: or concerning education.* Lexington, Mass.: D.C. Heath.

Savage, H. J. *et al.* 1929. American college athletics. *Bull.* **23.** Carnegie Foundation, New York: The Carnegie Foundation for the Advancement of Teaching.

Seaton, D. C., I. E. Clayton, H. C. Leibee, and L. Messersmith 1965. *Physical education handbook.* Englewood Cliffs, N.J.: Prentice-Hall.

Singer, N. 1972. *Coaching, athletics, and psychology.* New York: McGraw-Hill.

Tutko, T. A., and J. W. Richards 1971. *Psychology of coaching,* Boston: Allyn and Bacon.

Van Dalen, D. B., E. D. Mitchell, and B. L. Bennett 1956. *A world history of physical education.* Englewood Cliffs, N.J.: Prentice-Hall.

Wilson, P. K. *et al.* 1971. What do we mean by the expert in motor learning? *JOHPER,* (June): 24–25.

Wilson, P. K. 1967. Physical education, to be or not to be. *Phys. Educ.* **24,** 4, (December).

40

Tennis

Two articles on tennis were required to cover this fast-growing sport. Joanna Davenport begins with a brief summary of the historical development of tennis, alludes to the equipment used, and explains the nature of the game.

W. E. Murphy's article, written in 1960, covers class organization, progressive steps in teaching ground strokes, practice drills for use in teaching. These articles should prove helpful for those who teach or who are learning to play tennis. RBF

Tennis

Joanna Davenport

HISTORY

The modern game of tennis (or lawn tennis as it is formally known) was invented by an Englishman, Major Walter Clopton Wingfield, in 1873. Wingfield accomplished this task by taking elements of several older ball games and combining them with some clever innovations of his own. The next year tennis was introduced to the United States by Mary E. Outerbridge who brought the game home with her after playing it in Bermuda. It was literally a game to be played on grass and for many years was a leisurely game played by wealthy people who had large lawns or who were members of clubs which had courts. As the game developed, it became faster and more strategic. Soon tournaments were sponsored and it was evident that a national association was needed in order to standardize the game as playing conditions were different throughout the country. Consequently, the United States Lawn Tennis Association was founded in 1881, the first such lawn tennis organization in the world. This organization has been the dominant force behind amateur tennis in this country. Through its influence, the game has spread to schools and other institutions and has been adapted to courts which have surfaces made of something other than grass.

In 1900 international competition was inaugurated with the introduction of the Davis Cup, a cup contested for every year by men's teams of the world. This event resulted in the formation of the International Lawn Tennis Federation which encompasses all the tennis nations. Due to this federation, the rules and regulations for the game are standard throughout the world. There are now many other international contests in addition to the Davis Cup.

At present tennis is one of the most popular individual sports and is within the reach of all regardless of economic circumstances. There is a professional tennis circuit for both men and women and its successful growth is indicated by the fact that the yearly earnings of the top players is expressed in six figures. There are now over 11 million tennis players in the United States. It is estimated that new indoor facilities are being built at the rate of one a day. Whether tennis is played leisurely or strenuously or engaged in by a youngster or a person in later years, it is definitely a game for a lifetime.

EQUIPMENT AND FACILITIES

The only equipment needed to play tennis is a racket, balls, and tennis shoes. Until recently rackets were almost always made of wood, but are now also made of steel, aluminum, fiberglass, and graphite. They vary in price from relatively inexpensive to costly and are strung with either nylon, nylon composition, or catgut, the latter being the most expensive. Balls have traditionally been white but more companies are now manufacturing colored balls.

The usual outdoor court surfaces are concrete, asphalt, clay, and grass. With the present boom in indoor tennis, synthetic surfaces have been developed.

Most schools and public parks use concrete or asphalt on their courts. However, many excellent physical education programs operate without courts and basic skills are taught using whatever is available in the gymnasium or on the playground.

An ideal adjunct to tennis courts is a backboard against which players may practice in solitude. Schools which do not have backboards can substitute the walls of the gymnasium and the outside walls of the school. Other valuable teaching aids are ball-boy machines and stroke developers.

The traditional dress for tennis has always been white. Today, however, it has become acceptable to wear colors on the courts.

TENNIS CONTENT

Because of the new emphasis on carry-over sports in physical education programs, most upper level schools offer tennis as one of the activities. More and more communities are building public tennis courts; tennis camps and clinics are increasing in numbers; and most clubs, public or private, have a professional in attendance.

The basic skills in tennis consist of the forehand (Fig. 40.1), backhand, and serve. A beginner who acquires the rudiments of these three skills and learns the rules and how to score can play the game. The first element taught is how to hold the racket. The most common grip is known as the Eastern forehand grip which consists of grasping the racket in the same manner as in shaking someone's hand. This grip can be used by the beginner to start the ball (courtesy stroke) on the forehand and on the serve. For the backhand, the hand is moved slightly so there will be more power behind the racket. There are two schools of thought on this backhand grip: some teach that the thumb should remain around the racket, while others propose that the thumb should be up behind the racket. After the grip, the courtesy stroke is taught in order that the player may start the ball to an opponent or to the backboard. The forehand is usually taught next, as this stroke is the most often used in a game. The backhand should also be stressed early in instruction so that a person does not favor the forehand and consequently have a glaring weakness. The serve is taught last as it is considered the most difficult stroke in tennis. Its difficulty lies in the fact that there are two moving objects—a ball that is seen and a racket that is not seen—that must be so synchronized that they meet in the same place in the air space above the player. The importance of the serve cannot be overemphasized because it puts the ball in play for every point. As a beginner is learning the above fundamentals, it is important also to emphasize body position and footwork. Tennis players constantly place their bodies in good positions to hit the ball efficiently. They must be ever ready to move in relation to the force and angle of the ball. A good objective for beginning tennis players is to stroke through the ball so the swings become grooved.

Many authorities also teach the volley to beginners. Consequently, when playing doubles, even beginners would have one person at the net and one in the backcourt for the start of each point. The volley is considered to be the easiest stroke in the game because one does not need to allow for the

Fig. 40.1 The forehand stroke is usually the first one to be learned. Courtesy of Washington State University.

Fig. 40.2 The two-handed backhand shot has now been adopted by many top players. Courtesy of NCAA.

rebound of the ball from the court nor does one need to execute a full swing.

As players advance, they add to their repertoire of strokes the smash, the lob, and spin serves. The smash executed correctly is considered a sure point in tennis. The forcefulness of the stroke with its downward momentum is usually too powerful for the opponent to make a successful return. The lob is a most effective stroke and is usually not emphasized enough in instruction. It can be used not only defensively but offensively as well. A player who can lob well often forces an opponent to commit many errors due to the frustration of receiving slow, high balls. A serve with spin can be an invaluable weapon as the rebound of the ball is not certain and makes return difficult.

Strategies of play are learned through competition and analysis of opponents' weaknesses and strengths. Singles and doubles have unique strategies and it is a common contention that the games are entirely different. Doubles is a team effort in which two partners must work together to have a winning combination, whereas in singles players must rely only on themselves. As can be expected, doubles play is not as strenuous as singles and many people, as they get older, play doubles exclusively. No matter which game is played, the ultimate strategic objective is either to place the ball so the opponent cannot retrieve it or to force the opponent to make an error.

In conclusion, tennis is an activity that is easy, fun, and capable of being played by both sexes. The equipment is relatively inexpensive and play can now be indoors as well as outdoors. Tennis is played all over the world and participants can enjoy the game most of their lives.

REFERENCES

American Association for Health, Physical Education and Recreation 1967. *Ideas for tennis instruction.* (Rev. ed.) Washington, D.C.: AAHPER.

Barnaby, J. M. 1969. *Racket work: the key to tennis.* Boston: Allyn and Bacon.

Cummings, P. 1957. *American tennis.* Boston: Little, Brown.

Driver, H. 1964. *Tennis for teachers.* Madison, Wisc.: H. I. Driver.

Grimsley, W. 1971. *Tennis: its history, people and events.* Englewood Cliffs, N.J.: Prentice-Hall.

Hendrix, J. 1968. *Fundamentals of tennis.* Columbus, Ohio: Merrill.

Johnson, J., and P. Xanthos 1967. *Tennis.* Dubuque, Iowa: Wm. C. Brown.

Kenfield, J. F., Jr. 1971. *Teaching and coaching tennis.* (2nd ed.) Dubuque, Iowa: Wm. C. Brown.

United States Lawn Tennis Association, published annually. *The official USLTA yearbook and tennis guide.* Lynn, Mass.: H. O. Zimman.

Techniques for Teaching Tennis*
William E. Murphy

The instructor can most easily maintain interest and enthusiasm when teaching tennis to a group by employing a simplified method of instruction that progresses logically from easy to difficult, from simple to complex. The system should have clearly defined levels of achievement, which are well within the student's abilities, for the confidence that comes to a player when he attains proficiency at one level will encourage him to work hard toward the attainment of the next more difficult level. The mechanics of each stroke should be demonstrated and described for the student, and work toward the mastery of them should be presented in a specific manner. Definite levels of play, through which he can progress, should be defined for the student.

EXPLAIN, DEMONSTRATE

Teaching a sports activity begins logically with an explanation of the idea and purpose of the game. As knowledge of an activity increases so does interest and enthusiasm.

*   Reprinted with permission from *JOPER* **31,** 3, (March), 1960.

Next, the instructor explains and demonstrates the strokes used in play, starting with the forehand drive. Stand in the middle of the court, or near the baseline, and mark several dummy swings while explaining the basic technique of the stroke. Have a student toss a ball so that it bounces into your hitting area; then hit it over the net, using the forehand stroke. Make several such hits, at slow speed, to give class members a clear picture of the stroke. Emphasis should be placed on the importance of the follow through of the swing, with a demonstration of how the racket guides or steers the ball in the direction intended.

Explain the backhand stroke briefly and demonstrate it in the same manner, using a dummy swing first and then hitting a tossed ball.

Then explain and demonstrate the service, serving several balls from each side of the center mark. These serves should be made slowly at first, to give the students a clear picture of the technique involved, and then at greater speed to show what the complete or finished serve looks like.

Briefly explain and demonstrate the advanced strokes, including the volley, the half-volley, the lob, and the overhead smash, again by hitting tossed balls.

All explanations and demonstrations should be made as concise and brief as possible. Remember that in the area of motor skills, "telling isn't teaching," and that "we learn what we practice." Pupils are anxious to get on with the game and to start hitting balls. Prolonged verbal advice, particularly at this stage of the learning process, tends to decrease interest. "Explain, demonstrate, and practice" should be the order followed by the instructor, but the emphasis should be on practice.

After the simple demonstration of the strokes of the game, the group is ready to begin practice in the basic strokes. Learning is facilitated if members of the class are divided into small groups of equal, or near equal, ability. All may be beginners, but there will be differences in their ability to judge the flight of a tennis ball or to time the swing of the racket. A simple wall-test will reveal such differences. Have each student try to keep the ball in play against a wall when standing about 20 feet from it. Careful observation will enable the instructor to classify each group member with regard to his ability. The group can then be broken down into small homogeneous groups of either 2, 3, or 4 players each.

PROGRESSIVE STEPS IN TEACHING THE GROUND STROKES

In teaching the forehand stroke, the instructor should first describe, explain, and demonstrate the mechanical parts of correct form. Practice drills through which this form may be acquired should follow. These drills should move progressively from easy to difficult. The order used by many successful coaches is (1) the swing, (2) hitting a dropped ball, (3) hitting a tossed ball, (4) running to hit a tossed ball, and (5) rallying. The student should consider each level not an end in itself but an important step in the total plan. He should strive to acquire some degree of proficiency at each level before moving on to the succeeding one.

The Swing

When working with a group on simple swing drills, the instructor should have the group spread out on the court in the area surrounding the baseline. Each student should be 8 to 10 feet away from the class member nearest him in all directions, to prevent a clash of rackets or possible injury to someone. The group will be properly spaced if each member can turn completely around while holding his racket extended at waist level without touching another player's racket. The instructor should stand between the net and the service line, facing the students. Left-handed players should be to the left of the instructor, when the group is working on forehands, and to the right of the instructor when backhands are being practiced.

Lead the class through practice of the swing, emphasizing the main points of form. It is helpful to explain and demonstrate the backhand grip during the first lesson, because beginning students are curious about it. As the swing is practiced, walk among the students and check each student's swing, making necessary suggestions. The students can check each other's swings at this time, also.

Hitting a Dropped Ball

A good method of learning the feeder stroke (drop and hit) is for class members to hit the ball against the fence surrounding the court while working in pairs. One player hits while the other stands behind him and coaches him and checks his swing. The hitter stands about three feet away from the fence. With the racket in the racket-back position, he reaches out with his left hand toward what would be his right net post if he were standing on the baseline of a tennis court. With his palm held upward, he lets the ball roll off the tips of his fingers and drop to the ground. A few practice drops will show him how high he should hold his left hand when dropping, to make the ball bounce to about waist level.

He watches the ball carefully, and just before it reaches waist level, he steps toward it with his left foot, transferring his weight to this foot. He swings the racket forward, meanwhile, "through the ball" to the correct finish position of the stroke.

Spend time on the feeder stroke until students have become proficient at it. They can alternate hitting and coaching while the instructor moves along the line offering suggestions and checking each pair.

Hitting a Tossed Ball

The next step in the development of the stroke introduces a new technique for the player to master—timing the swing to the oncoming ball so as to meet it at the proper point of contact, just opposite the left hip. This will not be difficult to do if the correct swing has been learned and if the ball is tossed easily to the hitter. Correct timing becomes increasingly difficult as the speed of the toss and the swing is increased so it is best to begin with an easily tossed ball and with a very easy swing.

Begin by hitting against the fence. One player can hit, while his partners toss, coach and retrieve. Draw a line on the court about six feet in front of the hitter, who stands about 30 feet away from the fence. The tosser tries to toss the ball so that it bounces on the line.

Accuracy, rather than speed, should be stressed. Encourage accuracy by a contest to see who can first hit 10 consecutive balls back to the tosser. The instructor can make individual corrections, where necessary, in a student's swing.

When the majority of the class has learned to make several consecutive good hits by starting the swing from a hitting (sideways) position, all can begin to hit tossed balls by starting from a waiting position, facing the net. As the ball is tossed, the hitter turns into a sideways position by swinging his left foot forward and pivoting on the ball of his right foot. He swings the racket backward while making the pivot and then forward to meet the ball as it arrives opposite the hitter's left hip.

After a short practice session hitting toward the fence, students should practice hitting tossed balls while on the court. Here again, the class should be divided into small groups of two, three, or four depending upon class size and space available. The hitter stands about three feet behind the baseline; the tosser is on the opposite side of, and close to, the net. He makes the toss so that the ball bounces to the forehand side of the hitter, who merely pivots and strokes the ball toward the tosser. A retriever stands on the tosser's side of the net, against the fence, and returns the balls to the tosser by rolling them on the ground against the net. If necessary, a fourth player acts as coach for the hitter. When conditions are crowded and there is danger of the tosser being hit by badly aimed balls, he should kneel behind the net during the drill.

Running to Hit a Tossed Ball

During the tossed ball drills the students will get some practice in footwork as they turn from a waiting position to hit a ball. Additional practice in footwork is necessary, however, and can be provided by having the hitters run a few steps to a ball that is tossed eight to ten feet away from them. The instructor should stress the importance of doing the pivot and backswing simultaneously so that the running is done with the racket well on its way to the racket-back position.

The hitter will not always get to the ball with his feet in the proper hitting position, with the left foot forward. Quite often he will have to make some adjustments in his steps as he runs to the ball by taking small, short skipping steps as he nears the point at which he intends to make his swing. These short steps, if necessary, should be taken at the last moment by advancing the right foot forward to a position even with the left foot and then skipping the left foot forward to its proper position in the stance.

Court arrangement for this drill is similar to that used in the previous tossed ball drill. Hitter, tosser, coach, and retriever work as a unit. Spread the units sufficiently so there is ample room for running.

In all drills, rotate the groups frequently so that all players get equal hitting practice. Do not spend too much time working with one group; make certain each player receives some individual attention.

To prevent wasting time on retrieving balls, it is wise to have several dozen balls available for class use.

Rallying

The final stage in learning the groundstrokes is rallying. If the class is large and only a few courts are available, it is difficult and sometimes impossible for the entire class to rally at the same time. With a beginners class, four players to a court is the maximum number for safety reasons and for efficient learning.

Divide a large class into two or more sections. One group can rally on a few courts while the others, using only one court, can get additional practice on one of the other levels of development, dependent upon the instructor's judgment of what practice is needed. Rotate the sections from time to time, so they are allotted equal rallying time.

In rallying, the player stands a foot or two behind his baseline and, using the feeder stroke, drops and hits the ball to his partner, who is standing on the opposite side of the net, also a foot or two behind the baseline. All hits should be directed to a player's forehand, but if the ball goes to the backhand side the player should do his best to return it. In the early stages of the learning process, students remain near the baseline while rallying. Some balls will be played on the second or third bounce, while others will come to the player on the first bounce. In either case, the student learns to time and judge the ball. As he becomes more proficient, he should play every ball on the first bounce, moving forward to get into position to play a shot and immediately moving backward again to the vicinity of the baseline.

Concentrate on accuracy and steadiness at this time by having each group of two students count the number of times they can hit the ball before a miss is made.

THE BACKHAND

Development of the backhand proceeds along the same lines as the forehand, with one exception—the dropped ball drill can be eliminated. The position of the arms is such in dropping and hitting backhand that it makes for an awkward stroke. When rallying on the backhand, use the forehand drop-and-hit to start the rally.

THE SERVE

Practice drills for the serve differ somewhat from those used for the forehand and backhand drives. The dummy swing can be practiced as it was for the forehand and backhand, with the entire group spread out on the court. Hitting practice, however, is best begun by dividing the group into small units of two players. One serves the ball to his partner, who acts as a target by standing against the fence. The hitter stands about 36 feet from the target player, who catches the served ball or retrieves it when it comes to rest after bouncing off the fence, and returns it to the server. The server should stress control and accuracy; speed is unimportant at this stage of development. The instructor moves along the line of servers and coaches as necessary. Rotate the units from time to time so that all players get equal serving time.

Eventually students practice serving on the court, trying to serve the ball into the proper service area. Twelve players to a court, six on each baseline, can practice serving with no danger of injury to any player. Be certain that no player moves forward to the net to retrieve netted balls while other players on the same court are serving. The entire group on any one court serves or retrieves simultaneously.

THE ADVANCED STROKES

Class arrangements similar to those used for the basic strokes can be used when working on advanced strokes—the volley, the lob, the overhead smash. Begin with clear, concise explanations and demonstrations of these strokes. Hitting practice follows, with the group first hitting tossed balls and then hitting stroked balls. Emphasis in all drills should be on hitting practice and not on dummy swing drills or explanations and demonstrations.

41

Track and Field

Men's Track and Field

Wilton B. Wright and John T. Powell

INTRODUCTION

Track and field is one of the most popular sports on the international scene. No other sport in which individuals participate on an amateur basis has the universal popularity of track and field. It is contested on outdoor facilities during warm seasons and in recent years numerous indoor facilities have been constructed which make competition possible during colder, inclement seasons.

Many of the events that make up the sport are activities that are natural to life and find their roots in the activities of early civilizations as well as in early military tactics. Running, jumping, and throwing form the fundamental and functional movements of life beginning in early childhood and extending through adolescence, adulthood, and even old age.

Participation in the sport is increasing. This is due to the popularity and growth of programs for girls and women in schools. Another segment of the population being drawn into the sport is the over-40 group. Masters track and field programs have gained great popularity on a worldwide basis, even to the extent that world championships are held on alternate years.

Because of the diversified nature of the events in track and field (14–16 individual events in a meet) participants are found with varying body builds and physiques. A general classification places the heavier individuals in the throwing events, medium-weight individuals in the jumping events and the sprint events, and lighter individuals in the distance events. Few other sports offer the variety found in track and field.

Although the main purpose of competition is to defeat the other contestants in the event, winning is not the goal of most participants. Victory produces satisfaction, but only victory accompanied by greater height, farther distance, or faster time should leave the athlete with the feeling of accomplishment.

JAVELIN THROWING

This is the only true throwing event of field athletics—delivery action being very similar to that of the overhand motion of a baseball pitcher as he delivers the ball over the plate.

The javelin is thrown from behind a slight arc marked on the ground at the end of a run up of about 120′. The point of the javelin must strike the ground before any other part of the javelin hits the surface, but there is no need for the javelin to stick in the ground for a good throw to be recorded. Rules specifically state that the spear must be thrown over the shoulder, neither slung nor hurled, and that an athlete may not turn completely around (360°) in the process of the throw.

The modern javelin consists of a metal head, a shaft, and a cord grip. The shaft is made of either metal or wood. There are different lengths and weights of javelins, as well as many other dimensional differences for each age group. Some are given on the next page.

	Minimum length	Minimum weight
All girls, junior and intermediate boys	7', 2½"	1 lb, 5¼ oz
Boys 17–19	7', 6¾"	1 lb, 8½ oz
Men	8', 6"	1 lb, 12 oz
Women	7', 2½"	1 lb, 5¼ oz

To be thrown correctly the javelin must be held at the grip and, though there are three main ways of gripping, the pull should be exerted on the back of the binding so that the javelin will lie diagonally across the palm.

The athlete starts the run up with the implement above one shoulder, point of the javelin down, carrying arm bent.

The purpose is to accumulate speed gradually in the run, to place the spear as far behind the body weight as possible, and to turn the body into a position at delivery where the generated speed can be powerfully applied into the shaft, through as long a range as possible, to fling the javelin on its way. Three hundred feet is a world-class throw.

Excellent throwing depends upon controlled speed, coordination of many movements, and overall body condition. Much stress is placed on muscles and joints, and weight training is essential during the off-season. Pulley weights which can be progressively increased in poundage are particularly valuable. Their use will not only increase strength but aid with extension and range of joints. This apparatus (properly used) is of prime importance to the thrower who should include in the training regimen exercises for arms, shoulders, trunk, thighs, hips, and legs.

Sprinting and the hip mobility acquired through high hurdling are necessary. Very careful attention shall be given to the various aspects of the throw before it is blended into allout efforts in practice and competition.

Javelin throwing is strenuous and helps to create shoulder power and mobility, dorsal flexibility and strong lower limbs. Further, because it requires so much concentration on fine detail and blending of many movements into one continuous flow of movement, this event is not for the crude, powerful athlete, but rather for the more patient, careful, analytical type who is prepared to spend many hours perfecting details to have them blend into power application.

Injuries to the arm, shoulder, and trunk are common. The most troublesome injury to the elbow is called "javelin elbow." This is common to many sports and is frequently caused by poor condition. Athletes in poor condition cannot follow through after release because they are not strong enough to throw with such whip. Gradual throwing and *always* following through after adequate strengthening of the upper arm help prevent this complaint.

DISCUS THROWING

Actually, the discus is not thrown, but slung, by a straight arm from a cement-based circle 8′ 2½″ in diameter. The athlete must enter the circle from the rear half and usually performs at least a 360° turn in the circle before release of the implement which must land within a premarked 45° sector. After the sling the athlete retires from the rear half of the circle and each effort is measured by a nonstretch tape, unless the athlete has stepped onto or outside the circle in the process of the effort, or forward of the front half of the circle before the distance of the sling has been measured and recorded. Athletes usually are allowed six efforts each, the best effort of all winning the contest.

Although the circle diameter remains the same for all contests by either sex and for each age group, the weight of the discus, in each case, is different.

The dimensions of discuses are:

Men—4 lbs, 6.5 oz
Women—2 lbs, 3.2 oz
All girls, junior, and intermediate boys—2 lbs, 3.2 oz
Boys (17–19 years of age)—3 lbs, 5 oz

For the two heavier weights the diameter of the discus is 8″, otherwise its diameter is 7″.

A large hand to control the discus and well-developed arms and shoulders as well as powerful thighs for driving the hips into action before the release of the discus are essential elements in the makeup of the discus specialist.

Speed of reaction, loin mobility, and shoulder flexibility increase effectiveness. Muscular weight and height are of great advantage to enable an athlete of either sex to sail the discus through the air at an angle of about 35°.

The activity itself requires physical cleverness, great control and power for the best use of the driving turn which allows the body to transfer vast force, *at speed,* to the implement throughout a great range, before and at delivery. A low center of gravity, absolute muscular stability, and violent explosive power are all necessary to success in slinging the discus.

Much running, with short, sharp, repeated dashes, is a necessary component of training, as are all forms of weight training. Weight lifting is also advocated and power tests such as the vertical jump and the standing long jump, together with leg, back, and grip dynamometer tests are recommended.

As the event requires much control in a relatively small area, much practice in the circle, correctly dressed for competition with accurately weighed and measured impedimenta, is essential. The full action should be practiced and little time spent on standing efforts.

When a right-handed discus thrower performs, no one should be allowed in front of the circle to the athlete's right-hand side (left-hand side for left-handed throwers). Particular care should be taken that *no one* is allowed to throw a discus back, from where it landed, to the circle. Athletes should be deterred from practice throwing one to the other. Discuses should be carried or rolled back to the performer. The most sensible safety precaution is to have a discus (metal) cage made, behind which spectators and officials are sited for obvious reasons.

The activity itself does not develop great muscular strength or agility but both these qualities are necessary for successful performance of the activity. It should be understood that a person must get fit to perform an activity well and that it is not usually the activity which gives balance, power, agility, strength, speed, mobility, or endurance.

Before individuals even consider training for an activity such as discus throwing it is highly desirable that they be tested in all the areas mentioned above to detect weaknesses or strengths. When weaknesses are identified they can be worked upon, prior to training. Correct training will become purposeful and achieve its part in producing better and more consistent performance, especially in such a technical event as slinging a discus.

SHOT PUTTING

The shot is put by an explosive thrust of the shot from a starting position in which it is held between the jaw and the shoulder. The hand holding the implement may not be positioned behind the shoulder. The put is made from a 7′ circle which has a 4′ long, curved stopboard flush with the inner surface of the throwing circle. The shot must land within a sector of 45–60° (sector size determined by governing rules, i.e., AAU, NCAA) as scribed from the center of the throwing circle. The throwing pad should be constructed of concrete.

Linear momentum is gained by a glide across the throwing circle which places the putter in a position at the front of the throwing circle allowing the hips, trunk, and head to convert into a continuous rotary motion which gives impetus to the explosive thrust of the shot by the throwing arm.

A foul throw is recorded if

☐ the shot lands outside of or on the lines defining the landing sector
☐ the thrower touches the top of the circle or stopboard or any area outside of the circle with any part of the body
☐ the thrower leaves the circle after a put from other than the rear half of the circle or leaves the circle of balance immediately after or resulting from the throwing motion
☐ the finger, hand, or wrist are taped in an illegal supportive manner.

The shot, which is usually made of an iron- or brass-covered sphere for outdoor use (indoor shots are constructed of metallic pellets encased in a pliable plastic material covering), must conform to varying weights and diameters. The following lists the weights of the shots thrown in competition.

Men	16 lbs	Official weight—International, AAU, Collegiate
	12 lbs	High school
	8 lbs	Junior high school, elementary school
Women	8 lbs, 13 oz	All levels of competition

Factors essential to successful throwing are strength, speed of muscular movement, agility, and power. Large physical stature (weight and height) is of a great advantage in putting the shot.

In training for the event, large amounts of time are spent practicing the movements and techniques of the event. Aside from actual throwing, most shot putters spend considerable time training with weights to acquire power, particularly in their arms and legs. Short sprint work for speed development is also of value to shot putters.

A put of 60′ at any level is considered to be a world-class throw. Few athletes have reached distances of 70′.

HAMMER THROWING

The throwing hammer is a metallic sphere attached to a triangular handle by a strand of wire. The weight of the complete implement is 16 lbs, although a 12-lb weight is used for high school competition. The event is not contested in women's meets. Each segment of the implement (handle, wire, and ball) must conform to specifications of size as well as total weight. The maximum overall length of the implement is 3′ 11¾″. (Measurement is from end of ball to the inside of the grip portion of the handle.)

The hammer is thrown from a 7′ circle and must land within a 45° sector to be a legal throw. The surface material within the throwing circle should be constructed of concrete. The thrower may not make contact with the top of the restraining circle or the area outside of the circle during the throwing action with any part of the body. After the throw, the thrower must leave the circle by the rear half of the circle.

Momentum for the throw is built through a series (usually three) of 360° pivotal turns which position the thrower at the front of the throwing circle for the release of the hammer. Each turn should add to increased centrifugal force and speed. Good throws are a product of speed of the ball, effective radius of the ball from the rotational axis, angle of the release of the ball, and the power applied to the hammer by the thrower.

The throwing techniques of the hammer, as well as the construction of the implement, lend an element of danger to spectators of the event. The implement should not be thrown without a heavy-gauge wire cage surrounding the back and sides of the throwing circle. Caution should also be taken to

Fig. 41.1 Momentum of the hammer throw is built through a series of pivotal turns. Courtesy of Southern Connecticut State College.

keep spectators well back from the landing area as throws frequently land outside the legal 45° landing sector.

The complexity of throwing the hammer requires the athlete to spend hours of practice working on the particulars of the event. Since strength, power, speed, and balance are needed to throw the hammer, much of the practice time should be spent in training with weights, performing event-related agility exercises, and running short sprints.

While throwing the hammer does not add greatly to the physical fitness of the body, the training routines of lifting, running, and various other types of exercises do enhance an individual's physical prowess.

A throw of 230′ is a world-class throw. A few athletes have thrown in excess of 250′.

POLE VAULTING

History and Description

There is much evidence that pole vaulting originated in Ulverston, Lancashire, in England, where an ash pole of 16 feet was commonly used to enable men to cross the dikes to and from work. After a short run, the laborer planted the pole into the ditch (most were about 10-feet wide) and climbed the pole until his weight tipped it as he fell forward onto his feet from his sitting position. He then pulled the pole after him ready for the next effort.

The first competitions were for length, but modern vaulting is for height. J. Wheeler won the first English Championship in 1866 with an effort of 10 feet. In the United States, where championships were instituted in 1877, G. McNichol of the Scottish-American Athletic Club became the first titleholder at 9′ 7″. Climbing the long ash pole with a 3″ spike at its end, J. Stones won the United States championships in 1889 at 10', but directly after his victory a new rule was passed which stipulated that after the athlete had left the ground, his upper hand must not be moved nor may the lower hand pass above it. The rule pertains today. A. C. Gilbert of Yale University introduced the bamboo vaulting pole in 1902. The female bamboo was found preferable because the joints are wider apart than in the male bamboo, the whole pole is lighter in weight, and if it were to split, the break would be longitudinal, not transverse as in the male bamboo, thus lessening the chance of impalement and other injuries.

Later the steel pole was used, followed by the aluminum pole. Today, the vault is performed using a fiberglass pole which can bend as much as 90° with an athlete's full weight suspended from it—the action being more of a catapulting nature than a true vault. Present world-class vaulters exceed 18' in vaulting height.

Physical Qualities Needed

A pole-vaulter must possess courage and also have strength, particularly in the shoulder girdle, arms, and abdominal region. Ideally the athlete should be a fast sprinter, range between 5' 10" to 6' 2" in height, and have considerable gymnastic ability.

Specific mental as well as physical qualities are noted in the makeup of a vaulter. Highly intelligent and physically adept young men and women who are prepared to devote years to practice and competition are likely to succeed in the technically difficult event.

Actual practice and performance of pole vaulting will improve many of those abilities, but a great deal of diligent work is necessary to acquire sufficient skill and motor fitness to perform the event adequately.

Conditioning programs. Programs of fitness work should include:

- ☐ Much sprinting
- ☐ Sprinting with the pole
- ☐ High and long jumping, hopping, bounding, and vertical leaping to develop quick contractile power in legs, thighs, and hips
- ☐ Mobility exercises for the loin and dorsal areas
- ☐ Pole-planting practice—short and long runs
- ☐ Strong, progressive abdominal exercises of both the leg-raising and trunk-raising type. Each should increase in intensity by the lengthening of levers used, lifting or swinging additional weight, adding repetitions, and, to a lesser extent, increasing the speed of the performance
- ☐ Weight lifting and regular weight training

☐ Chinning (with the palms of the hands away from the face when grasping the high bar rather than with palms towards the body)

☐ Handstanding practice

☐ Horizontal bar and parallel bar work, tumbling and trampolining—all necessary for strength, agility, and the requisite kinesthetic awareness

☐ Rope climbing without use of legs

☐ Rope skipping from each foot and from both feet

Equipment. Poles are expensive but must be personal. Therefore, it is necessary to purchase one (preferably two) suitable to the individual's weight, height, and ability.

It is difficult to transfer a technique learned on a comparatively rigid pole to one which bends appreciably. While technique can be somewhat amended, it is better to learn on, practice with, and use known poles consistently.

Injuries. The most common injuries are sustained by the ankles. Ankle injuries occur when a pole breaks and the athlete falls either to the runway, onto the takeoff box, or awkwardly in the pit. Considering the height from which a fall will occur, the pits and surrounding area should be built up with suitably soft materials.

Other common injuries include:

☐ Shoulder joint strains, resulting from poor pole-vaulting technique.

☐ Neck and/or back injuries from falling awkwardly into an inadequately sized or builtup pit.

☐ Bruised heel as a result of inefficient takeoff position.

HIGH JUMPING

The standing high jump is no longer contested as a competitive event. However, L. Goehring of the United States leapt 5′ 5¾″ in 1915; R. C. Ewry, 5′ 5¼″ in 1901 and, as far back as 1898, Sgt. Chandler of Cork, Eire, sprang 4′ 11¾″.

The running high jump is an integral part of every modern track and field meeting. Men are now jumping over 7½′ and women are approaching the 6½′ mark. There are many techniques: scissors, back layout, Western roll, Eastern cut-off. The one with which the height of over 7′ 0″ has been cleared more than 100 times in competition is termed the straddle, where the athlete passes over the bar facing it. Since the 1968 Olympic Games the back layout has increased in popularity with both men and women.

There are two main types of straddle jumping. One, the straight-legged straddle, is taken from a very acute angle about 20° in which the jumper—usually tall—kicks along the bar with a straight leg and, in length, pivots around it. The other straddle is performed from an angle 40°, made with a fast run up of about nine strides. The performers appear to drape themselves around the bar, some parts of the body being over the bar before other parts have risen to it. In each case the landing in the builtup pit is usually on the athlete's side or back.

In both the Western roll (devised by George Horine in 1912 when he jumped 6′ 7″) and the straddle (used by David Albriton of the Ohio State University in tying the world record at 6′ 9¾″ in 1936) the takeoff is from the foot nearer the bar. It was only after the Berlin Olympics of 1936 that these techniques became popular because, prior to that date, international rules had banned any form of leap where the body crossed the bar prior to the lead foot; it was called "diving."

It is not essential to be tall to be a successful high jumper but it is an advantage to have a high center of gravity in relation to body height and weight. Expert high jumpers must be strong, particularly in the thighs and abdominal areas. High jumpers are usually good hurdlers (indicating sprinting ability and mobility) and often double in the long jump, although the basic techniques at takeoff are quite dissimilar; the last stride in high jump is long, whereas in the long jump it is somewhat shorter. The activity of high jumping develops a high coordinative skill and requires overall strength in shoulders, abdominals, hips, thighs, and legs.

Explosive power is particularly necessary as is quick reaction time. These are prerequisites to consistently excellent jumping for height. Weight lifting and weight training are especially recommended for high jumpers as are activities which raise the body weight such as chinning, wall ball exercises, rope climbing, vertical jumping, one-leg and double-leg hopping. An indispensable exercise, in and out of season, is prolonged and regular rope skipping. Mobility exercises are very necessary as is participation in basketball, squash, and/or handball. Every high jumper should enjoy sprinting; taking part in relay races is a splendid way of maintaining neuromuscular fitness.

The high jumper must practice assiduously and must understand that most faults in this event occur at takeoff. An excellent motto for any high jumper is "kick before spring" or "knee up, before spring." This ensures that the kicking leg travels from far back, on the last stride, to a very high position, above shoulder height, before the body mass has moved over the springing foot. If this is done vertical lift will ensue and then the athlete can concentrate upon the technique to be used.

It is also necessary for the athlete to learn the rules concerning the high jump, some of which are:

☐ Takeoff may be made from one foot only.

☐ An athlete may enter a competition at the height at which it has been decided to place the bar, or above that height.

☐ Three consecutive failures at any height, or heights, mean that the athlete is out of the competition.

☐ An athlete does not have to jump twice more at a given height even though he or she has failed once at that height.

☐ If there is a tie at a given height and no athlete has been capable of clearing a greater height, the *winner* is the one who cleared the bar with fewer failures at the height last cleared; if the tie still remains, the total number of failures up to and including the height last cleared are added; the one with fewer failures is the winner. However, the position for first place may still be undecided and the tying athletes and the Chief Field Judge decide whether the bar shall be raised or lowered one inch. The first to fail any height cleared by another receives second place. Track and field authorities continue to experiment in order to discover better ways of breaking ties.

It can be seen how very important it is for athletes to be so well trained and confident of their ability that it is possible to come into a competition later, or to pass a height, even though they may have failed previously.

High jumpers are so meticulous about training and warmup practices before training and/or competition that injuries are rare. The devotion to mobility exercises and strength generally keeps them free from injury.

TRIPLE JUMPING

Introduction

The event, previously known as the hop, step, and jump, is performed with the competitor taking off from a white-painted 8″ wide, 4″ thick, and 4′ long wooden board. The takeoff is from one foot, and the first landing is upon that same foot, the reverse foot is used for the second landing, and the third landing is on both feet in the pit. Measurement is the same as in the long jump.

Initially, the great performers came from Ireland and, in 1908, T. J. Ahearne created an Olympic record at 48′ 11¼″. The following year his brother Daniel, a naturalized United States citizen, created a new world record of 50′ 11″. Australians, then Japanese, and presently Europeans have dominated the event although in the past 60 years the world record has been increased by only five feet.

The triple jump is complex and physically very demanding. There is no known type of body build most suited to the event. The Irish were tall, slim men, the Australians exceedingly powerful, the Japanese were fast and slight, and the crop of European experts have all been noteworthy sprinters and muscular with magnificently developed legs and thighs.

Only one athlete of world-class has had the jump measure of the coordinated triple series of movements longer than either the step or the hop. It is accepted that the *hop* from one to the same foot is the longest distance, the step phase on to the other foot is the *shortest,* and the leap almost as long as the hop.

Fitness benefits. The effect the event has on its participants is the creation of controlled speed coupled with excellent coordination.

Conditioning programs. A physical conditioning program is of paramount importance. No triple jumper has been known to have exceeded 50′ without at least seven years of athletic experience. Women do not, as yet, compete in the event.

Physical activity should include:

- ☐ Sprinting
- ☐ Hopping for protracted distances on one foot to an even tempo
- ☐ Combining hop–step and step–jump activities into a pit to assist timing, balance, and hip mobility.
- ☐ Weight lifting (Olympic lifts)
- ☐ Weight training
- ☐ Rope skipping from one and from both feet
- ☐ Long jumping—standing and running
- ☐ Trampolining
- ☐ Vertical jump for height
- ☐ Volleyball
- ☐ Basketball
- ☐ Handball
- ☐ Squash racquets
- ☐ All forms of calisthenics

Physical qualities needed. The physical qualities needed prior to participation are speed, the ability to spring, leg and thigh power, good balance, and hip mobility. A sense of rhythm is all-important, especially in the learning stages of the event, for a cadence must be mastered and strictly adhered to in order to produce predictable distances for each phase of the effort.

Practices should be first upon grass, with each final movement made into a pit. The foot should be flat on landing so that the body weight can pass quickly over the supporting foot to enable it to drive the uprightly held trunk and forward-moving hips uninterruptedly onward. The arms, as power transmitters and balancers, must be well developed, yet the shoulders should be mobile.

Injuries. The most common injury is a "jarred" back caused by the stretching forward of the landing foot on impact after either the hop or step. There is a cessation of movement as the leg "buckles," having landed incorrectly on its heel.

Other injuries are:

☐ Muscular tears in the thigh

☐ Bruised heel

☐ Stubbed toes from loosely fitting shoes.

LONG JUMPING

The athlete runs, takes off from or behind an 8" white-painted 4" thick solid board and leaps for length into a pit (usually composed of sand and sawdust) the surface of which is on the level of the runway down which the athlete has run. The leap is measured with a nonstretch tape on a line perpendicular to the takeoff board. The distance from the forward edge of the board to the nearest indentation made by the athlete on landing constitutes the jump. Presently the men's world record is just under 29' 3" and the women's world record is just less than 23'.

This demanding sport requires—and thorough assiduous practice cultivates—sprinting ability, mobility of joints, vast explosive power, coordination and skill, powerful leg muscles, springing ability, and abdominal strength.

Most long jumpers are tall and wiry rather than stocky. They are invariably first-class sprinters.

To become fit for long jumping it is necessary to take part in activities which require a high degree of coordination and timing such as volleyball,

Fig. 41.2 Long jumping requires sprinting ability, vast explosive power, coordination, and powerful lower limb muscles. Courtesy of Luther College.

basketball, skiing, gymnastics, soccer, and weight training. Actual training for the event itself needs much patient practice at sprinting, acquiring the essential skills of running from the board, explosive extension of the hips, lower limbs, and erect trunk into the forward-upward action desired at takeoff, the cultivation of a smoothly balanced running-in-the-air action and an efficient landing position. These aspects should be learned in parts and be blended together gradually into a powerful yet continuously smooth action. Low hurdling has always been considered a useful activity for long jumpers, as have protracted hopping on one foot and abdominal exercises using weighted boots.

"Continuity" is the key word to success in long jumping. The run up is between 14–17 strides with gradual accumulation of speed; there is a settling on the last three strides with a reduction in the length of the last stride so that the body mass will pass quickly over the takeoff foot. This allows for a strong forward-upward drive from the board and preserves the speed and continuity developed. The running-in-the-air action or the "hang" style of some Europeans are the only two successful techniques used. Arms are used as balancers, and strong muscles enable first-class leapers to preserve an upright trunk throughout the action, as well as enabling them to keep the lower limbs well extended for a lengthy landing position.

Injuries are relatively few, except for bruised heel caused by the narrow takeoff board on which the athlete often catches the forward part of the heel. New treatment effects quick relief through use of ultrasonic rays.

RELAY RACING

For men and women the usual relay races are 4 × 110 yards, 4 × 220 yards, 4 × 440 yards, 4 × 880 yards, 4 × 1 mile or the corresponding metric distances and the one-mile medley sprint relay of 440–220–220–880 yards. There are also the shuttle hurdle relays of 4 × 120 yards for men and 4 × 100 meters for women, in which no baton is passed. In all relays other than shuttle races and those run around a curve, a baton is passed from hand to hand.

Except for shuttle runs, all other relays take place around a track, are most exciting, make a fitting finale to track and field athletic meets, and usually carry double the points of any other track or field event.

The speed of the baton is an important factor in relay racing, especially in the shorter races. If there is a poor baton exchange the baton's speed will be reduced and the team time will thus be greater. In all relays around a track a baton must be passed (not thrown) within a zone and, although international rules pertaining to relays have changed radically in the last 50 years, the handover of the 11¾″ hollow tube has always been made from person to person inside a given fixed area.

Fig. 41.3 Relay races are very appropriate as intramural activities. Courtesy of South Dakota State University.

In shuttle runs half of each team is at each end of the distance to be run or hurdled. Usually there are four contestants on each team so that the race will start and finish at the same line. In front of each team is a restraining line (about one yard away) and the outgoing athlete is allowed to move forward only when the incoming member of his or her team crosses it. Teams are assigned two lanes each and members of each team usually pass right shoulder to right shoulder.

The shuttle takes little space, can be adjusted to any age group, needs little organization and can accommodate large numbers of participants. Provided no baton is used or requirement made to touch an outgoing athlete by an incoming one, there are no safety hazards.

There are thus two main types of relays—the short dash type which demands little skill but great power and the endurance relays requiring pace assessment, tactical adjustment, and stamina—at speed.

The middle-distance relay runner's concern is the transference of sufficient oxygen to muscles and the ability to run well even with an oxygen debt. This athlete must learn to run fast without exaggerated movements and with great economy.

The sprint relay racer must train with others of the team so that adjustment can be made to the place within the zone where the baton is exchanged, the ideal place being where the outgoing runner is accelerating and the incoming athlete is still running fast, near the end of the zone.

Technically there are four major methods of baton passing but basically sprinters use a nonvisual pass, and longer-distance athletes—because of their comparatively slower speed and perhaps tiredness—a visual hand-over.

All coaches use relay races early in the season as team spirit-builders and as physical conditioners. Relay racing demands much of every participant and thus has exceptional training value.

An interesting aspect of 4 × 110 yards sprint relay racing is that each athlete in a team can run a different distance depending upon where the baton is handed over. These "legs" are from 90 to 130 yards. Therefore, there is a place in each foursome for the very powerful and smaller sprinter and the sprinter who, because of body mass, takes longer to attain velocity.

Any excellent teacher or coach will be able to calculate how far an athlete can run maximally and thus blend the team into an efficient running unit. Because of the fun element and the high competitive content, relays tend to produce the best in an athlete. They are excellent bases for the application of endurance at speed which is required in almost all other track and field events.

The most common injury is the torn hamstring of the short-dash relay runner. Adequate warmup, particularly of the antagonistic group of muscles of the front of the thigh, is indicated. Many relay teams are assembled suddenly at the end of a meet and participants are often weary from prior competition or have relaxed too much. As a result they may be ill-prepared for the muscular violence required of a heartily contested relay.

Relay groups should be chosen as part of the team, practice as a team and compete as a team for maximum satisfaction and safety.

HURDLE RUNNING

Hurdle races range from 50-yard indoor races to 440-yard outdoor races. The length of races and the height of the hurdles vary according to the age and sex of the runners. Table 41.1 lists data for outdoor hurdle events (indoor races are usually run at high hurdle heights over 50, 60, or 70 yards).

The relatively short distances of hurdle races make them events in which

Table 41.1

Race	Hurdle height in inches	Number of hurdles	Competitive level
120-yard high hurdles	42	10	Men—official
120-yard high hurdles	39	10	High school boys
440-yard intermediate hurdles	36	10	Men—official
330-yard intermediate hurdles	36	8	High school boys
180-yard low hurdles	30	8	High school boys
100-meter women's hurdles	33	10	Women—international
80-yard women's hurdles	30	7	Women—high school and college

Note: Metric distance for the 120-yard high hurdle race is 110 meters.
Metric distance for the 440-yard intermediate hurdle race is 400 meters.

sprint speed is a primary factor. Not all sprinters, however, are good hurdlers. In addition to sprint speed, an athlete must have other factors of flexibility, balance, and agility. Hurdle heights and stride patterns between hurdles, particularly in the official men's high hurdle race, are such that a taller athlete with sprinting ability is best suited for the event.

The runner must attempt to clear every hurdle in the lane. However, there is no penalty for knocking one down unless it is done intentionally. Both the lead leg and the trail leg must move over the top of the hurdle as the runner passes over the hurdle.

In the races which are of a definite sprint category (those fewer than 330 yards in length), the runner should leave the starting line at an all-out sprint. Starting block setting and length of initial strides out of the blocks should be adjusted in practice so that the dominant leg will be the lead leg over the hurdle. This leg should be kicked up so as to pass barely over the hurdle in a straight, yet not rigid, position. As soon as the lead leg passes over the hurdle, it should be forced down on to the track. The takeoff leg, or trail leg, should be recovered with the inside of the thigh, knee, lower leg, and foot all at the same level as the leg is snapped over the hurdle. This prevents the hurdler from gliding over the hurdle which may cause a delayed action in segmental progression. The tendency to take a short step with the recovery of the trail leg can be lessened by a high knee drive as the trail leg clears the hurdle.

As the hurdler drives into the hurdle, the upper parts of the body should lean into the hurdle. The leaning position aids in keeping the body low and close to the hurdle as well as aiding in more efficient lead leg snap and trail leg alignment. As the hurdle height decreases, the need for body lean over the hurdle also decreases.

Stride patterns are of great importance in hurdling. In that most hurdlers lead with their dominant leg and have little efficiency with a reversed leg action, a pattern of an odd number of steps should be developed between hurdles. In the high hurdles and women's hurdles, three steps are taken; in low hurdle races, seven or nine steps; and in the intermediate hurdle races, thirteen, fifteen, or seventeen steps should be the aim.

Training for hurdle races should include sprint training (start work through 330-yard distances) as well as middle-distance running, especially for intermediate hurdlers. Considerable work should be done over one, two, and three hurdles for form, balance, stride, quickness, and recovery. Weight training and flexibility programs are also essential for the hurdler.

SPRINT EVENTS

Two events in track are pure sprint events. These are the 100-yard and 220-yard dashes. The running of both events requires an all-out effort for the entire distance. The 100-yard dash is run on the straightaway portion of the

Fig. 41.4 The running of sprints requires all-out effort over the entire distance. Courtesy of Eastern Kentucky State University.

track. The 220-yard dash is started at the beginning of a curve and is completed at the end of the following straightaway portion of the track (preferred track layout).

Sprint speed, like most pure physical factors, is an inherited trait. It can, however, be increased with training. Prior to training, few athletes can run 100 yards at maximum speed and not tire and slow down before the completion of the distance. The 220-yard dash definitely requires considerable work to enable the runner to complete the distance at maximum sprint speed.

The training program of a sprinter should consist of working out of starting blocks, short bursts of intense sprint effort, running distances of 250–440 yards for increased endurance, weight training to aid speed through an increase in the strength of the legs and the arms, exercises and drills to increase the speed of neuromuscular reaction and movement, and large amounts of exercise for flexibility and total body muscle tonus. Flexibility exercises, particularly hamstring stretching, are important to a sprinter's training program, as the hamstring muscle is frequently injured in sprinting. Good running form, body lean, knee lift, heel lift, foot placement, and arm movement should receive careful attention during all running workouts as segmental efficiency adds to sprint speed.

MIDDLE-DISTANCE EVENTS

The 440-yard dash and the 880-yard run are the two intermediate distance events in a track meet. The 440, as run in world-class meets, may be considered a sprint as runners in peak condition can run the entire race at near maximum sprint speed. Regulation tracks in the United States measure 440 yards in length. Because of the distances, these two events are frequently referred to as one-lap and two-lap races.

Different physical and psychological traits are required for these events. The 440 is basically an event in which speed is the major factor. The main factor in the 880 is endurance. Many sprinters have the ability to run good 440s, but few can move up to the 880. Similarly, many one and two milers have achieved great success in the 880 but few are capable of producing the sprint speed needed to run a quality 440.

Training for both of the events should include running short sprints to cross-country distances. Speed workouts are of greater value to the 440 runner than to the 880 runner. The 880 runner, on the other hand, should spend a greater amount of training time on running distances longer than the actual distance of the race.

DISTANCE EVENTS

The distance events in track and field meets range from races of one mile to six miles. The one-mile run is contested in all track meets in which an official order of events is followed. The two- or three-mile distance is also run in men's meets. High schools usually run the two-mile distance while college and open meets usually run the three-mile distance. The six-mile distance is usually not run in other than championship meets.

Training for the distance events is very demanding. Distance runners, in order to be successful, must have a positive psychological attitude which motivates them to put in long hours of practice and drives them to continue a race even when almost exhausted. The training is perhaps more physically demanding than the training for any other track and field event. Runners have achieved success by following varied training philosophies. These philosophies include (1) running high repetitions of short sprints, (2) interval training emphasis, (3) long distance work of 15 to 20 miles, and (4) weight training for development of endurance. Many runners find that two practice sessions a day are necessary for maximum conditioning.

Distance running is a prime activity for the organic development of the body. The efficiency of the cardiorespiratory system is especially improved as a result of running. Little contribution is made to the increase in muscular strength and power of the body from distance running. This form of exercise has become one of the most popular forms of physical fitness development among middle-aged people.

REFERENCES

Doherty, J. K. 1971. *Track and field omnibook*. Swarthmore, Pa.: TAFMOP Publishers, p. 486.

———— 1963. *Modern track and field.* (2nd ed.) Englewood Cliffs, N.J.: Prentice-Hall, p. 480.

Gordon, J. A. 1972. *Track and field, changing concepts and modern techniques.* (2nd ed.) Boston: Allyn and Bacon.

Official handbook 1968. London: International Amateur Athletic Federation.

Powell, J. T. 1971. *Track and field fundamentals for teacher and coach.* (3rd ed.) Champaign, Ill.: Stipes, p. 225.

Pugh, D. L. 1967. *Javelin throwing.* (Instructional booklet.) London: Amateur Athletic Association, p. 36.

Women's Track and Field

Donnis H. Thompson

INTRODUCTION

Track and field may involve all levels of participation—from the woman who wishes to maintain physical fitness by running, to the female athlete who wants to become an accomplished international performer.

As an activity, track and field in and of itself cannot develop all the positive attributes needed by the female but it can provide an opportunity for a maximum expenditure of energy, which is what many women need today. It can provide physical, mental, and emotional development.

Track and field develops and helps to maintain the effective functioning of the heart and circulatory system, aids in relaxation and releasing nervous energy, improves digestion (probably by reducing tension), helps to control obesity, and improves the capacity of the respiratory system. It is valuable for all age groups, too.

Starting

Starting is the pivotal part of the race; it must be as smooth and rhythmical as any other movement in the race. The basic concern is to reach top speed as quickly as possible. Acceleration must follow the initial thrust so closely that it becomes part of the same movement. Thus, when the gun is fired the function of starting blocks is to give maximum efficiency to the thrust of the first drive forward.

Three commands are given in the start: "Take your mark," "Set," and "Go." Each requires a change in body positions.

"Take your mark." There are four points to remember when taking the stance for the start.

581

Fig. 41.5 Starting is the crucial part of the race. Courtesy of Washington State University.

☐ From a position well in front of the starting line, the runner stoops down and walks backwards into the block, pressing both feet firmly against the blocks, just touching the ground.

☐ The hands are placed behind the starting line exactly shoulderwidth apart and support the body with the fingertips.

☐ Arms should be straightened to keep shoulders high.

☐ The body is balanced between the hands and knee of the back leg, which is resting on the ground. The eyes are focused three to five inches in front of the line. The entire position should be one of comfort and alertness.

"Set." On the command "Set," all movements should be made slowly and deliberately so that the body's delicate poise is not disturbed.

Hips are slightly higher if the runner's blocks are closely spaced, and to the level of the shoulders if the blocks are farther apart. Body weight shifts forward six to eight inches so that the shoulders extend to, or a few inches beyond, the starting line. At this point, arm and finger strength is crucial. Only those who have developed this strength can successfully execute the necessary body lean. Both arms remain quite straight, but elbows are not locked. Feet remain in firm contact with both blocks. The head is naturally aligned with the body, neither dropping below body level nor rising above it.

"**Go.**" Action immediately follows "Go" or the firing of the starting gun. Concentration and repeated practice are the only ways to cut down reaction time and achieve consistently good starts. When the signal sounds, mind and body are tuned to instant response. One arm is thrust forward as if about to shake hands; the other is thrust back. Arm movements should be just powerful enough to balance the actions of the legs; if exaggerated, they will upset the body's balance. The thrust of the legs against the blocks occurs practically simultaneously. The back leg comes forward for the first stride; the front leg continues to push against the block until that leg is straight, thus providing maximum drive in propelling the body forward. Arm and leg motions follow each other within a split second and should allow the body to drive out of the blocks in a forward and upward movement. The body remains low for 10 to 15 yards.

Many beginners feel that they are losing their balance on the first few strides. This is frequently a good sign. To prevent falling, the knees should be raised higher and arms and legs moved faster. One should not stop suddenly when practicing starts but slow down gradually to a halt.

Sprints

Nationally, distances are run in either meters or yards. Locally, and for national girls (aged 14 to 17), sprinting races are 50, 60, and 75 yards. Actually, any race up to 200 meters (220 yards) is considered a sprint for the female.

There are two methods of getting from one place to another faster than an opponent:

☐ Moving the legs faster.
☐ Using a longer stride and one that carries the runner low to the ground.

Good sprint form. The following characteristics of good running form are not natural and must be practiced:

☐ high knee action
☐ good foreleg reach
☐ landing high on toes
☐ good arm action
☐ bouncing forward, not up
☐ good forward lean (20°)
☐ running tall, with back straight
☐ relaxation (loose hands and loose neck and face muscles)

Leg action: high knee action. All running should be performed with knees high. The runner should land high on her toes. Knees must be lifted high to obtain maximum power from the thighs and legs. When told to lift her knees, a beginner lifts the foreleg behind, almost hitting her buttock. This action is incorrect and should be avoided particularly in the early stages of learning; it should not be confused with high knee action.

Leg action: foreleg reach. When performed correctly, this technique can make the difference between a champion and a good sprinter. It is an advanced movement that should be carefully and diligently practiced by top sprinters rather than beginners. The coach should decide whether to emphasize it or not; if poorly performed, it could lessen the force of leg thrust, thereby reducing speed. The runner swings the foreleg forward while lifting the knee and from this position, brings the foot to the ground and touching high on the toes.

Arm action. Elbows should be bent at a 90 to $95°$ angle and arms should hang freely from the shoulders. All arm action should be forward and backward. On the forward thrust the hand should not be raised higher than the shoulders; on the backward thrust the wrist should not pass behind or below the hips. Arm action coordinates with leg action; arms always move as fast as the legs. If the foreleg reach technique is used, arms swing on the forward thrust no higher than the bust and no further back than the hip.

Body lean and posture. Eyes should be focused on the ground approximately 20 yards in front of the sprinter. This prevents the head from being held either too high or too low and inhibits head movement. It also helps to eliminate undue body lean or inefficient body straightness. Body lean should be approximately 20 to $30°$.

One should give careful consideration to a tall running appearance and avoid leaning only at the waist or "sitting down" in the run (the latter is demonstrated by protruding buttocks). The running action should be forward rather than up and down. Up and down running usually indicates that a runner has both feet simultaneously off the ground. This minimizes the force and power necessary for maximum performance because a body free in air cannot exert maximum force.

Middle-distance Running

The technique of the middle-distance runner (quarter and half-miler) differs slightly from that of the sprinter. Good form is more easily achieved than in sprinting. The greatest difficulty comes with insufficient conditioning to develop cardiorespiratory endurance and muscular strength. Both are needed to maintain speed over the great distances in these races.

Fig. 41.6 The middle-distance runner's stride is shorter than the stride of sprinters, yet longer than that of long-distance runners. Courtesy of Southern Connecticut State College.

The middle-distance runner's stride is shorter than the sprinter's, yet longer than the distance runner's, and must be developed by experimentation. There is less body lean and lower knee action than in sprinting, and a higher back kick than in distance running. Arms, in a relaxed position, are carried at about waist height. The action of the foot plant is on the balls of the feet rather than high on the toes as in sprinting.

Cross-country Running

In cross-country running, the emphasis is on endurance rather than on great speed and a long stride. The distance runner's knee action is much lower than that of the sprinter, and slightly lower than that of the middle-distance runner. Thus, the low knee action results in a short stride and lower speed. The less energy expended, the longer the runner can endure without tiring.

Arms swing freely from the shoulders in a forward and backward motion, at the same speed as the legs. Hands swing no higher than the shoulders on forward thrust and no farther back than the hip on the backswing. Fingers are flexed and the fist is relaxed, not tightly clenched.

Running Downhill on Uneven Terrain

Much cross-country running involves traversing uneven terrain, from slight inclines to steep hills. When running downhill, the pull of gravity works to one's advantage as the slope pulls the body forward. In these instances, the stride should be shortened to ensure proper footing; the body should remain relaxed and the run controlled. To prevent undue imbalance, the center of gravity should remain over the base of support.

Running Uphill on Uneven Terrain

Running uphill is a greater challenge than running downhill. The runner must lean forward, lift knees higher, lengthen the stride, and swing the arms harder. When nearing an incline, she must run to the top, increasing speed about five yards before the incline to help build up the momentum needed to mount the hill.

Relay Racing

A relay team composed of good sprinters can lose to a slower team that has superior ability in the baton exchange. The pursuit relay is the most popular and involves distances of 220 yards to a mile. The distances denote the total distance the four runners cover. The official national and international relays are:

quarter-mile (4 × 110)
half-mile (4 × 220)
mile (4 × 440)
the medley relay (110, 110, 220, 440)
two-mile (4 × 880)

Successful relay racing hinges on baton passing. Three methods are commonly employed in baton exchange.

☐ Conventional, nonvisual pass (Fig. 41.7): The baton is transferred from the incoming runner's left hand to the receiver's right hand. This is the most widely used exchange.

☐ Sprint pass: The baton is passed from the passer's left to the receiver's right hand (first exchange), from the passer's right to receiver's left (second exchange), left to right (third exchange). The receiver does not transfer the baton to her other hand.

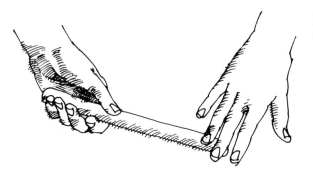

Fig. 41.7 Baton exchange: conventional, nonvisual.

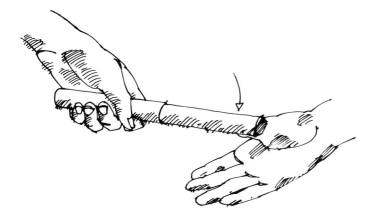

Fig. 41.8 Visual baton exchange. Passer and receiver's hand positions.

☐ Visual pass (Fig. 41.8): The baton is carried in the incoming runner's left hand and passed to the receiver's right hand. The receiver then transfers the baton to her left hand. This method is good when lanes are not provided and when speed of movement to the inside position is imperative.

Passing and receiving in the exchange zone. The baton must pass from one sprinter to another within a 22-yard passing zone. An 11-yard marker stands before and beyond each 110-yard point of the 440-yard relay; these mark the 22-yard exchange zone (Fig. 41.9). A restraining line is provided 11 yards before the beginning of each passing (or exchange) zone. The receiver may start on this restraining line so that she has a greater distance in which to build up momentum. Passing can take place only within the exchange zone, preferably within the last 15 to 18 yards.

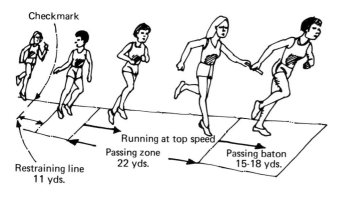

Checkmark

Running at top speed
Passing zone
22 yds.
Passing baton
15-18 yds.
Restraining line
11 yds.

Fig. 41.9 Passing zone and checkmarks.

FIELD EVENTS

The following basic principles are related to efficient performance in each field event:

☐ Maximum controlled momentum is built up in the approach.

☐ The action flows from this controlled momentum into the most effective power position from which to raise the body or thrust the implement.

☐ Follow-through results from the action that has taken place before rather than a separate consideration.

☐ Maximum performance is a result of a full-flowing total action rather than a segmented execution. The difference between these two lies primarily in the methods by which the principles are implemented.

Long Jump

The long jump consists of four elements:

☐ a fast run (approach)
☐ a high jump (takeoff)
☐ flight in air
☐ landing

Approach. The length of the run is determined by the shortest distance within which one can achieve optimum speed and still be prepared for the jump for height at the toeboard. Girls vary the length of their run from 80 to 115 feet.

This approach should be attempted ten to twelve times at each practice. Variables affecting the proper reaching of the toeboard (such as extreme wind, fatigue, a lengthened or shortened stride, and inconsistent strides) should be avoided. In the approach, strides must be consistent. Therefore, the long jumper must be aware of the stride lengths taken in each run.

Takeoff. In the last four strides of the run, attention should be shifted to jumping—not running at top speed—and to jumping as high as possible.

The takeoff foot (forward foot in starting block) hits the board almost flat-footed. The heel touches the ground slightly before the ball of the foot. Toes point directly forward, and the knee is slightly bent. At this juncture the center of gravity (point around which weight is evenly distributed) is directly over the foot. If the last stride is shortened, the center of gravity will be in front of the takeoff foot; if lengthened, the center of gravity will be behind. In either case, maximum jumping height will not be attained. Extending the takeoff leg must be coordinated with a raising and upward swinging of the free leg, and a rocking motion up onto the toes of the takeoff foot. At this time, the head and chest should be driven upward and the back should be arched. The action of the kicking leg (back leg in the blocks) involves lifting the leg vigorously, knee first, toward the shoulders.

Flight in air. There are three styles of form in the air:

☐ float (sitdown position in air)

☐ hitch-kick

☐ hang

It is impossible to increase body momentum after losing contact with the ground; therefore "running in the air" and various forms of hitch-kicking are used mainly to give the athlete aerial balance or to aid in elevating her feet. The most efficient and simple form for beginners is the knee-at-shoulders, or sitdown in the air, position—the "float" style.

In the float style, the knees are brought up toward the shoulders with great force; the jumper holds this position as she "floats" into the landing. From takeoff the chest and head must be held high and the back must be erect. The lead leg is thrust toward the shoulders and the takeoff leg follows in the same motion. When both feet are raised to a sitting position (knees at shoulder height), the body balances to keep the buttocks from touching the pit.

In the hitch-kick style, the jumper takes a stride and a half in the air. It is advantageous in that the jumper may maintain her balance in the air. The movement in the air does not increase momentum. The hitch-kick emphasizes lead leg action; the lead leg is driven forcefully upward and forward. As the takeoff leg is brought forward (also with great force), the lead leg drops back. Then, as the takeoff foot reaches its greatest height, the lead foot is again driven forward to its best position for landing.

In the hang style the athlete reaches maximum height with her chin and chest up, back slightly arched, and feet trailing behind the rest of her body. This form is greatly preferred because it further emphasizes the upward leap of the takeoff. After the board is cleared, the face points upward, the chin is lifted high, and the back arches. Quite naturally, the legs and feet drag well behind. Arms maintain balance. They are usually forward and out during flight. For an instant, the jumper seems to hang in the air. As she reaches the crest of her flight, there must be a forward swing of her hips to make it less difficult to lift her feet. As hips come forward, the legs are thrust ahead and the feet are brought up so that heels are about hip level. With arms also forward, there is now a slight forward curve of the back. In this sitting position, feet are about a foot apart and knees are slightly bent. When properly executed, this is a sound style that is used more frequently than any other by long-jump champions.

Landing. In landing, the jumper must continue in the forward direction. As she starts dropping toward the pit, she relies on strong abdominal muscles to keep her feet from touching too soon. The most practical method of landing is to extend the legs and spread the feet about a foot apart so that the body may go between the knees and over the feet when the pit is touched. The body should fall or pass beyond the point where the heel strikes the pit. Four techniques are used to get past and over the feet:

- ☐ dropping the chin on the chest
- ☐ leaning forward from the hips
- ☐ flexing the knees
- ☐ swinging the arms downward and backward

These techniques, taken in sequence, will prevent the jumper from falling back into a sitting position.

High Jump

The running high jump includes a run, a vertical jump, a layout over the bar, and landing. The style of the high jump is denoted by the position at the layout over the bar. There are five common styles:

- ☐ scissors
- ☐ Eastern cut-off
- ☐ Western roll
- ☐ straddle
- ☐ Fosbury flop

Approach. The run is an important part of high jumping and sets the pattern for the jump. If the run is weak or ill-timed, the jump will be equally so. The greater the height to be cleared, the more force (speed times mass) must be gained from the run. Perfecting the speed, rhythm, and coordination of the run is not merely helpful but also essential to great jumping.

The bar is approached from a 45° angle so that the kicking leg (back leg in the blocks) is the outside leg. The right-footed kicker runs from the left side. The simplest run is the seven-step approach, with the first step taken by the takeoff foot. During the run, emphasis should be directed toward acceleration and relaxation, not speed. The first four steps are slow, whereas

Fig. 41.10 The style of the high jump is denoted by the position at the lay-out over the bar. Courtesy of *JOPER*.

the last three must be smooth, quick, and progressively longer so that the takeoff foot is well ahead of the body weight. The only marks needed are the starting point and takeoff point, which is about arm's length from the bar.

Takeoff. The takeoff is concerned almost exclusively with jumping high. One must jump high first and then think about clearing the bar. The takeoff combines horizontal momentum with a vertical leap and includes the last few strides of the run. Since it establishes the direction and upward drive, the less it has to do with the method of clearing the bar the better. The concept of jumping high requires special practice. When done with a crossbar, it becomes confused with efficient clearance, proper form, and subconscious inhibitions. To explode upward with no concern for layout or landing is a technique that few jumpers have mastered.

Straddle style (layout). In the high-jump straddle style, the athlete straddles the bar on her stomach with her chest down. When taking off for the straddle clearance, the jumper should make certain that her outside arm does not come across her body. As in the Western roll, the kick should be along the bar and not over the center. These hints will prevent leaning into the bar at the takeoff. Again, not unlike the Western roll, a high pendulum kick turns the body toward the bar, but the takeoff leg does not tuck under. The secret in this style is to master the hip roll for the takeoff leg lift. **Note:** The takeoff leg (trailing leg) is most likely to hit the bar in this method of clearance.

At the top of the jump, head action plays a great part in lifting the trailing leg. Just before reaching the point of maximum height, the jumper turns the head back and slightly down, attempting to look at a spot close to the point of takeoff. At the instant the head starts to turn, straightening the trailing leg and simultaneously turning the toes on the left foot toward the sky assists the trailing leg in clearing the bar. During the clearance, the left hand is at the side. It must never get between the body and the bar. The landing is made on the kicking foot (right) and the outside hand (right). The athlete should let her momentum roll her over on her side into the pit.

Shot Put

The object of putting the shot is to push the sphere from the shoulder, not to throw it. To add momentum to the thrust, the athlete travels across a seven-foot circle before releasing the shot.

Shot putting is usually learned in the following sequence:

☐ the grip
☐ the put from a stand
☐ putting with total movement across the circle

Grip. The grip depends on the strength of the fingers. The shot should rest on the base of the fingers, as high as good control and strength will permit. Holding it too high stiffens the fingers, hands, and wrist; holding it too low deadens the "crack of the whip." The shot should be held low on the neck, with the elbow high.

The "O'Brien" method. One should keep in mind the principles of wholeness of action and continuous acceleration of motion across the circle throughout the following discussion of the "O'Brien" form in the shot put.

For a clear understanding of the action across the circle, the entire sequence of the shot put will be described in the following parts:

☐ stance in the rear of the circle
☐ shift
☐ impetus to the shot (release)
☐ reverse

Stance in rear. Action begins opposite the board, the putter placing her foot on an imaginary line that passes through the center of the circle and the middle of the toeboard. The foot can be either perpendicular to a tangent and touching the back of the circle, or turned at a slight angle. The shot is comfortably situated on the neck and held in the right hand. (The technique of putting the shot as described here is for a right-handed individual.)

Shift. With the body in balance, the putter now drops low over her right leg and drives; she maintains this low position to the center of the circle. During this drive, the weight of the hips is not over the right leg, but falls toward the toeboard, pulling the body off balance. The heel is the last part of the right leg to leave the ground. The leg is then quickly pulled under the body. The right foot of the putter should now be in the center of the circle, the left leg almost straight at the board. Shoulders and head still face the back of the circle. The putter is low and in a "power position."

Release. From here, the lift off the right leg begins. The hips and shoulders begin their rotation, the hips are driven up and around, the chest and head are also thrown up. This upward drive should be great enough to propel the thrower up on the toes of her feet. At the same time, the right arm pushes the shot upward and outward and it is released.

Reverse. Once the shot has left the hand, the reverse is executed quickly. The reverse is a result of the throw, not part of it. The right arm is across the body; the right leg is at the toeboard and bent, while the left leg is high in back, also bent. If necessary, the putter may have to drive her body away from the board by placing her fingers on the inside of the board (not on top) and pushing.

The main objective of practicing is not to establish "how far," but "how." It is best to work with two shots, with someone rolling them back to the circle. The puts should be taken with the idea of the whole action in mind, and all of the following points should be checked.

☐ position of the shot on the neck

☐ lowness in the back and center of circle

☐ glide to the center

☐ position of the right leg in the center of the circle

☐ lift of leg preceding rotation of hips

☐ chest and head position

☐ technique of reverse

Discus

Grip. The hand is placed on top of the discus, with fingers spread comfortably apart. The edge of the discus is in the first notches of the fingers as the discus rests against the palm. The farther the forefinger (right-handed thrower) is to the left of the center of the discus, the greater the rotating force that can be given, and the less chance of the discus slipping out. However, the forefinger must maintain its grasp and force the discus to rotate around it. The discus is released by closing the fingers, leaving the forefinger last, and rotating clockwise.

Turn. To build up momentum, the thrower starts a one-and-three-quarter turn at the rear of the circle, and continues through the reverse. The turn is one of the most difficult techniques to learn. Because of the necessity for maintaining balance, speed, and force during the turn, it is imperative that the thrower be secure in executing a throw from a stand.

The spin begins in the rear of the circle. The thrower straddles an imaginary line through the center of the circle, with feet no further apart than shoulderwidth. Head and shoulders should be level, with the weight on the right foot and the discus back and away from the hips. As the turn begins, the discus remains back and the weight shifts to the ball of the left foot, with the knees bent considerably. The left leg should be kept in contact with the ground as long as possible.

As the thrower lifts her right leg, it passes close to her left knee, which is still bent, but starts to rotate toward the center of the circle. With her head still level and arm still back, she drives off her left foot toward the center of the circle. At the same time, her body undergoes a 180° turn and her right foot falls into the center of the circle pointing toward the rear. After this 180° turn to the left, the body is now in the position practiced when throwing from a stand.

The right arm should now be in a cocked position, ready to come through quickly in a smooth, inclined plane; to immediately lift off the right leg, which was bent under the body; and to drive the left leg down to the ground as the hips lift upward and around pulling the arm through. Final impetus is given by the right leg and by the final wrist snap and finger force as the discus is released. If the spin is executed properly, the thrower will be forced into a quick and almost simultaneous reverse (a quick exchange of the feet).

Javelin

The javelin throw involves building up the greatest possible momentum without sacrificing the powerful body position from which maximum force and velocity can be applied to the delivery. There are three acceptable styles of throwing the javelin:

☐ American hop   ☐ Finnish   ☐ Russian

The American hop is practically nonexistent among experienced throwers because it involves slowing down while preparing for the throw and thus sacrifices optimum momentum. The Russian style is the most difficult to master, for it requires an arch of the back and whipping of these muscles for greater force in addition to the regular sequential movements. The Finnish style, when properly executed, is the most efficient and practical form; therefore, it will be used in this description. Here the athlete carries the javelin over the shoulder for running ease and uses a front cross-step to turn the trunk to a powerful throwing position.

Fig. 41.11 Javelin grips.

Grips. The two most acceptable grips are illustrated in Fig. 41.11. In both grips the javelin is placed diagonally across the palm, from the base of the index finger to the heel of the hand. The grip shown to the right is more desirable because the second finger can be strengthened beyond that of the first and the first finger can aid in slightly lifting the tail of the javelin. It is a comfortable grip that does not strain the arm.

Approach. Optimum momentum is provided by a running approach. The purpose of the approach is to initiate and accelerate the forward motion of the javelin. The length of the approach is determined by the distance in which the greatest speed can be attained and maintained in the cross-step. The approach must be rhythmical, smooth, and accurate before attempting to increase speed. A longer approach and more speed come with improvements in form and conditioning. Some coaches advocate three checkmarks, but the author recommends two:

☐ the starting point
☐ the place where the cross-step is to begin

Cross-step. From a run the athlete executes a front cross-step which allows her to turn her trunk to a powerful throwing position without sacrificing momentum.

The following count system is recommended for practicing the cross-step:

1. The left foot hits the second checkmark with toes facing forward; the javelin is starting to be pulled back.

2. The right foot lands in front of the checkmark with toes forward; the pull of the javelin to the back continues.

3. The left foot lands on the center line with toes pointing slightly to the right: the javelin is now well to the back.

4. The right foot crosses over in front of the left and lands parallel to the toeboard; the javelin starts forward, elbow leading.

5. The left foot goes into a long step and is planted just to the left of the center line with toes pointing forward in line with throw, the javelin continues forward.

After the fifth count the upper body is still going forward, but the left leg has checked the lower body and a whip action of the upper trunk is taking place. The javelin is pulled forward over and close to the head and is released in front of and about 12 inches above the head.

Follow-through (reverse). The follow-through or reverse results from the force built up from starting point until delivery. To check forward momentum (preventing a foul by touching or crossing the toeboard), the weight goes into the right leg, which has come forward after the javelin has left the hand.

Finally, speed is an important factor in throwing the javelin. The effective transfer of running speed into useful throwing force is essential and requires much practice to perfect.

REFERENCES

Thompson, D. H., and J. Carver 1974. *Prentice-Hall handbook of physical education activities for women.* Englewood Cliffs, N.J.: Prentice-Hall.

Thompson, D. H. 1973. *Modern track and field for girls and women.* Boston: Allyn and Bacon.

———— 1969. *Women's track and field.* Boston: Allyn and Bacon.

42
Trampolining

Jeffrey M. Austin

The exciting and exhilarating sport of trampolining has long been recognized by the entertainment profession as an activity with tremendous spectator appeal. Exploitation of the trampoline by European and American circuses brought an increased interest in it as a valuable addition to our recreational and competitive sports programs. The early pioneers of trampolining included such persons as George Nissen, Bill Sorenson, Larry Griswold, and Bob Fenner. These were all competent bouncers in their own right, as well as leaders in the field of trampoline manufacturing. It was the prodding, promoting, and trampoline exposure presented by these men that elevated the sport to what it is today.

Fig. 42.1 Jeffrey Austin and his family.

Like basketball and baseball, trampoline, as we know it, achieved its real beginning in the United States. Early versions of the trampoline were crude conversions of pipe, inner tube rubbers, and canvas assembled by performers for their own use. The best opportunity to enjoy trampolining had to be a family outing to the circus, or some outstanding European act on the Ed Sullivan Show.

In the 1940s, when trampolining was becoming popular, proponents of gymnastics, a sport also gaining popularity in the United States, felt that the

Fig. 42.2 The Austins perform their professional act.

trampoline was just what was needed to increase spectator interest in their competitions. Austin (1976) writes:

> Coaches used the glamor of the trampoline to lure prospective gymnasts into the gymnasium with the hope that they could encourage them to expand to other gymnastics events. This was particularly true in high school. Trampoline was given a prominent place in all competitions, usually the last event, to hold the crowds.
>
> With its audience appeal, trampolining catapulted into one of the nation's fastest growing sports. Backyards were being flooded with this new found sport. Investors were finding out that they could take advantage of the thrill and excitement of bouncing on the trampoline by selling jumping time on trampolines buried in the ground.

These were critical times for the sport. Gymnastics persons, oriented only to events included in the Olympic Games, were suggesting that, as a boost for the sport of gymnastics, trampoline may have outlived its usefulness. Prominent persons in the field of gymnastics used their influence to encourage the NCAA to remove trampoline from the collegiate portion of gymnastics competition. In 1967:

> ... under the pretext that trampoline was not safe, certain coaches reached our NCAA Executive Committee convincing them that trampoline should be removed from gymnastics competition. This was done in spite of outcries by coaches throughout the United States, especially the Midwest region. Opposition in large numbers rose to meet the decision squarely. Big 10 coaches, a majority of college and university gymnastics coaches, and the Illinois High School Gymnastics Coaches Association, voiced their opposition to the decision, but to no avail (Austin 1970, p. 204).
>
> The NCAA ruling, in 1967, at the time was felt to be the deathblow for a rapidly growing sport loved by so many. Olympic and NCAA committee members were subjected to continuous pressure to rescind their decision to remove trampoline from gymnastics competition, but the growth of United States gymnastics teams on the international scene prompted the collegiate powers to hold their ground.
>
> It was not until 1971 that some real significant changes were made in the future of trampoline. George Nissen, considered by many to be the Father of the modern day trampoline, assembled a Congress of trampoline coaches in Cedar Rapids, Iowa. "I have brought you together for the sole purpose of organizing the sport of trampoline. Separate yourselves from gymnastics. You are big enough to go it on your own. You need your own national organization," Nissen told us. The 33 members present put their heads together for two days and came up with The United States Trampoline Association (USTA), an organization for which I had the pleasure of serving as president from 1971–74. These outstanding coaches, known for their strong interest and enthusiastic approach to trampoline, took advantage of past mistakes in

other sports and molded a constitution for a sport which was quickly accepted by the competitors and remaining coaches throughout the country (Austin 1976).

The formation of the USTA provided the stimulus that revitalized the AAU's interest in trampoline competition, a sport they were previously letting die on the vine.

Trampolining as a sport and recreational activity is not without problems. In any activity where height and motion are involved, there are certain risks to which an individual is exposed. Most of these risks are quite obvious to those involved. Since most of the early exposure to trampoline occurs through watching television or performances by experts, first-time participants frequently do not take the time to learn the fundamental aspects of the sport. In short, they try to emulate what they see.

Many young athletes approach trampolining as a sport where there is no beginning. They broach their development largely through their courage rather than confidence inspired through many hours of preparation. Trampoline is unique in that people can achieve certain performance skills almost immediately without knowing all the fundamentals. For this reason there is a need on the part of trampolinists and coaches for a reliable reference.

THE TRAMPOLINE

The trampoline of today is quite different from the "nuts and bolts" versions of the early circus days. Modern engineering has brought standard models with refinements comparable to those of the automobile. Canvas beds and inner tube rubbers for springs were replaced with delicately sewn web beds and precision wound springs. Chrome plating, improved paints, and more durable materials converted the soggy trampolines of old to the modern versions presently used.

The standard competitive and recreational models are very much alike, with bed dimensions of 5' × 10', 6' × 12', or 7' × 14'. The steel rectangular

Fig. 42.3 The trampoline.

Fig. 42.4 Trampolinists in appropriate clothing.

frame is elevated two to three feet off the ground, well padded, with the bed, usually made of webbing, suspended by chrome springs. The trampolines designed for backyard use are almost identical to those designed for competition, with less expensive materials used to meet the highly competitive retail market.

Clothing

The clothing worn by the competitor consists of white pants and sleeveless shirts for men, and leotards for women, with white shoes required for both. Backyard bouncers lean toward more casual attire. The clothing selected has much to do with performance. Tight jeans and clothing that flaps up over the face while bouncing increase the chance of an accident. Tennis outfits or shorts made out of doubleknit fabrics work very well for women, with gym shorts and T-shirts for men. The feet should be covered with either socks or acrobatic slippers.

Safety

When a person is exposed to the heights and motion associated with trampoline, certain safety practices are essential (Austin 1970). A few rules that will make trampoline experiences pleasant are:

☐ Mount the trampoline carefully and always put a hand on the frame to get off. Never spring from the bed to the ground.

- ☐ Never bounce double except under experienced adult supervision.
- ☐ It is advisable that there be one person on each side and one on each end of the trampoline to act as spotters (give support) in the event a performer should lose his balance and get too close to the edge.
- ☐ *All* persons during their first trampoline experience must begin with the basic fundamentals before moving into anything complicated. Just learning to bounce is a good way to begin.
- ☐ *Alcohol and trampoline activity absolutely do not mix!*
- ☐ No street shoes on the trampoline.
- ☐ Always inform the persons around the trampoline as to what you intend to do. A spotter who knows what to look out for always does a much better job.
- ☐ Keep the turns short.
- ☐ Don't let the bouncers get overtired.

To sum up the points emphasized above, the presence of knowledgeable people, conscientious supervision, and properly maintained equipment will ensure the continued growth of competitive and recreational trampoline programs.

TRAMPOLINE SKILLS

The nature of competitive and recreational trampolining is one of mutual support and assistance. This activity seems to attract participants who are anxious to provide a coaching "tip" or lend support as a spotter when needed.

Beginners should be allowed to advance at a leisurely pace. Too often instructors are guilty of encouraging the novice to advance to somersaulting before mastering the simple bounce technique. When developing a trampoline program at the fundamental level, progressions should be used wherever possible. A beginner must develop a certain amount of air sense before getting involved in difficult tricks.

An established pattern which should be followed in the development of a suitable background for further trampoline learning includes:

- ☐ Familiarizing oneself with the springiness of the bed.
- ☐ Learning the proper technique of bouncing. The arm pattern is a sweeping motion of the arms, like swimming backwards. The arms should be swung horizontally to the outside and forced down into the bed at the bottom of the bounce. This will develop inertia. In a swinging motion, the arms are forced down next to the body and then forward of the body to the horizontal position to repeat the cycle. The arm pattern is performed for each bounce.

☐ Learning the technique for "breakfall." This is the movement of flexing the knees at the same time the bed is trying to force the performer in the air. The lift will be neutralized and the performer will end up motionless on the trampoline.

☐ Learning the "basic four" tricks that should be mastered before involving oneself in complicated maneuvers. They follow.

Seat Drop

Pick up the feet with the legs straight, knees together, toes pointed, hands beside the hips with the fingers forward, and the body leaning slightly backward. Try to land so that the seat and legs make contact with the bed at the same time. This is an excellent place to begin with fundamental instruction. Sitting down is something a student already knows how to do. Landing on the broad base of seat and legs develops confidence. The chance of error is minimized with a seat drop and the first experience is quite safe.

Knee Drop

On an appropriate bounce bend the knees, keeping the hips straight, the upper body vertical, and the head looking forward. The knees, shins, and the tops of the feet should make contact with the bed at the same time. Avoid sitting on the lower legs when making contact with the bed. Wait for the trampoline to lift you to your feet.

Front Drop

Lower the upper body and elevate the feet simultaneously to get the body in a horizontal position. Keep the head up, the elbows out, and hands in front of the face (palms down) to support the head and neck. The front surface

Fig. 42.5 Seat drop.

Fig. 42.6 Knee drop.

Fig. 42.7 Front drop.

of the chest, abdomen, legs, and feet make contact with the bed at the same time. Wait for the bed to push you back onto your feet. Keeping the elbows out helps prevent skinned elbows and allows for a more comfortable position.

Note: Encourage learning a "hand and knee drop" before trying the front drop. It is easier to understand. The beginner merely lands on the hands and knees, rather than the stomach. Encourage the student to keep knees under hips. Acquiring this progression first virtually eliminates the possibility of an injury if the pupil does not land perfectly flat on the front drop.

Back Drop

Although the back drop is relatively safe, there is usually some apprehension at first because beginners feel insecure when the body motion is backwards.

After a slight lift of the hips, elevate the legs to a 45° angle at the hips, simultaneously dropping the back and shoulders to a horizontal position. The

Fig. 42.8 Back drop.

small of the back, the shoulders, and the back of the head *all* should make contact with the bed at the same time. As the bed lifts you off your back, lift the hips, drop the legs, and raise the head and shoulders to prepare for a feet landing. Landing on the seat before the rest of the back will tend to make the back of the head slap against the bed. If the legs are not maintained at at least 45° at the hips, the legs will drop too early on the recovery and loss of lift will result.

It would not be unusual to spend four or five sessions on the "basic four" before advancing to other combinations. Usually the next step is to apply simple twists to the "basic four," such as a swivel hip, or cradle (Figs. 42.9 and 42.10).

Somersaulting (Flips)

Following the mastery of fundamentals, most bouncers progress to somersaulting, or "flips," forward or backward. Close supervision is necessary during this learning phase. I might add that it is unwise to allow a student to

Fig. 42.9 Seat: half twist to seat (swivel hips).

Fig. 42.10 Back drop: half twist to back drop (cradle).

attempt a somersault with nothing more than an explanation as to how to do the trick. Either hand spotting, or the overhead mechanic is recommended.

The Forward Somersault

From a normal bounce and arm lift, keep the head neutral on takeoff. Following a vertical lift, elevate the hips and drop the head. Extend the legs between two and three o'clock, allowing them to swing down for the landing. *Don't force the trick.* Open the hip angle and keep the chest high on the landing.

The Backward Somersault (To a Seat Drop)

From a normal bounce and arm lift, keep the head neutral, or perhaps slightly forward during vertical takeoff. One way to keep the head from dropping back early is to look at something in front of you. Following takeoff, fixate the shoulders and elevate the hips and shins. The knees will be tucked at this

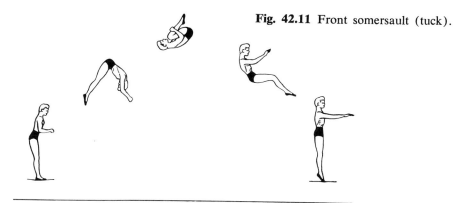

Fig. 42.11 Front somersault (tuck).

Fig. 42.12 Back somersault to seat drop (tuck).

point. Somewhere near the top of the bounce the head drops back while the shins move over the top. Open the legs between one and two o'clock. Straighten the legs, pull the legs through, and prepare for the seat drop landing. Frequently the student is taught to land on the seat to increase stability on the landing. The mechanics for landing on the feet are the same except the legs are not pulled through.

ADVANCED TRAMPOLINE

The United States has pocketed more world trampoline titles than all other nations combined, a surprising reality considering the removal of trampoline competition by the NCAA. In recent years our foreign competition has made rapid strides in the sport of trampolining. Were it not for the USTA formed in 1971, the European trampoline forces might have outstripped those of the United States to such an extent that recovery would have been difficult. At the same time the NAAU became concerned. They realized that if they did not revitalize their interest in trampoline, they might lose their control of international competition to the USTA. This proved to be a healthy situation. Strong individuals, holding membership in both organizations, integrated ideas for the promotion and development of trampolining. This proved beneficial to both parties as well as to the sport itself.

Advanced competitive trampolining has undergone some noticeable changes over the years. Gone are the days when the competitors performed their routines until they became so tired they could no longer continue. Interest in form and grace, as well as difficulty, now occupies a strong place in competition.

Development of routines and tricks has undergone pronounced advancement during the 1970s. Previously, competitors' routines demonstrated variety by landing on parts of their bodies other than their feet. The one and three-quarter backward somersault, cody (tricks off the stomach), and ball-outs (tricks off the back) were common. Paul Luxon, British World Champion, and Wayne Miller, United States World Champion, emphasized quality "feet-to-feet" work. With the introduction of the Axial Rotation System of difficulty scoring by Robert Bollinger, a system of rating trampoline difficulty presently used nationally and internationally, the emphasis moved away from the body landings. The new direction was toward multiple twisting *fliffises*. A fliffis is any double somersault with a twist. It was easier for competitors to increase the difficulty of their routines by performing a complicated fliffis rather than a bed landing. National and international competitors are programming their routines on the principle that fliffis combinations reign supreme. This is the direction advanced trampoline is going.

In the space of this article it would be impossible to explain the intricate coaching details of how to perform a fliffis, but I would recommend that one might learn the more popular ones in the following order:

☐ *Barani-Out Fliffis*   A double forward somersault, with a half twist on the second somersault.

☐ *½ In-½ Out Fliffis*   A double backward somersault, with a half twist on the first somersault and a half twist on the second somersault.

☐ *Barani-In-Full-Out Fliffis*   A double forward somersault, with a barani on the first somersault and a full twist on the second somersault.

☐ *½ In-Rudolph-Out Fliffis*   A double backward somersault, with a half twist on the first somersault and a full and one-half twist on the second somersault.

☐ *Full-In-Full-Out Fliffis*   A double backward somersault, with a full twist on the first somersault and a full twist on the second somersault.

I recommend learning the fliffises in the order above because the understanding of one fliffis aids in progressing to the next. Once you have advanced to the full-in-full-out fliffis, any twisting combination suggested will be easily understood and rapidly learned. I would recommend that most of these fliffises be learned with straight legs, or in the pike position. Frequently performers will elect to perform the more complicated fliffises in the "tuck" position (knees bent), but aesthetically it is not the most pleasing.

Twisting

A twist is any move where the body rotates laterally while at the same time rotating forward or backward. There are many ideas and techniques about twisting somersaults on the trampoline, but the results must still be the same. In both single somersault and fliffis work, where twisting is involved, there are a few basic theories which I would like to present (Austin 1976).

Twisting, to be of value in a routine, must be aesthetically correct. Twisting is a *full* body movement and performers should be instructed to realize that individual parts of the body, such as the head, arms, hips, and legs, do not by themselves make the trick work. Aesthetically, most twisting, particularly fulls, double-fulls, and triple-fulls, should be done with the body as straight as possible. Forward twisting and fliffis twisting offer exceptions to the straight body theory. I personally like to see straight legs on all twists, even including fliffis work.

Many times coaches will tell their bouncers that they have to "see the bed" on a twist. I believe this leads to confusion. It would be better described as "knowing where you are at". The body is more perceptive than a computer. The smallest glimpse of something will give the bouncers clues as to where they are. If they were to see every object go past and register each one, only confusion would remain. This is why first attempts at a twist are so mind cluttering. The brain has not had a chance to eliminate all the unimportant things the eyes see while attempting the twist. Repeated attempts will clear this up. This same point applies to all intricate maneuvers on the trampoline.

It is important that a trampolinist with aspirations to compete on an international level seek out competent and knowledgeable coaching. Bad twisting habits are difficult to correct and inhibit future development.

CONCLUSION

The sport of trampoline is in limbo at the moment. There is no question that this sport has a viable place in the sports society but its place has not yet been determined. There are many who ask if trampoline will be a part of the Olympic Games. This will be difficult because those making the decisions are concerned about the increased costs of international athletics. Some believe we have too many Olympic events already. There is an International Association for Acrobatics and many persons associated with the USTA and AAU suggest a merger with this organization. Foreign countries are stimulating expansion of their competitive trampoline programs faster than the United States is, leaving the Americans with the problem of sinking or trampolining back to the supreme position of world power it has always held. Organizations such as the USTA and the AAU have their members in important positions on the FIT Presidium (international trampoline governing body), but their powers are limited unless they have total support from the homeland.

In the United States the local trampoline clubs present the strongest case for the strengthening of trampoline competition. USTA, AAU, and club competition is increasing rapidly. Camps are once again incorporating trampoline in their programs. With the organizations, competitors, and media pushing hard toward fulfilling their objectives in a sport loved by many, its rise to even greater levels may be anticipated.

REFERENCES

Austin, J. 1976. *Winning trampoline*. Chicago: Henry Regnery.

———— 1970. Tumbling and trampoline removed from competition: its impact on gymnastics curricula. In G. George (ed.), *The magic of gymnastics*. Santa Monica, Calif.: Sundby.

Casady, D. R. 1974. Trampolining. In D. R. Casady (ed.), *Sports activities for men*. New York: Macmillan, pp. 437–451.

Culhane, M. J. 1969. Trampolining. In B. F. McCue (ed.), *Physical education activities for women*. New York: Macmillan, pp. 222–232.

LaDue, F., and J. Norman 1960. *This is trampolining*. Cedar Rapids, Iowa: Nissen Trampoline Company.

Szypula, G. 1968. *Beginning trampolining*. Belmont, Calif.: Wadsworth.

43
Volleyball

Three authors contributed to the material on the popular game of volleyball. F. E. Sills wrote about the nature, language and lore of the game, the playing court and the equipment needed. H. T. Friermood's classic article on volleyball instruction provides expert advice on fundamental techniques and instructional methods. A. Scates tells how "power volleyball" can be developed by teaching it properly to children. RBF

Volleyball
F. Eric Sills

LANGUAGE AND LORE

The game of volleyball has recently become recognized as one of the leading participative sports in the world. It is impossible to determine the exact number of people actually playing the game each year but estimates range from 50 to 80 million participants throughout the world. The game is played in over 80 countries, some 25 of which recognize the game as a major sport. When volleyball became a part of the Olympic Games in 1964, the game achieved the recognition it deserved. For many years before that, however, volleyball had an international quality with teams representing their respective countries in the Pan American Games, the European Championships, the Asiatic Championships, and the World Games.

The growth of volleyball in the United States has followed a somewhat different pattern. The game itself has an American origin, having been invented in 1895 by William C. Morgan, a student at Springfield College and later director of the YMCA at Holyoke, Massachusetts. The game was first called minonette, and it borrowed skills from tennis, handball, and baseball. Any number of players were allowed on each team and the object of the game was to hit or bat a rubber bladder from a basketball back and forth over a tennis net erected at a height of 6' 6" across the center of the gym. After Morgan moved to the Holyoke YMCA and revised his game he named it volleyball. Since that time, changes in technical rules and equipment occurred quite frequently, but the development of the game into a highly competitive sport was a lengthy process.

In the United States, volleyball is generally supported and controlled through the direction of the United States Volleyball Association (USVBA), which includes representation from the YMCA, NCAA, AAU, and AAHPER. The women's intercollegiate volleyball teams and tournaments are governed by the NAGWS rulings, which are similar to those of the USVBA. Internationally, the governing body is the International Volleyball Federation (IVF) which was formed in 1947 and held the first world's championship in Moscow in 1952. The IVF also governs the Olympic tournaments. The rules of the three governing bodies differ very little from one another.

PLAYING COURT AND EQUIPMENT

A net, the top of which is 8' for men and 7' 4¼" for women, divides the playing area into two equal parts. The court is 60' × 30' (Fig. 43.1). The volleyball is 26 to 27" in circumference, weighs 9 to 10 oz and is inflated to weigh between 7 and 8 lbs.

THE GAME

The official rules of volleyball call for six players on a team. Each team is arranged with three players across the front of the court near the net and three players behind them across the backcourt. The object of the game is to cause the ball to strike the floor on the opponent's court or to cause an opponent to engage in faulty play. Examples of faulty play are: carrying the ball, hitting the ball twice in succession (double hit), hitting the ball out of bounds, and one team hitting the ball more than three times before returning it over the net.

The game starts with the players facing the net and the right rear player (server) of the team which won the toss stepping out of bounds behind the court. In this serving area, each point begins when the server strikes the ball sharply causing it to fly over the net to the defensive team. There are two basic styles of serves: one, the floater used in competitive power volleyball, which is a forcefully hit overhand type of serve that is difficult to return; and two, the underhand serve, generally used in recreational volleyball, which is struck from an underhand swing and propels the ball in a high arc over the net. The receiving team must then field the serve and return it over the net using no more than three hits to do so. This pattern of three hits is basic to the game. The player receiving the serve must play the ball cleanly without letting the ball visibly come to rest or without making double contact with the ball. If the receiver must return the ball from above shoulder level he or she will use a two-handed pass, and if from below shoulder level a forearm pass or a "bump" pass. If the reception of the serve is successfully controlled, the ball will travel from the receiver to the player occupying the position in the center of the front line, normally called the setter.

Once the ball has traveled to the setter, there are many offensive maneuvers that may be employed. The success of each maneuver depends on the ability of the setter to place the ball in the desired position, above and several feet back from the net. One of the legal spikers then approaches the net, times the vertical jump to the position of the ball, and attempts to spike the ball forcefully into the opponents' court. Immediately after the serve, the serving team becomes the defensive team and should prepare to meet the offensive thrust or spike of the opponents by a series of defensive maneuvers. If the ball was skillfully served, the serve reception may be faulty and result in the setter of the offensive team being deprived of the ball. In the latter case, players move to predetermined positions to cover the court for the return. In the play situation previously described, however, where the ball has been well placed by the setter, the defensive team will attempt to have two or three of its front-line players jump high in the air, close to the net, directly opposite the spiker in an effort to block the ball (Fig. 43.1). During this action, the offensive spiker is attempting to utilize some type of offensive tactic that will "put the ball away" on the opposite side of the net. The spiker may attempt to hit the ball over or around the block on a hard driven spike, or the spiker may simply "dink" the ball (a soft lob) to an uncovered area of the opponents' court. The defensive team must endeavor to cover as much of its court as possible, utilizing the three or four players not taking part in the block.

If the spiker overcomes the block and the ball is not returned, the spiker's team gains the serve and the opportunity to score points. When the blocking team prevails and the ball is blocked back to the floor of the spiking team, the serving team has scored a point and wins the right to serve again.

Frequently the spiked ball hits the block and continues in play on the spiker's side of the court. If the ball is blocked back into the spiker's court, the players on that team will simply treat the situation as the start of a new play and will attempt to play the ball to the setter in the middle of the front line who, in turn, will set the ball up to the spikers. When the ball rebounds from the block into the court on the blocker's side of the net, the members of that team now have only two remaining hits to return the ball over the net. If the ball comes off the block high in the air and in or near the court, the next player to make contact with the ball becomes the setter and attempts to place the ball in a position to be spiked over the net on the third hit by a front-line player. The opposing team deploys its block and attempts to defend against this new offensive thrust.

Play continues until one team is unable to return the ball in the three hits allowed or until a foul is committed. Variations in defensive and offensive strategy are numerous, and the participants must learn to recognize the rapid changes from offense to defense and react accordingly. The basic plays in volleyball remain the same, however; players must become proficient in all skills including the serve, the forearm pass and dig, the two-handed pass or set, the spike, and the block for successful participation in volleyball.

Volleyball is well suited to today's living since it can be played and enjoyed by people of all ages. It also provides the opportunity to acquire a group of skills which may be used for many years in an almost injury-free

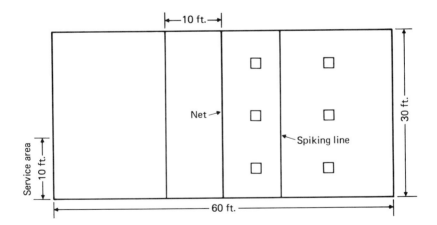

Fig. 43.1 Volleyball court dimensions. Net should be three feet wide and approximately 32 feet long. Uprights holding net should be three to four feet outside the court. There should be a minimum of six feet in back of each end line. Boundary lines should be two inches wide.

environment. At the same time it can provide a highly competitive, action-filled exercise pattern for large muscle groups. The level of competition and activity is regulated by the skill level of the players but it can be appropriately strenuous at all levels.

REFERENCES

Coleman, J. 1972. *Power volleyball: sports techniques.* Chicago: Athletic Institute.

Egstrom, G. H., and F. Schaafsma 1966. *Volleyball.* Dubuque, Iowa: Wm. C. Brown.

Slaymaker, T., and V. H. Brown 1970. *Power volleyball.* Philadelphia: W. B. Saunders.

Improving Your Volleyball Instruction*

Harold T. Friermood

Millions of people are playing and enjoying volleyball today because of its "relative" simplicity, but they are not playing well. Their instruction has been inadequate and they have not been indoctrinated with the full possibilities of the game. Volleyball ranks among the top half-dozen most popular team sports. It is played extensively in all branches of the armed forces, in industry, many schools and colleges, and other organizations. The game has been recruiting new players in foreign countries as well. Although originated 50 years ago in the Holyoke, Massachusetts, YMCA, its greatest growth has taken place during the two world wars.

Much good volleyball is played by women and girls. An occasional college-age young men's team is outstanding but by all odds, middle-aged businessmen, as a group, rank highest in experience and mastery of fundamentals. This need not be necessarily so. The game skills are readily acquired by young players when they are properly instructed. However, the conditions are much more favorable under which the older men learn the game, receive their instruction, and continue play.

They play indoors; nets are at standard height and stretched tightly; balls are properly inflated and kept clean and white; courts are clearly marked; convenient scoreboards are used to keep all players posted on the point standing of both teams; regular instruction and supervision are supplied, the players are in comfortable gym suits, wear gym shoes, and take shower baths follow-

---

* Reprinted with permission from *JOPER* **16**, 10 (December), 1945.

ing play; teams are usually limited to the official six players on a side; players take turns officiating thus aiding their own understanding of the game and sharpening up the observance and interpretation of rules; accurate ball handling and team work are stressed; they take part in leagues and see frequent matches between highly competitive teams. All these factors add to the prestige of the game and provide an incentive to play well.

In contrast to these conditions we usually find the informal playground, camp, or picnic game where a sagging net is hung between two trees or wobbly posts; some small stones and a few sticks roughly define the boundaries of the playing area; and no one is just sure about the rules or what the score is. Consequently disputes continually interrupt play; 10 or 15 players stand around on each side without having much chance of touching the ball unless they rush in and take it away from another player; there is little pass-work and much individualistic play. The ball is batted back and forth, aimlessly, over the net without directed purpose. Such a situation does little to develop playing skill and genuine interest in the game.

There are values in group fellowship where fresh air and fun together represent the major role but if in addition skillful play can also be enjoyed, the sport will be enhanced. Volleyball's chief value is that it is primarily a participant's sport. Players are able to continue play for many years. Like golf, bowling, swimming, and other sports, early training in fundamental skills and understanding of the game are important. How can this be accomplished? The three major factors are motivation, adequate instruction, and opportunity to participate, discussion of each of which follows.

MOTIVATION

The attitude of the teacher or coach plays an important part in influencing individuals and groups. If the instructor speaks well of the game, knows the fundamentals, and provides opportunities for play under favorable conditions where fun and learning occur, then a good start has been made. Equipment and playing space should be provided, and special periods should be set aside for individual and team coaching. Exhibition matches should be arranged where coached teams demonstrate play. Adequate explanation should be made to the observing players with opportunity provided for questions. Specialty events such as student vs. faculty teams, coed teams, recently returned veterans' teams or "singles" or "doubles" matches all create interest, as do scheduled leagues and tournaments. Visual aids such as photographs, diagrams, sketches, posters, and motion pictures should be utilized.

ADEQUATE INSTRUCTION

A volleyball, net, court, and twelve players will not result in a good game. Instruction, study, and coaching are also essential. Best results are secured when the players know what they are trying to do and want to do it. It is at this point that motivation and instruction join hands. When the readiness to learn has been created through a number of devices as suggested above then the specific steps of instruction can be successfully introduced. These functional fundamentals must be mastered: the serve, receive and pass, setup, "spike" or attack, block, net recovery, team work, knowledge of rules. The following outline may assist in locating a few points of emphasis for each:

The Serve

Stand in proper serving area with both feet *behind,* not touching, service line. Face direction of serve.

Serve underhand (most accurate and dependable), or overhand (as in tennis). May use open hand or closed fist.

Study opponents. Serve to "weak" or open spots. Far corners usually best.

Individual serving practice may be gained by serving against a flat wall. Mark serving line 30 feet away from wall and mark a line on wall eight feet above floor. Stand within 15 or 20 feet of wall and practice serving against wall so that the ball hits above eight-foot (net height) line. Keep moving back as accuracy and confidence are gained until the official 30-foot serving line is reached.

Receive and Pass

Stand with feet in walk stand position.

Face the ball as it comes over toward you. Try to handle the ball at height of chest or in front of face.

Elbows are half flexed (bent) and held well up (about height of shoulders).

Fingers are spread, palms are toward ball (away from face). Ball is handled (batted) with both hands—use fingertip control.

Pass should be high, spin taken off ball, and placed within one to three feet of spot desired.

Individual passing practice may be secured by passing (batting) ball in manner described above, against a flat wall, moving in to within three feet and back as far as six to ten feet, keeping the ball on the fly continually. Also, two players may bat the ball back and forth between them working for height, control, accuracy, and body balance. Also, a circle of players may keep a ball going up in the air with the use of this pass taking turns, no player hitting the ball twice in succession.

As judgment and ability are gained, hard, *thrown* balls, simulating a hard spike, should be received and handled by players. Practice should also be received in receiving underhand as well as in the overhand position.

Setup

Similar to pass but usually effected at net position, the pass or setup is made to the spiker or attack player.

Ball must be controlled; it must be put into position where attack player can strike it successfully with a powerful drive ("spike") or placement shot. A good setup should be passed four to ten feet above the net (depending upon the spiker's wishes) and placed so it will drop within six to twelve inches of the net (without a spin).

Individual practice in setting up may be secured by a player standing a few feet away from a basketball goal, tossing a volleyball into the air and as it comes down setting it up (batting it with both hands using the fingertips) so that the ball arches into the air and drops through the basketball goal without touching the hoop.

Another drill stunt for a single player is to stand with the right shoulder close to a wall, at least 15 to 20 feet high, and pass the ball high into the air close to the wall but without touching the wall. Keep this up. Then do the same with the left shoulder close to the wall. This develops control of eye, hands, and ball, wrist, and finger strength.

Spike or Attack

All players must serve, receive, and pass, but only tall players or those with a very good jump or spring can spike. Such players should be able to jump

Fig. 43.2 The block is an effective defensive technique. United States Army photograph.

and reach nine or nine-and-a-half feet into the air to be effective spikers (one or one-and-a-half feet higher than the net).

He must have an accurate setup man.

He must judge the ball and jump and hit at the proper time.

He must study opponents to discover "holes" in the defense and take advantage of openings.

He may spring from one or both feet (from two feet puts less strain on the jumping legs).

Use arms in getting more lift of body into air.

Keep head up and body erect in the air.

Legs spread in the air give stability for a hard drive.

Ball is driven with cupped palm for power and accuracy (closed fist is fast but less accurate).

Watch ball all the time to avoid being unprepared for blocked balls or quick return.

A newly developed mechanical "setup" machine makes it possible for a spiker to practice intensively with only one other player to trip the lever and recover balls.

Block

One-man block is not too effective. Two-man block can be developed to a high degree as a great defensive tactic.

Both blocking players must jump up simultaneously and reach high in front of opposing spiker. They must be close to net (within six inches) with their four hands and arms forming a wall against which the driven ball rebounds into the opponents' court to the consternation and chagrin of the spiker.

The blockers' hands should be tilted slightly backward to allow an unsuccessfully blocked ball to be deflected to the blockers' backcourt where it can be retrieved by the blockers' teammates; otherwise the ball might fall dead to the floor before the blockers.

Extreme care must be exercised by blockers to avoid reaching over or touching the net thus committing a foul.

Net Recovery

The difference between a good and a poor team lies in its ability to keep difficult shots in play. Many points can be scored by recovering balls driven into the net. As the coach throws the ball into the net, the player springs forward, his right shoulder toward the net, body crouched low and erect. He recovers the ball as it rebounds. The left shoulder approach is also practiced. The net is never faced for the ball would spring out directly at the player making recovery difficult.

Watch the net for recovery clues. A ball hitting near the top will drop to the floor. If the ball hits near the bottom, it will spring back two or three feet.

Team Work

There are six men, each with a specific position.

A team may handle the ball three times—never more—before returning it over the net. Make the most of these three hits by dividing the return in the three component parts: receive, setup, spike. It is illegal for a player to hit ball twice in succession.

Avoid collisions in wild attempts to recover the ball by calling for ball you intend to take as baseball fielders do on uncertain flies.

Develop the idea that every player is valuable, welcome, and has a part in making the game a success. People like to feel they "belong." Expect the best of each player. Everyone cooperates in getting this "best" from every player.

Knowledge of Rules

Study rules. Prepare true and false statements to check up on players' knowledge.

Take turns at officiating.

Know names of playing positions.

Have proper court markings.

Understand principle of rotation when side-out is declared.

Have manually operated scoreboards for players to use in marking up their own scores.

Have experienced players explain game to new players and give them coaching.

Opportunity for participation. Once a player has secured the general idea of play as a part of his motivation and has secured additional coaching in the component skills of the game, he must have an opportunity to participate in order to secure the fun that comes from satisfactory play and functioning as part of a group—the team. This is where regularly organized leagues play their part. Definite teams are arranged to ensure well balanced contests. The teams are formed in a manner that will cause no embarrassment to players who might be chosen last if players were selected in a class. If some teams are too strong, adjustments should be made to even up. Re-form teams and organize fresh leagues frequently to maintain interest. Emphasize fun, regular participation, and improvement in play.

Volleyball for Children*

Allen Scates

The main reason that "power" volleyball has been so slow to develop in the United States is that the basic skills and tactics essential to the sport are usually not taught to children in the elementary schools. It is much more difficult to teach older students and adults because they are self-conscious and afraid of looking uncoordinated and generally inept. Volleyball techniques do not come easy to people whose sports background has not incorporated similar movements. Children readily attempt to learn the techniques of the dive and roll while adults have a fear of going to the floor to retrieve a ball. We have strong age group programs in all of the sports that our country is successful in on an international level. The Eastern Europeans and Asians dominate international volleyball because instruction is available at an early age and the interest among young people grows as they mature.

While teaching elementary school I have found that coordinated kindergarten children can learn to use the forearm pass. High ability second graders are capable of using the overhand serve and can put the ball into the opponents' court 8 out of 10 times at distances up to 30 ft. On the other hand, I have made the mistake of frustrating children during their initial training period by attempting to teach skills beyond their reach. Unless they feel successful and have fun while they are learning, they will lose interest. Too much drilling without motivating lead-up games and tournaments can quickly turn into drudgery.

LEAD-UP GAMES

After the International Volleyball Association developed "mini-volleyball" in 1971, the Scientific Research Section of the Committee of Instruction and Popularization of the Japanese Volleyball Association carefully examined its possibilities. The Japanese have "taken a leading part in studying the volleyball rules for children and lead-up games that are considered a preceding stage of guidance to mini-volleyball" (Toyoda 1974a, pp. 38–41). In the course of study for volleyball in the elementary schools of Japan, students develop the capacities of catching and throwing as the first step in a progression to the fundamental technique of the overhand pass. The overhand pass is developed from the action of catching the ball in front of the body and

* Reprinted with permission from *JOPER* **46**, 9 (November–December), 1975.

immediately throwing it to a teammate over the net. The following stages are recommended by Hiroshi Toyoda, the Chief of Scientific Research of the Japanese Volleyball Association (Toyoda 1974b, p. 63).

- ☐ Throw and catch the ball.
- ☐ Hit the ball after bouncing it on the floor.
- ☐ Hit the ball without bouncing it.
- ☐ Do not catch the ball; at this stage the criteria for a held ball are not too severe.
- ☐ Do not catch the ball; criteria for a legally played ball are nearly those of the formal game.

Although there are many stages and styles of individual training at each of the principal lead-up games described in this article, the main point to stress is to move quickly in front of the oncoming ball. When players reach the receiving area the front foot should hit the floor first and *point in the direction of the intended pass*. It is very important to maintain a low body position to stop with good balance. The stop is made with the lead foot slightly forward and the trailing foot closing to maintain a balanced position.

The rules to the various lead-up games which follow are those that have worked for me at the elementary and junior high school level. Each instructor can devise modifications of these and other lead-up games to emphasize the fundamental techniques that need to be strengthened. It is important not to move too quickly in the progression of games or children will not experience success and feel that volleyball is too difficult for them.

1. *Net Ball* is played on a regulation court with a net or rope stretched across the center of the court. A team consists of six players or fewer when working with high ability groups of children; homogeneous groups may play with up to eight on a side. Any player puts the ball in play by throwing it over the net from the court or behind the court. The ball can be touched three times and must be caught and released quickly. Touching the ball two times in succession is a fault. If the ball flies out of the opponents' court or falls on the ground, a fault is committed and the opponents receive a point. Balls that hit the net are always in play. A game consists of 21 points.

2. *Newcomb* is played on a regulation court with the height of the net from 5 to 7 feet, depending on the size of the children. The game is played with eight players or fewer, depending on their ability. This game appears in many physical education curriculum guides throughout the country and can be introduced in the second grade. Instructors may want to continue this game with low ability fifth and sixth graders. All balls can be caught and quickly thrown to a teammate or into the opponents' court. Volleyball rules are in force with the following exceptions.

a) The server may throw or serve the ball to put it in play.

b) The server may stand as close to the net as necessary to complete a successful serve.

c) A back row player cannot throw the ball over the net. This rule is not in force when playing with four players or less.

3. *Modified Newcomb* is like Newcomb in that the first and second ball can be caught; but the ball that is returned to the opponents' court must be hit in a legal manner. A freer handling of the ball is allowed.

The children line up in the M formation to receive the serve. The player who receives the serve may catch it and throw it to the setter in the middle front. The setter sets or lobs the ball with two hands in an underhand toss to one of the spikers, who hits it over the net using any legal technique. The defense is also allowed to catch the first and second ball as long as the ball is hit into the opponents' court.

Hitting the Ball after Bouncing It

1. *Bounce Volleyball* is played on a regulation court with six players on a side. The ball is caught, bounced, and hit once in a regulation manner. The ball is still in play if a teammate catches the ball. The server has two chances to hit the ball over the net. Weaker servers may stand as close as 20 feet from the net.

2. *Option Volleyball* is almost the same as Bounce Volleyball. A player is allowed to hit the ball with or without bouncing it. The ball must be returned to the opponents' court within three touches. A game is 15 points with the teams changing sides at eight points.

3. *Volley Tennis* is played on a tennis court with a tennis net. A team consists of six to nine players. The ball is served from behind the end line and one assist can be made before the ball crosses over to the opponents' court. Although players are not allowed to catch the ball, they have the option of hitting it on the fly or letting the ball bounce once before playing it. The ball must be returned to the opponents' court within three touches. This is a good game to emphasize the spike.

Modified Volleyball

1. *Sitting Volleyball* teams consist of nine players or so, who all sit or kneel on the floor. A rope or net is drawn across the center of the court. The game can be played on mats and the size of the court is determined by the number of participants. Net height can be varied from group to group dependent upon their strength. Service is made from behind the end line, using an overhand pass. Rotation can be used if desired.

2. *Keep It Up* is played on a regulation court with four teams of three to six players. Each court is divided perpendicularly into two courts so that

there are two separate courts on both sides of the net. A front line player of a team puts the ball into play by using the overhand pass to direct the ball into one of the opponents' courts. If a team returns the ball over the net, the team is awarded one point. When an error is made, the team that made the error serves the next ball. There is no point awarded for serving the ball over the net. Each team is allowed three touches to return the ball over the net.

3. *Underhand Serve Volleyball* prevents a boring serving contest and encourages rallies. The most difficult technique for children to master is an accurate pass of a hard overhand serve. In this game an underhand serve is required into a smaller area of the court—the badminton court which seems to be marked inside of every volleyball court in America. This gives the server an area 20 ft. wide and 22 ft. long to serve to. Players on the receiving team align themselves into the area of the badminton court for service reception. The percentage of well-placed first passes will increase immediately. Since the first pass is the key to the offense, better sets and spikes also increase significantly. After the serve is received the boundaries extend back to the regulation 30' × 60' court. The children play on a net that is lowered until the average child in the game can touch the top of the net with outstretched fingertips from a standing position. This lowered net encourages spiking. Regulation rules are followed, but the criteria for handling the ball are determined by the capacity of the players.

4. *Bonus Volleyball* uses the same net height, serve, and criteria for ball handling as Underhand Serve Volleyball. Points are awarded in the normal way with the following exception: if a team scores using a pass, set, and spike they are awarded two points. A game is won when a team scores 21 points.

5. *Spike It Volleyball* was developed to teach defensive positioning. The ball is put into play by the attacker who hits the ball out of the Spike It. Each member of the attacking team hits the ball from the left side of the court before the Spike It is moved to the center and right side of the court. A point is scored on each play. The attacking team scores when the defense fails to block or return the ball over the net. The defense scores a point when the attacker makes an error or when the defenders return or block the spike into the opponents' court.

6. *Thriples Volleyball* is played on a badminton court with a lowered net. The underhand serve must be used and all players can block and spike. Two players stay deep in the court to receive the serve and the third player stays at the net in the center of the court to set. Players rotate from left back to setter to the right back or serving position. To increase the movement of the players and to encourage spiking, the regulation court can be used after the serve is received in the smaller confines of the badminton court. As skill level increases, the standard court can be used along with the overhand serve.

MINI-VOLLEYBALL

The Trainer Commission Committee on Mini-Volleyball of the International Volleyball Federation (FIVB) developed rules recommended for adoption by all national volleyball associations in 1971 (Baake 1974, pp. 36–40). These rules are for children from 9 to 12 years of age and are played by two teams of three players each. The rules enable children to grasp the technique and the elementary tactics and capabilities essential to the sport, such as swiftness, skill, jumping ability, and quick response, and they are able to learn all this while actually playing. The rules established for mini-volleyball were based on relevant experiences and scientific publications of many countries.

Rule Changes

The following rules were formulated by the FIVB Training Commission Committee on Mini-Volleyball (1971):

1. A team consists of three players; two substitutions per game are permissible.

2. The height of the net is 2.10 meters (approximately 6' 10") for both male and female teams.

3. The players of each team position themselves within their courts so that there are two front-line players and one back-line player at the time the ball is served. After serving the ball the back-line player may not spike the ball from within the attack area or attempt to hit the ball in the attack area unless the ball is below the height of the net.

4. The players of a team change their positions upon receiving the ball for service. The right front-line player becomes the back-line player and the left front-line player becomes the right front-line player.

5. A team wins the game when it scores at least 15 points and has a two point advantage over the opponents (15:13; 16:14 etc.)

6. A team wins the match when it has won at least 2 sets of the match (2:0 or 2:1).

7. The match is conducted by a referee who takes care that the rules are not violated and ensures that the match is played correctly and in keeping with principles of fair play. The referee has a teaching function.

8. The playing area is 4.5 meters wide and 12 meters long. A net divides the playing area in two equal parts. The spiking line is 3 meters from the center line. (**Author's note:** 4.5 m by 12 m is approximately 14' 9" by 39' 5". Since most school volleyball courts have badminton courts marked within their dimensions, I suggest you use badminton courts for mini-volleyball. This gives you an area of 20 ft. wide by 44 ft. long with a spiking line 6' 6" from the center line. I have used badminton courts for thriples volleyball with children up to the seventh grade with good results.)

Offense

Since the back line player cannot spike in the official version of the game, it is usually advantageous for the front row players to receive all the serves and have the back row player penetrate to the net to set. This allows the offense to run with two attackers. If players cannot pass accurately this system does not work.

I prefer to disregard the rule that prohibits spiking by the backcourt player and use a different formation and rotation. We place two players deep in the court to receive all serves.

The third player is placed at the net in the center of the court and has no receiving responsibility. This player's job is to set all passes for one of the other players to spike. All players are allowed to spike and block and players rotate from left back to setter to the right back or serving position.

Defense

Most children under 13 years of age are not capable of strong spikes. Therefore it is often best to keep all three defenders back to receive the spike. This leads to long rallies and great concentration and pride in digging techniques by the participants. The enthusiasm that is evident when children complete these long rallies is very stimulating for the participants and spectators. When players are capable of strong spiking, they should be opposed by one blocker.

MINI-VOLLEYBALL IN EAST GERMANY

About 1962 the East German Volleyball Federation began to assign some of their top volleyball coaches to work with children under 12 years of age. They were soon confronted with arguments that power volleyball techniques were too difficult to teach to children because of their insufficient physical development. However, their immediate success caused mini-volleyball to spread throughout Europe.

Today volleyball is an integral part of many national physical education programs; it is particularly strong in Eastern Europe and Asia. Teachers and coaches begin teaching mini-volleyball to children who are eight and nine years old. This experience would be difficult to duplicate in the United States since the overwhelming majority of children do not receive regular instruction from a physical education teacher until they are in the seventh grade. The chairman of the International Volleyball Council of Coaches, reporting on the East German mini-volleyball championships, states that "children possess already astonishing technical and tactical achievements and their enthusiasm is enormous" (Baake 1974, pp. 36–40). The chairman gives several reasons for this quick and successful development. First, technique is acquired quickly before puberty when the requirements of the game are modified to their possibilities. Second, the essential physical qualities of speed, mobility, and agility exist at this age or quickly develop. Third, children are enthusiastic about the game and its competitions. Fourth, the rich emotional content of mini-volleyball has strong attraction for children.

Children who train twice a week can learn the fundamental techniques in two or three months and after four or five months' training can successfully participate in formal competition. Since mini matches are the best two out of three games, children play in several matches in the same day without over-straining themselves. "For children, mini-volleyball is a complete, whole game, a struggle full of sense and joy, an event and, at the same time, a lesson. It is of paramount importance to stimulate the interest and the enthusiasm, to learn the movements of the game, to develop the physical qualities essential for volleyball both for all mass games of entertainment and the elite volleyball" (Baake, 1974, pp. 36–40).

JUNIOR HIGH SCHOOL VOLLEYBALL

In the physical education class, intramural program or extramural program at the junior high level, the student should have an opportunity to become a complete player. This means that all players should get to set and attack. Under our present system players are labeled setters or spikers and often fail to develop the fundamental techniques inherent in the other position. On our national teams there are setters who are poor attackers and spikers who are poor setters. In their development they missed the opportunity to become complete players.

At this level of competition one position on the court should be designated as the setting position. For example, if a team is running a two-hitter attack, every player who rotates to the middle front position should set the ball for the side-out attempt. If a team uses a three-hitter attack, the player in the right back position should set. This 6–6 system of offense forces all players to develop fundamental volleyball abilities. On defense the player should also play each of the six positions.

During the summer I have conducted coeducational volleyball classes which meet daily for two hours for a five- to six-week period. The children are entering grades six through eight and the first 24 students to sign up for the course are accepted without regard to ability.

We usually spend the first 20 minutes reviewing the last day's progress and establishing points of emphasis for the daily lesson. I have found that it is best to spend this time in the classroom where the students are not distracted by playground activities. The next 30 minutes are spent on drills with no more than two or three students to a ball. After the players learn a sufficient number of ball-handling drills, they should move from drill to drill rapidly so interest does not flag. Spiking and digging drills come last because these are the most satisfying and provide the best motivation as players start to become slightly fatigued. A ten- to fifteen-minute break is taken at this point to allow the players to get drinks and a snack if desired. Many students prefer to work with the ball during the break in unsupervised games of one-on-one or doubles. Others request· help with certain techniques, particularly spiking. After the break I align the class into various teams on two to three courts depending on the daily lesson. Older boys and girls are often invited into the class at this stage to challenge the better players in doubles or mini-volleyball while the majority of the class plays the other modified games. Heterogeneous grouping only succeeds when playing with six on a side. Smaller games need to be grouped by ability.

Since we play on the blacktop, the weather is a determining factor in the selection of the activity for the second half of the class. On particularly hot or humid days the students are divided into three teams so they can rest between games. We can play three games of underhand serve volleyball in 50 minutes, which gives every team two games. The more energetic players are allowed to play an unstructured game on the adjoining courts instead of resting. This type of practice is not designed to develop a school team, but rather to teach the fundamental techniques and instill interest in the sport.

In Eastern Europe and Asia children 12 to 14 years old train a minimum of 10–12 hours a week after school if they are representing a school team. Studies conducted by a prominent coach in Bulgaria indicate children are capable of playing a five-game match at this age and "began at the following day their meetings in a physical state fully restored" (Chakarov 1970, pp. 27–35). I have not been able to find similar studies in the literature, but my experiences with children of this age lead me to concur with the Bulgarian study.

REFERENCES

Baake, H. 1974. Mini-volleyball. *Technical Journal* **1,** 1. Scarboro, Ontario: Canadian National Volleyball Coaches Association.

Chakarov, T. 1970. Some questions of the maximum possibilities of playing of children in volleyball. *FIVB Bull.* **49–50** (March).

FIVB Training Commission Committee on Mini Volleyball 1971. Mini-volleyball rules for children from 9 to 12 years of age. M. Haley (trans.). Leipzig, December 27.

Toyoda, H. 1974a. Report to the Council of Coaches—FIVB. *Technical Journal* **1,** 2. Scarboro, Ontario: Canadian National Volleyball Coaches Association.

——— 1974b. Volleyball coaching seminar. *Technical Journal* **1,** 1. Scarboro, Ontario: Canadian National Volleyball Coaches Association.

44

Water Polo

G. Dintiman, L. Barrow, and B. Hutchinson

DESCRIPTION OF THE ACTIVITY

The game of water polo has been sufficiently refined in recent years to eliminate unnecessarily rough play and emphasize the more important skills of ball handling, dribbling, passing, shooting, play execution, and swimming endurance and skill. Water polo has been a popular sport in the training of military personnel due to its high contribution to general physical conditioning and development of advanced swimming skills. A steadily increasing number of institutions throughout the United States are incorporating water polo into their physical education and athletic programs. The necessity to master complex swimming skills, the great physical demands and value derived from competition, its spectator appeal, its competitiveness, and the pleasure of participation in the game will make water polo a popular sport of the future.

A team is composed of seven players—goal guard, left and right back, halfback, center forward, and left and right forward—with basic positions in the pool, or tank, fluctuating with the style and objectives of offensive and defensive tactics. To initiate play, teams assume a position parallel to their respective ends on either side of the goal guard, with the center forwards in the goal area. The whistle indicates play is officially started as the referee releases the ball in a neutral area in the center of the tank. Center forwards of both teams sprint for possession, pass the ball back to a teammate, and continue to their assigned positions in the offensive half of the tank. All players of both squads move to their areas as the ball is advanced toward the opponents' goal for an attempted score, which is accomplished by throwing or forcing the ball through the goal area by passing and dribbling maneuvers. The defensive team may use zone defense, whereby each player is assigned a specific area, or man-to-man defense, in which each player is assigned to an opponent, with the latter necessitating a skilled, highly conditioned, fast-break team.

A match consists of four 7-minute periods interrupted by 3-minute intermissions. One point is awarded each time the ball enters the goal area. In the event of a tie, two 5-minute periods, following a 5-minute rest period, with a 2-minute intermission between the two periods to allow for a change of ends are played. The third overtime period, if needed, is a "sudden death" extension in which the team scoring the first goal is declared the winner.

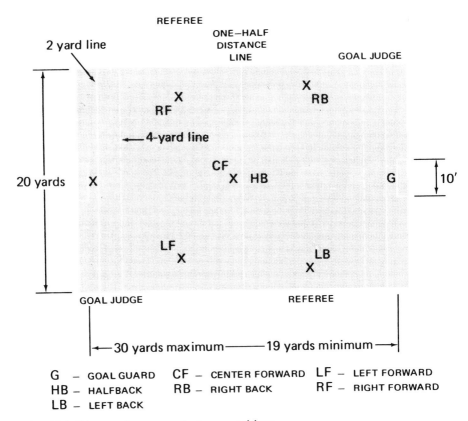

Fig. 44.1 Water polo area and player positions.

Referees, who are equipped with 12-inch square flags of various colors to indicate the type of infraction, wave a flag after each whistle. Goal judges are stationed at both ends of the pool to signal a score, corner, or goal throw.

Although the official tank must be adapted to available pool facilities, dimensions have been standardized. The recommended area, 30 by 20 yards, and positions of the players are shown in Fig. 44.1. The goal area, or cage, has a wooden or metal frame and a net cover and is 10 feet wide, 3 feet high, and 1 foot deep. An improvised goal area approximating these dimensions can be devised. The depth of the water must be a minimum of 3 feet for dual match competition and 5 feet for championship meets. A depth of 7 feet is recommended.

EQUIPMENT

The equipment required for water polo is the same as that required for competitive swimming. The suit must completely cover the buttocks, with the waist and leg lines parallel when viewed from a side position. Caps of contrasting colors, numbered 1 to 21, are used to readily distinguish teammates and opponents. Ear and nose plugs are permitted; however, the use of additional padding, rings, bracelets, and other jewelry or protruding objects that may cause bodily harm is prohibited. The body must be free from oil or other similar applications. The use of fins or masks is also a violation of the rules.

SKILLS AND TECHNIQUES

Water polo combines simple and complex swimming skills. Treading water with a scissor or breaststroke kick, with minimum expenditure of energy and maximum relaxation and use of body buoyancy, is one of the most essential skills that must be performed. Competitors must combine stroke efficiency with control of the body, balance, and the execution of passing, shooting, and blocking maneuvers at varying speeds.

Swimming

Crawl stroke. When speed is desired in pursuing an opponent or the ball, in maintaining spacing, or in dribbling, the crawl stroke is used. Form is altered somewhat by keeping the head above the water to aid vision. Initiating the stroke explosively is important and requires rapid arm movement to attain forward momentum and full extension of the body, to be followed by the flutter kick. The crawl stroke in water polo differs from the basic crawl in that the legs and feet are deeper in the water, there is a longer kick, a shorter underwater pull, and a more rapid abovewater recovery. The elbows recover high to provide maximum ball protection while dribbling.

Breaststroke. The breaststroke is actually a preparatory maneuver or a means of jockeying to maintain a position of readiness most conducive to the execution of all water polo skills. The head remains above the surface of the water in using this stroke to approach a loose ball, an opponent, or an area when speed is not a factor.

Backstroke. The backstroke provides an effective means of shooting from a back layout position, of evading an opponent, or of maneuvering defensively without losing sight of the ball or the opponents.

Underwater swimming. Underwater swimming, using the breaststroke and kick, is a legal maneuver that provides a means of secretly altering position when the player does not have the ball. Before the stroke is initiated, the body submerges from a vertical position, with the eyes remaining open throughout to permit accurate reentry.

Change of direction. A change of direction maneuver is used constantly and must be made with explosiveness, with a minimum loss of speed, and without aid from the sides or bottom of the pool. The stroke terminates by an extension of both arms outward, parallel to the shoulders, with the palms resisting movement and then rapidly performing a finning action. Utilizing the momentum of the stroke, the hips and knees are flexed and carried through and beyond the spot occupied by the hands, causing the body to change from a prone to a back position before rolling again to a prone position in the opposite direction. A turn to the left or right is less involved and requires a rotation of the shoulder and head as the strong arm pulls in the intended direction. Since the rules do not permit the use of the sides or bottom of the pool, the speed of a start is increased by a scissors or breaststroke kick.

Dribbling

The crawl stroke, with the head raised above the surface of the water, provides maximum speed and control in advancing the ball. To perform the dribble the eyes are focused on the ball, although teammates and opponents are kept in peripheral vision, and the control and forward push are performed by the face and upper arm on each forward arm movement. Keeping the elbow high serves to protect the ball from the defenders as well as to control and maintain position for the opposite arm stroke. Control is also increased by keeping the ball within the limits of the upper arm. An advanced technique, whereby the ball rides on the advancing wave created by the arm movement, may be used by highly skilled swimmers.

A *speed dribble,* with the ball being pushed four to six feet in front of the body, is useful on fast-break situations.

Lifting the Ball from the Water

The ball can be lifted and controlled by (1) placing the hand with widely spread fingers under the ball and scooping it upward, (2) placing the hand on top of the ball before rotating the wrist and arm downward, away from the body and under the ball (Fig. 44.3), and (3) applying a rapid downward

Fig. 44.2 Dribbling form.

Fig. 44.3 Lifting the ball from the water with downward pressure and wrist-arm rotation.

push with the wrist, while the hand is on top of the ball, and flexing the wrist back to control the ball as it rebounds upward from the water. In executing any of these three movements, a vertical or semivertical, rapid approach position is assumed with the hands and feet pushing the water downward in the breaststroke or scissors kick to elevate the body slightly out of the water to armpit level. The upward scoop is the surest means of acquiring control, followed by the rotating and pressure methods. Rapid movement from the approach to control and release of the ball in the form of a pass or shot is essential for the water polo competitor.

Receiving

In receiving the various types of passes, players should catch the ball at its highest peak and minimize interceptions in congested areas by meeting the pass and jumping upward and toward the ball, making it difficult for an interception from behind. The ball is caught with the fingers and cushioned by a slight give of the hand and body at impact. Control should be acquired quickly, followed by immediate release. The player should spin the ball on the surface of the water, with the arm extended to sweep and control the ball as the player moves between the ball and defender to protect the ball with his body.

Dry pass. A pass that approaches the player above the surface of the water is received by the player acquiring maximum height out of the water with a vigorous downward push of the free arm and kick of both feet as the receiving hand extends high above the water.

Wet pass. A pass that skims the water prior to being received also requires the player to raise the body above the water in the manner described above. The receiving hand, with comfortably spread fingers, rises a quarter to three-quarters of a ball length above the water to prevent the ball from going over or under by forming a trap pocket between the hand and the surface of the water. The body remains elevated through the use of a figure 8 sculling movement in preparation for a pass or scoring attempt.

Shooting and Scoring Techniques

No player·other than the goalkeeper may touch the ball with more than one hand at a time or strike the ball with a clenched fist. The types of passes described below are also scoring procedures with some providing more forceful, accurate attempts than others. The following suggestions apply to all passes and shots:

☐ Keep the fingers comfortably spread, avoiding contact with the palm of the hand.

☐ Maintain eye contact with the target until the follow-through phase has terminated.

☐ Learn to coordinate catching, lifting, and passing or shooting attempts into one continuous, smooth movement.

☐ Secure as much height above the water as possible to free the throwing arm completely.

☐ Incorporate the weight of the body into the toss when maximum speed is desired.

☐ Employ head, shoulder, and eye feints to avoid telegraphing the intended direction of a pass.

☐ Avoid spinning the ball in such a way that it may curve or present handling difficulties for the receiver.

☐ Adjust the speed of a pass to the distance of teammates and the proximity of the nearest defender.

☐ Use a quick trudgeon kick to move the body clear of a defender, lift the ball quickly and accurately, use a trudgeon kick to elevate the body and free the entire passing arm, and execute the pass or shot with concentration on the target area throughout the movement.

Back layout pass or shot. This common maneuver is performed by lifting the ball from the water using any of the three previously described methods. If the offensive player has his back to the goal or to a teammate, the player should turn the head and shoulders as he controls the ball and should elevate the body from the water to face the target area. To execute the toss efficiently, he should elevate the throwing arm from the water, flex the elbow slightly, snap the wrist sharply, and maintain fingertip control. As he makes the toss he tilts the upper body backward, away from the target. He should continuously maintain the body in a raised position by pushing the water downward and backward with the free hand and the feet.

Sidearm shot or pass. From a front layout, or modified breaststroke, position, with the head and neck clearly out of the water, the throwing hand is placed on top of the ball, with comfortably flexed fingers exerting a slight downward push. Pressure is then released resulting in a slight rebound which permits the hand, with the thumb underneath, palm and elbow away from the body and toward the target as the hand moves under the ball for control. The free hand and legs again must keep the neck and throwing arm completely free from the resistance of the water as the elbow extends forcefully toward the target, with a sharp wrist snap and fingertip control. The ball moves parallel to or somewhat forward of the body. Peripheral vision permits the necessary visual lineup and the use of appropriate feints.

The push shot or pass. Using the same hand placement, arm action, and movement of the free arm and feet as above, the elbow flexes and rotates outward away from the body; the back of the hand, which is slightly under and behind the ball, is approximately 18 inches from the face as the elbow extends rapidly, followed by a sharp wrist snap to propel the ball forward at a height approximately six inches from the water surface. Either a front layout, swimming, or vertical position can be used.

Backhand shot or pass. From a front layout position, form similar to that described for the sidearm pass is used. Hand placement is the same as the ball is lifted almost vertically and the elbow and wrist are extended to propel the ball backward at the desired level and speed. Sighting of the target area and use of feints are possible through peripheral vision.

Scoop pass. The scoop pass is a rapid means of throwing the ball over the head to a teammate who is behind or to either side. The control hand assumes a supinated, or palm up, position, with the elbows slightly flexed. It approaches the ball from underwater, rises quickly with a wrist snap and elbow extension, and actually scoops the ball out of the water to the target.

Defensive Block

The purpose of one-on-one defensive procedures is to block or deflect the ball, hurry the opponent, impair the opponent's vision, force a lob pass, change the throwing speed, or alter the accurate path of a pass or shot through other means. The defender must change from a rapidly approaching front crawl stroke to a vertical position, with all four extremities pushing water downward to elevate the body high above the water surface in preparation for the block. The hand nearest the ball is then extended rapidly toward the elbow of the opponent's throwing arm. The defender must move in close prior to an attempted block and must time his action with the opponent's throwing movement. This close position will permit the defender to rise vertically rather than at an angle to the passer at less than maximum height (see Fig. 44.4). Once a player takes hold of the ball, he may be impeded by being grabbed in any reasonable manner.

BASIC STRATEGY

Defensive Play

Tight man-to-man or zone defense may be employed. In one-on-one man-to-man defense the following positions can be used: (1) one-half man to one side of the ball, (2) "fronting" an opponent deep in the scoring area to shut off passing lanes and increase interception opportunities, or (3) playing be-

Fig. 44.4 Back layout shot or pass and defensive block.

hind an opponent who is not in a threatening position. Taking a position toward the ball side or fronting the opponent greatly increases interception opportunities and requires an aggressive, constantly changing position, a great degree of endurance, and excellent swimming ability. In order to thwart offensive attacks and maintain proper defensive balance in man-to-man defense, defensive players should help teammates by executing switches and recoveries to new assignments on break-through situations where the opponent gets by a teammate.

Zone defense is also effective and somewhat less physically demanding than man-to-man tactics. Although players are assigned to an area, it often becomes necessary to assist a teammate who is out of position or outnumbered due to overload offensive tactics. Man-to-man principles apply when an opponent with or without the ball enters a defensive player's area. A player must feel free to vacate his area to assist a teammate in difficulty and must retreat to the line of the ball or to a new area when the offense successfully passes the defensive player's area.

As a diversionary tactic, a defensive player may vacate his area and enter the scoring half of the tank for an attempted interception and possible score. Such a maneuver weakens the team's defensive end; however, it permits double-up tactics, in which there are two defensive players on the offensive player with the ball, and thereby increases the possibility of interception. Players should be encouraged to attempt interceptions by assuming positions that may include the element of risk. Should an assigned player manage to get by an opponent as a result of such a gamble, a teammate will immediately leave his area or man to pick up the free offensive swimmer. The defensive swimmer who was surpassed has the responsibility of immediately swimming toward the goal area to pick up the free man or fill an open area.

Offensive Play

Offensive teams should attempt to maintain proper spacing and cutting throughout the tank, setting up free-lance or pattern maneuvers by dribbling

and passing. A trailer generally follows a dribbler to provide a safety valve should a forward pass not be feasible when the defense attacks. As the six players initiate the attack, they assume proper spacing in preparation for both offensive and defensive action with the two most aggressive and competent swimmers taking the lead in the scoring half of the tank.

The *forwards* perform the majority of the scoring attempts through assists from the backs in setting up the plays. Forwards should be quick with their hands for shooting and passing, should be strong swimmers, and should be able to maneuver well. Forwards assume positions near the two corners of the scoring half and work within the 4-yard line.

The *center forward,* who sprints for the initial neutral toss in the center of the tank, should be a fast swimmer and an excellent passer and shooter. He assumes a position approximately six to eight yards from the opponent's goal to complete the three-lane attack consisting of the center forward and the left and right forwards. The center forward is responsible for setting up his forwards as well as shooting when the opportunity arises. He also covers defenders when a quick break-through occurs in an attempt to carry the ball into his scoring half of the tank.

The *center back* covers the opposing center forward and swims freely up and down the tank area. He should be the strongest, fastest swimmer and should be capable of analyzing the opponent's offensive and defensive intent. The center back maneuvers for the pass from the goal guard to initiate the attack by passing to his forwards. Defensively, he protects the goal area by stopping feed passes from the opposing center forward to the opposing for-wards.

The *guards* are generally larger, stronger players with long extremities since a defensive role is the preliminary function. The guards combine with the goal guard to protect the goal area aggressively and to initiate the attack when the ball is recovered. They must be able to diagnose offensive intent and must have skill in the breaststroke and in blocking tactics.

The *goal guard* should be the tallest player on the team, with long arms and quick reactions. He must use his extremities explosively to push the water forcefully downward and elevate the body high above the water before raising both hands high, with elbows extended, in preparation for blocking a shot or pass. He uses a breaststroke or scissors kick to provide the vertical momentum out of the water. The goal guard must keep his eyes on the ball throughout the blocking attempt, must be proficient in the breaststroke, and must be physically capable of treading water for long periods of time. His position around the goal area varies according to the angle of the scoring attempt; therefore, he must master the knowledge of which position to take with each angle of attempt if the dangerous portions of the goal area are to be decreased and adequately covered for all attempts. The goal guard also has the function of initiating offensive attack with a quick, accurate outlet pass to the center back or guards. He is not permitted to throw the ball beyond the center of the tank.

Basic Systems

Both offensive and defensive styles of play will vary according to the abilities, strengths, and weaknesses of the team and of the opponents as well as with special situations, for example, one team being short or up one player.

Stationary, man-in-the-hole pattern. This stationary, man-in-the-hole pattern is commonly employed by beginning, inexperienced teams. As shown in Fig. 44.5, left, right, and center guards group in a triangle around the goal area and utilize a zone defense to supplement the efforts of the goalkeeper. Each is responsible for his defensive area and will vacate this basic position for offensive tactics only on rare occasions. The right and left forwards are responsible for moving the ball to the scoring half of the pool after receiving a

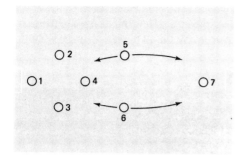

Fig. 44.5 Stationary, man-in-the-hole pattern. From Charles Hines, *How to play and teach water polo.* Association Press, New York, 1967.

pass from the guards. The center forward, or man-in-the-hole, is stationed in front of the opponent's goal area and is mainly responsible for shooting after receiving a pass from the forwards.

This system of play requires a minimum level of skill and conditioning since each player is required to master only his specialty—the guards, defensive ability; the forwards, speed and the abilty to handle the ball; and the center forward, scoring or shooting ability. The stationary pattern does possess the obvious disadvantages of limited movement, limited strategy, lack of variation, and a three-man attack that is often thwarted by close coverage of the hole forward.

Combination zone/man-to-man defense. The combination zone/man-to-man defense is commonly employed against teams using the man-in-the-hole offense. The three guards utilize zone principles in covering their respective areas. The right and left forwards also apply zone principles when possession of the ball changes. Man-to-man tactics are employed by the player guarding the man-in-the-hole. Any one of the three basic defensive positions—behind, fronting, or overplay—described previously can be used depending upon the location of the offensive player. When the man-in-the-hole assumes a position at the 2-yard line, fronting is recommended in order to force him into the illegal area as well as to close passing lanes.

Continuity pattern. The continuity pattern represents the other extreme of offensive attack and is only employed by experienced, well-conditioned players of great ability. The players swim and move the ball continuously in and around the opponent's goal area, with two trailing players also entering the scoring triangle as well as an additional player moving toward the middle of the scoring half of the tank ready to react depending on the offensive or defensive situation. This system represents a five-player offensive continuity that requires a well-balanced team. All three forwards move in a triangle, alternately swimming in front of the goal. The three guards provide defensive stability by assuming positions in the defensive half of the tank and continuously moving to the right before sprinting toward the scoring half, entering the scoring triangle, and returning to their original defensive positions. Constant movement by the forwards toward the scoring area, combined with the breaking into scoring position, by a fourth player (a guard), and a strong defensive balance make a wide variety of movements possible. Constant passing and movement by all six players provide the key to success.

The advantages of the continuity pattern include (1) a defensive balance; (2) the rapid movement of the ball requiring continuous adjustment by the opponents, including the constant altering of head and body position by the goalkeeper to acquire and maintain the ideal defending angle; (3) a five-man attack; (4) the ability to exploit a defensive weakling; (5) control of the tempo, or pace by a highly conditioned team that can keep up with any opponent and slow down when it is strategically necessary to do so; (6) constant pressure on the opponent to swim continuously, which may prove advantageous in the final minutes; and (7) the psychological advantage of mastery of basic skills and attack and defensive patterns conveyed to the opponent forcefully by the rapid movement and the appearance of organization.

Full pool, man-to-man press. The full pool, man-to-man press is undoubtedly the most effective and demanding defensive technique in water polo today. It provides an excellent defensive system against teams utilizing the continuity pattern and requires immediate, tight coverage in the overplay position as soon as possession of the ball changes. This defensive tactic requires the players to be in excellent physical condition and represents a highly organized style of defensive play. As indicated previously, players must maintain a helping atmosphere and must have exceptional ability in switching and recovery to new assignments. Imperative to success are the use of double-ups, in which two defensive players rapidly move to impede an offensive player in possession of the ball and close all passing and dribbling lanes; splitting, in which the remaining players not involved in the double-up adjust their positions by moving one-half man toward the ball to intercept a forced lob pass; and jump switching, in which players delay defensive intent when an offensive player approaches with the ball until the final second, at which time they perform a quick switch and vacate their assigned man.

Player advantage attack. A player advantage attack is employed when the opponents are short one man. The regular offensive system should be immediately discarded at this time and a set offense employed that exploits weaknesses by outnumbering the opponents in the scoring half of the tank. Two forwards are stationed on the 2-yard line to occupy the goalkeeper and the two additional opponents who may be forced to use man-to-man tactics. Four additional players form a semicircle around the goal area to outnumber the three remaining defensive opponents. Rapid, accurate, and patient passing among these four players generally produces a scoring opportunity.

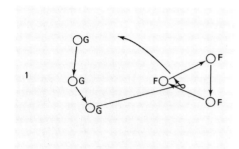

Fig. 44.6 Continuity pattern. From Charles Hines, *How to play and teach water polo.* Association Press, New York, 1967.

Defense against a player advantage attack generally necessitates zone tactics in front of the goal area to force a short passing attack and possible fumble or interception. A combination zone/man-to-man or man-in-the-hole defense may also be used.

HELPFUL HINTS

☐ Initiate body movement by moving the arms and legs rapidly and simultaneously.

☐ Master the fundamentals of water polo with both hands.

☐ Learn to dribble at varying speeds with rapid and frequent changes of direction.

☐ Remember that wet passes are dangerous and slow since the ball must first be lifted up and controlled prior to being shot or passed. Avoid wet passes in congested areas or to a teammate who is closely guarded unless excellent position has been attained.

☐ Perfect lifting, receiving, and passing or shooting actions into one continuous movement without loss of control, speed, or accuracy.

☐ Although a high lob pass with little spin may be effective in some situations, in general make passes relatively short and snappy so that they remain in the air for a short period of time, thereby reducing interception and deflection possibilities.

☐ Use the dribble sparingly. Dribble to force a defender to commit himself and thus free a teammate, to advance the ball when you are unguarded, to attack when receivers are covered, and to outswim an opponent. The ball is more rapidly and safely advanced through accurate passing and should not be dribbled when receivers are free.

☐ Play the dominant or strong side of the offensive player.

☐ Do not shoot from great distances where the probability of scoring is low.

☐ Remember that short passing attacks are more effective than long, dangerous attempts that more often result in turnovers or loss of possession.

☐ Do not throw the ball to voices following interceptions and fast-break situations.

☐ Learn to meet the pass when you are closely guarded.

☐ Fake prior to any offensive move with or without the ball.

☐ Learn to move effectively without the ball and break for open areas to receive a pass.

☐ Avoid turning the head when returning on defense or in pursuing an opponent without the ball.

☐ Keep hands flashing when applying tight pressure to the passer.

☐ On fast-break situations by the opponent, retreat to the line of the ball and continue toward the goal area to pick up a new assignment from the "inside out" by the opponent nearest the goal area.

☐ Maintain proper spacing to facilitate offensive maneuvers.

☐ Use the backstroke when sprinting down the pool and unable to see the ball.

☐ Master the "egg-beater," or frog kick, moving the legs alternately from a vertical position to propel the body upward out of the water. Lean forward at the hips to initiate the upward motion.

SAFETY PRACTICES

Water polo should be restricted to competent swimmers, with qualified, firm supervision and officiating provided to control and eliminate rough, dangerous play. Officials should be trained swimmers and should serve as both mediators and lifeguards, prepared to enter the pool at any time. Strict enforcement of the rules and application of procedures governing the use of the swimming area in general will eliminate much of the danger associated with water polo. Penalties requiring the removal of a player from competition should be retained and strictly enforced. All jewelry must be removed, toes and fingernails cut short, and the body free from grease.

ETIQUETTE

Competitors should observe swimming rules specific to the area being used. Rough play of any type in the form of holding an opponent under water, kicking, hitting, and scratching should be avoided. The potential danger of the surroundings should be respected and reflected through sportsmanship and regard for the safety of opponents.

QUESTIONS AND ANSWERS ON THE RULES

1. *Q.* Do timers stop their watches when the ball is dead?

A. Yes. The clock is stopped when the ball enters the goal area and crosses the goal line on a corner or goal throw. It remains stopped until it leaves the hand of the individual executing the throw-in.

2. *Q.* How is the ball put in play following an action causing it to leave the area of play?

A. The player who is nearest to the point at which the ball left the tank at the sides and who is on the team opposite to the one causing such an action puts the ball in play with an unopposed throw-in. A ball that rebounds from the goalposts or crossbar into the pool remains in play.

3. *Q.* What are the common fouls or rule infractions?

A. Personal

Touching the ball simultaneously with both hands.

Touching the goalposts, nets, or rails at any time for the purpose of pushing off or resting.

Holding, pulling, or pushing off an opponent, swimming on the back of his legs, or impeding a player without the ball in any way.

Using the side or bottom of the pool for forward or vertical momentum in any way, other than at the start of play following a dead ball, to obtain possession or tackle an opponent.

Unsportsmanlike acts such as splashing water in the face, kicking at an opponent, or throwing the ball directly at an opponent within two yards of the goal.

Technical

Walking on the pool bottom or touching the bottom to advantage other than for resting purposes.

Holding the ball underwater when tackled.

Hitting or striking the ball with a clenched fist.

Assisting a teammate in any way at the start of the game or following a dead ball.

Initiating movement before the official blows his whistle or touching the ball before it strikes the water following the toss.

Failing to comply with the rules of goalkeeping by moving more than four yards from the goal line, taking a goal attempt improperly, or throwing the ball beyond the center of the pool.

4. *Q.* What types of infractions are classified as willful or intentional fouls?

A. a) Stalling through wasting time or failing to assume normal positions in a reasonable amount of time at the onset of both halves, b) as-

641

suming a position within two yards of the opponent's goal line, c) changing position after the ball is declared dead and before it is again put in play, d) failing to maintain the normal action or progress of the game when on the offensive and e) refusing to obey an official.

5. *Q.* What types of penalties are imposed for the various rule infractions?

   A. a) A player who commits a willful violation is removed from the water and may not reenter the game until a goal has been scored regardless of the intervening intermissions. Special permission from the official may be granted to reenter the game in a new period of play. b) For each foul, a *free throw* is awarded to the nearest player of the opposing team from the spot of the infraction. Other players must hold their positions prior to the referee's whistle. c) A *penalty throw* from any point on the 4-yard line is awarded to a player who is willfully fouled within four yards of the goal area of his opponent. The offending player is removed from the pool and reenters the game only after a goal is scored. At the signal of the referee, the throw is immediately initiated. d) A *corner throw* is awarded to the offensive player nearest the point of exit at the side of the pool where a defensive player causes the ball to go over his goal line. e) A *free goal throw* is awarded if the attacking team causes the ball to go over the opponent's goal line. The goal guard initiates the throw from within the goalposts to a teammate located beyond the 2-yard line. As the ball crosses the goal line in a corner or goal throw, the whistle is blown, requiring all players to maintain their respective positions until the throw-in is executed. All throw-in attempts must occur within five seconds after the referee feels play should resume.

6. *Q.* How many time-outs are permitted?

   A. Three time-outs per team are permitted in regulation play and one additional for each overtime period to be called by any player in control of the ball. The goal guard puts the ball in play following the time-out period.

7. *Q.* Is substitution permitted?

   A. Yes. Substitution is permitted to replace an injured player or a player who has committed four personal and one major foul and is removed from play.

8. *Q.* What constitutes a legal goal or score?

   A. The ball must pass fully over the goal line between the two posts by means of a pass, dribble, or projection from any part of the body. The ball must first be handled by two players, playing the ball with the palm side of the hand, at the start and restart of the game before a goal can be scored.

9. *Q.* How many players constitute an official team?

A. An official team has seven participating players and four substitutes. Five players per team is recommended in very small pools.

10. *Q.* What restrictions govern the use of the hands?

A. Only the goalkeeper may touch the ball with more than one hand simultaneously.

11. *Q.* What restrictions govern the area within the 2-yard line?

A. No player may enter the area within the 2-yard line unless the ball enters first, in which case he may follow to recover and shoot. If the ball is thrown out of this area, he must vacate the area immediately.

12. *Q.* What restrictions govern tackling?

A. When an opponent has acquired control of the ball, he may be impeded in any reasonable manner, with interpretation left to the officials.

13. *Q.* How far may the ball be thrown by the goalkeeper?

A. The goalkeeper may not throw the ball beyond the center of the pool. He may also not swim beyond this point at any time.

REFERENCES

Cureton, T. K. 1949. *Fun in the water.* New York: Association Press.

Gabrielson, M. A., B. W. Gabrielson, and B. Spears 1961. *Aquatic handbook.* Englewood Cliffs, N.J.: Prentice-Hall.

Hines, C. 1967. *How to play and teach water polo.* New York: Association Press.

Lipovetz, F. J. 1950. *Swimming, diving, and water sports.* Minneapolis: Burgess.

NCAA official swimming guide, water polo rules. (Latest ed.)

Rajki, B. 1959. *Water polo.* New York: Pitman.

Smith, C. J. 1956. *Illustrated fundamentals of water polo for player and coach.* In cooperation with the swimming department, Springfield College. Springfield, Mass.: Springfield College.

45
Waterskiing: Basic Instruction

James J. Lampman

Waterskiing is by far the fastest growing, most dynamic sport in the world. It appeals to the entire family for recreation, fitness, and competition. Two-year-olds as well as seventy-year-olds have learned the fundamental skills of standing on two skis while being pulled behind a boat.

It is estimated that in the United States alone, over 9 million people participate in this aquatic sport. Annual surveys of the Outboard Boating Club of America and the American Water Ski Association show conclusively that, even though an estimated 500,000 pairs of water skis are sold annually in the United States, accidents and fatalities have been the lowest among all other aquatic sports.

The sport of waterskiing has developed in many directions. From the original sport of "aqua-planing" behind a powerboat, today's skiers are being towed by boats, jeeps, and even airships. Skiers use two skis, one ski, shoe skis, no skis, surfboards, kites, and balloons!

PRELIMINARIES

Swimming ability is not a prerequisite for waterskiing but all skiers should have fundamental water survival skills. Life belts, or preferably life jackets, are a must for all who water-ski.

Fig. 45.1 The sport of waterskiing has developed in many directions. Courtesy of *JOPER*.

A good ski boat is relatively light, highly maneuverable, and utilizes higher horsepower than comparable boats used for cruising, fishing, and general family boating.

Ski boats should carry all required Coast Guard equipment as well as a speedometer, wide-angle rearview mirror, rear facing observer's seat, extra towline and a boarding ladder. It is important that the towline be hitched to the boat in such a way as not to become fouled in the propeller. Many hitches attach to the transom with a floating bridle, while others are installed inside the boat forward of the motor.

Proper towline is essential for safety. Polyethylene towline which floats on the surface has exceptional lasting qualities and can be braided and spliced in the same manner as manila line. Although there is some initial stretching, this towline does not recoil and can resist rotting.

Skis vary as to material, bindings, shape, and size. The beginner should probably select a combination ski (rear binding on one ski) with an adjustable binding. This will allow the beginner to double ski and drop a ski when preparing to slalom. Because of the adjustable binder, other skiers may also use the ski.

Anyone who has skied will attest to the fact that skiing is a physical activity requiring strength, agility, endurance, and balance. Waterskiing has various levels requiring different degrees of these fitness components. There is no comparison between the strength, endurance, and agility required by an individual starting barefoot in deep water and a beginner making a shallow water start on two skis.

Fitness for waterskiing requires good general fitness with an emphasis on strengthening certain muscle groups such as legs, back, and grip. In preparation for the waterskiing season one should concentrate on these muscle groups as well as cardiorespiratory endurance exercises. Such activities as jogging, swimming, rowing, handball, paddleball, and squash are excellent means of accomplishing this goal. When actual skiing begins, the skier will find that the best method of attaining fitness for waterskiing is to water-ski. Being towed behind and crossing the wake of a speeding boat makes more stringent demands in terms of isotonic and isometric muscle contractions than almost any other sport.

The beginner should experience many short periods of instruction at the onset of learning and avoid becoming exhausted before giving the signal to return to the dock. Serious accidents can happen if the skier is exhausted.

BEGINNING INSTRUCTIONS

Waterskiing is taught individually or in small groups at many clubs and ski schools. However, at camps and colleges it sometimes becomes necessary to teach larger groups. The number of boats and instructors, the facilities, the time, and the type of student are all factors which must be considered when setting up an instructional program. Several techniques which could be adapted or combined to meet the particular situation will be mentioned here.

The most important ingredient in learning to water-ski is desire. Seriously crippled children and adults, including amputees, are among the thousands who are learning to water-ski each year. Recently groups of mentally retarded and blind students began learning to ski.

Beginners should start with a water test to determine their ability to swim and survive in the water. Next, familiarization with a life belt or jacket and maneuvering and retrieving skis in deep water should be practiced. This will cut down on valuable time when actual skiing begins.

Land drills with skis and towline are next. Learners should learn to put on a life jacket and skis and be able to adjust them properly that they fit snugly. Next, with the towlines held by the instructor, the beginner sits on the back of the skis with feet flat, knees against the chest and arms straight while holding the handle. The instructor pulls the towline gradually, and as the line tightens, the beginner rocks forward on the heels and stands up, keeping the feet flat in the binders. Back and arms should remain straight with legs slightly bent for balance and to act as shock absorbers once on the water. It is important to emphasize that arms remain straight. The legs bring the body up out of the water. When reaching the upright position, the arms remain straight with the hands at waist level. The shoulders are forced back and hips forward so that the beginner is upright and not leaning toward the boat.

Of the several methods of getting a beginner to his or her feet I believe the most effective and useful to be the side-by-side technique. Other techniques that could be used include: (1) trial and error, (2) sitting on dock (3) instructor behind, and (4) a tow bar extended from the side of the boat.

The trial-and-error method is probably the most utilized method with the average weekend boater and skier. There is approximately a one in six probability that the beginner will get up on the first try and most people can catch on to the technique of getting up in four or five attempts. Unfortunately many of these skiers never achieve the proper form and rarely progress to an intermediate stage unless they receive instruction from an experienced skier.

If time is a factor in teaching or if a professional ski school is used, the side-by-side technique is utilized. This cuts the time required for each student and ensures the attainment of proper technique and form early in the instruction.

In the side-by-side technique, two separate towlines of the same length are rigged from the boat harness on a special teaching line 50–75′ long, divided for the last 20 or 30 feet into two lines with handles. The instructor enters the water alongside the beginner. The beginner then sits back in the water, places the tips of the skis just out of the water and has the towline between the ski tips. Knees should be tucked up close to the chest and arms held in close to the knees. The tow handle should be grasped with both hands keeping the thumbs down. The instructor should be alongside with a firm grip under the near upper arm to assist the beginner in assuming the proper position.

The command "in gear" should be given. At this time the towboat will tighten the line and begin to move the skier through the water. When the correct takeoff position is set the words "hit it" are given. As the boat moves out, the skier should maintain the starting position and allow the pull of the boat to plane him or her. The weight should then be shifted to the balls of the feet and the legs used to gain an upright position. The arms should be kept straight. Bending the elbows will cause one to pull on the line and create slack which will spill the skier. Once the beginner has gained the upright position the instructor should suggest necessary adjustments in form. Correct form includes back moderately straight, arms straight, skis about shoulderwidth apart, knees flexed and bent, and eyes straight ahead.

Once up on skis, the beginner should concentrate on form and relaxation. At first it will take a tremendous amount of energy to maintain the proper body position but with practice and time the tenseness will disappear and the skier will begin to feel relaxed. Early lessons should be devoted to short rides with emphasis on starting, stopping, and retrieving the skis and towline.

If a beginner should fall on the first few attempts the instructor should drop the line immediately and render assistance in preparing the student to restart.

Teaching from behind, which supplies maximum control and support, is an excellent technique in teaching the mentally retarded, physically handicapped, and those who have a poor sense of balance or low motor ability. The instructor should use trick skis and use two towlines equal in length. The instructor takes a position behind the student placing his or her arms under the student's arms for maximum support. After the beginner is assisted to the standing position, the instructor should step to the side and continue support in the side-to-side position.

The last method of teaching skiing is the tow bar extension. The towline is attached to a bar which extends six to seven feet from the side of the towboat. The beginner grasps the bar and the boat begins to move forward. The student assumes the correct starting position with the ski tips slightly above the water, maintains this position until the skis plane on the water, and rises to a standing position. After the corrections are made in form and the student becomes accustomed to this new experience, the student grasps the tow handle located at the end of the extension pole. From the boat the instructor may give directions and, by means of a pulley system, let out additional line to place the skier behind the boat. However, there is danger in skiing in front of or alongside the propeller. Also, as the towline is reeled out, the skier must cross the boat's wake from behind.

At this point the skier should follow a progression of beginner stunts.

(1) Ski inside wake, with two skis, (2) ski outside and back in one wake, (3) ski across both wakes, (4) jump wake, (5) hold one hand on tow handle, (6) falling technique, (7) stopping technique, (8) signal with ski, (9) skier's salute, (10) dock takeoffs, (11) ski a zigzag course with two skis, inside the wake and outside the wake.

ADVANCED TECHNIQUES

The advancement from two skis to the slalom ski should follow extensive practice in the beginner's stunts, experience as a boat observer, and knowledge of safe boating and skiing practices.

Initial attempts to slalom should occur while on two skis. Shifting all the weight to one ski and raising the other ski in a skier's salute should be practiced extensively.

Most instructors recommend dropping one ski in learning to slalom. This will quickly acquaint the skier with the balance required to maintain good slalom form.

To accomplish the drop, the binder on the ski to be dropped should be loosened so that the drop can be accomplished without difficulty. When dropping a ski the time of the drop and its location should be considered in advance. Designated drop areas should be determined and precautions taken by boat drivers and skiers in that area.

To accomplish the drop the skier's weight is transferred to the slalom ski and the other foot is quickly lifted out of the binder, heel first, toe pointed down, so as not to disturb balance. The free foot is carried above the water briefly and then should simply be placed on the back of the ski until proper balance is achieved. The back foot should next be gradually moved into the rear binder. If the novice falls from the position a second ski may be handed from the boat for a second attempt or the fallen skier can be taken into the boat and returned to the ski dropoff area.

Another method, very often used by ski schools, is one in which the instructor with trick skis assumes a straddle position behind the student with a second ski rope or split training line. This is similar to the technique utilized at the beginner's level when additional support and control are necessary.

To start in deep water on a slalom ski takes a considerable amount of strength in the legs, back, and hands. As proper technique and timing are developed less effort is required to get up out of the water.

Some instructors advocate both feet in the ski while starting but the one foot to the side technique gives much more balance and is preferred by most instructors. The skier sits in the water with the tip of the ski out of the water or if a split line is used, the tip of the ski is positioned between the line. When the skier is ready he or she calls "in gear." As the slack is taken out of the line and tension increases, the skier yells "hit it." At this time it is important that the boat driver accelerate smoothly but quickly to get the skier out of the water and planing as soon as possible.

The skier's starting position in the water is similar to a two-ski start. One knee should be bent and near the chest, arms straight, and shoulders well back. The free leg should be bent slightly with the toe pointed down. When the command "hit it" is given, the skier must remain rigid and allow the boat to move him or her through the water. The moment the ski is lifted to the surface, the leg is straightened with the free foot still in the water. As soon as the upright position is achieved, the free foot should be placed on the back of the ski, preferably in the rear binding. Most beginners do not remain rigid when the boat begins to move forward but allow the boat to pull their shoulders forward, and thus lose their balance.

Once upright, the skier should keep both knees slightly flexed with the weight evenly distributed on both feet. The back should be fairly straight and shoulders back. The handle should be placed in front of the waist.

TESTS AND QUALIFICATIONS

There are two national organizations that test and certify skiers. The American Water Ski Association rates its skiers as novice, third class, second class, first class, expert, and master. The novice rating deals with basic two ski and slalom fundamentals. The remaining classes are geared to the three areas in competition skiing: slalom, jumping, and trick riding. A skier must be an AWSA member, and also have an AWSA instructor's rating or AWSA judge's rating to compete. The master's examination must be taken in conjunction with an AWSA-sanctioned tournament or a Canadian Association-sanctioned tournament. Ratings are also available for instructors, kite-flyers, and barefoot skiers. Additional information and official tournament rules are available on request, at no charge, by contacting the American Water Ski Association Headquarters, P. O. Box 101, Winter Haven, Florida 33880.

The National Water Ski Association, Inc., has developed a national certification rating and a teaching packet primarily for camp programs. Its purpose is to provide a safe, systematic progression of skiing fundamentals that will aid camp directors and educators in conducting summer camp water-ski programs. The achievement levels of the NWSA are beginners, intermediate, advanced and expert. Each level has a certificate of completion and decorative patch.

The NWSA expert certification tests can be administered by any camp director and consist of slalom starts, some jumping if available, backward skiing, and skiing on shoes and disk.

Instructor's manual, progression charts, safety hints, awards, and other teaching aids can be obtained by writing the National Water Ski Association, Inc., P. O. Box 2811, Fort Myers Beach, Florida 33931.

PREVENTION OF ACCIDENTS

Instruction in the prevention of skiing accidents embraces five areas: equipment, facilities, driver, observer, and skier.

Essential to any proper skiing is safe equipment. This includes boat, towline, skis and life jackets. The boat should be adequately equipped with a wide-angle rearview mirror, rear facing seat to enable the observer to maneuver quickly back to a fallen skier. To do this the boat must have adequate power. Too much power is as dangerous as too little power. Towlines should be in good shape and not frayed or worn. Skis should have no rough edges and be in good working order.

The water facilities become a serious safety hazard especially when several boats are pulling skiers in the same area. Special traffic patterns should be observed or designated areas assigned to each skier. Shallow water, rocks, stationary fixtures, other boats, and bathing areas should be avoided.

The boat driver carries most of the responsibility for safe boating and safe skiing. Standard safety and operating procedures for power boats and pulling water skiers must be observed as well as "rules of the road" for small craft.

The responsibility for transmitting instructions and signals to the skier is the responsibility of the boat observer. It is essential that he or she be constantly aware of the skier's position behind the boat, especially when the skier takes a fall.

Due to the nature of waterskiing, the skier must observe safe and sensible practices. Along with basic swimming skills, the skier must be familiar with the commands and signals used in skiing and must keep alert and be aware of stationary objects or unusual wave or wake conditions which might arise. Common sense and proper progression of skills are the keywords in skiing.

REFERENCES

Bartlett, T. 1959. *Guide to water skiing.* Philadelphia: Philadelphia Chilton Co. Book Division, pp. 31–34.

Dorwin, T., and W. Pearsall 1971. Water skiing. In W. Barton (ed.), *The sportsman's encyclopedia.* New York: Grosset and Dunlap, pp. 602–607.

Hardman, T., and W. Gifford 1968. *Water skiing fundamentals.* New York: Hawthorn Books, pp. 29–42.

Hester, R. 1965. *Instant water skiing.* New York: Grosset and Dunlap, pp. 10–13.

Liebers, A. 1962. *Complete book of water sports.* New York: Coward and McCann, pp. 18–27.

McDonald, H. S. 1968. *Safety in water skiing.* Winter Haven, Florida: AWSA, pp. 1–6.

Pratt, J. L., and J. Benagh 1964. *The official encyclopedia of sports.* New York: Watts, pp. 315–316.

Tyll, A. 1970. *The complete beginner's guide to water skiing.* Garden City, New York: Doubleday.

46
Whitewater Sport
Len and Jan Wolcott Cormier

HISTORY

From the earliest days of civilization, watercraft have been instrumental in the development and survival of innumerable cultures. Pirogues, log dugouts fashioned by burning and scraping, date back to the Stone Age and a refinement with an outrigger has long been the ocean vessel of the South Seas. Two designs which evolved from these primitive beginnings, because of the necessity of environmental adaptation, are the classic Canadian canoe and the Eskimo kayak. These more familiar craft are the subject of this work.

North American Indian tribes traveled on lakes and twisting streams

Fig. 46.1 A C2 mixed slalom team sprints to the finish. Courtesy of the authors.

and therefore required a craft which was lighter in weight and much more maneuverable than the pirogues. A frame of thin strips of hardwood was formed, covered with tree bark (usually birch) and sealed with pitch to provide a strong, resilient, watertight hull. Modifications of the basic design with higher sides and ends were well suited to travel on large lakes where a sudden squall could whip up waves of impressive height. Lengths of 22 to 35 feet were common for freight canoes and the typical 22-footer with a 60-inch beam could transport an incredible weight of 5000 pounds!

The development of the canoe has taken place almost entirely in South America and, while it has maintained its utilitarian nature in this country, its primary attribute is in its value to recreation. Several basic designs dictated by ultimate usage are available. The greatest development has been in the use of advanced materials and construction techniques. Of these, the use of fiberglass-reinforced plastic is the most significant.

Farther north beyond the woodlands and wilderness and into the barren Arctic, Eskimos compensate for the total lack of wood by using sealskin to make their watercraft. An Eskimo umiak is an open boat similar to the Canadian canoe but made of sealskin stretched tightly over a ribbed frame and used primarily for freight. The kayak was developed because of a need for a completely closed hunting craft which would not be swamped by the high seas and which could be rolled upright after overturning.

The kayak was introduced in Germany as a sporting craft in the early 1900s. It was constructed of rubberized canvas over a collapsible frame in single- and two-place designs. The relative ease with which it could be assembled attracted those driving small European automobiles to the Alpine rivers and pleasant seas on their holiday. The original touring designs were somewhat modified by individuals of a competitive nature who wanted faster boats for downriver and flatwater racing and more maneuverable boats for the new sport of slalom racing. Kayaking as a sport became so popular in Europe that flatwater racing was introduced in the 1936 Olympic Games, whitewater slalom in the 1949 World Championships, and wildwater racing in the 1955 World Championships. World War II provided exposure to the sport for Americans and, since the postwar period, advances in materials, construction, and paddling technique have been rapid. Competition in open canoes in whitewater downriver events and, more recently, in slalom has achieved national championship stature.

Competitively, European paddlers have consistently dominated the sport. East Germany, in the 1972 Olympics, chose whitewater slalom as one of its optional events. To the surprise of the entire world, a bronze medal for the United States was won by Jamie McEwan in C1. The United States has been demonstrating its rapidly growing expertise in each successive world championship, particularly in the women's classes.

WHITEWATER SPORT DEFINED

Whitewater, first of all, is generally the white, frothy waves generated by rocks, ledges, and other inconsistencies in a river. Their severity varies from slight riffles in a river current, without any traces of "white," to severe tortuous twists, drops, hydraulics, waterfalls and other, sometimes unnavigable, characteristics. Rivers are usually categorized into six classes of difficulty based on frequency, severity and length of the rapids, on volume of water flow, on ease of rescue, and river gradient. The American Whitewater Affiliation* lists these classes as follows:

Class I   Moving water with a few riffles and small waves. Few or no obstructions.

Class II   Easy rapids with waves up to three feet, and wide, clear channels that are obvious without scouting. Some maneuvering is required.

Class III Rapids with high, irregular waves often capable of swamping an open canoe. Narrow passages that often require complex maneuvering. May require scouting from shore.

Class IV   Long, difficult rapids with constricted passages that often require precise maneuvering in very turbulent waters. Scouting from shore is often necessary, and conditions make rescue difficult. Generally not possible for open canoes. Boaters in covered boats should be able to Eskimo roll.

Class V   Extremely difficult, long, and very violent rapids with highly congested routes which nearly always must be scouted from shore. Rescue conditions are difficult and there is significant hazard to life in event of a mishap. Ability to Eskimo roll is essential for kayaks and canoes.

Class VI   Difficulties of Class V carried to the extreme of navigability. Nearly impossible and very dangerous. For teams of experts only, after close study with all precautions taken.

Obstructions in the river are what present the challenge. They may take some of the following forms:

Large boulders Scattered throughout the stream, they can be seen well in advance. The current splits around them and, therefore, the paddler would be wise not to do likewise!

Smaller rocks Sometimes not as easily seen, especially when paddling into

---

* AWA Safety Code 1974, *American whitewater, Journal of The American Whitewater Affiliation* **19**, 4 (July–August).

the sun, they present no less of a problem to the paddler. A proliferation of these little devils is known as a "rock garden" and, in a fast current, can be quite a challenge even to an expert.

Ledges Actually small-scale waterfalls at abrupt drops in the river. If a spot can be found where the river runs through a notch in the ledge with sufficient volume, it can usually be run by a canoe.

Pillows A smooth area of water running over a submerged rock, sometimes a very difficult obstacle to spot and a threat to the integrity of any hull.

Standing waves When the current is disturbed by a submerged rock or other obstruction, it is deflected upwards and exhibits itself as a decreasing series of wave crests and troughs. The height and severity of these waves are basically determined by the velocity of the current and the nature of the obstruction. Larger waves can roll or swamp a boat.

Rollers and stoppers Roughly speaking rollers are a severe stage of standing waves, the chief characteristic being that the tops of the waves curl back upstream. They look like ocean waves breaking but maintain a stationary position downstream of the obstruction causing them. The upstream component at the top of the wave can sometimes impede the downstream movement of a boat and thus is known as a *stopper*. These are generally to be avoided by open boats and to be driven through with vigor for an exciting ride in a covered canoe or kayak.

Hydraulics-reversals This very serious threat to the boater develops when fast water falls a vertical distance over a dam, ledge, or waterfall. Some of the current falls to the bottom of the river and continues downstream while a large amount curls up and forms a tight, foaming roller at the base of the drop. These can be "keepers" which will hold a boat or paddler rolling them over and over. Escape is effected by the unnatural trick of diving to the bottom and washing out with the downstream current. Hydraulics are generally to be avoided by all boats.

Eddies When the current splits around a rock, a backwash is formed on the downstream side of that rock. It is an area of relatively calm water actually flowing upstream back toward the rock much like the vacuum formed by a trailer truck or racing car at speed. The eddy can be a refuge in a turbulent rapid where a paddler can rest and study the next course of action or use the currents flowing in different directions to help in turning the boat. The separation between the current flowing downstream and the eddy current is called the eddy line. Eddies vary from diffuse to extremely sharp and turbulent and are avoided by wildwater racers who are trying to stay in the fastest downstream current.

Sharp curves, undercut cliffs, downed trees, fences, and pinned or submerged boats are just some of the additional obstructions that can pose a serious threat for any boater. Most of these should be scouted and, if they are deemed navigable, a safety crew should be stationed on shore for possible rescue attempts.

Equipment

Boats. The basic piece of equipment to be chosen is the boat. While this may appear to be a relatively simple task, a quick glance through a canoeing magazine will reveal the many types, designs, and construction available. The popular types of crafts used in running whitewater are the *canoe,* the *kayak,* the *C1*, and the *C2*. The canoe to which we refer is the classic Canadian style usually run as an open boat. In more extreme conditions, a spraydeck is sometimes fitted in order to reduce the possibility of swamping. It is paddled by one or two people in a kneeling-squatting position, never from a seated position. The kneeling position provides a stable base for the paddler in the boat and also lowers the center of gravity, an important consideration in whitewater. Single-bladed paddles are used to propel the craft. The kayak, on the other hand, is a totally enclosed boat and is paddled by an individual from a sitting position with the legs outstretched. A double-bladed paddle is used. A sprayskirt is fitted around the paddler's waist and also around the cockpit rim in order to make the boat watertight. The C1 is similar in appearance to a kayak but, like the open canoe, is paddled from the kneeling-squatting position. A single-bladed canoe paddle is used as is the kayak type sprayskirt. Mastery of a C1 requires the development of precise technique and demands higher strength outputs. The C2 is a two-place version of the C1. The two paddlers of a successful slalom racing team must be well-coordinated, compatible, and mature.

Each of the types of boats above is available in variations suited to particular needs. Racing designs run the gamut. A wildwater (downriver) boat is as long as the rules will allow and has a sharp V cross section. Its purpose is to progress downstream at the fastest possible speed. It is not meant to turn but just to follow the current. Extreme tippiness results from its hull's shape. At the other end of the gamut, we have the slalom boat. Unlike the wildwater boat, it is designed to turn with ease and, as a result, it is slower when paddled in a straight line. The less extreme of the slalom racing designs are generally preferred for running rapids because of their maneuverability. Somewhere in between are hundreds of compromises. If one has difficulty choosing a boat, one should consult an expert who paddles the kind of boat in which one is interested. Learning how, and in what type of water, one uses it will help to determine its suitability.

Paddles. A paddle is usually chosen on the basis of personal preference and "feel." The rough rule-of-thumb for open-canoe paddle length is about chin

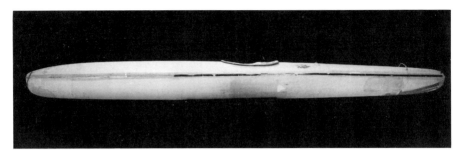

Fig. 46.2 Note the rounded lines of a slalom kayak designed for ease of turning. Courtesy of the authors.

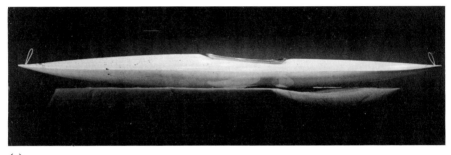

(a)

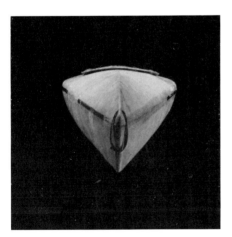

Fig. 46.3 A wildwater C1 is built to travel fast in a straight line: (a) side view, (b) end view. Courtesy of the authors.

(b)

high for the bow paddle and about nose or eye high for the stern paddle. Solo paddling the open canoe generally requires the latter or even a couple of inches longer in order to get the required "reach" from the center of the canoe. Wooden, beavertail-shaped paddles are still quite common and inexpensive. They are being replaced by those made of synthetic materials, with the preferred construction being an aircraft-type of structural aluminum shaft covered with fiberglass and epoxy resin. Squared-off blades and "tee" grips permit far more precise blade-angle control. Racers still sacrifice durability for the "feel" of specially constructed wood paddles for which they must pay a premium. Kayak paddles have a blade at each end of the paddle shaft. One takes alternate strokes on either side of the kayak facilitating travel in a straight line or turning with efficiency. "Feathered" blades (one 90° to the other) reduce the windage of the blade out of the water. Just stand outside on a windy day holding a kayak paddle over your head and you will become the most novel weather vane on your block! Kayak paddle blades are also available "spooned" (slightly curved in two planes). While they are more precise for boat control, mastery of the technique for their use requires slightly more effort. "Take-apart" touring paddles are not strong enough for whitewater use but they may be considered if one wishes to carry a spare for an emergency.

Life jackets. A life jacket should always be worn when running whitewater in any kind of boat! It should be the "over the shoulder" type and, when considering the purchase of one, it would be wise to get a Coast Guard approved jacket. This is required by law in most states.

Helmets. Covered boat paddlers should always wear helmets in whitewater. It takes longer to separate from a kayak than from an open canoe after an upset. Besides, a kayakist should make several attempts to roll the boat up before exiting and this increased time spent underwater increases the risk of head injuries. Research is presently being done in order to establish impact resistance specifications.

Clothing. Unfortunately, the prime canoeing season is during the spring runoff of mountain snows. Water and air temperatures combined with wind conditions make hypothermia a real threat. Wet suits, mittens, and booties will often prevent a moderate upset from becoming a disaster. Woolen underclothing beneath a windproof padding suit works well, particularly if energetic paddling is to be done.

SAFETY AND ETIQUETTE

The most important thing paddlers can bring to a river is a profound respect for the forces of nature. Paddlers can work with these forces to their advantage, but the forces will easily overpower anyone who tries to fight them. Recently, there was a drowning in a Class II stream. A paddler was trapped in a most unusual position in two feet of water with well over a hundred people instantly attending to rescue. It took a full six minutes to clear his head from the water. And all this only five feet from shore!

The prime requirements for personal safety are the ability to be completely in control of the boat and to be aware of one's limitations at any level of expertise. Control of one's boat means not only the ability to steer it down the river but also the ability to stop, go slowly, ferry, eddy out, etc. Individual limitations will change with experience. What may be casual playing for an expert may be an incredibly hair-raising ordeal for a novice.

All applicable safety equipment should be *worn!*

Open boat Life jacket, wet suit (if conditions require it), helmet (if Class IV water)

Covered boat Life jacket, helmet (always), wet suit (optional) or multi-layered clothing and paddlng suit, sprayskirt.

Equipment in boat Flotation, grab loops or painters, spare paddle, dry clothes.

Group equipment Rescue rope, first aid kit, emergency kit (knife, matches, etc.)

A degree of etiquette should be observed on the river in order to facilitate organization and efficient implementation of rescue if necessary. The following rules are suggested for group trips:

☐ Never pass the lead boat and stay in front of the assigned last boat (sweep)

☐ Respect and observe the judgments of those in the lead boat who are familiar with the river

☐ Always keep the boat behind you in sight and be prepared to assist in any situation

☐ Do not stray from the group and explore other channels

☐ Portage when your judgment questions your ability to negotiate a particular drop

☐ If a capsize occurs hold onto your paddle, grab the painter, and go to the upstream end of the boat.

In heavy or dangerous rapids, abandon your boat for your own safety, float on your back, keep your feet *high* and pointed downstream to ward off obstacles, and work your way to shore. If your own safety does not compel you to leave your boat, stay with it, always at the upstream end, and work it gradually toward shore by pushing or pulling the upstream end toward the shore you are heading for, being careful to keep it aligned with the current.

Covered boaters should be able to execute a reliable Eskimo roll in any water in which they paddle. If several attempts at a roll fail, the precautions above should be observed.

Other boaters can and should provide immediate aid to anyone in the water. Attend to people first and equipment second. If one is not familiar with rescue technique in the water and other more experienced paddlers are immediately available, stand by to assist as improper rescue technique can present an additional hazard to the victim.

PADDLE STROKES

Canoe In running downstream, beginners should rarely paddle forward but rather place the canoe so the currents take it downstream and around obstacles. Paddle strokes should be quick, neat, and decisive.

Back paddle or backstroke Used by both partners. Keep strokes parallel to keel.

Draw Used by both partners. Reach out perpendicular to the keel of the canoe and draw the boat to the paddle keeping the shaft of the paddle vertical. This draws the canoe sideways.

Cross-draw Used mainly by the bow and is more powerful than draw. This stroke is used so as never to switch hands. Twist the body to draw on the "off" side keeping the hand on the grip low to the gunwale. This stroke is used in lieu of a pry especially in shallow water.

Cross-backstroke Used mainly by the bow and more powerful than the back paddle. Same principle as the cross-draw but with more twist to the body so as to face upstream.

Pry Used mainly by the stern and is the stern's most powerful stroke. The paddle is sliced into the water against the side of the canoe. Using the side of the canoe as a fulcrum, pry the boat away from the water thus moving the canoe sideways in the opposite direction. To pry left, paddle is on the right side of the canoe with the left hand on the grip and the right hand on the throat.

Paddle brace A very important stroke for bow and stern. It is not really a stroke but, as indicated, a brace for the canoe. Turning the blade and shaft of the paddle to about a 40° angle to the current and the water and actually leaning on the paddle to stabilize the canoe by giving it another point of support, the effect is that of a South Sea island canoe with an outrigger. Keep the paddle in the water as much as possible in rapids even to go from one stroke to another by feathering the paddle through the water. In this way the brace can easily and quickly be employed to stabilize the canoe in case of a sudden, unexpected lurch.

Reverse sweep Used mainly by the stern where the paddle is placed close to the stern and swept powerfully out until at 90° angles to the body.

Inverted sweep Used primarily in solo canoeing.

J-stroke Used by the stern for directional control. The paddle blade is turned outward at the end of the forward stroke pushing the stern away from the paddling side; an essential skill for solo canoeing.

Scull Used as a gentle draw, during a brace and in solo canoeing. Make figure 8s in the water using the side or edge of the paddle.

Rudder Used by stern for simple steering although minor course corrections may also be used by the bow.

As skill increases, more aggressive forward paddling will permit the same negotiation of such obstacles as standing waves, stoppers, and strong eddy lines.

C1 and C2 strokes

Generally "C" boats, i.e., covered canoes which have developed along the lines of the kayak, require much more skill and finesse than an open canoe. They are much more maneuverable. The same basic strokes are used with them as with the open canoe except that all paddling is done without changing sides and crossover strokes are generally avoided. In C2, the most frequently used strokes are forward, backstroke, forward and reverse sweep, draw, pry, and low brace. In addition the bow must develop a strong high and low brace.

C1 paddling is also done on one side only. The J-stroke must be developed to perfection in order to steer a straight course. Again, the same strokes are used but they require much twisting of the body to make the boat respond properly and efficiently. One important fact must be remembered when paddling C1, C2, or kayak. Any time you are not running parallel to the current, lean the boat away from the current!

Fig. 46.4 A high brace in a C1. Courtesy of the authors.

Kayak strokes

What would appear to the neophyte to be a simple move, the forward stroke, is usually the least perfected stroke in a paddler's repertoire. Development of this technique results in the ability to hold a course and in the efficient use of muscular energy. Jay Evans, former United States Olympic Whitewater Coach, describes the forward stroke as follows.

> We can divide the forward stroke into three closely interrelated parts—the dip, the draw back through the water, and the withdraw/recovery.
>
> *1. The dip.* Lean slightly, but not too far, forward. Extend the right arm forward as far as possible toward the bow and insert the right blade completely in the water. Meanwhile the left wrist should be at ear level, the left elbow pointed down and slightly away from the kayak to provide maximum leverage. The fingers of the left hand may be fairly relaxed on the shaft at this point.
>
> *2. The draw.* With full muscular effort, draw the blade straight back to the midpoint of the kayak *but not beyond.* The right wrist is straight, but the right elbow flexes as the blade comes directly back alongside the kayak. To utilize more power, don't hesitate to turn the body and shoulders a little to the right as the blade is drawn back. Put the body into the stroke, because if the arms do all the work, they'll soon tire.
>
> While the right hand was dipping and drawing back, the left hand (which controlled the other half of the paddle) pressed straight forward toward the center line of the kayak at eye level. This movement of the left arm and hand is not unlike putting the shot in field events, or delivering a straight left to the jaw of an opponent in boxing.
>
> Don't allow the dip-and-draw arm to do all the work in each cycle of strokes; if you paddle this way you'll soon be fatigued (maybe after only a quarter-mile of paddling). Instead, think of the power of the forward stroke as coming from two distinct sources: about 65 percent from the dip and draw, and about 35 percent from the forward punch with the other hand— while rhythmically moving the body and shoulders at the waist to the right and left to complement both draw and push. Both power sources working in harmony together not only produce an amazingly efficient forward stroke with which you can paddle for miles, but they also create a graceful movement that is completely satisfying aesthetically.
>
> *3. Withdraw/recovery.* The right hand smoothly lifts the paddle from the water in a natural upward movement after the right blade passes the cockpit. The left hand is now in a position to begin the dip of the left blade near the bow of the kayak to complete the stroke cycle.

Other strokes used are the sweep, draw, backstroke, and high and low brace. These are used on both sides. The all important Duffek stroke is simply spectacular as explained by Evans (1973).

This great stroke revolutionized the sport of kayaking. It was developed by Milovan Duffek, a Czech kayaker who first demonstrated the move at the 1953 World Championships in Geneva. Ever since his innovation, kayakers have not had to rely on the boat itself for stability: the paddle becomes the primary means not only of support but also for *turning the kayak while in brace position.*

What a nifty stroke it is—particularly in whitewater! But first learn the basic idea in flatwater; otherwise you'll spend a good share of the time upside down wondering what went wrong.

To simulate moving current in flatwater it is best to get going very fast —almost full speed in a forward direction. Then lean out as far as you can to the right. With the face of the blade at an angle of about 45° to the forward direction of the boat, insert the blade at about two o'clock or approximately three feet away from the bow. Without stroking at all, hold your blade right there while your left hand is held high above your head. Presto! The kayak will spin around to the right with the paddle acting as a pivot.

The exact blade-angle to use depends upon your speed, how far you lean, and how abruptly you wish to turn. The Duffek turn can often be finished with a firm but short draw stroke to redress your balance.

If you wish to perform a Duffek turn to your left, simply hold your right hand high above your head and use your left hand to insert the left blade properly.

This is one of the most exciting moves in kayaking, but get the idea of it in flatwater, then try your luck in moving current, and then advance into eddies, etc. As an added bonus you'll be pleased that a Duffek properly done does not cut down your speed appreciably.

In flatwater—on a lake or gentle river—you can come steaming up to a dock or other chosen point on the shore, pull a Duffek, and bring your kayak into a snappy landing right on the button. You'll have earned the right to hotdog it for the folks on shore.

Expert paddling is simply a blending of these individual strokes, sensitivity, and a dash of good judgment resulting in precision, efficiency, and pure enjoyment of the sport.

RIVER MANEUVERS

The techniques described below are suggested for beginners but, as skill increases, paddlers may be able to execute maneuvers paddling on either side of the canoes.

The following describes a few of the basic river maneuvers which should be mastered.

Ferrying. Going from one side of the river directly across toward the opposite bank.

Fig. 46.5 Proper execution of the forward kayak stroke. Note that the upper hand is pushing forward level with the eye. Courtesy of the authors.

Fig. 46.6 A reverse sweep and low brace is used to turn a kayak. Courtesy of the authors.

Setting. (Back ferrying, downstream ferry)
Facing downstream, the upstream end of the canoe (stern) points toward the bank to which you want to go. The stern back paddles on the upstream side of the canoe. The bow twists the body around one-quarter turn to face upstream so that the bow can see and keep the proper angle of the canoe with the current (approximately 20–40°). The bow paddles on the downstream side of the canoe and uses the cross-backstroke which is a forward stroke with a pry.

Upstream ferry

Same purpose and principle as setting except the canoe is facing upstream. The bow is now the upstream end of the canoe and it points toward the bank to which the boat is going. The bow paddles ahead on the upstream side of the canoe. The stern's main job is to keep the proper angle of the canoe and current as the stern paddles on the downstream side using a forward stroke with a pry.

Ferry glide. Going from one side of the river to the other while *moving* downstream. In a setting (ferrying) angle with the current, in order to go right (or left) but also drifting downstream, the stern (upstream end) points toward the bank to which the boat is heading. The bow uses a draw stroke or cross-draw on downstream side, stern uses a back paddle or pry on the upstream side.

Tight S-Turn. To spin the canoe around an obstacle with the center point of the canoe as the axis and the midpoint of a gunwale next to the obstacle, the bow does a draw or a pry to set the angle, the stern helps the bow by doing the same stroke. Both paddle ahead. When the midpoint of the canoe is next to the obstacle the bow either pries, cross-draws, or draws. To straighten the canoe, the stern pries or draws as the stern end of the boat clears the obstacle.

Running backwards. Sometimes a canoe will "pinwheel" and the boaters will find themselves going down the river backwards. If they have time, both partners should simply turn around in their "seats" to face downstream. If there is not time, they should run the rapid backwards until they find a spot to turn the boat around.

Stopping. Always bring the upstream end of the canoe to shore first (same principle as ferrying or ferry glide).

Eddy set

First pry or draw the stern into the eddy as close and as soon as possible after the rock. Bow then draws, back paddles, or cross-draws into the eddy.

Eddy turn

Example A—set angle, bow then reaches out into the eddy at the inside of the curve and uses a draw or a high brace, then paddles forward as the current whips the stern downstream and into the eddy. The stern uses a powerful forward sweep. It must be remembered that at the moment the canoe passes the boundary line of the slow eddy current and the fast mainstream current, the canoe will stop quickly with a tendency to roll to the outside of the curve! Therefore, the stern counteracts this with a pry and both lean to the inside of the curve. Leaving the eddy, the bow upstream ferries out of the eddy paddling on the downstream side, then reaches out and draws downstream when the bow wishes to turn. The stern paddles forward on the upstream side of the canoe but right after the bow begins the turn, executes a powerful forward sweep, and then rudders to be parallel with the current.

Example B—set angle, bow slices the paddle into the water and uses a pry stroke remembering to lean away from the paddling side, then paddles forward into the eddy. The stern uses a back sweep. Leaving the eddy, the bow upstream ferries out of the eddy paddling on the upstream side and pries when he wishes to turn, leaning well away from his paddling side. The stern also pries or uses a low brace, and then rudders to be parallel with the current.

COMMANDS THAT ARE "HOLLERED"!

Back paddle!
Draw right! (or left, could also mean cross-draw)
Pry right! (or left)
Set right! (or left)
Ferry glide right! (or left)
Eddy set right! (or left)
Eddy turn right! (or left)
Upstream ferry right! (or left)
OK! (bring canoe parallel with current and go with it)
Land right! (or left)

The ideal, most enjoyable method of canoeing is for each partner to sense what the other partner is doing and therefore have as few commands as possible between each other.

GUIDELINES FOR RUNNING THE RIVER

☐ Picking a channel. Follow the main current whenever possible. Choose your route well in advance!

☐ Always keep the canoe parallel with the current unless maneuvering.

☐ Always move faster or slower than the current.

☐ Do not drift through a rapid. Paddle aggressively. Go faster through heavy drops so there is speed for steering.

☐ Read the water and pick your course well in advance. As you go, constantly shift your attention from the near to the more distant problems.

☐ The stern decides the general course; the bow decides the immediate!

☐ To make a perfect eddy turn, aim for the rock, slow down, set the correct angle, drive the bow across the eddy line into the water, and let the boat swing. Lean and brace as the stern "hits" slow water then paddle ahead into the best part of the eddy.

☐ Learn to read your partner's movements. The stern cannot see the immediate problems, but responds to the bow's maneuvers. Shouting does not help.

☐ When possible, in maneuvering a very tight S course, the stern should have the paddle on the downstream side of the canoe in order to use the most powerful stroke against the force of the current—the pry stroke.

☐ In a tight S course, the bow should help the partner immediately *after* the bow end of the boat has passed the obstacle.

☐ Remember always to bring the canoe back to a parallel position with the current *as soon as possible!*

The boat maneuvers are basically the same for kayak as for the open canoe. However, the strokes used to effect these moves are those appropriate to the craft as described in the "Kayak Strokes" section.

COMPETITION

As in most sports, the zenith of performance is usually attained through competition. The development of higher level motor skills is only one of the rewards of dedicated training. Improved self-image, maturity, and camaraderie are the true prizes. Whitewater competition takes three basic forms, *whitewater* (*downriver*) *racing, wildwater racing* and *slalom racing.*

Whitewater racing. A downriver race, usually in Class I, II, and sometimes III water, the purpose of which is to get from point A to point B in the shortest possible time. The course length is anywhere from 4 miles to over 40 miles. Basically oriented toward open-canoe racing, it is often run by covered boats also. The obstacles presented to the paddler by these classes of river are, of course, to be avoided in the process. The racer will usually run the boat in the fastest water in order to maintain best possible speed. Eddies are to be avoided as we must remember that eddy water actually flows upstream and will spin a downriver boat in a flash. Standing waves are a major source of concern to the open-boat racer as water in the canoe tremendously increases the load on the paddler in addition to rendering the canoe quite unstable. Swamping, at best, requires stopping to empty the boat or else it results in a "did not finish." Large standing waves can be run over their shoulder keeping away from the steep areas yet avoiding the slow water or eddy usually at the edge of the wave. There is a substantial temptation to cut the corner at a bend in the river. The major current runs the outside of the bend and "cutting" requires paddling in shallow water causing "bottom drag" (slowing of the boat), something that is best demonstrated by actual experience. To be successful, the boater must know every whim of the river along the course so that no decisions or hesitations occur during the race.

Whitewater racing is governed by the American Canoe Association. Many local races are held throughout the country, which permit novices to try their hand at the game. A Whitewater Open Canoe Circuit allows expert paddlers to accumulate points toward a National Championship.

Various classes are usually run: OC 1, open canoe, one paddler; OC 2, open canoe, two paddlers; OC 2M, open canoe (mixed), two paddlers, one female, one male. There is additional categorization by several boat length groups.

Methods of starting vary from one to five boats started at one minute intervals to a mass start that somewhat resembles feeding time in the monkey cage. Elapsed time over the course is computed and the fastest time in each class determines the winners.

Wildwater racing. Wildwater racing, as its name implies, is a much more rigorous version of a downriver race in rapids. The course, of about four to five miles, is in a minimum of Class III water and, more typically, it is in as much Class IV water as can be found. Entries are necessarily limited to covered boats only and classes usually run are: K 1, men's kayak, single paddler; K 1W, women's kayak, single paddler; C 1, men's covered canoe, single paddler; C 1W, women's covered canoe, single paddler; C 2, men's covered canoe, two paddlers; and C 2M, covered canoe, one female and one male.

Paddling technique is essentially the same as for whitewater racing. A wildwater racing boat is fast but of a very unstable design and is prone to being rolled over in heavy water at the slightest error in balance. Boats are usually started singly at one or two minute intervals. Covered boat competition is governed by the International Canoe Federation, and administered in this country by its member organization, the American Canoe Association. All major races up to and including World Championship events are sanctioned by this group.

Slalom competition. To some minds, slalom is the pinnacle of the sport not only requiring expert navigation in the rapids but extremely precise maneuvering in heavy water. The slalom course only vaguely resembles that of a ski slalom. Supporting wires are hung across the river and from these are hung "gates"; each gate consists of two wooden poles with a minimum width between the poles of 1.2 meters. Championship races will have from 25 to 30 gates in Class III to IV water while novice races are designed with about 12 to 20 gates in Class I and II water. Proper course design necessitates the use of the features of the rapids in order that a boat may "make" all the gates. Three types of gates are used, the forward gate, paddled through in the downstream direction; the reverse gate, while the boat is traveling downstream it is turned so it passes through the gate stern first, and the upstream gate, positioned in an eddy so that the boat coming downstream must snap a turn into the eddy, paddle up through the gate, then turn out into the current and continue to the next gate. The maximum length of the course consisting of mostly forward and upstream gates and with a minimum of four reverse gates is 800 meters.

Classes run are usually the same as for wildwater although open-canoe slalom is becoming more popular. Only one boat is started at a time and scoring is based on the time of the run with penalties accrued by improper negotiation of any of the gates. Penalties in the form of 10, 20, or 50 seconds are added to the running time for each error. The time required to run a course averages from two to five minutes. The goal is to have the fastest running time with no penalties. Thus, slalom requires not merely speed and strength but also technique, finesse, and use of every feature of the river so that one may achieve a fast, "clean" run. Penalties are basically judged as follows:

50 sec—a gate missed or negotiated in the wrong direction
20 sec—a gate touched from the outside before negotiation
10 sec—a gate touched from the inside during negotiation

Hitting either or both poles of a gate with any part of the boat, paddle, or body is considered a "touch." Gates are numbered in order of required negotiation and marked with an indication of the proper direction of travel through the gate. There are much more complicated penalty situations and for a com-

Fig. 46.7 Slalom competitor and United States World Team member, Ned Jose "peels" out of an upstream gate. Courtesy of the authors.

plete description one should refer to the ICF Slalom Rules (American Canoe Association).

GETTING STARTED

Even if one is not considering competition, knowledge of slalom technique will develop a mastery of techniques which will prove valuable in running any whitewater river. A few basic guidelines for getting started in slalom follow:

1. Reasonable physical condition should be maintained. If you have any questions about your health before the start of training, by all means consult a physician. A balanced diet tailored to your needs is necessary in order to efficiently develop the strength, endurance, and flexibility required to compete. Casual racing necessitates only moderate conditioning while top-level competition demands intense and dedicated training. Proper body weight should be maintained. It is of little use to paddle a lightweight racing boat if you are ten pounds overweight. Diet off that excess!

2. One of the best ways to gain familiarization with slalom is to attend races in your area. Volunteering as a worker will accelerate the process.

3. When running whitewater rivers for recreation, "play" the river. When you are comfortable making all sorts of maneuvers in heavy water, you can race with the prime concentration being negotiation of the course rather than apprehension about the water.

4. Review and perfect all basic paddle strokes and develop a strong, instinctive roll.

5. Train in the boat as much as possible. Even one or several gates hung over a pond or a Class I stream will provide valuable development of precision and finesse. As a matter of fact, this is the preferred method of initial training and is used continually by experts to stay sharp. Once these important skills are developed, one may move training to heavier water.

6. Equipment should be the best and matched to your degree of competency. Very advanced "boats" are to be avoided by most novices as they may find themselves upside down a good part of the time! Again, talk to the good racers about equipment and weigh their suggestions against your ability.

There are no shortcuts to becoming a good racer; no secret diets or training sequences, only hard work, dedication, and love of the sport.

RACE TECHNIQUE

Before you start, you should memorize the course so that you can run it practically blind. Take all the practice runs you can manage in order to learn every intricacy of the course. Warm up before entering the water and again when in your boat.

The start. The boat is held, usually at the stern, by a starter at the edge of the river. When the timers and paddlers are ready, a countdown from five is given. During this countdown the paddler should be slightly stroking in rhythm so that on the command "go" the paddle will be in the water starting the first stroke. If a rock or other suitable feature is available, the racer may "push off" with the paddle in order to accelerate the boat. Because a slalom boat is meant to turn easily, the first stroke will tend to turn the boat quite a lot. Two remedies for this problem are first to aim the boat a little away from the intended course and, second, to take only a moderately strong first stroke.

The forward gate. If possible, paddle through the gate without interrupting stroke rate. In the interest of efficiency, approach the gate in a way that permits proper alignment for the next gate. Know the precise stroke to take upon leaving one gate to ensure immediate and correct approach to the next.

The reverse gate. Turn as close to the gate as skill permits. Too early a turn will result in a long approach during which the boat tends to drift off course. Generally power through the gate in order to maintain control except when a tight spin is required upon leaving the gate. In this case, slow the boat in the gate and initiate the turn while still in the gate. Exit the gate at the correct angle for proper approach to the next gate.

The upstream gate. Enter the eddy at full speed to minimize the disturbing effect of the eddy line and to permit a quick, efficient turn. Ideally, upon completion of the turn, a couple of feet of the bow will be in the gate. Follow this with a powerful drive just high enough to clear the gate.

The finish. After the last gate there is usually a 25-meter sprint to the finish line. Develop the habit of paddling "through" the finish line. By relaxing and not driving the last bit of the course, you will lose valuable seconds from your time. Know exactly where the finish line is!

At the end of the run, you will be required to remain in your boat until the next two or three boats finish. This provides the necessary rescue effort for paddlers who have capsized on the course. Failure to do this can result in disqualification because safety is of prime importance. You may be assigned timing, scoring, gate judging, or other duties while other classes are running. These should be attended to conscientiously as everyone must work together to run a slalom race.

REFERENCES

American Canoe Association. *Competition rules.* 4260 East Evans Ave., Denver, Colo. 80222.

Evans, R. J., 1975. *Fundamentals of kayaking*. Brattleboro, Vt.: Stephen Greene.

————, and R. R. Anderson 1975. *Kayaking*. Brattleboro, Vt.: Stephen Greene.

———— 1973. *Whitewater coaching manual*. Ledyard Canoe Club of Dartmouth.

Granek, I. 1969. *Paddling kayaks and canoes*. Elizabeth, N.J.: Robin Printing Co. Available from American Canoe Association, National Paddling Committee, East Riverside Road, Rt. 1, Box 83, Buchanan, Mich.   49107.

McNair, R. E., 1972. *Basic river canoeing*. (3rd ed.) American Camping Association, Inc., Bradford Woods, Martinsville, Ind.   46151.

Urban, J. T. 1971. *A whitewater handbook for canoe and kayak*. Boston: Appalachian Mountain Club.

47
Wrestling: Basic Instruction

Buel R. Patterson, Ray F. Carson, and Art Griffith

The scope of wrestling instruction encompasses teaching holds and moves for controlling an opponent as the means of winning. The element of control is inherent in every phase of the sport. Each contestant is continually striving to either gain control, maintain control, or terminate the control of the opponent.

Fig. 47.1 Wrestling encompasses teaching holds and moves for controlling the opponent. Courtesy of Eastern Kentucky State University.

There are four broad areas of instruction in wrestling. The first area (takedowns) consists of maneuvers employed from a neutral position for the purpose of taking an opponent to the mat and gaining control over him. After gaining control, the wrestler in the position of advantage must work to maintain it. Rides, then, constitute the second area of instruction. They are techniques used to keep control. The third area of instruction includes escapes and reversals. The wrestler (1) in the position of disadvantage is constantly working to terminate the control the opponent (2) has over him. Escapes occur when (1) gains a neutral position. A reversal occurs when (1) gains the position of advantage on top of (2). The ultimate in control is the fall. This is realized through holds known as pinning combinations. They are applied in turning the opponent over onto his back and constitute the fourth area of wrestling instruction.

There are literally thousands of wrestling holds and variations. All of them, however, can be divided into two broad categories: those performed from standing and those performed from the "down" position on the mat. For purposes of greater clarification, they can further be classified according to their general purposes.

There are four general headings under which holds employed from a standing position can be divided. These headings are as follows:

☐ Moves used to take an opponent to the mat when facing him;
☐ Moves used to get behind an opponent;
☐ Moves used to take an opponent to the mat after having gone behind him;
☐ Moves used to get free when an opponent has gone behind.

Mat wrestling can be divided into three parts:

☐ Moves used to control an opponent while on top in order to bring him into a position where a pinning hold can be applied;
☐ Moves used from underneath to get free of, or reverse positions with, an opponent;
☐ Moves used to pin an opponent.

The instructing of wrestling requires that a certain amount of discretion be exercised in the selection of techniques. Any technique which requires the wrestler to place himself in one of the following positions should be avoided:

| On his back | On his buttocks | On his side |
| On his stomach | On one or both knees | |

The methodology used in first presenting a wrestling technique should not include a complex description. Early emphasis on details is undesirable.

Only the basic movement pattern required to perform the technique need be explained.

After the technique has been explained and then demonstrated at the speed and in the manner it is expected to be performed when mastered, the learner should immediately be given the opportunity to try it. Until he has tried it, the advisability of offering additional guidance is questionable. The temptation to tell everything about the technique should be resisted. A few minutes of practice is worth thirty minutes of explanation.

Only after the general movement pattern has been learned should more details be introduced. Areas needing emphasis should be pointed out. Demonstrations on the mechanics of performing the technique should be frequently repeated. Repeatedly calling the wrestlers together provides the opportunity for presenting progressively more detailed instruction on the finer points of properly executing the technique.

During the times the technique is being practiced individual instruction should be provided for those experiencing difficulties. When a common mistake is spotted it should be brought to the attention of the entire group.

Demonstrating a mistake in slow motion, while the attention of the group is focused upon it, is one of the best means of effecting improvement. At times, it may be necessary to isolate that part of the technique that is causing the greatest difficulty. Overcorrection by repeated exaggeration of the proper movement is an effective method of eliminating the mistake.

The methods used for teaching a new skill should provide the learner with confidence in his ability to use the maneuver. When the learner is first learning the skill, his partner should not offer undue resistance.

The learner, after watching the technique demonstrated, should practice it slowly in an attempt to get the feel of the desired movement pattern. It is essential that movement through a new skill be slow at first since this is the only way to learn proper body position. The partner, in this learning situation, should try to resist only to the extent necessary for the learner to get the feel of the hold. As the learner improves, his partner should resist more actively.

If efforts to execute any manuever continually fail, no real learning occurs. Therefore, counters to techniques should not be taught until a reasonable degree of proficiency is attained. When tried before being mastered, against someone who knows the counters, they will likely fail. The consequences are that the learner will lose confidence in the techniques and they will remain undeveloped.

Emphasis in the teaching of wrestling should be on a progression in skills. Instruction should begin down on the mat with forward and backward rolls. Stress should be on keeping the arms and legs bent. This will reduce the chances of injuries. Since takedowns from standing are generally taught first, it is important that safety in properly falling to the mat be given high priority.

Fig. 47.2 Emphasis in the teaching of wrestling should be on a progression of skills. Courtesy of *JOPER*.

Fundamental to the successful execution of any wrestling technique is the setup. This entails a plan of action requiring the initiation of a move or series of moves with the intent of getting the opponent to react in a predicted manner and thereby place himself in a weakened position. If he reacts as anticipated he becomes vulnerable.

The ultimate in executing a technique skillfully is the ability to "bait" an opponent into assisting in its application. Baiting is a clever means of tempting, enticing, or luring an opponent into making a move that from all outward appearances would seem to be an excellent opportunity for improving his chances of winning. He is thus drawn to an attractive opening for which a counter has been prepared. Unwittingly he assists in its application.

Success in competition is largely dependent upon continuity, speed, and an uninterrupted sequence of movement. Only by merging or linking individual isolated techniques into uniform series can the most positive results be realized. The time lapses between moves is thus kept to a minimum and the opponent is given little time to adjust to a repeatedly changing set of circumstances. The ability to employ techniques in this manner makes the sport of wrestling a practical means of self-defense.

Wrestling is also an excellent conditioner and all-round body builder. Some of the major physiological changes resulting from a properly conducted conditioning program are as follows:

☐ Cardiovascular efficiency becomes greater. The heart's ability to pump a sufficient supply of blood to working muscles improves. This improvement is reflected in the fact that a given amount of work is accomplished with less effort.

☐ Wrestling lowers the heart rate. This means that the heart refills more fully after each beat and has a more complete evacuation with each stroke. This permits a longer resting phase between strokes and accounts for a lower heart rate.

☐ Muscles are enlarged, stronger, and tougher. Their ability to contract repeatedly without experiencing early fatigue is partially attributed to their increased capacity for work. When working muscles tire, rested ones take over. This permits more prolonged activity.

☐ Cardiorespiratory function improves. The lungs inflate more fully and the oxygen–carbon dioxide exchange is more complete. This results in a greater supply of oxygen and fuel being transported to working muscles and a larger amount of waste products being removed. This permits muscles to work longer and more vigorously prior to the onset of fatigue.

Collegiate wrestling is conducted in ten weight classes:

| 118 lbs | 134 lbs | 150 lbs | 167 lbs | 190 lbs |
| 126 lbs | 147 lbs | 158 lbs | 177 lbs | Unlimited |

Competition at the high school level is divided into twelve weight classes:

98 lbs	119 lbs	138 lbs	167 lbs
105 lbs	126 lbs	145 lbs	185 lbs
112 lbs	132 lbs	155 lbs	Unlimited

Both a simple and practical method of determining the lowest weight class in which a boy should wrestle is to pinch the skin at the midline of his stomach and compare it with the thickness of the skin pinched on his forehead. When the amount is identical the boy is at his minimum weight.

Wrestlers are not characterized by highly mesomorphic builds or great bodily strength. Somatotyping of wrestlers' physiques suggest they do not differ greatly from the average.

Most champions seem to develop their individual styles in accordance with their natural attributes. Consequently, no one standard build typifies these champions.

REFERENCES

Brown, R. L., and T. E. Robertson 1967. *Illustrated guide to the takedown in wrestling.* West Nyack, N.Y.: Parker.

Camaione, D. N., and K. G. Tillman 1968. *Wrestling methods.* New York: Ronald.

Clayton, T. 1968. *A handbook of wrestling terms and holds.* Cranbury, N.J.: A. S. Barnes.

Keith, A. 1968. *Complete guide to championship wrestling.* West Nyack, N.Y.: Parker.

Martin, G. 1962. *The mechanics of wrestling.* Madison, Wisc.: College Printing and Typing.

Maertz, R. C. 1970. *Wrestling techniques: takedowns.* Cranbury, N.J.: A. S. Barnes.

Parker, C. W. (ed.) 1972. *The official national collegiate athletic association wrestling guide.* Phoenix, Ariz.: College Athletics Publishing Service.

Patterson, B. R., and R. F. Carson 1972. *Principles of championship wrestling.* Cranbury, N.J.: A. S. Barnes.

Rasch, P. J., and W. Kroll 1964. *What research tells the coach about wrestling.* Washington, D.C.: AAHPER.

Spackman, R. R. 1970. *Conditioning for wrestling.* Springfield, Ill.: Charles C Thomas.

DANCE

Introduction

Section 2 on dance has been treated somewhat differently from Section 1 on sports. A number of individuals with experience and expertise in teaching dance pooled their knowledge, made suggestions as to the organization and presentation of the material, and then delegated the task of writing to Dr. M. Frances Dougherty.

The section is divided into five chapters: (1) *Dance—A Cultural Force*, (2) *Dance—An Educational Force*, (3) *Dance Is . . .* , (4) *Theater Forms*, and (5) *Recreational Forms*. The growth of dance as an art form, its influence in education, and its increasing acceptance by men as well as women are treated in the opening paragraphs. The history of dance in education is briefly presented and the struggle to justify it as a valid educational subject discussed.

The "dance explosion" of the last half century is explained and its rising support, both as a performing art and as an educational activity, is related. The place of dance in educational programs is reviewed and its "value objectives" enumerated. The ultimate recognition of dance as a vital part of the total educational experience is told.

Under Chapter 51, *Theater Forms*, modern dance, ballet, ethnic dance, and jazz are examined. The discussion of Recreational Forms includes folk dance, square dance, and social dance. *RBF*

Section Editor

M. Frances Dougherty is professor emeritus, department of dance at the University of Oregon. She obtained her B.S. and MS. from the University of Northern Colorado at Greeley and her Ph.D. from New York University. During her teaching career, she has been a teacher of physical education at the elementary level in Greeley and at the secondary level in Denver, an associate professor in health, physical education, and dance at the University of Northern Colorado, an instructor in dance at the New York University Graduate Camp, and head of the department of dance, the University of Oregon.

Dr. Dougherty was vice-president of AAHPER and chairperson of the dance division (1967–1970), chairperson of the theatre section, AAHPER dance division (1966). More recently (1970–1973) she was editor of the Proceedings and Conference Reports, WSPECW.

In addition to contributing many articles on dance and related activities to professional journals such as *JOPER,* Ms. Dougherty authored "Dance and Physical Education" in A. Chujoy and P. W. Manchester (eds.), *The Dance Encyclopedia,* published in 1967 by Simon and Schuster.

48

Dance:
A Cultural Force

INTRODUCTION

The intent of this section is to discuss dance as a cultural force, to review the role of dance in public education and to define the forms of dance most frequently included in current educational programs. The portion on forms contains some historical background, comments on social significance, and defines general movement characteristics. No specifics in content or methods of instruction are included.

The references for this section of five chapters is found at the conclusion of Chapter 52. MFD

Among the influences that have restricted the role of dance in American culture are those stemming from colonial Puritanism, asceticism, and even antitheater laws once imposed by the Continental Congress. An even greater impact from the past may have been the absence in this country of a royal house to subsidize performing artists. In spite of these restrictions, all forms of dance have realized amazing growth both as a performing art and as a valid educational endeavor. Emphasis in education occurs at all levels from preschool to preparation for professional careers as performers, teachers, researchers, ethnologists, and therapists. Tangent to dance as an art form are expanded career opportunities for historians, dance critics, notators, composers, designers, theater technicians, and filmmakers. This has come about in the past 40 years in what has been called "a dance explosion."

Dance as an art product has enjoyed rapid growth in popularity on the part of participants, professional performers, and students. It has also received increasing attention from the reviewers of dance theater forms and film. Existing and more recently formed professional companies conduct extended tours in cities throughout this country and abroad. Professional dance has enjoyed broad audience appeal and has been assisted financially by substantial governmental and private agency support. Representative of such support are those legislative programs providing educational undertakings in the arts and humanities administered by the United States Department of Health, Education and Welfare, Office of Education, the National Endowment for the Arts, and the National Council on the Arts. Among private foundations increasingly supportive of dance as one of the arts worthy of consideration for funding are the Ford Foundation, J. D. Rockefeller III Foundation and the A. W. Mellon Educational and Charitable Trust, Bethsabee de Rothschild Foundation, the Guggenheim Foundation and the Rebekah Harkness Foundation.

An example of governmental support for projects in which dance plays an important role is Project IMPACT (Interdisciplinary Model Program in the Arts for Children and Teachers). The program funded through the United States Office of Education (EPDA Arts Education Program) established programs in five sites across the country to "humanize the setting and the instruction program of the school with aesthetic concerns as the principal learning core." The center focus was the development of aesthetic/affective response through instruction and participation in the arts, specifically music, visual arts, drama, and dance as well as the arts which utilize the written language. These programs were funded for three years and evaluations now available indicate an overall gain in achievement of educational objectives defined for children participating in these programs.

State and regional councils on the arts have stimulated interest and participation in dance by providing financial and service assistance in the promotion of performances, workshops, special classes, newsletters, bulletins, and other types of support. One example of this type of effort is a document published and distributed through state arts councils which lists touring dance companies available for residency programs in schools. Guidelines for sponsors give details of application, funding, program content and particulars about dancers in the companies.* Some states supplement this with similar listings of companies and sponsors in that state. *The California Dance Directory,*† prepared and distributed by the California Arts Commission, is an example. The "Index to Dance Companies" included in this publication lists 177 dance companies with a diversity of specialty: Ballet (48), Modern (59), Afro-American (9), Ethnic (30), Environmental (12) and Other (19).

---

* *Directory of Dance Companies.* Dance touring program: guidelines for sponsors. Coordinated residency touring program. National Endowment for the Arts.
† C-C News from The California Arts Commission, Sacramento, Calif., 10-24-72.

Technological accomplishments related to various communicative media, transportation, and exploration have given renewed direction to all of the arts. To dance this direction is evident in a number of ways, some of which are: (1) the use of dance movement and film in the art of what is called by some "cine-dance"; (2) a tremendous expansion of the viewing audience for dance; (3) accessibility of performances of ethnic dance forms not previously available to all; (4) acceleration of research in dance ethnology; (5) accumulation of a vast wealth of archival and research material on film, tape, and notated scores.

Perhaps of even greater consequence to expanding a cultural orientation to dance, is that all of the advancements cited above serve to inform, evoke curiosity and stimulate the desire for understanding. Young people today seek experiential understanding of themselves and the expanding world in which they live. As related to dance, some of the ways in which this is evidenced are: 1) dance programs are flourishing in number and kind; 2) there is increased cultural acceptance of the role of men in dance; 3) there is greater awareness of the interrelationship of all the arts; 4) many non-professional performing groups are in existence; 5) higher standards of performance and production prevail for all dance endeavor.

Walter Terry (1975, pp. 94–97), foremost dance critic, writes of the realization of the prophecy of Isadora Duncan, "I see America dancing." He relates the saga of Americans suffering from a "mammoth inferiority complex" about their dance to arrive at a position of worldwide recognition and profound respect. Americans are dancing their dance around the globe; the world is dancing in America. A respectful reciprocity exists in international arts of the dance.

Fig. 48.1 Dance programs are flourishing in number and kind. Photos courtesy of *JOPER*.

49

Dance:
An Educational Force

The foregoing discussion on dance as a cultural force in our society has implications for dance in education as reflected in the past, evident in the present and predictive for the future.

HISTORY OF DANCE IN PUBLIC EDUCATION

The nature of education in a culture at a given time reflects social forces directing change in pedagogy and curricular content. In America, periods of changing emphases for educational responsibility in terms of goals might be grossly designated chronologically as follows: (1) acquisition of basic academic fundamentals (reading, writing, arithmetic); (2) development of skills in areas other than academic such as art, music, physical education, vocational subjects; (3) social adjustment for a democracy; (4) adaptation to worldwide technology; (5) creativity, self-awareness, and personal involvement. It is difficult to predict what influence the current educational concern for accountability through competency-based programs will have on the arts.

Certainly dance has had a place in the formal and informal education of most cultures, including those of Western civilization, since recorded time. Education in America during the centuries of colonial rule was obviously patterned on that of the European homeland. Those colonies that deemed some training of the physical being worthy of consideration for education usually included dancing as an activity beneficial for its hygienic value. In addition, dancing was often thought to be important for developing gentility and social graces. It is evident that the need for the quality of grace was often incompatible with more demanding needs of frontier life, particularly for men; however, that quality was thought to be essential for "womanliness." Little wonder that the idea that "dancing is for girls" was fostered in America when it is almost nonexistent in other world cultures. This prejudicial attitude, stemming from an assigned cultural role stereotype, has been slow to change in education as opposed to entertainment and other commercial fields where such prejudice does not appear to exist. It must be pointed out, however, that many early leaders in education and physical education have advocated the desirability of dance for both men and women.

In American public education, dance instruction has been fostered largely under the aegis of physical education. With some notable exceptions, this curricular placement prevails in elementary and secondary schools; the trend in colleges and universities is today strongly toward separation from physical education to the status of an independent discipline or inclusion in a grouping of the performing arts.

Most professional publications concerned with aims and principles for programs of physical activity include dance as contributing to the values proclaimed to be inherent in such programs. Authorities in education and physical education have endorsed dance as a desirable activity for both sexes and at every level. The history of dance in education since the 19th century has evolved in content emphasis as related to sociopsychological and cultural values appended to goals paralleling those for education generally. From 1880 through the mid-1930s, the content for dance was imbued with inherent value objectives. Value intentions for dance were: (1) to help young children acquire poise and grace (1800–1825); (2) as a form of musical exercise beneficial to the health (1850–1900); (3) as "aesthetic dance" derived from Delsartian theory for expression; (4) as "gymnastic dancing," an adaptation of aesthetic dance but more appropriate for boys and men (1880–1920); (5) as "folk or national dance" yielding intercultural and recreational benefits (1880–1920); (6) "clog, tap, and character" dance valuable in developing coordination and response to rhythm (1920–1935); (7) "natural" dance, using natural movements to evoke creative response, with music providing the emotional stimulus (1900–1925); (8) "creative dance" using free movements and aesthetic expression but based on scientific movement principles and a philosophical rationale for dance as art (1920–1930); and (9) "modern dance," an art form eclectic in origin emphasizing freedom but a freedom with exacting discipline.

Dance in schools during the early years of the 20th century included several of the forms above existing concurrently in curricular offerings. Proponents of each form and those largely responsible for educational leadership in these forms are: natural dance, Gertrude Colby and Bird Larson; creative dance, Margaret H'Doubler, Martha Dean, Ruth Murray, and Dorothy La-Salle; folk and national dance, Mary Wood Hinman, Elizabeth Burchenal, and Louis Chalif; clog, tap and social dance, Marjorie Hillas, Mary Jane Hungerford, Anne Schley Duggan, Edith Ballwebber, and Helen Frost; modern dance, Mary O'Donnell, Martha Hill and Mary Josephine Shelley. Melvin Ballow Gilbert founded and directed the Gilbert Normal School of Dancing. These educational pioneers and others following them succeeded in establishing a climate in which dance might flourish as a viable force in American schools.

Modern dance dominated the content of dance programs in education from the mid-1930s to the present time. The dance impetus evident in theater and professional dance occurred as well in education, or perhaps because of the acceptance of modern dance in education. In any event, a relationship of mutual need existed between professional dancers pioneering the then new dance form, and the establishment of receptive and enthusiastic audiences and students for this form. Youth, and teachers of youth, were receptive to learning the movement technique and experiencing the exhilaration of an art form so adaptable and appropriate as an expression of American culture.

Earlier work of American dancers Isadora Duncan, Ruth St. Denis, Ted Shawn, and Helen Tamaris led to the later artistry of Martha Graham, Doris Humphrey, and Charles Weidman and their amazing pioneering efforts in establishing "a truly American dance form." Considerable influence was afforded from the dance concepts and techniques of Mary Wigman and Hanya Holm in Germany. These professional dance artist-teachers, together with such gifted composers as Louis Horst and Norman Lloyd, articulate writers like John Martin, Ruth Lloyd and Ted Shawn, historian Curt Sachs, and anthropologist Franz Boaz, led to what amounted to a revolution in the arts and resulted in the birth of a new dance form. John Martin (1967, p. 44) succinctly captures the essence of the idea and defines the new form:

> The movement itself was a composite of individual inspirations, discoveries, and adaptations, frequently divergent and even antagonistic but all impelled by the exigencies of the time (hence, perhaps legitimately to be called modern), and rooted in the specific heritage of Isadora Duncan.

The social and cultural climate in America in the period between the two World Wars was conducive to a reorientation to the arts; educational theory and practice were immersed in the trend for progressive education. Together these phenomena strongly influenced the role of dance as an art form to be taken seriously by consumer and practitioner alike.

Some of the resulting developments were of particular significance to education: (1) establishment of the first university dance major program at the University of Wisconsin in 1926 under the leadership of Margaret H'Doubler; (2) founding of "Orchesis" dance club, again by Margaret H'Doubler; (3) establishment in 1934 of the Bennington School of the Dance at Bennington College in Vermont under the direction of Martha Hill and Mary Josephine Shelley. Other major programs were established; many Orchesis clubs became activated; education accepted and supported the new art. The impetus was begun; artists, students and teachers explored together the volcanic force of the "new dance." These developments led to widespread inclusion of dance as a discipline appropriate for inclusion in higher education and revealed a thirst for learning the new art which education found compatible with progressive educational philosophy and theory. It was education

Fig. 49.1 Great advances in their dance programs are evident in institutions of higher education. Courtesy of *JOPER*.

in general, and physical education in particular, that fostered and supported gatherings of artists, teachers, and students as a part of curricular, cocurricular, and extracurricular activities in the school. A new generation of artiste and audience was born.

Certainly much credit for the expansion and acceptance of modern dance in America must be given to those dedicated women in physical education who implored, cajoled, and demanded of administrators that modern dance become a valid educational endeavor. They were successful in gaining the support of most of the leading men in the field, either through philosophical conviction or by demonstration that as an activity modern dance technique could achieve the physical objectives of increasing flexibility, strength, and coordination. It should be pointed out that these men were not insensitive to the aesthetic values that dance offers, but they were more impressed with the physical demands made obvious in performance of technical skills.

During the time modern dance was replacing earlier forms of aesthetic and natural dance in school programs, the social and recreational forms continued flourishing because of compatibility with goals for general education then oriented to adjustment for democratic living. Square dance was stressed in particular, and folk and social usually were given lesser attention; tap and clog all but disappeared. At the elementary level, creative dance or rhythms received greater attention than the traditional singing games. Here too, square dance was thought by some to be appropriate for young children.

The foregoing review of the history of dance in American education seeks to point out that dance as a physical activity was compatible with the aims and objectives held valid for engagement in physical performance of all kinds. It met the criteria for the objectives of organic, neuromuscular, and psychosocial development. Meeting the criteria for recognition as an art form, however, was not so apparent to academia. A shift in educational focus from appraising behavior as significant to the social group, to self-realization and avoidance of conformity, necessitated concerns for changing from an emphasis on the physical and intellectual climate for learning to the sensate climate; to inculcate sensitivity and awareness; to expand experiences in all the arts as modes of nonverbal communication and self-actualization. This required a new look at the place of dance in education.

CURRENT STATUS OF DANCE IN EDUCATION

Current programs of movement education—physical education—include activities broadly classified as games, sports, dance, aquatics, and equitation. The trend toward greater specialization implies that each of these classifications has important categories receiving greater or lesser attention from program to program. This is true for dance. Dance programs in public education generally include the social/recreational, creative, and theater forms of dance.

Dance in public education today has achieved its current status as a result of many social forces and changing concepts of the purposes of education reflecting these forces. Dance is recognized as a vital part of the total motor learning, nonverbal experience to be promoted and supported at all levels of education. Two general types of programming exist; (1) in general education, to be made available to all students; (2) in professional education, selected as to kind and amount for purposes fulfilling personal need or career designation.

Programs in elementary and secondary schools fall largely into the first category, where a variety of dance forms are offered with instruction or elective as extracurricular. The same situation exists at the university level where classes may be elected as a matter of choice or to fulfill an activity requirement. Professional programs are largely restricted to those established in colleges or universities, or in schools and academies, whose primary concern is professional preparation in the arts. Several such of the latter type of institution are supported by public funds and at least two are designed for talented secondary school students: the High School of the Performing Arts in New York City and the North Carolina School of the Arts in Winston-Salem. Several private schools for secondary students combine academic programs with specialization in the arts. One of these in which dance is an independent area for study is the Interlochen Arts Academy in Michigan.

In elementary schools, dance is generally regarded as an important adjunct to developmental goals. Surveys have been conducted, however, which reveal dance instruction to be given less consideration than the other arts in the curriculum and to further suffer from a lack of quality instruction. The status of dance in elementary education will be detailed elsewhere in the publication.

In junior and senior high schools, dance is usually taught by women physical education teachers and the programs are designed primarily for girls. Practices and content vary from place to place. An unpublished study by Joan

McGinley and Richard Kraus, *A Comparative Study of Trends in Dance Education,* revealed significant findings from a nationwide study of these practices (Kraus 1969, p. 276). Another study on the status of dance in secondary education is currently being conducted by the Dance Curriculum Construct, a substructure in the National Dance Association of the American Alliance for Health, Physical Education and Recreation. From survey findings available, it appears that at the junior and senior high school level little progress has been made in extending the scope of dance in the curricula beyond conceiving of content as nothing more than an activity in which minimal skills are to be acquired. Allocations of time to dance are meager compared with time allotted other activities, and variety in content generally limited, with less of both time and content provided for boys. Some of the reasons cited for this paucity of dance opportunity for youths are: (1) dance is viewed as a minor skill area in the broader spectrum of physical activities; (2) "dance is for girls" is an idea enforced by the fact that most existing programs are taught by women; (3) physical education teachers lack motivation to give priority or equal attention to teaching dance; (4) dance is not viewed by administrators on the same basis as the other arts; (5) only a few special teachers of dance are available because of limitations of state certification.

Obviously, in spite of the above, many good secondary dance programs are emerging where interdisciplinary curricula in the arts provide opportunity for advanced study. Some of these programs certainly have developed through inspirational leadership of physical educators; others may be coordinated as a part of drama, art, or music.

It is in institutions of higher education that the greatest advances have been made. They have provided opportunities to study dance as an art form and as an academic discipline, in multifaceted professional programs or as general education. Programs in general education are too numerous to cite with any degree of accuracy. The seventh edition of *The Dance Directory* compiled by the National Dance Asssociation of AAHPER lists 164 colleges or universities with professional preparation programs of which 49 offer degree-granting graduate programs.

Professional dance programs are often differentiated as to specialization for performance or teaching. One of the recent developments in dance at the college level is the large number of dance workshops offered during the summer throughout the country. Most of these grant academic credit. Curricular emphases for graduate programs in dance tend to stress dance as an academic discipline and major choreographic and production projects are in many instances regarded as valid research.

A significant development in graduate dance programs is specialization in dance-movement therapy, which is a young profession in the field of mental health. Obviously, such programs have an interdisciplinary orientation to psychology and psychotherapy as well as prerequisite background in anatomy, kinesiology, and theories of nonverbal communication. At the present time the study of dance therapy places greater emphasis on the psychosocial attributes of dance for therapeutic use. However, Marr (1975, p. 65) defines the broader scope of dance therapy:

> Dance can be used in many forms of therapy; for the physically handicapped, the mentally retarded, and the emotionally disturbed. Dance for the blind and the deaf is receiving wider application in recent years.

The institution of dance ethnology programs in interdisciplinary ethnic studies in colleges and universities is another development in graduate and undergraduate dance curricula. Current emphasis on an extension of cross-cultural understanding at all educational levels makes the study of dance of greater significance. A valid rationale is that in many cultures dance serves as the matrix of the arts and social order as reflected in beliefs, customs, and rituals giving form to patterns of individual and group behavior. Through the study of movement parametrics (choreometrics) it is possible to make cross-cultural comparisons not necessarily revealed in other means of classification.

While dance in education at all levels has evidenced growth, many problems still have to be resolved in order for it to be generally included as an important ongoing means of realizing the goals for education. Some of the problems toward which continuing effort needs to be directed are: (1) stereotyped attitudes about dance as a meaningful experience; (2) lack of certification for public school teaching; (3) tendency for dance specialists to isolate their efforts from others in the academic endeavor; (4) need for greater interdisciplinary diversification in professional programs; (5) resolution of curricular affiliation at all levels.

Solutions to these problems and other concerns of dance educators are being studied by as many as eight or more national professional organizations dealing with subjects such as research, standards for performance, curriculum construction, certification of teachers, etc. Since this publication is prepared by the American Alliance for Health, Physical Education and Recreation, it is appropriate to cite one of these dance organizations in particular, the National Dance Association, a member of the Alliance.

Dance educators, largely from the field of physical education, formed a National Section on Dance in 1930, with Ruth Murray as the first chairman. In 1965 Division status was granted to the Section with Mary Ella Montague as Vice President of AAHPER and Chairman of the Dance Division. With the reorganization of AAHPER in 1974, the Dance Division became the National Dance Association. Structural components include six districts to include all the states and United States territories, Curriculum and Program Resources Divisions and eleven specialized units and/or committees. Evelyn Lockman became the first president of the Association.

50
Dance Is....

Dance is the stylization of human movement which exists in space, consumes time (apportioned into intervals of emphases and duration), and is usually organized into a structural form. As an art form, the body is the instrument and movement the medium used for purposes of human expression. Dance may also be performed for social, ritual, recreational, therapeutic, or entertainment purposes.

The meaning of dance may be said to depend on perception, as modified by individual and cultural experiences which determine function. Experience may range from the simplest kinesthetic response to patterned, rhythmic externalization of feeling states, to a powerful rite of profound importance to the entire social group; from a statement of significance concerned with human values, to the presentation of moving designs through space enhanced by feats of spectacular performing skill. There is no common meaning or purpose to the many existing forms of dance.

Dance is a part of the cultural heritage of all races, for people have always danced. They have danced for many purposes and in many ways. The

Fig. 50.1 The body is the instrument and movement is the medium used for purposes of human expression. Photos courtesy of the University of Oregon.

following forms are ways of dancing most commonly found in American culture and broadly classified as theater forms and social/recreational forms.

51
Theater Forms

MODERN DANCE

Modern dance or "contemporary dance" is that dance form which was created, nurtured and established as a valid art of the twentieth century. McDonagh (1970, p. 1) terms it "the only form of serious, indigenous, theatrical dance developed entirely outside the tradition of classical ballet." Through the medium of dance, artists reflect on their perceptions of, and reactions to, the environment of their ever-enlarging world. The American dance heritage from the classical and ethnic past was felt to be too static and restrictive in terms of this environment. The first to actively seek a more fitting mode of dance expression was Isadora Duncan (1878–1927). However, there is little similarity between the form and style of her dancing and the modern dance viewed today. By the 1970s there have been three generations of dancers who have been responsible for the developments that have occurred. Some of these developments are (1) technical training designed to extend the performing range of the body, and the development of an awareness of natural body movements as the medium of dance; (2) validity of movement as an expressive form independent of ties to music or poetic metaphor; (3) performance orientation to spaces other than the proscenium theater; (4) choreography achieved through improvisation or creativity as opposed to rules for movement organization; (5) use of human movement as one component in multimedia dimension, made possible through adaptation to modern technology in artistic endeavor.

As each generation of artists needed to search anew for technical and choreographic means to adequately reflect the way in which their world was viewed, the work of the preceding generation became a point from which to depart—some to be saved, some to be extended and some to be discarded. As is true with all the arts, some of the best of each period withstands the tide of time, or at least is recognized for the artistic validity the work reflects.

The following is a somewhat simplistic description of the components that may go into creating a "modern" dance. Skill in dance requires the following: a responsive instrument—the body; awareness of many kinds and qualities of materials—movement; practice, knowledge and good judgment in the selection and organization of these materials—composition or chore-

Fig. 51.1 A trained dancer's body should be strong, flexible, coordinated, and capable of meeting great energy and endurance demands. Courtesy of *JOPER*.

ography. A trained dancer's body should be strong, flexible, coordinated, and capable of meeting great energy and endurance demands. Much modern dance stresses technique designed to achieve these goals. However, it should be pointed out that recent directions in choreography stress the need for an awareness of the body's natural movements as appropriate media for meeting desired choreographic ends.

The range of bodily movements is extended by attention to the quality or exposure of a movement and its suitability to purpose. Quality depends upon the way energy is released in executing a movement or in suppressing movement. The energy aspect controls as well the size or amplitude of movement. The motivation for a movement may stem from an idea or a feeling or it can stem from a perceptive response to any stimulus.

Choreography, or dance composition, means the selection and organization of dance movements into a form. This may be a process of problem solving involving but a few movements for a single dancer or many complex movements for a large group of dancers. There are no absolute rules for this kind of problem solving. Each dance artist must work in his or her own way. It usually is a process of exploration to consciously organize movement into shapes, mass, forms, patterns or designs; it may be a process of selecting variables which would modify movement to see what form might emerge. Emphasis may be given to the process of moving rather than to development of a precise form. Improvisation may be a process in movement selection or it may be the entire choreographic approach to finalizing a dance.

Developing the body for artistic expression, selecting movement materials or modifying variables affecting movement, and determining the form that is intended to be perceived are all parts in the making of *a* dance.

Various systems of dance notation exist which make it possible to record particular dances in minute detail for future reconstruction. Special training is required to read or write dance scores which are to be preserved. The most commonly used system is Labanotation. The Dance Notation Bureau, with offices in New York, makes available various kinds of services such as providing notators to record dances, training teachers in the system, conducting workshops for students, and assigning personnel who serve as teachers and adjudicators for the reconstructed dances intended for public performance. While the system is not restricted in its use to dance, it is the most common application of notation at this time.

The approach to modern dance found in schools is as varied as the number of persons teaching dance. However, the preparation of most teachers is highly eclectic and rarely reflects a single approach to either technique or choreography. Many students of dance in private studios choose to work with a number of artists during the time they are studying modern dance. If they become members of a performing company, they are more apt to become advocates of the theories employed by that company.

Fig. 51.2 Choreography means the selection and organization of dance movements into a form. Courtesy of the University of Oregon. Photo by John Descutner.

BALLET

Ballet is the oldest classical form of dance in Western culture. The term "ballet" is derived from the Italian words *ballare* meaning "to dance" and *ballo* meaning "dance songs." The diminutive of the latter is the word ballet. The original meaning was simply patterned dances; however, by the middle of the 18th century the term came to mean a theatrical event related to a narrative theme.

Ballet stems from the European court dances of the 16th and 17th centuries. It began in Italy but it was in the French court of Louis XIV that ballet reached a high point of development and gave us ballet as we know it today. This development included establishment of specific rules for performing the movements. The French terms remain relatively unchanged and are used to identify steps of ballet wherever it is taught or performed.

The movement of ballet has been likened to architecture since the technique evolved from a geometric analysis of human movement in space, characterized by linear placement and "aplomb" or balance. Movements for ballet include conventional poses or positions for the feet, the arms and hands, the body; all positions are done standing in place, springing or leaping into the air, or traveling through space. There are five positions of the feet and five positions for the arms. The seven basic movements in ballet dancing are defined by the following French verbs: *plier,* to bend; *étendre,* to stretch; *relever,* to rise; *glisser,* to slide; *sauter,* to jump; *élencer,* to dart; *tourner,* to turn around.

Fig. 51.3 Ballet is the oldest classical form of dance in Western culture. Courtesy of the University of Oregon. Photo by John Descutner.

Practice for body control in execution of the movements is performed in sequences of exercises called *barre*. A hand support to assist balance is provided by a rail or bar upon which to place the hand. When the sequences are performed without the support, they are referred to as *au milieu* or "center practice." *Adagio* is a term meaning a combination of slow, sustained movements. It also includes certain poses such as the "arabesque" and the "attitude." The term may also refer to that portion of a ballet performance usually danced by the principal female dancer, the "ballerina," and the principal male dancer, the "danseur," and is generally conceived to be a romantic interlude. *Allegro,* on the other hand, refers to quick movements through space, often into the air, by means of leaps, jumps, and turns. Rising onto the toes is referred to as "dancing on pointe." A chorus of dancers is called the *corps de ballet.*

Classical ballet choreography is closely related to the music and tends to use the conventional "tutu" costume for women and tights and tunic for men. Modern ballet, however, often departs from the traditional movement codes and uses accompaniment in a variety of ways, much as does modern dance. Modern choreography for ballet may employ electronic sound and decor or scenic effects derived from technological aids. Ballets are usually composed by choreographers rather than performers.

To master the technique of ballet requires many years of training usually beginning at an early age. An appreciation of ballet as a form of dance art is made more meaningful and enjoyable by experiencing some of the movement techniques. The main purpose of ballet is exclusively performance, although the technical training has been used successfully to strengthen and correct some kinds of physical disabilities.

Most public elementary and secondary schools do not include ballet in instructional programs. Exceptions are those schools specializing in curricula allied with the arts. To a lesser extent, the same situation exists for colleges and universities. Most professional dance programs contain some ballet instruction; an increasing number of these programs provide for specialization in ballet.

ETHNIC DANCE

There is considerable disagreement among dance theorists as to the precise meaning of the term "ethnic dance." However, proponents of this form generally designate it to be the indigenous dance arts of a race which have come to be recognized as the classical theater form of the art. Other characteristics deemed essential for ethnic identification are that the form be an expression familiar to all the population, that there is a specific terminology for its technique and that there is a recognized school of instruction.

The qualifications above would differentiate ethnic dance from folk dance which is designed for participation by members of the community. However, when folk dance is choreographically transposed for theater presentation, it may be conceived to be ethnic dance, or at least appropriately included in the repertoire of ethnic theater.

The orient is most representative in the possession of ethnic dance art. Some examples are the Indian Natya (meaning dance and drama) encompassing at least five styles, Japanese Noh and Kabuki, and Hawaiian Meles.

Ease of worldwide transportation has increased the availability of ethnic companies for the American theater. Certainly television has made it possible to view ethnic dance filmed in traditional settings. These factors, together with tourism, have provided motivation for study of ethnic dance forms in conjunction with music and art in cultural context. Ethnic dance companies are touring extensively, workshops are given with college or community

Fig. 51.4 Ethnic dance consists of indigenous dance arts of a cultural group. The dance arts evolve into a recognized theater form. Courtesy of the University of Oregon. Photo by Stan Green.

sponsorship, and the appointment of ethnic dance teachers as guest faculty is common procedure.

Several dance organizations are conducting conferences, sponsoring research and publishing materials concerned with dance ethnology. At least one program in dance ethnology is now established (University of California, Los Angeles). Other programs offer courses in the subject or conduct special workshops in the ethnic techniques. It is predicted that this area of specialization will continue to expand.

JAZZ

Jazz dance, like jazz music, has its origin in African cultures where dancing is done for utilitarian and social purposes and is performed by all rather than only by the specialist. This is true of many cultures where dance is functional; the entire community participates. As these cultures became displaced, the dance remained, usually changed in content, meaning, and purpose, and reflecting influences or conditions from the foster environment.

The history of jazz dance as we know it in the United States has existed in several forms: (1) religious expression, as reflected in spirituals and gospel songs; (2) theater minstrel or vaudeville forms; (3) social dancing, creating popular "fad" dances such as the Charleston, Shimmy, Bugaloo, and many ohers; (4) as theater form in night clubs and musical theater; and (5) concert, by many fine black dance companies and brilliant dance artists. Negro dance routines were known to have been performed in America early in the 19th century and forms of jazz have strongly influenced musical theater since that time. It is in the area of concert dance, however, that American blacks have earned justifiable acclaim. Since the establishment of a school by Katherine Dunham in 1931 for the study of black Caribbean dance to the formation of Arthur Mitchell's Dance Theater of Harlem in 1968, black dance artists, both dancers and choreographers, have excelled in both modern dance and ballet (Moss 1975).

Because of the many expressions of African dance in these and other expatriated forms, no single style or technique is defined. The following, however, might be said to be characteristic: complex, syncopated rhythms, isolation of parts of the body, the bending of the body toward the earth and use of foot movements into the earth, and a high degree of improvisation in the selection and performance of movements.

Like other movement art, jazz dance will continue to change in form and style. Certainly it is more than syncopated "modern" dance, in spite of adopting "warm-up exercises" to increase range of bodily movement, and the use of the language of "ballet" as a convenience for describing movement. It has tremendous appeal to most students since it relates directly to their listening, seeing, and media-controlled world.

52
Recreational Forms

FOLK DANCE

The 20th-century technology and the "jet age" have resulted in a one-world concept and have made it possible for all people to know more about varied and differentiated cultures. People in far-off lands are no longer strangers. Instead they are neighbors to visit and understand. We can share with them the joy of dancing purely for exhilarating participation; folk dancing is non-restrictive in terms of age, sex and ability.

Folk dance is one means of reflecting the art, music, customs, and life-style of a people. A sense of personal identity and group unity is transmitted along with dances, legends, customs, and costumes. Many of the folk dances known today had their origins in rituals celebrating the forces of life influencing mankind, the family, and the community. Dances are created out of the life experience of the people. There are happy dances and sad ones, dances of imitation and of ritual, dances requiring little skill and others of great difficulty. The original meaning of many of the dances has been lost through the years, but the pride, the strength of character, and the feeling of unity exhibited by the dances of a particular culture are apparent when the dances are performed today.

Fig. 52.1 Folk dance is one means of reflecting the art, music, customs, and life-styles of a people. Courtesy of the University of Oregon. Photo by Stan Green.

Current interest in a return to the natural and the folk arts has resulted in heightened interest in folk dance. Many folk dance clubs or groups exist for purposes of social and recreational satisfaction. These community or collegiate groups enjoy participation in a variety of international dances; others may specialize in dances from a particular country.

There is a proliferation of folk dance camps or workshops held during the summers throughout this country and elsewhere. They are characterized by concentrated study of dances, music, cuisine, costumes, geography, and history. Generally specialists/teachers serve as instructors, all of whom feel a responsibility to perpetuate and preserve their country's dances. Among the many talented individuals engaged in this kind of work are: Andor Czompo (Hungary), Yaakov Eden (Israel), Bora Ozkok (Turkey), Atanas Kolarovski (Yugoslavia), Ingvar Sodal (Norway), and Vyts Beliajus (Lithuania).

The movements and steps used in folk dancing, and the style in which they are performed, are as varied as can be imagined. The walk, for instance, is generally a simple mechanical act, but to walk in the style of an Israeli dance which has a Yemen influence is physically, culturally, and emotionally very different from performing the "shuffle" walk used in the Appalachian Big Circle dances.

Folk dancing implies dancing with others. Some folk dances are done by couples; others are done by groups of people. The grouping may be in a single, double, or concentric circles, which move clockwise or counterclockwise. The dance grouping may call for single, double, or multiple lines, with dancers side by side or one behind the other, with lines moving forward, backward, or in serpentine pattern. Each folk dance has a design of its own, although similarities exist among dances of a particular country and other countries which have shared common cultural influences. Many of the basic steps are similar, but the total design for each dance is unique, depending upon the way in which steps are combined, how dancers are grouped, and the style of the movement underlying the purpose of the dance. Most traditional folk dances once had a purpose, although as they are done today that purpose may no longer have meaning for the dancers.

Folk dancing provides desirable outcomes which are social, recreational, or physical in nature. Dancing with others and assuming individual responsibility for a part in a group have social significance; recreational outcomes are realized through the satisfaction enjoyed; physical outcomes are exhibited by improved states of physical well-being. Folk dancing is for everyone and enjoyable for all. In addition to the many dances inherited from other cultures, an American folk dance form has emerged by adapting parts of that inheritance. That form is square dancing.

SQUARE DANCE

Square dancing is known as the folk dance of America. Some of the dances brought to the colonies from Europe were the *quadrille* and *contredanse*. The European forms of these dances changed little by little in their new environment. Jigs and reels from the British Isles became the lusty square dance. Clog dances from England and Ireland became the basis for the fast footwork contained in the famous "running sets" characteristic of the Appalachian mountain region.

The gold rush of the western United States brought an intermingling of cultures and dances from those cultures. An evening program of dances might include quadrilles, contres, round dances, and called figure dances—the square dance. It was the added element of the "caller" which was uniquely American.

A caller does not dance but directs the interchanging movements of dancers into patterns called "figures" which make up the design of the dance. Several variations exist in the grouping of dancers; and characteristic groupings, styles, and movements are associated with various parts of the country. The most common formation is that of four couples arranged with the "head" couple standing with their backs to the caller at the beginning of the dance. The other couples are numbered two, three, and four in a counterclockwise direction around the square. Couples number one and three are known as "head" couples, and numbers two and four are the "side" couples.

Variations also exist in the steps used for square dancing. Walking, shuffling, and light running steps are used to move the dancers through intricate interweaving figures. The caller defines the movement and the figures to be danced and indicates which dancers are to execute the call.

The movements most commonly used in making up figures are *circle* (left or right), *swing your partner, allemande* (left or right), *grand right and left, right and left through, ladies chain, do-si-do, do-sa-do,* and *do paso.* The style used in performing these movements varies, depending on that which is popular regionally, the particular group of dances, the nature of the call, and the use of a figure designated by the caller.

The earliest American square dance called for a different figure to be performed by each couple, while the other three couples waited their turn. Today a caller may have all eight dancers moving at the same time in the most intricate patterns. There are two general kinds of square dance calls in popular use today; the singing call and the patter call. In the singing call, the lyrics of a song are the call directions arranged in rhythm and set to be a specific melody; the song is the call. The patter call consists of rhythmic, rapidly spoken directions for dance figures, mingled with humorous or nonsense phrases. The patter call is often used to create a fast dance with many changing figures. Dancers must pay close attention to the call to avoid entanglement in the interweaving of patterns and figures.

Square dancing is enjoyed by people of many ages. It can be relatively simple requiring little specialization of dance skills. However, enjoyment is increased as more difficult figures are introduced and as footwork becomes smoother and more intricate. Square dancing is included in many school programs but currently seems to have less appeal for school age participants than other forms. However, square dance continues to be a very popular community recreational activity with a great many clubs in existence throughout the country. As is true with other social forms, excellent performing groups are formed for purposes of entertainment.

SOCIAL DANCE

Social dancing, like other recreational forms, is done almost exclusively for personal pleasure. This dance form is also known by the terms "ballroom" and "popular" dance. These terms came about because certain dances were done on social occasions in a room designated a "ballroom."

Social dancing, as we have come to know this couple dance form, in America, was imported to the colonies from the European courts of France, Italy, Spain, and England. The dances were modified and refined versions of the more vigorous peasant dances. These were called court dances and included such dances as the courante, the pavana, the allemande, the gavotte, the gigue, and galliard. The 18th and 19th centuries fostered the contredanse, quadrilles, and cotillions from which the American square dance evolved. Many European couple dances of the nineteenth century remained relatively unchanged in America. These included the polka, the schottische, the mazurka, and the waltz. These dances were popular in essentially the European form until they were influenced by syncopated music, first known as "ragtime" and later "jazz." This influence, too, was an import from Africa and brought to America by Negroes.

Recreational dance in any historical period has always been closely related to the popular music of that period. The popularity of jazz music in America led to many long-lasting dance innovations during the first three decades of the 20th century. Today jazz provides the major dance music for social dancing over much of the world. Dances called the turkey trot, the bunny hug, the one-step, and the fox trot were popular in the early part of the 20th century. Dances of the 1920s reflected the black influence in movement and music. Popular dances included the Charleston, the shimmy, and the black bottom. The thirties and forties saw the evolution of the jitterbug, jive, and swing while the 1950s and 1960s fostered rock and roll and discotheque. Other music and dance imports to America came from Latin America. The tango was popular early in the 20th century and the rumba was introduced in the 1930s. The 1960s saw the rise of such dances as the cha-cha, the meringue, and the bossa nova. Moreover, in the 1960s popular dancing took a different direction. Emphasis was placed on the individualistic style of discotheque dancing. Dances from this period include the twist, the watusi, the swim, the monkey, and many others. The 1970s appear to be another transitional period in which the influence of "rock" and "soul" music creates a dance response which is either individualistic, "do your own thing," or a return to the partner-touching, close-embrace position with little attention given to intricate step patterns.

Social dancing in America has always shown the tendency for innovation in the creation of dances. It has provided a way for young people to reflect their own ideas instead of the ideas of an earlier age. Some of the ways of dancing created by youth are retained and become a part of our social dance heritage; others quickly lose their appeal and are dropped. New dances will continue to be created out of the same material, since there is really nothing new in social dancing, only new ways of using the same basic material. Each generation leaves a heritage of social dance only to be discarded by the next generation until such time as some cyclic motivation returns an earlier form to regenerated popularity.

REFERENCES

General

Haberman, M., and T. Meisel 1970. *Dance: an art in academe.* New York: Teachers College Press.

Kraus, R. 1969. *History of the dance in art and education.* Englewood Cliffs, N.J.: Prentice-Hall.

LaMeri, 1967. Ethnic dance. In A. Chujoy, *The dance encyclopedia.* (Rev. ed.) New York: Simon and Schuster.

McDonagh, D. 1970. *The rise and fall and rise of modern dance.* New York: Outerbridge and Dienstfrey.

Marr, M. 1975. Where do they go when the dancing stops? *Dance Magazine,* September.

Martin, J. 1967. American modern dance. In A. Chujoy and P. W. Manchester (eds.), *The dance encyclopedia.* New York: Simon and Schuster.

Moss, R. F. 1975. The arts in black America. *Saturday Review,* September 15: 12–15.

Nadel, M., and C. Nadel 1970. *The dance experience.* New York: Praeger.

Reed, G. (ed.) 1971. *Dance directory* (7th ed.) Washington: AAHPER.

Sorrell, W. 1967. *Dance through the ages.* New York: Grosset and Dunlap.

Terry, W. 1975. America's impact on the arts—dance. *Saturday Review,* December 13.

——— 1971. *Careers for the 70s dance.* New York: Macmillan.

Ballet

Denby, E. 1965. *Dancers, buildings, and people in the streets.* New York: Horizon.

Kirstein, L. 1970. *Movement and metaphor.* New York: Praeger.

———— 1952. *The classic ballet.* New York: Knopf.

Maynard, O. 1959. *The American ballet.* Philadelphia: Macrae-Smith.

Sparger, C. 1970. *Anatomy and ballet.* London: Adam and Charles Black.

Vaganova, A. 1969. *Basic principles of classical ballet.* New York: Dover.

Dance Ethnology

Boaz, F. 1944. *The function of dance in human society.* New York: Boaz.

———— 1940. *Race, language and culture: the origin of totemism (1910).* New York: Macmillan.

Committee on Research on Dance 1972. New dimensions in dance research: anthropology and dance. *Proceedings of Third Conference on Research on Dance.* New York: CORD.

Lomax, A. 1968. *Folk song style and culture.* Washington, D.C.: American Association for the Advancement of Science, No. 88.

Merloo, J. 1960. *Dance from ritual to rock and roll.* Philadelphia: Chilton.

Rust, F. 1969. *Dance in society.* London: Routledge and K. Paul.

Standard dictionary of folklore, myth, and legend 1950. New York: Funk and Wagnall.

Dance Therapy

American Dance Therapy Association 1968. *Third Annual Conference Proceedings.* Columbia, Md.: ADTA.

———— 1970. *Fifth Annual Conference Proceedings.* Columbia, Md.: ADTA.

———— 1972. *Sixth Annual Conference Proceedings.* Columbia, Md.: ADTA.

———— 1973. *Seventh Annual Conference Proceedings.* Columbia, Md.: ADTA.

Committee on Research in Dance 1970. *Workshop in dance therapy: its research potentials.* New York: CORD.

Criddle, K. (ed.) 1974. *Focus on dance XII: dance therapy.* Washington D.C.: AAHPER.

Schoop, T. 1973. *Won't you join the dance?* Palo Alto: National Press.

Folk Dance

Gilbert, C. 1969. *International folk dance at a glance.* Minneapolis: Burgess.

Joukowsky, A. M. 1965. *The teaching of ethnic dance.* New York: J. Lowell Pratt.

Lidster, M. D., and D. H. Tamburini 1965. *Folk dance progressions.* Belmont, Calif.: Wadsworth.

Wakefield, E. 1966. *Folk dancing in America.* New York: J. Lowell Pratt.

Jazz

Cayou, D. K. 1971. *Modern jazz dance.* Palo Alto: National Press.

Emery, L. 1970. *Black dance in the United States from 1619 to 1970.* Palo Alto: National Press.

Stearns, M. W. 1968. *Jazz dance: the story of American vernacular dance.* New York: Macmillan.

Modern

Lockhart, A., and E. E. Pease 1973. *Modern dance: building and teaching lessons.* Dubuque: Wm. C. Brown.

McDonagh, D. 1970. *The rise and fall and rise of modern dance.* New York: Outerbridge and Dienstfrey.

Penrod, J., and J. G. Plastino 1970. *Modern dance for beginners.* Palo Alto: National Press.

Shurman, N., and S. L. Clark 1972. *Modern dance fundamentals.* New York: Macmillan.

Square Dance

American Square Dance Society 1971. *Sets in order handbook series.* Los Angeles.

Jensen, M. B., and C. R. Jensen 1968. *Beginning square dance.* Belmont, Calif.: Wadsworth.

Phillips, P. A. 1968. *Contemporary square dance.* Dubuque: Wm. C. Brown.

Social Dance

Kleinman, S. 1968. *Social dancing: fundamentals.* Columbus: Merrill.

Kraus, R. G., and L. Sadlo. 1964. *Beginning social dance.* Belmont, Calif.: Wadsworth.

Youmans, J. G. 1969. *Social dance.* Physical Activities Series. Pacific Palisades, Calif.: Goodyear.

RELATED ACTIVITIES

Introduction

Some of the activities in Section 3 could be classified as sports, depending on the definition employed and the circumstances under which they occur. However, as they are described in this volume, some of them are recreational in nature, some are wilderness activities, and others are variations of personal self-defense. Relaxation, yoga, and weight training have still other objectives.

All the activities in Section 3 are found in some physical education programs. Their inclusion as educational subjects is increasing rapidly. Students who have previously disliked traditional physical education classes have become highly enthusiastic about activities such as backpacking, orienteering, sailing, and rock climbing.

The needs of some students for solitude, peace, and relaxation are being met by several of these courses. Some of the more challenging activities are particularly helpful in self-discovery and the development of a desirable self-concept. The important objectives of fun and joy are being achieved in activities such as roller skating, surfing, ice skating, and canoeing. All of these activities can make contributions to an individual's mental and physical well-being. *RBF*

Section Editor

Frank D. Sills is professor of physical education at East Stroudsberg State College, an institution of which he was president (1968–1971). He obtained his B.S. and M.S. from Pennsylvania State University and his Ph.D. from the State University of Iowa.

Dr. Sills is listed in *Who's Who in American Education* and numbers among his many honors the R. Tait McKenzie award from the AAHPER and the Iowa AHPER American Heart Association Award and has been cited in *Phi Epsilon Kappa* as the "Noteworthy Person in the Profession." He is a member of the American College of Sports Medicine; the American Alliance for Health, Physical Education and Recreation; the American Academy of Physical Education; the International Society for Biomechanics, and the American Association for the Advancement of Tension Control.

In addition to holding numerous chairmanships in national, district, and state sections of the AHPER, ACSM, and other organizations, he is past president of two AAHPER districts and chairman of the Board of Pennsylvania Affiliate AHA.

Dr. Sills has assisted with the solicitation and editing of articles dealing with sports and related activities.

53
Angling and Casting

David L. Engerbretson

INTRODUCTION

Fishing, which began as a search for food by primitive peoples, has become one of the world's most popular leisure time activities. The first written record of this sport is found in Aelian's *De Natura Animalium* which was written in the 3rd century A.D., and describes artificial flies used to imitate the insects Hippurus found on the River Astraeus in Macedonia.

Fig. 53.1 Fishing has become one of the most popular leisure time activities. Courtesy of Springfield College.

The first major work in the English language dealing with angling was the "Treatise of Fishing with an Angle" found in the *Second Book of St. Albans* written, according to legend, in 1496 by Dame Juliana Berners, a prioress of the Sopwell nunnery.

Several books on angling appeared in print during the next 150 years, but the first of major significance was not published until 1658 when Izaak Walton wrote *The Compleat Angler.* Walton's book, with a subsequent addition in 1676 by Charles Cotton, remains one of the best known works of angling literature with over 300 editions existing in the English language alone. To this day, Izaak Walton is known as the "patron saint" of the angler.

Following *The Compleat Angler,* angling literature began to appear with regularity, and, at the present time, more books have been written on angling than any other form of sport. An excellent discussion of angling literature is found in *McClane's Standard Fishing Encyclopedia* (1965).

Early attempts at catching fish for food undoubtedly involved the use of crude spears and traps. For thousands of years the techniques did not improve beyond a hook and line attached to a stick. Angling, as it is known today, was impossible prior to the development of the fishing reel. The use of a reel allowed anglers to extend their line and bait or lure beyond their rods and made possible the landing of large fish on a relatively weak line.

The first "reels" were nothing more than two pegs protruding from the grip of the rod around which the line was wrapped by hand. Next, wooden spools were fitted with handles and mounted on the butt of the rod which allowed the line to be wound in after a cast. Casting, however, was not done "from the reel." Instead, the line was stripped off by hand and coiled on the ground, the bait was then cast with a side-arm swing of the rod. Even these crude reels were not in common use until about the year 1700 in Britain, and about 1750 in the United States.

The forerunner of the modern day revolving spool reel was the British "Nottingham Winch" which was built in about 1750. The next major advance in reel building came with the introduction of a geared multiplying reel in 1810 by George Snyder, a Kentucky watchmaker. Improved geared reels were subsequently built by other Kentucky watchmakers such as Jonathan and Benjamin Meek, John Hordman, and Benjamin Milam.

The first American click type fly reels were developed by J. L. Sage of Frankfort, Kentucky, in 1848, and the modern era of the narrow, ventilated spool fly reel began with the introduction of such a reel by C. F. Orvis in 1874.

The first prototype of the fixed spool, or spinning, reel was built in 1884 by Peter Malloch of Perth, Scotland. The technique of spinning was introduced in the United States from Europe in 1935, but did not receive wide acceptance until the post–World War II years.

Angling was first introduced in the college physical education curriculum in 1931 by Charles M. Sprague at Stanford University (*Campus Report*

1972). Courses are now being offered by more than 200 institutions through-out the United States and, in addition, many workshops and clinics have been conducted by the AAHPER and various fishing tackle manufacturers.

OBJECTIVES

Primary objectives of classes in casting and angling are to teach students the wise use of leisure time and to help them learn a valuable lifetime sport skill. In addition, the student gains an understanding and appreciation of conservation, ecology, and the relationship between humans and their environment.

Casting and angling can provide a direct contribution to general education through their relationship to other disciplines such as biology, entomology, physics, history, and literature. The sport also provides an excellent vehicle for teaching motor skills and is an ideal activity for the handicapped. Casting is a competitive sport with opportunities for amateur and professional competition available locally, nationally, and internationally.

CASTING AND ANGLING IN THE SCHOOL CURRICULUM

A variety of methods exists for integrating casting and angling into the school program. Most commonly the course is offered as a regular class elective. The sport may be sponsored as a club activity in angling, fly tying, or target casting, or as a competitive activity through the intramural program. Units on angling can be included in general outdoor education classes. Casting, angling, and fly tying are often popular additions to evening adult education or summer recreation programs.

Fig. 53.2 Classes in angling and casting teach students the wise use of leisure time.

Class Organization

Casting and angling classes can be organized in several different ways. The following arrangements have been used successfully, and the method ultimately selected is best determined by the individual situation.

Bait, spin, and *fly-casting* involve teaching the skills of casting with minimal consideration given to other aspects of angling. In some cases students use one method exclusively, while in others they rotate in groups from one casting technique to another. After the proper casting techniques are learned, students may play various casting accuracy games. Records of scores are maintained and ladder tournaments and other forms of competition arranged.

Angling classes deal with a wide range of fishing theory. Topics include angling literature, construction and repair of tackle, temperature and structure theories of angling, entomology, aquatic biology, cleaning and cooking of fish, conservation, and angling techniques for various species. Such classes can effectively utilize guest lecturers, and readily lend themselves to interdepartmental cooperation.

Fly-fishing classes are similar to those in angling, but deal exclusively with the techniques, theories, and literature relating to fly fishing. *Fly-tying* classes are often used as a follow-up to courses in fly fishing, and provide an opportunity for a more detailed study of entomology and instruction in the techniques of constructing artificial fishing flies.

Fig. 53.3 Winter is no problem for those hardy souls who know how to enjoy it. Courtesy of Michigan Conservation Department.

Equipment and Materials

Ideally, each student should have a rod, reel, line, and practice plugs or flies. When equipment is shared, one student casts while his or her partner serves as a coach and scorekeeper.

Many schools provide all of the required equipment. It is not necessary that the equipment be the most expensive, but moderately priced equipment is usually of significantly better quality and durability than inexpensive tackle. Care should be taken to select well-balanced outfits so that rods, reels, and lines are not mismatched. Manufacturers' guidelines should be followed carefully.

If students provide their own tackle, they should be counseled regarding the selection of equipment prior to the start of casting instruction. Expenses can be reduced and an educational experience provided by allowing the students to construct their own rods from inexpensive kits. Consult resources listed at the conclusion of the chapter.

In addition to casting outfits, a number of casting targets should be provided. These may be constructed of ¼″ exterior grade plywood, or may be open hoops or rings. A typical tournament casting arrangement requires five targets.

A fly-tying class requires both permanent tools and expendable materials such as hooks, thread, feathers, and fur. Some schools supply all of the equipment and materials, and charge a nominal class fee to cover the cost of replacing expendable materials. Other institutions furnish the tools, but require the students to purchase material kits. If students are expected to provide their own tools and/or materials, the instructor should purchase the items in bulk and make up kits to be sold to class members. In this way all students will have the proper materials.

Activity Area

Maximum class enrollment should be determined by the dimensions of the meeting area. Care should be taken to avoid overcrowding. Each casting station consists of five targets at distances of 40 to 80 feet for bait-casting and spinning, and 25 to 50 feet for fly-casting. It must be remembered that fly casters require at least as much free space behind them as in front. Targets should be spaced so that they can all be used simultaneously. Thus each teaching station can service five or ten students. The *classroom for fly-tying* should contain worktables that are thin enough to allow vises to be attached, and the area should be well lighted.

Instructors

Many schools offer classes in casting, angling, and fly-tying despite the fact that no members of the physical education faculty are qualified to teach them.

Often members of other departments are experienced fishers and are willing to assist as are local resident "experts" within the community. Extensive use can be made of members of local sportsman's clubs as well as state and local offices of conservation, wildlife, fish and game, and pollution control. Proprietors of local fishing tackle shops, and field representatives from most fishing tackle manufacturing companies are generally happy to serve as guest speakers and demonstrators.

RESOURCES

Teacher's Guides and Instructional Manuals

Casting and Angling, AAHPER, 1201 16th St. N.W., Washington, D.C.

Fly and Bait Casting Guide, Am. Casting Assn., Paul Jones, Executive Secy., Box 51, Nashville, Tenn. 37202.

Fly Casting, Fenwick/Sevenstrand Tackle Mfg. Co., Box 729, Westminster, Calif. 92683.

To Cast A Fly, Scientific Anglers, Inc., Box 2001, Midland, Mich. 48640.

Films, Teaching Aids, and Tackle Manufacturers

American Fishing Tackle Manufacturers' Assn., 20 N. Wacker Drive, Chicago, Ill. 60606.

Cortland Tackle Mfg. Co., Box 1362, Cortland, N.Y. 13045.

Fenwick/Sevenstrand Tackle Mfg. Co., Box 729, Westminster, Calif. 92683.

Scientific Anglers, Inc., Box 2001, Midland, Mich. 48640.

Fishing-rod Kits and Fly-tying Materials

Buz's Fly Shop, 805 W. Tulare Ave., Visalia, Calif. 93277.

Fireside Anglers, Inc., Box 823, Melville, N.Y. 11746.

Herter's Inc., R.R. #1, Waseca, Minn. 56093.

E. Hille, The Angler's Supply House, 815 Railway St., Williamsport, Pa. 17701.

The Orvis Company, Manchester, Vt. 05254.

Reed Tackle Co., Box 390, Caldwell, N.J. 07006.

REFERENCES

Bates, J. D., Jr., B. Hall, M. Marshall, F. P. Rice, and M. Sosin 1971. *Tacklebox library.* (5 volumes.) New York: Harper & Row.

Brooks, J. 1972. *Trout fishing.* New York: Harper & Row.

Campus report **4,** 4, (October 1972). Stanford University.

Dalrymple, B. 1968. *Sportsman's guide to game and fish.* New York: Harper & Row.

Harvey, G. W. (Undated). *Fly-tying.* Harrisburg: Pennsylvania Fish Commission.

Lucas, J. 1962. *Lucas on bass fishing.* New York: Dodd, Mead.

McClane, A. J. 1965. *McClane's standard fishing encyclopedia.* New York: Holt, Rinehart and Winston.

McNally, T. 1970. *Fisherman's bible.* Chicago: Follett.

Slaymaker, S. R. 1969. *Simplified fly-fishing.* New York: Harper & Row.

54
Backpacking

James E. and Jean B. Genasci

INTRODUCTION

Backpacking is really nothing more or less than taking a hike with the idea in mind that one will stay overnight, sleep comfortably, eat reasonably well, and carry all necessary items in a pack. One must, therefore, be self-propelled, self-contained, and self-reliant.

The few remaining natural areas in the United States and in the world are rapidly becoming filled with backpackers. An attempt to group them is almost futile, but it may help to use the following categories: the conquerors, the enjoyers, and the utilizers.

Conquerors

Any number of hikers and backpackers seem to have need to prove themselves, perhaps to overcome some persistent, nagging deficiency. They use the environment to determine how high they can climb, or how far they can walk under various conditions and constraints. There is a sense of accomplishment in the activity, and although it is often perceived as an individual effort and fulfillment, the accomplishment appears to take on greater significance when the feats are compared to another's, and discovered to be of greater magnitude. Thus, the conquering spirit is joined by the gauntlet of a challenge, breeding a competitiveness. The conquerors set out to conquer themselves, others, and the natural environment.

716

Enjoyers

A second group is composed of those who immerse themselves in the environment, wishing to be at one with the mountain, the desert, the trees, and the flowers. To ask them how high or how far they hiked is futile. They will know the answer and will inform the inquirer, but to this group the most meaningful question is: "Did you enjoy yourselves?" It is difficult for the enjoyers to verbalize their experiences and to communicate the joy of being at one with nature.

Utilizers

Still another group includes hunters, fishermen, photographers, soldiers, and others who can be considered utilizers, for they use the environment to produce something—fish, deer, a victory, or a picture—resulting in ends which are sometimes noble and other times ignoble.

HISTORY

It seems appropriate to divide the development of hiking and backpacking into three diffuse yet distinct periods of time—antiquity, early modern, and modern.

Antiquity

In the days of antiquity, backpacking was motivated by necessity rather than pleasure, and we see some rare instances of this today. Among some nomadic peoples such as the reindeer herders of Lapland, movement of belongings and food over long distances is still a necessity. Even in remote areas, however, technology has brought electricity, helicopters, and snowmobiles, as well as nylon cloth and rope which have altered lifestyles drastically.

Early Modern

There was a time prior to ultralight, sturdy equipment, and rapid mass transportation, when the hearty backpacker enjoyed natural areas with different skills and heavy equipment. The old skills of building a bough bed and pit fire, felling a tree, burying trash, and building a leanto are still known, but solely as novelty skills. If used, these practices are frowned upon unless they are needed for survival in an extreme emergency. The last campfire at the end of a long day's hike has not yet died out, but in many areas fire building is restricted because of wood shortage. The early modern period, with its careless use of natural resources, is over although the nostalgia will linger on.

Modern

The presently evolving modern period is characterized by two major influences—technology and conservation. With the advent of aluminum tubing,

717

arc welding, foam rubber, ripstop nylon, freeze-dried food, artificial fibers, and liquid gas, there has been introduced to backpacking a new era of ease and comfort. Accompanying this technological surge has been the development of rapid and efficient transportation which can move backpackers into desirable natural areas quickly. To fly by jet in a few hours to the Rocky Mountains, or take a bus via interstate highway to the trailhead for a week or more of hiking is common in this era of easy transportation and ultralight, serviceable equipment. For example, it is quite possible for a troop of boy-scouts to travel from New Jersey to New Hampshire and hike into the Presidential Range all in one day.

A second dimension of the modern period concerns conservation. Modern technology and the desire to return to nature have made remote areas easily accessible to huge numbers of people. The human impact on the fragile environment has begun to destroy the very conditions which make backpacking attractive. The problem has reached serious proportions. The backpacking ethic supports conservation of the natural environment from the saving of a single stream to the passage of necessary congressional legislation.

THE ACTIVITY

The greatest amount of hiking and backpacking activities occurs in three places—the mountains, the valleys, and the deserts.

Mountains

When entering mountainous regions for the first time, one must be prepared to expect changes in temperature and oxygen. As one gains altitude, there is generally a corresponding drop in temperature (as much as several degrees for each thousand feet) and a drop in the percentage of oxygen in the air becomes noticeable around 8000 feet. Hikers must be equipped for cooler weather as they continue to ascend and must also rest more frequently. In the Sierras, hikers have found that the "hundred-half-steps-and-rest" technique enabled them to climb over a crest at 11,000 feet without excessive strain. Only in emergencies is it necessary to race up or down a trail. High mountains may have sudden summer storms; therefore, in addition to concerns about temperature changes and the need to rest frequently at high elevations, the mountain hiker must also be prepared for rain.

Deserts

Desert hikers are confronted with extreme daytime heat and scarcity of water. It is recommended that desert hikers equip themselves with a current map, which shows updated water locations, and approximately a gallon of water per person. When one stretches out at night under a brilliant blanket of stars, it is comforting to know that one has an adequate water supply to meet the needs of the coming day. Desert hikers should rest during the extreme heat at midday in a shaded area. They should be prepared to make awnings of their own in the event that no natural shade is available.

Valleys

Valley hiking has its particular pleasures and precautions. In New England, hiking on old wood roads is popular. On occasion the roads fade away or fork and it is quite easy for the inattentive hiker to veer off the intended route. This can also happen when following animal paths. The authors found delight in following migratory reindeer paths while backpacking through the great valleys in northern Sweden.

THE SEASONS

Winter

Winter brings snow, ice, and extreme cold, but despite, or because of, this, backpackers continue to journey outdoors, and winter backpacking is growing in popularity. Technology has produced ultralight, warm clothing, and serviceable equipment; thus, many backpackers have acquired these items and added snowshoes, crampons, or skis to the boots allowing them to make trips into natural areas.

Because winter conditions require not only special gear and clothing but also special techniques for living in the cold, persons interested in cold-weather packing should:

☐ gain experience in backpacking at mild temperatures which would allow basic skills to be practiced under less harsh and less hazardous conditions. Basic equipment can be acquired, to which the specialized equipment can be added.

☐ take part in workshops, clinics, or beginner programs taught by winter backpacking experts who can turn what could be an extremely hazardous situation into an enjoyable, rewarding experience. Most hiking clubs sponsor such clinics or workshops during the winter season. In addition, there are private organizations such as Outward Bound, Inc., and National Outdoor Leadership School which provide courses in winter backpacking, as do many colleges and community agencies.

☐ read extensively before and after undertaking each winter trip. Books, articles, essays, and reports (particularly the accident reports found in the magazine, *Appalachia*) are not only helpful, they are essential to an understanding of the many conditions encountered in winter hiking, and the reasons why some hikers have succeeded while others have failed.

Spring, Summer, and Fall

Summer hiking in the southwestern desert, wet spring hiking in New England, and high altitude fall hiking in the Rocky Mountains each presents its own particular problem. Problems notwithstanding, each season has its own special attraction. Fall hiking in New England gives one a fantastic experience—the crunch of fallen leaves underfoot, the sun streaming through the red, yellow, and gold leaves still clinging to the branches, and the clear crispness which permeates the air. Spring hiking when the deserts of the southwest are in bloom brings a different exhilaration as does the cool, low-humidity hiking in the high mountains during midsummer. Refreshing, invigorating? Words are inadequate! When proper skills and equipment have been acquired, backpacking through the four seasons holds the potential for many pleasurable experiences.

SKILLS

Map and Compass

Topographical maps prepared by the United States Geologic Survey are basic for orientation, and are available for all sections of the country. Hikers should be able to read map markings such as contour lines, power lines, types of roads, wet lands, etc., and be able to estimate hiking time between points. The ability to orient map and compass for direction and to recognize key features in actual surroundings designated on the map are other important skills. Another vital consideration is the ability to plot a hike as one expects to complete it, including the scouting of entrance and exit points as well as allowing for alternate routes should it be necessary to abort the trip.

Trail Signs

Hiking trails are generally marked with blaze marks painted on a tree, post, or rocks. Man-made piles of rocks, called cairns, are generally used above the tree line and in other nonwooded areas. The blaze marks are usually placed in the line of vision as one is hiking along the trail; this necessitates their being blazed in both directions. The mark is color-coded and has a particular shape for a given trail. When using several trails on a given trip, one may be following white blaze marks of a rectangular shape in a vertical position, and at a trail intersection, the next trail may be marked with orange circles. When following a trail of any kind, a change is designated by a double blaze mark, one over the other. This double marking simply indicates a change, usually in direction, but it does not indicate which direction or exactly how soon it will take place. Upon seeing a double blaze mark, the hiker is alerted to the fact that there will be some change in the trail, and that it is wise to be watchful. When hiking along some trails, such as those which follow old wood roads, it is very easy to be lulled into following the road and not paying attention to the marks. Suddenly one realizes that the blaze marks have disappeared, and it is impossible to remember when the last one was seen! Such a predicament requires backtracking until the blaze marks and the place where the trail departed from the wood road can be found again. Blazes are usually in the line of vision, and visible from one mark to the next. Because of overgrowth and insufficient trail maintenance, and also foresting, this is not always the case. When trail markings cannot be found, it is necessary to scout out the next blaze mark. If the hiker is in a group, a few members of the group can fan out in search of blazes and then return to the point of departure before going on, once they have located blaze marks and trail. If the hiker is alone, the last blaze mark can be used as the focal point. The hiker then fans out in a series of ever-expanding semicircular patterns until the next blaze mark is found.

Cairns are recognized as rocks piled in a particular way, one on top of another. Small cairns may be arranged with three rocks, usually the smallest on top. Large cairns may take the shape of a cone or pyramid. The majority of cairns are found at high elevations. Dense fog, which is a frequent condition hikers encounter when following a high-altitude trail, often makes it impossible to see from one cairn to the next. When this happens, it is necessary to have one hiker scout the next cairn and maintain contact with the waiting group by voice only.

Guidebooks

Most of the major United States trail systems are described in detailed guidebooks. Beginning backpackers should acquire the guidebook which describes the trail system they wish to hike. Detailed written descriptions, maps of various sections of the trail, and helpful advice are included in most guides. They can be purchased from hiking organizations or from stores specializing in backpacking equipment.

Weather Information

For local hikes, backpackers should check with regular forecasts in order to determine weather patterns which will be in effect during the time of the planned hike. For week-long hikes, a call to the national weather service is in order.

FIRST AID

Prevention of Trail Miseries

If blisters, sore muscles, a twisted ankle or knee, sunburn, headache, hypothermia, heat exhaustion, dehydration, hypoxemia, abrasions, nausea, diarrhea or similar conditions can be prevented, an enjoyable hike can be experienced. On the other hand, any one of these miseries, or a combination of them, can turn what could have been a pleasurable outing into a miserable experience.

Blisters. A hot spot is recognized as the first sign of a blister. When one occurs, hikers should stop immediately and check socks for wrinkles and the inner boot for any irregularities. In addition, they should place moleskin directly on the hot spot, straighten or change socks, remove from the boots any irregularities such as sand, pebbles, or twigs, and cover inner boot protrusions, such as a cobbler's misplaced nail, with a piece of sponge rubber. They should be especially careful to keep feet clean and dry, as well as to remove boots and socks during rest or lunch stops when time and weather permit. These precautions will help them avoid blisters.

Abrasions. Abrasions (scraping away of the skin) occur most frequently on the shoulders. They are caused by improperly fitted or unpadded shoulder straps. Improperly adjusted hip belts can cause abrasions on the front of the hips. Modern frame packs are designed to carry the bulk of the pack weight on the hips, with the belt placed below the crest of the ilium (hip bone). Abrasions can usually be avoided by using both padded shoulder straps and padded hip belts.

Wearing a frame pack correctly can help to avoid the discomfort of abrasions. When putting on a frame pack, hikers should hunch the shoulders and cinch the hip belt firmly below the hip bones. As the shoulders are relaxed, the pack weight is borne on the hip belt, and the shoulder straps are just snug enough to act as lateral stabilizers. There is little or no weight carried by the shoulder straps. No single setting is ideal. Fine adjustments of hip belt and shoulder straps go on constantly throughout a hike.

At the first sign of abrasion, hikers should cover the sensitive skin area with moleskin. Hiking pants should fit so that a belt is unnecessary, thus avoiding the possibility of irritation. Some women wear tank tops and halters that do not have shoulder straps in order to reduce the occurrence of shoulder abrasions.

Muscle cramps. Eating well-balanced meals, salted to taste, and drinking plenty of water will help to reduce the possibility of muscle cramps. In order to relieve the muscles of the feet and legs during short, standing rest stops, turn and face the opposite direction of an incline. Hikers hiking uphill should turn and face downhill, and vice versa. Reaching back with both hands and lifting up on the pack will relieve strap pressure. For sitting rest stops with pack on, prop it so that its weight is resting on the ground, a boulder, or a log, and for a rest stop with the pack off, stretch out and enjoy a snack or drink.

When hiking uphill, hikers should use the whole foot and the large muscles of the buttocks and thigh by consciously taking a shortened step, placing the whole foot down, and driving the knee back. This technique of walking when ascending under full load requires some practice. Stretching, massage, and rest are the immediate procedures to relieve a cramped muscle, while proper hiking technique and nutrition are long-term considerations.

Hypoxemia. The inability of the respiratory system to supply adequate oxygen for muscle metabolism may occur at elevations above 7000 or 8000 feet. It may also occur due to poor physical condition or incipient heart or chest disease. Before engaging in strenuous hiking activities persons should check with their physicians to be sure that they have no limiting physical deficiencies.

For those who are on occasion out of breath, the following suggestions are offered:

- □ rest frequently
- □ establish a rhythm and pace commensurate with individual capacity
- □ condition before setting out on a trip
- □ be examined regularly by a physician who will test body responses under stress conditions. A number of physicians are becoming aware of the need to examine cardiorespiratory responses under maximum stress conditions.

Dehydration. Body fluids are lost quite rapidly during exertion, and need to be replaced. Dryness of the mouth and throat or drippy perspiration are not always indicators of how much fluid is lost, for the loss may occur when hikers are seemingly not perspiring or breathing hard. This constant evaporation and periodic draining process, plus the excessive perspiration and labored breathing during exertion, require hikers to drink liquids throughout the day.

Desert hiking, in particular, may cause dehydration. To avoid this, each hiker should have at least a gallon of water per day. Salt tablets should be available in special circumstances where fluid loss might be excessive. However, for routine hiking, salt tablets are not necessary. Ample salting of the food works well for most normal, healthy people even in the desert. In any event, the body merely eliminates any excess salt should it be taken in.

Hypothermia. Hypothermia is a hiking hazard which occurs when the body gives up heat under conditions involving rain, cold, and wind or a combination of these, so that the core body temperature starts a downward trend. This loss of body heat which lowers core body temperature can occur in any season, and must be a concern of any hiker or backpacker regardless of season or apparent weather conditions at the start of the hike. The three admonitions for prevention of hypothermia are: stay warm, stay dry, and stay nourished!

Not only must the hands, legs, and torso be kept warm, but also the head and neck, for a considerable amount of body heat is radiated from the head, face, and neck. Staying as dry as possible is a must! Wet clothing loses its heat retention capacity, and even worse, it "wicks" body heat to the atmosphere very effectively, thus causing the body to lose warmth rapidly.

High energy foods should be available to the hiker for consumption when fatigue is setting in and the weather conditions are wet, windy, and cold. It is essential to be able to prepare hot drinks quickly when uncontrollable shivering, slurred speech, and fumbling fingers impede the ability to think and act efficiently. If this occurs, one is clearly in danger, and must take immediate action to get dry, warm, and nourished!

A few final preventative suggestions which may help to avoid discomfort are included for hiker consideration:

- □ select properly fitted clothing, pack, and boots.
- □ condition before setting out, including testing boots on at least a few occasions to determine their comfort.
- □ eat well for at least a week before setting out on a long hike, and plan adequate meals for the trip.
- □ take special care of the food, as well as cooking and eating implements while on the trail.
- □ pace with a steady rate, allowing for intermittent rest stops. A variety of rest stops—some short, some long, some to sit, others to lie down with boots and pack off—proves helpful.
- □ drink water regularly as long as it is available.
- □ treat all water suspected of pollution with Halizone or boiling for ten to twenty minutes. Almost all water at the present time is suspect.
- □ carry an extra set of dry clothes.
- □ take special care of the feet, cleaning and drying them daily.

Care of trail miseries. As careful as one tries to be, conditions do occur which need immediate attention. In anticipation of this need to provide first aid, at least four recommendations are in order:

1. Take a first-aid course or review the fundamentals of first aid for the conditions discussed previously.
2. Hike with different groups under competent leadership and observe closely how trail miseries are handled.
3. Attend a few workshops on hiking sponsored by hiking clubs. First aid is usually on the agenda.
4. Carry a first-aid kit on every hike, even a short one. When hiking in a

group, it is necessary to carry group first-aid supplies in addition to personal first-aid items. A complete kit is recommended for every four to six persons. The contents of a sample kit are listed below:

Matches	Vitamin pills
Halizone	Two elastic bandages
Aspirin	Wash and dries
Gauze	Pain pills
Adhesive bandages	Moleskin
Rubber bands	Ammonia
Safety pins	Tweezers
Bactine	Needle
Dimes	Foot powder
Space blanket	Sponge rubber piece
Snake kit (optional)	Adhesive tape

THE TRAIL

Etiquette

Survival of the environment, of others, and of self depends on the degree to which those who enter the natural areas respect and follow the rules of the trail.

The Green Mountain Club, Inc., headquartered in Rutland, Vermont, makes available a wallet-sized card with suggestions concerning clothing and equipment, and several rules to be followed when hiking and backpacking. The Green Mountain Club requests that those who follow the trail *respect the environment* by agreeing to (1) protect living plants by leaving them in place and unharmed, (2) use a portable stove for cooking, (3) camp or build fires in designated areas only, (4) use only dead wood and extinguish fires completely, and (5) walk on rocks rather than on delicate alpine plants above timberline.

Hikers should *respect others* by agreeing to (1) carry out what is carried in, (2) use toilet facilities where available, (3) wash in an area that is removed from the water supply, (4) share facilities with others and limit stay to two nights at a shelter, (5) leave the site in better condition than it was upon their arrival, and (6) limit group size to ten, with one leader for four youths.

Hikers should *respect themselves* by agreeing to (1) plan carefully within their limitations, (2) inform others of planned trip, (3) pack sufficient food, clothing, and equipment, and (4) take time for the experience to be a meaningful one.

It is crucial that a reverence for the land be cultivated among those who enter the natural areas, as well as among those who do not! Our past record is not an enviable one in this regard, for as an old Wintu Indian woman said in speaking of the white man's destruction of the land, "Everywhere the white man has touched it, it is sore." (McLuhan 1972)

Solo

The solo hiker should contact someone who is not hiking and give information as to when the hike will start, where it will be taken, when return is expected, who should be contacted and what should be done if the hiker does not return as expected. The same procedure should be followed for group hikes, but with two or more hikers there is always the possibility of sending a well hiker for help in the event of an accident or illness.

Reconnaissance of the area and information regarding the local conditions are necessary before solo hiking. Consultation with those who have intimate knowledge of the area, particularly if they are experienced at hiking there, is important. Topographical maps of the region to be hiked should be carefully examined. Visual observation of the general area and its major features should be accomplished prior to starting the hike.

Groups

Most organizations recommend a group size of from four to eight, with no more than eight per leader. Larger groups can be organized into smaller units, each with a designated leader. Prior to the hike, leadership and lines of responsibility must be clearly established. Injury, illness, and mitigating circumstances may alter the lines of authority, but each leader must know those for whom he or she is responsible, and each member of the group must know to whom he or she is responsible. Those acting as group leaders must be knowledgeable, experienced, and able to make prudent and judicial decisions, often in consultation with group members. Above all, the leader must place the enjoyment and the survival of the group before self-aggrandizement, bravado, or personal achievement.

Mountain Hiking

When planning for backpacking, it is most common to think of going up and down a mountain. We tend not to think of canyon hiking, which is down and up, or of valley hiking which is over and back.

In mountain hiking, fortunately, the heaviest load is carried up the trail when one is generally freshest. When coming down at the end of the hike with fatigue setting in, the load is usually lighter because of food consumption. Either way, some careful planning and practice are helpful. Pacing and rhythm should be practiced and employed consciously. The pace should be steady and the rhythm regular. A good question to ask oneself starting up the trail in a rested state is, "Could I be comfortable ten hours from now hiking at this pace?" For most novice backpackers, the answer will be no. The old hands will answer yes. Experienced backpackers set a pace which is one they could continue all day and all night if necessary. In addition to pace, rhythm is also important. In scientific terms, we know that when a body is in motion, it tends to remain in motion until acted upon by some force. A body at rest tends to remain in the state of rest until moved by a force. In other words, it takes more energy to start and stop or to hike unrhythmically than it does to hike rhythmically. Perhaps the best word to describe it is flow. When legs, heart, lungs, mind, and soul are all synchronized on the trail, one feels as if one could climb forever! It really does happen, but the techniques must be learned, and the chief ingredients are pacing and rhythm.

On the ascent, the large muscles of the thigh and buttocks must be used in favor of the smaller muscles of the calf and foreleg. There are two simple techniques which must be employed to accomplish this. First, one should consciously shorten the stride. Although steepness will make one do so, one should think about shortening the stride and do it before being forced. Second, learn to push the knee back into a full leg extension. This forces one to activate the large gluteal muscles and the large quadriceps or thigh muscles. In achieving full leg extension, there is a momentary transmission of the body and pack weight through the bones of the leg (femur and tibia) which relieves the muscles briefly from having to carry the weight. When one considers the number of steps that are necessary for most mountain hikes, those momentary muscle resting periods at each step are going to be greatly welcomed at the end of the day. This is not a natural walking pattern. It will feel uncomfortable at first, if not downright awkward. It is a mountain hiking technique that should be practiced until it can be done skillfully and efficiently. It requires one to shorten the stride and plant the foot down solidly, forcing the knee back completely.

On an extended hike in northern Vermont, for example, it was necessary to shorten the stride to less than six inches on a particularly steep ascent of Jay Peak, but by doing so and using the mountain hiking technique, the top was reached with climbers in good condition and able to enjoy the fruits of the climb.

Canyon Hiking

The reverse of mountain hiking is canyon hiking, where the beginning is down and the end of the trip is up. This also requires planning, pacing and rhythm.

Heat is often a complicating factor in canyon hiking. On a summer three-day trip into Grand Canyon, it was found that hiking between the morning hours of three and seven was preferable to hiking during the remainder of the

Fig. 54.1 Fording a stream while back-packing is real adventure. Courtesy of Mott Community College.

day. The intense heat of midmorning continued long after sunset. The temperature was so high that relief was obtained on one day by sitting in the creek for hours, coming out only for brief periods to dry off!

Wet Trails

Those who hike in the southwest have little experience with wet trails, while those who hike in New England encounter these frequently. In areas where one might expect wet conditions, essential items are a rainsuit, rain cover for pack, and extra dry clothing wrapped in plastic bags. Every effort must be made to keep self, equipment, and extra clothing dry. One can manage reasonably well for one or two days in rain, but continuous rain for longer periods really tests one's ability to stay dry. Special care must be taken to keep sleeping bag and clothing dry, because even in the summer months, there is the danger of hypothermia. To illustrate, after five days of continuous rain on the Vermont Long Trail, a small group of hikers arrived at a shelter area experiencing the preliminary symptoms of hypothermia—uncontrollable shivering, and difficulty with both speech and thought patterns (the slurred speech, fumbling fingers stage). The ambient temperature was 42°F, but there had been continuous rain for five days. Fortunately, the sleeping bags were still dry, and immediately everyone was told to get into their bags while hot soup, tea, coffee, and chocolate were made quickly and served continuously.

In approximately 45 minutes, recovery was sufficient for hikers to start getting up and about. The body temperature had been raised. Following this, a deluxe supper was prepared using all the special treats which had been saved on the hike. The next day, it was necessary to abort the hike when it was learned that the rain was predicted to continue for another three days! Backpackers in the west are rarely treated to such wet trail hiking.

Dry Trails

The need to prevent sunstroke, heat exhaustion, and sunburn, as well as to replace body fluids is imperative when hiking in extremely dry, hot areas. Plenty of water, a food supply amply salted, loose-fitting clothing and a brimmed hat are recommended for hiking under these conditions. A bandana soaked in water and placed over the head helps to cool the hiker as the water evaporates, and is a welcome relief when hiking in extremely dry areas.

No Trails

Sometimes the hiker travels across boulder fields, or up and down rivers, either in water or on dry river beds. Because the footing in such areas is very uneven, and because movement of the pack can cause one to lose balance, it is important to be especially cautious with each step in order to avoid twisting an ankle or knee. A staff or hiking stick can be of great assistance under these conditions. If a fall does occur, the body can be injured and the packframe bent or broken.

CLOTHING

Comfortable, durable clothing, appropriate for conditions encountered, should be selected. A suggested basic list will serve as a guide:

Rain pants and jacket	Long pants
Wool hat and gloves	Short pants
Down sweater	Long-sleeved shirt
Brimmed hat	Short-sleeved shirt
Wool sweater	Socks (2 or 3 pairs)
Sneakers or moccasins	Hiking boots
Briefs (2 or 3)	Bandana

The following comments regarding specific items included in the clothing list indicate personal preferences:

1. Long-sleeved, button shirt—sleeves can be rolled up or down for varying conditions (bugs, sun, wind) and the front can be opened and closed for similar reasons.

2. Vibram-soled, ankle-high boot—gives good traction under a variety of wet and rocky conditions. The thicker sole prevents stone and bone bruises to the bottom of the foot when hiking on irregular terrain with a heavy load. The ankle-high boot gives lateral stability to the ankles which is needed for the twisting, turning, and slipping which are bound to occur on uneven, slippery, root- or rock-strewn trails.

3. Long and short pants—both should be fitted so that they can be worn

without a belt. Short pants should have a slit at the sides to allow for lifting the thigh without binding. Long pants should allow for ample knee action. The blue-jean generation may not wish to affirm this preference!

4. Down sweater—this item is better than down vest or jacket because of its wider range of use. It can be stuffed into a small compact package and can be used as needed as a pillow. Synthetic fiber may be preferred over down by those concerned about wetness. Down loses its fluff when wet, and becomes useless for retaining warmth. Even in New England with adequate care it is possible to keep down dry while hiking in continuous rain for several days. Nevertheless, synthetic products are attractive for wet conditions.

5. A brimmed hat—not only is this good for shading the head but it also makes a good dipper-dripper on hot days. Just dip it in the stream and put it on the head, full of water. It makes the next half hour of hiking quite pleasant! Then, for rainy days, turn the brim down permitting the rain to drip off the back without running down the neck. It is also useful as a pot holder, bug swatter, fan, and seat cushion.

EQUIPMENT

Frame Pack

The variations of both frame and pack are so numerous and technology is changing the materials so rapidly that it is mind boggling! Therefore, only a few general principles will be considered.

The frame should be contoured, sturdy, and so constructed that if accidentally dropped with full load, the parts and pieces will not spring loose or

Fig. 54.2 Students who wish to backpack must pay careful attention to the details of packing. Courtesy of the University of Utah.

fracture easily. The frame size should match body size. The means of pack attachment should be such that the total load is distributed as evenly as possible to avoid stress points where the pack might split under the pressure of the load. There should be some fine adjustments possible such as the width of the shoulder strap setting, and the tension of the back support. The pack should have a sufficient number of outside pockets (four or five preferably) to carry the numerous small items as well as the immediate access items such as water bottle, flashlight, snacks, map, and compass. The opening to the interior of the pack should be quick and easy; whether zipper or string arrangement, it makes little difference under most circumstances. The material, however, must be water repellent and tear resistant. For wet weather conditions, a rain cover for the pack is a necessity.

Several pack designs are available, but the basic ones are either the full-size or the three-quarter, where the sleeping bag and tent are tied on the frame rather than stuffed inside the pack. Some packs are divided into separate zippered compartments for special equipment storage, and some are divided inside for organizational possibilities. Since the pack and frame will be used for a long time under a wide variety of conditions, it would be wise to consider these possibilities before purchase. Both the frame and pack need to be rugged and durable for regular backpackers.

Kitchen

Simplicity in kitchen equipment, utensils, and food is recommended by most seasoned backpackers. The novice is usually surprised to learn how simply meals can be prepared and served on the trail.

Stove. A small, portable backpacking stove fueled by nonleaded liquid gas, or pressurized gas such as butane or propane is most common. There are several of these small stoves on the market. When purchasing one, be cognizant of the following:

- [ ] total weight of stove and fuel
- [ ] ease with which flame can be lighted and regulated
- [ ] length of burning time of fuel and manner in which the fuel is to be carried
- [ ] the stability of the stove when set up with pot of food
- [ ] protection of flame from wind
- [ ] the number of component parts necessary to assemble in order to use the stove (the fewer the better)
- [ ] ease of repair when 300 miles from the store and 30 miles from the nearest road

☐ the contour of the whole package when it must be carried in pack until the next use

Cooking over an open wood fire is nostalgic, but currently it is being prohibited in more and more areas. A total ban on any open wood fire is now in force in some areas, and the need to restrict fires is growing each day.

Utensils and food. Eating is such an idiosyncratic activity that it is impossible to say much about it. The backpacker can eat anything desired, but should remember that the food, equipment, and the utensils must be carried in and out. The bare essentials are a cup made either of plastic or metal with heat-resistant rim, a spoon, and two nesting pots. It is not necessary to carry more. One-pot meals, if food is to be cooked, are the order of the day; on the trail food should be nourishing, palatable, easily prepared, and lightweight.

A sample day's menu is included which can be modified to suit individual tastes. As one gains experience, other foods and combinations can be tried to give a varied diet.

Breakfast
    Dehydrated orange drink
    Oatmeal
    Brown sugar
    Bacon bar

Lunch
    Cheese
    Crackers
    Canned meat
    "Bird seed" (cereal, raisins, nuts, chocolate candy)
    Powdered drink

Dinner
    Freeze-dried dinner
    Vegetables
    Dried fruit
    Powdered drink or hot chocolate

Snacks
    Space sticks
    Hard candy
    Prunes or other dried fruit
    Chewing gum

Sleeping

Bag. A good quality sleeping bag which can be stuffed easily into a small nylon sack is essential. It should be of down or synthetic fiber and adapted to the temperature range of expected use. Before buying the bag, close attention should be given to the covering material, the zipper and air baffle arrangement, the internal construction (slant, box, V tube, and sewn through) and cost, weight, and bulk.

Pad. A sleeping pad is needed as a temperature barrier and for comfort. There are three kinds in use at the present time–air mattress, open-cell pad, and closed-cell pad:

☐ an air mattress is heavier than the other two and requires inflation and deflation daily, but has other possible uses such as a raft or a makeshift easy chair.

☐ an open-cell pad is lighter in weight, and provides good padding, but it is bulky when rolled and absorbs ground or body moisture which may require drying out after use.

☐ the closed-cell pad is the lightest in weight, and is the least bulky. It provides the most effective temperature barrier and does not absorb moisture. However, it does not pad as well as either the air mattress or an open-celled pad.

Tent. Where weather conditions are changeable and shelters are not available, or where insects are plentiful, a small, light, breathable, ripstop nylon tent with a detachable fly is advised for restful sleeping. Several basic features which may be helpful with either rental or purchase are:

☐ waterproof flooring extending several inches up the sides

☐ access in and out of both ends

☐ openings completely covered by mosquito netting

☐ detachable fly

☐ separate tent poles which contain shockcord internally so that they snap open

☐ sidewall pullout tabs

☐ catenary cut for stability in wind

Survival

In addition to the survival items already mentioned, it is wise to have available:

☐ knife, preferably a Swiss Army type with multiple tools which can be obtained with a wide range of options

☐ candles

☐ matches in waterproof container

☐ nylon cord (50′)

☐ flashlight with spare batteries

☐ map and compass

☐ whistle

There are additional items which would be needed for special conditions, depending upon where the trip was planned. In country where one would expect to come across large animals, it is recommended that a bell be hung on the pack to serve as a warning of approach. This simple signal gives animals time to move out of the area.

Equipment survival lists can be very specialized, and it is prudent to gain experience under a normal range of conditions before attempting a very specialized trip, such as that requiring crampons and ice axes, or carabiners and rope.

Play and Pleasure

The dividing line as to whether an item is essential equipment or optional is shadowy on occasion. Sample items in this category could include binoculars, camera, dice, playing cards, a paperback, or a small musical instrument. While one person might consider an item optional, another might consider it essential. For some hikers, the use of binoculars or camera could contribute immensely to their enjoyment of a hiking trip, and could help to enhance their appreciation of nature. The need to experience pleasurable activity is human, and most hikers and backpackers derive a sense of pleasure from spending extended periods of time in natural settings. Colin Fletcher, an authority on walking, sees this need to spend time in natural settings as an absolute necessity. In any event, sunrises, sunsets, cloud formations, foliage, flowers, mushrooms, and birds, to mention only a few of nature's delights, can play a major role in the pleasure and recreative benefits of hiking and backpacking.

BASIC SOURCES

The basic sources of backpacking information listed here are intended to lead the reader to more detailed or specialized sources. The list will be rather brief and limited to organizations, suppliers, and publications which are comprehensive.

Organizations and Agencies

Appalachian Trail Conference
P. O. Box 236
Harpers Ferry, W.V. 25425

The Green Mountain Club, Inc.
P. O. Box 94
Rutland, Vt. 05701

National Audubon Society
950 Fifth Avenue
New York 10028

The Sierra Club
1050 Mill Tower
San Francisco 94104

United States Geologic Survey
1028 General Services,
Administration Building
Washington, D.C. 20240

National Wildlife Federation
1412 16th Street
Washington, D.C. 20036

United States Forest Service
Washington, D.C. 20240

The Wilderness Society
2144 P Street, N.W.
Washington, D.C. 20037

Suppliers

L. L. Bean, Inc.
Main Street
Freeport, Me. 04032

Co-op Wilderness Supply
1432 University Avenue
Berkeley, Calif. 94702

Camp Trails
P. O. Box 14500
Phoenix, Ariz. 85063

Eastern Mountain Sports
1041 Commonwealth Avenue
Boston, Mass. 02215
        and
Route 9, Amherst-Hadley Line
P. O. Box 12
Amherst, Mass. 01060

Holubar Mountaineering
P. O. Box 7
Boulder, Colo. 80302

Recreational Equipment, Inc.
1525 11th Avenue
Seattle, Wash. 98122

Kelty
1801 Victory Boulevard
Glendale, Calif. 91201

Ski Hut
1615 University Avenue
Berkeley, Calif. 94703

Publications

Books

Fletcher, C. 1974. *The new complete walker.* New York: Knopf.

Manning, H. 1973. *Backpacking: one step at a time.* New York: Vintage.

Rethmel, R. C. 1974. *Backpacking.* (5th ed.) Minneapolis: Burgess.

Wood, R. S. 1972. *Pleasure packing—how to backpack in comfort.* San Francisco: Condor.

Magazines

Backpacker. A magazine published six times yearly. Subscription address: 28 West 44th Street, New York 10036.

Wilderness Camping. A magazine published six times yearly. Subscription address: 1597 Union Street, Schenectady, N.Y. 12309.

REFERENCES

Appalachia. Appalachian Mountain Club, 5 Joy Street, Boston, Massachusetts. 02108.

The Green Mountain Club, Inc., P. O. Box 94, Rutland, Vermont. 05701

McLuhan, T. C. 1972. *Touch the earth.* New York: Pocket Books.

55
Boating

Charles J. Smith

The "small boat" is a specific term that generally refers to boats less than 15 feet in length. The rowboat is usually found in varying lengths up to 15 feet, and in some instances 16 feet.

Several thousand years before the laws of floating and immersed bodies were first enunciated by Archimedes neolithic peoples had observed and had begun putting to their own uses the phenomenon of buoyancy. Undoubtedly, the first craft was a floating log used to assist those with imperfect natural swimming powers. People soon improved on this primitive device, for dugout canoes, rafts, skin boats, and even planked boats are in evidence as far back as history goes. Many sorts of boats evolved from these simple vessels, although essentially primitive craft are still found in remote corners of the world.

The floating log became the dugout canoe. Eventually, the planked boat came into popular use. The planked boat is formed of numerous narrow wooden planks laid upon a number of wooden frames. Today, most boats are constructed of molded fiberglass, plastic, or aluminum.

Most of the boats found in the United States were copies or modifications of European prototypes introduced by the first settlers. Variations in the original designs were not uncommon in the boats built in the new land, since the special requirements of function and environment and the availability of boat-building material and tools, as well as the skill of the craftsman, largely determined the size and shape of the finished craft.

Fig. 55.1 Flat-bottomed boats are stable and inexpensive. Courtesy of Springfield College.

There are several basic designs of the rowing craft:

☐ *The flat-bottom boat* designed for protected waters. Such boats are stable if they are wide enough. They are inexpensive to build.

☐ *The V-bottom boat.* V-bottom or dead-rise boats are more seaworthy than flat-bottom craft and are less affected by crosswinds. The wide beam at the water line gives great initial stability.

☐ *The round- or arc-bottom boat.* Round-bottom rowing boats are generally more seaworthy in rough water than either the flat- or V-bottom boat if the weight is kept low. They lack the initial stability of beamy flat-bottom boats, but they row easily if they are well designed.

With few exceptions, rowing craft are designed for protected waters. They are comparatively light, and the greater part of the bulk is above the waterline. Consequently, the load—including the occupant's weight—should be kept as low as possible and distributed to keep the boat properly trimmed.

TYPES OF ROWING BOATS

Dory Dories are deep, narrow, flat-bottom, keelless rowing craft with sides that flare out to a relatively wide beam amidships.

Dory-skiff Dory-skiffs are shallower than the dories and have a wider bottom and transom.

Skiff Skiff is a general term given to the common square-stern rowboat.

Pram Prams are flat or slightly V-bottom boats made of metal, wood, or plywood. The transom bow is slightly narrower than the transom stern.

Dinghy Dinghies are short, beamy, round-bottomed craft and are frequently rigged for sail.

Punt Punts or scows or johnboats are narrow, shallow flat-bottom wood or metal craft with identical square, overhanging ends.

Trainer Multipurpose training boats are designed for training in rowing, sculling, sailing, and outboard motor operation. They are constructed of marine plywood, with flotation built in along the gunwale line for extra buoyancy.

Oars

Ash and spruce are generally selected for making oars—spruce for lightness, ash for durability—but length and balance are of primary importance in choosing a pair of oars for any given boat.

The oar as it rests in the rowlock (or oarlock) represents a first-class lever. The first-class lever is a lever of balance or equilibrium, and speed. It is essential, therefore, that the rower select the proper length oar to avoid unnecessary fatigue in handling the oar. The distance between the rowlocks is the basis for determining the proper length of oars. A leverage ratio of 7 to 18 is preferred by most oarsmen, but individual preferences and also the height of the freeboard may be reasons for slightly altering the ratio.

The balancing point should fall between 8 and 12 inches outboard from the rowlock or the button. Even a heavy oar, if properly balanced, can be held clear of the water just by the weight of the hands during the recovery phase of the stroke.

Types of Rowlocks

Many types of rowlocks, or oarlocks as they are sometimes called, have been developed, but the average boatman is likely to encounter only a few.

The *open socket* equipped with chain and toggle and the *David patented lock* are favored by most boatmen. The open socket lock can be removed completely. The socket and the rowlock should fit snugly but not bind. A loosely fitted rowlock will often drop forward from the vertical during the pull and allow the oar to jump out. This can be dangerous as well as embarrassing.

The *ring rowlock* must be removed when the oar is boated, and it is usually fitted to the oar before the leather collar and the button are put on.

The *pin-type rowlock* is permanently fastened to the oar by a pin through the loom and riveted to the horns of the rowlock. The arrangement makes good rowing impossible, and the type is mentioned only because of its widespread use.

The *swivel rowlock* is found mainly on yacht tenders and other finely built rowing craft. It has a flat base that fits onto a flanged plate.

The *box-type rowlock* is favored for surfboats. It is functional and less hazardous than a projecting type in case of capsize. The notch in the sheer strake is usually lined with metal.

Hardwood thole pins were formerly used in workboats, but they have almost disappeared. Single pins with rope grommets are still found in some areas.

Most rowlocks are made of malleable iron and are heavily galvanized, but bronze and aluminum alloys also are used. Cast-iron rowlocks are brittle and may break under stress.

Location of rowlocks. Rowing proficiency depends, in part, on the correct location of the rowlock in reference to the seat or rowing thwart. The standard setting is approximately 8 inches from the afteredge of the seat or rowing thwart.

ROWING

The proper distribution of weight is important to good rowing. Fore and aft trim should approximate the level of the empty boat's normal waterline. The weight should also be balanced with reference to the centerline to prevent listing to the side.

Assuming that the rowboat is properly fitted out for rowing, with foot braces, rowlocks, rowing thwart, and oars, rowers position themselves on the proper rowing thwart without causing the boat to list or lose its normal trim. Then, in the following order:

1. The rowlocks are shipped and secured to prevent loss.

2. The feet are braced so that when the rower is sitting erect on the thwart the thighs are nearly level, with perhaps a slight decline toward the knees. The knees are slightly flexed and fairly close together, as are the feet.

3. The oars are shipped and extended outward at right angles or directly abeam of the boat. At this time determination should be made as to how deep in the water the blades will be during the stroke and also how well they are balanced. This is done by lowering the blades edgewise into the water until they reach their floating depth. When the weight of the hands is removed from the handles, approximately seven-eighths of each blade should be submerged at its proper depth for stroking. If the oars are well balanced, the blades will clear the surface by merely returning the weight of the hands and arms to the inboard ends of the oars.

"Dress" the oars before beginning the stroke by holding them horizontally in the rowlocks at right angles to the boat with the blades vertical. The hand-grips are adjusted so that the forearms and the back of the hands are in alignment. The trunk is held erect with the shoulders squared, head up, and eyes level. The elbows drop naturally to the sides. The handles may overlap, if preferred.

The rowing stroke is divided into the following oar positions: catch, pull, finish, feather, and recovery.

Catch. To make the catch from the "dress oars" position, drop the wrists to bring the blades to a near horizontal position (feather) and, at the same time, rock forward (toward the stern) from the hips and simultaneously extend the arms. Do not round the back, but keep the head up and eyes at horizon level. The tip of the blade should be no higher than necessary to clear the surface as it travels toward the bow of the boat to the catch position. The catch is made by straightening the wrists and relaxing the downward pressure of the hands on the handles to allow the blades to drop to their edgewise floating depth. The point of entry is approximately 45° toward the bow from the rowlock.

Pull. The pull or power part of the stroke develops smoothly from the catch, as the body swings back toward the vertical. At the same time, extra power is generated by driving with the legs. The back and arms remain straight, and the eyes level, as the trunk goes into the layback position, where the arms finish the pull, with elbows low, as the hands come in toward the chest. The angle of the trunk from the vertical in the layback is approximately 20–25°.

Finish. At the end of the pull (tips of the blades are approximately 45° aft of the rowlock), a slight downward pressure on the handles will glide the blades from the water to finish the stroke. Almost simultaneously, the wrists are flipped to feather the blades.

Recovery. The trunk swings forward from the hips for the recovery as the hands are thrust toward the stern. To avoid water resistance in case of contact with a wave and also to reduce wind resistance, the blades remain feathered during the recovery until the point for the catch is reached.

Rowing a Straight Course

Crosswinds, currents, a warped or improperly trimmed craft, or faulty rowing techniques can cause a boat to deviate from its course. If there are no wind, wave, or current effects, the boat can be held on course by keeping the transom squarely lined up with an object on shore.

If the boat is making leeway or is being carried off course by crosscurrents, rowers establish a "range" on shore by picking out two objects that are in line and adjust their heading to keep the range "closed." An occasional glance over the shoulder should be made in both instances to check the course ahead.

Rules of the Road

Manually propelled craft have right-of-way over power boats, but canoeists and rowboaters should be familiar with the boat traffic regulations and should avoid maneuvers and practices that may confuse other boat operators or cause a dangerous situation to develop.

All craft should keep to the right in narrow channels and when meeting other vessels. Other manually propelled boats have right-of-way when they are being overtaken or when they may be on a converging course from the right of another rowboat or canoe.

Regardless of who has the right-of-way or privileges over others, all craft are charged with the responsibility of doing whatever is necessary to avoid collisions. It should be remembered that large vessels respond slowly to rudder action and cannot stop quickly and therefore should be given a wide berth by the more maneuverable small craft.

Except for emergency reasons, it is against federal and state regulations to moor to channel markers and other navigational aids.

At the present time there are no races organized for rowboats. There is great national and international competition for the skill of rowing as used in single sculls up to eight-man sculls. This type of competition is organized on a high school and college level. International lifeboat races are popular in California and Australia. The tremendous number of boating enthusiasts found in this country are those who use boats and rowing skill for pleasure and sport fishing.

REFERENCES

Basic rowing 1964. The American National Red Cross, (February).

Colliers encyclopedia **4,** 1966. Crowell Collier and Macmillan.

56
Camp Aquatics

Thomas K. Cureton, Jr. and Richard H. Pohndorf

The aquatic program is a major area of physical activity in any American or Canadian camp. Literally thousands of college students serve as waterfront counselors or directors or assist as swimming teachers, boating counselors, lifesaving instructors, pageantry directors, diving instructors, or in some way assume part of the waterfront responsibility. The program offers basic instruction in all of these areas, doing what few schools can do for youngsters below high school age. In addition to the many skills that it teaches, the program is good for general physical development. Intramural swimming meets offer opportunity for friendly competition and add lively interest to the summer in camp. In many summer camps a large part of the total program centers on the waterfront.

VARIOUS TYPES OF CAMPS

There are many types of camps. Agency camps such as Boy/Girl Scout or YMCA camps generally operate in two-week shifts. Most of the private camps, of which there are many hundreds, operate for eight-week periods. The type of program planned must meet the restrictions of the time available.

Fig. 56.1 A well-equipped waterfront layout for teaching camp aquatics. Courtesy of Camp Sunapee, New London, N.H.

There are also camps where itinerants may stay a day or two and want a place to swim safely. Such itinerants may also ask for "tutoring" in swimming or lifesaving. A combination twosome, guard and instructor, may have a busy summer, guarding and instructing transients in motel pools, adult camps, at beaches and waterfronts. There are also stations where scuba instruction and certification can be secured, as those are in great demand. Camps which provide boat rental must also make provision for the care and repair of the boats as well as enforcement of water safety regulations.

PRECAMP PLANNING

Arrangements must be made in advance for suitable direction, guards, instructors, and equipment. The waterfront must be checked over and repaired or replaced as necessary. An overall plan should be drawn up and approved by the owner of the establishment. Posters or charts, advertising materials, and record books should be obtained and made ready. Test sheets and certification cards need to be secured or lines of communication established so that awards, certificates, buttons, and badges may be quickly available. Institutional camps, which have affiliation with Boy Scouts, Girl Scouts, YMCA or YWCA, Catholic Youth Organization, 4-H Clubs, etc., should obtain such materials from, and operate according to the standards of, the sponsoring organization. Equipment and waterfronts will vary widely, depending upon local conditions and financial resources. Minimal standards of safety and efficiency should be enforced.

QUALIFICATIONS FOR LEADERSHIP

The top leader of the waterfront should be at least 21 years of age, have good eyesight, be physically fit, and preferably athletic and strong. He or she should have all necessary qualifications to pass or fail candidates for lifesaving certification and the graded levels of swimming. This leader should conduct a precamp training period for the assistants so as to become acquainted with their abilities and qualifications. It may be necessary to test some of them and to brief them all in safety procedures and instructional techniques. Each person employed should have appropriate credentials (American Red Cross Water Safety Credential, YMCA or CNCA Certified Aquatic Director or Certified Aquatic Instructor, etc.).

GENERAL ADMINISTRATIVE STANDARDS

Ratio of waterfront leaders to campers. There should be one qualified leader for every 50 campers, with an assistant for every ten campers using the waterfront at any one time.

The waterfront director's housing. This should be located as close to the waterfront as possible. The waterfront director should be free from counseling or other administrative duties so as to be able to give adequate attention to the waterfront: facilities, docks, boats and canoes, bulletin boards, check system, preparation of staff, safety devices, and reports.

The waterfront director's duties. Duties should be specifically described in writing. They include:

☐ Preparing of the waterfront facilities
☐ Enforcing procedures
☐ Planning instructional program
☐ Following procedures in case of emergencies
☐ Awarding of certificates, cards, recognitions
☐ Facilitating trips and planning for safety
☐ Administrating exhibitions and pageants
☐ Keeping equipment, boats, canoes, and all craft in good repair
☐ Preparing reports to be made, keeping records, using forms
☐ Maintaining bulletin boards
☐ Overseeing use and protection of equipment
☐ Posting and making campers aware of health rules

THE WATERFRONT LAYOUT

☐ To facilitate simultaneous instruction of sections and to eliminate hazards, the swimming area should be separated by suitable markers from the boating and canoeing area.

☐ The swimming area should be arranged so that diving does not conflict with swimming instruction, beginners are separated from intermediates, and advanced competitive swimming and lifesaving are separately located. If the latter is not possible, these activities should be offered at different times to eliminate conflicts and ensure proper leadership coverage.

☐ A beginners' shallow water area should be clearly marked off with *float markers* and *ropes*. Depths and danger areas should be clearly marked.

☐ A *lookout tower* or lifeguard station should be established from which the entire waterfront can be viewed.

☐ The entrance to the waterfront should be a *control gate* located near the *check-in-out board* so that both may be supervised by one person.

☐ There should be firm construction to avoid broken planks; exposed nail

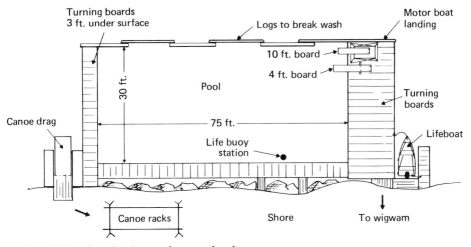

Turning boards
3 ft. under surface

Logs to break wash

Motor boat
landing

10 ft. board

4 ft. board

Turning
boards

30 ft.

Pool

Canoe drag

75 ft.

Lifeboat

Life buoy
station

Canoe racks

Shore

To wigwam

Fig. 56.2 Swimming layout for a rocky shore.

heads should be carefully driven in; all cans, broken glass, dangerous rocks, pointed or sharp objects should be removed or fenced off in the appropriate manner.

☐ An airspace of at least one foot should be underneath all platforms. Supports should be of ample strength, firm and free from broken boards, irregularities, looseness, or unusual projections (see Fig. 56.1).

☐ There should be sufficient teaching space, deck surface and/or land area for warm-up drills as well as instruction.

☐ The depth of the water for the 3-meter diving board or tower should be

Fig. 56.3 A jungle float adds to the fun of camp aquatics. Courtesy of Camp Sunapee, New London, N.H.

at least eight feet immediately in front of the board and ten feet under the board.

☐ Exposed and projecting ladders should be removed from lanes in which swimmers swim, to avoid the possibility of a broken arm or other injury.

☐ *Lifeboats* should be located outside the swimming area to avoid conflict and *throw buoys* should be appropriately located around the swimming area.

☐ Overcrowding should be avoided. Fifty square feet should be allowed each swimmer at any one time and swimming should be taught in sections if necessary. Running, diving on top of swimmers, dangerous pranks at the waterfront, holding swimmers under water against their will, swimming over a person, and throwing objects in a hazardous way must be prohibited.

☐ A hold-on *kick rail* should be provided for the beginners' area.

☐ The waterfront rules should be conspicuously posted.

☐ A first-aid kit should be conveniently located at the waterfront. It should contain tape, iodine, gauze, petroleum jelly, sunburn lotion, eyewash, several nose clips and sets of earplugs, first-aid book, aromatic spirits of ammonia, absorbent cotton, adhesive bandages, sterile pads, bandages, a triangular bandage, and lamb's wool.

THE WATERFRONT AND AQUATIC PROGRAMS

Broadly considered, the program should include *swimming instruction* (beginners' level, intermediate level and prelifesaving, advanced and competitive swimming, lifesaving instruction and qualification), *boating instruction, canoeing instruction, swimming meets* and *pageants* and *exhibitions* (diving, lifeboat drills, evolution of swimming strokes, teaching beginners, relays, canoe races, scuba demonstrations, rescue exhibitions, etc.).

CLASSIFICATION OF SWIMMERS

At the very beginning of the season, every swimmer should take a test for classification as:

☐ Grade E: *Nonswimmer.* One who has not passed the beginner's test.

☐ Grade D: *Elementary swimmer.* One who has passed the beginner's test but is not a lifesaver or advanced swimmer.

☐ Grade C: *Advanced swimmer.* One advanced enough to take lifesaving instruction or to practice advanced swimming and diving, scuba, and advanced water games.

☐ Grade B: *Qualified lifesaver.* The same as Grade C plus advanced classification in one other area of swimming or diving.

☐ Grade A: *Qualified lifesaver.* The same as Grade B plus established advanced rating in three other areas of swimming, diving, scuba, advanced water games and stunts, membership on the camp swimming team or exhibition in water games or pageantry.

☐ Grade A+: *Grade A rating plus instructor's rating in one area.*

WATERFRONT SAFETY SUGGESTIONS

☐ The waterfront director should assign leaders to particular areas and jobs for each scheduled swimming class to: man the lookout tower, operate the check-tag system and board, teach in designated areas, be a member of roaming safety patrol, and serve as beach aid for first aid or for individual help.

☐ If swimming is permitted outside designated areas, a lifeboat should be manned to patrol the free swimming area.

☐ Instruction should be given about excessive sunburn and treatment if needed.

☐ The "Buddy System" should be regularly employed and strictly enforced.

☐ If possible, a first-aid counselor should be designated.

☐ Swimmers should be required to stay in their classified areas or locations.

☐ Preliminary warm-up drills should be held on cold days.

☐ There should be an official set of signals: (1) to begin swimming (water entry), (2) to stop swimming and leave the water, and (3) for danger (which means *hold the hand of your buddy as quickly as possible*).

☐ Air and water temperatures should be posted before each class.

☐ Before-breakfast dips may be optional as announced but with a lifeguard always on duty at the waterfront.

☐ All area markers, life buoys, and depth markers should be painted bright orange or white.

☐ One lifeboat should be in place, ready for immediate use, fully equipped with oars, bailing can, life buoy, rescue ropes (with shoulder loop at end), underwater goggles, anchor, etc.

☐ Grappling irons should be available but kept at the waterfront out of sight.

☐ All instructors should be drilled as to their duties in case of a "man lost" or "emergency" signal.

☐ All canoe trips should have a qualified lifesaver in each canoe and a commander designated for the entire trip.

☐ In case of a lightning storm, all swimmers should come out of the water.

☐ The use of scuba equipment and dangerous equipment or gadgets by unqualified persons should be restricted.

BOATS, CANOES, AND WATERCRAFT

Preferably, boats, canoes, sailboards, and all types of watercraft should be under one counselor, who should also serve as instructor in this area. Locations should be selected which are not in conflict with swimming. Rules for the use of all such craft should be posted. Tests should be administered for classifying individuals in the following categories: (1) basic instruction, (2) use under supervision, (3) unrestricted use. (Some camps have a list of "responsibles" who may have the unrestricted privilege, provided they observe waterfront safety rules.)

Dory-type skiffs are usually used for basic boating instruction. Campers should learn names of all parts; correct versus incorrect positions; entry and debarking; techniques of rowing, sculling, and feathering; landing; emergency procedures in case of swamping or capsizing; and improvised sailing. Care of equipment is important.

Aluminum canoes are the most practical in camps as they are relatively

Fig. 56.4 One of the newest forms of watercraft is the sailboard. Sailboarding (or wind surfing) requires a vast array of skills and techniques all of which must be flawlessly synchronized. Courtesy of Camp Sunapee, New London, N.H.

Fig. 56.5 Kayaking is a fast-growing camp aquatics sport. Courtesy of *JOPER.*

impervious to the scratches, gouges, and rips which afflict canvas canoes. Proper racking and handling as well as proper techniques for launching and landing must be taught to all campers. Canoe-capsize drills should be practiced under supervision and at the very outset of the program, with a check on swimming safety requirements. Instruction includes carrying for portages, paddling (see Chapter 57, *Canoeing*), and duties of the bow paddler and the stern paddler. Circling outside and inside, canoe-over-canoe, and kicking ashore a swamped canoe are all practiced. Stunts such as paddling on gunwales, jumping onto gunwales, and jump-pushing a canoe may also be taught. After the other basics are learned, sailing a canoe, packing and tripping with a canoe, and one-man, two-man and multiple-man carries are practiced. Canoe tilting is fun.

Instruction can also be offered in kayak paddling and flipping and righting with a paddle. Races, including those with a war canoe, may also be held.

WEEKLY AQUATIC MEETS AND EXHIBITIONS

It is stimulating to put on a weekly swimming meet, and also to combine it with an exhibition of some other kind for those who are not taking part in the competition. This can be an intramural meet or competition with another camp. A pageant, a boating rescue demonstration, or a canoe race may be used. Such exhibitions will add interest and will motivate campers for their preparatory instructional work. Water polo, water kickball or water basketball make good exhibition games. Relays can involve a large number of participants.

It is suggested that, in order to involve as many as possible, campers should be allowed to participate in only one event and a relay. Lifesaving

Fig. 56.6 This canoe was dubbed *Roses Afloat* during a camp aquatics exhibition. Courtesy of R. H. Pohndorf.

contests for those not in the swimming contests or relays may also count as an event.

The announcer (master of ceremonies) should be equipped with a megaphone and the referee with a whistle. All officials should be instructed in their duties by the referee in advance of starting the meet.

A counselor should be in charge of each group if several age classes are involved. This counselor should have a list of those for whom he or she is responsible.

Events for the youngest campers should be first on the program, and provision made for their protection from wind and cold. On cool days they may be allowed to dress and then return to watch the rest of the events.

During the meet and exhibition a safety patrol should be on duty and be ready to issue proper warnings or to render help if needed.

CANOEING STUNTS AND EXHIBITIONS

Headstand in canoe. Stand on the head, resting head on the bottom of the canoe or on the seat of the canoe, with hands holding onto the gunwales rather than on the bottom.

Aquaplaning a canoe. Stand with one foot on each gunwale, well toward the rear of the canoe. Propel the canoe forward by alternately rising and squatting in rapid succession. A paddle, held crosswise for balance, may be used if needed.

Canoe over canoe. Empty canoe in deep water after swamping. Working with a partner, lift the end of the swamped canoe over the rescue canoe; when the upset canoe is halfway over the rescue canoe, flip it upright and slide it into the water. This whole maneuver may also be done by one person.

Getting into canoe. On a given signal, partners vault out on opposite sides of the canoe, change places and then get back into the canoe. Signals should be used to coordinate balance.

Tilting or mopping. Using a padded mop or tilting pole or broom, the bow paddler tries to push the bowman of the opposing canoe overboard.

Hand paddle race. Stage a race with the participants lying prone on the seats of the canoe. This can be either singles or doubles.

Front end race. Participants in this race sit astride the bows of their canoes and paddle with their hands.

Man overboard race. At each signal of the whistle the paddlers in each canoe jump overboard and then get back in as quickly as possible. Continue this sequence until the finish line is crossed.

Canoe filling contest. Each canoe has a crew of two people, one a paddler and one a pail handler. The pail handler in the bow tries to fill the opposing canoe by dipping water and throwing it into the other canoe. The first to sink is the loser.

Canoe tug-of-war. Contested by one canoe against another, or by any number tied together.

Paddle-swim-run combination race. As the name implies, contestants compete on a carefully laid out and defined course.

Submarine race. Paddle to a given place, then upset the canoe and while underneath kick and swim the canoe to the finish line.

TERMINOLOGY

Parts of a boat Bow, stern, center board box, center board, seats, gunwales, chocks, keel, skag (or skeg), washboards, beaching strip, rowlock sockets, cleats, centerboard peg, dock blocks, deck pullup, hatch, rudder, bowline, stern line.

Sails and spars Mast, mainsail (sheet), boom, reef points, lace line, halyard, rings, jib sail.

Boat equipment Rudder, tiller, oars, bailer, life belt (preserver), marlin, anchor, throw buoy.

For further information in regard to aquatic skills and instruction, reference is made to the following articles in this volume.

Basic Swimming Instruction, R. K. Stallman, pp. 475–485

Waterskiing, J. J. Lampman, pp. 644–650

The Instructional Aspect of Competitive Diving, G. E. Darda, pp. 485–504

Lifesaving and Water Safety, T. K. Cureton, Jr., pp. 504–507

Canoeing, K. J. Cureton, pp. 753–763

Skin Diving and Scuba Diving, B. E. Empleton, pp. 508–513

Survival Aquatics, T. K. Cureton, Jr., pp. 513–515

Swimnastics, M. G. Sholtis, pp. 516–525

Synchronized Swimming, J. L. Smith, pp. 526–530

REFERENCES

AAU. (223 Broadway) New York 7, N.Y., *Handbook of swimming.* (Current year.)

American Camping Association 1962. *Camping for American youth: a declaration for action.* Association Press.

——— 1960. *Camping is education,* Chicago: Association Press.

——— 1968. *Legislation affecting camping.* Martinsville, Ind.: Association Press.

——— 1966. *Standards report for accreditation of organized camps.* Martinsville, Ind.: Association Press.

American National Red Cross 1968. *Swimming and water safety,* Washington, D.C.

Anderson, L. A. 1969. *A guide to canoe camping.* Chicago: Reilly.

Bloom, V. W. 1961. *Camper guidance: a basic handbook for counselors.* Martinsville, Ind.: American Camping Association.

Boy Scouts of America 1963. *Aquatic program.* (Rev. ed.) New Brunswick, N.J.

Emmett, J., and J. Seiville 1967. *Boating for sportsmen,* New York: Outdoor Life.

Gabrielson, M. A., B. Spears, and B. W. Gabrielson 1960. *Aquatics handbook,* Englewood Cliffs, N.J.: Prentice-Hall.

Lane, C. D. 1961. *The boatman's manual.* (Rev. ed.) New York: Hartaen.

Pohndorf, R. H. 1960. *Camp waterfront programs and management.* New York: Association Press (with Editorial Committee: T. K. Cureton, Jr., H. T. Friermood, E. I. Griffin and R. H. Pohndorf).

Pyle, B. 1974. *Small craft* (an instructor's text). Kendall/Hunt.

Silvia, C. E. 1970. *Manual and lesson plans.* Springfield, Mass.: Privately published.

Smith, H. M. 1962. *Water games.* New York: Ronald.

57
Canoeing
K. J. Cureton

THE SIGNIFICANCE AND SCOPE OF CANOEING
IN NORTH AMERICA

Canoeing is one of the oldest modes of aquatic transportation. It has been used almost universally by primitive people throughout the world when there was a need for traveling on rivers, lakes, or oceans. The Indian dugout and birchbark canoes, the Eskimo kayak, and the outrigger canoes used by the inhabitants of the Pacific islands are all characteristic of these cultures. The canoe played a significant role in the early exploration and development of North America by European explorers and fur traders who quickly adopted Indian canoes for expeditions and travel on rivers and lakes in the interior of the continent. The history of the canoe has been well covered in the American Red Cross textbook, *Canoeing* (1956).

Although the canoe is still used as the necessary mode of transportation by park rangers and others who travel on lakes and rivers in remote regions,

Fig. 57.1 Canoeing is an important phase of aquatic activity at summer camps. Courtesy of *JOPER*.

its predominant use is for recreation and sport. Canoeing is an important phase of aquatic activity at summer camps. The American Camping Association, the Boy Scouts, the Girl Scouts and the Camp Fire Girls all have published canoeing standards for their organizations (New England Camping Association 1958, Perry 1954). Other independent standards for camps are also available (Perry 1948). The American Red Cross has included canoeing in its water safety programs for many years and, since 1948, canoeing instruction has been offered at National Small Craft Schools to prepare instructors for the Red Cross Basic Canoeing Course (American National Red Cross 1956).

Canoe camping or tripping is popular in many regions of the United States and Canada and pamphlets describing canoe routes are available from several states (Grinnell 1956, Illinois Department of Conservation 1970). The canoe is also used for hunting, fishing, and just cruising by persons with little formal training in canoeing. Whitewater canoeing has recently become a popular activity in some areas of the country and information about aspects of this exciting activity may be found in the journal, *Whitewater,* or in several books (McNair 1972, Whitney 1960). (See also article 46, *Whitewater Canoeing.*)

Canoeing is often taught in colleges and universities as a part of water safety or as a basic canoeing course, although its offering is restricted to areas where a suitable body of water is available. This activity is included in the professional physical education curriculum recommended for an "aquatic specialist" (AAHPER 1970).

Formal competition in canoeing in the United States is directed by the American Canoeing Association, which holds regional and national championships each year on an age-group basis for men and women and organizes the selection of the team sent to the Olympic games every four years. Flat-water racing includes two types of racing: Canadian canoe racing and kayaking. Canoeing differs from kayaking in that canoeists kneel rather than sit, use a single-bladed paddle as opposed to a double-bladed, and steer with a paddle instead of a rudder. The kayak is generally a faster craft than the canoe. In the Olympics there are five men's 1000-meter flat-water paddling events: kayak singles, doubles and fours, and canoeing singles and doubles; and two women's 500-meter events: kayak singles and doubles. Whitewater slalom was also added to the Olympics in 1972 (Rademaker and Welbourn 1972). In addition to formal canoeing competition, informal canoe racing is held at many camps and recreation centers.

CANOES AND PADDLES

Modern canoes have followed the prototype of the Indian birchbark canoe. The traditional canoe and the type used almost exclusively in this century

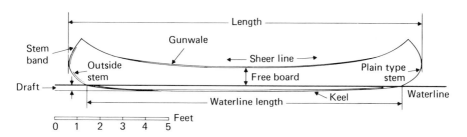

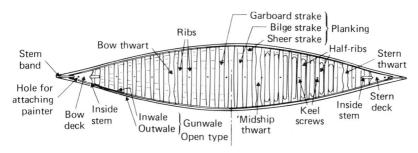

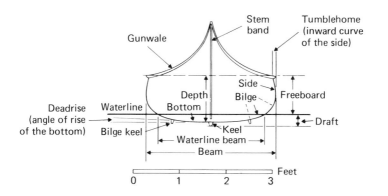

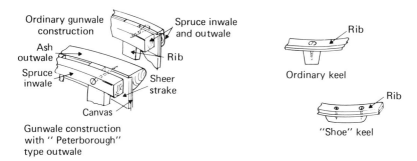

prior to 1948 is the canvas-covered wooden canoe. This canoe is preferred by canoeing purists for quiet water because of its performance, quietness, and aesthetic appeal. Today, in the United States (but not in Canada) the wood and canvas canoe has largely been replaced by aluminum and fiberglass canoes because of their lower price, lightness, durability, and minimal maintenance requirements. Although aluminum canoes are now the most popular with sportsmen, camps, and rental agencies in this country, these canoes have some disadvantages. They are relatively noisy, hard to repair on a trip, absorb heat, and are therefore uncomfortable on hot days. Fiberglass canoes that are completely decked over except for cockpits and shaped for optimal maneuverability have proven to be the best for whitewater canoeing and slalom racing. The advantages and disadvantages of the different types of canoes and the effect of size and shape on their stability, speed, and maneuverability are discussed in recent canoeing books (Angier and Taylor 1970).

Canoes used for recreational purposes are 12 to 18 feet in length, 32 to 36 inches in width and 12 to 14.5 inches deep. Canoes 16 to 18 feet in length are recommended for canoe tripping and camping. *Freight* canoes, ranging in length from 18 to 22 feet and 46 to 62 inches in width may be obtained for transporting heavy loads. *War* canoes, ranging from 24 to over 30 feet in length are often seen in summer camps and are useful for transporting large groups and for racing. A variety of special canoes are available. These include

This is used for pageantry and all other utility purposes. It consists of two or more canoes lashed together, using three wooden (or metal) beams. Lash the center beam to the center canoe first, then to the other canoe(s). Follow by lashing the remaining beams in place, then lashing the platform. If a thwart is missing, pass the lashing around the hull. Note that the canoes must be absolutely parallel and that with heavy loads or choppy water, the canoes should be left open for bailing; otherwise, the platform can be solid.

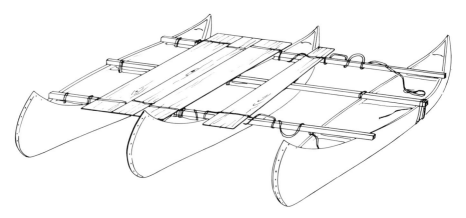

those constructed for formal racing, many types of kayaks, and canoes that may be adapted for rowing and sailing.

Paddles are manufactured from several types of wood, in many lengths, and with a variety of blade shapes. Paddles made from softwood, such as spruce or cedar, are light and are often preferred for recreational uses; however, these paddles split easily if they are used for pushing off rocks or poling and do not hold up well on canoe trips. Hardwood paddles constructed from maple, ash, or cherry are stronger and more durable and are preferred for tripping. The beavertail paddle with a short blade and rounded tip is usually recommended for the beginning canoeist. Paddles with rather long blades and square ends, often referred to as *traders* or *voyageurs,* are best for tripping and are good blade shapes for sterning a canoe. Paddles used for racing have wide blades and square tips that will pull large amounts of water with each stroke. Double-bladed paddles are used with kayaks and sometimes with canoes, but rarely for recreational purposes.

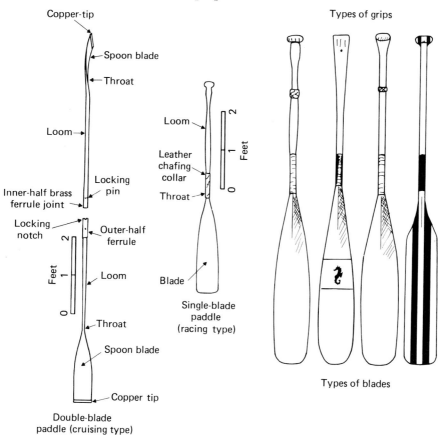

Double-blade paddle (cruising type)

Single-blade paddle (racing type)

Types of grips

Types of blades

INSTRUCTION AND STANDARDS

Canoeing instruction involves developing competencies in and appreciation for (1) safety practices and rescue techniques; (2) basic abilities in the canoeing strokes, paddling style, and methods for launching, landing, stowing, portaging, and handling a canoe in wind, waves, currents and rapids; and, (3) care for the canoe and paddle. The actual techniques used in teaching canoeing depend upon the size of the class, the number of canoes, the body of water, and the organizational setting. In general, many of the techniques are analogous to those used in teaching swimming.

Material normally taught on shore includes the origin and history of the canoe; types of canoes, construction, and parts of the canoe and paddle; proper methods for caring for and repairing canoes and paddles; and safety practices. At the shore or on the dockside, instruction is given in paddling positions; effect of balance and weight; methods of loading, launching, and emptying a canoe filled with water; and demonstration of the paddling strokes. Initial practice in paddling is usually obtained by learning the bow stroke and paddling tandem either with the instructor, with another experienced paddler, or with another member of the class sterning. Other basic strokes, singling, and more advanced skills are added as competency increases.

Learning to control a canoe with precision under a variety of conditions is accomplished only by extensive practice and a variety of canoeing experiences. Canoe trips, in particular, are valuable for gaining experience in sterning a canoe effectively, for developing efficient stroke mechanics, for controlling a canoe in wind, waves, rapids and along winding courses, and in portaging a canoe overground. Canoe regattas and races are effective adjuncts to basic instruction, teaching special skills, balance under varied conditions, and the importance of strength, stamina, and skill in developing optimal canoeing speed over a given distance. There are an endless number of novelty events and stunts that can be done with canoes.

Fig. 57.2 To control a canoe under a variety of conditions requires practice and experience. Courtesy of *JOPER.*

Many sets of standards have been developed to judge proficiency in canoeing. The most widely known are those of the national organizations of the American Camping Association, the Boy Scouts and Girl Scouts of America, the Camp Fire Girls, and the American Red Cross. The standards of Perry (1948) are widely used in Canada and, along with the American Camping Association standards, are the most detailed, providing graded classifications of canoeing skills and knowledge.

Below is presented an outline of knowledge and abilities expected at different levels of canoeing competency, reflecting requirements established by the American Camping Association and by Perry. This outline is intended to indicate progression in teaching as well as competencies expected at different levels.

GRADED CLASSIFICATION OF CANOEING SKILLS AND KNOWLEDGE

I. Class C—Elementary Canoeing

Emphasis is placed on developing knowledge of fundamental techniques and on safety knowledge.

A. *Prerequisite*

Demonstrate minimal swimming ability: jump or dive into deep water, swim at least 25 yards, tread water for at least one minute.

B. *Knowledge*

1. Essential safety requirements, canoeing *don'ts,* and what to do if a canoe upsets.

Fig. 57.3 Those who canoe should be familiar with essential safety requirements. Courtesy of Camp Monomoy.

2. Parts of a canoe and paddle; how to select a paddle; how to care for a canoe when launching, landing, or stowing.

3. The importance of balance and weight distribution in the canoe.

C. *Abilities*

1. Launch and pull up a canoe (with assistance).

2. Demonstrate the proper method for getting in and out of a canoe from the dock or shore.

3. Demonstrate bow, middle, and stern paddling positions.

4. Demonstrate the bow, sweep, draw, backwater, and "J" strokes.

5. Bow satisfactorily with good rhythm on both sides for a distance of one mile.

6. Paddle alone a distance of at least 200 yards in smooth water.

D. *Privileges*

Take out a canoe alone in a supervised area. Go on an overnight canoe trip.

II. Class B—Intermediate Canoeing

Emphasis is placed on the development of techniques and principles of safe and efficient canoeing.

A. *Prerequisites*

1. Swimming test. Jump into deep water fully clothed, disrobe, swim for 15 minutes using elementary backstroke, sidestroke, breast-stroke, or a combination of these.

2. Pass requirements for Class C canoeing test.

B. *Knowledge*

1. Different models of canoes, their uses, and how to select a canoe for different purposes according to size, shape, and construction.

2. How to make emergency repairs to a canoe or paddle.

3. When to use different strokes.

4. Theory of paddling in wind, waves, currents, and rapids.

5. How to portage a canoe.

6. How to handle upsets under different conditions.

C. *Abilities*

1. Jump out of canoe into deep water and reenter; demonstrate how to "splash out" a canoe filled with water; demonstrate how to paddle a water-filled canoe with hands; demonstrate how to hang

onto an upset canoe for extended periods of time; empty a swamped canoe on shore or at a dock.

2. Demonstrate ability to launch and land a canoe on a beach or at a dock with proper care for canoe and paddle.
3. Demonstrate bow rudder, crossbow rudder, crossbow draw, sculling, and Indian strokes.
4. Paddling single: cover a course of at least one mile in quiet water with good paddling style.
5. Paddling tandem: stern and bow around a winding course; demonstrate ability to paddle on both sides with steady rhythm; show ability to handle canoe in rough weather.
6. Stern a canoe with four paddlers.
7. Participate in a canoe race.
8. Paddle a total of ten miles in one day.

D. *Privileges*

Take out a canoe alone with a person of equal class within terms of local safety regulations. Stern a canoe on a trip under observation. Take out a paddler of the class below with permission.

III. Class A—Advanced

Emphasis is on more definite skill in all phases of canoeing and broader knowledge than in class B with experience in teaching individuals and small groups.

A. *Prerequisites*

1. Hold a current lifesaving certificate.
2. Pass requirements for Class B canoeing test.

B. *Knowledge*

Be able to discuss with assurance the following topics: canoeing safety requirements; importance of the paddling strokes; history of the canoe; canoe types and their uses; care and repair of the canoe and paddle; use of the pole as a means of propulsion in shallow water; the theory of wind, wave and rapid paddling; the organization of canoeing expeditions, regattas, or displays; weather forecasting; the canoe as a means of recreation; canoeing literature.

C. *Abilities*

1. Handle a canoe alone in rough water.
2. Demonstrate each of the 12 paddling strokes with expertise and describe their usefulness.

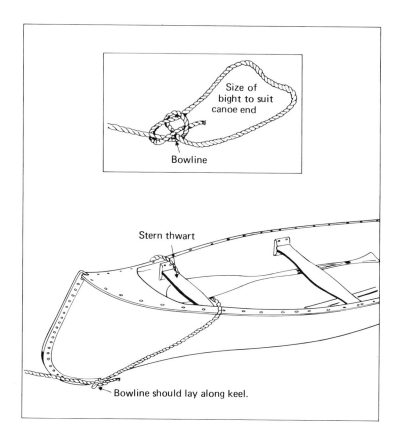

Size of bight to suit canoe end

Bowline

Stern thwart

Bowline should lay along keel.

3. Show excellent canoeing style under all conditions.

4. Paddle a figure 8 within a 25-yard square.

5. Paddle Indian stroke successfully for ¼ mile.

6. Demonstrate ability to bow and stern in rapids (not required).

7. Demonstrate ability to portage a canoe alone and with a partner.

8. Upset a canoe, shake it out, and climb back in.

9. Demonstrate ability to repair a damaged canoe.

10. Submit proof of having paddled 100 miles.

11. Instruct at least six persons in paddling so they pass the tests for their class.

D. *Privileges*

Unlimited. The canoeist should be completely at home in a canoe.

REFERENCES

American National Red Cross 1963. *Basic canoeing.* Washington, D. C.: American Red Cross.

———— 1956. *Canoeing.* Garden City, New York: Doubleday.

Anderson, L. A. 1969. *Guide to canoe camping.* Chicago: Reilly and Lee.

Angier, B., and Z. Taylor 1973. *Introduction to canoeing.* Harrisburg, Pa.: Stackpole.

Boy Scouts of America 1968. *Canoeing* (Merit Badge Series). North Brunswick, N.J.: Boy Scouts of America.

Camp, R. R. 1971. Canoeing. In *The sportsman's encyclopedia.* New York: Grosset and Dunlap.

Conference on Professional Standards for Aquatic Education 1970. Washington, D.C.: AAHPER.

Elvedt, R. 1964. *Canoeing A–Z.* Minneapolis: Burgess.

Grinnell, L. I. 1956. *Canoeable waterways of New York State and vicinity.* New York: Pageant.

Illinois Department of Conservation 1970. *Illinois canoe guide.* Springfield, Ill.: Illinois Department of Conservation.

McNair, R. E. 1972. *Basic river canoeing.* (3rd ed.) Martinsville, Ind.: American Camping.

New England Camping Association 1958. *Canoeing standards, graded classifications: canoeing manual.* 4th ed. Sommersworth, N.H.: Sommersworth.

Perry, R. H. 1953. *Canoe trip camping.* Toronto, Canada: J. M. Dent and Sons.

———— 1948. *The canoe and you.* Don Mills, Ontario: T. H. Best.

Pulling, P. 1954. *Principles of canoeing.* New York: Macmillan.

Rademaker, S., and J. L. Welbourn 1972. *Canoeing* (The Little Known Olympic Sports Series). *JOHPER* **43:** 43–45.

58

Cycling

David A. Field

AN INTRODUCTION

Note that this section is entitled "Cycling" rather than "Bicycling." This was done intentionally because the sport is too broad today to be limited by the concept that normally surrounds the word bicycling.

Had this section been written two centuries ago, it would have pertained only to adults using a vehicle that had two wheels placed in tandem fashion to help the rider to move from one place to another with greater speed. Had it been written one century ago, the script would have concentrated on affluent adults riding socially on a vehicle having one large wheel in front and a small one behind it. Should it have been written 50 years ago, the text would have focused on a vehicle used to propel youngsters around their neighborhood or aiding their delivery of newspapers after school. However, in current parlance, the word cycling has acquired a greater breadth of meaning.

For the preschooler it is the "trike" that affords an initial opportunity to move along a sidewalk or driveway with great fun and alacrity. For the teenager the bicycle helps to extend geographical limits. The collegian sees it as a practical way of getting across the campus to reach a class on time. From the family viewpoint, the father sees a "ten speed" as a means of saving money. The grandmother finds an adult tricycle in vogue in a retirement environment, and a more sophisticated exercisor serves to rehabilitate the grandfather after a heart attack. Still another looks at cycling from the eyes of the unicyclist who rides across a tight wire high in the air or across the stage with a partner on his shoulders. An increasing number look at cycling as a healthful diversion within a neighborhood or while enjoying a weekend or longer vacation in recreation. Let's see how it all began.

Recent anthropological diggings reveal that the human species has existed for more than three million years. Presumably throughout the centuries *Homo sapiens* has assiduously searched for easier ways to accomplish routine tasks. One of these tasks involved self-transport from one place to another. Not until 2500 B.C. were humans able to grasp the implications and "know-how" related to the development of the wheel. They placed wheels side by side on an axle, and attached this device to trained animals. Thus they eased their movement over the terrain.

An insatiable desire to constantly improve devices, however, eventually led to placing the wheels in tandem fashion one behind the other. Around 1791, a Frenchman named Chevalier de Sivrac constructed something which resembled a contemporary hobbyhorse. Its two wheels were connected by a wooden block upon which a seat was mounted. This permitted the rider to sit and move straight ahead by pushing alternately with each foot. But the rider was unable to steer de Sivrac's vehicle. This disadvantage was overcome in 1816 when a German, Baron Karl Drais Von Sauerbron, made two distinct contributions to the bicycle: (1) an arm and chest rest which permitted the body to lean forward and thus give a better mechanical advantage for push-ing with the feet, and (2) a pivoting front wheel to enable the rider to change direction. Thus, the "Draisine" was born, and although it was heavy and cumbersome (close to 70 pounds), its 8–10 mph on level terrain was vastly superior to a walking gait. Two years later it was patented and called the "velocipede." Comparative speeds for hilly conditions will not be made!

Tricycles were in vogue for a while, but then attention returned to the bicycle. Kirkpatrick MacMillan in England introduced foot pedals to the front wheel of the hobby horse in 1835. It had taken nearly a half century to get the rider's feet off the ground. At first this innovation was called a "bone shaker" because of the effect given the rider when the iron wheels rolled over the rocky roads of those days. The first bicycles with rubber tires were not manufactured until 1869. Later on these bicycles were termed "ordinaries" because they were so common. There were fifty thousand of them in 1878. Ten years later over two million were sold! For a while the rear wheel was made with a larger diameter (about 30″) than the front wheel (about 24″). The rationale was that speed could be increased with such a ratio now that pedals on the front wheel were connected to the rear wheel with two long lever arms.

Tricycles and quadcycles driven by one and two riders came on the scene, and cycling became the "in" thing of the day. Wagenvoord (1972, p. 6) reports that shortly after the Civil War "seventy-one velocipede design and manufacturing patents were granted by the U.S. Patent Office." Included was a new idea—that of increasing the circumference of the front wheel and de-creasing the rear wheel to a minimal 17″ to 20″, merely enough to aid in balancing the vehicle. The front wheel often was 60″ or whatever the length of the driver's legs would dictate. Pedals were attached to the sprocket of the front wheel, and the rider sat just behind the center and over the front wheel.

In spite of the popularity of the "ordinaries," the public became aware that the machines were dangerous. Roads were built for horse-drawn vehicles in those days, and the potholes and cobblestones provided unexpected dangers for the rider. In an effort to improve the roads, the League of American Wheelmen was formed in 1880, and in ten years attained a membership exceeding 80,000 which proved a formidable voice for road improvement. This was the forerunner of our modern automobile clubs.

Fig. 58.1 The "ordinary" bicycle. Courtesy of Schwinn.

This organization could not do the whole job, however, and it took the ingenuity of another Englishman, H. J. Lawson in 1873, to take the ideas of André Guilment, a Frenchman, and incorporate them into the design of a new bicycle called the "safety." Both wheels of the safety were of equal size, and the machine was chain-driven from the rear. It had wire wheels and spokes to replace the wooden ones. All features made the "safety" much safer than its predecessor, the "ordinary." At last, if need be, the driver could easily dismount from the seat with little fear of injury.

Fig. 58.2 The "safety" bicycle. Courtesy of Schwinn.

Since the turn of the 20th century the mechanical changes have been basically far less radical than those of the preceding 50 years. The crossframe has been replaced by the diamond, the weight has decreased to about twenty to thirty pounds, the derailleurs and many accessories have been created to increase the comfort of the cyclist. Other improvements such as the bicycle's pneumatic tires, ball bearings, chain drive, and brake controls all contributed to the rapid development of the automobile.

As the automobile emerged on the American scene, the bicycle's popularity began to wane. American bicycle manufacturers like Ford and Duryea turned to the manufacture of cars, and never returned. Names like Columbia, Pierce, Schwinn, and Huffman succeeded them.

The bicycle was invented to meet the need for improved transportation. Within a short time it met the challenge and was used to move soldiers, physicians, school boys, passengers, and countless commodities to and from the marketplace. Many activities which today are considered to be sports, such as riflery, skiing, parachuting, scuba diving, archery, fishing, catapultery, and swimming, were at first engaged in for purely utilitarian purposes. Cycling, too, underwent the same metamorphosis. Private schools sprang up to teach neophytes how to cycle.

The bicycle boom of the 1960s and 1970s far outstripped anything seen in the industry before. In 1972 about 8.7 million bicycles were sold in the United States. For the first time since the advent of the automobile, bicycle sales were greater than automobile sales. Table 58.1 shows the ups and downs of the domestic bicycle industry in this century.

Bicycling today has captured the interest of all segments of the population, children and adults, men and women. Contributing to this upsurge in interest is: (1) the "back to nature" ecological mood of the individual and

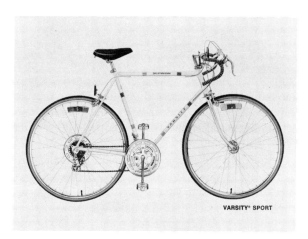

Fig. 58.3 The "ten-speed" touring bicycle has helped to make cycling a popular activity in the 1970s. Courtesy of Schwinn.

VARSITY® SPORT

Table 58.1*
United States Bicycle Market Statistics 1895–1975

Year	United States resident population (thousands)	Domestic industry shipment bicycles	Exports United States bicycles	Imports United States bicycles	Total United States market (apparent consumption)			
					Bicycles	Bicycles per 1000 populace	Domestic industry % total market	Imports % of total market
1895	69,580	800,000			800,000	15.1	100.0	
1905	83,820							
1915	100,549							
1925	115,832	260,000	7,710		252,296	2.2	103.0	
1935	127,250	657,000	1,120	13,000	668,880	5.26	98.2	1.9
1945	132,481	554,655	13,609	3,675	544,721	4.11	101.8	0.7
1955	164,303	1,794,968	7,217	1,223,990ᵃ	3,011,741	18.33	59.6	40.6
1965	194,483	4,617,743	3,503	1,038,884	5,654,124	29.06	81.6	18.4
1974	212,200	10,161,291	34,741	3,979,225	14,105,775	66.5	71.8	28.2

ᵃ Includes bicycles from Communist-dominated countries
* *Schwinn Reporter,* February, 1975

the country, (2) the increase in the cost of gasoline, and (3) a desire to improve one's physical fitness, particularly to combat the cardiovascular disorders related to the sedentary life-style.

Data indicate that sports participation rises with level of education and the increase in income. Since these are on the rise in the United States, it is logical to assume the cycling trend will continue.

Municipalities have affirmed their faith in the movement by erecting appropriate street markings for bicycle paths, routes, or bikeways. Federal regulations have intensified efforts to make bicycles safer, and commercial products are aimed at improving the cyclist's safety. The industry has produced training wheels to shorten the time in which to learn how to ride a bicycle. The unisex fashion movement has made it easier for women to play a larger role in cycling. The industry has promoted the derailleur bicycle through all the media to emphasize the fun and ease in which *adults* can tour 50–100 miles a day. The 1973 Federal Highway Act allotted 120 million dollars for bikeways. The 1976 Bikecentennial helped to add momentum to the interest in bicycling. These are a few reflections of the nation's interest in cycling.

Transportation agents for bus, train, and airplane trips now accept bicycles as legitimate baggage and can accommodate the passenger who desires to bring a bike to explore the countryside often unseen from cars or buses.

A variety of racks for automobile trailers and motor homes have made the transporting of the bicycle "standard operating procedure" for the "young at heart" who frequent crowded campgrounds. With the increased building of nationwide federal roads to accommodate fast-moving automobile traffic, more secondary roads will be available for safer riding by cyclists.

Our population's gradual increase in age should not mean a decline of the total use of bicycles during the rest of this century. More commuter-cyclists and business persons are recognizing the health and financial savings accrued by cycling reasonable distances to and from work.

In many countries throughout the world the bicycle is the principal means of transportation. In other countries bicycle racing is a major spectator sport. In the United States its time has come as a viable form of recreation for all.

SCOPE OF CYCLING

Racing

It takes but a short while after a vehicle has been invented before drivers compete to determine who is most skillful. These are some miscellaneous times and distances recorded over the years:

☐ The first "ordinary" race was conducted in the United States in 1878. The winner was Will Pittman who cycled the mile in 3:55.

☐ In 1883 a mile race was won in 1:53.

☐ When professional racing was conducted at Madison Square Garden in the 1890s on a one-tenth of a mile track, one man cycled 1983 miles in six days' riding time.

PROFESSIONAL
TRACK PARAMOUNT*

Fig. 58.4 Bicycle used in Olympic track competition. Courtesy of Schwinn.

- The first long-distance bicycle race was between Paris and Rouen in 1869 with the 83 miles being covered in 10.25:00 by James Moore.
- Alfred Letourner covered a mile behind a racing car in 0:33:05 at the rate of 108.92 miles per hour (motor-paced type of racing).
- Charles Murphy rode a mile behind a locomotive in 0:57:08 on June 30, 1899, on the Long Island Railroad between Farmingdale and Babylon, New York.

Road competition. Usually road competition consists of a race between two cities about thirty to several hundred miles apart. The principal types of road races are:

- Criterion: Completed over a route of a few miles and on a road in which other traffic is prohibited.
- Handicap: A race in which, to equalize the competition based on previous racing times, the slower riders are given an earlier start.

Most racing is done on the open road for distances up to one hundred miles. The terrain over which open-road races are conducted differs widely. Consequently it is impossible to make valid comparisons between riders. Nevertheless, speeds of around 25 miles per hour are common. A predetermined number of seconds is usually subtracted from a competitor's elapsed time if he is the leader at the end of the first day, second day, etc. The best known example of road racing is the Tour de France which covers about 2500 miles and was first conducted in 1903.

Some selected United States Cycling Federation Official Road-Scratch Competition Records as of January 1, 1976, are as follows:

Men		*Women*	
Distance in miles	*Time*	*Distance in miles*	*Time*
1	2.02.0		
2	4.43.2		
3	7.18.2		
5	11.38.0		
15	34.14.6		
20	45.22.0		
25	55.04.4	25	1:00.31.5
30	1:08.05.1		

Track racing. This is the other principal type of racing but is seen less often in the United States than in Europe because of the dearth of velodrome facilities. Most indoor tracks have a high bank (about 30–55°) and are about 300 meters in distance—slightly less than half of a typical college quarter-mile track found within a football stadium. Outdoor velodromes have a bank of about 10 to 25° and are about 400 meters long. The principal ones in the United States are in California, Illinois, New York, Pennsylvania, Georgia, Washington, Michigan, and Wisconsin.

Typical track races are normally over one to thirty miles or one to twelve hours when done by individuals. Most recent times and distances for selected track races as furnished by the United States Cycling Federation are as follows:

Men		*Women*	*Men*	
Outdoor banked track unpaced miles vs time			Outdoor banked track distance vs time	
Miles	*Time*		*Miles*	*Time*
1	2.13.6		25M 4185′	1 hr
2	4.27.9	4.45.1	50M 1760′	2 hr
3	6.42.1	7.16.3	72M 3960′	3 hr
5	11.10.5	12.05.3	103M 4250′	5 hr
10	22.21.4	24.07.2	195M 717′	10 hr
15	38.59.2	36.17.0		
20	45.22.1			
25	56.48.3	60.28.4		
30	1:08.24.2			

Pursuit racing. One team (or individual) begins the race on one side of the track and the opponent(s) on the opposite side. The race continues until one catches up to the opponent.

Miss and out race. Cyclists go around a track, and after each lap, the last competitor drops out until only one remains.

Time trials. Merely a race in which the first one across the finish line wins.

Cyclo-cross racing. This is principally an off-season (winter) event in racing in which the riders repeat a one- to two-mile course until five to fifteen miles have been ridden. The terrain is purposely ill-suited to cycling so that the cycle must be carried for part of the time. Cyclo-cross racing calls for maximum fitness. Though such races were held at the beginning of the century in France, it was not until they were revived in 1950 on an official world championship basis that they captured the interest of many in northern Europe.

Touring. Unquestionably, touring is the area of cycling that has shown the most growth in recent years. Several factors are responsible for this: (1) the cycling industry's promotion of the "ten-speed" derailleur bicycle that makes traveling over hilly terrain much easier than it is on a one-speed bicycle, (2) the desire of young adults to "go back to nature" by engaging in such activities as backpacking, spelunking, skiing, etc., and (3) the public's insistence that their municipal, state, and national governments improve cycling routes.

Everything should be done to provide the rider with an almost sensual experience if trips are to be repeated. Should a journey be unduly tiring and have constant interruptions due to poor planning or suboptimal fitness or be undertaken on a bicycle that does not meet the rigors of the occasion, the rider will hesitate to repeat the experience.

Cycling trips must be carefully planned. It is necessary to find a destination within the physical capacities of *all* riders, to allocate time for the jaunt, to have sufficient "in pocket" money to take care of the expected—and reasonable "unexpected" expenses, and to inform families of the riders about destination and estimated time of arrival in case emergencies arise which call for immediate contact.

One may have to be conditioned prior to the trip in a manner commensurate with its demands. It may mean riding a series of progressively longer distances to condition the cardiovascular and muscular systems to withstand excessive fatigue. Clothing must be selected which is appropriate to face the heat, rain, and chill that often confront cyclists. Sleeping and eating accommodations must be arranged prior to the trip.

Fig. 58.5 Cross-country racing and touring have shown remarkable growth in recent years. Courtesy of *JOPER*.

Supplying one's fluid needs is essential. Burke *et al.* (1975) write, "Since thirst can be an inaccurate mirror of body water needs, cyclists must learn to consume fluids at regular intervals—perhaps one-half pint every fifteen minutes."

Which kind of bicycle should be employed for this particular trip is a question to which careful thought must be given. For example, for the terrain to be covered, does the bicycle have sufficient gears? Does it have a spare tire, repair kit, and pump if one is needed? Is the seat fitted to the rider's proportions and is the clothing appropriate? Will the carrier withstand the weight of the equipment? Are there sufficient reflectors for reasonable safety in case one is late reaching the destination? Finally, has the vehicle been given a thorough inspection and met A-1 touring standards several days before the departure? These are questions which must be faced by any cyclist who seeks maximum enjoyment on a tour. The demands made upon a touring bicycle are quite different from those made on a bicycle used to merely go to the store, deliver papers, or ride around the neighborhood block. Depending upon the scope of the tour, touring bicycles may also need to carry bike flags, water bottles, carriers, spare parts, saddlebags, toe clips, and detailed maps.

Etiquette (rules of the road). Cyclists may neglect the rights of others on the road and thus become the objects of wrath of both the pedestrian and the motorist. Two simple rules should be observed by the cyclist: (1) give the pedestrian the right of way, and (2) follow automobile traffic rules.

PERTINENT RESEARCH

Kenneth Cooper (1970) has examined thousands of servicemen and civilian men and women and has devised a popular and reasonably valid test to diagnose an individual's physical fitness. The criterion is primarily the ability of one to use oxygen, and the test has a 0.90 correlation with more scientific measurements done on a treadmill.

In brief, Cooper says that if a man (he has no figures for women) runs the following distances, he will consume the stated milliliters of oxygen per kilogram of body weight per minute:

Distances covered in miles	*Oxygen consumption (ml/kg/min)*
less than 1.0	less than 25.0
1.00 to 1.24	25.0 to 33.7
1.25 to 1.49	33.8 to 42.5
1.50 to 1.74	42.6 to 51.15
1.75 or more	51.6 or more

These five categories of fitness were established for men:

	12-Minute Test for Men			
Fitness category	(Distance in Miles Covered in 12 Minutes)			
Age:	Under 30	30–39	40–49	50+
I Very poor	<1.0	<.95	<.85	<.80
II Poor	1.0 –1.24	.95–1.14	.85–1.04	.80– .99
III Fair	1.24–1.49	1.15–1.39	1.05–1.29	1.00–1.24
IV Good	1.50–1.74	1.40–1.64	1.32–1.54	1.25–1.49
V Excellent	1.75+	1.65+	1.55+	1.50+

These five categories were established for women:

	Women's Optional 12-Minute Run			
Fitness category	(Distance Walked and Run in 12 Minutes)			
Age:	Under 30	30–39	40–49	50+
I Very poor	<0.95	<0.85	<0.75	<0.65
II Poor	0.96–1.14	0.86–1.04	0.76–0.94	0.66–0.84
III Fair	1.15–1.34	1.05–1.24	0.95–1.14	0.85–1.04
IV Good	1.35–1.64	1.25–1.54	1.15–1.44	1.05–1.34
V Excellent	1.65+	1.55+	1.45+	1.35+

Cooper recommends that the individual who is interested in maintaining reasonable physical fitness should have a complete medical examination. Pending the physician's approval, a self-administered twelve-minute run test can be conducted. If the individual has been living a sedentary life, the *starter program should be taken*. See Table 58.2.

After one has taken the 12-minute running test and has been classified according to fitness category, a more intensive cycling program is recommended to improve or maintain reasonable physical fitness. The reader is advised to read either of Cooper's books (1970, 1973) for a more thorough regimen training program.

The bicycle is an excellent medium for attaining physical fitness; particularly fitness of the lower body and cardiovascular conditioning. It is recommended by Hellerstein (1973) that the cyclist ride "relatively slow for the first three to five minutes, followed by periods of faster cycling for five to six minutes, followed by interspersed two to three minutes of slower cycling." This method of interval bicycling allows the muscles to perform more effectively with a small oxygen debt, lower lactic acid accumulation, less fatigue and, in general, better performance. Road conditions permitting, the speed of the interval periods can be increased, to increase strength.

Bicycling is also conducive to weight loss by burning off calories. Below is a table calculated by Hellerstein that gives a rough estimate of the potential weight loss at various speeds.

774

Table 58.2

Individuals using the starter program *who prefer bicycling* as their means for improving physical fitness should follow this regimen:

Week	Miles	Time (min)	Frequency per wk	Week	Miles	Time (min)	Frequency per wk
		Men under 30				Women under 30	
1	2	10:00	5	1	2	12:30	5
2	2	9:00	5	2	2	11:00	5
3	2	7:45	5	3	2	9:45	5
4	3	11:50	5	4	3	16:00	5
5	3	11:00	5	5	3	14:30	5
6	3	10:30	5	6	4	20:00	5
		Men 30–39				Women 30–39	
1	2	10:30	5	1	2	13:00	5
2	2	9:30	5	2	2	12:00	5
3	2	8:30	5	3	2	10:00	5
4	2	7:45	5	4	3	17:00	5
5	2	7:30	5	5	3	15:00	5
6	3	11:50	3	6	4	22:00	5
		Men 40–49				Women 40–49	
1	2	11:00	5	1	2	13:30	5
2	2	10:00	5	2	2	12:30	5
3	3	15:00	5	3	2	10:30	5
4	3	14:00	5	4	3	17:30	5
5	4	19:00	5	5	3	15:30	5
6	4	17:30	5	6	4	23:30	5

The exercise sessions should be about 30–45 minutes three or four times a week, and the intensity should be at least 70 percent of the person's maximum heart rate.

Approximate calories expended during bicycling at various speeds:

Average bicycle Speed mph	55 lbs calories per		110 lbs calories per		165 lbs calories per	
	Minute	Hour	Minute	Hour	Minute	Hour
5.5	1.6	95	3.2	190	4.8	285
9.5	2.5	150	5.0	300	7.5	450
13.1	3.9	235	7.8	470	11.8	750

Since it takes a loss of 3500 calories to lose one pound, one can see that a 165-pound individual who cycles recreationally for thirty minutes a day

DELUXE EXERCISER

Fig. 58.6 The exerciser is being used for fitness and therapeutic purposes. Courtesy of Schwinn.

four days a week at a brisk 13.1 miles per hour speed loses 1500 calories. If the caloric intake was reduced by a similar amount, it would take about six months for the individual to sensibly lose thirty pounds if need be.

The bicycle ergometer is being received more positively in scientific circles for measuring certain physical fitness parameters. When compared with the more conventional treadmill, it has these advantages: (1) it isolates the work requirement to the thigh muscles, (2) little or no learning is expected of the subject prior to testing, (3) the subject holds himself in one position with little extraneous movement which permits the collection of data in an easier manner, and (4) testing cycling ergometers range from about $500 to $600 as compared to $2000 to $8000 for the treadmill.

REFERENCES

Burke, E., D. Costill, and P. Van Handel 1975. When drinks can be hazardous. *Bike World* **4:** 33 (February).

Cooper, K. H. 1970. *The new aerobics.* New York: M. Evans and Company.

Cooper, M., and K. H. Cooper 1973. *Aerobics for women.* New York: M. Evans and Company.

Hellerstein, H. K. 1973. Bicycling for fitness and fun. *Schwinn Reporter* **23:** 6–7, (September).

Schwinn Reporter, February, 1975.

Wagenvoord, J. 1972. *Bikes and riders.* New York: Van Nostrand.

59
Equitation
Betty L. Brunson

Horses have long been one of our most useful animals. They were first used to do heavy work on farms and ranches and to provide transportation. Although machines have replaced most of our horses in the work field, the use of horses for recreation and companionship has grown more and more popular.

Those of us who admire these wonderful animals enjoy just being with them, while riding or caring for them. People learn to ride for many reasons: for exercise, to be outdoors, for relaxation, to be with people with a similar interest, or for the competition of an event such as a horse show.

Team work is all important in riding a horse. The rider who is experienced enough to convey a message to the horse will usually call forth a desired response from the animal. Horse and rider must work together and understand each other in order to perform well.

STYLES OF RIDING

There are many styles of riding. Some common ones are referred to as follows: *Western* riding, often associated with the cowboy; *forward seat* riding, used primarily by those who jump their horses; *saddle seat* riding, mostly used with the elevated action of saddlebred show horses; and the *balanced seat* where the rider is balanced in the middle of the saddle and able to convert to any of the other styles as the occasion requires or suggests. Forward seat, saddle seat, and balanced seat are all referred to as English styles of riding (Fig. 59.1).

The *Western rider* sits in the middle of a Western saddle with long stirrups, legs slightly bent at the knees and heels lower than the toes as the ball of the foot rests on the stirrup. The reins are reasonably loose, held in the left hand and used to turn the horse by a method called neck reining. The horse is cued in addition by shifts in weight and pressure from the legs of the rider. Western gaits are the walk, jog, lope, and gallop. The rider sits in the saddle for all gaits, never standing in the stirrups nor posting (Fig. 59.2).

Most of the terminology used in this discussion stems from the English styles of riding. The basic principles apply to Western riding but it will be helpful to understand the Western counterpart of the English term. An En-

Fig. 59.1 English styles of riding:

(a) saddle seat

(b) balanced seat

(c) forward (or hunt) seat

Fig. 59.2 Western seat.

glish girth is a Western cinch. The Western saddle has a horn on its pommel; the English saddle has none. A saddle pad is used under the English saddle, a saddle blanket under the Western saddle. Most English bridles have a brow band and nose cavesan, most Western bridles have neither. Sometimes the English style of handling reins is referred to as draw reining; the Western rider neck reins the horse.

The *forward seat* rider shifts the weight of the trunk forward as the horse progresses from the walk into the trot and gallop. Both hands are on the reins and held low near the horse's withers. The stirrups are short with knees and ankles bent. As the rider approaches a jump, he or she assumes an extreme forward position in order to give the horse its head in going over the jump. Weight is centered on inner thighs and legs, head up and hands held low.

The *saddle seat* style of riding hits the rider in the middle of an English saddle, erect at all gaits. The reins are held in two hands and the hands held higher than any of the other mentioned styles because this seat is used when riding horses that carry their heads high with arched necks. The stirrups are long with knees slightly bent.

The *balanced seat* is exactly what the word implies; the rider is in balance with the horse when sitting in the middle of the saddle. Stirrups are measured at the ankle, neither long nor short. Hands are held slightly above the withers of the horse and the reins are held in two hands. This seat is the most adaptable for any kind of horse.

If a rider uses a balanced seat the weight is in the middle of the saddle where the horse can best carry it. As the horse is already top heavy, it does not need, under normal circumstances, the weight of the rider over its neck. The rider should incline the body weight forward to free the horse's hind quarters to jump, but after the jump come back again to the middle of the saddle where the horse can best carry the weight. In contrast the rider should not be pushed back to the cantle of the saddle to hinder the horse as it propels its body forward with its haunches. Such a rider will cause a horse to end up with a sore back.

In all styles one should choose the horse best suited to a particular way of riding in order to achieve the best performance.

The position of the hands, whether high or low, is very important and is determined by the horse's head carriage. In other words, the rider's arms should be a continuation from the horse's bit through the reins in a straight line. Riders using reins in any style should use a gradual pull to slow down and stop, never a jerk.

It is common to all styles of riding that the rider's heels are down and away from the horse. In no style of riding does the rider sit on the cantle or back of the saddle.

LEARNING TO RIDE: A BASIC APPROACH

☐ Decide on the style of riding that suits your needs and interests and get instruction in this style at a professional stable. Be aware of the other styles also.

☐ Learn to mount and dismount properly. More injuries occur during mounting and dismounting than in actually riding the horse.

☐ Learn the proper use of aids, both natural and artificial.

☐ Learn and observe safety rules around horses, whether riding in the ring or on the trail.

☐ Learn about the care of horses and a little about the animals themselves. In understanding your horse you will be able to communicate better with it.

Mounting and Dismounting

Approach the horse from its left side. Horses are traditionally approached from the left to mount, dismount and tack and are accustomed to this procedure. When mounting, hold the reins in the left hand which should be placed on the horse's withers preferably holding a good piece of mane along with reins. The hand must be anchored to the mane or withers because a jerk on the reins, in addition to hurting the horse's mouth, could make the horse move backwards or even rear up. Turn the stirrup toward you with the right hand and insert the left foot in the stirrup all of the way to the heel of the boot or shoe so that it will not slip. Point the toe toward the girth so as not to kick the horse in the side. Put the right hand across the cantle (back) of the saddle and spring from the ground foot up into the saddle. Never pull the weight up, as it will strain the horse's back. Sit down lightly in the middle of the saddle. Avoid dragging the foot across the horse's rump.

Dismounting should be done slowly so as not to frighten the animal. Hold the reins in the left hand along with a piece of mane or on the withers. Push the weight up with the right hand on the front of the saddle (pommel) with weight on the left foot as you remove the right foot from the stirrup to swing the right leg over the horse's rump. Remove the left foot and pause for a second as if on a balance beam with both legs together and the body balanced over the saddle, then slip quietly to the ground. When using Western tack the rider does not pause, but swings the right leg all of the way to the ground and then removes the left foot from the stirrup.

Aids

The aids used in riding are both natural and artificial. One should always use natural aids before the artificial ones. Aids are used gradually as needed. Keep remembering that you are riding a sensitive animal. Why frighten it with a spur when a gentle nudge will serve as well. Horses are as individual as people and what works with one on one occasion will not necessarily work with the same horse on another day or with another horse.

Natural aids. The natural aids most commonly used are the hands, legs, body weight, and voice.

The *hands* on the reins are used to guide the horse's direction, to slow it down, to stop it, and to aid in collection. Slight contact with relaxed arms will give the animal confidence. A steady pull on the reins deadens the horse's mouth and is heavyhanded. Riding with a loose rein is not "good hands"; it is "no hands." How can one avoid being abrupt in asking the horse to slow down or stop when one must shorten the reins twelve inches or more before the message reaches the horse's mouth? To shorten reins, reach over with one hand (left) and catch the opposite rein with thumb and forefinger behind the other (right) hand, then pull to the desired length. To lengthen the reins, simply let the reins slip through the hand until the desired length is reached. The reins must, of course, be held so each side is the same length.

Never underestimate the use of the *legs* in the control of the horse's hind quarters. Forward movement is initiated by slight pressure of the legs to the horse's sides. Use the leg at the girth to help the horse to bend. Pressure with the calf on one side will move the horse in the opposite direction; i.e., away from the pressure. Use the heels to signal the horse in the canter departure for the correct lead. The leg aids are frequently overused, making a horse listless or stubborn. A rider who keeps the calves in a horse's side all of the time can hardly expect the horse to respond to a leg aid.

Body weight is of great importance in riding any horse, and its importance is often underestimated. Just carrying the trunk sideways while riding will give the horse a sore back. Shifting the weight from left to right or back and forth can control the horse's direction and speed as well as its way of going.

In my opinion, the best horses on which to learn to ride are the *voice*-trained animals. Using the voice as a natural aid can be very effective and pleasant for the horse as well as the new rider. The horse does not then get confused by different signals from each new rider. However, the day may come when a verbal command is not enough and stronger natural or artificial aids will be needed.

Artificial aids. The ordinary riding *crop* is the only aid a rider in training should ever use.

Artificial aids are numerous and they are for the use of the professional only. The long *whip* can be used to touch a horse on the rear legs in the canter to make it increase the use of its hocks and improve a rough canter to a pleasurable gait. *Spurs* can be a wonderful aid in training the young, lazy horse in a canter departure or to respond to leg aids. There are many kinds of *martingales* which can be helpful in training a horse to control the position of its head.

INTO THE SADDLE

There are no "ninety-day wonders" in the equestrian world. No matter how gifted and athletic individuals may be, it will still take them time to learn to ride well. Teachers who take shortcuts will produce weak riders.

A good riding teacher emphasizes the importance of a walk. Much is learned at a walk; correct position, guiding, and feeling the movement of the horse's head through the reins. Until riders learn to feel the horse's mouth, they have not learned to ride, despite their ability to post or sit the canter. Too much movement in following the natural movement of the horse in the walk can cause bobbing of the horse's head. Riders should learn at the walk to let the horse lead them.

Next riders learn to trot their horse. With slight collection the horse will usually trot if the riders apply slight pressure with the knees, or on verbal command, depending on how the horse is trained. At this gait, riders post. Riders post by simply allowing the horse to thrust them up and forward with its haunches while the riders tighten their knees and inner thighs, then briefly touch back down in the saddle to rise again in rhythm with the horse's movement. Posting should be a smooth movement executed close to the saddle. In posting, riders follow a diagonal pair of the horse's legs, rising with one foreleg (and thus the opposite hind leg) and sitting as that forefoot comes to the ground. This is known as a diagonal. When riders are synchronized with the left front leg, i.e., up when it is forward and down when it is back, they are said to be on the left diagonal. When riding on the straightaway either the right or left diagonal can be used, but when riding in the ring the rider must use the outside diagonal to keep the horse in balance. A simple method of checking the diagonal is to observe the horse's shoulder on the outside, or rail side, of the ring. As it moves forward, riders should start to sit in the saddle. If they find that they are incorrect, they simply sit a beat (stop posting for a beat) and begin posting again. Using both diagonals can keep the horse from overdevelopment of one shoulder.

The next gait learned should be the canter. Riders must not progress to this until the posting trot has been perfected. This means that their hands are motionless while posting (the horse's head does not move in the trot) and do not interfere with the horse's head. They also must be able to change diagonals smoothly.

The horse nods its head in the canter. Therefore it is imperative that riders have a relaxed arm and hand. Being relaxed as they sit in the saddle is also important. Standing in the stirrups or hanging on with the legs and bumping against the natural movement are very abusive to the horse.

In the canter it is important that the horse leads in its stride with the correct foot. In this gait the two left feet follow the two right feet with the inner set leading or ahead of the outer set. When the horse is traveling clockwise, its right feet lead keeping it in balance on the curve. The incorrect lead could cause a horse to trip or stumble. The obvious leg to check in this is the inner foreleg which should reach the ground sooner than the outer foreleg.

To begin the canter from the walk, riders collect their horses slightly to prepare them to canter. The most popular lead departure signal is to angle the horse's body away from the side with which riders intend it to lead and apply a leg aid by pressing strongly behind the girth on the opposite side of the horse. The horse should move away from the pressure of the rider's leg and thrust its opposite legs ahead as it is aided in this decision by its body being angled to put the inside set of legs ahead of the outside ones. A horse can be trained to obey almost any command if it understands what is expected of it. If a horse cross canters, for example, right front lead and left back lead, it should be stopped immediately and started again. As riders go back to a walk from any gait, they should release the reins a bit.

In order to slow down a horse in the canter, tension on the reins is increased on the back stroke while following the movement of the horse's head. This will shorten the horse's stride, thereby slowing it down. Pulling straight back only results in the horse breaking into a trot, as the rider has interrupted the natural movement of the horse's head at the canter.

Rider and horse can also move backwards, i.e., back up. No one actually pulls the horse back with the reins. Instead, the horse has to be trained to back with a given signal. Moving a horse forward a few steps gets it in motion and encourages flexibility of the neck. Then applying gentle pressure on the reins and guiding it with the legs will cause the horse to back in a straight line.

Trail Riding

Trail riding is not for the beginner, as the horse might see unfamiliar things and shy (step sideways quickly), bolt, or otherwise unseat the rider. No matter how competent the teachers, they cannot control the horse for the rider. However, in the ring, teachers can at least see the riders and tell them what to do or even step out and stop the horse if necessary.

One of the first rules of trail riding is to always walk the horse a good distance after leaving and before returning to the stable. Walking after leaving promotes circulation of the blood and limbering of the horse's muscles before it trots. Returning at a walk relaxes the horse and prevents acquisition of the vice of running back to the stable.

Riders should always have at least one trot before they canter. A horse that bucks off in its canter probably feels good and has not had sufficient exercise. This is not the horse's fault.

Riders on a horse that rears should lean over and grasp the horse's mane or neck, keeping the reins in their hands. This will throw the rider's weight forward which encourages the horse to stop rearing, and helps the rider to keep on balance. Riders *should never* catch their balance on the reins. This act encourages the horse's upward movement, sometimes even causing the horse to fall completely over backwards.

Runaways are usually caused by the rider who lets the horse get out of control in the canter. This might seem like fun for a bit, but the horse gets excited and might not respond to the rider's signal to slow down. The horse should be under control at all times. In checking the runaway horse, the rider should restrain and release rather than use a steady pull which would tend to numb the horse's mouth and result in no response. Riders can try to turn the horse in short circles which will slow it down. The rider should try not to tense up and get excited as feelings are relayed to the horse and may make it go faster. Other riders in a group should not try to catch up with the runaway horse as this will also make it run faster. It would be better for the group to stop completely. Horses are herd-bound animals and the runaway will be less apt to go very far should every other horse stop.

Horses do not like to be crowded while under saddle, even though they may stand in the pasture touching each other. Whether on the trail or in the ring, riders should stay a horse's length from any other horse. This will prevent collisions, injuries caused by kicking horses, and the misbehavior of one horse upsetting other horses.

On the trail or even in the ring, the enjoyment and well-being of an entire group of riders are greatly affected by the horse and rider in the lead. On the trail the leading rider will warn the others of anything unusual ahead such as an approaching car, a dog, other animals, a person with an umbrella, a baby carriage, a low hanging limb, or a wet or boggy spot on the trail. The riders need to be aware of things the horse might not understand. If the lead rider gets the horse to cross a bridge, this will encourage the others to follow. The lead rider sets a comfortable pace for the others. The lead horse should be an aggressive horse that enjoys leading. Riders should not force a horse and demand of it what it is not able to give. Riders should try to train horses not to be afraid by using gentle pressure with their legs and a reassuring voice. Even though all horses do not make good leaders, most of them want to do what is asked of them. It is up to the rider to get the message across to the horse.

Horses should not be allowed to graze or drink from a stream while the rider is mounted. Only when the rider is on an endurance ride or is planning to ride for several hours is watering the horse necessary. It is bad for the bridle for the horse to drink or graze and could encourage it to roll with the rider on its back. Grazing will lead the horse to the vice of eating while under saddle. It can be very annoying to a rider to have a horse trying to dive for leaves or blades of grass.

When riding up inclines, riders should lean slightly forward to free the horse's hind quarters with which it pushes itself up the hill. Moving downhill, however, riders should not lean forward, but sit upright, as the horse is already top heavy and does not need extra weight over its neck. Riders should always walk the horse downhill to keep it from stumbling and to discourage the buck it is likely to do if it goes up an incline on the other side.

Unless the rider is expert, it is unwise to change horses on the trail. Horses which were easy to mount at the stable might be quite different on the trail. Also the owners of the horse may have put a particular rider on a particular horse for a reason. It is very important to match horses and riders.

When riding along a road, riders should generally ride facing the traffic, with all riders on the same side of the road, allowing as much room for passing cars as possible. On a curve, ride on the outside of the curve in order to be seen more clearly. In crossing the road, all riders should cross at the same time.

Riders should be considerate of others when riding with a group. They should not break into a canter without warning the others. If riders are going to stop or slow from a canter to a trot or walk, they should hold out their hands to signal those behind. If riders find it necessary to pass, they should ask permission, then trot slowly by.

Think Horse: General Riding Information

In the team of horse and rider, it is the rider who has the larger brain; the horse, the greater brawn. Humans are the ones capable of figuring out the horse and changing their riding style or signals. Riders should not expect the horse to change with each new rider. Many problems can be avoided, much satisfaction gained, if riders will think about the horse. If they encourage a horse to gallop and then get frightened when it won't stop, it is not the animal who has caused their plight. Perhaps the horse is accustomed to a slow canter and in getting out of its pattern, it became excited. Horses are creatures of habit.

If the horse bites or kicks when the girth is tightened, the girth may be too tight, twisted, or tightened with the forelegs back under the horse causing a painful wrinkle in the skin under the girth. The girth should be tightened a little when the horse is first saddled and finished just before the rider mounts. It is wise to check the girth after the horse has been ridden a few minutes.

Uncomfortable tack can cause a horse to misbehave. The bridle should be suitable for the horse. The bit should come well up in the corners of the horse's mouth, causing a slight wrinkle, and should be just wide enough to comfortably come outside of the mouth; not so wide as to have excess bit nor so narrow as to pinch the lips. A rider should stand on the ground beside the horse, grasp the reins directly behind the bit, and gradually pull. If the horse steps back slowly, the rider has sufficient control. If it doesn't move, there will be no way the rider can control the horse while on its back. On the other hand, if the horse runs backward with this test, the bit is too severe. The bit should be chosen for the individual horse according to its needs.

Riders should think horse each time they ride. They should consider when the horse was last ridden or exercised. A horse should be ridden, turned out in a pasture or paddock, or lunged at least every other day. An old horse is much better off with a little exercise every day than with several days of rest followed by two or three hours of work on one day.

A horse can also misbehave because the rider is asking it to do so. Perhaps the reins are too tight because of the rider's fear of the horse. A rider sometimes hangs on with the lower calves, causing the horse to become nervous. Sometimes a rider rides with toes turned out so as to be constantly kicking the horse with the heels. A rider carrying a crop on a horse that is afraid of a crop, or simply doesn't need a crop, will have an unpleasant ride on a frustrated horse.

"Thinking horse" is a continuing thing and learning to do this is as important as learning to walk, trot, and canter. Riders should always be cognizant of their animals and how their environment (which includes the riders) affects them.

Getting More Involved: Horse and Rider

Advanced riders are fluent in basic skills and can apply them under a variety of circumstances. A more important characteristic of advanced riders, however, is that they are advanced enough to never stop learning about a horse. Each experience with each new horse teaches them something.

Advanced riders let the horse "talk to them." It is always telling them something. If they will listen, or perceive, they will understand the animal and get the best possible performance. They are intelligent enough to know when they have gotten the horse's best, and stop there. Good riders use various aids and signals according to the animal's vocabulary, never forgetting that each horse is an individual.

Advanced riders should never turn down the opportunity to broaden their knowledge. They try every style of riding. Some horses cannot be ridden in a particular style or seat. For example, the American Saddle bred should not be asked to move on a relaxed rein for Western pleasure, nor could a brilliant five-gaited performance be obtained from a steady quarter horse trained to work cattle.

An advanced rider should be able to train a colt, keeping in mind the goal of making its introduction to the rider a pleasant one. The colt should anticipate its work as fun and look forward to its association with people. The skilled rider will work the horse for short intervals and not sour it.

A lot of ground work is necessary with a young horse. The colt should be able to walk, trot, and canter on the lunge before being mounted. The advanced rider must learn to handle the horse from the ground before stepping into the saddle. A bitting harness properly used will help teach the horse to flex. Working the horse in a small ring will teach it to bend its body. When the colt is ridden, it should be ridden with other horses. The colt will like this, and the experience will be good for it. When it is introduced to the trail, riders should make sure that the colt goes out with an old reliable horse in the lead or beside it closest to passing cars. In all phases of training it is impossible to overemphasize the importance of giving the horse a pat on the neck after it has done a new thing well. Trainers talk to the horse and touch it constantly.

The advanced rider should be able to stabilize the gaits of any horse: the walk, seated trot, posting trot, extended trot, collected canter, and hand gallop, all at different speeds appropriate to that particular gait's movement. The use of a cavaletti, a series of logs or poles spaced on the ground a distance apart determined by the horse's stride, is very beneficial in stabilizing the trot, making the horse use its shoulders, and discouraging stumbling.

The cavaletti can also be used as an exercise in teaching the horse to jump. It is used for short periods of time so as not to sour the horse.

The advanced rider will be able to work a horse in small circles, figure eights and serpentines (a series of half circles connected by an imaginary straight line) executed in the walk, trot and canter. These exercises improve the horse's muscular development, balance, and flexibility. The rider uses a great deal of leg aid in these exercises. Riders of each style of riding perform these exercises differently. Forward seat, saddle seat, and balanced seat riders are required to change diagonals in trotting figure eights and serpentines; Western riders do not post but sit the trot. Saddle seat riders halt in the center of the figure 8 and between half circles of the serpentine when cantering, whereas riders of the other seats perform the flying change (changing leads without breaking the gait).

Horses can be used in games for the gymkhanas or other exercises by a skilled rider, but care must be taken that the horse is not abused. Some animals used for games never recover and when mounted they expect to be jerked and spurred and are unable to be ridden as a pleasure horse.

Some dedicated horse people go on to dressage. Dressage is collection at different levels. Only expert riders should try this with their animals. Too many riders end up only pulling on their horse's mouth because they do not understand flexing of the horse and collection itself, which comes from the rear or hind quarters of the horse.

Equipment and What to Wear

What horse and rider wear varies with the style of riding. For the beginner in any style a pair of jeans and a sturdy shoe or boot are quite suitable.

The Western rider wears the traditional western hat, western type shirt, western (cowboy) boots and chaps. A poncho can be tied on the saddle.

Informal attire for the saddle-seat show rider includes Kentucky jodhpurs. These are high waisted jodhpurs, form fitting all the way to the lower calf where they flare to the bottom. The coat is long and vented in the back and sides with inverted pleats. The pants and coat together are called a habit and can be made from any material, but should be of a conservative solid color. A white or colored shirt with a mannish collar is worn with the habit along with a tie (four-in-hand), leather or string gloves, jodhpur boots and a hard crown derby. Men and boys sometimes wear a short brim sport type hat.

Formal show ring clothes for the saddle seat rider comprise jodhpurs with solid braid down the outer legs; an extra long tuxedo coat with satin lapels, a tuxedo style winged collar shirt with formal front, a bow tie, preferably white, a satin cummerbund, leather gloves which can be white or a dark color matching the habit, jodhpur boots of black or brown patent leather and a high top silk hat. Ladies should wear their hair in a net and off their faces. The formal habit should be made of a thin material and be dark in color.

The balanced seat rider usually wears the same clothes as the saddle seat rider in the show ring.

Informal attire for the hunt rider includes either jodhpur pants, styled with snug fitting legs from knee to ankle where there is a cuff, or breeches. Breeches are knee length and worn with high top boots. As an informal coat the hunt rider wears a plaid, tweed, or saltsack coat. A ratcatcher shirt or stock is acceptable. Gloves are always worn, also a hard crown hunt cap.

The hunt rider's formal clothes consist of fawn color breeches, a white shirt with a neck band and a white stock tie, a black melton coat, leather gloves, plain black high top boots and a hard hunt cap.

The horse's attire is called tack and includes a saddle, bridle, girth, saddle pads, halters, leads, and any other equipment used in riding or handling the horse. Each horse should have its own tack properly adjusted to it.

Several types of saddles are in common use. The one chosen will depend on the style of riding and on individual taste or preference within this style. The *Western saddle* was designed for working cattle and is heavier, larger, and more sturdy than most of the other saddles. It has a deep seat with a prominent pommel and a saddle horn that is used when roping stock. The *forward seat saddle* is also deep seated but lacks the horn (as do all saddles except the Western saddle). It is built to sit the rider in the forward position. A flap of leather extends forward at the knee position to protect the rider's knee which is bent at a greater angle than in the other seats. Knee rolls are built into the saddle to provide greater security when jumping. The *park saddle* is neither deep seated nor very flat. It is used for pleasure riding in the saddle and balanced seat. The *show saddle,* more like the park saddle than any other, but with wider flaps and a flatter seat, is used mostly in horse shows by saddle and balanced seat riders. The wide flaps protect the rider's attire. The shallow seat of this saddle shows off the top line of the horse, while its pommel is cut back to show off the horse's neck. Another type of saddle is the *dressage saddle,* a moderately deep-seated saddle with knee rolls that are lower than the forward seat saddle. This saddle encourages the rider to sit erect rather than forward and is designed to give the rider's legs support and facilitate their ease in collection.

Whichever saddle is used, it is imperative that it fit the particular horse using it. A low-pommeled saddle on a high withered horse can cause a fistula, an infection of the withers which is seldom cured. A saddle too high off the horse's withers can easily slip sideways while being used in riding.

A saddle pad or saddle blanket should always be used under the saddle for protection of the horse's back. In teaching beginners to ride it is good to use two pads. The pads or blankets must be kept clean as a dirty blanket can cause a sore on the horse.

The bridle is a horse's head gear for riding. It may be a hackmore which is fitted around the horse's nose for control. Most likely it will have a bit or two bits which need to be properly adjusted and selected according to the horse's needs. The reins are part of the bridle (they may be single or double), as are the cheek and crown pieces to keep the bit(s) in place. Some bridles have a nose cavesson to keep the horse's mouth closed over a bit and a brow band to keep the parts of the bridle that run over the horse's poll in place around the ears.

There are many kinds of bits and we will discuss some of the common ones. A horse should be bitted with a bit that gives the rider control without hard pulling, yet is as light as possible on the horse's mouth.

The *snaffle bit* is a mouth piece that is jointed in the middle. It does not have a shank nor a chain or strap to run under the horse's chin; hence most of the pressure from the rider's hands goes on the horse's lips. The snaffle is an extremely mild bit that is used mostly in training colts. Some people use this bit outside of the riding ring, which can prove a mistake if the horse becomes excited or frightened.

The *curb bit* has shanks which vary in length according to the need of the individual horse. The longer the shank, the stronger the bit. A half-circle rise is in the middle of the mouth piece and this too varies in size according to the needs of the horse. The curb bit acts on the bars of the horse's mouth rather than the corners of the lips. It is used with a curb chain or leather strap under the chin which when properly adjusted aids in control of the horse.

The *pelham bit* is in between the snaffle and curb in severity. Two sets of rings are on the bit; one at the mouth piece, as in the snaffle, and the other at the end of the shank as with the curb bit. Two sets of reins can thus be used with this bit.

The bridle is selected according to the bit to be used: a snaffle bridle for a snaffle bit, etc. The *full bridle,* consisting of both a curb and snaffle bit, is used mostly for showing horses. The purpose of the two bits is to set a horse's head in a desired position. On this bridle the snaffle bit and reins are called the bridoon. The bridoon lifts the head while the curb ducks the chin. The little finger is kept between the two reins in the rider's hand with the less severe and more used bridoon on the outside. This bridle should not be used by the novice. It is used with leg aids to teach the horse to flex at the poll.

A *martingale* is often used when riding a horse. The *standing martingale* is a strap coming from the noseband to the girth. The *running martingale* comes from the girth and divides at the chest and ends with two rings through which the reins slide. The martingale is used for various reasons; it will keep a horse from tossing his head or carrying it too high (usually a standing martingale) or to help a horse to learn to flex (running martingale). Bear in mind that individual horses respond differently to the aids.

Using tack or equipment correctly is very important and should start with putting it on correctly. Ill-fitting tack can cause a horse to misbehave. When bridling and saddling a horse the handler should do it the same way each time. A horse becomes confused when things are out of pattern.

The horse should be approached from the left side. To bridle the horse stand at the horse's left side near its head, lift the reins over the horse's head, and slide them down around its neck. The horse may be steadied by holding the reins close under its neck. The bridle should be lifted toward the horse's head with the right hand on the crown (top) pieces and the left hand on the bit. Place the left thumb in the corner of the horse's mouth, where there are no teeth, so that the horse will open its mouth. By gently raising the right hand, the bridle is brought over the ears, which should be put in one at a time. While the right hand raises the bridle into position the left guides the bit into place. Note that the bit is not bumped or pressed against the horse's teeth until it opens its mouth, rather the pressure of the left thumb on the bars of the horse's mouth asks it to open its mouth. The throat latch should be buckled loosely to allow the horse to arch its neck more comfortably. The nose band should fit snugly as its purpose is to keep the horse's mouth closed and make the bit more effective. The curb chain should be loose enough to allow the insertion of two or three fingers, but again this will vary with the individual horse.

The saddle should be slowly raised to the horse's back and gently placed forward at the withers, then slid back to settle at the horse's middle. The girth should then be tightened one notch to keep the saddle from falling if the horse should become frightened and shy. Then walk around the front of the horse to the other side and raise the saddle skirt on the right to be sure the saddle pad is not wrinkled, or the girth twisted. Returning to the left side, make sure the left forefoot of the horse is slightly forward keeping the skin under the girth area from wrinkling, and tighten the girth a bit more. Actually, the girth should not be completely tightened until the horse is mounted. The rider should be able to put a hand under the girth comfortably, that is not have to wiggle the fingers to get them between the horse and the girth. It is a good practice for riders to check the girth after they have ridden for a few minutes. It is just as bad to get the girth too tight as too loose. A girth that is too tight could cause a horse to misbehave, one that is too loose will allow the saddle to turn.

The technicalities of the aspects of equitation presented here could comprise chapters or even books in themselves. These few basics are things that I have learned from a lifetime of experience which have proved effective in the teaching of equitation.

One last thought I'd like to leave with those of you who would like to learn to ride a horse. Try to remember you have the intelligence that the horse lacks. If you work with the horse, rather than master it, you will find your ride much more enjoyable and your association with this animal more complete.

TERMINOLOGY

Bite of the reins The part of the reins from the hand to the end of the reins. In English riding the bite is between two hands in front of the body.

Cantle The back of the seat of the saddle.

Cinch Western term for the strap that runs under the horse's body to keep the saddle on the horse.

Colic A common and serious ailment of the horse. It is an intestinal upset, often a blockage in the intestine, complicated by the fact that the horse cannot regurgitate.

Collection As the word implies it means pushed together. A collected horse has its hocks up under it and is alert, head up, flexed at the poll and ready to move.

Dressage Extreme collection and performance of moves such as those executed by the Spanish Riding School of Vienna.

Floating of teeth Filing off sharp points of the teeth. The horse chews with a circular motion, grinding its food and needs smooth teeth.

Founder An inflammation of the internal hoof. The walls of the hoof become rigid and the sole drops. The causes are not completely understood although overfeeding is a frequent cause. The damage to the hoof is permanent. Also referred to as laminitis.

Gaits The different patterns of movement of the horse's feet combined with the rate at which it is ridden in each pattern. Examples: walk, trot, extended trot, canter, gallop, jog, and lope.

Gelding A male horse that has been castrated.

Girth English term for the strap that runs under the belly of the horse to keep the saddle in place.

Good hands Tactful, sensitive hands which feel the horse's mouth to make it respond. It takes a long time to develop good hands. They are paramount for a good rider and a happy horse.

Green horse An unschooled horse.

Hack To ride for pleasure, usually across country.

Heaves A chronic respiratory condition in which the air sacs of the lungs have broken down. The horse does a lot of coughing and exhales twice for each inhalation.

Heavy hands A rider who has stiff, rigid hands and arms and controls the horse by force rather than feel and responsiveness.

Lead In the canter and gallop, the horse puts both of its right or left legs down ahead of the opposite legs. This set of legs which is ahead is the lead, i.e., right or left, that the horse is on. When traveling clockwise in a circle the right lead should be used and vice versa.

Lunge To exercise or school a horse in a small circle at the end of a long rein or rope. Also spelled longe.

Near side Left side of the horse.

Neck reining The Western rider holds the reins with the left hand and moves the reins against the horse's neck to turn it. The horse is trained to move in the opposite direction from the side of the neck that is touched by the rein.

Off side Right side of the horse.

Pommel The mid-front section of the seat of a saddle.

Poll The part of the horse's neck directly behind the ears where the flexion of the neck is evident.

Post The rhythmic movement to the trot performed in English riding.

Thrush A disease of the frog or center of the horse's hoof, which is characterized by a strong-smelling discharge. If not treated, it can cause the whole sole of the foot to deteriorate. Often caused by dirty stalls.

Withers The part of the horse at the base of the mane where its back begins. The withers are slightly raised from the level of the back.

60
Ice Skating

J. F. Gasparini, in his article, touches on the origin and development of skating as recreation, discusses its teaching and learning, and gives some sound advice regarding equipment. K. J. Wolf follows with a discussion of class organization, appropriate attire, and the operation of a skating program in colleges. The two articles complement each other. RBF

Recreational Ice Skating
John F. Gasparini

Skating probably dates back to the first time people put runners on their feet to glide on ice. There are indications that people skated as far back as 2500 years ago, 500 B.C., in Greece. The first really authentic story of ice skating is dated 1396 when a young woman in Schiedam, Holland, seriously injured while skating, lived so beautiful and patient a life that she was canonized as Saint Siedwi. Thus, skating is the only sport to have a patron saint.

Undoubtedly, the sport of ice skating has since gained much popularity

Fig. 60.1 Recreational skating has been with us for a long time. Courtesy of *JOPER.*

along with ice hockey, a sport which developed as an offshoot of recreational skating. In the states of Minnesota and North Dakota alone over the last decade, 100 artificial arenas have been developed. Naturally, with this increase in the amount of ice time available, there has been an upswing in the number of hockey participants but, more important, there has been an increase in ice-skating classes for those wishing to participate for the sole purpose of recreation. Recreational skating should be a pleasure and its primary aim, fun. There is a realization today that everyone should have some outside interests and must have the opportunity to fulfill those needs. Recreational skaters, whether their interest is in free-style skating, figure skating, ice dancing, pair skating, hockey or speed skating, participate because it is an exciting and challenging activity for them.

AT WHAT AGE SHOULD A CHILD START SKATING?

There isn't any definite answer to this question as all children differ in their ability and their power of concentration. Theoretically, once children can walk firmly, they can start skating. The important thing to keep in mind is the psychological readiness of the children. They must be able to overcome the fear of falling. Surprising as it may seem, skating is a safe sport. The natural elasticity of the ice absorbs much of the force in a fall. Advanced skaters, as well as beginners, have falls and the sooner they can accustom themselves to these falls and the getting-up procedures, the sooner they will be at ease on the ice. The age at which children can reasonably be expected to learn to skate will vary from four to eight years. One is never too old to learn to ice skate. If one has adequate coordination, one can learn to skate. Assuming reasonable motor ability, success depends largely upon confidence.

IS ICE SKATING DIFFICULT TO LEARN?

Recreational skating is like all physical activities; the more proficient one becomes, the greater the degree of enjoyment. There is no instant formula for success. No matter what the age, learning to ice skate can be as frustrating as learning to play golf. If one wants to learn to skate with good technique, lessons are essential. In the case of children, lessons increase the speed with which self-reliance is acquired. This is not necessarily true with adults, but their progress is accelerated. The desire to make steady progress can be satisfied only by skating a minimum of three or four times a week. Skating once a week brings progress, but it is slow as a person is striving to maintain proficiency rather than improve. Learning a new skill is not as important as is the ability to maintain balance while skating. If, for a person, learning means to be able to skate nicely around the rink, then that person has reached

Fig. 60.2 The more proficient one be-comes, the greater the degree of enjoy-ment. Courtesy of *JOPER*.

his or her goal; but there are very few skaters who want to stop at this point. Further progress depends on the following:

- [ ] Physical aptitude
- [ ] Type of equipment used
- [ ] Amount of time devoted to practice
- [ ] Instruction and its quality
- [ ] Desire on the skater's part

SELECTION OF EQUIPMENT

Since one's ability to skate depends completely on the skates one is wearing, skates are undoubtedly the most important equipment for hockey players, figure skaters, speed skaters, and even recreational skaters. The quality and fit of the skate are directly related to proper skating technique.

Good skates are expensive but, if at all possible, the best skates should be purchased. However, if this is not possible, there are many types of skates at a lower price range which are satisfactory. When purchasing skates, the buyer must insist upon correct size and proper fit. Proper skate size and shoe size do not necessarily correlate. Usually skate boots will be a half size to a whole size smaller than walking shoes.

The only way one can check the fit of a pair of skates is to try them on. The key to a proper fit is snugness. Therefore, if the skates are close to the correct size, it may be necessary to force them on. Only one pair of socks should be worn. Anything more will cancel out any support that a skate gives by putting too much padding between the skate boot and the foot. When lacing the skate up, tap the heel of the foot snugly into the slot before standing up. There should be at least 1–1½″ over the instep between the eyelets on opposite sides of the skate boot. This will provide maximum support through the lacing, which should be tight, especially in the top four or five eyelets over the ankle joint. With the skates tightened in this manner, the heel of the foot back into the slot of the boot, the toes all the way to the front of the boot, and no wrinkles from the instep back to the heel, the skate should fit properly.

There is really no such thing as weak ankles, in the opinion of the author. If the skates fit and provide good ankle support, it is surprising how weak ankles disappear. Lack of strength in ankles is usually due either to poor skates or an inadequate fit.

Young children, whose feet are still growing, will probably need a new pair of skates each year. This may represent a large expenditure, but if children are to improve their skating ability and progress, this is necessary. It is a poor idea to buy skates two or three sizes too large. A child wearing skates which are too large will develop poor technique and, as a result, will not enjoy skating.

SOME POINTS TO REMEMBER

☐ Proper equipment—good skates aid in developing good skaters.

☐ Good posture—feet should be shoulderwidth apart with back straight for good balance.

☐ Knees bent—provides for greater leg strength in skating stroke.

☐ Push from edges—use blade edges by toeing out when stroking forward.

☐ Head up—don't watch your feet, look where you're going.

☐ Be relaxed—there is no such thing as a stiff skater.

REFERENCES

Button, D. 1964. *Instant skating.* New York: Grosset and Dunlap.

Ogilvie, R. S. 1968. *Basic ice skating skills.* Philadelphia/New York: J. B. Lippincott.

Owen, M. V. 1960. *Figure skating: a primer of the art–sport.* New York: Harper & Row.

Proctor, M. 1969. *Figure skating.* Dubuque, Iowa: Wm. C. Brown.

Richardson, T. D. 1962. *The art of figure skating.* New York: A. S. Barnes.

Van der Weyden, E. 1957. *Instructions to young skaters.* London: Museum Press.

Ice Skating Instructional Programs*

K. J. Wolf

The Health and Physical Education Department of Queens College has developed off-campus courses for the past two years, including bowling and skiing. This past year the Department also included ice skating. The course was conducted at the New York City Building on the site of the World's Fair grounds. The facility, an indoor rink, was used for public skating under the direction of the New York City Department of Parks.

Administration and departmental representatives approached the Commissioner of Parks expressing the desire to use the ice rink for Queens College classes. Permission was granted and the rental fee for the year was paid.

Since this was the first experience of this type with the Department of Parks, it became necessary to place a few additional restrictions on the students. Aside from following already existing rink rules, the regulations pertaining to safety, the correct entrance and exit to be used, and the proper areas for parking were stressed. The city made it possible to use their sound system, and Queens College furnished records and tapes.

In order to use a facility of this type, it was necessary to program the rink for the off hours. The college uses the rink from 8:00 A.M. to 12 noon on Monday, Wednesday, and Friday. Two sections are offered—8:00 to 9:30 on Monday and Wednesday and 9:30 to 11:00 on Wednesday and Friday.

At the first meeting of the class car pools were arranged for the return of students to campus after the early class. Car pools were also used to and from the rink for the second class. Arrangements are being made to use a shuttle bus in the future.

Students enrolled in the class supplied their own skates; this ensured the proper fit. It was suggested that students purchase inexpensive skates initially; if they enjoy skating, a better quality could be purchased later.

The instructor should have the ability to demonstrate figure, hockey, and speed skating. The blade of each skate type is different, and the use of the

---

* Reprinted by permission from *JOHPER* **39,** 9, (November–December), 1968, pp. 75–76.

edges for each skate has a definite purpose and should be taught separately. All skates should be taken to a skate shop for sharpening to assure the proper edge. Racing, hockey, and most figure skates have stainless steel blades. The blades of some figure skates are made of white metal. This type figure skate should not be purchased, since the edge will not last for any length of time. The edge on the skate is part of the key to proficient skating.

The correct shoe fit will aid those with weak ankles. Instructors should spend time explaining the process of lacing skates so they will fit properly. The laces should be pulled tight from toe to top lace, especially at the ankles where the shoe bends.

Another factor to be considered is the type and number of pairs of socks to wear. Regular street socks or one pair of thermal socks is all that is needed to keep the feet warm. Emphasize that many pairs of socks will not keep you warm. In fact, they will cause the feet to perspire. This moisture actually causes the feet to cool. Perspiration will accumulate, and the feet may possibly freeze.

It is also not necessary to wear excessive clothing while teaching or for the students to do so while skating. This will hinder movement, and surprisingly, the body gets cold much faster. Shirt, tie, and sports jacket is a typical costume for teaching. For speed skating, a nylon jacket is more comfortable for easy movement.

On figure skates, the instructor should develop a course of study bringing the beginners to the stage of skating forward followed by backward, doing crossovers, and, where possible, three turns. For the advanced students, the goal should be set for spins, jump turns, dance routines, and combination routines. The degree of difficulty depends on each student's ability and rate of progression.

With the speed skaters, the fundamentals of conditioning must be stressed along with the proper method of cutting corners. The correct use of the skate edge for balance and the power pushing necessary for short bursts of speed must be included.

The popularity of this sport has drawn many students. In the second semester class numbers increased from 40 to 70 per class. This increase was accommodated by the addition of another teacher. By doing this it was possible to instruct two teaching stations during the same class period.

As the classes progressed, it was necessary to set aside a definite time and day for teaching speed skating to allow the teacher to orient himself from figure skates to racing skates. Valuable teaching time is lost when the adjustment is done during the same teaching days. One class per week should be for speed skating and one for figure skating.

Where possible, it is advisable to have three different sections—one for beginners, one for advanced figure skating, and another for speed skating. In this manner one instructor can teach all three levels in a given class.

Classes were conducted on an informal basis and started with the instructor presenting and demonstrating the lesson for the day. The students asked questions and then went to separate places on the rink to practice on their own, each at his own pace of learning. Because some students learn a new skill much quicker and are ready to progress, the instructor must know the mechanics of each skill to be taught. This method of mechanical breakdown can be used for correcting students as they experiment with new steps.

A survey was made of the area surrounding New York City to determine where ice rinks existed. In discussions with either the owner and/or manager of privately owned rinks and the superintendent of the municipality or state operated rinks, it was apparent that they would welcome schools or colleges to use their facilities during off hours. They felt that use of these facilities under a program similar to that at Queens College allowed for more people to develop an interest in skating, as well as making use of the rinks when they were normally empty. When working with a private company, the manager should be contacted to make all arrangements. The municipally or state operated rinks have either a local commissioner of recreation or a state assistant commissioner in a county office who should be contacted. The fee will depend on the number of hours the facilities are to be used and the operating costs. It is recommended that an arena be rented on a two-year basis with a renewal option to guarantee that no other school or agency will be using the facility at the same time.

61
Judo
Ju-Ho Chang

ORIGIN OF JUDO

The origin of judo is not thoroughly established. Many historians and judokas believe that origin of the oriental "martial arts" was China. In ancient China during the Chou Dynasty (1122–256 B.C.) physical education was greatly emphasized. "Six art" Chinese self-defense was the important part of their program (Wu 1967, pp. 32–33).

Je-Hwang Lee (1969, pp. 91–94), author of the *Spirit of Yudo* (Judo), said the uniform of Korean yudo has its origin in the period of the Triple

Kingdom (108 B.C.–A.D. 935) especially in the Silla period. Yudo, in the intrinsic form, began to emerge when the Koryo Dynasty (A.D. 268) established it as its official military art. According to *Muyae-dobo-tongji,* a book of military arts, an annual yudo contest was held in May every year. According to the same book, the contest was conducted in three categories: the use of waist, the use of hands, and the use of feet. In addition to the three ways of using the body, the contest also included 25 other skills as it does today. Yudo as an official military art was kept secret and handed down by word of mouth until the early period of the Lee Dynasty. When the Lee Dynasty seized power, it began to organize yudo in a systematic and scientific manner. During the Hideyoshi Invasions in the year of Imjin (1592), Korean yudo was brought to Japan along with the cultural institution (Lee 1969).

> According to the book of *Illustrated Kodokan Judo,* judo of today is based on the traditional jujitsu, or Jujutsu of old Japan. The origin of jujitsu is lost in mists of antiquity. *The Chronicle of Japan,* a history compiled by Imperial Command in A.D. 720 refers to a tournament of Chikara-Kurabe, a contest of strength held in the seventh year of the Emperor Suinin, 230 B.C.
>
> According to the same book, jujitsu was originally introduced to Japan by a Chinese, named Chen Yuan-ping, approximately in 1644–48, or in 1627 according to the KoKushoji document. (Kotokan Institute 1962, pp. 1–2, 6)

In this brief historical and cultural background, it is really hard to say which is the historically verified birthplace of the ancient form of judo as the origin of this sport.

MODERN HISTORY OF JUDO

Modern judo has its roots in the ancient art form and method of defense called jujitsu. In the latter part of the 19th century, Jigura Kano, founder of modern judo as a form of competitive sports, combined the vigorous physical activity of the rough and tumble jujitsu with a concept of gentleness and self-defense into a new sport form which provided recreation, a feeling of achievement and self-confidence, and a challenge for all in a competitive setting. Kano opened a school in order to pass on to others his new approach to jujitsu (judo) in 1882. The first competition between schools took place in 1886. Thus began the sport we now call judo. The success of Kano's students led to the rise of judo as a replacement for the older jujitsu. By 1911 the sport had become a part of the Japanese school curriculum (Bowen and Kim 1970, pp. 128–132).

Judo in the United States

One of Kano's disciples, Y. Yamashita, brought judo to the United States in 1902 and taught it to the West Pointers. It found its way into some colleges along the west coast in the 1930s. Before Kano's death in 1938 it had spread throughout the world. However, the sport found little favor in the United States prior to World War II. The return of American servicemen from the orient marked the first influx of a large group who had been exposed to the sport and this led to an expanded development (Kim 1969, p. 64).

In late 1949, Henry A. Stone, wrestling and judo coach at the University of California at Berkeley, and other judo leaders of northern California submitted a plan for reorganization so that judo could be practiced as one of the sport events in the AAU. At first, judo was a substructure of National AAU Wrestling. The popularity of judo in the early 1950s made possible the formation of an independent National Judo Committee under the AAU in 1953. There were five yudanshakais: (Central California, Northern California, Southern California, Seattle, and Hawaii) which formed the Amateur Judo Association in 1953. This was later called the Judo Black Belt Federation of the United States, or the JBBF, and is now known as the United States Judo Federation (USJF). The USJF is presently composed of 23 black belt associations.

An agreement between the AAU of the United States and the USJF was made whereby the USJF recognizes the AAU as the sole governing body of all amateur judo contests and exhibitions conducted in the United States. Furthermore, the AAU is the United States representative to the International Judo Federation. The AAU in turn recognizes the USJF as the sole organization within the United States qualified to make belt awards for proficiency in, and understanding of, judo. More than 80,000 judo players are registered with USJF (AAU–USJF 1970, pp. 35–37).

The National Collegiate Judo Association is the governing body for college judo competition and the organization most concerned with the promotion of judo at the college level. Little has been achieved toward the development of competitive judo as a sport within the high school program. The future of judo as a competitive sport in schools appears to lie in the development of competent instructors who can teach and coach at the high school and college level.

The International Judo Federation (IJF) is the world organization for judo. IJF has 92 member countries with five geographical unions: European Judo Union (29), Asian Judo Union (17), Pan-American Judo Union (23), Oceania Judo Union (7) and African and Madagascan Judo Union (16) (IJF 1972a).

PHILOSOPHY OF JUDO

The word *ju* means "flexibility" or "gentleness" and *do* means "way" or "principle." Ancient oriental philosophers such as Lao-tze and Confucius often contrasted the state of being flexible and the state of being rigid; the former was understood as something virtuous, harmonious, and dynamic, while the latter was regarded as a symbol of grudge, aggression, or hostility. They understood physical flexibility or gentleness to be superior to rigidity. And Chinese Emperor Moon-Moo-Wang also compared the principle of gentleness to a willow sprig or sprouting bud with promises of eternal vitality in its growth process.

The surest way to grasp the deeper meaning of the philosophy and principle of judo is to study the written words of its founder, Jigura Kano (IJF 1972b):

> The principle of maximum efficient use of mind and body is the fundamental principle governing all the techniques of judo. But it is also something more. The same principle can be applied to the improvement of the human body, making it strong, healthy and useful, and so constitute physical education. It can also be applied to the improvement of intellectual and moral power, and in this way constitute mental and moral education. It can be applied to the improvement of diet, clothing, housing, social intercourse, and methods of business, thus constituting a study in living. I gave this all-pervading principle the name "judo." So judo, in its fuller sense, is a study and a method of training in mind and body as well as in the regulation of life and affairs. . . . The final aim of judo, therefore, is to inculcate in the mind of man a spirit of respect for the principles of maximum efficiency and mutual welfare and benefit, leading so to practice them that man individually and collectively can attain to his highest state, and at the same time, develop the body and learn the art of attack and defense.

PLAYING AREA AND EQUIPMENT

Practice Hall (Dojo)

The practice hall or main indoor playing area is called dojo, meaning meditation hall. The dojo must be clean and have a solemn atmosphere. In the dojo free exercise (randori), contests, and other functions of judo events such as lectures and clinics are conducted. Just as importantly, the dojo is also used as a place for teaching the philosophical and intellectual aspects of judo. In this way the objective of judo—the most efficient use of both mind and body—can be achieved.

The floor of the dojo should be covered by tatami, judo mats, or similar material. The walls should also be covered by panels or mats about shoulder high, and angles of pillars should be padded to prevent any injury.

Judo Attire (Judogi)

The white cotton judo attire shall be worn while practicing or participating in contests. It consists of a jacket, trousers, and belt. The sleeves of the jacket should extend halfway down the forearm to protect the elbow and the trousers should extend to a point slightly below midcalf. The color of the cotton belt indicates the degree of proficiency, or the rank, of its wearer. The belt is worn over the jacket and tied in front in a square knot.

Judo Ranks

Kyu (Beginners) Ranks
6th to 4th Kyu grades—white belt
3rd to 1st Kyu grades—brown belt

Dan (Advanced) Ranks
10th to 9th Dan grades—red belt
8th to 6th Dan grades—red and white belt
5th to 1st Dan grades—black belt

TECHNIQUES OF JUDO

Fundamental Stance

There are six fundamental stances in judo, classified as follows:

Natural stance (Shizentai)
Basic natural stance
Right natural stance
Left natural stance

Defense stance (Jigatai)
Basic defense stance
Right defense stance
Left defense stance

In the natural stance the body is upright and straight, feet spread about twelve inches apart. The shoulders, joints of knees, and lower trunk are relaxed. The arms are held loosely at the side. The natural stance consists of three positions: basic with the feet parallel, right with the right foot about 12 inches forward and left with the left foot forward.

The defense stance is similar to the natural stance except that the legs are wider apart (approximately 30 inches) and the center of gravity of the body is lowered by bending the knees. The defense stance also has the three basic positions: with the feet parallel, and with one or the other foot advanced about 26 inches.

Breaking the Stance and Balance (Kuzushi)

In judo, to throw an opponent who is standing in the natural or defense stance is almost impossible. First one must break the opponent's stance or balance. This is done by pushing or pulling in different directions until the opponent is off balance. This method of "off-balancing" is called kuzushi. It is an indispensable element in the techniques of judo.

(a)

(b)

(c)

Fig. 61.1 (a) Tsukuri, (b) foot and technique, and (c) costumes (judogi). Courtesy of *JOPER*.

There are eight different directions in which kuzushi can be applied using the basic natural stance. They are front, back, right or left side, rear oblique right or left side, and front oblique right or left.

After kuzushi is accomplished, you then move in or "fit in" very swiftly for the throw. This is called tsukuri. After you have made a good tsukuri, you then throw (kake). Kake (meaning attack) is the final stage of the throw. These three movements should be executed in one smooth act to complete the technique of the judo throw.

Breakfall Techniques (Ukemi)

Falling (ukemi) is the most important basic skill which you have to learn before practicing free exercise in judo. Ukemi is a reflex action which enables you to land safely when you are thrown. Ukemi is also a protective technique to avoid shock or injury from violent impact against the mat when you are thrown down by your opponent.

There are five kinds of basic breakfall: falling forward and backward, to the right and left side, and a forward somersault fall.

The Throwing Techniques (Nagewaza)

The throwing techniques enable one to throw an opponent to the mat by breaking his stance or balance. There are about fifty basic throws and innumerable variations of each. Generally nagewaza is divided into two major groups: (1) the art of throwing in standing position (tachiwaza) and (2) the art of throwing in a lying position (sutemiwaza). The art of throwing in a standing position is further subdivided into three sections. They are (1) the hand technique, (2) the hip technique, and (3) the foot and leg technique. The art of throwing in a lying position is subdivided into two sections: (1) throwing with one's back on the ground and (2) throwing with one's side on the ground.

The Grappling Techniques (Kotame-Waza)

The grappling techniques enable one to pin down an opponent, to choke him, to bend or twist the joints of his arms or legs so as to cause him pain and thus disable him. They are generally divided into three groups: the art of holding (osaekomi-waza), the art of choking (shime-waza), and the art of bending and twisting the joint (kansetsu-waza).

The Art of Attacking Vital Points in the Body (Ate-Waza)

These techniques are taught only to advanced judoka because of the dangerous nature of the skills. Most of the vital points of the body are the target points for hitting, chopping or kicking with the fists, fingers, knife edge of hand, elbow, ball of foot, and heel.

METHODS OF PRACTICE

Practicing throws (uehikomi). Uehikomi involves practicing the throw without actually throwing or releasing the opponent. Many repetitions of maneuvers are required to attain perfection and speed in technique.

Free practice (randori). In free practice two judokas take turns throwing each other. This method should be introduced after the student has learned the falling method satisfactorily. The randori practice is done in a spirit of cooperation and is only practice, not actual competition.

Forms (katas) of judo. Forms of judo are other methods of practicing skills in judo. Form (kata) is a system of fundamental techniques. The emphasis in this method is on understanding and practicing correctness of technique. All the forms are executed in a formal manner and often used in demonstrations. There are five kinds of forms in general practice. They are forms of (1) throwing (nageno-kata), (2) grappling (katameno-kata), (3) gentleness (ju-no-kata), (4) counterthrowing, and (5) self-defense (kimeno-kata).

THE CONTESTS (SHIAI)

Contest area. The contest mat area should be 10m × 10m or about 30 × 30 feet (50 tatami mats) and must be indicated by a red band parallel to the four sides of the contest area. Also the area must be mounted on a resilient platform.

Length of contest. The time limit of the bouts is set before the contest begins. It is usually between three to ten minutes but could extend to twenty minutes.

Start of contest. Contests of judo are generally held between judoka of the same rank (dan or kyu) but they are confined to people in certain age groups and weight divisions. The contest must always start with both contestants in a standing position approximately twelve feet apart facing each other with the referee standing midway between them. After salutation, the contest will be started immediately with the command, "Begin," by the referee.

Scoring system. The scoring system is simple since each bout is won by one point, or ippon. Ippon is scored by a well-executed forceful clean throw, a hold down lasting thirty seconds, or lock or choke in which loser signifies defeat by tapping out.

Sometimes a competitor may be judged victorious on the basis of a half point or even on superiority of skill and good judo attitude.

Referee and judges. One referee is on the contest mat at all times and two assistant judges are at the corners of the mat.

REFERENCES

AAU–USJF 1970. *Official judo handbook.* National AAU Judo Committee, United States Judo Federation.

Bowen, R. T., and D. S. Kim 1970. A new role for an ancient art. Detroit: AAU–USJF Official Judo Handbook by USJF.

IJF 1972a. *Contest rules of the International Judo Federation.* London: Purbrook and Eyres.

IJF 1972b. *Handbook of the International Judo Federation.* London: Purbrook and Eyres.

Kim, D. 1969. *Judo.* Dubuque, Iowa: Wm. C. Brown.

Kotokan Institute 1962. *Illustrated Kotokan judo,* Tokyo: Dai Nippon.

Lee, J-H. 1969. *The spirit of yudo.* Seoul, Korea: Kyo-Mun.

Mifune, K. 1962. *Canon of judo principle and technique.* Tokyo: Seibundo-Shinkosha.

Wu, W-C. 1967. *The history of physical education in the last hundred years in China.* Taipei, Taiwan: Commercial Press.

62

Karate

Tchang-Bok Chung

INTRODUCTION AND HISTORY

Karate is the most vigorous of the methods of weaponless self-defense known. It is a complex art which has always addressed itself to the simultaneous development of mind, body, and spirit. More recently, it has become for many a sport. The origins of karate show it to have been a system of self-defense which relied on precise techniques of a highly disciplined body to block or thwart an attack and to defensively counterattack the aggressor by punching, striking, or kicking.

Inspired by the popularity of such TV series as "Kung Fu" and accompanied by the new-found desire of many Americans to be prepared to defend themselves, karate today enjoys a new surge of interest. It is becoming increasingly popular not only on television programs and in motion pictures but in schools and colleges as well. According to Hennessy, a prominent publisher in the martial arts field, the United States in 1975 could boast about 164,800 karate and Kung Fu *dojos* (schools, studios, or training halls).

Fighting as an art has probably existed as long as human history. It originated with the need for self-defense, for survival, not in any one country but instead as a natural development in many different areas. It was influenced in its development of hundreds of styles over the ages by local characteristics of culture, environment, and physiology. According to the most popular legend, the Indian Zen priest Dahlma is credited with its birth, having introduced it in A.D. 517 to China. By the 16th century a Buddhist named Chuehyuan mastered the 18 lo-han movements that had originated with the five original frolicking exercises under the monk Hung-yun in the Shao-lin Monastery. Later he expanded the 18 movements to 72, and further expanded them, with the great masters Pai Yu-feng and Li in the Lo-yang Monastery, to include 170 exercises to be divided into five different sets under the names of "dragon," "tiger," "leopard," "snake," and "crane." This is an origin of what today is known as Kung Fu.

From China karate found its way to Okinawa and subsequently was modified and developed into many styles. There were two distinct schools which contributed to the martial arts in China: one was the Sou Rym Temple School which originated and developed in the south, and the other was the Chang Sam Bong School which grew and developed in the north. The art of the Sou Rym Temple School was characterized by active, light, and speedy circulating movements. On the other hand, the Chang Sam Bong School was characterized by stable, heavy, and powerful defensive movements. Later in its development, about 340 years ago, the school of the Sou Rym Temple spread to Okinawa. About 60 years ago, Okinawan karate was systemized and further developed into the present-day Japanese style by Master Gichin Funaloski who was president of the Shotokai, of which he was a founder. The northern Chinese art of the Chang Sam Bong School was introduced through Manchuria to Korea by Grand Master Hwang Kee in 1945. The present Korean style called Tang Soo Do is under the leadership of Grand Master Hwang Kee, president and founder of the Korean school and brotherhood of martial artists called Moo Duk Kwan. Since 1961, many schools of Korean karate have adopted the name Tae Kwon Do and have been organized under the Korean Tae Kwon Do Association.

America was introduced to karate in 1952 by the Japanese master, Masutatsu Oyama. Its popularity here was immediate and was reinforced by the thousands of American soldiers returning home who had studied karate while on duty in Japan, Okinawa, and Korea. A *Black Belt Magazine* survey in 1971 showed that the Korean style predominated in the United States and was used by 51 percent of all practitioners. This was followed by 34 percent as students of the Japanese style, Okinawan 9 percent, and all others 8 percent. A national YMCA karate survey in 1974 showed Korean style 52.9 percent, Japanese style 21.7 percent, Chinese style 12.3 percent, and all others, 13.1 percent.

Karate, in 1972, and Tae Kwon Do, in 1974, became official sports in the Amateur Athletic Union. Since then many experts have been working to make karate more a sport, just as judo is a martial art that has become a sport.

THE GAME

The perfection of techniques is the goal in karate. Karate is practiced in two ways: basic skills and form (*hyung* or *kata*) exercises which permit the individual to practice the techniques alone, and sparring which involves two persons. In contests, to increase the objectivity of evaluations and to further the standardization of achievement levels, judges evaluate on the basis of the following: power control, tension and relaxation, speed and rhythm control, direction of movements, spirit or attitude, power of technique, precision of movements, and intentness. In addition, kata sequence, understanding kata technique, and distinctive features of the kata are essential for a form contest, The size of the match area for sparring is eight meters square (26.1 square feet) and for kata exercises no less than 20 × 20 feet. Wood floors which are flat, smooth, and clean are required.

A sparring match usually lasts two minutes for eliminations and three minutes for finals. In practice, however, there are many variations in tournament rules and regulations, scoring systems, number of judges, qualifications of judges and referees, and even in the duration of a match. A form sequence may consist of as few as twenty predetermined moves for beginners to as many as two hundred for advanced students. The time for completion may therefore vary from 30 seconds to several minutes.

The objective of sparring in the true spirit of the martial arts is to practice defensive and offensive techniques with a partner using basic skills and forms that have become conditioned reflexes. The emphases in sparring practice are:

☐ defense techniques over offense techniques

☐ speed

☐ straight movement over round movement

☐ heavy movement over light movement

☐ long movement over short movement

☐ concentration

☐ hand techniques for upper body attack and foot techniques for lower body attack

☐ low center of gravity over high center of gravity

☐ knowing yourself first and your partner second

☐ keeping your mind from too much concern over winning or losing

☐ using your head, not your emotions

The karate form exercise, Korean *hyung* or Japanese *kata* is an established, clearly defined set of steps, blocks, kicks, and thrusts. Basic forms consist of one block followed by a thrust or strike, and turns patterned to develop control, rhythm, power, and speed. As they progress, the katas become increasingly complex in the variety and sequence of blocks, kicks, thrusts, jumps, and turns. One advanced form may take years of daily practice and intense concentration to master. Perfect form, the exquisite fusion of mind and body, is a high art and a thing of beauty. However, the form is not an end in itself. As an exercise it is that part of the progression in the art which conditions the mind, body, and reflexes for the stresses of free sparring and ultimately the realities of defensive conflict. The sequence of moves may simulate responses to many kinds of attack, strategies for defense against a number of attackers, and the control of one's space in dealing with the direction of attacks. The "form tournament" is a demonstration and judgment before acknowledged masters of individual achievement in the practice of forms. Individual participants declare their level of achievement within their belts or ranks and then compete against their own previous performances in attempting to match the skill of the masters. The declaration of achievement, or choice of form to be performed, is itself a matter for evaluation. Preliminary to success is the student's accuracy of perception in estimating his own level of achievement. The basis for comparison, the criterion of success, is the perfect form which combines precision, control, focused power, speed, rhythm, and concentration. Implicit in the judgments is the evaluation of the quality of schools and instructors—their thoroughness and dedication in preserving and perpetuating the art.

The sport of karate has no season and can be practiced indoors or out, without special equipment.

TERMINOLOGY Korean/Japanese

Basic skill *(ki sul/waza)* A variety of precise stances, blocks, punches, kicks, and combination techniques.

Breaking *(kyok pa/tameshiwari)* A small part of karate, breaking techniques requiring great self-confidence, concentration of mind, body, and spirit, breath control, and speed. Students should learn these techniques under a well-qualified instructor's direction and leadership. Injury results easily if the emphasis is strictly on brute force.

Dan/dan A rank in black belt system.

Do bok/gi A pajama-like uniform which consists of a coat, pants, and belt.

Fig. 62.1 The ability to kick high and hard in all directions is important in karate. Courtesy of the University of Utah.

Do jang/dojo A place where the martial arts are practiced, often called a school, studio, or training hall.

Form *(hyung/kata)* A traditional, well-established, and clearly defined set or sequence of steps, blocks, kicks, and thrusts.

Gup/kyu A rank in the non-black belt system.

Sparring *(dae ryun/kumite)* A method of practicing the various techniques that have been mastered during basic skills and forms exercises with a partner under preplanned, semiplanned, or unplanned conditions.

Various Ranks in Karate

Generally, throughout the world, karate ranks in two systems: the 10 gup/kyu ranks of non-black belts and the dan or black belt ranks. This is the most common practice of color belt rank in this country although the system of colors may vary in different styles.

In the gup/kyu style of karate, ranks are indicated by belts of the following colors: red, from 1st (highest) to 3rd; green, from 4th to 6th; orange, from 7th to 8th; and white, from 9th to 10th (lowest).

In the dan style the ranking is reversed with the 1st rank being lowest and the 8th, highest. All practitioners wear belts of black or midnight blue.

OUTLINE OF KARATE SKILLS

New skills are introduced as students demonstrate their readiness. The idea behind each new skill is explained so that they can understand the rationale and integration of the old and the new.

1. Basic Skills

  a) Stances
      ready   mount
      front   others
      fighting

  b) Blocks
      low   inside to outside
      high   side
      middle   knife hands
      outside to inside   others

  c) Punches
      low   elbow
      middle (See Fig. 62.2) back fist
      high   spear-hand
      side   U-punch
      vertical fist   others

  d) Kicks
      front (See Fig. 62.3) spinning back
      side   jumping front
      roundhouse (See Fig. 62.4) stamping
      back   others
      knee

  e) Combination techniques
      block-punch   kick-punch
      block-kick   others

2. Forms

    basic   advanced
    intermediate

3. Sparring

    basic sparrings   1-step sparrings
    3-step sparrings   free sparring (See Fig. 62.5)

4. Breaking

    wood board breaking   brick breaking

TEACHING TECHNIQUES

There is an orientation for beginners to eliminate misconceptions about karate. Students should learn that karate requires perseverance and discipline, and that it is impossible to expect everybody to like this sport or to be ready for the self-control it requires.

Fig. 62.2 Middle punch.

Fig. 62.3 Front kick.

Fig. 62.4 Roundhouse kick.

Fig. 62.5 Action in free sparring.

Along with dispelling the prospective student's misconception that karate is a belligerent or aggressive activity, the instructor must take the time to explain the logic of the moves and the principles of physics which underlie the forces which can be released. Instructors must therefore be familiar with Newton's laws of motion and the principle of equal and opposite actions and reactions.

It is recommended that the number of individuals in a karate instruction class not exceed fifteen. Classes larger than this, even with a good instructor, result merely in organized exercise without detailed instruction. Karate classes should be scheduled for at least two 90-minute periods a week. Each period should include warm-up exercises, basic skills exercises, lesson plan activities, wrap-up, and meditation.

The principles in basic skills practice are:

☐ Strong and well-executed techniques of both defense and offense depend on a balanced and stable stance to a large extent.

☐ The center of gravity is to be kept as low as possible to establish a more stable state of equilibrium.

☐ All muscles of the body become focused and concentrated at the moment of impact.

☐ The fist and feet move directly toward target in the shortest distance at the fastest speed.

☐ A sharp breath is exhaled at the instant of execution of the movement and is inhaled as soon as completing it.

☐ The abdominal muscles are tensed at the moment of impact.

☐ The eyes and mind are kept on the target always, even though it may be imaginary.

Each student is evaluated for promotion at the end of each term (most commonly in the United States a term is three months). All students are informed after a pretest about what they excel in or about what skills they should practice. The basic element in evaluation should be skill performance. In addition to the evaluation of skill performance, other elements that must be considered are accuracy of self-evaluation, physical proficiency, emotional development, social adjustment, improvement in performance, and effort. For higher rank, it is common practice to require teaching experience in addition to time in rank.

Following is the system for gup promotions developed by the YMCA National Ad Hoc Committee on Karate, Tchang-Bok Chung, Westfield, New Jersey, Chairman. Different styles or schools of karate have developed achievement levels which are less demanding, some which are more demanding. For terminology and detailed descriptions of moves, forms, and sparring the reader is referred to the definitive works of Kee Hwang (1970) and Masatatsu Oyama (1967).

Skills to Be Completed for Promotion

10th Gup (all beginners)

Stance:	1. ready	2. mount	3. front
Block:	1. low	2. high	3. middle a) from outside b) from inside
Attack:	1. low	2. high	3. middle
Kick:	1. front	2. side	3. roundhouse

9th Gup

Stance:	1. fighting		
Block:	1. low X-block	2. side	
Attack:	1. vertical-fist	2. side	3. elbow strikes
Kick:	1. back	2. knee	
Form:	1. basic form 1		

8th Gup

Combination techniques:

low block-reverse punch	front kick-lunge punch
high block-reverse punch	front kick-reverse punch
low block-front kick	low block-high block-middle punch
high block-front kick	low block-reverse punch-front kick

Kick:	1. jumping front kick	2. stamping kick	
Form:	1. basic form 2		
Sparring:	1. basic sparring		

7th Gup

Block:	1. low knife hands	2. middle knife hands	3. two-fist middle
Attack:	1. high attack with knife hand	2. spear-hand straight thrust	
Kick:	1. jumping side kick	2. jumping roundhouse	
Form:	1. basic form 3		
Sparring:	1. 3-step sparring		

6th Gup

Attack:	1. close punch	2. U-punch	3. back-fist
Kick:	1. spinning back	2. jumping back	
Form:	1. pyung-ahn form 1		
Sparring:	1. 1-step sparring		

5th Gup

Form:	1. pyung-ahn form 2	
Sparring:	1. 1-step sparring	2. free sparring

4th Gup

Form:	1. pyung-ahn form 3	
Sparring:	1. 1-step sparring	2. free sparring

3rd Gup

Form:	1. pyung-ahn form 4	
Sparring:	1. 1-step sparring	2. free sparring

2nd Gup

Form:	1. pyung-ahn form 5	
Sparring:	1. 1-step sparring	2. free sparring

1st Gup

Form:	1. pyung-ahn form 5	2. bassai form	
Sparring:	1. 1-step sparring	2. free sparring	3. sparring against two opponents

ETHICS AND ETIQUETTE

Karate is mental and moral exercise as well as excellent all-round physical exercise. There is a concerted effort to unite mind, spirit, and body in exercise. A translation of the charter of Moo Duk Kwan, a leading Korean Karate Association, presents this philosophy:

> Reverence for life is as important as offense and defense within the Moo Duk Kwan. Our basic charter charges all members to protect life, even that of an enemy. Developing reverence for nature, with emphasis on Beauty, Speed, and Rightness of Action, is a training goal held forth by the charter.

The Japan Karate Association also emphasizes character-building aspects, in which respect for one's opponents or sportsmanship is the cardinal principle. The moral and ethical aspects of the art are summarized in the karate students' code adopted by the Westfield YMCA Martial Arts Committee.

The karate student:

☐ Speaks courteously and acts considerately.

☐ Does not bully or boast.

☐ Does not criticize other martial arts styles.

☐ Competes only against his own previous performance.

☐ Promotes nonviolence.

☐ Bows to show his respect for skill and his belief in the perfection of form.

☐ Learns concentration through silent meditation before and after practice.

☐ Learns self-control in precision noncontact sparring.

☐ Accepts karate's challenge and discipline as a way to self-knowledge.

☐ Applies the principle of focused power in his daily life.

Karate is seen as contributing to the well-rounded development of all its practitioners as responsible citizens in oriental countries as well as in the United States. The discipline of karate helps students learn self-control and builds confidence in youngsters who are reluctant to defend themselves. Moreover, boys who enjoy rough and tumble sports find in noncontact sparring a way to release aggressive feelings in a socially approved activity.

RESEARCH

Chung concluded in his study, "Mechanical Analysis of Forefist Straight Punch in Karate," that the force is inversely proportional to the square of time taken by the motion. In other words, for a given weight and length of arm, the force exerted in 0.05 second is four times greater than the force exerted in 0.1 second. The force exerted in the technique with twisting waist is six times greater than the force exerted in the technique without twisting waist.

Lerch's case study identified the personal construct system of an adult male beginning karate student at the University of Florida and evaluated changes in his construct relationships after karate instruction using the Repertory Grid. After ten weeks of instruction the following major changes in the subject took place:

1. He experienced greater self-confidence in being able to physically defend himself.

2. His identity with what he considered to be a masculine sport challenged him to become "mentally purged" during workouts which, once completed, fostered a sense of relaxation.

3. The type of activity and atmosphere enabled him to leave his personal problems outside the training room.

4. The subject's self-concept and ideal self-concept emphasized the unique and complex response of an individual engaged in an activity.

REFERENCES

Chung, T-B. Should judo-karate programs be put on the same level as YMCA competitive swimming? *J. Phys. Ed.* **71**, 2: 36.

Dreika, P. 1975. Karate: Open hand . . . open question. *Family Safety* **34**, 2: 12–13.

Hu, W. C. 1974. Will the five animals of Kung-Fu please stand up? *Black Belt* (May): 60–62.

Hwang, K. 1970. *Soo bahk do (tang soo do) dae kam.* Seoul, Korea: Sam Kwang.

———— 1971. *Introduction to moo duk kwan.* Seoul, Korea: Korean Soo Bahk Do.

Kim, D., and T. Leland 1971. *Karate and personal defense.* Dubuque: Wm. C. Brown.

Lerch, H. A. 1973. An analysis of the personal constructs of a beginning karate-ka using the repertory grid. *J. Phys. Ed.* **70**, 6: 135–136.

Nishiyama, H., and R. C. Brown 1969. *Karate: the art of "empty hand" fighting.* Tokyo: Charles E. Tuttle.

Oyama, M. 1967. *Advanced karate.* Tokyo: Japan Publication Trading Co.

Uyehara, M. 1972. Karate hits an all-time record. *Black Belt,* (October): 74–78.

Westfield YMCA Martial Arts Committee 1974. *Karate form championships.* Westfield, N.J.: The YMCA.

63

Orienteering

Howard G. Knuttgen

Orienteering is a sport activity based on topographical map reading ability and consisting of progression on foot to predetermined control points. The heart of orienteering is the process of route selection and the ability to progress through forest terrain with a confidence in one's geographic location at all times.

There are a number of different forms of participation which permit persons to engage in the sport for pure recreation or on a wide variety of levels of competition. Persons of all ages and skill levels can participate and, because of the virtual absence of required equipment, they can participate at minimal expense.

The most common form of orienteering involves a person reporting to a starting area and receiving a topographical map together with certain basic instructions regarding the location of control points laid out by a "course setter." The information will take the form of a list of short, written descriptions of each numbered control (e.g., 1. The knoll, south side.) and the location area of each control being designated in color (usually red) as a circle and number superimposed on the map (see Fig. 63.1.). The participant must locate the controls in the order designated by the numbers. Consecutive controls on the map are joined by straight lines printed in the same color as the circles. The standard procedure for confirming the orienteer's successful location of a control is the procedure of "punching in." A plastic punch device is located at each control and is used to perforate with a coded symbol the "control card" that each orienteer carries.

The course map, a list of control descriptions, and a control card are all that a person requires as minimal essentials for orienteering. A compass, however, is virtually essential to all orienteers and is considered to be an integral part of the sport. A plastic map case (available at nominal cost) is usually employed to protect the map from moisture. The orienteering "uniform" a person might select is subject to great variation in personal choice and imagination and will be further discussed under the section on Equipment. In any case, the uniform can very well involve little or no expense.

The choice of route to each new control involves decisions each person must make individually. The need to know one's exact location at all times and to continually match natural features with the corresponding map

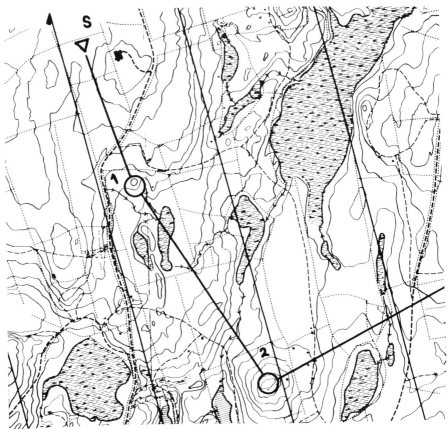

Fig. 63.1 Sample portion of a black and white orienteering map with the locations of the starting area (triangle and S) and the first two controls of a course superimposed on the base map (map section reproduced by permission of the New England Orienteering Club). Control descriptions would be: (1) (CB) the knoll, south side; (2) (LR) top of the hill. CB and LR are the code letters the orienteer would find on the control markers. North/south lines are drawn to magnetic north.

designations requires a high level of mental alertness. When a person develops sufficient map-reading skill to be able to run from one control to the next, the sport then combines high-level challenges both to the mental processes and to the physiological mechanisms enabling large muscle endurance performance, i.e., oxidative energy release and cardiovascular fitness.

HISTORY OF ORIENTEERING

Orienteering had its beginnings in Scandinavia as an exercise for military messengers called upon to traverse unknown terrain. There are records of events involving military messenger competition in Stockholm, Sweden, in 1893, and in Bergen, Norway, in 1897. The first recorded nonmilitary competition took place on skis as a relay event between the towns of Bollnäs and Härnösand, Sweden, in 1900. This same year saw a competitive event take place in Oslo, Norway, where the term "orienteering" was employed for the first time.

Participation in orienteering in both Sweden and Norway was limited and sporadic during the early 1900s although certain events were conducted with an impressive number of participants. For example, over 200 competitors took part in a meet held outside Stockholm in March, 1919. International competition probably had its origin when a team representing Sweden met a Norwegian team in an event held in 1932 outside Oslo.

It was in the early 1930s that an equipment innovation occurred in Sweden that had a great impact on orienteering's future. The Kjellström brothers, Björn and Alvar, together with Gunnar Tillander, developed a simple, one-piece protractor compass. Now available in a variety of models, this basic "orienteering compass" facilitated the operation of establishing direction of route, particularly while walking or running.

Other significant dates in the history of orienteering include the first national championship competition in Sweden in 1935 and in Norway in 1937. The year 1938 saw the establishment of the first national organization in Sweden (*Svenska Orienteringsförbundet*) and of regular national team competition among Sweden, Norway, and Finland. Of particular note is the inclusion of orienteering as a mandatory subject in the Swedish schools since the year 1942.

Since the 1930s, orienteering has grown rapidly and attained a high degree of popularity in all of the Nordic countries. As of 1976, active orienteers numbered approximately 65,000 in Sweden, 35,000 in Finland, 25,000 in Norway, and 10,000 in Denmark. A 100-kilometer relay race run annually in Sweden (the "Tio Mila") attracted 387 ten-man teams in 1975. An international five-day event (called "O-ringen") also held in Sweden on an annual basis attracts over 10,000 participants from approximately 30 countries.

Orienteering was introduced to North America in the mid 1940s. In 1946, Björn Kjellström held a demonstration meet at Indiana Dunes State Park. In 1948, meets were held in both Montreal and Toronto. Activity in each country resulted in the formation of the Canadian Orienteering Federation in 1967 and the United States Orienteering Federation in 1971. The first Canadian national championship meet was held in Gatineau Park outside Ottawa in 1968 while the first United States championships were hosted by Southern Illinois University in Carbondale in 1970. In 1971, the first North American championships were held at Quantico, Virginia, with the intention of being held every other year with Canada and the United States alternating as hosts. The North American Championships of 1973 were held in Gatineau Park, Ontario, and 1975 at Bear Brook State Park, New Hampshire.

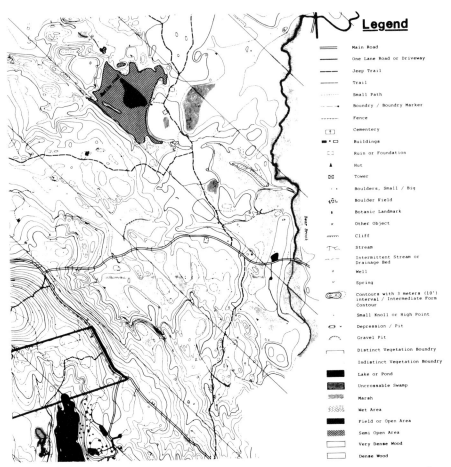

Fig. 63.2 Sample portion of an orienteering map with legend. The original map is printed in color and has brown contour lines. Blue indicates water; brown shading, fields and open areas; green shading, dense woods; white areas, easily traversable forest; and black, roads and various symbols for objects. Reproduced by permission of the New England Orienteering Club.

Orienteering has developed rather extensively in Canada. Numerous local clubs have formed and provincial associations now exist throughout the country. The first provincial associations were developed in 1967 in Ontario and Quebec. Competition exists on the local, regional, and national levels. Progress has been less extensive in the United States. Clubs and local competition exist at a variety of locations throughout the country, with the greatest amount of activity found in the mid-Atlantic and Northeastern states. Considerable support has been given through Reserve Officer Training Programs on college and university campuses throughout the country.

Switzerland became the first European country outside of the Nordic group to take up the sport. Organized competition began in that country in 1948. Considerable activity was generated in other European countries as well and, in addition to the formation of national organizations, the International Orienteering Federation was formed in 1961 in Copenhagen by Sweden, Norway, Finland, Denmark, Switzerland, Bulgaria, Czechoslovakia, Hungary, East Germany, and West Germany. The first European Championships were held in Løten, Norway, in 1962. The first World Championships took place in Fiskars, Finland, in 1966 and are held every second year. To the list of ten original member nations of the International Orienteering Federation have been added over a dozen additional nations, including Canada and the United States.

Types of Orienteering

There is a variety of forms of competitive orienteering. In the most common form, a "course setter" will set out a number of controls and the participants will locate and punch in at each control in a designated order before returning to a finish area. A more elaborate description of this type is presented in the section, A Competitive Orienteering Event.

In large competitive events, a number of courses are laid out with varying degrees of difficulty and overall distance. Competitive categories are organized on the basis of both sex and age and courses are designed as appropriate to maturity and skill level. For example, a meet might be organized with women and girls broken down into the following age groups: 14 and under, 15–16, 17–19, 20 and over, and 35 and over. For men and boys the breakdown could be 14 and under, 15–16, 17–19, 20 and over, 40 and over, 50 and over. In each case, the 20 and over group would be considered the championship class and persons eligible for the other groups would be eligible to select this category for competition. Countries where extremely large numbers of persons participate employ greater numbers of age groups involving smaller age ranges as well as A, B, and C categories within the age groupings to further differentiate by skill level.

Score orienteering is a popular variation although it is rather uncommon to other than local competitive events. Controls are laid out with assigned point values, the point value of each control varying in direct proportion to the distance from the area used for starting and finishing. A time limit is usually designated for locating controls and exceeding it results in penalty points. No order is specified for locating the controls so that each competitor chooses a unique route to locate and punch in at the controls chosen in the effort to accumulate the greatest number of points possible within the time limit. Order of finish is calculated on the basis of net points (points earned minus possible penalty points). Score orienteering can be run as an individual event, or, in various forms, as a team event.

Line orienteering is performed with a map on which no controls are indicated. Instead, a route is indicated by a drawn line on the map which each person must follow. If the participants are accurate in following the designated route, they will come upon the controls as they move along. Order of finish is determined by a combination of number of controls located and speed around the course.

While the above constitute the most common forms of orienteering presently employed, additional variations exist and even others will be developed as innovative persons think of ways to use map and compass and nature. For example, other varieties of orienteering include *night orienteering, bicycle orienteering,* and *ski orienteering.* Night orienteering involves the additional features of all participants wearing a special headlamp (or carrying a flashlight) and the control markers consisting of small lamps illuminated by a flashlight battery and bulb. In bicycle orienteering, the participants cycle from control to control. In ski orienteering, they proceed cross country on skis. Bicycle orienteering is conducted where smooth surfaced roads are available with minimal auto traffic. Ski orienteering is characterized by longer legs between controls, longer courses, and placement of controls beside trails.

All forms of orienteering described can be performed as team events and/or relays. Participation by pairs of participants or in small groups can be used advantageously during the first stage of learning orienteering skills.

Rules. The rules and regulations governing competition are simple and straightforward. While progressing from one control to the next, an orienteer may not purposefully follow another participant, may not use vehicles for transport, may not swim across lakes or rivers, and may not cross agricultural growing areas. Participants should not survey or study an area prior to competition. In fact, championship meets are held in areas not previously used

Fig. 63.3 "Go!" Four junior orienteers have been given the starting signal after receiving their maps, control descriptions, and control punch cards. Photo by K. Samuelson, Lidingö, Sweden.

for orienteering. A participant in such a meet does not receive a copy of the newly printed map until the start.

When given the start signal for a standard orienteering event, the participant must take the controls in the designated order. This is a rule that can, under certain circumstances, be violated. It can, however, also be monitored. Failure to adhere to this rule may result in disqualification.

The procedure of punching in at the controls is something that the participant cannot compromise even though no one is present to supervise the punching-in procedure. The key letter, symbol, or number of each punch is not known to the competitor until the control is located and the appropriate box of the control card punched.

When the numbers of participants involved are great, or high-level competition is involved (e.g., district, national, or international championships), more elaborate directives and regulations are obviously required as regards course setting, eligibility, starting order, etc. Such sets of rules and regulations are available from the various national organizations and from the International Orienteering Federation (IOF).

As for the basic procedure of orienteering, a person begins at a designated starting area, locates controls according to the directions for the type of orienteering being conducted, and returns to a designated finish area. It is difficult to find events of other organized competition with rules that are so straightforward and uncomplicated.

The author has found the following guide, prepared for the New England Orienteering Club, to be very helpful in organizing a group for orienteering:

A Beginner's Guide to Getting Started

1. Place the *map, control card,* and *control descriptions* in a plastic map case so that important parts of the map are not covered; e.g., the control card and map can be placed back-to-back.

2. Hold the compass in one hand (the right hand is "handy") and attach the compass string to the wrist. Hold the map in the other hand.

3. Use your compass needle to determine *magnetic north* and face that direction. If the sun is out, note the relation of the sun's position to magnetic north for future reference.

4. Check the compass rose and north arrows on the map and find where magnetic north lies.

5. Determine your present location and compare the features and contours shown on the map with the natural features that surround you.

6. Establish your correct compass bearing to get to Control 1:
   a) Holding the map flat in front of you (or placing it on the ground), align the side of the compass with a line drawn from the starting point

to Control 1 (with the *outside* or *directional arrow* of the compass pointing in the direction you will go on the map!).

b) Keeping the compass in the same position on the map, dial the *inside* or *north arrow* so that it points to magnetic north on the map (you can also align the inner lines of the compass with the magnetic north lines on the map). Make sure the north arrow points to north on the map and not south.

c) Without moving anything else, turn the entire compass so that the north end of the compass needle (red) coincides with the inside or north arrow. The outside or directional arrow now *points the way* to the first control.

7. Place your thumb on the map at your present location (the starting point of the course as indicated by a triangle) and hold the map so the first control is directly ahead; i.e., it is *not* necessary to hold the map so that north is at the top. Fold the map so that you can carry and study it as you proceed.

8. Proceed toward Control 1 with the compass in your right hand showing the direction and the map in your left hand, the thumb placed exactly where you are located.

9. Note the features on the map that should be seen to the left and right as you proceed. Check them as you go along so you are sure of your exact location at all times.

10. Successfully reaching the red and white control marker (we knew you'd make it!): a) make sure the control code on your control description matches the letters on the control marker ("XR") and b) punch your control card in the box marked "1" with the special punch hanging at the control marker.

11. Repeat as in direction 6 above: establish the new compass heading to get from Control 1 to Control 2, locate your location on the map with your thumb, and proceed. Observe the natural features around you as you go and compare with the map. Punch in at Control 2.

12. Complete all the controls in numerical order and return to the Finish (double circle on map). If you lose your way and cannot find a control: a) return to the last control you found and try to determine what went wrong, b) pick up a physical feature you can locate on the map and determine the correct compass heading, or c) ask a friendly orienteer!

A COMPETITIVE ORIENTEERING EVENT

A competitive event can be organized by one or two persons for 50–100 participants or, as is true on the international level, can involve thousands of participants and require hundreds of persons to organize and conduct a local

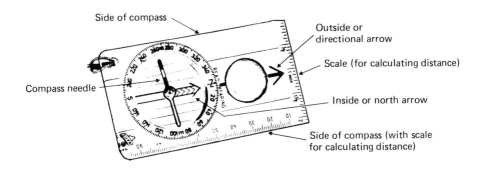

competitive event. A description will be presented of a meet to be organized for approximately 100 participants coming from a small geographic area and representing various ages and skill levels. For such a "local meet," the international classification system for age and sex will not be employed. Instead, we will describe a meet where four courses will be laid out and identified by color. The lengths and numbers of controls for the courses are variable and optional and those specified below are presented as appropriate examples.

White Course

Length: 1:5 km
Number of controls: 5
Designed for beginners

Yellow Course

Length: 3:0 km
Number of controls: 7
Designed for advanced beginners

Orange Course

Length: 5.0 km
Number of controls: 9
Designed for persons with such orienteering experience, map-reading skill, and compass facility that they have had success on "Yellow" courses in previous meets

Red Course

Length: 7.5 km
Number of controls: 11
For experienced orienteers only

The "meet director" must first either secure or make a map of good quality regarding accuracy, detail, and clarity. The map must be reproduced in sufficient quantity to meet the demands of the expected registration. Some weeks ahead, the meet director must secure permission to use the area and begin planning the courses. Course planning includes a study of the map for potential control locations as well as field checking. The latter involves covering the courses on foot to evaluate the suitability of each location and to confirm the accuracy of the map. Strips of surveyor's tape are often employed to designate the points at which control markers might eventually be hung.

When the four courses have been laid out and all control points determined, the meet director will then either prepare master maps for each course or print the courses onto maps to be distributed to the participants. If master maps are used, a participant will copy the course onto his or her map, usually after the start signal has been given. Printing involves superimposing a course (usually in light red) with the aid of a special printing device on the topographical maps to be used by the participants.

As a final step in this phase of the meet director's preparation, control description lists will be prepared for each course in sufficient quantity that each participant will have a listing of the following information for each control on a particular course: the numerical order designation, the code identification found on the control flag (letters or numbers), and a brief description of the location of the control, e.g., the stream junction, top of the hill, south edge of the marsh. The control description list is given to each participant at the time of registration and is carried along with the map while following the course.

Other considerations for the meet director are the locations and organization of a registration area, a start area, and a finish area. Additionally, an adequate number of helpers must be recruited to carry out the registration procedures, the timing, and the recording of results.

Preregistration is usually not necessary for local meets and, therefore, all a participant need do is to report to the registration area during the time period previously announced for registration and starting. Registration will involve signing in (and usually payment of a nominal participation fee), selection of an appropriate course, receipt of a copy of the map, the control descriptions for the course selected, and the control punch card (usually available in the color of the course selected). The control card will have a main portion where the participant's name and starting time will be recorded as well as numbered squares to be used for punching in at the various control points. The remaining portion (or stub) of the card will also have a place for the name of the participant and a box for eventually recording elapsed time. The stub is torn off and retained at the registration table and transferred to the finish area while the person is out on the course.

Each participant will be given a starting time either at the registration table or at the starting area. The starting area is usually located at some distance from the registration area, especially if a large number of participants is expected.

Fig. 63.4 A junior competitor punches in at a control (identified by the code number 84 on the marker) and begins to plot the route to the next control. Photo by K. Samuelson, Lidingö, Sweden.

Fig. 63.5 Competitive orienteering demands a high level of cardiovascular fitness. With map case in one hand and compass in the other, an elite competitor presses on to the next control attempting to save precious seconds along the way. Photo by L. Månsson of Bildbyrån, Hässleholm, Sweden.

At the starting area, each participant is given sufficient warning before the signal to begin the course is given. If the course has been printed on the map, the participant immediately sets out for the first control. If not, the participant must copy the course from a master map (usually after the start signal has been given). Persons going out on different courses can start simultaneously but those on the same course will start with intervening time intervals so as to diminish the chances of participants progressing together within visual contact range.

To select a route to each control, each participant must determine his or her exact location on the map and make the decision whether to follow trails, go directly cross country, or embark on some variation. Good orienteering courses are designed to challenge the participant with options. For the less experienced orienteer, selection of a route involves establishing direction with the compass, estimating distances with the aid of the map scale, and pace counting. The latter is usually accomplished by counting every other stride and knowing the relationship between such double-strides and the actual distance for a particular speed; e.g., at a fast run a person may take 40 double-strides each 100 meters. As it is very important to know where one is located on the map at all times, the participant will be constantly checking natural features such as trails, knolls, streams, and hills with the features indicated on the map. Very often, certain features along the way will be selected as informal checkpoints by the participant along the route to a control. If such a feature located in the vicinity of a control is employed for a final directional and distance determination, it is referred to as an "attack point" for the control.

A control marker consists of a small, three-sided flag (presently red and white in color; see Fig. 63.4) hanging from a branch, small tree, bush, or constructed wooden support. Hanging together with the marker will be a plastic punch device that contains small teeth that perforate the person's control card with a number, letter, or symbol. On locating the first control, the person will punch in on box 1 of the control card to give evidence of having located the control. The route to the next control is then selected, distances are checked, and the compass is reset.

Under competitive circumstances, route selection is of great importance. Decisions must be made with great speed so that time is conserved. Route selections must be amended if the terrain turns out to be different from that expected from reading the map. Trail running is usually much faster than heading cross country through woodlands. However, the available trails might involve much greater distances than the direct route or involve excessive changes in elevation so that the increase in fatigue and elapsed time will make a more direct compass route preferable.

If after embarking on a direct, cross-country route a person finds the progression impeded by dense undergrowth, fallen logs, or uneven terrain, an alternative plan that preferably does not involve backtracking must be adopted

Fig. 63.6 Large events demand a great amount of organization. For this international meet, five finish points are located at the end of five chutes to better handle the thousands of competitors as they return from a variety of courses. The courses are laid out on the basis of competitive categories as designated by age level, sex, and degree of proficiency. Photo by K. Samuelson, Lidingö, Sweden.

on the spot. Similar demands for route revision can result when other hindrances (such as marshy areas or unfordable streams) appear unexpectedly or when obviously easier terrain appears to the side of a chosen route. Major errors (e.g., getting lost!) will require reestablishment of location and designation of a new plan so as to get back on course.

In any case, the participant must locate each control in the numerical order designated, punch the appropriate box at each control and, finally, return to the finish area as designated on the map by two concentric circles. As the participant crosses the finish line, a finish judge will record the time and note this on the person's control card. Elapsed time will be calculated and recorded on both the control card and the stub. The stub is usually used by the meet organizers to post the results for each competitive course.

TERMINOLOGY

The following is a listing of terms commonly employed in orienteering as either a recreational or competitive sport:

Aiming off To deliberately choose a route that will lead to a predetermined side of a checkpoint or control for the purpose of coming on a prominent natural feature that leads directly to the control.

Attack point A natural feature located in the vicinity of a control from which an orienteer will take a final bearing and make the approach on the control.

Checkpoint A natural feature along the route chosen to a control used by the orienteer to confirm location and successful progression. The term can also be used as a synonym for control.

Control A natural feature chosen by the course setter to be located by the participants in an event.

Control marker A small, three-sided flag which is hung at a control point. At present flags are red and white but will, in the future, be orange and white.

Course A series of controls laid out by a course setter each of which must be located by the participants in numerical order.

Handrail A linear feature such as a path, stream, or ridge that an orienteer can follow to assure accurate progression along a route.

Leg The section of a course between consecutive controls.

Magnetic north (compass north) The direction indicated by the northseeking portion of a magnetic needle as being the magnetic pole of the earth located in the northern hemisphere.

Map scale The relationship between distance on the map and actual geographic distance. The most commonly employed scales are 1 : 10,000; 1 : 15,-

000; 1 : 16,667; 1 : 20,000; and 1 : 24,000. For a scale of 1 : 10,000 each mm on the map is equal to 10m and for 1 : 20,000 each mm is equal to 20m across the earth's surface.

Miss a control To fail to find a control on the first attempt.

Pace counting The practice of counting strides to keep track of distance covered.

Precision compass The determination of an exact compass bearing which is then followed with little regard for changes in the terrain or the occurrence of natural features.

Reading by thumb The practice of folding the map so that the thumb can move along the map in direct relationship to a person's progress; i.e., the thumb always indicates on the map the person's exact location.

Rough compass The following of an approximate bearing; usually includes adapting the line of progression to take advantage of easier terrain, less dense undergrowth, etc.

Run by needle The practice of approximating the appropriate direction by quick orientation to compass north and, therefore, without going through the steps of setting a bearing with the aid of map and compass.

Spike a control To arrive perfectly at a control on the first approach.

Take a bearing The procedure by which an orienteering compass and a map are used to determine a precise compass direction. The procedure results in the directional arrow on the compass housing pointing to the desired route direction.

Topographic map A map on which natural contours are shown by lines which join portions of the earth surface having identical, predetermined levels of altitude and various natural or man-made features (lakes, streams, paths, buildings, etc.) are indicated by specific symbols.

True north The location in the Arctic corresponding to one of the imaginary points of an axis upon which the earth rotates.

EQUIPMENT

The single item that is essential to the various forms of orienteering is a topographical map. Such maps are prepared from contour maps by persons experienced in this form of cartography. Symbols are added to the contour maps to designate buildings, fences and walls, large boulders, lakes and ponds, swamp areas, gravel pits, cliffs, etc. Maps are usually carried by the participating orienteers in inexpensive plastic map cases.

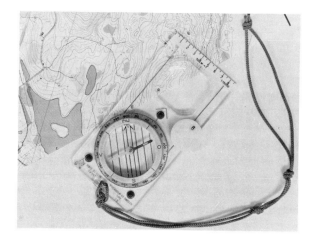

Fig. 63.7 An orienteering compass typical of advanced models used for recreational and competitive orienteering. Note the following features: transparent construction of most of the compass to facilitate map reading when the compass is placed on the map for course setting, the magnification section for easier identification of map features, a counter to aid in recording distance traveled, a wrist cord, and a distance scale, in this case 1:15,000.

While not absolutely essential to orienteering, a compass is invariably carried by all participants. In addition to keeping track of general headings, the protractor compass especially designed for orienteering permits rapid determination of rather precise bearings. Experienced orienteers depend much more on an ability to "read themselves across a map" (to follow their progression continuously on the map while running) and a knack of knowing in which direction north lies at all times. For the beginner and intermediate, however, the establishment of rather exact bearings is important and, therefore, the compass is essential.

The typical orienteering compass is found in a variety of models and available within a broad cost range. All models have a circular compass housing held by a rectangular plate of transparent plastic. The housing (also transparent) contains the magnetic needle bathed in liquid (for shock damping). The rectangular plate will have one or more scales etched along its borders for estimating distance and a directional arrow to indicate headings. More expensive models will include such features as a built-in magnifier to facilitate map reading, a small counter to aid in pace counting, and interchangeable scales to accommodate the various scales of reduction found on orienteering maps. (See Fig. 63.7.)

The clothing a person wears is completely a matter of personal choice. For persons who plan to walk around an orienteering course, typical hiking apparel is completely suitable. For persons planning on rapid progression, especially running, much lighter garments and footwear are highly advisable. In warm weather, a simple T-shirt is all that is needed for the upper body. When competing in cold weather, an additional layer plus arm cover becomes necessary. Lightweight orienteering pullovers constructed of porous synthetic fiber materials are available for those wishing to make the investment. In addition to the thermal qualities, such garments facilitate movement through dense forest and undergrowth by warding off twigs, branches, thorns, and the like.

The lower extremities are usually covered by sweat pants, orienteering pants (of synthetic material), or a combination of knickers and kneesocks. Kneesocks with padded front section are available for added protection against undergrowth, rocks, and stumps. Persons usually do not participate without leg cover because of the dangers of scratches and cuts from branches and thorns and the skin irritations caused by such plants as poison ivy and sumac.

Most running shoes function well for orienteering use although synthetic materials are more appropriate if wet terrain will be encountered. Lightweight footwear especially designed for orienteering of synthetic material and constructed with a molded cleat sole is now available.

In summary, a map is provided each participant at an event. A plastic map case is desirable and an orienteering compass rather necessary. Footwear and other clothing involve items of personal choice. Simplicity seems to characterize the sport of orienteering.

Information about orienteering can be obtained in the form of brochures and information sheets from local and national organizations, books which can be purchased, and films which can be rented. The principal organization in this country is the United States Orienteering Federation, the present address of which is Post Office Box 1081, Athens, Ohio 45701.

REFERENCES

The following books describe various aspects of map reading, compass use, and competitive orienteering:

Bengtsson, H., and G. Atkinson 1976. *Orienteering for sport and pleasure.* Brattleboro, Vt.: Stephan Greene.

Boy Scouts of America 1974. *Orienteering.* New Brunswick, N.J.

British Orienteering Organization 1973. *Mapmaking for orienteering.* Matlock, Derbyshire: Lea Green.

Disley, J. 1973. *Orienteering.* Harrisburg, Pa.: Stackpole.

———— 1971. *Your way with map and compass.* London: Blond Educational. Available through American Orienteering Services and Canadian Orienteering Services.

Gilchrist, J. W. 1975. *Teaching orienteering.* Canadian Orienteering Services.

Hellman, P.-Å., R. Kaill, L.-U. Rystedt, and L. Gustavsson 1971. *Competitive orienteering.* Canadian Orienteering Services.

Jägerstrom, E. 1973. *Course planning*. S. Harvey (trans.). The British Orienteering Federation: Matlock, Derbyshire: Lea Green.

Kjellström, B. 1967. *Be expert with map and compass: the orienteering handbook*. New York: Scribner's.

Ontario Orienteering Association 1972. *Introduction to orienteering*. Canadian Orienteering Services.

Pirie, G. 1968. *The challenge of orienteering*. London: Pelham.

Watson, J. D. 1973. *Know the game: orienteering*. Wakefield, Yorkshire: E. P. Publishing.

Films and information on equipment are available from the following:

American Orienteering Service
308 West Fillmore
Colorado Springs, Colo. 80907

Canadian Orienteering Services
446 McNicoll Avenue
Willowdale, Ontario
Canada M2H 2E1

Educational Film Distributors, Ltd.
285 Lesmill Road
Don Mills, Ont. M3B 2V1

International Film Bureau, Inc.
332 South Michigan Avenue
Chicago, Ill. 60604

Silva, Inc.
2466 State Road 39 N.
North LaPorte, Ind. 46350

64
Relaxation

Josephine L. Rathbone

UNIVERSALITY OF THE PROBLEM

It is easy to write about relaxation because most people are ready to hear about it. It is difficult to write about relaxation because a great many of those who are writing about it are not technically qualified to do so and are either trying to promote partial methods of achieving it or to present panaceas which they believe everyone needs. Relaxing is an individual matter and a skill which is often difficult to learn.

The noise and rush of our highly industrialized society, the bright lights and exhilaration at night, the demanding competition by day, and the distorted values common in today's society are all conducive to tension for which relaxation is an antidote. Even agrarian society in many cases produces almost as much tension as industrial living. Its members also feel driven to accumulate this world's goods and to advance themselves and their families. They live with tension, as do their landlords, their religious leaders, and their medicine men.

It sometimes appears as if all the peoples of this world are caught up in a state of tension. Money and the things money can buy, or status which individuals believe they are entitled to elevate, are often controlling factors of life today. Few people are willing to live without striving to outdo their peers in the accumulation of material possessions. Young people as well as those who are older are prey to conditions which keep them highly stimulated and we in physical education are expected to help both children and adults to relax.

RESPONSIBILITY OF PHYSICAL EDUCATORS

The physical educator of today needs to know how to help people overcome tenseness, not by eliminating economic, political, and emotional stresses but by helping them offset these by changing themselves and/or by getting the rest necessary to allay them. Physical educators have studied physiology and know how the body works. They have studied psychology and understand how the mind works. They also need common sense and good judgment and an appreciation of what is really worthwhile in life. Only in this way can they intelligently assist those who are too tense.

One purpose of physical education in the schools is to offset indirectly the strains of the rest of the program. One way of doing this is to make daily programs less stressful. Adolescents can be shown how much better they will perform if they are not tense, and how much more quickly they can recover from extreme effort if they have periods of relaxation. They can learn that academic work is tensing and that periods of relaxation are needed by all of us.

Another purpose is to assist students to learn how to relax consciously. In classes of physical education for adults and senior citizens, techniques in relaxation will be appealing, because by this time in life everyone has become aware of the consequences of tension and is longing for something to allay it.

In the field of therapy there is an acknowledged need for relaxation techniques. Even if some doctors are willing to dismiss patients, whom they know need to relax, with prescriptions for depressant drugs, they realize that such treatment is only palliative and never curative. The causes of tension are so varied, its symptoms so diversified, and methods of relief so time-consuming that physicians sometimes write prescriptions knowing that their patients will have to return repeatedly as long as they live.

EDUCATION AND MEDICINE IN COOPERATION

Education can help medicine in the search for relief from this common complaint—tension. Education can function either through classes, before symptoms get bad enough to warrant the attention of a physician, or through group psychotherapy which may enable individuals to understand the causes of their current tension. In this way they can be helped to forestall problems which might be ahead of them.

Physicians have already set up cooperative relationships with nurses, physical therapists, and leaders in recreation and sports. It is almost axiomatic in medical circles that relaxation is needed for cardiovascular patients and for some who suffer from gastrointestinal disturbances. It has made its contribution in the offices of dentists. Witness the calming, "relaxing" music coming over the loudspeakers. Observe also the relaxing techniques offered before surgery and the prescription of back massage in the hospitals. Much progress has been made in the use of relaxing exercises to help women prepare for childbirth. If one can be taught to relax the skeletal muscles, the relaxation will be reflected in the cardiac and smooth muscles. This explains its beneficial effects for conditions as different as dysmenorrhea and spasms of the esophagus. This is one thing all physicians understand.

PSYCHOPHYSICAL NATURE OF TENSION

All tension is psychophysical. As Henry James said, "Mind and body are one," and never more so than when a person is tense. When the psyche is disturbed, the reacting tissues of the body—glandular and neuromuscular—are affected. When the glands are disturbed in their functioning or the skeletal or smooth muscles are tense, the "person" will be apprehensive and emotionally on edge.

Tension accompanies any intense effort. This is not bad, if it does not last too long. Nothing in this world can be accomplished without tension, but tension can be exhausting and so rest pauses and devices to release tension are needed. All of us can become tense if we work too hard and too long or if we take ourselves too seriously. All people should learn, while they are young, how to offset accumulated tension and so live a well-balanced life, with release from tensions alternating with periods of effort and accomplishment. In that direction lie sanity and success. When individuals value rest and sleep in proportion to effort and activity, they will never become too tense.

NEED FOR SLEEP

The amount of sleep one gets and one's vitality seem definitely related. On minimum rations of sleep, for a limited time, one may be able to accomplish a great deal of work because of the hyperexcitability of the nervous system; but one cannot maintain a high standard of efficiency indefinitely without sufficient sleep. Adults seem to vary in the amount of sleep they need and some even argue that they can get by on four hours a night. This idea arose because Thomas Edison was credited with needing only that amount. The truth is that he got a great deal more in every 24 hours.

Edison did his sleeping in a very different manner and with a different rhythm from the majority of people. He had a cot in an alcove in his laboratory, and he slept several times during the 24 hours, his various naps ranging from 20 minutes to four hours. The great inventor considered his "catnap" sleeping sensible, because he felt that it was not wise to push fatigue too far. He believed that one should rest just before becoming weary; thereby relieving any tension or excessive strain. Edison is a good example of the efficacy of sleep and relaxation; he put in many hours of hard work and accomplished much.

COUNTERACTING CAUSES OF TENSION

Doctors sometimes find it necessary to deal with functional problems in a patient by prescribing a tranquilizing drug for symptoms but they often regret having to do so and usually limit such treatment to only a few days. Doctors keep searching for the real cause of the symptoms, and desire to treat it directly. Tranquilizers are not curative as quinine is for malaria or penicillin is for pneumonia. Doctors never suggest tranquilizers as a substitute for a full doctor-patient relationship. Whereas teachers of physical education or coaches are not authorized to provide tranquilizers, they may supply heat and massage. Since pain inevitably causes tension, it goes without saying that all devices to relieve pain are indicated in the treatment of excess tension related to pain. Heat and massage are frequently offered.

Heat can be given in the form of salves which serve as counterirritants and draw blood to the surface of the body where it will feel warm. Other forms of heat are heating pads, cloths wrung out in hot water and applied as wraps, or an immersion in very warm water.

Massage is one of the very finest means of tender loving care (TLC). Vast claims have been made for massage—that it pushes blood along toward the heart, that it removes waste products from tissues, that it reaches internal organs which are not functioning properly. None of these effects is direct although each may be indirect with skillful massage. However, massage done properly does soothe sensory nerve endings in muscles and joints thereby lessening pain. The question: "Why is massage effective in helping people to relax?" can be answered, "Because it makes them feel better." When one feels better, one can more easily relax.

PSYCHOLOGICAL TREATMENT

Individuals cannot get rid of their tension unless they face the causes of their distress and modify their way of life to rectify those causes. The author has found that the safest and easiest way for her to help a person to face reality and to establish a new set of values and a new pattern of conduct is through group discussion of the problems that she has found to be quite universal in her own trainees. In a group, it is worthwhile to discuss nervous mannerisms that are to be observed in one's acquaintances, and to admit those individuals find in themselves.

Group members should list their physical complaints. They may see immediately a relationship between their held positions and their aches and pains. They may associate their discomforts with old injuries or operations of which they are still being protective or with posturing at their desks while on their jobs.

In connection with one's daily occupation, the most important factor as far as tension is concerned is a person's schedule. Everyone has 24 hours in every day, and those who arrange that time wisely are free from distress and tension.

As to eating, in our culture *when* we eat is usually more important than *what* we eat. Of course it is essential that we drink enough milk, for the calcium in milk is important for the proper functioning of nerves and muscles. Stimulating drinks, like coffee and soft drinks with high caffein content, should be kept to a moderate amount.

Concerning relaxants like wine and beer, the group leader must be careful not to moralize. In group discussions about such topics everything and anything can be aired, but nothing should be condemned unless the entire group makes that decision. As far as liquor is concerned, the dependency of some people on the cocktail hour, to offset the tensions of the day, may be offered in discussion. The leader may inject some indication of regret that these people are so unresourceful as not to be able to find other more creative and less destructive devices for letdown, devices which allow them to remain in control of themselves.

A session on the likes and dislikes of the members of a group can be amusing, as well as enlightening—amusing because what other people dislike tends to be funny, and enlightening because it becomes obvious that one's own dislikes must seem funny to someone else. One individual may have an aversion to eating berries out of a glass sauce dish; another, to sitting in a room with green wallpaper; and still another, to picking up a burnt matchstick. These aversions may be great but revealed as personal idosyncrasies they often vanish.

Some individuals experience tension because they are uncomfortable with their own physical self-image. Individuals may be able to face their own feelings about their own bodies better after a group session in which disturbing dislikes are brought into the open for discussion and are shown to be quite normal, quite general, and often culturally induced.

At the end of any series of sessions in group counseling for tense people, it is not strange that the group members usually come around to discussing their basic attitudes toward life, their fellow creatures, love, and toward ultimate religious and philosophical questions.

RHYTHMIC EXERCISE TO OFFSET TENSION

For feelings of fatigue and even for residual tension, rhythmic exercise, preferably out of doors in the sunlight, will bring considerable relief. Walking is great medicine for it takes one's mind off work as other ideas intrude on consciousness. Dancing, swimming, or running in a ballgame are also beneficial. However, there appears to be some special efficacy in rhythm itself. It surely upsets held, tense positions.

Here are a few exercises that can be done in one's own room.

☐ Lying on the back with arms close to side: *alternate* arm and leg flinging upward until the hand touches the floor beyond the head and the foot is raised as high as possible. This exercise is the most simple approximation to the usual *alternation* of the extremities in walking. The exercise should be done rhythmically, and the arm and opposite leg should move in unison.

☐ Lying on the back with the arms abducted; (1) single leg raising with knee straight, (2) trunk twisting, aiming to touch opposite hand with the raised foot, (3) return of leg to the vertical position, (4) return of leg to starting postion. Alternate legs.

☐ Assuming a position on all fours with the knees separated a few inches, with thighs perpendicular to the floor, with the shoulders the same height as the hips and the elbows bent slightly: (1) humping the back and letting the head hang down, (2) extending the spine with the head held high. Emphasis should be placed upon humping or flexing in the lumbar region and lowering or extending in the dorsal region of the spine.

☐ The exercise above may be made a little more difficult by swinging the trunk forward and backward, pushing the hips back as the chest is lowered and the head is held high, and swinging the trunk forward as the head is lowered and the back is humped.

After performing the movements in third and fourth exercises a few times, one should sit back on the thighs and swing the arms forward and sideward, brushing the thighs on each swing.

STRETCHINGS

Movements that encourage flexibility of joints, and positions which tend to pull the tightness out of muscles will help to counteract residual tension. It is contrary to common sense to suggest exercises to increase tonus of muscles in a chapter stressing techniques in relaxation. The positions to accomplish the muscle stretchings for release of tension have no relation to the development of tonus in the antigravity muscles. These stretchings for comfort, in relation to relaxation, must be maintained for several seconds, at least, with no expectation of assuming a strong position after the stretch.

Everyone has noticed how natural it is to stretch the arms up over the head and out to the sides when a tensing task has been completed and it is time to "let go." It is in the mood of these stretchings that one gets release from tension.

An excellent practice is to start stretch of the muscles in whatever position one finds oneself when there is time to get rid of tension and discomfort. Why not start in a sitting position? Just pay attention to the complaints of the body. If the hands feel tight, interlace the fingers and stretch them apart. If the back of one hand is uncomfortable make a strong fist or bend the wrist down to get a slight cramp out of muscles that have been used in writing. If one side of the neck feels tight, lower the head to the opposite side, and place the hand on that side across the head in such a way as to stretch the side of the neck that felt tight. Maybe it will actually hurt more now. Don't worry. Make it hurt even more. Wait in that position until sensation somewhere else in the musculature is more uncomfortable. Maybe that will be in the center of the back, so lean forward in the seat and let the arms fall by the sides and the head hang down in front. Maybe then you will want to straighten out one or the other leg, because of tightness behind the knee. This will mean getting down on the floor.

Your private series of stretching positions for each session of relaxing will help to take the tight places out of muscles. This treatment is not actually comfortable while it is going on, but it will result in a sense of well-being afterward. You can do it just as long as you wish.

RELAXING THE BREATHING MECHANISM

Exercises for chest flexibility and relieving tension in the diaphragm are particularly important for relaxing. When individuals are tense or anxious, they hold their breath. Many people have to be taught to let out breath forcibly, so that there is a slight rebound after the exhalation. The system of exercise which has put most attention on therapeutic exhaling is yoga. Yoga, it must be understood, is a system of discipline, so the one simple exercise suggested here must be done precisely. Exercisers are to count in about the rhythm of the normal heartbeat. Then they are to take four counts to inhale, four counts to hold the breath, four counts to exhale, and four counts to hold the breath again. An absolutely full breath must be inhaled and exhaled each time. This skill takes a little practice. Also the rhythm can be changed to (1) inhale for six counts, (2) hold for two counts, (3) exhale for six counts, and (4) hold for two counts; or (1) inhale for eight counts, and (2) exhale for eight counts. For variation one can select any entertaining rhythm, but the counting must be regular and precise.

CONSCIOUS RELAXING

Before completing any lesson plan for physical relaxation, you must direct some muscles to do nothing. If you truly relax thoroughly any part of the body, the whole will benefit. This is because proprioceptive sensations are shut off from the area relaxed and fewer impulses are entering the central nervous system. When we wish to train the muscles to relax at will, it becomes necessary to assume a position in which no muscle tonus is needed. The horizontal position on the back is best, on a firm couch or on the floor. It may be more comfortable to have the neck supported by a firm roll, and the lower back supported by a small, firm cushion. The knees can be raised slightly on other rolls or cushions, so that the drag of the legs from the lower back will be relieved. The thighs should rotate upward, and the arms should not be pressed close to the body. The arms may be bent at the elbows, and placed in the winged, rolled-out attitude of an infant as it sleeps on its back.

Through the ages, a number of practitioners have postulated systems for relaxing various regions of the body. No suggestions are more helpful than those of Edmund Jacobson (1957), a Chicago physician. The Jacobson technique demands great determination on the part of the subjects and depends entirely upon their conscious cooperation or control. Subjects do not have to put faith in anyone else nor learn any complicated routine. Under the observation of a helper, usually at first, subjects contract certain isolated muscles and muscle groups until they are sure they recognize tension. Then subjects "go in the negative direction." Whatever they do or do not do, as they begin to relax, they are to continue on and on, past the point when the part seems to them to be perfectly relaxed. When the subjects are practicing in solitude, they are not to contract before relaxing, that is, they are to begin in whatever stage of tension they happen to be. Subjects learn to localize tensions wherever they occur, and to relax them away.

One can think clearly of only one thing at a time. It is difficult to concentrate on even two sets of muscles located near each other. One must bear this in mind when learning to relax. Disturbing thoughts often create tension. Ridding oneself of such troublesome thoughts assists the organism to relax. It is difficult, if not impossible, to think of the grade one received in algebra, whether or not one will make a team, losing one's job, financial difficulties, or similar subjects when giving full attention to relaxing a specific set of muscles in one's body. Conscious relaxation of muscle groups not only relieves tension of the body but also relaxes the mind.

Swinging one's arms and legs eliminates tension in those appendages. Stretching one's joints will relieve discomfort in them. Getting rid of excess tension in the respiratory apparatus will increase flexibility in the chest. If one can consciously get rid of tension in any muscles, but particularly those along the spinal column and around the shoulders, in the forehead, and around the eyes, and in the mouth and throat, one will definitely become relaxed. This is the perfect way to rest, either with or without sleep.

To do nothing is not as easy as it sounds, particularly if the knack has been lost or has never been acquired. Yet it is doing nothing or relaxing which permits the body to recoup its losses after periods of effort or even wakefulness; it is reducing effort, in the direction of doing nothing which induces sleep. To be able to relax consciously is an ability worth all the time put into learning how to accomplish it.

REFERENCES

Jacobson, E. 1964. *Anxiety and tension control: a physiological approach.* Philadelphia: Lippincott.

———— 1957. *You must relax.* (4th ed., rev.) New York: McGraw-Hill.

65
Rock Climbing
Chris Gulick

HISTORICAL OVERVIEW

Rock climbing for the sake of rock climbing has been an activity in its own right for a relatively short time. It has grown as a sport from the overall field of mountaineering. In the early days of mountain exploration, the peaks were often climbed by their easiest routes. The purpose was primarily to get to the top, although there were people who climbed for the pure pleasure of it. This was often hidden under the guise of "scientific experiments." As people began climbing more and more for the sport of it, they began to attempt more difficult routes up the mountains. These routes were quite often on the steep faces rather than the easier snow and ice slopes first used. The face routes are often steep climbing on rock and ice in a very exposed position.

British climbers began rock climbing in the early 1900s in preparation for their summer climbs in the Alps. Accordingly, this training led to an enjoyment of rock climbing in itself. Climbers such as John Menlove Edwards began climbing as a sport, very often attempting to explain their pleasure and addiction to climbing to a public who thought it lunacy.

Up to this time, climbing had been primarily for the wealthy men and women who would pay to be dragged up some precipice. With some advances during the two World Wars, the late 1940s saw climbing open up more and more to the general public. Some of the more important advances, socially and physically, were pushed by people like Don Whillans and Joe Brown.

All this time the climbs were getting harder and harder. They now involved more balance, physical conditioning, and a heightened awareness of one's body. These were predominately free climbs, in which climbers used just the rock for holds and did not rely on artificial aids for upward progress. The superb climbers of today seem to be dancing up rather than climbing some exhausting route.

Rock climbing in the United States had one of its most avid proponents in Fritz Weissner, a German immigrant who had climbed extensively in the Alps before bringing his expertise to America. One can usually find at least one route he put up in almost any climbing area of the United States.

The prime development in eastern United States climbing occurred during the early 1950s at the Shawangunks in New Paltz, N.Y. The majority of the climbs were put up by a group known as the Vulgarian Mountain Club, a rather colorful, rebellious group of excellent climbers with a decided preference for martinis. They weren't rebellious from a climber's viewpoint but more likely considered so by the passers-by who happened to witness one of their nude climbs. During their heyday, they put up some of the finest routes to be found in the "Gunks." Many of them still climb today at a consistently high standard.

In the western part of the United States there was a similar development. This was centered primarily in the Yosemite Valley of California's High Sierra. Some of the basic techniques were introduced into the valley during the 1930s. The average height of the valley walls provided the impetus for the development of today's modern pitons and other aid climbing techniques. In the East the emphasis had been primarily on free climbs while in the West the oft-times blank, overhanging rock required additional techniques. As free climbing had not yet attained to the high standards it has today, most of the routes required some or all aids. These aid techniques were not new to mountaineering but were brought closer to perfection in Yosemite.

After the 1930s, climbing proceeded to develop on its own in the United States. It began to hold a certain metaphysical quality for the climbers who climbed to extend themselves beyond what was once thought possible. Free climbing was beginning to receive more attention and some demanding lines were being put up in the United States. Some long-commitment wall climbs were being put up in the West, combining a high standard of free climbing mixed with fiercely hard aid climbing.

In times past climbing had been pretty much ignored by the general public which considered the activity to be strictly for eccentrics. In the East it had been frowned upon by those who happened to encounter the Vulgarians. But on October 23, 1970, Warren Harding and Dean Caldwell began an ascent of El Capitan, which they called "The Wall of Early Morning Light." This was by no means the first ascent of "El Cap" but it was to be the most publicized. Their estimated 12-day climb turned into a 26-day epic which was given national TV coverage. Suddenly, thousands of Americans realized that superb opportunities for climbing were available in their own country and that there was no reason for them to travel to the Alps or Himalayas in order to participate.

The main impetus of rock climbing over the past few years has been towards producing hard free climbs. This has included putting up lines on seemingly impossible faces and free climbing routes that had previously required aid. Another important development was the elimination of the piton from the free climber's equipment. It was found that the continued placement and removal of pitons was causing gross, irreparable damage to the rock. Climbs that previously had tenuous fingertip holds now had large buckets from the continued use of the hard steel pitons. A climb that had at one time required a gymnast's finesse could now be ascended as if it were a ladder. And so the use of *chocks* evolved.

British climbers started the practice of using chocks or nuts as they are now called. They would pick up stones on their way to climbs and would later use them as a means of protecting themselves from a fall. By placing the stones in a crack and running their rope behind the stones, they would prevent falling all the way to the ground. They would also place a sling on the chockstone, then run the rope through the sling to keep the rope running in a straight line which minimized the amount of rope drag. The stones could later be removed without causing any damage to the rock. In many cases they were left in for the use of the next climber.

In the Yosemite valley, Royal Robbins, Tom Frost, and Yvon Chouinard began a movement to discourage the use of pitons in almost all situations. Chouinard and Frost designed and manufactured a series of aluminum nuts of varying shapes and sizes that could be placed quite securely in any number of cracks. They now market them quite successfully. In recent years, pitons have rarely been utilized by free climbers. Surprisingly, many people spend years climbing before they even realize that pitons are still used in some situations.

WHAT ROCK CLIMBING IS

Rock climbing's name is self-explanatory. To maintain a measure of safety, the basic requirement is a nylon climbing rope. This can be, quite literally, the difference between life and death. It is also, when used on a multipitch climb, the only connection to the outside world. But one can always pull up the rope and untie the knot. Control of the rope allows one complete control of oneself. It provides the perfect escape. It is for this reason that there is a hard and fast rule: "Don't step on the rope!" It is taken very literally and is the basis for all the unwritten rules forbidding any mistake.

All climbers must have enough common sense to recognize their individual limitations. What may be easy for one climber may be impossible for another. Climbers should not be embarrassed or feel inferior in acknowledging their limitations. If a climb is too difficult for them, they should back off. An understanding of individual limitations can be gained only by climbing. Climbers who get scared out of their minds, can't figure out what they're doing up there, and really don't want to be there have limitations. They should come down.

Those who have experience and are in a position to teach others to climb have considerable responsibility for the safety and welfare of their students. It is essential that beginning climbers are made aware of the hazards involved and how to prevent serious injury. When they have learned basic climbing techniques and safety measures, they should be encouraged to climb and discover their own limitations.

There is a strong freedom, an anarchist's ethic to rock climbing, the responsibility to yourself alone. It is for this reason that a lot of climbers would probably agree that there are certain ways of doing things that have proven effective but that there are no rules. This is why the Vulgarians were important in the development of climbing. A great deal of their spirit is still embodied in climbing and it is essential that it remain. It might even be the reason people start climbing in the first place.

LEARNING ROCK CLIMBING

If you want to try rock climbing, find someone who knows how to climb. Gain an understanding of the techniques involved by observing demonstrations and by practicing. The fact that firsthand experience is superior to any other method of learning cannot be overemphasized. Your continued climbing could very well depend on your grasp of basic techniques. Once the mechanics are understood, the major part of your progress in climbing will come only from you and your commitment to it. The harder climbs are accessible only to those willing to continually raise their standards. Many climbers train rigorously just to maintain the standard they have achieved.

Once you've learned to set up a *belay* and how to belay, you have the basic skills to try rock climbing on your own. It's helpful to climb with someone who's better than you are. You can learn by watching the better climber.

It's essential to learn how to use certain holds, to find out which moves will work. The first time you see someone accomplish something that you couldn't even get off the ground on, you'll realize the possibilities inherent in climbing, in pushing. The first time you achieve something that you couldn't get off the ground on the year before, the seemingly impossible may begin to look possible. This may sound romantic but the fact remains that present day climbers are putting up routes that are four grades higher than those put up 10 or 15 years ago.

For an activity that stresses the individual's freedom, there is a strong code of ethics. There are a few things which are not to be done, ethically. Actually, the code is constantly in flux as differing opinions strive for equilibrium. However, there are some things which are generally accepted. As might be guessed, one of the more important ones has to do with the placing of pitons and expansion bolts. Climbs which have been done free should not have pins and bolts placed on subsequent ascents. Also, when this hardware is used, it should be used with discretion and "cleanliness" in mind. A climber caught violating this ethic might possibly elicit some sort of violence from other climbers.

Placing a bolt seems to be a more serious offense than placing a piton. Bolts offend the sensibilities more because they appear to constitute a permanent change.

The code calls for climbers to do their own climbing. If you are climbing for enjoyment, there is nothing more annoying than having someone at the base of the climb telling you which holds to use. If, however, you are attempting a specific move such advice may be helpful.

There are really no rules which are to be followed explicitly. Enough words. Use your own head.

EQUIPMENT NEEDED

The basic tool, assuming the climber has some expertise, is a rope. With a rope alone you can belay someone, they can belay you, you can rappel off a climb. These are the basic movements up and down. It is also advisable to have some nylon slings and a few carabiners, locking and nonlocking. With these it is easier to set up smoother and to keep the rope over the line being climbed. This equipment is needed when you are climbing on a top-rope.

Fig. 65.1 The author leading the climb called "Ego Buster" which is rated 5.8. Note the nuts carried at his side. When possible, he will wedge them in cracks for protection. Photo by John Krakauer.

Fig. 65.2 The author leading a climb, rated 5.8, called "YMC" at Ragged Mountain, Connecticut. Note how the rope runs through carabiners attached to a piton that has been placed in the cracks permanently. Photo by John Krakauer.

When leading a climb, invest in some nuts and more carabiners. You'll also want additional slings to place between the protection and your rope. The slings are quite limp so that the upward motion of the rope doesn't pull the nuts out of the cracks. The slings are also used to keep the rope running in a straight line and cut down on the friction which is known as rope drag. A protection system can develop enough friction, if not properly slung, to make it almost impossible to drag the rope through.

In some areas, like the Shawangunks, it's necessary to carry only a few nuts and mostly slings. Climbing has been going on here for so long that many of the existing routes are filled with resident pitons. Resident pitons are *meant* to be there. They are not to be removed. The same goes for resident bolts.

If you start aid climbing, it may be necessary to buy some pitons for the places you can't use nuts. A lot of climbs can be done using just nuts. A few years ago, the face of Half-Dome was climbed using nuts alone. Again, on many existing aid climbs there are resident pins. These should be examined closely, as they should on free climbs, as it's often hard to tell how long they've been there. Any planned climbs that will take over a day may require a hammock, a haul bag for extra equipment and food, and most likely a pair of jumars (mechanical devices used to ascend a rope). As you try longer and more committing climbs, the amount of equipment and expertise you will need will increase. There is a lot of equipment available in climbing shops, some useful and necessary, some just nice to have along. It all depends on how much you're willing to carry. The right equipment can certainly help to ensure success on a climb but the major commitment will still have to come from you.

The success of a climb depends on many factors. If you're going out for the day to some local crag, then all you'll need is a nice day. If you're going into a more mountainous area, you will need to be prepared for sudden changes in weather. The more remote areas will require either large amounts of packing or air drops. It's important to be familiar with the area you'll be in. Talk to people who have been in the area before you and find out what to expect. How long did other parties take, what were the difficulties encountered? It's also important to figure out ahead of time how you'll get down. Another consideration when climbing in remote areas is that you'll be a long way from any medical facilities. On a long, remote, alpine climb, a broken arm could set off a chain of events that could have a disastrous end. This same broken arm in a local climbing area would probably not lead to any of the complications you might expect in an alpine setting. Consequently, these factors will have much to do with how far you're willing to extend yourself on certain climbs.

RATINGS AND CLASSES

Climbs are rated according to their level of difficulty and the amount of time they're expected to take. The rating system currently used in the United States is known as the Yosemite decimal system. The decimal system is used to divide Class 5 climbing.

Class 1 is walking on level ground. Class 2 is steeper walking. Class 3 is steep scrambling without a rope. Class 4 is steep scrambling with a rope but no belays. Class 5 is roped, belayed climbing.

Class 5 is presently divided into thirteen ratings ranging from 5.0 to 5.12. The higher the number, the harder the climb.

Climbs involving aid are rated according to how difficult the actual climbing is and to how difficult it is to make the aid placements. The aid rating presently ranges from A1 to A5.

Climbs are also graded according to the amount of time involved. These ratings run from Grade I to Grade VI. A Grade I climb requires an hour or so. A Grade II about a half a day. A Grade III will take most of a day. A Grade IV is a full day's climbing. A Grade V is a hard multiday climb under good conditions. A Grade VI is a climb of several days under strenuous conditions.

Fig. 65.3 The author following a 5.10 climb called "Anticipation" at Ragged Mountain, Connecticut. Note the four wired nuts with carabiners attached, placed in the crack for protection. The second climber removes the nuts and carabiners in climbing past them. Photo by John Krakauer.

A route on a small cliff would be rated I, 5.6 while in Yosemite a long wall climb might be rated V, 5.9, A4. The rating should carry all the information you need for the climb. Still there are some discrepancies. Ratings tend to differ from place to place. Even in the same area, climbs of the same rating will be far apart in terms of difficulty. Very often a 5.10 in the Shawangunks will be different from a 5.10 in Yosemite. This is partly because different types of climbs are involved but also because different climbers rated the climbs. And though it may not be apparent, there is an intense amount of competition between climbers. Some climbers might rate a climb 5.9 when in reality it's probably closer to 5.10. They might do this for a couple of reasons. Either they're bent on one-upsmanship or they've climbed their climb so often it no longer seems hard. Underrating is known as "wiring" a climb.

There's a lot to be gained by climbing and a lot to live down. Enjoy yourself.

TERMINOLOGY

aid climbing using holds other than the rock for progress.

belay the act of holding the rope for a climber and pulling it in or letting it out while he or she climbs. Also the act of holding the rope taut when the climber falls.

bolt a metal stud that is pounded into a hole drilled into the rock. Used for passing blank sections of rocks or as belay points on long crackless friction climbs.

bucket a large, solid hold.

carabiner a metal snap link, usually forged aluminum, that has countless uses. Prevents nylon/nylon contact which could result in instant melting. Locking carabiners have a screw gate which increases their strength and prevents their opening accidentally.

chocks pieces of metal of varying sizes that are slung on perlon or wire and placed in cracks to prevent a long fall. Climbers will fall only twice the distance they are above the chock, providing it doesn't pull out.

chockstones stones of any size that are lodged in a crack.

clean climbing refers to climbing without the use of pitons or bolts, leaving no trace of the climber's passing.

free climbing climbing using the rock itself for holds. The rope is there to hold the climber in case of a fall.

lines another word often used instead of route.

nuts same as chocks.

perlon a type of rope consisting of a braided core and a woven sheath.

pitch one roped length of climbing.

piton a metal spike of varying sizes that is pounded into cracks to protect the leader from falling. Used primarily in aid climbing.

rating a method of grading a climb to let a climber know how hard it is, what to expect on it, and how long it will take.

sling a loop of nylon webbing, usually one inch wide, used in conjunction with nuts. The sling is clipped to the protection sling by means of a carabiner and then to the rope with another carabiner. The upward movement of the rope is taken up by the limpness of the carabiner thus preventing the rope from pulling out the nut. Slings are usually 18″ to 3′ long. Their length depends upon their intended use.

top-rope climbing with the rope running up the cliff to the belayer. Another option is running the rope up through carabiners that are attached to a sling that is firmly anchored and then back down to the belayer. This is a popular way of climbing as there is not much risk of a serious fall involved. If climbers do fall, they can just hang on the rope and can be lowered or resume climbing.

wall an unusually large cliff.

REFERENCES

Eder, S. 1976. Learning on the rocks. University of New Hampshire wilderness experience program for education students. *American Education* **12:** 3, (April): 16–21.

Greenbank, A. 1963. *Instruction in rock climbing.* London: Museum Press.

Manning, H. (ed.) 1967. *Mountaineering: the freedom of the hills.* (2nd ed.) Seattle: The Mountaineers.

M.I.T. Outing Club 1956. *Fundamentals of rock climbing,* Cambridge, Mass.: Massachusetts Institute of Technology.

Rebuffat, G. 1971. *On ice and snow and rock.* Evans (trans.). New York: Oxford University Press.

Robbins, R. 1971. *Basic rockcraft.* Glendale, Calif.: La Siesta.

———— 1973. *Advanced rockcraft.* Glendale, Calif.: La Siesta.

Rowell, G. 1974. Climbing Half Dome the hard way. *National Geographic* **145:** 6, (June): 782–791.

Scott, D. 1974. *Big wall climbing.* New York: Oxford University Press.

Starnes, R. 1974. Peril point at fifty-some-odd: rock climbing. *Field and Stream* **78:** 10, (April).

66
Roller Skating Skills*
Herbert C. Price, Jr. and Claire B. Koch

Roller skating was initiated as an activity at the Barrington Junior High School, Barrington, Illinois, in 1955 as a means of improving the noon hour recreation program for seventh and eighth grade boys and girls. It was decided that certain skills should be mastered by the students before skating could become desirable recreation in the school situation, and so roller skating was added to the physical education curriculum.

Roller skating instruction at the school is now begun in later October. The incoming seventh grade students are taught the basic fundamental skills at

---

*   Reprinted by permission from *JOHPER* **31,** 3, (March), 1960.

Fig. 66.1 Group skating helps social adjustment of junior high school pupils as well as developing their coordination and skill. Courtesy of *JOPER.*

Fig. 66.2 Roller skating is another enjoyable activity that provides vigorous action for boys and girls. Courtesy of *JOPER.*

this time, while the eighth graders begin experiences in more advanced skills. In the early stages of instruction, one period each week is devoted to the teaching of roller skating. Instruction is reduced to one period every two weeks as skills are achieved. This plan adds variety to the activities normally presented at this time of year and at the same time helps the students become successful roller skaters.

Skating skills can best be taught on an individual progression basis. Skills are grouped by order of need and difficulty in categories or achievement levels. Each student learns at his own rate and is checked on his ability to perform each of the skills in the progression.

ELEMENTARY SKILLS

Skills that the boys and girls must learn for good skating and enjoyment during their noon hour involve ability in forward skating, stopping, corner turns, partner skates, group skates, backward skating, and procedures for various novelty skates of the mixer type.

Students must learn two methods of stopping, the drag stop and the turn stop. The dragging of the four wheels of the outside skate provides a gradual stop which should be used by the skater as he leaves the floor.

Drag Stop

1. Put weight on inside skate.
2. Point toe of the outside skate to the outside at at least a 45 degree angle, with the heels nearly together.
3. For even wear, the wheels must all be in contact with the floor.
4. Add pressure to the drag skate as you reach the stopping point.

Turn Stop

1. Perform this stop by employing the skating fundamental known as the "eagle" (gliding with skates pointed in opposite directions).
   a) Point toes of outside skate forward and slightly to the inside of the floor.
   b) Point toe of inside skate backward and to the inside of the floor.
   c) Maintain weight equally on both skates and lean in and describe a circle with the skates.
2. The "eagle glide" may also be done as a method of turning corners or on a straight-away if the joints are loose and limber.
3. May be practiced in partners with hands joined facing partner and pushing with rear skate for momentum until an eagle glide in a circle can be done.

Forward Skating

Forward skating is best mastered by having the opportunity to practice skating. Once the basic ideas are in mind, the student must skate and skate some more until he gains confidence and coordination.

1. Point toes slightly outward from center.
2. Have weight forward and over the center of the skates.
3. Try first to "run and slide on the ice."
4. Next try pushing from one skate and gliding on the other repeating with each skate.

Corner Turns

Cross-over turn

1. Outside skate crosses in front of the inside skate until the corner is managed.

2. Lean in.

Two-foot leaning turn

1. Inside skate is placed in front of the outside skate on the floor.
2. Lean to the inside.

One-foot leaning turn

1. Glide on the inside skate.
2. Bring the outside skate around from the back to the front of the body gradually as the turn is made.

The above skills should also be done in the opposite skating direction around the floor.

Partner Skates

Partner skates are presented to help the boys and girls in their rhythm and social relationships. Emphasize skating to rhythm and coordinating movements with partner's skates.

Positions

1. The side position is assumed with the girl on the right of the boy, hands joined in the familiar skaters manner (right to right, left to left).
2. Partners may also skate in a position with left hands joined in front and right hands joined from the rear and to the outside of the girl's waist.

Two step

1. In partners, step left, bring right together, step left, kick right forward.
2. Repeat, using opposite feet.

Group Skates

Various group skates are popular with the boys and girls, because they involve more people. Boys particularly find strength in numbers when inviting girls to skate.

Trio

1. Formation—two girls with one boy between, or vice versa.
2. Hook elbows to avoid being widespread.

Conga

1. Formation: two girls and two boys in a line, holding on to waist of person in front.
2. Take three skates forward and one kick sideward. (Can also be done in partner formation.)

Backward Skating

To prepare for skating to a waltz, backward skating must be mastered. This skill is both popular and challenging. The fundamentals of backward skating are opposite to those of forward skating.

1. Lean slightly forward.
2. Point toes in and push from one skate to a glide on the other.
3. Corners may be turned by crossing the inside skate behind the outside skate.

Waltz

1. Social dance position is assumed by the partners.
2. One partner skates forward, the other backward.
3. Partners may change positions by performing an eagle.

INTERMEDIATE SKILLS

Intermediate skills are presented to the more accomplished skaters. These skates furnish more variety to the recreation period as the skating season progresses and help to maintain the interest of the boys and girls in the program.

Quadruple skate

1. Formation: two boys with two girls between and side by side.
2. Link elbows tightly.

Crazy trio

1. Formation: sets of three skaters.
2. The trio reverses direction at a signal.
3. The inside member of the trio pivots in as the other members turn to the inside, at a signal.

Polka

1. Cross right leg in front of left while dipping left knee slightly.
2. Cross right leg in back of left while dipping left knee.
3. Two step right, left, right.
4. Repeat the above crossing with the left leg and dipping the right knee. Variations can be added to suit the polka rhythm and the experience of the skaters.

Individuals may practice the polka using wall for support.

Waltz

1. Partners forward and backward and turn at the ends of the floor.

2. Backward partner turns by stepping forward onto left skate skating counterclockwise.

3. Forward partner eagles at the same time until he reaches the backward skating position.

ADVANCED SKILLS

Advanced individual and group skills are presented to the superior skaters. Some of these may well be practiced using a wall for support.

Advanced conga

1. Right knee raised and pointed toward left, right knee points toward right.
2. Right leg kicks sideward, hop on left.
3. Skate right, left, right, and kick left.
4. Repeat the above using the left knee.
5. Knee in, knee out, kick, hop, skate 2–3 kick.

Schottische

1. Position: assume a tandem position with boy behind girl, left hands joined sideward and boy's right hand under girl's right arm.
2. Corresponding skates must operate together.
3. Skate left, right, left, hop left and skate right, left, right, hop right.
4. Skate left, hop left, skate right, hop right.

Collegiate

1. Position: partner skate position.
2. Boys skate regular, girl's opposite skate coordinate with boys in front, using a cross-over step.

Dip or splits

1. Skate on back wheels of forward skate and front wheels of rear skate.
2. Spread the feet as far backward and forward as possible.

   This can be done on corners, straightaway, and in partners.

Spiral or scale

1. Balance on one foot with the other leg and body parallel to the floor.
2. Partners may do this holding hands going forward and backward.

Through the teaching of roller skating skills in our physical education classes, we have been able to add variety to the physical education curriculum and have discovered another enjoyable activity that provides vigorous action for boys and girls. Skating has helped the students to improve their coordination, balance, rhythm, poise, and self-confidence. It has proved to be an excellent social activity as we find that boys will mix socially with girls more readily in skating than in dancing. We believe that roller skating would be an excellent addition to any school's physical education program.

67
Rope Jumping*
Theresa Anderson

A group of girls at North High School in Des Moines, Iowa, is improving the century-old art of rope jumping. They are doing so much with it, with so much enthusiasm that they make it an important part of a physical education program of the school.

Almost any elementary school girl knows the rudiments of rope jumping but the North High School girls have taken this childhood pastime and developed it into a precision event which reduces audiences to wide-eyed amazement.

Rope jumping has long been considered by athletic coaches an excellent activity for body conditioning and agility. Boxers and wrestlers have found it particularly advantageous. It is also an activity through which the techniques of creative endeavor and democratic self-management may be learned and practiced. In addition rope jumping is fun.

The girls work with small ropes which they themselves swing inside the big ropes, turned by other members of the group. This is the basis of their routine. Many variations are worked out. First, one girl jumps three jumps inside the big rope with her small rope, while the long rope turns once. Then another girl, also with a small rope, comes in. In one instance, the big ropes are swung crosswise; in another they are swung parallel but in opposite directions—in eggbeater fashion. Girls with small ropes jump inside these big ropes.

In order to reach the highest proficiency in rope jumping, high motor ability, excellent rhythm, precision of movement, cooperation, perseverance, and a high degree of concentration are required. North High School rope

---

*   Reprinted by permission from *JOHPER* **15,** 4, (April), 1944.

jumpers, in addition to mastering an interesting activity, have reached top flight popularity on school and civic programs in Des Moines.

The equipment is very inexpensive. Small ropes require nine feet of ordinary ⅜-inch rope. Large ropes require twenty feet of ½-inch rope. Work may be conducted en masse, with small groups, or individually.

The following are single techniques with small ropes. These may later be combined with large ropes. In the titles given below, forward means that the rope passes from back to front over the head. The list given below includes only those in which the rope moves forward. All these and others may be done with the rope moving backward. Techniques 1, 2, 4, 5, 6, and 7 are fairly simple; techniques 8, 9, and 10 are more difficult; and techniques 3, 11, and 12 are the hardest to do.

1. Forward two-count jump. The performer jumping on both feet, jumps twice on each circle of the rope, once over the rope, once between.

2. Forward one-count jump. The performer jumping on both feet, jumps once only, on each circle of the rope.

3. Forward one-half count jump—doubles. The performer jumping on both feet, jumps once while the rope makes two complete circles.

4. Forward run. The performer runs in place. The rope passes under the feet on each step.

5. Forward hop run. The performer runs in place taking an extra hop on each step. The rope passes under the feet on each step.

6. Forward double hop on left (or right) foot. The performer, standing on the indicated foot, hops twice on each circle of the rope, once to clear the rope, once between. The performer changes feet after each two hops.

7. Forward single hop on left (or right) foot. The performer, standing on the indicated foot, hops once on each circle of the rope to clear the rope.

8. Forward hop skip. The performer performs a hop skip on alternate feet. The rope passes under the feet on each hop.

9. Forward squat jump. The performer, in a squat position, jumps on both feet on each circle of the rope.

10. Forward crosses. The performer jumps on both feet on the first circle of the rope in the usual manner. She then crosses the hands in front of her and jumps the second circle of the rope. She continues alternating.

11. Tap steps. Various tap dance steps may be done while the rope is being swung.

12. "Slips." This is used as a device or break so that the direction of the rope may be changed, or a change made to a different type of jump. It is

done by the performer swinging the rope to one side while she maintains the same rhythm in jumping as though the rope were passing under her feet.

Various interesting combinations may be developed:

☐ Two or three persons may work in the same small rope. One turns the rope while all jump it.

☐ All of the techniques with the small rope may be combined with one large rope. The tempo of the small rope may be kept the same as the large rope or it may be accelerated to twice the speed of the large rope (Fig. 67.1).

☐ Many of the techniques with the small rope may be combined with two large ropes crossed at right angles (Fig. 67.2).

☐ The "eggbeater" type of turning is interesting. Two turners use two long ropes, turning them in opposite directions. One or two performers jump

Figure 67.1

Figure 67.2

between the two ropes (Fig. 67.3). It is also possible for a performer with a small rope, to jump inside the two long ropes if she faces one of the turners.

SUGGESTED PATTERNS

The following are merely suggestions. Students will soon learn to work out their own combinations.

1. The big rope is turned by two persons. A performer with a small rope, runs in and jumps both ropes, using first a two-count jump and then a one-count jump (Fig 67.4). For variation, the jumper may speed her small rope to two or three times the tempo of the large rope.

2. The big rope turns once while two performers each with a small rope, jump two-count and then one-count rhythm on their small ropes (Fig. 67.5).

3. The same as No. 2 except that the jumpers jump backward. The two are then combined.

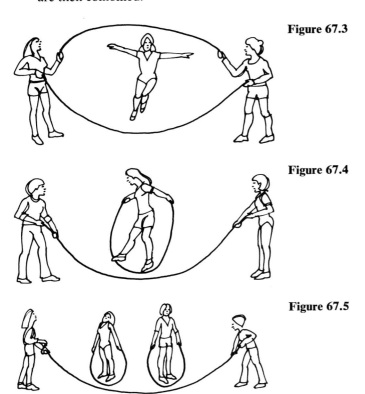

Figure 67.3

Figure 67.4

Figure 67.5

4. The big rope turns once while the performer jumps two-count and one-count rhythm with her small rope, first using crossed ropes forward and then backward (Fig. 67.6).

5. The same as No. 4 except the performer stands facing one of the turners.

6. Three performers jump in one small rope. The middle one swings the rope. Both one-count and two-count jumps are used (Fig. 68.7).

7. The big rope is turned in double tempo while the performer does the one-half count jump (doubles) with the small rope.

8. The trot is done by the performer running in place with the small rope. The tempo of the big rope is increased to meet the tempo of the performer with the small rope.

9. The big rope turns once, while two groups of two performers each jump, using one small rope to each group. Two-count and one-count jumps are used (Fig. 67.8).

10. In the "eggbeater," two long ropes are held parallel and turned in opposite directions. A performer or two go in and jump between the ropes.

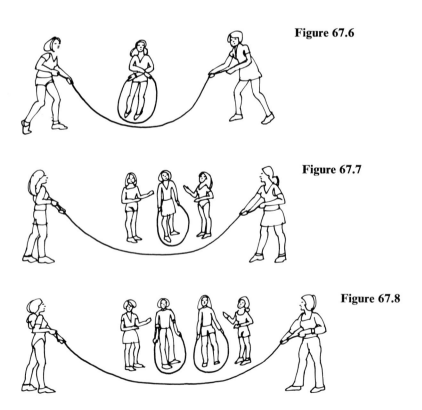

Figure 67.6

Figure 67.7

Figure 67.8

In a variation of this, a performer goes in with a rope and faces one of the turners, and does plain jumps, crosses, and doubles. (Fig. 67.9).

11. Two long ropes are crossed at right angles to each other. (Fig. 67.10).

   (a) A performer goes into the center with a small rope and jumps two-count and one-count rhythm.
   (b) Two performers go in with one rope and do the same.
   (c) A performer goes in with a small rope and does crosses, forward and backward.
   (d) A performer goes in with a small rope and jumps doubles (one-half count jumps).

GENERAL SUGGESTIONS

1. Ropes should be swung with wrist action.
2. In jumping, the body should be pushed up from the floor. Beginners often merely bend the knees to get the feet off the floor.

Figure 67.9

Figure 67.10

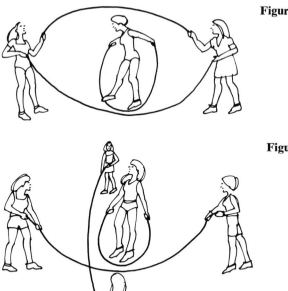

863

3. The importance of good turners should be emphasized in the group work. Their rhythm must be excellent. They must cooperate with the jumpers.

4. In teaching a beginner to run in to the big rope, with a small rope, both ropes should be turning in the same direction.

5. In jumping front or back crosses, the hands reach completely across the body just above waist height.

6. In teaching "doubles," caution the performer to continue fast swinging of the rope. While learning, it helps if the jumper takes two or three single jumps between each "doubles."

68
Sailing

William L. McIntyre

Sailing, in all of its aspects, has played an integral part in our nation's experience. A primary and continuing theme in our history has been our involvement with the sea and, consequently, the activity of sailing. The voyages of the Norsemen, the exploits of John Paul Jones, the Gloucester fishing schooners, Bedford Whalers and Baltimore Clippers may appear to be many years removed from the Star and Lightning classes, the 12-meter America's Cup defenders and the hundreds of thousands of everyday competitive, cruising, and day sailing enthusiasts of the present, but the feelings and attitudes of both groups are extremely similar. Every time a sailor, whether a renowned class champion or a duffer, takes the tiller or wheel, there is the promise of a unique adventure and a personal challenge.

According to the *Encyclopedia of Sailing* by the editors of *One-Design and Offshore Yachtsman* (1971), the idea of sailing pleasure craft is as old as Cleopatra; however, in times past such pleasure was reserved for the elite only. The word "yacht" comes from the Dutch term "jaght," meaning "to put on speed" or "to hunt." It appeared in the English language in Stuart England. Samuel Pepys records his yachting experience aboard the *Charlotte* owned by Sir William Batten, in 1663. The world's first yacht club, the Water Club of Cork Harbour, Ireland, was formed in 1720.

Like many Anglo-Saxon traditions, sailing for pleasure came to America's shores long before the Revolution. We know that John Paul Jones cruised for pleasure prior to becoming the father of our navy, and that a Dr. John Jeffries obtained a pass from British authorities to go sailing for pleasure, fishing, and shooting. It was a Salem, Massachusetts, sea captain and merchant, George Crowninshield, Jr., who began in 1801 to build boats solely for the owners' enjoyment.

Small boat sailing for pleasure is a fairly recent development, commencing shortly after the American Civil War. However, the real growth came with the development of one-design craft after the turn of the century. An example of this is the Snipe class boat. Designed to be home-built for under $100, it was 15½ feet overall with a centerboard, weight 440 lbs, and had a sail area of 116 square feet. The first one was built in 1931. Today, over 15,000 Snipe class boats are sailed in more than 510 clubs in 32 nations. The boating industry has hundreds of examples of such growth, especially after World War II.

The combination of several factors—increased leisure time, growth in per capita income, development of less expensive and more easily worked and maintained materials, and a greater awareness of the potentialities of participation in sailing—has created an explosive growth in the industry in the past 20 years. While this growth is not limited to small boats, certainly a great part of it is in the area of easily transportable type craft. An example of this is the Sunfish, much in evidence at roadside rentals, which first appeared in the early 1960s. Ten years later there were over 75,000 of these craft.

The range of sailing activities is limited only by one's imagination and pocketbook. The ocean-racing circuit features boats valued at hundreds of thousands of dollars. Often owned by syndicates, they are organized and manned by amateur participants. The same enthusiasm which prevails in this group is displayed by every racing class down to the nine-foot El Toro prams. In fact, the greatest pride in the sailing fraternity is most often shown by one-design sailors for their class. It is not, however, the racing buffs who concern us here. With the dedication, enthusiasm and closeness of each class, the sailor who enters the sport through such membership will be well cared for until experience has been gained. But for every sailor belonging to a well-organized group, there are many more who will learn haphazardly. Keeping in mind that for less than $1000 one can buy one's own yachting adventure or for less than $20 a day rent it, there is a clear-cut need for programs in boating, boating safety, and sailing. It is this thought more than any other which has provided the impetus for this article. I direct this, therefore, toward the layman, beginner, novice, and occasional sailor, with the firm belief that all persons should have some fundamental instruction in boating and sailing before ever being allowed to cast off onto any of our nation's waterways.

THE ART AND SCIENCE OF SAILING

While the basic skills needed to sail a boat are relatively easy to learn, the art of sailing is much more than simply making the craft execute its few simple maneuvers. Beginners with only a few hours of instruction under their belts will probably execute a tack in the same manner as a veteran of 30 years at the helm with little observable difference; but follow the same two sailors for a short two-hour cruise and little doubt will remain as to what is meant by the "art of sailing." There is no substitute for experience and time spent on the water. This does not mean that mishaps do not happen to veteran sailors. They do. The difference is in how they are anticipated and handled.

With these thoughts in mind I have organized this article in terms of basic sailing skills (with the emphasis upon simple mechanics) and fundamental knowledge and skills (a noticeably greater emphasis on the art of sailing). Because my own teaching techniques invariably reflect my own philosophy of sailing, it is difficult to separate completely the science from the art. I can, for example, go through a step-by-step explanation of how to tack (strictly a mechanical procedure) but at the same time, some comments about shifting of weight, body position, changing of hands and visual and mental perceptions will enter into the explanation. These comments, varying from sailor to sailor and instructor to instructor, constitute that art which is inseparable from the science.

FUNDAMENTAL KNOWLEDGE AND SKILLS

Prospective sailors should have an understanding of and respect for the environment in which they will operate plus a continuous concern and watch-

Fig. 68.1 There is no substitute for time spent on the water. Courtesy of Camp Monomoy.

fulness for safety. The responsibility that they accept in operating a sailing craft necessitates a mature attitude. They must be made conscious of water, wind and weather for all three directly dictate what they will be doing.

The first rule of sailing is to know the limits of the boat's capabilities. Sailors must not go out when the weather elements exceed these limits or are even marginal. How does one know this? Scanning the horizon, sniffing the wind, getting a general feel of the atmosphere will give some indication. The old timers, those of great experience and skill, are the most careful and faithful listeners to daily weather and tidal information. It is the first and most carefully heeded topic among boatmen. Prospective sailors should: (1) read the daily weather forecast, (2) listen to radio weathercasts frequently prior to and during activity on the water (many wise boaters have the frequencies written and secured in a quickly accessible spot along with other emergency numbers and call signals), (3) check with knowledgeable people along the water area, (4) make certain that some responsible person is aware of their itinerary or plans, and (5) *always* be conscious of changing or potentially dangerous conditions.

Some general observations can be determined immediately. These would include:

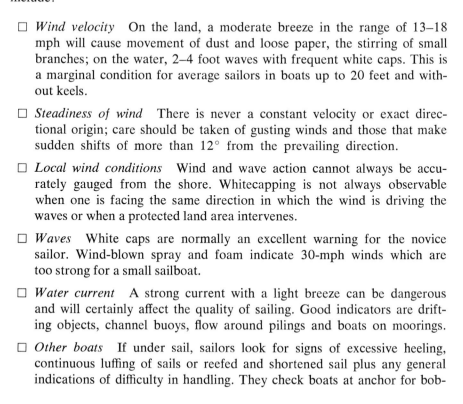

☐ *Wind velocity* On the land, a moderate breeze in the range of 13–18 mph will cause movement of dust and loose paper, the stirring of small branches; on the water, 2–4 foot waves with frequent white caps. This is a marginal condition for average sailors in boats up to 20 feet and without keels.

☐ *Steadiness of wind* There is never a constant velocity or exact directional origin; care should be taken of gusting winds and those that make sudden shifts of more than 12° from the prevailing direction.

☐ *Local wind conditions* Wind and wave action cannot always be accurately gauged from the shore. Whitecapping is not always observable when one is facing the same direction in which the wind is driving the waves or when a protected land area intervenes.

☐ *Waves* White caps are normally an excellent warning for the novice sailor. Wind-blown spray and foam indicate 30-mph winds which are too strong for a small sailboat.

☐ *Water current* A strong current with a light breeze can be dangerous and will certainly affect the quality of sailing. Good indicators are drifting objects, channel buoys, flow around pilings and boats on moorings.

☐ *Other boats* If under sail, sailors look for signs of excessive heeling, continuous luffing of sails or reefed and shortened sail plus any general indications of difficulty in handling. They check boats at anchor for bobbing and swinging. During these conditions the average sailor should exercise caution and the novice should stay ashore.

☐ *General weather* Storm warnings are imminent with heavy, black clouds, a sudden drop in temperature and a radical change in wind direction and steadiness. Boat radios will emit static and interference and, even better, a weathercast.

It is impossible to overemphasize the importance of developing a sound knowledge of wind and weather. These are the elements which allow the boat to sail. Those in pursuit of nautical excellence must learn to read these elements. When it can be a matter of survival there is simply no excuse for failing to familiarize oneself with every aspect. Beginning sailors will not learn all there is to know about wind, water, and weather but by recognizing their importance, competence will come with reasonable speed. Youngsters will gain it more slowly but they will, it is hoped, be sailing under closely supervised conditions with experienced adults.

Safety Training

Initial comments concerning weather and elements are a necessary part of any safety instruction. However, some specific areas of knowledge come under the category of safety skills. These include (1) swimming and lifesaving competence, (2) being aware of minimum required safety equipment and procedures, and (3) training and practice in capsize situations, rescuing persons who fall overboard, and coping with emergencies in equipment breakdown and bad weather conditions.

Swimming. All persons sailing in small boats, 20 feet or less, should be able to pass the Red Cross Beginner's Test. An excellent additional requirement is the ability to put on a life jacket securely while in the water. Many people will carry a life jacket with them in the boat but will not put it on. A sudden emergency may require them to put it on while in the water under what might be confusing or chaotic circumstances. It should be mandatory for nonswimmers, weak swimmers, small children and those with health problems to wear life jackets at all times. All persons in small sailboats should follow this rule. My choice leans toward the sailing-vest type approved by the United States Coast Guard.

Safety equipment and procedures. Without exception, each sailor should be familiar with the safety equipment required by the United States Coast Guard. Beginning sailors should go beyond the minimum requirements and use the following equipment:

☐ United States Coast Guard approved personal floatation devices—one for each person in the boat plus at least two extras.

☐ A small anchor and line suitable for depths in which one would be sailing; length should be a minimum of four times the average depth.

☐ Paddles or oars, usually five to six feet in length.

☐ One working flashlight—batteries should be kept separate and condition checked each time out.

☐ A sound device—preferably a hand foghorn; other acceptable substitutes would be a whistle, an airhorn, or a bell.

☐ A small compass and a chart of local waters.

☐ A repair kit—items of personal choice will be added through experience but a basic list would include: a screw driver, pliers and needle nose pliers; water-proof tape; sail patches (tape type); spare parts (such as clevis and cotter pins), a small block on swivel eye, a jib snap or two and, if used, extra sail slides; and two to three feet of fine wire coiled neatly. Anytime an emergency repair is made, full repairs should be attended to promptly after arriving ashore.

☐ Boats equipped with outboard motors will need an additional spare kit containing such items as spare plugs, shear pins, a starter cord, and gasket material.

☐ All sailors should carry a small knife. Aboard boat, there should be at least one and preferably two knives ready at hand.

Emergency situations. First priority should be given to instruction in "capsize" and "man overboard" situations. The procedures in both cases should be explained in the first lesson. However, the practical application is better postponed until some skill in boat handling has been acquired. It would be well to include additional instruction in emergency weather conditions or equipment breakdown throughout the learning experience. What is wanted is a commonsense attitude about safety. Experience is the key to developing it.

BASIC KNOWLEDGE OF SAILBOATS

With progression in instruction comes the realization that sailors, like many other specialists, have a terminology all their own. It is not necessary to master this language before sailing a boat but one must eventually do so, for verbal communication and rapid understanding are an integral part of good sailing.

Chances are that one will begin nautical adventures in a small monohull (one hull) type of boat carrying either one (cat rig) or two (sloop rig) sails (Figs. 68.2 and 68.3). The sail rig will normally be jib-headed (triangular), gaff-headed (four-sided), or a lateen (triangle with two booms) (Figs. 68.4, 68.5 and 68.6). The lateen rig is popular for sailboard types of boats but not

Fig. 68.2 Cat rig.

Fig. 68.3 Sloop rig.

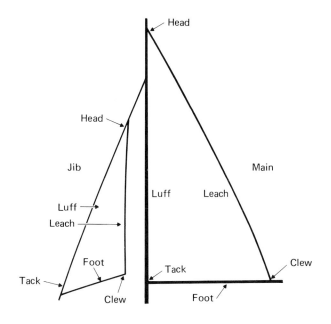

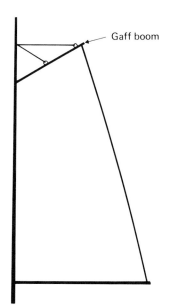

Fig. 68.4 Main jib head or marconi-type sails.

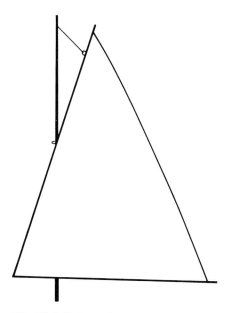

Fig. 68.5 Gaff head rig.

Fig. 68.6 Lateen rig.

limited to them. Workboats, older designs or replica classic types of boats generally employ the gaff rig. The most common sail rig used in the United States today is the jib-headed type.

The four major areas of a boat with which one must be familiar are the *hull*, the *rigging*, the *helm*, and the *sails*. The hull refers to the actual shell of the boat and all of the parts which are permanently attached (Fig. 68.7). The rigging is the apparatus which is used to support and control the sails. The *mast* and *boom* are usually called *spars*, wire supports to the mast are known as *stays* and those on either side referred to as *shrouds*. These may be supplemented with other stays and in their entirety are called the *standing* rigging. Lines controlling the sails are *running* rigging and involve two primary functions: those raising and lowering the sails are the *halyards* and the others responsible for the side to side angle of the sails are the *sheets*. The *helm* is the entire apparatus for steering the boat through the water and consists of the *rudder* and *tiller* (or wheel). The function of the rudder is to direct the movement of the boat by increased or decreased pressure from water flow while the tiller (used by almost all small sailcraft) controls the movement of the rudder.

One part of the hull of especial importance is the *keel* or *centerboard*. This fixture reduces the sideslip of the hull and provides some degree of bal-

Fig. 68.7 Main parts of a boat.

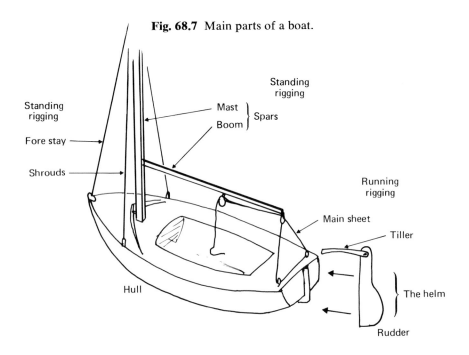

last (weight to maintain the boat in an upright position). The several types available include:

- *Centerboard* Most common in small sailboats. Housed in a covering or box, it is found well along the centerline of the boat and usually just behind the mast. It is lowered or raised into position by means of a line or lever and rotates around a pin (Fig. 68.8).

- *Keel* Less popular among sailors. It is permanently affixed to the underside of the hull along the centerline and, consequently, limits the depth in which the boat may be operated (Fig. 68.9).

- *Dagger board* Similar to a centerboard but simply slid up or down in the well. This is often a choice on sailboard type boats (Fig. 68.10).

- *Leeboard* A centerboard device attached to the side of the hull. Small prams or dinghies give this preference as it allows for more open space within the hull (Fig. 68.11).

The parts of the sails are indicated in Fig. 68.4.

Knots. There are numerous sources from which one can learn to tie the knots necessary to basic sailing skills (see references). The five most commonly used are:

- *Bowline* A good permanent mooring knot and one with which to secure the end of a line to an eye, ring, or spar of some type.

- *Round turn with two half hitches* A knot used often for mooring and securing the end of a line in situations similar to the bowline but not as permanent as the bowline.

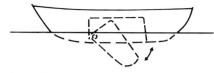

Fig. 68.8 Centerboard.

Fig. 68.9 Keel

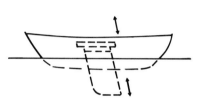

Fig. 68.10 Dagger board.

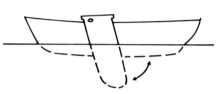

Fig. 68.11 Leeboard

□ *Square knot*   Used to join two lines of the same diameter together, often for reefing (although most boats seem to have a roller type of reefing now).

□ *Clove hitch*   A temporary knot usually securing the line about a spar type of object; this knot needs tension on the line or it loosens.

□ *Figure 8 knot*   Used in a line to stop it from passing through an eye or fair lead.

In addition to the knots described above, the aspiring sailor must know how to properly *cleat, coil* and *heave* a line. Two types of cleats most frequently used are the open standard and the jam. On both, the line should be taken one compete turn around the cleat with complete contact and no gaps; then, in the case of the jam cleat, pulled tight into the jaw and one more turn completed. After the full turn on the standard cleat, continue a half-turn further before one complete figure 8. Finish with one full turn. It is not advisable to "lock-hitch" any lines on a cleat. This may cause jamming in emergency situations, usually ending with the line being cut. All excess lines should be kept neatly coiled and ready to run free. Heaving a line properly takes practice but is worth the effort to avoid some embarrassing moments. Start by putting a quick figure 8 knot (loosely) in the end of the line. Place the coiled line lightly in your nonthrowing hand and the end with the knot in your other. Keep the coil hand open rather than closed for gripping. Draw both arms back in an underhand motion with the throwing hand making a much greater arc; then throw, swinging both arms forward with the throwing hand moving faster than the coil hand and releasing earlier. Always make certain you have plenty of line. To fall short is amateurish, and a backlash can hurt you!

BASIC SAILING SKILLS

Boarding and preparing to sail. There are three possible ways to board a small boat: from a dock or float, from the beach, or from another boat. It is important during boarding to keep in mind several points. Make sure there is enough water under the boat so that the weight of passengers and equipment does not ground you. Step quickly and lightly into the cockpit area, keeping close to the centerline of the boat. To insure safe balance, maintain three points of contact (two hands and two feet are four points so any combination of these will suffice). Remember that the boat is floating and will move with any shift of weight. When adding additional persons or gear, shift the weight as needed to maintain balance. It is often a good practice to lower the centerboard to near the halfway point. This will increase stability.

Do not jump into a boat unless you want to chance a sprain or laceration. *Never* allow arms or legs to hang over the side. The typical sixteen foot fiberglass sloop weighs between 300 and 500 pounds and could cause serious injuries to the luckless person whose arm or leg is dangling when the boat comes in contact with another solid object.

It's not wise to step into a small boat with hands and arms full of gear. Avoid stepping onto the narrow side decking (foredeck) unless you enjoy swimming and hearing humorous stories about yourself!

Two additional points one will find helpful: it is wise to rig dinghies and sailboard types of craft before boarding. They are small, extremely tippable and usually require some heavy or awkward movements to install spars. Also, when bringing the boat close to a dock or float, it is proper to "fend off" while loading; that is, keep the two from banging together. The simplest remedy is to place a temporary fender or other soft padding at the collision point. Arms and legs are *not* recommended as fenders nor are life jackets. The latter can be torn and rendered unserviceable.

Once in the boat, each person should be assigned specific tasks stowing gear and readying the boat for sailing. It often helps to do this prior to embarking. Movement must be kept consistent with proper weight distribution. The skipper should make a final check of equipment and location of stowage. Life jackets should be donned prior to sailing and preferably before coming onto the water. Rudder and tiller are now installed. Care should be exercised to prevent pinched fingers or hands. When necessary, the boom crutch should be secured and stowed. *Always* check to ensure that the helm functions properly and does not foul sheets or other gear. With centerboard down, all other gear ready, stand to bending sails. It is imperative that the skipper and crew carefully check all equipment. Any that is found faulty or dangerously worn should be replaced before setting out.

Bending the sails. This term simply means to attach the sails to the spars and rigging. In the case of a mainsail, the foot should be secured to the boom clew first, then the tack to the gooseneck. The luff should be fed a short way (one to two feet) up the mast until all are secured and the head attached to the main halyard. If the sail is designed with battens, and most are, these should be slipped into the pockets and secured. It is bad for the maintenance of the sail and the performance of the boat to leave the battens out. Also, unless reasonably secured, they can work out of the pocket in turning maneuvers. *Test the sail and halyard to be sure they will operate freely and as intended.* Check for twists and any gear that may bind or impede the hoisting of the sail. The jib should be attached tack first, then luff-clipped to the forestay. Next, the head is attached to the halyard. Last, the jib sheets should be attached to the clew. Again, battens should be inserted if called for, and the sails, halyard, and sheets double-checked for free and normal functioning. All sails should be loosely furled (accordion-style folding) in position to be hoisted and secured lightly with shock cord or light line.

All sheets should be cleared, coiled, and ready for free running. The gear needed for leaving the dock or float should be handy and the cockpit and decks cleared ready to get under way.

Getting under way. As in flying, getting under way and landing are two rather critical periods. Below are the three general situations that will face you when getting under way.

☐ *From a dock or float,* it is unwise for the novice to hoist the sails until clear from congested areas. Cast off the lines, carefully, attempting to place them where they can be easily picked up upon return. Using a paddle, oar, or motor, maneuver the boat into reasonably clear water and head the bow directly into the wind. Recheck those sails again for free movement, then hoist them from the aftermost to the foremost sail (main to jib). Allow the sails to luff until halyards are secured before trimming the sheets (again, main to jib). By adjusting the angle of the sail to the wind, the boat is allowed to bear off (ease away from the eye of the wind) as it picks up movement through the water. Under certain conditions, you may use the wind in the aftermost sail to ease you from a dock but if the area contains piles and other boats or fixtures, you may tear your sails and cause damage to your craft.

☐ *Leaving a mooring* (a fixed anchorage away from docks and floats) is usually a simpler process. If surrounded by many other moored boats, care must be taken not to foul the boat or collide with them. While still fastened to the mooring line, hoist the mainsail (again, the aftermost) and permit it to luff freely. The wind will hold the boat swinging bow first on the mooring line. Decide upon the best direction for leaving the mooring area. After a quick check to ensure that all running rigging is functioning freely, push the tiller in the direction you wish to go. The boat will swing on its mooring line in that direction. Once it is headed in that direction cast the mooring well clear in the opposite direction. Ease the tiller back slightly past the centerline, taking care not to foul the mooring. Trim the main sheet, allowing the mainsail to fill away. ALL of these operations should be done almost simultaneously. If you are alone, there is a slight time interval between casting off the mooring and adjusting the tiller. But the beginner *should not* be leaving a dock or mooring alone! When under way, hoist and trim the jib. A word of caution is in order. While mooring areas may appear to be less congested than dock areas, things that will foul or entangle you are floating both on and under the water. Only sharp observation will keep you from running over and fouling mooring equipment—especially your own.

☐ *Sailing from a beach* will most often be done with sailboard and dinghy types of craft. The preparation of the boat is basically the same with these exceptions:

1. Do not install the rudder until after the sails are bent and hoisted.
2. Dagger or leeboards are not lowered until under way.
3. Almost all preparation is done while standing outside the boat.
4. As in all car-top or trailerable boats, the mast will have to be installed (stepped).

Always keep the bow of the boat facing into the wind while preparing to shove off. When ready to get under way, the rudder and tiller are set in position to operate and the dagger board readied (if heading to windward when starting) but allow the sail to luff. Normally, you will push off the bottom with your feet while at the same time you will be pulling yourself into the craft. Once aboard, make the necessary rudder, tiller, sail trim, and board adjustments.

Sailing under way. Once you are under way, the basic mechanics and maneuvers are relatively simple. Three important points should be mentioned concerning the mechanics:

1. The relative heading of the boat determines the point of sailing which in turn dictates what one will do in the boat. The relative heading means the direction in which the bow is pointed in relation to the direction from which the wind is blowing (Figs. 68.12, 68.13, and 68.14).
2. The action of the tiller and rudder determines the turning of the boat. The rudder turns the boat but it is the tiller that controls the rudder. As the boat moves forward, the bow turns in the opposite direction from the tiller, i.e., tiller moved to starboard (right), the bow moves to port (left). The actual pivot point is at the center of lateral resistance, the centerboard or keel. When the boat is moving astern (backward) the bow will swing in the direction the tiller is pointed. The turning of the boat is due to the change of water flow over the rudder blade. The more rapid

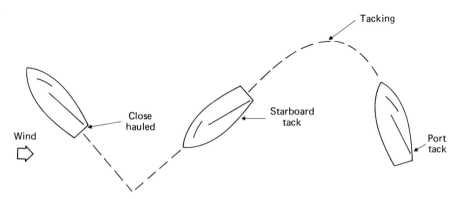

Fig. 68.12 Beating to windward.

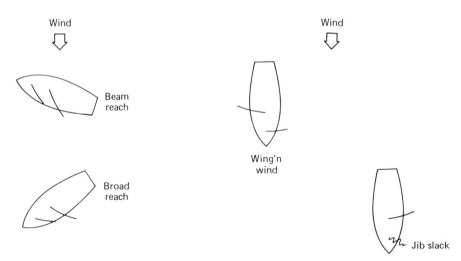

Fig. 68.13 Reaching.   **Fig. 68.14** Running.

the flow, the more quickly the boat will turn. The rudder will not affect the movement of the boat unless the boat has way (movement through the water).

3. The trim of the sails affects the actual driving force of the wind. To trim means starting (slackening) or trimming (tightening) the sheet. This adjusts the leading edge and the plane of the sail to the relative direction of the wind. Most sails are now cut so that there is a curve to the plane or surface. This creates an aerodynamic effect similar to that of an airplane's wing. Best results are achieved at about a 45° angle to the wind and, except when running ahead of the wind, the foot of the jib should always be about parallel to the foot of the main.

The three basic points of sailing are *running, reaching,* and *beating.* Running is the position where the wind comes from dead astern (behind). The mainsail should be let out as far as possible and the jib blanketed (shielded from the wind) unless sheeted on the opposite side of the main; this is then called *running "wing and wing."* On this point of sailing, which is not the fastest, the centerboard should be raised at least halfway to reduce drag and possible tripping in a jibe (see below). Caution must be exercised especially in three specific danger situations:

☐ An accidental jibe when the wind gets behind the sail with the leach crossing the eye of the wind. This will result in slamming sail and boom to the opposite side of the boat running the risk of injury to passengers, heavy damage to spars and other equipment and even capsizing or swamping.

Fig. 68.15 Running "wing on wing." Courtesy of *JOPER*.

☐ With a heavy following sea, the chance of accidental jibe is still ever-present with the two accompanying dangers of swamping and pitch-poling. These latter two can result from poor weight distribution fore or aft, too much sail, and the combined effect of cresting, breaking waves.

☐ A more remote possibility experienced mostly by catboats with extremely long booms occurs when the end of this boom catches in a heavy sea causing a violent broach (turning sideways into breaking waves) with resultant swamping.

The running position is a tough one to sail effectively as the wind is moving with you and its vagaries are not as detectable. Also, great skill at the helm and in weight distribution is demanded by the wave action.

Reaching is the point of sailing where the wind is abeam. It is the fastest and generally the easiest point of sailing. (Most beginners spend too much of their time enjoyably on reaching.) Allow the sail to luff, then trim it in just slightly. The center board may be raised a little and moveable weight shifted slightly aft. Take care if a heavy sea is running from a 90° angle to dead astern (quartering seas). These can swamp you if you are careless.

Beating refers to the position in which the boat is headed as close as possible to the direction of the wind. It is sometimes identified (inaccurately) as tacking. Tacking is only the turning maneuver while sailing on a beat. It is the turning of the bow into and across the direction of the wind. Some call it the close-hauled position because the sails are trimmed tight with the boat headed at about a 45° angle to the wind. To maneuver the boat against the wind involves the process known as tacking and is often referred to as work-ing to windward. The full centerboard will normally be needed and, as wind velocity increases, the boat will heel more continuously and at a greater angle. This heeling necessitates shifting moveable ballast (human type) to the wind-

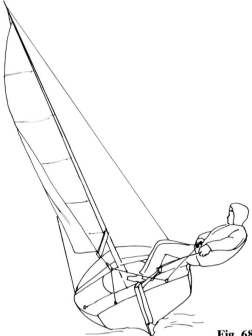

Fig. 68.16 Hiking out.

Fig. 68.17 "Hiking out" over the side to keep hull as upright as possible is necessary in heavy winds. Courtesy of *JOPER*.

ward (wind'ard) side of the boat and in heavy winds "hiking out" over the side to keep the hull as upright as possible (Figs. 68.16 and 68.17).

To jibe is the act of turning the boat so that the stern (back) and leach of sail cross the eye of the wind. When intentional, it is called a controlled jibe; when unintentional, it can be a disaster. This is the procedure to be followed:

☐ Raise the centerboard almost all the way.

☐ Put the tiller over and at the same time, take in the main sheet as rapidly as possible, trying to get your mainsail aligned along the fore-aft axis of the boat.

☐ Keep your eye on the leach of the sail; as it crosses the wind, it will form an S curve. Let it run out in the new direction rapidly.

☐ Ease the tiller on the new heading and trim your sheets.

When jibing, turn the jib sheet loose and allow it to luff throughout the entire maneuver. In a heavy wind if the centerboard is down, it can trip the boat. Prior to and during this operation, it is essential that the main sheet runs freely and does not jam. One last and important point is that of shifting the ballast at the moment the mainsail crosses the wind. This is true in both tacking and jibing and becomes increasingly important as the wind force increases.

Mooring and putting the boat to bed. Picking up a mooring is generally the easiest of the three landing procedures. Until one has a good feeling of the boat, it is wise to make one or two practice approaches for any landing. Head in from the leeward (downwind) side. Keep in mind that every boat will fetch (glide) some distance after the driving force is stopped. With the mooring upwind, an approach from either tack enables you to turn head into the wind allowing enough distance to glide up to the buoy or float holding the mooring line (see Fig. 68.18). It is important to start your sheets and to allow the sails to luff. Lower the jib as soon as the mooring line is secured.

A dock or float landing is not difficult if there are no obstructions. Approaching from the leeward, turn using the glide to gain a position alongside allowing the sails to luff. Keep in mind that the boom must be brought inboard to prevent hitting the dock and causing damage. It is wise to get the jib in just before making the final approach leg. If the area or setup is too difficult, dowse the sails in a clear area and use motor or muscle to dock. There are so many variables to consider, I believe it is best to have an experienced sailor practice dock landings with beginners before they attempt them.

Beaching a small boat is relatively the same as a float landing and very easy because there should be no congestion or obstruction. Also, the sailboard fraternity expects to spend some time in the water up to their waist everytime

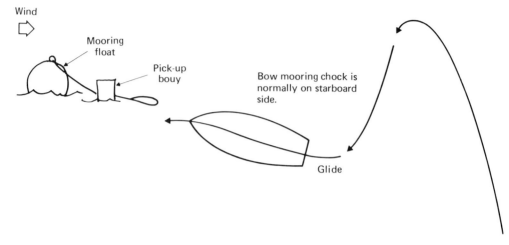

Fig. 68.18 Proper approach to mooring.

they go out so this simplifies the landing. However, two points must be emphasized: (1) get the dagger board and rudder up and out to prevent major damage, and (2) take care in disembarking. The landing and disembarking of sailboards are the most frequent sources of minor scrapes and bruises. The novice should not take these maneuvers too lightly.

Putting the boat to bed or securing it is essentially preparation in reverse. Here, again, there are several important things to remember:

☐ Always wash the decks, hull and equipment, with fresh water when possible.

☐ Leave the bilge dry. Bail it out before you leave.

☐ Secure everything to something permanently affixed to the hull. Wind and wave action have a tremendous wearing effect on loose and swinging parts. Occasionally, in foul weather, loose gear in a moored boat will be lost.

☐ Allow for adequate rise and fall of tide, where applicable, when adjusting mooring lines.

☐ Check for any repairs needed and get to them immediately, if possible.

SETTING UP A PROGRAM

Personnel and equipment. The first requirement for any program is the selection of the right person to run it. The editors of *Sports Illustrated* emphasize this point. "... finding such a man ... is often the determining factor in the success or failure of the program." The assistants or instructors necessary in programs of any size are a very important element. While sailing master at the Cape Cod Sea Camps, the author worked with between 20 and 40 young sailing counselors each summer. With a few exceptions, they were successful because they knew how to sail well, were interested in helping others, and were attractive, personable youngsters. This latter point may seem trivial but keep in mind that the instructor works with students in a confined cockpit for several days, two to four hours daily.

The minimum capital equipment for any program should include:

☐ Two boats equipped with outboard motors plus one spare motor.

☐ A fleet of sailboats—preferably 14- to 16-foot small sloops. If the fleet is limited to fewer than six boats, it is recommended they be sloops. If possible, part of the fleet should include small prams or dinghy sailboats, a few boardboats, and a catamaran or two.

☐ A building of some type with stowage area, maintenance and repair area, and space for classroom work. The sail stowage, the motor stowage, and the classroom should be separated from the work area because noxious fumes could be present.

☐ Many small items such as replacement parts, extra sets of sails, safety equipment for each boat, lifesaving equipment and first-aid kit, a fire extinguisher, and a set of general tools, and boat maintenance items such as varnish, paint, and fiberglass patching.

☐ Teaching aids which should increase over the years: chalkboard, bulletin board, mock-ups, windboards, toy boats, nautical charts, and a small

Fig. 68.19 If possible, part of the fleet should include dinghy sailboats. Courtesy of Camp Monomoy.

library of books, periodicals, and nautical games. It is very helpful to have access to film and slide projectors.

Whenever possible, be looking at ways to teach or supplement on land everything you expect to teach in the boat on the water. For example, use a flagstaff to practice with a spinnaker or perhaps mount a dinghy on a cradle attached to a turntable made from a wooden telephone cable reel. There is, however, *no* substitute for learning in the boat.

Program content and application. The principles of developing and implementing a good sailing program are essentially the same as any teaching or learning program. These are the salient points:

- [ ] Decide what the objectives and limits of the program are to be.
- [ ] Ensure that the program is adaptable to the type of students anticipated.
- [ ] Build in a system for responding to the individual differences among the students.
- [ ] Develop, write, and disseminate an outline or booklet covering the program, its objectives, skills, and concepts to be learned, suggested teaching methods, a system for determining progress, and evaluation procedures. Use one basic reference book. Alan Brown (1968) or P. Royce (1969) is highly recommended.
- [ ] Keep all learning in a progression but at the same time, capitalize on any unexpected learning situation which may arise. For example, if weather conditions change and dictate a reduction in sail, that is the moment to demonstrate a quick reef or other method of taking in sail—but not a detailed lesson normally planned for a certain time period. On-the-spot demonstrations drive a point home most effectively!
- [ ] A last and most important suggestion is to constantly vary the instruction and evaluations. Don't overlook good old "under the longboat" yarn sessions. In the evening or during a flat calm, get the group together and encourage them to talk about their experiences in the program. This is the way the art of sailing becomes real to them.

Preparation for instruction. As in all teaching, preparation improves the chances of success. Each session should be planned. However, as the weather is the dominant factor, it is wise to have two or three different plans each day. The more experience an instructor has, the easier this becomes.

Indoor programs. No one can truly learn to sail without being on the water. Yet too many opportunities pass by over the winter or during extended periods of foul weather. It is possible to run a half-year sailing elective in public school physical education classes. During February, March, and even

April, much valuable instruction can be given. For example, a multipurpose room could be set up with these suggested learning stations:

- [ ] A dinghy mounted on a homemade turntable could be used for several teaching experiences from points of sailing to identification and correct use of various parts of a boat. A large electric fan can be used to simulate wind.

- [ ] Poles used normally for volleyball nets with typical floor mountings and stays could be used for demonstrating how to bend sails, reef or even handle a spinnaker (again, making use of a floor electric fan for wind effect).

- [ ] Sailing games at tables can serve as an aid in learning the "rules of the road" and racing techniques.

- [ ] Charts, boat models, navigational aids, and compasses can be utilized at other tables. For that matter, students could be designated a boat and instructed to work their way through a room designed as a simulated sailing area.

- [ ] Ropework (knots, cleating, and heaving lines) can be set up using railings, mock-ups and targets (heaving lines).

- [ ] If a pool is accessible, boardboats and dinghies may be used for teaching capsize procedures, man-overboard rescue drills, necessary swim skills, and even some points of sailing.

- [ ] Audiovisual equipment can be utilized in many ways; for example, they can produce sound effects to create realism.

It is assumed, of course, that such an indoor program would culminate with a warm May and June series of sessions utilizing local lakes, creeks, rivers or bay facilities with actual boats. If such facilities are not available, a physical education unit in boating safety or some similar course might be offered.

REFERENCES

Book of junior sailing 1964. New York: Sports Illustrated, J. B. Lippincott.

Book of small boat sailing 1960. New York: Sports Illustrated, J. B. Lippincott.

Brown, A. 1968. *Invitation to sailing.* New York: Simon and Schuster.

Calahan, H. A. 1968. *Yachtsman's omnibus* (10th ed.). New York: Macmillan.

Encyclopedia of sailing 1971. By the editors of *One-design and offshore yachtsman.* New York: Harper & Row.

De Fontaine, W. H. 1961. *The young sportsman's guide to sailing.* New York: Thomas Nelson.

Royce, P. 1969. *Sailing illustrated.* Newport Beach, Calif.: Fashion Press.

———— 1950. *Sailing technique.* New York: Macmillan.

69

Surfing

James E. Odenkirk

INTRODUCTION

Surfing in some form has been enjoyed for more than one thousand years. However, recorded accounts date back to only 1778 when Captain Cook, the British explorer, sailed to Hawaii and saw men who appeared to be "flying over the water." The sport of Hawaii's ancient kings was surfing—sliding down the slope of a breaking wave. According to legend, King Kamehameha and his Queen, Kaahumanu, surfed side by side on the great Hawaiian waves.

During the 19th century, the sport almost disappeared and by 1900 a wave, a board, and a man were seldom seen together on the foamy edges of Hawaii's green islands. But early in the 1900s a revival of interest in surfing took place. The late Duke Kahanamoku, Hawaii's premier surfer, popularized the sport by encouraging the formation of surfing clubs. In May, 1908, the Hawaiian Outrigger Canoe Club was founded for the purpose of "preserving surfing on boards and in Hawaiian outrigger canoes." By 1912, Duke Kahanamoku inspired the growing colony of surfers in southern California and in 1915 he introduced board surfing to Australia. Kahanamoku was considered surfing's worldwide ambassador.

During the 20th century, surfing has spread to New Zealand, South Africa, England, Israel, France, Peru, areas of South America, and along both coasts of the United States.

Surfing received added attention when Big Surf, an artificial wavemaking operation was developed and built in Tempe, Arizona, in 1969. Big Surf is a surfing facility which provides three-to four-foot waves over a four-hundred-foot lagoon. The waves are generated through fifteen underwater gates which spring open by hydraulic force, and propel water over a three-foot baffle and toward a sand-covered beach 400 feet inland. The size of the wave is controlled by the amount of water pumped into the reservoir behind the gates. No two surfing curls are exactly the same. The water in the lagoon is nine feet deep where the wave begins and becomes more shallow as it approaches the shore.

Surfers descend stairs built in each of the lagoon sidewalls and enter the water every two minutes as a new wave develops. Eight to ten surfers may ride each wave.

The Physical Education Department at Arizona State University offers surfing classes each semester to aspiring surfers and the course has proven quite popular. Big Surf projects a new dimension for surfing, previously associated only with certain coastal regions and the natural waves formed by the oceans.

Accompanying the surfing boom were attempts to develop better equipment for the surfer. The earliest boards were made of wood—redwood at first and balsa later on. Experimentation continued on new materials for surfboards, and in the late 1950s, a new material was developed. The material was polyurethane foam which formed the core of the new surfboard and it was covered with a combination of woven fiberglass cloth and liquid resins.

From this point on there were no more limitations on surfboard designs and the sport grew rapidly as did the formation of surfing clubs, publications, associations and an increasing number of competitive events.

The Makaha International, The Duke Kahanamoku Invitational Classic, both in Hawaii, the Peruvian International, and the World Surfing Championships attract top surfers and worldwide attention. Numerous surfing groups such as the Eastern United States Surfing Association, Western United States Surfing Association and the Hawaiian Surfing Association are actively promoting the sport in their respective ways.

Surfing has now become a worldwide sport, especially attractive to younger age groups. Modern transportation assists the surfer in reaching favorable surfing areas. Films, television, lectures, and written materials are "messengers" for promoting a sport which allows the participant to enjoy the thrills of conquering nature and extending human physical capabilities to their zenith.

Surfing Contests

Point system for judging surfing. The *basic rule* of the International Surfing Federation states, "A surfer will receive the maximum amount of points for

Fig. 69.1 Surfing has now become a worldwide sport, especially attractive to younger age groups. Courtesy of *JOPER*.

traveling the greatest distance at the greatest speed in the most critical part of a wave." Greatest distance means the distance traveled on a wave utilizing all curling and breaking sections, not the distance from takeoff to shore. Greatest speed and critical part of wave mean the section of wave directly in front of the white water, where the greatest speed can be obtained.

Judges also take into account the following:

☐ Wave judgment, the quality and utilization of each wave selected.

☐ Functional maneuvers, maneuvers which change a rider's position, direction, or speed so that he or she may maintain a favorable position in the most critical part of a wave. These maneuvers are turns (top and bottom), cutbacks, climbing and dropping, trimming, stalling, and squatting under critical sections.

☐ Form and board control, the manner in which a surfer handles the surfboard while executing a maneuver with the ability to blend together elements of style in a display of graceful control.

☐ Safety, a surfer's ability to hold onto the board while executing pullouts, kickouts, proning, keeping in mind that a surfer who does not attempt to hold onto the board is a danger to one who does hold onto the board.

☐ Wave right-of-way, a surfer in position catching a wave has the right-of-way over anyone else who may be dropping in or out of position. Points will be deducted from a rider who, in the judge's opinion, interferes with another surfer's ride.

10 Point modification for each wave. Three points for difficulty. Judges consider wave size, type of break (fast, slow), position in wave (shoulder, curl).

Three points for form, style, and safety (see above).

Four points for execution. Functional manuevers on the board and in the wave. Each ride is scored from 0 to 10 points. The five highest wave scores are used to obtain a total score. Regular heats last 30 minutes and the final heat lasts 45 minutes.

TERMINOLOGY

Angling Crossing a wave instead of riding it into the beach.

Backhand turn A left turn for a "natural" rider, a right turn for a goofy-footer.

Bailing out Jumping off a surfboard quickly to avoid being wiped out.

Beach break Waves that break close to shore rather than over sandbars or reefs.

Blowhole surf A surf breaking over holes in a lava bottom, creating a boiling surface.

Body surfing Catching a wave with the body.

Bombora Offshore reef surf, usually big and powerful.

Catching a rail Akin to catching an edge in skiing; the down-wave rail, or edge, of the board digs into the water and throws the surfer.

Close out Occurs when heavy surf breaks along the entire length of a beach, making surfing impossible.

Coffin ride A surfer lying on his back on a board is enveloped in the curl of the wave.

Cornering Traveling sideways across a wave.

Critical A wave reaches a critical stage when it is extremely upright and is about to break.

Curl The curved portion of the wave, usually the top section of a semihollow or hollow wave.

Deck The top surface of the board.

Ding A chip or hole in a surfboard.

Dumper A powerful wave that breaks in shallow water and which, instead of breaking slowly from the top, falls suddenly in an arc.

Face Surface of a wave, usually the front part of an unbroken wave.

Glass Short for fiberglass used in board production.

Green waves Smooth waves steep enough for riding.

Goofy foot Surfing with the right foot forward.

Ground swell Swell which has traveled a long distance from the place of its origin.

Gun Large surfboard designed for big surf.

Hang ten Walking to the nose of the board and putting ten toes over the edge; hang five is self-explanatory.

Heavies Big waves.

Hot dogging A flashy surfing style.

Inside The area between the beach and the breaking waves.

Jamming Obstructing or blocking the ride of another surfer.

Kick out When, at the end of the ride, a surfer steps to the back of the board and swings it 180° around, letting the waves pass by.

Lining surf A wave that stretches a long distance from end to end and provides a long ride.

Locked in Surfing inside the curl.

Mushing wave One that breaks in the top and dies out quickly, leading to a very short ride.

Offshore wind Wind blowing from the land toward the sea.

Onshore wind Wind blowing from the sea toward the land.

Outside 1 A surfer riding outside another surfer who is closer to the curl; 2 seaward beyond the break.

Nose Front of the surfboard.

Peak The highest point of a wave before it breaks.

Pearling The nose of the board digs into the water and submarines, causing the surfer to lose control and get wiped out.

Point break A break activated by land jutting out into the ocean.

Popout Production model board.

Pullout To get off a wave.

Quasimodo Riding crouched with one arm forward, the other arm back.

Rail The edge of the board.

Reef surf Surf breaking on a reef.

Rip Current of water running to sea.

Rocker Curve, banana, or lift of a surfboard shape.

Set A series of good waves, usually three or four coming along in a group.

Shooting the tube Riding through the hollow part of the curl, usually in a crouched position near the nose.

Shore break A surf which breaks on the shore or close to it.

Skeg The fin at the bottom rear of the surfboard that gives the board stability and makes it maneuverable.

Slide To move down or across the face of a wave.

Soup The foamy, broken part of the breaker.

Stringer The strip or strips of balsa running the length of a board.

Surf's up! There is big surf.

Taking gas Falling off the board.

Taking off To catch a wave.

Tandem Two people riding the same board.

Trimming Positioning the surfboard on the wave.

Tube Sometimes when a wave breaks it forms a tunnel between its face and its curl. Occasionally a surfer can get a ride in the tube—one of the supreme thrills of surfing.

Undertow Current of water traveling below the surface.

Wall surf A wave-face which seems to stand vertically like a wall.

Wind swell Waves created by wind.

Wipe out Taking gas.

SURFING FOR BEGINNERS

Waves and the surfer. What happens when surfer and board combine to capture the energy of the surf? There are certain basic forces coming into play that, if they are understood and appreciated, will help the new surfer to grasp what is happening. The first of these natural forces is the movement of the surf toward the shore. The next factor is the force of gravity pulling the breaking wave downward. The surfer's sliding, forward momentum on the face of the wave helps to overcome gravity and stabilize the board. On a smooth, fast wave, stability is greatly increased. Waves with steep slopes tend to break faster than those waves with a moderate slope. The degree of slope steepness will influence the surfer's choice of location in relation to the wave. At a beach where the bottom starts the wave breaking at one end, instead of across the whole face of the wave, catching a wave is easy. The portion of the wave just in front of the break is called the shoulder. Waves with a well-formed shoulder are ideal for the beginning surfer, provided the waves are not too large. When the ride is started close to the breaking portion of the wave, near the white water, only a few strokes are needed to begin the slide.

Getting started. To reach the state of ability where a good ride is usually the rule takes a lot of work and knowledge. Much learning comes from watching other surfers, but watching doesn't develop strength or balance.

It takes strength to paddle a board out through the surf, burst through incoming waves, then kick it around and sprint paddle to catch a wave.

Paddling is the best way to train for paddling. A good paddler will be able to control the board, get more speed for the takeoff, and use less energy going out time after time.

The two basic paddling techniques are done in the prone and kneeling position. The secret of paddling well is to achieve proper balance and to bring as many muscles into play as possible. A good paddling position will keep the nose of the board slightly high. If the nose is low, it will dig in and submarine. Keep the nose an inch or two above the surface of the water. On rough choppy days the nose should be raised a little higher so the board will not take water over the front. If the nose is too high, the tail will drag and the board will be harder to paddle.

The head is held high and the chin is up. This chin-up position helps the surfer to see better and to arch the back so more muscles work when stroking. If a combination of arm, shoulder, and back muscles all work together, the result is more power with less overall effort. For long-distance paddling, slow gliding strokes are best. Some distance paddlers feather their hands at the end of the stroke to reduce resistance to the water. This is done by turning the hands parallel to the rails of the board just before the recovery of the arms. If the arms stay relaxed during the recovery, they will not become stiff so quickly.

Knee paddling requires a little more balance, but if the board is not too narrow or does not tip, knee paddling is easy. A lot of younger surfers seem to paddle only on their knees. It is really a matter of preference. Some surfers believe a kneeling position is better for the takeoff due to the faster starts achieved.

Surfers sit on their heels between strokes. When they paddle, their bodies rock forward and the weight shifts from the center of balance forward to the nose. The hands dig in and the body is rocked back. Both the muscles and the momentum of the body in a rocking position aid the force of the stroke in the kneeling position takeoff. When paddling down the wave on the takeoff, it is sometimes necessary to move the balance point forward or backward. Moving the balance point forward increases the downward tilt of the board and will help speed the slide. Moving the weight back will reduce the slide angle and sometimes prevent pearling. A good paddler will feel comfortable either prone or kneeling and can change from one to the other without missing a stroke. Champion paddlers can paddle continuously for hours by changing positions and bringing different muscles into play while other muscles rest.

Another skill related to paddling is turning the board. Slight, slow turns are done by leaning toward the direction in which the turn is to be made. Some surfers drag a foot to help turn the board. Dragging the right foot while paddling will turn the board to the right. A radical 180° turn is made by sitting at the tailend of the board and raising about two-thirds of the board out of the water. The nose of the board can then pivot around the tail. Both the arms and legs help turn the board around in the pivot turn. To turn right, both legs rotate counterclockwise; to turn left they rotate clockwise. Many surfers face out to sea waiting for a wave and spin around quickly as the wave comes. At the end of the turn they throw their weight forward and start to paddle. This sudden shifting of weight forward accelerates the start and results in the wave being caught with fewer strokes.

Paddling out. Much can be learned about surfing from watching waves. Even a new surfer can recognize that on a certain day the waves will come shoreward with a certain definite pattern, or set. There's no reason to waste energy fighting through broken surf when in a few minutes the sets of waves will diminish and a calm period will follow. It's always a good idea to watch the surf for a while before going out. This is the time to spot the best place to catch a wave, look for possible hazards, and judge the easiest way of getting outside. On some days, for example, after a storm, waves will roll in continuously and there won't be a period of calm, or lull, between sets. On such days, the surfer usually tries to find a channel of calmer water in which to paddle the board. At most surfing beaches it is also possible to paddle around the break. At beaches where the surf humps up due to a rocky point or reef, there will be an area of calm water on one side of the break. It's better to try going around the break rather than paddling through it. Going around the end will take less fight, reduce the chance of getting hit by another board, and frequently take less time than a direct route out.

If it isn't possible to get around the surf on days when the surf is breaking big and rough, the surfer must push through. Waves often roll in at 15 or 20 miles an hour. To move through the advancing white water (the soup),

Fig. 69.2 Position, wave judgment, and paddling skill are needed for successful surfing.

893

the board must be paddled fast enough to achieve sufficient momentum to meet the shock of the wave without being pushed back. Just before smashing into the wave, rise to a push-up position. This posture allows the water to pass between the body and the board.

As waves grow bigger (over four feet) the surfer can't develop enough thrust to overcome the shock of the wave. In this type of surf, the board can be used as protection from the crash of the surf by "turning turtle." This term means flipping the board upside down and hanging on while the wave passes overhead. If the surf is large, it is best to wrap the legs as well as the arms around the board. However, the body hanging to the board acts as a sea anchor and stops the board from being washed back too far by the force of the wave. When the board is overhead it is also a protection from other boards coming at one from any angle. It is a rough trip to fight through six or seven waves, paddle hard, and then "turn turtle" again and again. Good physical condition pays off in such situations.

Catching the wave. Position, wave judgment, and paddling skill are needed for successful surfing. Beginners may find catching broken waves much easier as the white water supplies the necessary push to get them moving. In catching broken waves, surfers should assume a position on the board so that the nose is clear and slightly out of the water. They should face directly toward shore and take a few paddles just before the "soup" hits. As the white water rolls into them, they should grab the rails of their boards, lean back, and hold tight. After the initial push they may want to slide themselves slightly forward to stay with the wave. At this point beginners are ready to stand.

Catching unbroken waves. The position of the surfers depends on the type of wave they are riding. If they are at a beach break where the waves break over a sand bottom, they can sit just about anywhere, and it's merely a matter of luck that they'll be in the right spot at the right time. As they become more experienced they'll be able to spot the waves and tell exactly where they're going to break. Then they can paddle to meet the waves and thus get many more rides. If they're riding at a reef break where the waves consistently break in or near the same spot, they should position themselves near this point of initial breaking and a little outside (seaward). They should always try not to interfere with others, and if possible, select the wave that has no one riding on it. Positioning is mostly a matter of experience and expert surfers can spot a hump on the horizon and know almost exactly where it's going to break.

After surfers have positioned themselves in front of an oncoming wave, their procedure in catching the wave is to face shore and begin paddling before the slope of the wave or white water reaches the back of the board. They paddle directly toward shore, not at an angle to it. As momentum is gained, surfers will pass the point at which paddling becomes a drag rather than a pull. At this point they have almost caught the wave. One of the most common mistakes made by the beginner is not taking an added stroke or two to move down the face of the wave before it gets too steep. The tendency is to stand up at the first indication of a moving wave beneath you. This is the reason why many first rides end with either nosing into the water at the bottom of the wave (pearling), getting dumped from the top of the wave in the white water (over-the-falls), or standing up after the swell has passed (most common).

Standing. When the wave has been caught and pearling has been avoided, surfers stand up by pushing up with their hands beneath their chests (some prefer holding the rails). The hands keep balance as surfers rise to their feet. If the balance feels correct, surfers remove their hands and stand up. The faster the stand, the less chance there will be of falling.

Standing up on the board can be done at any time during the initial part of the ride. Experts move to their feet quickly, turn the board at the right moment, and slide away. The beginner may want to wait until the board is turned and riding smoothly before standing up.

Standing can be done either by coming directly to the feet in one smooth motion or coming to the knees or a crouch and then standing up. Most surfers take a standing position with the left leg forward and the right foot back. Some reverse this stance and earn the name of "goofy foot." It's the back leg that transmits changes of body balance to the board. The further back the weight is placed and the greater the lean toward the face of the wave, the faster the board will turn. An extreme movement of this type will produce the pullout. Moving the weight forward toward the nose will drop it until it digs in and pearls. This is another type of pullout. A carefully balanced forward position will result in the best speed, but it is hard to maintain. In the basic stand-up position the feet are usually spread about 18 inches apart and the rear foot is turned almost at right angles to the center line of the board. The body can face directly forward or be turned about 45° off the center line. Many different positions are used, depending on the wave, the surfer, and the surface condition. Practice will help determine which position is best for the individual.

Falling and stopping. Surfers who start to fall try to fall on or alongside of the board, grabbing it as they do. A loose board is dangerous as it may pop up and hit its rider or another surfer inside the waves. Holding onto the board also eliminates unnecessary swimming. If the wave is large, the surfer who is in for a wipe-out should dive to the inside (toward the wave) or away from the direction of the board.

Turning. Once the techniques of standing have been mastered, beginners naturally want to start turning and maneuvering their boards. Although there are many different styles of turning, they are all derived from the same basic maneuver. By digging the left rear, surfers get a left turn. To do this, one foot should be in front of the other. This is the lead foot. The lead foot is the balance foot; the trail foot, the turning foot. Surfers keep most of their weight on the lead foot until a turn is desired. A right turn is made by applying pressure with the trail foot on the right rear of the board. A left turn is made by shifting the trail foot to the left rear of the board and applying downward pressure. For a kick-out or a turn over the top of the wave, surfers apply weight through the trail foot on the rear of the board—to the right side if going right—to the left side if going left. The front foot is used as a guide as the board comes up and through the wave. To accelerate the board, surfers step foot over foot toward the nose. This technique is called "walking the nose" and is an extremely popular technique used by hot-doggers. If the wave is breaking or the board is headed for a pearl, surfers backstep (back paddle) foot over foot until rear control is regained. Turns are very valuable in regaining proper wave position as well as keeping the surfer from riding out of the wave.

SOME OF THE DANGERS

Drowning. Surfing, even in small waves, requires that the individual be at ease in the water. Waves over four feet high require a high level of swimming ability as well as a good level of conditioning. "Big waves," over eight feet, require excellent conditioning and swimming knowledge as well as knowledge about the hazards of surf, e.g., undertow, rip currents, method of traveling around and/or through surf.

Coral. Many of the best breaks occur over coral reefs which have many sharp edges on which to cut feet, hands, or any other body part which comes in contact with them.

Jellyfish. All types of jellyfish are equipped with stinging cells. The severity of the sting depends on the type of jellyfish and the number of times a person has been stung. Some jellyfish move with the currents and cannot actually swim. This kind of jellyfish can be avoided.

Rays. Stingrays are equipped with a stinging tail which can cause severe pain. Rays are not known to attach to a person. If you see one, give it plenty of room. "Attacks" are generally haphazard encounters.

Sharks. The shark is a primitive animal, a life form which has existed 320 million years. There are about 1300 species. The shark has a small and primitive brain which mostly services its olfactory sense. A shark can smell blood from great distances. Sharks are highly unpredictable. They prefer warm water but can be found anywhere. Sharks may attack anything, especially if in a feeding frenzy. They can attack from any position and do not have to roll over to bite.

Attacks often occur in the warmer months when water is between 60 to 70°F. Most attacks are made on bathers in two to three feet of water, which of course is where most bathers are. Injury is greatest to the legs and buttocks. Mortality is as high as 70 percent because of shock and the loss of blood.

The size of a shark makes little difference. An eight-foot hammerhead, the species associated with most attacks, can tear flesh out of your leg just as well as a 24-foot white shark, only in smaller bites.

Sharks are more likely to be found in warm, calm water where there are many small fish to eat but may appear anywhere at any time. If you are surfing and you see a shark, slowly move in the direction of the beach and catch the first wave in. Sit on the beach and enjoy the sun.

Sea urchins. Sea urchins are small animals with spines of calcium carbonate about two to six inches long. Urchins most commonly live around coral reefs where they feed. If you step on or put your hand on an urchin, the needle-sharp spines go straight in and break off at the surface of the flesh. The spines contain a weak poison. While the result is not severe, it is painful. If you are going to step down, watch where you step.

RULES OF COURTESY AND COMMON SENSE

- ☐ The person on the inside of the wave has the right-of-way. If there is any danger of getting in their way, do not take off.
- ☐ When paddling out, try to go around a break. Pick a rip, which is a channel or deep place where waves are not too big. This method is safer for you and other surfers.
- ☐ Try to stay with your board at all times. A loose board is dangerous.
- ☐ If you are riding a wave and someone else is paddling out, it is up to you to avoid a collision, as the surfer on the wave has more maneuverability than a paddler.
- ☐ Look back before you turn back.
- ☐ Give yourself plenty of room. Try to perceive future dangerous situations and plan your actions accordingly.

EQUIPMENT

The primary requisite, of course, is waves which one can ride. As the sport of surfing grows throughout the world, more and more good surf spots are discovered. The type and size of break one tries to surf will depend on a person's individual ability. For beginners, a well-formed and glassy wave of about two to three feet is ideal. Inexperienced surfers will not only have difficulty in larger waves but can also run a great deal of risk.

The second piece of equipment would be suitable swim wear such as baggies, which are loosely fitted swim trunks designed to allow maneuverability. In colder weather and/or cold water, a wet suit may also be desirable to protect one from the cold.

The third piece of equipment is a surfboard. Of course body surfing does not even require this piece of equipment. The board one chooses will vary with the size of the individual, the size of the wave, and the shape of the wave. Examples of body weight and recommended board size are:

Body Weight (lbs)	Board Width (in.)	Board Length (ft/in.)	Board Weight (lbs)
112	20 1/2–21	9–3	22–27
126	21–21 1/4	9–6	25–30
140	21 1/4–21 1/2	9–9	27–32
154	21 1/2	10–0	30–35
168	21 1/2–21 3/4	10–3	32–37
182	21 3/4–22	10–6	35–40

Wax is needed to keep the surface of the board from being too slippery to stand on. Some form of skin lotion is also advisable.

REFERENCES

Allan, J. 1970. *Locked in, surfing for life*. South Brunswick, N.J.: A. S. Barnes.

Bascom, W. 1967. *Waves and beaches: the dynamics of the ocean surface*. Garden City, N.J.: Anchor Books, Doubleday.

Cunningham, G. 1967. *How to keep warm*. Denver, Colo.: Outdoor Sports.

Edwards, P., and B. Otlum 1967. *You should have been here an hour ago*. New York: Harper & Row.

Farrelly, M., as told to C. McGregor 1967. *The surfing life*. New York: Arco.

Finney, B. R., and J. D. Houston 1966. *Surfing: the sport of Hawaiian kings*. Rutland, Vt.: Charles E. Tuttle.

Gross, M. G. 1967. *Oceanography*. Columbus, Ohio: Merrill.

International Surfing Magazine. A bimonthly publication.

Severson, J. 1964. *Modern surfing around the world*. Garden City, N.Y.: Doubleday.

Surfer. A bimonthly magazine.

Wagenvoord, J., and L. Bailey 1968. *How to surf*. New York: Colber.

70
Weight Training

Philip K. Rasch

The desire for strength and the use of weight training to achieve it must be nearly as old as the human race. Prior to the early 1940s, however, American coaches discouraged its practice on the grounds that it would make a practitioner slow and "musclebound" and that it was "bad for the heart." Consequently this type of training was largely left to professional strongmen, "professors" selling correspondence courses, some athletic clubs, and a comparatively few enthusiasts working in the privacy of their own homes. However, one writer of this period, Alan Calvert (1875–1944) is considered "the father of weight training in America."

During World War II a physician, Thomas L. DeLorme, applied weight training techniques to the physical rehabilitation of wounded servicemen with such success that Hellebrandt (1946) remarked:

> The recent demonstration of how much can be done to expedite the return of normal function by the systematic use of judiciously administered exercise, graded in dosage, is one of the important contributions of the period to human knowledge.

Subsequently the use of weight training methods to develop muscular strength has become one of the principal modalities in departments of physical medicine and rehabilitation throughout the country.

Weight trainers may be divided roughly into five classes:

1. Seekers of health and improved physical condition. These individuals usually claim that they use weights to obtain "better health," or "to keep in condition," although some researchers have suggested that their underlying motivations are largely vanity or feelings of inferiority. A survey conducted in 1972 revealed that seven percent of the adult population questioned owns weights, although only three percent uses them regularly.

Following the war there was a tremendous boom in the so-called health studios featuring weight training. Some were organized into nationwide chains. Most of them proved ephemeral and quickly faded from the scene, often with considerable financial loss to their clients. By the 1970s most of the fly-by-night operators had left the professional field and the situation with regard to the "health spas" had become better stabilized. A noticeable development

Fig. 70.1 Coeds around the world are becoming interested in weight training. Courtesy of Old Dominion University.

was the effort made to attract the female trade. The emphasis has remained on the hiring of salesmen to operate these spas, rather than trained physical educators, but even so the results have not been markedly successful. The 1972 survey found that only 3 percent of the adult population patronizes spas, YMCAs, or community agencies.

2. Athletes. Shortly after World War II coaches began to profit from the medical approval of weight training and by the late 1950s it had become an integral part of most athletic conditioning and rehabilitation regimens. Athletes practice weight training as a means of improving their performance in their specialized activity. With them it is strictly a means to an end. Emphasis is largely on three factors: (1) improved performance from increased weight and strength; (2) prevention of injury through greater strength, and (3) more rapid and complete rehabilitation following injury. Elaborate training programs have been devised for the various sports, particularly football, track, and swimming. Jesse (1971, 1968) gives examples of the degree to which such specialized training has been developed.

As an offshoot of the athletes' interest in weight training, the 1960s progressive resistance exercise courses, classes, and clubs had become common in colleges and universities and, to a lesser extent, in high schools. Physical educators in general, however, tend to discourage weight training by younger individuals.

3. Olympic weight lifters. When the Olympic Games were revived in 1896, weightlifting was included as part of gymnastics. After a somewhat uneven career it was organized on an international level with the founding of the Federation Halterophile Internationale in 1920. In the United States the Amateur Athletic Union assumed control of the sport in 1927, with Dietrich

Wortmann serving as National Chairman until his death in 1952. In the early years, competition usually included five lifts: one-hand snatch, one-hand clean and jerk, two-hand clean and jerk, two-hand press, and two-hand snatch. In 1935 the one-hand lift events were discontinued and the remaining events became known as the Three Olympic Lifts. These were further modified in 1972, when the press was discarded from future Olympic and world competition. The AAU subsequently dropped it from national competition.

During the decade between 1946 and 1956 Americans were in the thick of the competition for world championships. Much of their success was due to the enthusiasm and financial support of Bob Hoffman. After that period, supremacy went to the Soviet Union. In 1972, for the first time in modern history, the United States failed to win an Olympic medal. Intensive efforts to develop lifters in the United States are now being made through the AAU Junior Olympic Weightlifting Program, the Age Group Clean and Jerk Program, the National Coaching Scheme, teenage training camps, etc. Spasmodic efforts to promote weightlifting as an intercollegiate sport have met with little success.

4. Power lifters. Power lifting arose among men who were interested purely in maximal muscular strength and considered that the Olympic lifts were not a satisfactory means of determining or demonstrating it. Various "odd lift" contests were organized, the exact lifts differing from meet to meet. These were discouraged by the AAU which desired to emphasize Olympic lifting. However, it finally bowed to the inevitable and assumed control of powerlifting on January 1, 1965. Competition has since been standardized on the squat, bench press, and dead lift, contested in that order. At the present time it appears to be more popular than Olympic lifting.

While powerlifting has been a distinctively American development, its adherents are working diligently to promote it on an international basis. The first World Championships were held at York, Pennsylvania, in 1971. Only the British sent a team, but increased participation by foreigners is anticipated in the future.

An untoward development in this form of lifting has been the frequent appearance of high blood pressure in the superheavyweights. This appears to be related to their excessively heavy bodyweight.

5. Body builders. In 1903 Bernarr McFadden sponsored a contest to determine America's most perfectly developed man. He conducted similar contests from time to time during the next twenty years, as did other individuals and groups. In 1939 local AAU sanction was secured for a Mr. America contest in connection with the national weightlifting championships. The following year John C. Grimek won the first title awarded under national AAU auspices.

Fig. 70.2 Weight training in preparation for sports participation and for general physical development is now common practice. Courtesy of Physical Education at the United States Military Academy.

Fig. 70.3 Lifting weights, when properly executed, will develop muscles in all parts of the body. Courtesy of Physical Education at the United States Military Academy.

These contests are held in conjunction with the Senior National Weightlifting Championships and have become more popular than the lifting itself. Contestants are evaluated by a panel of either five or seven judges and may be awarded a total of 80 points, based on

a) Symmetry—25 points,

b) Muscularity—25 points,

c) Presentation (manly good looks and posing ability)—25 points, and

d) Interview (poise, personality, education and character)—5 points.

Subdivision titles are awarded for best arms, back, chest, legs, and abdominals, and a trophy is awarded to the Most Muscular Man. Curiously enough, the competitors are not required to do anything with their muscles.

The title "Mr. America" has also been awarded in non-AAU-sponsored competitions. As a result considerable confusion has been created over the identity of the rightful title holders.

Research in Weight Training

Prior to World War II, there was very little scientific research in weight training. Since that time it has been the subject of numerous papers. These may be most conveniently located by referring to the annual volumes of *Completed Research,* published by the American Alliance for Health, Physical Education and Recreation (AAHPER). In general they tend to show that in order to achieve maximal muscular strength and hypertrophy, weight training should be practiced at regular intervals, must be strenuous to the point of maximal exertion, and must be progressive in nature. However, this activity does very little to improve cardiovascular and respiratory functions.

REFERENCES

AAU weightlifting rule book 1971. Indianapolis, Ind.: AAU.

Hellebrandt, F. A. 1946. Recent advances in methods of hastening convalescence through exercise. *Southern Medical Journal* **39:** 397–401.

Jesse, J. 1971. *Strength, power, and muscular endurance for runners and hurdlers.* Pasadena, Calif.: Athletic Press.

——— 1968. *Explosive muscular power for championship football.* Pasadena, Calif.: Athletic Press.

Rasch, P. J. 1966. *Weight training.* Dubuque, Iowa: Wm. C. Brown.

Sills, F. D. *et al.* (eds.) 1962. *Weight training in sports and physical education.* Washington, D.C.: AAHPER.

71
Yoga (Hatha Yoga)
Louis E. LaGrand

INTRODUCTION

William James, father of modern psychology, wrote:

> I wonder whether the yoga discipline may not be, after all, in all its phases simply a methodical way of waking up deeper levels of will power than are habitually used, and thereby increasing the individual's vital tone and energy.

Yoga is one of the six systems of Indian (Hindu) philosophy the exact origin of which is unknown, although some authorities claim that it was in existence 4000 to 5000 years before the birth of Christ. In its traditional form it is a way of life, a particular style of living, not a religion, although today its goals are shared by many of different religious persuasions. Yoga is a composite of several different branches or pathways, each an individual system of its own.

The word yoga comes from *yuj,* a Sanskrit root which means a yoking, joining, a union or, in the Indian tradition, "the marriage of matter and spirit." While the word yoga is commonly used to denote the physical yoga or hatha yoga in Western culture, it is in fact a very general word that refers to several different forms that are interrelated. For example, bhakti yoga focuses on the qualities of love, devotion, and being other-centered; jnana yoga, on knowledge, intellect, and study. Karma yoga places action, work, and activity as the medium for uniting the finite with the infinite or matter with spirit. Raja yoga is considered to be the ultimate form of union and liberation or the royal yoga in which the aspirant attains very high levels of consciousness through introspection, meditation, and concentration. These and other forms (mantra yoga, yantra yoga, shakti yoga, laya yoga, dhyana yoga, kundalini yoga, samadhi yoga) are considered to be different paths to the same goal. Their variety meets the temperaments, needs, and levels of development of those who seek to transcend the mundane. The goal of all yoga is union, a complete self-knowledge that surfaces only by each individual's meticulous search. Reaching this level of knowledge brings the aspirant in unison with the supreme consciousness (or God, cosmic consciousness, truth, reality, supreme self, etc.), a merging of the individual spirit with the universal spirit. The yogi subjugates the mind through the practice of yoga to become one with the Infinite.

Hatha yoga, in Eastern thought, is a stepping stone to reach the higher forms of union (yogas). One must gain perfect control of the body through the mind. Some authorities claim that there are over 800,000 different postures. It is believed that the body must be prepared to release and conduct forces essential for higher attainment and union. A force called kundalini, thought to lie dormant at the base of the spine, is, when activated, the medium through which oneness is achieved. In addition, there are certain moral prerequisites, called *yamas* or "abstentions" and *niyamas* or "observances," which must be practiced and which precede initiation into yogic discipline.

Pantanjali (200 B.C.), an ancient Indian author of works on grammar, medicine, philosophy, alchemy and other subjects, is considered to be the father of yoga, having placed in writing many of the earliest classic yoga concepts. Before this time the basic tenets of yoga had been passed down through the ages by word of mouth. From all indications, hatha yoga may be considered as the oldest system of exercise known; some of the postures practiced today are similar if not identical to those practiced in antiquity— but for quite different reasons.

YOGA (HATHA YOGA) IN THE WEST

The practice of hatha yoga in Western culture is a product of diffusion and is characterized by numerous variations in content and method from such classic texts as *Siva Samhita, Gheranda Samhita,* and *Hatha Yoga Pradipika.* It is quite likely that there are as many forms of hatha yoga today as there are teachers teaching it. Each instructor adds his or her own particular teaching style, as is the case in so many subjects. This yoga consists of breathing techniques, exercises or postures (asanas) and techniques of deep relaxation, having excluded the cleansing practices of Eastern circles. The use of breathing techniques, simultaneously with the execution of the asanas, is an essential condition of practice.

Aside from the philosophical implications, hatha yoga contributes a number of unique benefits to the physical, mental, and spiritual well-being of the individual. As practiced in the West, the emphasis is utilitarian. That it has contributed to these practical goals is borne out by the increased practice of this movement form by millions of Americans. Hatha yoga is now being taught in many schools and colleges, including elementary and junior high levels, as well as in community centers, adult and continuing education programs and YWCAs and YMCAs. Television series depicting the techniques and exercises are viewed daily in homes throughout the country, while yoga centers (such as the Sivananda Vedanta Center in New York) are established in many large and small cities across the land.

Despite this widespread interest, and much empirical evidence supporting the benefits of participation, the subject remains highly controversial in many quarters of the educational enterprise, particularly among professional educators. It is controversial for three primary reasons. First, the word yoga itself connotes a montage of misconceptions and stereotypes based on bits and pieces of information, some totally false. Many people associate yoga with the occult, black magic, or fortune-telling. Others conjure up pictures of the Indian rope trick, grotesque contortions, sleeping on a bed of spikes, or standing on hot coals. These stereotypes are not unlike those which pervade the unknown of many other forms of activity such as ballet, dance forms for men, or foil fencing—stereotypes based on a lack of knowledge and understanding. Cultural differences, coupled with Western civilization's pressurized pace of life, make the controlled, low-key approach to hatha yoga difficult to accept.

Secondly, there are many unfounded claims as to the benefits which accrue from participation and the exact nature of these benefits. For example, a number of texts purport to show that practice of particular postures will "massage the glands, beautify the body, and cure many ailments." Still others claim aid for "insomnia, inner organs, jaw lines, or bust line." To the scientific community and those skeptical of unwarranted claims without supporting data, such statements create suspicion and negative attitudes toward the entire discipline. Many physical educators charge gimmickry and sensationalism in the presentation of hatha yoga. This brings us to the final source of controversy—a lack of quality research.

There is a paucity of research available on any of the current positive results which many people report as a consequence of their practice of hatha yoga. While there are scattered reports in the literature, much of what is available is of dubious quality or outdated (with the exception of the work by deVries in the 1960s). The lack of convincing data is a hindrance to acceptance of hatha yoga as a bona fide movement form which contributes to total fitness. Here is a fertile area for research as there are many participants who report increased sensitivity to muscular tension, ability to recognize and release neuromuscular hypertension, increased trunk and hip flexibility, increased strength in various muscle groups, ability to balance, more energy, and on and on. That hatha yoga contributes to one's development is academic; but the scope, type of physical change, and other specific contributions desperately need documentation.

GUIDELINES

Unlike conventional movement forms, hatha yoga is devoid of all actions of impulse, quickness, strain, or forcing. Each movement is controlled, slow and deliberate; in effect, participation is in slow-motion. The class atmosphere is one of quietness, with few of the sounds which normally fill the gymnasium or playground. Therefore, the choice of teaching station is critical. The usual gymnasium setting is not appropriate unless complete quiet and a minimum of distractions can be guaranteed. An area more conducive to participation is the wrestling or tumbling room where mats are available and traffic into and out of the room is easily controlled. The quiet surroundings are important to the concentration and focus which accompany movement and the awareness of physical feelings. Class should never be conducted on a hard floor. A mat, rug, or folded blanket, about one inch thick, is best for use in any indoor or outdoor area. Adequate ventilation must also be provided. Hatha yoga can be practiced for as little as a few minutes up to an hour or more depending on the level of skill, time available, and individual preferences. However, like the learning of any motor skill, regular practice for short periods of time is preferred over one- or two-hour sessions once a week. This highlights the need to encourage short practice periods at home outside of class.

A class or individual session usually consists of (1) mental-physical preparation, (2) short relaxation phase, (3) asana (exercise) phase and (4) deep relaxation phase. Most sessions include asanas in sitting, standing, kneeling, inverted, prone, and supine positions. Proper breathing technique is emphasized.

Mental-Physical Preparation

Phase one consists of forming the habit of positive thinking about involvement in the session. In any of the sitting postures, the student contemplates his or her session as a time to escape from the hustle and bustle of the day, scan physical feelings, recognize states of neuromuscular hypertension, and begin to focus internally. The importance of concentration is emphasized; it is essential to the mental and physical control and execution of the asanas. The idea is to develop the *habit of concentration* both for participation and mental practice. This is accompanied by deep abdominal breathing. Then, in a sitting or standing position, the student begins to test and loosen muscles in a systematic way. Muscles of the arms, hips, shoulders, legs, abdomen are all stretched and contracted by way of a series of asanas called the Sun Salutation or by more conventional warm-up activities, all executed in controlled fashion.

Relaxation Phase

In phase two the student assumes on the mat a reclining position called the Corpse or Sponge (*Savasana* in Sanskrit) and based on the warm-ups again scans the physical self for feelings of neuromuscular hypertension, discomfort, or relaxation and prepares for the execution of the asanas. Relaxation is crucial in the control of body parts and specific movements. Students are instructed to read the physical messages of warmth, coldness, position, stretch and strain concentrating on the release of unnecessary neuromuscular tension. While relaxation after warm-up may seem contrary to conventional standards, the relaxation response is used often throughout the session after execution of one or more of the asanas. The use of this technique is important to establish in the mind of the student the differences in feelings of stretch, contraction, relaxation, overstretch, and excessive tension in voluntary muscle. In this and all phases of a session increased kinesthetic awareness is sought.

Asana Phase

Phase three represents the major part of the session and includes emphasis on control of movements, mechanical efficiency, breathing and concentration, and the contraction and stretching of muscle and connective tissue. By way of the asanas chosen, muscles and joints are activated at various angles and for specific durations of time. The intensity of execution of the asana or exercise depends on the length of time the student takes (counts) going into, holding and coming out of a particular position and the repetition of that asana.

Relaxation Phase

Each session closes with the Corpse or Sponge position and is held for a much longer period of time than occurred in phase two. A minimum of six to ten minutes is suggested with the purpose of assisting the student to develop the neuromuscular skill of deep relaxation. Concentration, so important in all motor activities, is stressed throughout the session, particularly in developing the relaxation response.

It is important to note that some teachers may vary the length of time of any of these four phases. However, every session should end with an opportunity for deep relaxation.

TERMINOLOGY

While much of the terminology in hatha yoga is of Sanskrit origin, an equal amount, depending on course objectives, is centered on the biophysical values and relationships of physical activity. Much information on anatomy, physiology, and mental health blends naturally with any course presentation. Following are a selected group of terms that are associated with the teaching of hatha yoga and are used in relation to the learning and maturation level of the class, as well as the objectives of the individual instructor.

Arteriosclerosis A condition of the arteries characterized by a loss of elasticity and a hardening and/or thickening of the walls of the artery.

Asanas The Sanskrit name given to the postures or exercises of hatha yoga. (The pronunciation of the first syllable is "ah.")

Atherosclerosis A condition in which deposits collect on the walls of arteries and result in the narrowing of the circumference or lumen of the artery.

Counts Refers to the time in seconds for breathing and the performance of an asana. A five count would mean to hold for the time it would take to silently say 1001, 1002, 1003, 1004, 1005, or om one, om two, etc.

Bhagavad Gita A Hindu book of religious poetry which explains the concepts of reincarnation, reaching heaven, and the tenets of yoga.

Biofeedback The control by thought processes of involuntary processes, such as heart rate, brain rhythms, blood pressure, and body temperature. The use of special equipment provides information which the subject uses to learn how to control internal conditions.

Cardiorespiratory endurance The ability of the heart and lungs to function at a highly efficient rate during sustained, vigorous exercise.

Extension A type of movement of body parts in which there is an increase in the angle between bones. Straightening one's leg is an example of extension.

Flexibility The condition of using a muscle and joint through the fullest possible range of movement. The degree of flexibility depends on the length of muscles, condition of connective tissue, and the bone structure of joints.

Flexion A type of movement of body parts in which there is a decrease in the angle between bones. An example would be bringing the hand up to touch the shoulder, thus flexing the arm.

Hatha Yoga Pradipika One of the classic books on the physical postures and breathing.

Isometric The static contraction of muscles without the movement of an object. An example would be the state of a muscle while pushing against any immovable object.

Isotonic Muscle contraction in which an object is moved and the length of the muscles changes as in lifting weights or running.

Mental practice The act of thinking about and performing a skill mentally without actually doing the skill. This sometimes helps in the development of physical skill.

Observation Focusing on the feelings and reactions of the body to the various asanas.

Om A mystic syllable used as a mantra and considered the name of the Divine Power or God. Sometimes repeated in Western circles as a form of counting.

Osteoarthritis Degeneration of the cartilage between bones, causing bone surfaces to rub together with resultant imflammation, swelling, and sometimes irregular bone growth and spur formation.

Pranayama The science of control and regulation of breathing.

Progressive exercises The gradual increase in duration, intensity, and/or difficulty of specific exercises for the purpose of increasing beneficial effects.

Psychosomatic Indicating a physical symptom or disorder of the body caused by, or originating with, the emotions.

Siva Samhita A classic and detailed work on hatha yoga.

Static stretch Placing a muscle in a position which is longer than its normal resting position. This results in an increase in muscle length and flexibility.

Stretch reflex A protective reaction of muscle when stretched beyond its normal length. The reflex contraction helps prevent injuries to muscle if overstretched.

Yogi The accomplished male practitioner of yoga.

Yogini The accomplished female practitioner of yoga.

SKILLS: TEACHING TECHNIQUES AND FUNDAMENTALS

The teaching of hatha yoga should be based on the scientific methods applicable to the learning of any motor skill. The importance of the instructor's role in creating a class atmosphere conducive to participation is important. A widely held theory of psychologists is quite applicable here: people tend to erase unpleasant experiences from memory or to avoid them completely. This is readily seen in one's tendency to forget traumatic experiences such as accidents or those sore muscles after overexertion in a particular task or sport. Many individuals are lost to regular activity because of a lack of early success and the physical unpleasantness associated with particular movements.

Hatha yoga is unique in its application, as one of its basic tenets is that the participant is in competition with the self only but, and much more important, there are immediate gains and each period ends with the Corpse or Relaxation pose which provides for an unusually refreshed feeling. *Class always ends on a strong positive note.* Pleasant experiences and early successes, which are inherent in this medium, are the building blocks for strong and continued motivation. *We can learn and have fun in doing so.* Learning does not necessarily have to be difficult or anxiety producing; neither is it a continuous joy. There is obviously a middle ground; a teacher can find that middle ground and take advantage of it in helping students enjoy what they are doing. However, the contrast between feelings of fatigue at the conclusion of conventional physical activity and the feelings of added energy and vigor at the close of a yoga session (owing in part to the release of neuromuscular hypertension and the quiet, relaxed class atmosphere) has special significance for teacher and student alike. Learning is best served when success predominates over failure. Such intrinsic motivation, as one experiences progress, is the dynamic force behind positive attitudes and responses of participants. The retention of pleasant memories of participation and the association with the instructor who is sincere, interested, and who can *relate hatha yoga to daily living patterns* provide the climate for continued interest and positive involvement.

Students and teachers alike should take note of the following observations and recommendations for class participation.

- ☐ Clothing should be loose and stretchable to permit freedom of movement. Belts, bracelets, watches, or other jewelry which would move during exercise should not be worn. Eyeglasses should be removed.

- ☐ Patience in the execution of asanas must be continually stressed. Never force movements or overstretch muscles.

- ☐ There should be a gradual increase in the repetitions of the asanas and the time each is held. The tendency is for the student to do too much or for the teacher to present too much in the initial sessions. Pacing must be stressed. The instructor must plan for progression.

- ☐ Only those muscles needed for execution of the asana should be used, working toward release of others not directly involved in the movement.

- ☐ Should one feel dizzy or nauseated at any time during participation, the asana should be terminated. Relax in Sponge or Corpse posture. (See Fig. 71.1.)

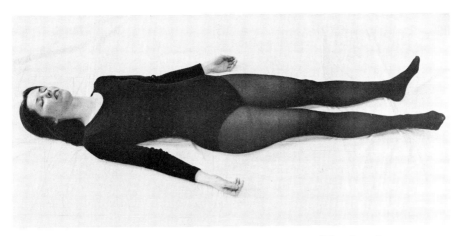

Fig. 71.1 The Corpse or Sponge position. Courtesy of SUNY at Potsdam.

- □ Routines should not be practiced directly after eating.
- □ All stretching movements should be controlled and passive. Never bounce during warm-ups or execution of any asana.
- □ Breathing techniques generally accompany the asanas: inhaling going into the posture and exhaling coming out of it.
- □ When beginning participation after illness, the length of holding time and repetitions of the asanas should be reduced; the student should never begin again at the previous level but gradually work up to his or her original competencies.

Safety Considerations

Assuming that the choice of room, mat, lighting and ventilation has been made, and distractions have been eliminated, the instructor should next be sure that students with a history of high blood pressure are not allowed to execute any of the inverted postures. In addition, students with previous back problems should obtain specific clearance from their physicians before participating. Continuous emphasis on *not* overstretching or trying to do too much is essential. The student should terminate a movement if pain is felt at any time.

Breathing and the Asanas

The use of various breathing techniques has both mental and physical implications in the practice of hatha yoga. Focusing on breathing is an aid to concentration and performance; it is also an index of inward conditions as our breathing is closely associated with emotional states. Traditionally, the yoga practitioner believes there is a life force in the air as in all things in the universe, and that the more life force, called *prana,* which can be utilized and controlled, the greater the possibility of reaching the goal of union.

The lungs may be listed among the most vulnerable organs of the body in spite of the fact that the individual has direct control, in most instances, over biological insults to the lungs; these are in the form of dust, aerosol sprays, gases, burning wastes, cigarette smoke, and other air pollutants. The act of breathing occurs more than 14,000 times daily and is both a voluntary and involuntary act. Most people are shallow breathers, not fully utilizing total lung capacity. Deep breathing *may* strengthen and stretch the diaphragm while more completely utilizing the lungs, but there is no evidence that it increases vital capacity or the ability of the lungs to process oxygen. It is clear that *hatha yoga does not provide changes at the cellular level which lead to a high level of cardiorespiratory endurance.* Furthermore, there is no evidence that deep breathing increases maximum oxygen uptake and hence the amount of oxygen reaching the brain. Inasmuch as the blood is nearly 98 percent saturated during normal respiration, the only increase in oxygen level occurs when one breathes pure oxygen under pressure. There is, however, room for research on the purported claims of increased efficiency and the effect on lung structure and function. For example, it may be possible to increase the efficiency of the pulmonary membrane, through deep breathing, with an expansion of the total surface. This, plus a strengthening of all the muscles involved in respiration, may provide some modest gains. Whatever the case, the breathing procedures of hatha yoga *do* assist the participant in relaxation, concentration and total involvement with the exercise as well as restoration of composure after anxious moments. The element of transfer is quite applicable in this regard from in-class to out-of-class situations. Furthermore, the topic of breathing is an excellent point of departure for discussing the important role of the lungs, their structure, and their use or abuse.

There are numerous names and a variety of styles or techniques of breathing found in the literature. Names such at vitalic breathing, alternate nostril breathing, bellows breathing, cleansing breath, or deep abdominal breathing are frequently listed. Most commonly used with execution of the asanas is diaphragmic or deep abdominal breathing. This is performed as follows with the mouth closed and all air drawn via the nose through the back of the throat.

□ When inhaling, the stomach muscles are relaxed and the abdomen distended as the student visualizes the filling of the lower section of the lungs.

□ Part two focuses on the middle portion of the lungs filling, the widening of the intercostal muscles, and the expansion of the diaphragm.

□ Inhalation terminates as the student visualizes the completion of the filling process. The breath is then held from one to five seconds.

□ On exhalation the process is reversed as air is released slowly from the top part of the lobes. This process must not be rushed, as often happens, if the breath is held too long.

□ The middle portion of the lungs is now emptied as the muscles of the rib cage shorten.

□ In the final phase of exhalation the abdominal muscles are gently contracted, expelling a bit more air.

It is emphasized that the shoulders should not be raised when breathing nor should one strain to increase the depth of inspiration or expiration. The time in seconds for inspiration, holding, and expiration is gradually increased with a corresponding increase in the time taken to go into a posture and come out of it. A common starting point is a 5-2-5 or a 6-2-6 count. Deep breathing may be used in any of the sitting postures or when executing other asanas as well as when in Corpse or Sponge position.

The Asanas

The *Gheranda Samhita* states that hundreds of thousands of asanas were originally described and that 84 are of special significance. Among these 84 are 32 which are of the most practical benefit for the individual. There are hundreds of different asanas listed in the literature on yoga today with many of these variations of the more classic postures. The variations that teachers can create or develop are almost limitless and provide a very individualized approach for particular classes or individuals.

Perhaps the most versatile group of asanas, possessing implications for conditioning as well as warm-up, is a series of twelve postures called the Salutation to the Sun. Traditionally, this was performed on rising and is a greeting to the sun which was believed to be the "deity for health and long life." The series is characterized by specific order and continuous, flowing movement. From a practical viewpoint the Sun Salute activates most of the major muscle groups in the body. It can be executed several times and at different speeds depending on individual preferences, although some authorities have indicated that repetitions would range from a minimum of twelve to as high as sixty on a given day. Two or three repetitions suffice as a warm-up; for conditioning, increased speed and repetitions are employed. (See Fig. 71.2.)

SALUTATION TO THE SUN

1. Standing position, palms together in front of chest. Inhale and exhale pressing palms together.

2. Inhale, bring arms up extended over head. Bend backward at the waist arching back.

3. Exhale, keep arms extended and bend forward touching fingers to toes or palms to floor keeping legs straight. Let forehead touch knees.

4. Inhale, bend knees and extend right leg back keeping left knee close to chest, palms on mat. Lift head back.

5. Retain breath, bring other leg back and extend both legs keeping back straight. Arms are extended in "push-up position." Head up.

6. Exhale, lowering body to floor so that toes, knees, chest (not abdomen), hands and forehead (eight points) are touching the mat.

7. Inhale, straightening legs and allowing abdomen to touch floor as you contract muscles of the back and lift upper part of the body as in the Cobra posture.

8. Exhale, extending arms, raising hips with heels on floor, head between extended arms. Body is in a capital lambda (Λ) position.

Fig. 71.2 Sequential positions 1 through 12, the "Salutation to the Sun." Courtesy of SUNY at Potsdam.

1

2

3

4

5

6

7

8

9

10

11

12

9. Inhale, bringing right knee up to chest and extending left leg back, hands on either side of right foot. Lift head back.

10. Exhale, bringing feet together bending at hips with legs straight and touching fingers to toes or palms to mat as in position 3.

11. Inhale, stretching arms and fingers and lifting arms up over head as in position 2. Arch back.

12. Exhale, bringing arms down, straightening back, placing palms together in front of chest or allowing arms to hang loosely at sides.

Some Classic Asanas

The asanas are executed by way of both isotonic and isometric muscle contractions; as the student goes into the posture isotonic contractions occur while isometrics are employed during the holding phase of the movement; parts of the body, and the angle at which they are held, act as the medium for overload. The asanas also provide the static stretch necessary for increased flexibility; this fitness parameter is of special significance in view of the established fact that a muscle not worked through its full range of movement will shorten, sometimes resulting in bouts of spasm or cramps.

Below are eight classic asanas used with elementary or secondary students.

1. *The Forward Bend* (pachimottanasana)

   a) In a sitting position with legs extended slowly inhale, raising both arms overhead and stretch toward the ceiling. Hold breath two or three counts.

   b) Exhale, slowly bringing arms down, sliding hands on sides of legs out toward toes.

   c) Bend forward as far as possible observing the feelings of stretch in the upper and lower back and the hamstrings. Hold the position from thirty seconds to three minutes. See Fig. 71.3.

   d) Do not bounce to increase ability to stretch. Passive stretch and patience are important. Visualize bringing the stomach down to contact the thighs.

2. *The Cobra* (bhujangasana)

   a) Lie in a prone position, toes pointed with hands, palms down on mat directly under the shoulders.

   b) Inhale and slowly lift head off the mat, then gradually elevate the upper back visualizing the contractions of muscles around each vertebra.

Fig. 71.3 The forward bend (pachimott anasana). Courtesy of SUNY at Potsdam.

Fig. 71.4 The Cobra (bhujangasana). Courtesy of SUNY at Potsdam.

c) The lower half of the body maintains contact with the mat.

d) At the top of the asana, the face points toward the ceiling, arms are extended but not locked and eyes are looking upward and back. See Fig. 71.4.

e) This asana is not a push-up, although the arms have to be used for support. The objective is to ever so gradually transfer weight from the arms to the erector spinae muscle to lift the upper body.

f) Hold the uppermost position from three to ten seconds. Reverse the lifting procedure to return to starting position, the forehead coming to rest on the mat at the completion of the movement.

3. *The Plough* (halasana)

a) Lying in a supine position draw the arms along the mat to a parallel position above the head.

b) Inhale, push the small of the back down and into the mat and slowly elevate the legs bringing them up and over to a position where they are resting on the mat. Toes may be curled or extended. If unable to touch the mat, go only to the point of stretch short of overstretching. This should be emphasized in all asanas. See Fig. 71.5.

c) Breathing normally, the position is held from three to thirty seconds.

d) When coming out of the position, exhale, bend the knees and touch the forehead, then gradually lower the hips to the mat. Finally, extend the legs, press the small of the back into the mat, and lower the legs to starting position.

e) An alternate position is to place the hands, palms down on the mat, at the sides and go into the position described in a) and b) above.

Fig. 71.5 The Plough (halasana). Courtesy of SUNY at Potsdam.

4. *The Bridge* (sethu bandhasana)

a) Lying in a supine position, bend the knees and draw the legs up placing the heels close to the buttocks, feet on the mat.

b) Grasp the ankles, inhale, and slowly elevate the hips as high as possible arching the back. Do not go up on the toes—keep heels on mat. Hold from three to fifteen seconds. Breathe normally. See Fig. 71.6.

c) Exhale, slowly bring hips back to the mat, release ankles and return to resting position. More advanced procedure demands keeping the feet and legs close together, not spreading or pointing the toes to the sides.

5. *Full Shoulder Stand* (niralamba sarvangasana)

a) Lying in a supine position, press the lower back down and into the mat, inhale and slowly elevate both legs up and overhead.

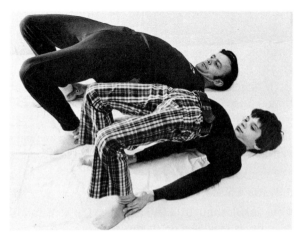

Fig. 71.6 The Bridge (sethu bandhasan). Courtesy of SUNY at Potsdam.

Fig. 71.7 Full shoulder stand (niralamba sarvangasana). Courtesy of SUNY at Potsdam.

b) Hands move to support hips as they are elevated and brought in line with the legs in a vertical position. Chin touches notch in the chest, toes are pointed. See Fig. 71.7.

c) Position is held from thirty seconds to five minutes or more. Breathe normally. Reduce feelings of fatigue in the legs by not pointing toes.

d) When coming down, bend knees and slowly lower hips to the mat. Then bring legs slowly back to starting position.

6. *The Bow* (dhunurasana)

a) Lying in a prone position, flex the knees bringing heels up toward buttocks. Grasp the ankles with the hands. See Fig. 71.8.

b) Inhale, extend arms, lifting head, chest and thighs off the mat balancing on stomach and hips from three to ten seconds. Breathe normally.

c) Coming down, exhale, and slowly allow chest and thighs to come back to the mat, then head and lower legs. Do not let the legs "drop" to the mat.

7. *The Stomach Lift* (uddiyana banda)

a) In a standing position, inhale and exhale normally. On exhalation, bend knees slightly placing palms down on thighs.

Fig. 71.8 The Bow (dhunurasana). Courtesy of SUNY at Potsdam.

b) Contract the abdominal muscles drawing them up and in visualizing the attempt to touch the muscles to the spine. Hold for an eight- to ten-second count or until the need to inhale is necessary. See Fig. 71.9.

8. *The Spinal Twist* (ardha matsyendrasana)

a) Sitting with both legs fully extended, draw the left leg up placing the sole of the foot on the inside of the right thigh, heel close to the groin.

b) Place the right foot directly in front of the left knee, sole of the foot on the mat.

c) Placing the left elbow over the right knee, rotate the lower arm back to grasp the right ankle.

d) Swing the right arm around the waist palm out, exhale, and turn the head looking over the right shoulder. Hold the position from three to fifteen seconds. See Fig. 71.10.

e) Release hand on the ankle to gradually come out of the posture. Repeat to the opposite side. Several lead-up movements may have to be practiced before this asana is correctly performed.

The asanas not only have the potential for strength development but obviously elongate muscles and increase flexibility. Numerous amateur and professional athletic teams use the asanas, called by Americanized names, to develop flexibility as a preventive factor in muscle pulls or tears by way of static stretching. Full muscular contraction and/or stretch, within one's limits, is essential for improvement, which can usually be seen within ten practice sessions. Also, the asanas do increase circulation to muscle tissue; while isometric contractions tend to slow or reduce blood flow, movements into and

Fig. 71.9 The stomach lift (uddiyana banda). Courtesy of SUNY at Potsdam.

Fig. 71.10 The spinal twist (ardha matsyendrasana). Courtesy of SUNY at Potsdam.

out of an asana aid circulation. This is particularly true of the inverted postures, the Salutation to the Sun and others which activate major muscle groups.

Teaching Progression

Following is a list of 25 asanas presented in teaching progression for elementary, junior high, or secondary school students. All of these asanas can be found in most hatha yoga books on sale in book stores. If called by more than one name they are listed accordingly.

1. Easy posture, tailor posture
2. Corpse, sponge, or supine relaxation position (Fig. 71.1)
3. Tension reliever, full body contraction
4. Single leg pull, head-knee pose sitting
5. Forward bend, sitting forward bend
6. Backward bend
7. Cat stretch
8. Tree pose

9. Neck rolls
10. Warrior pose, over shoulder hand clasp
11. Cobra
12. Plough
13. Half shoulder stand, reverse posture
14. Fish pose
15. Full shoulder stand
16. Crow pose
17. Spinal twist
18. Lion pose
19. Triangle pose
20. Archer, shooting bow pose
21. Camel, rabbit pose
22. Abdominal lift
23. Tripod stand
24. Bridge
25. Turtle, fetal pose

The Salutation to the Sun and warm-up asanas, like the single and double leg lift, should be introduced early to the class. Deep abdominal breathing should also be presented during the first or second period. Numerous variations of the above may be introduced depending on the length of each class and the amount of time devoted to the entire unit.

Strategies

The strategies or basic principles which guide the learner in the practice of hatha yoga and the instructor who teaches it are as follows:

☐ Never force a movement. Work toward slow, flowing, integrated performance.

☐ All movement should be accompanied by visualization or mental imagery. Positive inner conditions are necessary.

☐ Competition is with the self; an exploration of potential and limitations. Inner performance (what transpires in the mind when meeting the adversities of performance) is more important than outer performance (how one looks to others).

☐ One can learn to master and control the physical self and does not have to be dictated to by physical feelings alone.

☐ Patience, particularly in the execution of static stretching, is essential. Never rush.

☐ Participate with the goal of gradually increasing the time of entering, holding and coming out of a posture.

☐ Repeat exposures to particular postures toward the goal of increasing kinesthetic sense. Listen to the body.

☐ The emphasis during a class or routine is on personal commitment and effort, not on the degree of skill shown. The latter will be forthcoming if the former is constantly employed.

☐ Never bounce to increase reach or flexibility. Static stretching and holding are emphasized.

☐ Learn to transfer skills and knowledge learned in class to situations outside of class. The instructor should suggest situations where what is learned in class can be applied to circumstances outside of class.

☐ Frequent practice, if only for a few minutes, on a daily basis is a realistic goal. Practice should become a part of everyday living just as one eats, sleeps, reads, or enjoys music.

Teaching Techniques

1. *What to expect and the goals of participation are important to basic and concomitant learnings.* Therefore, the first class should be carefully planned to characterize the nature of hatha yoga and its goals, and to dispel the misconceptions and stereotypes. Self-awareness (increased kinesthetic sense, realization of the delicate body-mind relationship, knowledge of anatomical structure and function) and skill (heightened sensitivity to neuromuscular hypertension and ways to release it, performance of asanas for strength and flexibility purposes, and ability to induce deep muscular relaxation) must be spelled out to the class both verbally and by written course outlines; attention to logical spacing and sequence of material is demanded. Human potential is the subject matter; hatha yoga, the method of realization.

2. *Suggest that students keep a yoga notebook on their reactions to each class.* Also, on the first day, if time permits, allow them to list their weight, waist measurement, blood pressure, resting pulse rate and measurements on one or two flexibility tests. They should also note *feelings* of weakness or strength in various body parts. Comparisons of these initial entries, with others later in the course, provide some interesting differences for discussion purposes.

3. *Use lead-up movements when necessary.* Each asana is modified to fit existing limitations. The student performs within existing capacities. The numerous variations and lead-ups for beginners should be demonstrated be-

fore each full demonstration. Lead-up movements are essential for many beginning students and provide opportunities for self-discovery.

4. *Use other resource people in the school or community who practice yoga or have an expertise which fits into the program.* There are usually a number of individuals who, as guest lecturers, can provide added interest and technique helpful to the class. Observation of their expertise is a necessary prerequisite before your invitation to speak to the class.

5. *Introduce asanas and develop routines which produce opposing effects.* For example, if the primary action of one asana is to flex the trunk then the next to be executed should extend the trunk. This procedure should be followed, insofar as possible, for a more complete utilization and development of muscle groups.

6. *Emphasize movements outside of class which complement the asanas.* For example, when bending over to pick up a very light object from the floor, such as a pencil or paper clip, straighten the legs and gently stretch the hamstrings. Many similar movements can be devised to both contract and flex muscles, yet are everyday actions that can be a source of developing fitness parameters and speed individual progress.

7. *Speak in class in a very calm, relaxed manner.* Shouting instructions only serves as a deterrent to concentration and individual involvement. The instructor's voice, empathy, and mannerisms are essential in creating confidence, security and continued interest.

8. *At various times during a class, ask students to compare their physical feelings at that moment with how they felt before class started.* Are there differences? Can they characterize those differences?

9. *Introduce fitness concepts related to the subject of hatha yoga.* The concepts of flexibility, strength, endurance (especially cardiorespiratory), low back syndrome and osteoarthritis, to name a few, have relevance to a subject which focuses so intensely on the mind-body relationship.

10. *In assisting students in mechanically correct execution, manipulate the limb or body part into position within limits of the students' existing capacities.* Again, never force. Indicate that the correct techniques often feel "funny" or different and that continued practice will eliminate this very normal response.

11. *Remember that many students feel self-conscious and nervous in the performance of motor skills when they realize others are watching them.* This is particularly true in a hatha yoga class. Prepare for quietness, privacy, and reduction of distractions at your teaching area.

12. *Evaluate on both an individual and group basis.* A major goal of education is change in behavior; that is, changes in living habits, skill acqui-

sition, mental attitude and ways of meeting adversity. In hatha yoga, evaluation and feedback may come after each session. The instructor should include this is the plan for each class. Written responses, after just a few classes, can provide much information for the instructor in terms of reinforcement or changing method and content. A final evaluation at the close of the course or unit can be either by way of open-ended responses or by checking specific items on an evaluation form. These data are always of value to future planning.

UNUSUAL FEATURES

There appear to be several unusual features associated with the practice of hatha yoga that deserve mention, though not claiming exclusiveness or originality.

Increased Self-awareness

Of all the questions which people ponder early in life the question, "Who am I?" often looms as the single most important one. Theorists in mental health have referred to the Socratic principle "know thyself" as an important part of attaining peace and happiness. Sport, dance, and games are agents for self-understanding and discovery of mental, physical, and spiritual potentials. In hatha yoga, the total focus on execution of movements in relation to thinking about feelings, provides a unique combination for experiencing the body and its sounds, rhythm changes, and sensations in a very intense way. One of the readily apparent outcomes in transition from specific asanas to the relaxed position, referred to as Corpse or Sponge, is the experiencing of changes in heart rate, skin temperature, and the contraction and relaxation of various muscle groups; further, the location of neuromuscular hypertense areas, with the attendant relaxation of these areas, is a common learning experience. According to Jacobson, a pioneer in scientific relaxation techniques, recognition of such tension is essential for employing specific relaxation methods. The observation and reporting of sensations are similar, if not identical, to what is requested of the hatha yoga aspirant. Few people can learn to relax unless they understand what neuromuscular hypertension really is, for many fail to recognize its signs or symptoms.

The intricate relationship of mind and body is experienced very early in participation as one realizes how auditory and visual cues affect physical changes within the body. That one's mental-emotional state influences physical changes and disease processes is a long established medical principle. Electromyography objectively demonstrates changes within muscle tissue due to changes in emotional states. Like the Greek physician Galen, medical doctors today agree that over half of the patients they treat suffer from psychosomatic illnesses. Hostility, depression, anxiety, fear, and anger have their counterparts in fatigue, insomnia, headaches, stomach trouble, backaches, and ulcers. Here is where creating a dialogue between the brain and physical feelings associated with muscular activity can provide data for making appropriate changes. Classes are structured to create a learning environment which can help students develop needed muscular sensitivity and provide opportunities and guidance in developing "physical outlets for emotional stimuli."

A type of biofeedback is, therefore, a part of every session. It has long been known that yogis have been able to control, with amazing accuracy, involuntary processes such as heart rate and blood pressure. Today, biofeedback generally implies the use of sophisticated electrical equipment which monitors internal changes and provides information to the learner, who then utilizes the data to initiate internal changes by thought and action. This requires training in the interpretation and use of data. This is also true with respect to feedback from proprioceptors, audiovisual cues, and the positive mental attitude which accompanies participation in yoga. There is much to be said for the power of the central nervous system to control tension states of muscle tissue and physical feelings. Controlled experimentation, for example, indicates that meditative states can reduce oxygen consumption to a greater degree than sleep or hypnosis, producing a lowered metabolic rate. In addition, the rate of respiration decreases, changes in electrical activity in the brain take place, and a general hypometabolic state ensues. The biophysical and mental-physical relationships inherent in the practice of hatha yoga are integral parts of increased self-awareness for the participant; they provide opportunities for self-discovery and self-realization.

Reclaiming the Nonactive

What a student perceives as a threatening situation, the teacher may not. This often evolves into reduced communication between student and teacher, a lessening of interest in the subject, and a redirection of student energies toward avoiding the threat. In physical education this translates into avoidance of participation and the loss of numerous learning experiences. There are many who for reasons of poor coordination, lack of peer approval, embarrassment, overweight, or insecurity have shunned most forms of activity. However, early success, noncomparisons, self-testing, muscular relaxation, and concentration in hatha yoga provide a setting for the reintroduction of activity into the style of living of many people. The experience of being able to relax in a physical education class is a most unusual happening for them. The setting provides the much needed acceptance of individuals as they are, with no requirements or prerequisites in motor learning. This opens up new avenues of learning and eliminates the negative attitudes and stereotypes which they have long associated with physical activity. The unpleasant experiences of the past become lost in the enjoyment of the present.

Interest in Biophysical Subjects

The major subject matter of hatha yoga is the person. While a holistic approach to teaching is highly recommended, the very nature of participation generates interest in how and why the body works and reacts as it does. The interest is quite spontaneous as one feels bodily limitations while in positions in which mechanical advantage overburdens existing strength levels or in which accumulated flexibility loss necessitates increased effort and curtails movement. Questions centering on the cause for existing limits, how these can be expanded, and what movement does for the body are the catalysts for deeper understandings of physiology and anatomical structure. Anatomy charts are excellent teaching aids for the study of particular movements. Lung structure and function are subject matter that evolves from discussion and practice of the various breathing techniques. Body alignment, with discussion of the weight-bearing joints, also provides interest for individual or class discussions.

Prevention and Relief of Back Problems

Traditionally a number of asanas focused on the spinal column as a source of dormant energy which could be tapped by way of the physical and mental discipline associated with the asanas. From a very practical point of view in modern times, some of the asanas prove to be excellent exercises for the prevention of back problems caused by a loss of strength and flexibility. This is of special importance when it is estimated that some six million Americans suffer from backaches. The therapeutic function of the asanas is also apparent in the reduction of low back syndrome, as several medically prescribed exercises are identical to movements of particular asanas. Hatha yoga appears to be one of the few systems, if not the only system, of exercise which systematically flexes, extends, and rotates the large number of muscles of the entire spinal column as well as other muscle groups directly affecting the back.

IN RETROSPECT

Even though hatha yoga does little to improve cardiorespiratory endurance, suffers from a multiplicity of stereotypes, and lacks valid data to support many of the beneficial claims attributed to its practice, the system has a place in programs of physical education. One of its most apparent contributions is the development of skill in neuromuscular relaxation at a time in which pressured styles of living and sensory overkill are at a dangerously high level. DeVries places the responsibility for meeting these challenges squarely on professional educators when he states, "Physical education has pursued knowledge for developing more strength, more power, and more endurance in muscle tissue, but the future will demand emphasis in our curricula upon how to relax muscles, as well as how to tense them." This movement form can meet that challenge.

Not to be overlooked is the vast learning potential within the affective domain. Education in this area is a natural outgrowth of organization, class presentations, and interaction of student with student and student with teacher in a *unique activity setting*. To allow the lack of sharp, quick movement, or conversely, the abundance of slow motion patterns and quietness of the hatha yoga class, to act as deterrents to its inclusion in physical education programs is to fall victim to narrow and inflexible attitudes which educators should seek to eliminate. Better yet, perhaps all educators should remind themselves that genuine learning experiences are closely related to personal and interpersonal relationships. Such relationships are significant factors in the development of self-esteem and provide opportunities for self-expression so essential for personal growth. Hatha yoga facilitates this growth; there are many paths to the same goal.

REFERENCES

Benson, H. 1975. *The relaxation response*. New York: William Morrow.

Bernard, T. 1968. *Hatha yoga*. New York: Samuel Weiser.

Corbin, C. B., D. J. Linus, R. Lindsey, and H. Tolson 1970. *Concepts in physical education: with laboratories and experiments*. Dubuque, Iowa: Wm. C. Brown. Concept 17, Tension and relaxation, pp. 109–114.

Devi, I. 1963. *Renew your life through yoga*. Englewood Cliffs, N.J.: Prentice-Hall.

DeVries, H. A. 1974. *Vigor regained*. Englewood Cliffs, N.J.: Prentice-Hall.

———— 1966. Relief from muscle soreness. *Am. J. of Phys. Med.* **45**: 119.

———— 1962. Improved joint mobility and flexibility. *Res. Quart.* **33**: 222.

Folan, L. M. 1972. *Lilias, yoga, and you*. Cincinnati: WCET TV.

Friedman, L., and L. Galton 1973. *Freedom from backaches*. New York: Simon and Schuster.

Hewitt, J. 1969. *Yoga and you*. London: Tandem.

Hittleman, R. 1968. *Yoga U.S.A.* New York: Bantam Books.

Jacobson, E. 1962. *You must relax*. New York: McGraw-Hill.

———— 1956. *Progressive relaxation*. Chicago: University of Chicago Press.

Kraus, H. 1965. *Backache, stress, and tension*. New York: Simon and Schuster.

————, and W. Raab 1961. *Hypokinetic disease*. Springfield: Charles C. Thomas.

LaGrand, L. 1974. *Hatha yoga in health and physical education*. Potsdam, N.Y.: State University of New York.

———— 1974. Threatening or nonthreatening models. *The Physical Educator,* (March).

———— 1972. On relating to students. *School Health Review,* (January–February).

Lamb, L. (ed.) 1974. Osteoarthritis: degenerative or wear and tear arthritis. *Health Letter* **4,** 10, (November).

Luby, S. 1974. *Yoga is for you.* Englewood Cliffs, N.J.: Prentice-Hall.

Lyon, W. 1974. Notes on teaching yoga. *JOPER* (March–April): 95–97.

Lysebeth, A. 1972. *Yoga self-taught.* New York: Harper & Row.

Miller, S. 1973. New directions in sport. *Intellectual digest,* (September): 48–50.

Rawls, E., and E. Diskin 1967. *Yoga for beauty and health.* West Nyack, N.Y.: Parker.

Selye, H. 1974. Four words to live by. *Reader's Digest,* (February): 69–72.

———— 1974. *Stress without distress.* New York: J. B. Lippincott.

———— 1956. *The stress of life.* New York: McGraw-Hill.

Stearn, J. 1968. *Yoga, youth, and reincarnation.* New York: M. Evans.

Vitale, F. 1973. *Individualized fitness programs.* Englewood Cliffs, N.J.: Prentice-Hall. Chapter 8, Handling stress and tension, pp. 199–222.

Wallace, R. K., and H. Benson 1972. The physiology of meditation. *Sci. Am.* **226,** 2, (February): 84–90.

Biographical Appendix

Richard Abrahamson is captain of the 1976 U.S. Olympic Handball team and was a competitor on the team in 1972. He is a member of the U.S. Olympic Athletes Advisory Committee. Mr. Abrahamson graduated from the University of Oregon, where he majored in political science and business and captained the basketball team in 1969. He is presently working as a marketing representative in the Greater Washington, D.C., area.

Philip E. Allsen is professor of physical education at Brigham Young University, where he is involved with research as well as teaching. He has formerly served as director of professional program and athletic coach at Ricks College in Rexburg, Idaho; as a physical fitness officer with the U.S. Navy; and as director of athletics in the Gardena, California, school system. Dr. Allsen has authored three books and twenty-seven articles. His honors are numerous, and his professional memberships include the American College of Sports Medicine, AAHPER, and NCPEAM.

Jay Arnold is head of the department of health and physical education at Valdosta (Georgia) State College and chairman-elect of the College Physical Education section of the Southern District AAHPER. He taught and coached in the public schools of Maryland and New York and, after receiving his Ed.D. from Temple University in 1969, was on the faculty of the University of South Carolina. Dr. Arnold was assistant convention manager for Southern District AAHPER in 1970, and has served as chairman of a special AAHPER task force on club sports from 1973 to 1975.

Jeffrey M. Austin has been varsity gymnastics coach at Triton College, River Grove, Illinois, since 1968. His high school championships were in the area of wrestling, but as an undergraduate at the University of Illinois he turned to gymnastics and proceeded to win numerous titles, among them the National AAU Tumbling and Trampoline Championships in 1957. Mr. Austin earned his master's degree at the University of Illinois, and for ten years was a member of the faculty at Proviso

West High School in Hillside, Illinois. Jeff and his wife, Susan—also a former national trampoline champion—have appeared throughout the country with their professional trampoline act, "The Austins."

Carolyn E. Baker earned her M.Ed. from East Stroudsburg (Pennsylvania) State College in 1973 and since then has been an instructor of aquatics and swimming coach at Southwest Texas State University, San Marcos. As an undergraduate at East Stroudsburg, she lettered in both swimming and lacrosse, and went on to play for the New Jersey Women's Lacrosse Association in 1968 and the Westchester Women's Lacrosse Association from 1969–72. She competed in USWLA National Tournaments from 1968–72 and was selected to New England I in 1970 and to New England II in 1971 and 1972.

Dick Bertrand is coach of Cornell's Big Red hockey team, and the record he has achieved during his first six years is unmatched by any other coach in college hockey. With a winning percentage of 0.740, his teams have won three Ivy titles, one Eastern title, and a second and fourth in the nation. Mr. Bertrand is a native of Connaught, Ontario, and a graduate of Cornell, where he was a wing and tri-captain of the Big Reds' undefeated (29-0) national championship club.

Richard W. Bowers is affiliated with the department of health and physical education at Bowling Green (Ohio) State University. His membership in AAHPER dates back to 1962, and he is a member of its research council, as well as a fellow in the American College of Sports Medicine. Mr. Bowers is also on the Board of Associate Editors of *Research Quarterly*.

Daniel L. Canada is a faculty member in the department of community and outdoor recreation at Springfield (Massachusetts) College. Since 1962 he has been continually involved in the field of leisure services. His positions have included that of recreation leader for the San Jose Park and Recreation Department; recreation intern with the California Division of Beaches and Parks; assistant superintendent of recreation in Natick, Massachusetts; and recreation director for the Warrensburg, Missouri, school district. Mr. Canada has also taught part time at Central Missouri State University and the University of Connecticut.

Ray Carson has more than 20 years' experience in the field of wrestling. From interscholastic and intercollegiate competition he has gone on to teach, officiate, and coach that sport, and to instruct judo/karate and physical education as well. He was educated at Augustana College, the University of Illinois, and Indiana University, from which he holds a bachelor's, a master's, and a director's degree, respectively. Mr. Carson has authored four books on wrestling, and a fifth is due to be published shortly. He is currently affiliated with the Grossmont Union High School District in California.

Ju-Ho Chang has worked extensively with YMCAs in Korea and the United States. He received his M.A. from Seoul National University, studied for a year at Sydney (Australia) Teachers' College, and earned his M.S. in physical education from Springfield (Massachusetts) College in 1973. He has instructed judo for the Eighth U.S. Army in Korea, the Australian Judo Federation, and at YMCAs in Norwalk, Connecticut and Springfield. A participant in Olympic Games at Sapporo and Munich, Mr. Chang has been involved in many Korean professional organizations.

Tchang-Bok Chung is senior program physical director for the YMCA in Westfield, New Jersey, where he serves also as a member of the Special Physical Education Committee of the public schools. He received his B.S. from Seoul (Korea) National University in 1965, his master's degree from Springfield (Massachusetts) College in 1971, and his Ed.D. from New York University. Dr. Chung has done much to advance the sport of karate in the United States; his many professional involvements include service as judo and karate commissioner for the Middle Atlantic region and YMCA representative to the National AAU Karate Committee.

John W. Cobb, Jr., is professor of physical education at Texas Tech University, where he has served on the faculty since 1958. He formerly taught and coached in the public schools of Corpus Christi, Texas. After receiving a B.S. from the University of Corpus Christi and an M.Ed. from Texas Tech, he studied at Indiana University and earned his Ed.D. in 1958. Dr. Cobb is a past national president of Phi Epsilon Kappa, and his numerous other professional memberships include AAHPER, NCPEAM, and the American College of Sports Medicine.

Janet Wolcott Cormier's whitewater experience stems from ten years' association with the Appalachian Mountain Club. Elected whitewater canoeing chairman in 1973, she conducted numerous kayak and canoe clinics and served as whitewater instructor at Springfield College for three years. **Leonard Cormier** started paddling in 1958 and has primarily been coaching, boat building, and consulting for youth groups and outdoor programs. As director and slalom chairman of the Westfield Wildwater Canoe Club, he established one of the major races in New England. Recognizing the competitive urge, he began racing C1 in 1973.

That same year, Len and Jan Wolcott teamed up for C2 Mixed competition. They have not only achieved national ranking as "B" competitors but also have become husband and wife in the process. They are currently divisional vice-champions in the C2 Mixed class in both slalom and wildwater.

Jan has a B.S. in physical education from Boston University and is now completing her Masters at Springfield College. She utilizes her skills in teaching an alternative physical education program.

Len is in occupational education as an instructor of television operations and production and is production director at a regional telecommunications center.

Kirk J. Cureton is instructor of physical education and research assistant in the Physical Fitness Research Laboratory at the University of Illinois at Urbana-Champaign. He is a doctoral candidate in the area of exercise physiology and the scientific aspects of physical fitness and performance. He received a B.A. in biology from Carleton College in 1969 and an M.S. in physical education from the University of Illinois at Urbana-Champaign in 1972. He taught at Ball State University in Muncie, Indiana, from 1971–1973. During the summers from 1965–68 he was counselor and assistant waterfront director at the Taylor Statten Camps in Algonquin Provincial Park, Ontario, Canada.

Gerald E. Darda has been diving coach at the University of Wisconsin since 1964. He holds a Ph.D. in physical education with emphasis in the area of biomechanics. Dr. Darda has coached four international teams, including the 1972 U.S. Men's and Women's Olympic Diving Team and the 1975 U.S. Pan-American Team. At Wisconsin he also instructs physical education and each summer conducts four two-week sessions of an intense diving training program for serious male and female high school divers.

Joanna Davenport is presently the director of women's athletics and an associate professor of physical education at Auburn University, Auburn, Alabama. Her special interest is in the history of sports, and she has done extensive research in the history of tennis. A former tournament player, Dr. Davenport devoted her master's thesis to "The History of Tournament Tennis in the United States and the Career and Contributions of Hazel Hotchkiss Wightman." This research was continued with her doctoral dissertation, entitled "The History and Interpretation of Amateurism in the United States Lawn Tennis Association." Dr. Davenport has written several articles on tennis, and portions of her dissertation are quoted in the history section of *The encyclopedia of tennis*.

Dorothy Deach is currently professor and coordinator of women's intercollegiate athletics at Arizona State University, where she served as professor and chairman of physical education for women from 1967 to 1975. She was associate dean at Texas University College of Health, Physical Education, and Recreation for six years, and chairman of physical education for women at the University of Maryland for thirteen. Ms. Deach is a Fellow of the American Academy of Physical Education, the American College of Sports Medicine, and AAHPER.

George B. Dintiman is currently chairman and professor of HPER at Virginia Commonwealth University. He has authored seven books and two syndicated columns (*Champion athlete* with John Unitas and *Driver Ed and Edna* with John Dintiman; both distributed by Transworld News Service, Washington, D.C.). Dr. Dintiman took his B.S. degree in health, physical education and sports from Lock Haven State College, his M.A. from New York University, and his Ed.D. from Columbia. His athletic background includes winning 12 letters in football, basketball, and track and becoming Little–All American halfback and draft choice of the Baltimore Colts and Montreal Aloquettes. He was basketball coach at Inter American University of Puerto Rico (1959–64) and Southern Connecticut State College (1965–68).

Edward T. Dunn is professor of physical education at Springfield (Massachusetts) College, where he has served on the faculty since 1947. From 1958 until 1975 he was Springfield's head football coach, and was named New England College Football Coach of the Year in 1965. Mr. Dunn received his B.A. from Colgate University in 1942, saw duty with the United States Air Corps for the ensuing 39 months, and subsequently earned his M.A. from Springfield in 1949. His professional memberships include AAHPER and Massachusetts AHPER. He has served on the committees of numerous organizations.

Marigold A. Edwards, a New Zealander, is associate professor at the University of Pittsburgh, where she has been teaching since 1962. With undergraduate degrees from the University of Otago and the University of Canterbury in New Zealand, she earned the M.Ed. and Ph.D. at the University of Pittsburgh. Dr. Edwards has published articles in professional journals on competition, racquet sports, conditioning, and tension control. In squash she won the Canadian Singles in 1970 and 1971 and has reached the United States finals three times. Currently ranked third, she also holds the National Senior Singles and Doubles titles.

Henry Eichin is currently chairperson of physical education programs at the University of Wisconsin at Green Bay, where he also coaches soccer. While on active duty with the U.S. Air Force, he served as officer-in-charge of boxing at the Academy. His responsibilities included an activity course for cadets and the coaching of intramurals, and here he also conducted the wing open boxing championships. Mr. Eichin holds a bachelor's degree in physical education from Springfield (Massachusetts) College and a master's degree from Columbia University.

Bernard E. Empleton is currently executive director of the Council for National Cooperation in Aquatics, under whose auspices he chaired the team that wrote *The new science of skin and scuba diving* and its four revisions. Educated at Springfield (Massachusetts) College, he received his B.S. in physical education and served with several major YMCAs over a 34-year period. From 1953–57, Mr. Empleton edited the *YMCA Journal of Physical Education.* His professional memberships include the American College of Sports Medicine and the Undersea Medical Society, and he is the recipient of several service awards.

David L. Engerbretson earned his Ph.D. from Pennsylvania State in 1970, and has served on the faculties of Northeastern University, Macalester College, and Washington State University. In addition to teaching human anatomy, physiology, kinesiology, and exercise physiology, he has taught many clinics and workshops in casting and angling and is a master clinician for the Outdoor Education Project of the AAHPER. As a freelance outdoor writer/photographer, Dr. Engerbretson has authored as many as 75 articles in various national publications. He is a member of the Outdoor Writers Association of America and is a licensed fishing guide.

Carl E. Erickson is dean of the School of Health, Physical Education, and Recreation at Kent State University, Kent, Ohio, where he has served as a professor and director of athletics since 1957. His undergraduate as well as postgraduate education was at Boston University, and he earned his Ed.D. there in 1953. Dr. Erickson has chaired and served many committees of AAHPER and NCAA; his lengthy list of professional memberships includes NCPEAM, the American School Health Association, and the American College of Sports Medicine. He has co-authored or contributed to two textbooks, numerous periodicals, and is active in community service.

Peter W. Everett was educated at the University of Iowa, where he earned his B.S., M.A., and Ph.D. and also taught for three years. In 17 years at Florida State University he has seen service as chairman of his department as well as of the graduate program. Dr. Everett has been President of the Florida Association for HPER and the Southern District of AAHPER, of which he is a Research Council member. He has received Honor Awards from both associations and has published articles in the *Research Quarterly*.

Paul S. Fardy is a member of the faculty at Case Western Reserve University, Departments of Medicine and Physiology. He earned his M.S. and Ph.D. in physical education at the University of Illinois in 1964 and 1967, respectively. His undergraduate studies were at the State University of New York, College at Cortland. Dr. Fardy formerly taught at California State University at Fullerton, and from 1971–72 was a National Heart and Lung Institute Fellow, Institute of Occupational Health, Helsinki, Finland.

David A. Field has been the department head of men's physical education at Ball State University (Indiana) since 1971. Prior to this he served 18 years as Director of the Arnold College Division, University of Bridgeport. Dr. Field was educated at the University of Illinois, where he received his B.S. in 1940 and M.S. in 1946. He subsequently became assistant professor of physical education at the University of Maryland and earned his Ed.D. there in 1951. Throughout his career he has been active in AAHPER and NCPEAM.

K. John Fisher is deputy head of physical education at the Beaufoy School, London, England. He was born in Sydney, Australia, in 1947, studied at St. Luke's College, Exeter, Devon, and received his B.E. from Exeter University in 1974. He completed his postgraduate study at the University of Oregon, earning his M.S. there in 1975. Mr. Fisher's coaching distinctions include that of M C C Cricket Coach (1969) and the Rugby Football Union Award (1975).

Harold T. Friermood retired in 1967 as senior secretary for physical education on the National Board YMCA Staff, a position which he had held for 24 years. He earned bachelor's degrees from George Williams College and the University of Chicago, an M.S. from the University of Wisconsin, and an Ed.D. from New York University in 1954. His professional involvement with the YMCA dates back to 1920, and among many accomplishments he originated the National YMCA Health Service Clinic. He has served in leadership capacities and is active in numerous organizations, including the United States Olympic Committee, CNCA, AAHPER, AAU, and the National Health Council.

Harry Fritz is the executive secretary of the National Association of Intercollegiate Athletics. He served as chairman of the Division of Men's Athletics of AAHPER from 1970–72 and during 1975–76 was President of the National Association for Sport and Physical Education. A 1946 graduate of Transylvania College, he earned his master's degree from the University of Kentucky and his doctorate from the University of Indiana in 1954. Dr. Fritz has held positions of prominence on the faculties of Bemidji (Minnesota) State University, Western Illinois University, and the State University of New York at Buffalo.

Frank H. Fu is currently director of the testing and appraisal program at the Ottawa, Canada, YM-YWCA, as well as an instructor in physiology at Algonquin College. He received his B.A. degree from Dartmouth College and continued his education at Springfield (Massachusetts) College, where he subsequently earned the degrees of M.S. and Ed.D.

Maxwell R. Garret has been associate professor of recreation and parks and fencing coach at Pennsylvania State University since 1972. He graduated in 1939 from City College of New York, and began coaching and teaching at the University of Illinois in 1940. In 27 years as a member of the faculty at Illinois his teams won 17 Big-Ten Fencing Championships and 2 NCAA titles. Mr. Garret's coaching activities include work in Israel, and his list of accomplishments and honors both there and at home is extensive.

John F. Gasparini was born and raised in Fort Frances, Ontario. In 1964 he was awarded a hockey scholarship from the University of North Dakota, where he has been associated in either a student or a professional capacity ever since. It was here that he lettered four years in hockey and graduated with a B.S. degree, returning in 1969 to earn his master's degree in physical education and administration. Mr. Gasparini is presently an assistant hockey coach and instructor in the Health, Physical Education and Recreation Department at the University of North Dakota.

James E. Genasci is professor of physical education at Springfield (Massachusetts) College, where he coordinates courses in hiking, backpacking, mountaineering, skiing, whitewater sport, and winter alpine activities. He received his B.S. and M.S. degrees from Springfield, earned his Ed.D. at the University of Colorado in 1960, and has served on the faculties of the University of Maine, the United States Air Force Academy, and the University of Northern Colorado. Dr. Genasci is the former assistant director of graduate studies and summer Peace Corps director at Springfield and is treasurer of the Philosophic Society for the Study of Sport. He is coauthor of *Skiing: a resource manual.*

Jean Boutwell Genasci earned her B.S. from Springfield (Massachusetts) College and her M.A. from the University of Northern Colorado in 1963. Currently a substitute teacher in the Springfield and Longmeadow public school systems, she has served as a high school librarian and worked extensively in YMCA, private camp, and town recreation programs. Mrs. Genasci is an accomplished backpacker, camper, and skier, and has pursued these interests in both eastern and western parts of the United States. She is coauthor of *Skiing: a resource manual.*

A. John Geraci is a fencing master of the United States Academy of Arms and the Academie d'Armes Internationale, with over 39 years' experience as a teacher, coach, competitor, and international referee. He has been head coach at the United States Military Academy since 1965, and has guided the cadet fencing teams to over 100 victories. Mr. Geraci served as fencing master of the United States senior World Fencing Teams at the World Championships in 1973 at Goteborg, 1974 at Grenoble, and 1975 at Budapest. He is editor of the professional magazine, *The Swordmaster.*

Harry R. Groves has a professional record that speaks for itself: in 22 years of coaching, he has never known a losing season! Since 1968 he has been exercising his skills as head track and cross-country coach at Pennsylvania State University. Prior to that he was at William and Mary, and with the Army at Ft. Eustis, Virginia, from 1953 to 1954. Mr. Groves's colleagues last year elected him to the presidency of the coaches' associations for both cross-country and track, distinguishing him as the first individual to hold these offices simultaneously. In 1975 he was named National Cross-Country Coach of the Year.

Chris Gulick lives in Amherst, Massachusetts, where he works full time in a mountaineering supply store. Mr. Gulick has been climbing fairly consistently during the past few years, mostly around New England. Climbing has become an important part of his life in a surprisingly short amount of time, and he hopes his interest continues and grows in this vein.

He also has a conflicting obsession with trout fishing and hopes some day to find a mile high granite face rising from a model trout stream.

Mary F. Heinecke received her B.A. from Valparaiso University in 1952 and her M.Ed. from Miami University of Ohio in 1963. She is currently an associate professor of physical education at Lawrence University in Appleton, Wisconsin, where her position includes the coaching of men's and women's tennis and fencing teams. She formerly served as acting chairman of the department of physical education at Milwaukee Downer College, and as a field and camp director for the Girl Scouts. A member of the National Fencing Coaches Association of America and AAHPER, Ms. Heinecke is also on the board of directors of the American Badminton Association.

Roland Hess is associate professor and physical education department chairman at Hanover College, Hanover, Indiana. He received his B.S. at East Stroudsburg (Pennsylvania) State College and his M.S. from Springfield (Massachusetts) College in 1957. His Ed.D. was earned at West Virginia University in 1969, and he has done post-doctoral study at the University of Maine, as well as Ball State, Michigan State, and Colorado State Universities. Dr. Hess instructed and coached at Johnson State College in Vermont and at the University of Rhode Island before joining the Hanover faculty in 1969.

Ruth A. Howe, professor of physical education at Bemidji (Minnesota) State University, holds a B.S. and an M.Ed. from the University of Minnesota, and an earned doctorate in physical education from Indiana University. She has been a member of the Bemidji faculty since 1957, and there was introduced to the game of curling. As a member of the Bemidji Women's Curling Club, she has served as vice-president for one year, president for two years, and as a member of the executive board for six years. She instructs curling classes for Bemidji State University at the Curling Club. Her dissertation, "A History of Curling in the United States," has provided the basis for speeches, articles, and clinics.

Fred Hushla is chairman of the United States Olympic Luge Committee and serves as Coach/Manager of the Olympic Luge Development Teams, training in Sweden, Italy, Germany, Australia, and the United States. In 1972 he coached the United States Olympic Luge Team in Sapporo, Japan. A former president of the Niagara Association Amateur Athletic Union, he has been its chairman of registration for 10 years. Mr. Hushla was chairman of the National AAU Luge Committee from 1970–74.

Burris F. Husman received the B.S. and M.S. degrees from the University of Illinois and earned his Ed.D. degree from the University of Maryland. He has had over 20 years of experience as a teacher, coach, researcher, and administrator in college physical education programs. His writing and research have been in the area of psychology of sport. Active in professional organizations, he has served as president of a state and district organization as well as of NCPEAM. Dr. Husman has received honor awards from the State, District, and National AAHPER.

Howard G. Knuttgen is professor of physiology and associate dean for academic affairs at the Sargent College of Allied Health Professions, Boston University. He has published widely both research articles on the physiology of exercise and general articles on sports and physical conditioning. Dr. Knuttgen is a past president of the American College of Sports Medicine. An active orienteer, he holds membership in the United States Orienteering Federation and serves as chairman of the Competitive Program for the New England Orienteering Club.

Louis E. LaGrand is professor and director of health and physical education at the State University of New York, College at Potsdam. His undergraduate degree is from the State University of New York, College at Cortland. He holds advanced degrees from Columbia University, the University of Notre Dame and Florida State University. Dr. LaGrand is the author of three books, the most recent of which is *Hatha yoga in health and physical education,* and has written numerous articles for professional journals.

James J. Lampman earned his M.A. in health and physical education in 1967 while coaching the freshman swim team at the University of Florida at Gainesville. Since then he has been on the faculty of Miami-Dade (Florida) Community College, where he is swimming/water-polo coach and aquatic consultant. During his undergraduate years at the State University of New York, College at Brockport, he swam competitively and captained the team as a senior. Mr. Lampman served with the United States Marine Corps and taught drownproofing on several bases including Camp LeJeune, N.C., and Camp Sukiran, Okinawa.

Marie R. Liba is a member of the American Academy of Physical Education, Research and Measurement Councils, and AAHPER. Her articles have been published in the *Research Quarterly* and the *American Education Research Journal*. With Donald Casady, Ms. Liba coauthored the book *Beginning bowling*.

William L. McIntyre holds a B.S. from Towson State College in Baltimore and three graduate degrees from California Western and Johns Hopkins Universities. His involvement in sailing dates back to the age of 10, and in the past 30 years he has cruised and raced on the Chesapeake, the mid-Atlantic Coast, San Diego's Mission Bay, and Kaneohe Bay in Hawaii. College summers were spent as a sailing counselor on Cape Cod, where he returned after service in the Marine Corps to direct the Cape Cod Sea Camps' sailing programs for 10 years. By profession he is a social studies teacher in the Baltimore County school system, but sailing continues to be the pastime of the McIntyres and their six seaworthy children.

Lloyd Lowell Messersmith was chairman of the physical education department at Southern Methodist University from 1945 until 1970. He received his B.A. at DePauw University, his M.A. from Columbia, and earned his Ed.D. at Indiana University. Dr. Messersmith has served in leadership capacities in numerous organizations including the Indiana and Texas State Physical Education Associations and the Southern District AAHPER, all three of which granted him Honor Awards. He is a member of the Dallas Chapter of Phi Delta Kappa and the American Academy of Physical Education.

Carole L. Mushier received her B.S. from Sargent College, Boston University, her M.A. from Columbia University Teachers College, and earned her Ph.D. at the University of Southern California. She has taught on the high school and college levels and is currently professor of women's physical education at SUNY College at Cortland. She has taught and coached women's lacrosse at all levels, including the USWLA national teams.

James E. Odenkirk presently serves as professor and chairperson of the physical education department at Arizona State University. In the last 25 years he has taught and coached at Bowling Green (Ohio) State University, Central Missouri State University, and the University of Dubuque, as well as in public school systems. Dr. Odenkirk has been president of the Arizona Association for Health, Physical Education, and Recreation, from which he received the Honor Award, and of the Southwest District of AAHPER. He has held various offices in NCPEAM, and is the author of some 15 articles published in national professional journals.

Arne L. Olson earned his Ph.D. from the University of Oregon after attending the Universities of Iowa and Northern Iowa. He has done post-doctoral study at the University of Illinois with Dr. Cureton and is currently golf coach at East Stroudsburg (Pennsylvania) State College, where he has developed a unique golf analysis laboratory. His former faculty service includes the universities of Oregon and Illinois, as well as Temple University. Curriculum, evaluation, and biomechanics are Dr. Olson's special professional areas, and he has been a research consultant for AAHPER.

Patrick O'Shea is a graduate of Michigan State University with a doctorate from the University of Utah. He is a professor of physical education at Oregon State University. His teaching interests are highly diversified—from exercise physiology to ski mountaineering. He has authored a textbook in the area of strength physiology and published over 40 research and technical papers dealing with a wide variety of subjects. His pursuit of mountaineering has taken Dr. O'Shea and his wife from the lofty Cascades of the Pacific Northwest to the high reaches of Alaska's Mount McKinley.

Buel R. Patterson retired in 1972 after coaching for 20 years at Kansas State University, three years at the University of Nebraska, and 20 years at the University of Illinois. He was manager of the 1952 United States Olympic Wrestling Team. Mr. Patterson is enjoying his retirement in Bradley, Oklahoma.

Alfred F. Pisano, Jr., has been head coach of lacrosse at the United States Miiltary Academy at West Point since 1969. He received his education at the State University of New York at Cortland, where he lettered four years in lacrosse and captained the 1961 and 1962 teams. After a year as graduate assistant in physical education and freshman lacrosse coach at Pennsylvania State University, Mr. Pisano taught and coached in the Massapequa, Long Island, school system and returned to Cortland as an instructor of physical education and head lacrosse coach for five years.

John Talbot Powell has for ten years served the University of Guelph (Canada) College of Biological Science as its director, school of physical education, and chairman, department of human kinetics. His former positions include that of head track and field coach at Cambridge University, England, and Rhodes University, South Africa. Dr. Powell taught seven consecutive years on the Canadian National Track and Field Coaches Clinic, and since 1949 has designed and/or conducted 127 track and field coaching courses. He is the author of *Track and field fundamentals for teacher and coach* and *Rugby—the team game*.

Herbert C. Price, Jr., is principal of the Barrington Middle School in Barrington, Illinois, and has been a school administrator for nine years. He formerly taught physical education, with emphasis on alternative activities and the development of individual achievement standards for students. His articles have been published in *JOPER* and the *Illinois Education Journal*.

Philip J. Rasch retired in 1972 from his position as chief of the physiology division, Naval Medical Field Research Laboratory, Camp Lejeune, N.C. His B.A., M.A.,

M.Ed. and Ph.D. degrees were all earned at the University of Southern California, and he is author or coauthor of such books as *Kinesiology and applied anatomy, Sports medicine for trainers,* and *Weight training,* as well as a substantial number of other publications. Dr. Rasch is enjoying his retirement in San Pedro, California.

Josephine L. Rathbone earned her B.A. at Wellesley College in 1921 and her M.A. and Ph.D. at Columbia Universty Teachers College in 1936. Since then she has held assistant professorships and consultant positions at Wellesley, the Payne Clinic at Cornell Medical Center, Springfield (Massachusetts) College and Columbia. There she helped initiate programs to train physical therapists after World War II. On the 200th anniversary of the founding of Kings College of Physicians and Surgeons at Columbia, Dr. Rathbone received a citation.

Peter H. Raymond has coached at the Naval Academy and Harvard University, and currently edits the *Oarsman,* the official publication of the National Association of Amateur Oarsmen. He rowed at Princeton University in 1968 and was a member of three national teams.

William W. Richerson has taught physical education and coached football at college and high school levels for 20 years and is presently the division chairman for health, physical education, and recreation at the Northeast Missouri State University. His former experience includes five years as an assistant professor and football coach at the University of Wisconsin at Madison. Dr. Richerson received his B.S. and M.A. degrees from Northeast Missouri and earned his Ph.D. at the University of Utah.

Allen Scates has led the UCLA Bruin volleyball team to eight national championships, including 1974, '75, and '76. A member of four Bruin teams (1960–63), he was named USBVA All-American five times and competed on three United States men's national teams (1965–67). In addition to coaching the UCLA team, Mr. Scates is an elementary physical education specialist with the Beverly Hills school district. He has served as head coach of United States, Pan American, and Olympic volleyball teams and has authored two books, one of which is appropriately entitled *Winning volleyball.*

Maryanne M. Schumm is an associate professor in the physical education department at East Stroudsburg State College in Pennsylvania, where she is archery coach of a team that has earned two National Championship titles and ten All-America Archers. She is codirector of the World Archery Center in Marshalls Creek, Pennsylvania, former editor of the *DGWS Archery Guide,* and a former tournament director and official for U.S intercollegiate archery championships. Ms. Schumm serves as archery representative to the United States Olympic Committee–International Olympic Academy Committee.

Don Cash Seaton's career in health and physical education includes military, academic, and public offices. He was in charge of the Fourth Naval District Physical

Fitness Program and Rehabilitation 11th District for the Navy. At the University of Illinois, Dr. Seaton taught physical education and coached varsity track and cross country. His public offices include those of Illinois State Director of Health, Physical Education and Safety and Illinois Civilian Defense Director of Physical Fitness. He was associated with the Sanford B. Perkins Fellowship Center for Safety Education at N.Y.U. and coordinated the *Safety Education Bulletin* of the New York public schools. More recently Dr. Seaton was chairman of the department of physical education at the University of Kentucky. He is the author of seven textbooks and numerous bulletins and articles.

Thomas M. Scott earned his B.A. and M.A. in education at the University of Florida, where he has taught since 1949. He is responsible for the programs of adapted physical education, golf, and weight training in the general physical education department. Mr. Scott's broad teaching experience includes individual, dual, and team sports.

Herman B. Segrest is professor and coordinator of the physical education service program at Texas Technical University in Lubbock. Director of required physical education, he spent 17 of his 39 professional years with Texas A&M University. He has worked with Air Force cadets and directed numerous summer camp programs. After receiving his B.S. and M.S. degrees from North Texas State University, he went on to earn an M.Ed. at Texas A&M and an Ed.D. at Baylor. Dr. Segrest is a member of TAHPER, AAHPER, NCPEAM, and SEOA, and has held several state and national offices.

Armond H. Seidler originated the game of flickerball, with the help of Dr. H. E. Kenney. Currently a professor of physical education at the University of New Mexico, he has coached football and basketball in Illinois and Iowa and taught at the universities of Illinois, Arkansas, and New Mexico Highlands. Dr. Seidler earned his B.S., M.S., and Ph.D. from the University of Illinois. Among his accomplishments is the development of the Seidler system of bayonet fighting, used by the United States Armed Forces.

Carl W. Selin has served as director of physical education for the United States Coast Guard Academy since 1959. A member of the permanent commissioned teaching staff, he has also coached baseball, football, and has been director of athletics. In 1963 he was named Coach of the Year in New England by the College Baseball Coaches. Capt. Selin earned his Ph.D. at the University of Iowa and has taught and coached at the University of California and Aurora College. Currently he directs the Maine Wilderness Canoe Basin/Deer Isle Sailing Center for boys and *Les Chalets Français* (French Camp for Girls) on the coast of Maine.

Emery W. Seymour was in 1966 named director of the division of graduate studies at Springfield (Massachusetts) College, where he has been a member of the faculty for 20 years. He is a member of AAHPER (Research Council), NCPEAM, and a former member of the American College of Sports Medicine. Coauthor of *Administration of health, physical education, and recreation for schools*, Mr.

Seymour has also published a number of articles in professional journals. Prior to 1956 he was associated with Emory University.

Irene Shea is the director of athletics for women at California State University at Sacramento. For five years she was employed at the SUNY College at Brockport. While she coached there the softball team became the NYSAIAW State Champions three times. Ms. Shea is the national president of the NAGWS Softball Academy and represented the sport of softball in ABC's "Superstars Competition." Her amateur softball experience was for the most part with the 13 time National Champion Raybestos Brakettes and present World Champions. She was selected All American in each of the national tournaments in which she participated. Ms. Shea presently plays professional softball for the Connecticut Falcons of the Women's Professional Softball League.

Jenepher Shillingford is assistant chairperson of the physical education department at Immaculata (Pennsylvania) College, where she also serves as business coordinator for basketball. Her own sports career included the United States Field Hockey Team from 1955–57, and she is a former national hockey and basketball official. Ms. Shillingford earned her M.Ed. from Temple University in 1959 and has been active in numerous professional as well as church and community organizations. Her articles have appeared in several publications, and she is a camp director as well as the wife of a pediatrician and mother of three children.

M. G. Sholtis teaches swimnastics as a part of the professional recreation and leisure education curriculum at Southern Connecticut State College in New Haven. Recognized as one of the nation's outstanding authorities in the field of swimnastics, she has organized and conducted swimnastics programs in recreation departments and for clinics at state, regional, and national conferences in health, physical education, and recreation.

F. Eric Sills, a doctoral candidate and former teaching associate at Temple University, is now an assistant professor at Bridgewater State College, Bridgewater, Massachusetts, where he teaches exercise physiology and mechanical aspects of movement. He has been a physical education instructor and coach of soccer and track and field in the Gloucester public school system. Mr. Sills is presently developing a Stress Testing Center in the physical education department at Bridgewater State College.

Charles J. Smith is associate professor of physical education at Springfield (Massachusetts) College, where he serves as assistant swimming coach and varsity diving coach. He earned his B.S. and M.S. at Springfield and did further study at the University of Connecticut. Prior to joining the Springfield faculty in 1966, Mr. Smith taught and coached for ten years at Windham High School, Willimantic, Connecticut. He is a life member of AAHPER, a Fellow of the American College of Sports Medicine, and the author of *Water polo fundamentals.*

Joanne L. Smith received her B.S. from SUNY, at Brockport, and her M.S. from Penn State. She has over a decade of experience as a producer of water shows and as a natagrapher. Ms. Smith has participated actively in AAU synchronized swimming, IAAA symposia, and NICA functions. She has coached a college competitive swimming team for the past eight years which has produced several All-American swimmers.

Frank Spechalske is director of athletics at Eastern Montana College. He currently serves on the Board of Directors of the National Association of Collegiate Directors of Athletics, and as associate secretary general for North America for the International Amateur Basketball Federation. Dr. Spechalske is secretary of the United States Amateur Basketball Association and chairman of the Basketball Committee Amateur Athletic Union. A member of the Governor's Commission of Physical Fitness, he is a past chairman of the United States Olympic Basketball Committee and has twice received the National Association of International Athletics Award of Merit.

Robert K. Stallman has worked with YMCAs, the Red Cross, the Boy Scouts, the Royal Life Saving Society, camps, municipalities, and schools in the United States and Canada. He has coached water polo and has coached several university national champions in swimming and diving. Dr. Stallman has conducted clinics in instructor training, lifeguard training, coaching, and the preparation of officials and has contributed a variety of conference presentations and publications in the field of aquatics. Presently an assistant professor in the department of human kinetics at the University of Guelph in Guelph, Ontario, Canada. Dr. Stallman estimates that he has personally taught swimming and lifesaving to 10,000 people!

D. K. "Dutch" Stanley founded the College of Physical Education, Health, and Recreation at the University of Florida, and was its dean until 1969. His association with that university dates back to 1931, when he began his collegiate teaching career as assistant football coach there. After serving as head football, track, and tennis coach, as well as director of intramurals, he left in 1939 to become assistant football and track coach at Duke University. Seven years later he returned to Florida, where he continues to serve today as professor of professional physical education.

Donnis H. Thompson received her Ed.D. from the University of Northern Colorado in 1967 and currently serves as women's athletic director and associate professor at the University of Hawaii. She has coached ten national champions, six Olympic participants, and two world record holders. Dr. Thompson is chairperson of the AIAW Cross-Country and Track-and-Field Committees, and has authored two books on the subject of track and field.

JoAnne Thorpe is chairperson of the women's physical education department at Southern Illinois University in Carbondale. After studying for her B.S. at Florida State University, she earned her M.Ed. from the University of North Carolina at

Greensboro and her Ph.D. from Texas Women's University. Dr. Thorpe taught in Florida public schools for three years. In 1958 she began her affiliation with Southern Illinois, where she teaches kinesiology and methods of research and advises graduate research.

Adrian Martin Underwood was educated at Saint Luke's College, Exeter, England, where he has since joined the faculty as a senior lecturer in physical education. A member of the English Rugby Coaching Panel, he is responsible for the production of "Better Rugby" and played for England from 1962–64. Mr. Underwood's recent summers have been spent at McArthur College in Kingston, Canada, teaching rugby, gymnastics, and track and field. Commencing in 1978, he has been appointed lecturer in education at the University of Exeter.

Mildred Vanderhoof did her undergraduate work at Panzer Normal School and Trenton (New Jersey) State College, where she received her B.S. in 1931. Her M.A. was earned at Columbia University. She was for many years chairman of the girls' health and physical education department at the Kenosha, Wisconsin, High School. Ms. Vanderhoof is a member of Delta Kappa Gamma and is noted for her work in swimming programs, particularly her initiation of the Kenosha High School Swimming Ballet. She has been active in Girl Scout and camp work.

Irving F. Waglow received his B.S. and M.Ed. degrees from Springfield (Massachusetts) College and earned his doctorate at New York University. His professional life has been devoted to YMCAs, Boys' Clubs, Army Air Force physical education, and university service. He has been department chairman at the University of Florida for 13 years. Dr. Waglow has published 65 articles in professional journals and has authored or coauthored three books, which have appeared in three editions. He is listed in *Who's who in American education* and other biographies.

Lyle Welser served for 25 years as professor of physical training and volunteer gymnastics coach at Georgia Tech. He received his B.S. and M.Ed. from Springfield (Massachusetts) College in 1933 and 1934, and studied further at the University of Illinois. Among his many professional accomplishments were the founding and developing of the Georgia Gym Association, of which he is a life member. Mr. Welser also founded the first gymnastic clinic in Daytona, Florida, which later became the first National Gym Clinic, Sarasota, and is its Honorary Life President. He holds numerous honors and awards, and an NACGC research grant has been named for him.

Philip K. Wilson is professor and director of the human performance laboratory and lacrosse cardiac rehabilitation program at the University of Wisconsin at LaCrosse. He received his B.S. and M.S. in physical education from Illinois State University, where he subsequently taught and coached in high schools from 1965–67. In 1969 he earned his Ed.D. from the University of Northern Colorado. A Fellow of ACSM and member of AAHPER, Dr. Wilson has published more than

20 articles, coauthored an anatomy/physiology manual, and edited *Adult fitness —cardiac rehabilitation.*

Janet Wolcott. See **Janet Wolcott Cormier.**

Jerry P. Wrenn has the administrative responsibility for all undergraduate programs in physical education at the University of Maryland, where he is assistant department chairperson and teaches a basketball class for physical education majors. His B.S. was earned at East Carolina University, his M.S. at the University of Tennessee, and his Ph.D. at the University of Maryland. Dr. Wrenn's 15 years of teaching and coaching experience have included all academic levels from kindergarten through junior and senior high schools, to his present position.

Wilton B. Wright is chairman of the men's physical education department at Southern Connecticut State College, where he coaches cross-country and track and field. He has been with the faculty of Southern Connecticut since 1963. During these 13 years his teams have represented well within the New England region and have posted consistently winning records.

Index

951